# INTERNATIONAL FINANCE

## Exchange Rates and Financial Flows
## in the International Financial System

Heather D. Gibson

LONGMAN
LONDON AND NEW YORK

**Longman Group Limited,**
Edinburgh Gate
Harlow
Essex
CM20 2JE, England
*and Associated Companies throughout the world.*

*Published in the United States of America*
*by Longman Publishing, New York*

© Longman Group Limited 1996

First published 1996

ISBN 0 582 218136 CSD
ISBN 0 582 218128 PPR

**British Library Cataloguing-in-Publication Data**

A catalogue record for this book is
available from the British Library

**Library of Congress Cataloging-in-Publication Data**

Gibson, Heather D., 1961–
    International finance : exchange rates and financial flows in the
international financial system / Heather D. Gibson.
        p.   cm.
    Includes bibliographical references and index.
    ISBN 0–582–21813–6 (hard) : £40.00. — ISBN 0–582–21812–8 (pbk.) :
£17.99
    1. Foreign exchange administration.   2. Capital movements.
3. International finance.   I. Title.
HG3851.G5   1996
332'.042—dc20                                                        95–32423
                                                                         CIP

Set by 8 in 10/12 pt Ehrhardt
Produced through Longman Malaysia, CLP

To Euclid

# CONTENTS

# LIST OF FIGURES

# LIST OF TABLES

# ACKNOWLEDGEMENTS

I first began to teach a course in international finance to post-graduate students at the University of Kent in October 1987. Over the years, the course developed in response not only to my own research interests but also as a result of comments and questions from these students. The first draft of the book was tried out on MA students in the Department of International and European Economic Studies at Athens University of Economics and Business this year. I would like to express my thanks to all my students who have contributed to making the book what it is.

A number of people gave of their time to make constructive comments on my ideas at various stages of the production of the book. In particular, I would like to thank David Llewellyn, Eric Pentecost and Nuno Cassola e Barata for commenting extensively on the proposed outline. I am also grateful to Peter Sanfey, Pat Fraser, and two anonymous referees for the comments and recommendations they made on various chapters of the book.

Felicia Stanescu helped me enormously in collecting both statistics for the numerous figures and tables which are included as well as in compiling the bibliography for a number of the chapters. Her efficiency and enthusiasm were much appreciated.

Finally, my greatest gratitude is to my partner, Euclid Tsakalotos. He gave me the love, support and encouragement necessary to my task. In addition, he spent a substantial amount of his time reading the whole of the book, making extensive comments and suggestions, and discussing many of the topics with me. Without his help, I can say that the book would have been a much poorer effort.

*Heather Gibson*
*May, 1995*

We are grateful to the following for permission to reproduce Figures and Tables:

Academic Press Ltd for Fig. 2.1 from the article 'The capital transfer mechanism of the 1970s' by D. T. Llewellyn from *The International Financial Regime* edited by G. Bird (Surrey University Press); Blackwell Publishers for Fig. 1 from the article 'A dynamic model of forward foreign exchange risk, with estimates for three major exchange rates' by M. P. Taylor from *The Manchester School*, 56 (1988), copyright Victoria University of Manchester; Brookings Institution for Table 3 from an article by R. N. Cooper from *Brookings Papers on Economic Activity*, 1982, 1; Financial Times for a Table from *Financial Times*, 12.5.94; Gower Publishing Limited for Table 6.1 from *The Quest for Economic Stabilisation* by T. Killick (Gower in association with Overseas Development Institute, 1984); IMF for a Table from *International Financial Statistics*, December 1993; Kiel Institute of World Economics for Table 1 from the article 'Money Creation in the Euro-Currency Market' by M. Willms from *Weltwirtschaftliches Archiv*, vol. 112, 2, 1976; Macmillan Press Ltd for Figs and a Table from *The Eurocurrency Markets, Domestic Financial Policy and International Instability* by Heather D. Gibson (1989); Oxford University Press for Figs from *The Economics of Monetary Integration* by P. De Grauwe (1992), a Fig from *International Money: Post-war Trends and Theories* by P. De Grauwe, and Figs from the article 'Monetary policy and international competitiveness' by W. H. Buiter and M. Miller from *The Money Supply and the Exchange Rate* by W. A. Eltis and P. J. N. Sinclair.

We have been unable to trace the copyright holder in Fig. 1 from the article 'Asset markets and relative prices in exchange rate determination' by W. H. Branson from *Sozialwissenschaftliche Annalen*, Band 1 (1977) and would appreciate any information that would enable us to do so.

# 1 THE INTERNATIONAL FINANCIAL SYSTEM

The history of the international financial system is a complex one. Many different systems have been adopted with varying degrees of co-operation between individual countries. Throughout this century there has been an increase in international linkages through both trade flows and capital movements. This has led to a rise in the degree of interdependence between different countries. As a result, the form which the international financial system takes has become more important in influencing standards of living in all countries throughout the world. As well as determining the extent to which countries trade with each other it also influences the ability of countries to attract financial flows which allow investment and development.

In this opening chapter we want to introduce some of the theoretical issues which are relevant to the design of any international financial system and to discuss briefly some historical aspects. We focus on the problems of adjustment and financing which any system of international financial relations has to address. We argue that the smooth functioning of any system requires the development of appropriate institutions which can oversee its running, ensuring that the 'rules of the game' are adhered to and that disputes between members are settled. Only in this way can the benefits of greater interdependence be truly realised while the costs of greater interdependence, if not eliminated, are, at least, managed.

In the first section, we examine the questions of adjustment, international money and liquidity in the international system. We discuss each concept from a theoretical point of view. This prepares the ground for the second section where we discuss the possible theoretical ways in which the international monetary system could design mechanisms to deal with these questions.

Finally, in the third section we provide a brief history of the international monetary system from the late nineteenth century onwards. We focus in particular on how the questions of liquidity and adjustment have been dealt with at a practical level. We draw on the experiences of the Gold Standard, the inter-war period and the post-war Bretton Woods settlement. We conclude with a brief outline of some of the stylised facts of the international monetary system since the breakdown of Bretton Woods. It is these facts that we seek to shed some light on in the following chapters.

## Adjustment, international money and liquidity

Adjustment of the balance of payments and the means by which international transactions in goods, services and assets are undertaken are the core issues that must be addressed by any international financial system. In this section, we examine some basic theoretical concepts underpinning these two issues. In particular, we discuss what exactly we mean by adjustment and why it should be a matter of concern for either the government or the monetary authorities of any particular country. We then go on to introduce the concepts of international money and liquidity, emphasising the problems that arise in the development of an international means of exchange. Finally, we conclude the section by outlining various ways in which the international financial system can be organised and discuss at a theoretical level the means by which different types of organisation seek to deal with the problems of adjustment and liquidity.

*Adjustment*

Since the balance of payments accounts always sum to zero, the concept of disequilibrium and hence adjustment arises from consideration of particular segments of the balance of payments (see Box 1.1). The general equilibrium view which uses the intertemporal approach of neoclassical economics to analyse the economy provides a good first approximation to understand the origins of balance of payments disequilibria. A surplus/deficit on the current account is simply the result of the decisions of private individuals to save or dissave.[1] In the absence of any controls on international transactions, the principle of comparative advantage and the operation of free competition will prevent chronic structural problems on the balance of payments from arising. Instead, there will only be (temporary) deviations from equilibrium depending on whether individuals wish to consume now or later. We can see this more clearly by employing the familiar national income identities:

$$Y \equiv C + I + G + X - M \tag{1.1}$$

Output and national income (Y) is composed of consumption (C), investment (I), government spending (G) and net exports $(X - M)$. At the same time we know that income can either be consumed (C), saved (S) or used to meet tax commitments (T):

$$Y \equiv C + S + T \tag{1.2}$$

Combining equations (1.1) and (1.2) and subtracting consumption from both sides:

$$I + G + X - M \equiv S + T \tag{1.3}$$

and rearranging we obtain:

$$(X - M) \equiv (S - I) + (T - G) \tag{1.4}$$

That is, any current account imbalance should be identically equal to the private sector's imbalance plus the government's budget position. Assuming all sectors are initially in balance, what happens if individuals decide to consume more? The private sector will go into deficit (S < I) and this will be reflected in a current account deficit (X < M). The ensuing deficit will be financed through borrowing from abroad. That is, a capital account surplus (deriving from the capital inflow associated with borrowing) will ensue. Ultimately individuals will decide that they have borrowed enough (or alternatively, the rest of the world will be unwilling to extend further loans) and the process will go into reverse. Thus balance of payments disequilibria are simply the manifestations of individual desires to consume either now or later and need not cause concern. The issue of adjustment simply disappears.

It is interesting to note that this conclusion does not depend on whether the exchange rate is fixed or flexible. We discuss this in more detail later, but we can note

---

[1] See, for example, any textbook which takes an intertemporal approach to macroeconomics: Sachs and Larrain (1993, Chapter 6); Abel and Bernanke (1992, Chapter 7); or Blanchard and Fischer (1989, Chapter 2).

---

### BOX 1.1   Concepts of Balance of Payments Equilibria

| | |
|---|---|
| 1. Trade Balance: | which is equal to visible export earnings minus visible import payments. This is the narrowest definition of a balance of payments disequilibria, but is little used especially for countries where invisibles play a major role. |
| 2. Current Account: | exports minus imports. This is an important concept because current account deficits need to be financed by borrowing from abroad. Equivalently, current account surpluses imply a build-up of assets held abroad. |
| 3. Basic Balance: | exports minus imports plus long-term capital flows. The argument here is that we can include the long-term capital account because it is more stable than other parts of the capital account, including as it does foreign direct investment and long-term portfolio investment. This concept thus measures the basic balance of payments performance of a country abstracting from short-term (and often volatile) capital flows. |
| 4. Total Currency Flow: | exports minus imports plus the long-term and private short-term capital account. In other words, this concept adds to the basic balance definition short-term *private* capital flows. It is a very broad definition of the balance of payments, effectively omitting only the changes in reserves. Hence it gives us some idea of the pressure which a government is facing at any one time if it is managing the exchange rate. |

Not surprisingly, these different concepts are useful in different contexts, depending on the question which is being addressed.

---

here in passing that our example of borrowing from abroad does not necessitate an exchange rate change. The outflow associated with the current account deficit is exactly matched by the inflow from the capital account surplus.

Few economists take this approach as a description of the way in which the global economy works in practice. Indeed, even a cursory glance at history suggests that it is an inadequate account of the adjustment process. In order to understand why this is the case, we need to delve deeper into the central questions of exactly how, why and when this process will occur. In doing so, we can point to a number of problems with this general equilibrium world of atomised individuals.

Firstly, how is the process by which deficits/surpluses are reversed co-ordinated? In an uncertain world, where those who are dissaving and saving are perhaps not the same individuals, then it is unclear how we can be sure that automatic correction will be forthcoming. Moreover, if the deficit persists for some time, the debt buildup in aggregate may become greater than the economy can bear. If individuals believe this and the deficit begins to take on 'crisis' proportions then agents will anticipate a devaluation/depreciation and this could encourage large speculative flows. The response to such a criticism may be that rational forward-looking agents will be aware that the process is only temporary and should eventually adjust itself – there is therefore nothing to be gained by precipitating a confidence crisis in the currency. However, a recent body of literature on rational speculative bubbles suggests that it may be in the interests of rational agents to precipitate a crisis since there is a large opportunity for short-term profits. All these issues are themes which we take up in this book.[2]

The second problem with the general equilibrium approach to balance of payments disequilibria is that it pays insufficient attention to the causes of disequilibrium. The national income identity equation tells us only that *ex post* the deficit will show up as either an excess of investment over savings or alternatively government spending over taxation. In other words, national savings (the sum of $(S - I)$ and $(G - T)$) are insufficient. However, this does not necessarily imply that *ex ante* this resulted from too great a desire to consume. Instead national income could have fallen because of some exogenous shock (for example, a fall in demand for our exports). Using the traditional aggregate supply and aggregate demand diagram, we can explore further the impact of this. Assume the economy is initially at full employment (Yf) on the vertical part of the aggregate supply schedule. A negative shock to the economy which reduces our exports will cause the aggregate demand schedule to shift in to $AD^1$. Income falls and with a marginal propensity to consume of less than 1, consumption falls by less: a balance of payments deficit thus results. With full wage-price flexibility, the deficit could be corrected by a fall in wages and prices, thus restoring competitiveness. In terms of Figure 1.1, the aggregate supply schedule shifts downwards, restoring full employment. However, in a world of sticky wages and prices the aggregate supply schedule will not adjust and the deficit will persist. Since the deficit has not arisen because of individuals' desire to dissave, there is no presumption that it will automatically adjust and indeed a further cut in consumption is not the appropriate response. In such a situation there is an adjustment problem and the government may well wish to respond in order to seek to correct it.

The final problem that arises with the general equilibrium approach is that it ignores that fact that actors other than just rational individuals have a large role to play in international transactions. In particular, we can emphasise here the role played by governments and financial institutions. Financial institutions primarily act as intermediaries between those who wish to save and those who wish to borrow. However, they are also autonomous actors in their own right and will pursue their own interests and goals. Thus if they anticipate a depreciation/devaluation of the exchange rate, they can call on a large volume of funds which will make such an outcome self-fulfilling.[3]

The government may become concerned about the deficit and potential exchange rate movements for a number of reasons. They may fear a speculative bubble which could take the exchange rate away from the long-term fundamental value warranted by the competitive position of the country. With financial institutions (and also large multinational companies) becoming increasingly important, such an outcome is not unlikely. Additionally, exchange rate changes influence price expectations and thus

---

[2] For example, history tells us that individuals often take on more debt than they could reasonably repay and lending institutions do not always act to prevent overborrowing and we examine this in Chapters 8 and 9. The literature on rational bubbles and speculative crises is discussed in Chapters 3 and 4.

[3] We discuss this in some depth in Chapter 4.

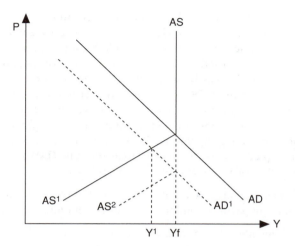

**Figure 1.1**   *An exogenous shock: a fall in demand for domestic exports*

may impinge on a variety of macroeconomic variables. Thus, for example, deprecia-
tion/devaluation is likely to cause expectations of price increases/greater inflation
with their consequent impact on wage claims. Finally, it may be necessary for the
government to react to the actions of other governments who may be unwilling to
allow the deficit to resolve itself naturally. In short, in a world comprising not just
atomised agents who have little individual impact on the balance of payments, but
also large actors such as governments, companies and financial institutions, there can
be no presumption that the balance of payments will be self-correcting. Thus the
government may not be indifferent about balance of payments disequilibria and may
be keen to initiate adjustment itself.[4]

Thus in a world characterised by problems of co-ordination, a number of actors
with potentially diverging interests, and a variety of market failures, the problem of
adjustment becomes a central concern of governments and more widely the international financial system. Different institutional structures address the problem of
uncertainty which arises in the real world through the adoption of varying rules of
the game or social norms. These rules or norms should not be seen as obstacles to the
operation of the market. Rather they are the means by which the uncertainty of free
markets is reduced and in this way they make the market work better. The chosen
institutions need to address a number of questions. In particular, how should adjustment be fostered and what role is there for the exchange rate? Given that balance of
payments problems are necessarily two-sided, that is there are at least two countries
involved, the question arises as to who should be responsible for adjustment. What
role is there for financial flows in financing imbalances whilst adjustment takes place
(the so-called recycling problem)? And, finally, how should more long-term imbalances associated with the development process be financed? Different types of
systems seek to deal with these questions in different ways. But before going on to
look in more detail at these issues and the form that international institutions take,
we turn now to examine the issue of international money, the provision of liquidity
and the role of financial flows.

---

[4] We discuss the methods by which adjustment may be undertaken later in the text.

*International money, liquidity and financial flows*

International money can be defined as the commodity or currency in which international transactions in goods, services and assets are undertaken. In fulfilling this role, it acts much like a nationally circulating money: it is a unit of account (for quoting prices in international trade); a medium of exchange thus eliminating the need for barter which is costly and inefficient); and a store of value.

As McKinnon (1979, p.3) argues, if a national currency is to become an international currency, then it needs to be convertible. The extent of its convertibility represents an example of the idea that institutions can try to impose different 'rules of the game', implying uncertainty is reduced to differing degrees depending on the rules adopted. The International Monetary Fund (IMF), for example, in Article VIII of its articles of agreement defines convertibility as:

> No member shall, without the approval of the Fund, impose restrictions on the making of payments and transfers for current international transactions . . .

> Each member shall buy balances of its currency held by another member if the latter, in requesting the purchase, represents:

> (i) that the balances to be bought have been recently acquired as the result of current transactions
> (ii) that their conversion is needed for making payments for current transactions . . .

> The buying member shall have the option to pay either in the currency of the member making the request or in gold. (Or, in practice, in an internationally acceptable currency such as United States dollars).
> (quoted in McKinnon, 1979, pp.4–5)

In other words, the IMF emphasises current account convertibility – the ability to convert national currency into other currencies for the purposes of trade in goods and services. The problem with this definition is that, whilst some capital account transactions may be allowed to finance current account trade, by and large, capital account transactions are not included. A broader definition of convertibility would thus grant all residents the freedom to buy and sell foreign currency in any quantity and for whatever purpose[5] – for current or capital account transactions.

Under what we called above the general equilibrium approach to the balance of payments, clearly full convertibility of national money is required. Otherwise, the debt build-up required to finance the desire to dissave would not be possible – free access to foreign currency is required for repayment when it becomes due. Individual agents can then conduct whatever transactions they wish – convertibility effectively allows all currencies to be equivalent to international money.

To confine our definition of international money simply to the issue of convertibility is to miss some of the essential characteristics of international money and some of the problems associated with its provision. As Laidler (1993) has argued, money is essentially a social institution: Robinson Crusoe did not require money and even when Man Friday made his appearance, money was still redundant. In other words, money requires at least three individuals (and three goods) before it can help to eliminate the costly inefficiencies of barter. As a social institution, money is subject to a

---

[5] We can note that it is not necessary that the rate at which foreign currency can be bought and sold is fixed – a narrower definition of convertibility might specify such a condition; a wider definition requires only that transactions be undertaken in a unified foreign exchange market (see McKinnon, 1979, p.6).

variety of social conventions and rules and these, as we shall see later in this chapter, have differed historically depending on the organisation of the international monetary system.

The need for social conventions and rules in respect to the provision of money (both nationally and internationally) derives, in part, from a number of market failures which are associated with its provision. Thus in order to understand more fully the problems with the provision of money at the international level, we need to examine these failures more closely.

De Grauwe (1989) points to a number of failures: the public good nature of money; the existence of economies of scale in its provision; and the role of confidence. We consider each of these in turn.

Firstly, money has to have the characteristic of a collective (or public) good – as we noted previously, the benefits of money derive from the fact that other individuals use it. The market, however, generally undersupplies collective goods because of the difficulty of getting individuals to pay voluntarily for its provision and at the same time, it is difficult to exclude those who have not paid. Usually collective goods are provided by some central authority which pays for their provision through general taxation. However, in the case of money, this need not be the case. To understand why, we need to introduce the concept of seigniorage. This is defined as the difference between the value of a particular coin or note and its production costs: a $1 bill, for example, costs considerably less than $1 to produce. Thus the producer of money gains monopoly profits and, in this way, the users of money can be made to more than cover the costs of its production.[6] Given the existence of these monopoly profits, however, there is a case for public rather than private provision.

This case for public provision is strengthened by the second market failure associated with the provision of money – it is subject to economies of scale. The more people who use a particular currency, the greater the utility that is derived since the opportunities for exchange between individuals increase. Thus most countries have moved from a system of competitive supply of money (with different currencies perhaps circulating in different regions) to the monopoly supply of money. For all the usual arguments about the potential inefficiencies of private monopolies, the state has normally taken on the role of the sole supplier of money in any economy. However, at the international level, there has never been a central provider of international money. Clearly the same benefits would be obtained – currency would become more useful to individual traders and, at the same time, the supplier would benefit from the monopoly profits (seigniorage). However, in spite of this, the supply of international money remains competitive.[7] De Grauwe (1989) gives two possible reasons. Firstly, there is no international government and hence no obvious central authority which could take over the supply.[8] Secondly, national governments still retain a monopoly over the supply of national currencies and this makes it difficult for an international currency to displace this. The consequences, however, of the continued

---

[6] For this to be true, money should pay a below market interest rate. In general notes and coins do not pay interest. In this way, De Grauwe (1989) argues, holders of money can be made to pay for its provision.

[7] We can note here that even with rival currencies the public sector of each economy whose currency is used internationally benefits from seigniorage.

[8] We can note here that Triffin's proposals in the 1960s (see, for example Triffin, 1968, for a resumé) went some way to establishing the principle that international money should be provided centrally, in his case, by the IMF. Recent moves towards monetary union in Europe can also be seen as attempts to get the benefits from one currency.

competitive supply of money at the international level is increased volatility and the potential for crises. The same phenomenon was observed at the national level before governments or central banks took over the central provision of money. For example in the UK commercial bills issues by a variety of companies (not necessary financial institutions) were used as money. If suppliers got into difficulties, then the value of these bills fell dramatically and exchange was frequently disrupted.[9] At the international level such disruptions take the form of changing actual exchange rates or expectations regarding future exchange rates which cause holders of international currencies to reappraise their portfolio composition.

The final problem associated with the provision of money identified by De Grauwe is the question of confidence. Ultimately individual agents in an economy are only willing to hold money if they believe that they will be able to exchange it at some time in the future for either a good, service or asset. Critical to this is the idea that money should act as a store of value and that individuals have confidence that the supplier will not do anything that might undermine its value. This could be achieved by guaranteeing that money can be exchanged into some commodity (the supply of which is beyond the control of the authorities) at a fixed price. Convertibility into other currencies is one way in which this could be achieved at the international level. However, there is a fundamental problem with such a commitment that has been identified in the literature on time inconsistency.[10] Assume a country seeks to build confidence in its currency by fixing the rate at which it can be exchanged into other currencies. The costs of doing this are that monetary policy can no longer be used to meet domestic aims.[11] At some point, however, there may be a benefit to the authorities from reneging on their commitment (for example, monetary policy could be used to respond to a national shock; alternatively there may be benefits from changing the exchange rate in response to an external shock). Rational, forward-looking agents will realise this potential benefit from cheating on the commitment and hence the commitment will lack credibility. Thus whilst confidence is crucial in both national and international spheres, it is difficult to achieve and periodic crises are thus likely to occur.

We can therefore conclude our discussion of international money by noting that the problems of supply necessitate a much greater role for national and possibly international institutions. As with adjustment, it is not simply a matter of allowing full convertibility and leaving individual agents to get on with their own decisions. Instead, various conventions and adherence to certain 'rules of the game' will be of paramount importance in determining the stability of the international monetary system.

Up till now we have been discussing the provision of an international means of payment. The concept of liquidity is broader than that of (international) money, although it can be argued that money represents absolute liquidity. National monetary systems comprise not only notes and coins but also other financial assets with differing degrees of liquidity as well as offering the potential for access to credit (i.e. borrowing). Liquidity is usually defined as the ease and cheapness with which

[9]  See, for example, Kindleberger (1984, Chapter 5).
[10]  See, for example, Kydland and Prescott (1977) and Barro and Gordon (1983).
[11]  We can think of this result as stemming from a simple Mundell–Fleming world with perfect capital mobility. The national money supply becomes completely endogenous if the authorities wish to maintain a fixed exchange rate.

financial assets can be converted into a means of payment which can be used to meet current liabilities or the ease with which agents can get access to a means of payment through borrowing.

At the international level, liquidity has traditionally be confined only to the level of international reserves held by national monetary authorities.[12] Indeed, government access to liquidity is crucially important internationally. At the national level, the government has no liquidity problems – they can always print money to meet their national obligations. However, internationally governments must be able to present foreign exchange to meet their obligations (balance of payments deficit) abroad unless, at least in theory, they allow the exchange rate to float. Williamson (see Milner, 1987, Ch. 5) goes beyond the government and defines international liquidity more broadly as the ability of a country to meet its international obligations or to finance a balance of payments deficit.[13] Williamson refers to this as a functional definition of international liquidity. We define it even more broadly to include liquid assets held by all agents (individual private agents, companies, financial institutions, or governments) in an economy. In this way, international liquidity is critically bound up with financial flows in the world economy: the way in which funds are recycled from surplus areas in the world economy to deficit areas; the role of speculative movements of capital; international portfolio transactions; etc.

We can identify a number of aspects to international liquidity. At a national level, an individual's (company's or government's) portfolio of assets can be said to become more liquid as assets with a longer maturity are exchanged for assets with a shorter maturity. Such a portfolio alteration can be thought of as vertical switching between maturities: the currency of denomination of the assets remains the same. Internationally, we can also introduce the concept of horizontal switching where an individual substitutes an asset of the same maturity but a different currency. In this case, liquidity could have increased, decreased or remained unaltered, depending on the currency now held and the composition of the agents's liabilities. With many currencies in the international system, some may be more liquid than others, with the thickness of the market determining the degree of liquidity. Indeed, horizontal switching is easer between those currencies that have a thicker market because this implies greater marketability of existing holdings as well as lower transactions costs associated with the sale or purchase of the holdings. Thus it is easier to alter the liquidity of a portfolio.

We can divide international liquidity sources into a number of branches, each of which have their associated types of international financial flows. These are illustrated in Figure 1.2. International liquidity can either be held privately (by international banks, multinational companies, private individuals etc) or officially (by the monetary authorities of the country concerned). It can be obtained from either official sources or private sources. Figure 1.2 suggests four possible combinations. One of these, however, is largely redundant: privately held – officially obtained liquidity does not play any role in the international monetary system and thus we can ignore this. The other three possibilities are, however, rather important.

---

[12] See, for example, Hirsch (1967) and Crockett (1977, p.112).

[13] For example, international liquidity can include the foreign exchange holdings of commercial banks, because they also settle international obligations.

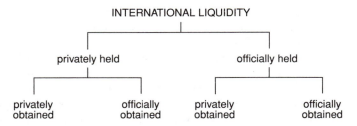

**Figure 1.2**  *Types of international liquidity*

With regard to the privately held – privately obtained liquidity, individuals, banks and firms are the main protagonists. Funds are obtained through the foreign exchange markets either from trade transactions or transactions in assets. In the past, governments have sought to buy up all this privately held international liquidity: they controlled its issue through exchange (or capital) controls. By the late 1970s, after the advent of floating exchange rates, exchange controls were scarcer or less strict among the major industrialised countries and private financial intermediation grew rapidly. As a consequence private holdings of privately obtained international liquidity increased dramatically, and, as we shall see later, this was associated with an increase in private financial flows.

The second category of international liquidity is that which is officially held but privately obtained. The growth of government borrowing in international capital markets was one of the major features of the post-1973 oil price shock. Many countries borrowed extensively to supplement their existing holdings of foreign exchange reserves and finance their current account deficits.

Finally, we have the more traditional measure of international liquidity: that of officially held and officially obtained international liquidity. This includes foreign currencies derived from balance of payments surpluses, reserves at the IMF, Special Drawing Rights (SDRs) and gold.

These various categories of international liquidity and financial flows will prove useful in our discussion of how different types of international systems deal with the problems of the provision of international liquidity and the question of recycling. Over time, the importance of each of these different categories has changed rapidly and drastically.

**Adjustment and international liquidity: various systems**

At the international level various different types of system deal with adjustment, liquidity and financial flows in differing ways. Before going on to examine that actual history of the international monetary system, it will be useful first to outline analytically the various kinds of system and how their associated institutions seek, in theory, to solve the adjustment problem and provide international liquidity. In doing so, there are a number of questions that we can usefully ask about any particular system. With respect to adjustment the critical questions are who is responsible and what techniques should be used to facilitate the removal of balance of payments disequilibria. With respect to liquidity there are the issues of which currency (currencies) is (are) used and whether this is achieved through coercion or through voluntary commitment (to use De Grauwe's (1989) distinction). With respect to both adjustment and liquidity, a crucial issue is that of symmetry. In other words, does a particular system lead to equivalent pressures being brought to bear both on deficit and surplus countries (in the case of adjustment) and on reserve centres and others (in the case of liquidity)?

We can identify four main systems that we will discuss in turn.[14]

  (i)   automatic mechanisms
 (ii)   the $(N-1)$ system
(iii)   a system relying on policy co-ordination and multilateral mechanism
 (iv)   monetary union.

We concentrate here on how each system should operate in theory. The reality of these different systems along with various criticisms that can be made is left until the historical section of this chapter.

*Automatic mechanisms*

There are two systems which can be described as automatic: a freely floating exchange rate system and a fully fixed commodity standard. We deal with each in turn.

Under a freely floating exchange-rate system, there should never be any balance of payments problems. Any disequilibrium leads to an automatic adjustment of exchange rates. We can illustrate this with reference to Figure 1.3 which shows the demand and supply for foreign exchange in any one country. The demand curve derives from the desire by domestic residents to purchase foreign goods, services or assets. Demand is negatively related to the exchange rate. A depreciation of the exchange rate (i.e. an increase in the domestic price of foreign exchange)[15] causes

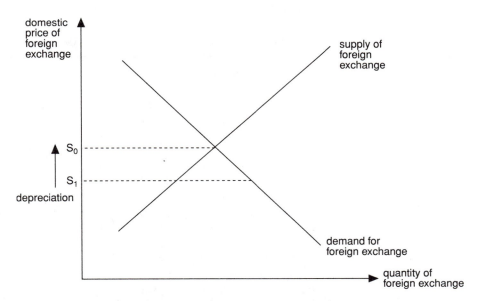

**Figure 1.3**  *Automatic adjustment with freely floating exchange rates*

---

[14]  These differing types of system have been identified by Llewellyn (1990).
[15]  Throughout the book the exchange rate is quoted as the domestic price of a unit of foreign currency. An increase in the exchange rate is therefore a depreciation of the domestic currency, whilst a decrease is an appreciation.

foreign goods etc to become more expensive in domestic terms and hence demand falls. The supply of foreign exchange arises from nonresidents demand for domestic goods, services and assets. A depreciation of the domestic currency causes domestic goods etc. to become cheaper abroad and hence demand increases – more foreign exchange thus becomes available as we move up the y-axis.

Assume the exchange rate is at $S_1$ – there is therefore an excess demand for foreign exchange. This is equivalent to a deficit on the balance of payments, since residents wish to purchase more goods etc. from abroad than nonresidents demand from the domestic country. The domestic price of foreign exchange therefore rises. This depreciation should make the country more competitive – demand for foreign goods etc. by residents falls, whilst demand for home goods from abroad increases. The result is automatic correction of the balance of payments. If the exchange rate is left freely floating, it should settle at $S_0$, that is, the balance of payments will be in equilibrium. Any exogenous shock which shifts the demand or supply schedules will simply cause the exchange rate to vary and equilibrium to be restored.

Liquidity in this system is unnecessary provided adjustment occurs immediately. International money, the currency in which international trade is generally conducted, is not explicitly specified. Presumably, given the advantages of having only one money, only a few currencies will be widely used as international means of payment. The point for our purposes here is that no specific currency is nominated as the international means of payment – instead it (they) simply emerge automatically.

The second type of automatic mechanism is the fully fixed commodity standard. The main characteristic of this system is that fiduciary money[16] circulating within any economy is backed by a particular commodity (for example, gold or silver). Additionally, the ratio of fiduciary money to reserves of the commodity are fixed and the monetary authorities guarantee free convertibility of circulating money into the commodity. Since all countries within the system set a fixed price between their national currencies and the commodity, in this way all national currencies are tied together: exchange rates are fixed. The potential for arbitrage ensures this and to see why it is useful to take an example. Assume we have two countries with currencies X and Y. Assume further that 1 unit of currency X is freely convertible into 1 unit of the commodity; whereas 2 units of currency Y are freely convertible into 1 unit of the commodity. The exchange rate between X and Y will be 1:2, that is, 1 unit of X equals 2 units of Y. What happens if the exchange rate is not 1:2? For example, assume it is 1:1. In this case there is the potential for profitable arbitrage. Residents of country X could take 1 unit of X, convert it into 1 unit of the commodity; ship the commodity to country 1 and exchange it for 2 units of Y which at an exchange rate of 1:1 can be converted into 2 units of X. They have therefore made a profit of 1 unit of X.[17] However, the action of selling Y and purchasing X will cause the exchange rate to change – the price of X in terms of Y will rise towards 1:2. Only when the exchange rate is 1:2 will there be no further opportunities for arbitrage.

In such a system, the commodity is essentially the international means of payment and of course because each national currency is freely convertible into the commodity effectively national currencies become potential international means of payment. Thus *de facto* in this system, the benefits of one international money are realised.

[16] That is, currency – notes and coins in circulation.
[17] We ignore transport costs for simplicity here.

If exchange rates are fixed, how are balance of payments disequilibria eliminated? As with freely floating exchange rates, the adjustment mechanism is automatic. Assume country X experiences an exogenous decline in the demand for its exports. A current account deficit then ensues. The monetary authorities in country X must settle this deficit by shipping the commodity to country Y. The reserves of the commodity in country X automatically fall, thereby necessitating a contraction of the money supply. With fully flexible prices, the fall in the money supply causes the price level to fall thus restoring country X's competitiveness and eliminating the balance of payments disequilibrium. In the surplus country, country Y, the opposite occurs. The inflow of the commodity causes the money supply to increase. Thus adjustment, in theory, is two-sided – the system is symmetric in this respect. We can note that if country X does not allow its money supply to fall to maintain the fixed ratio, then its reserves of the commodity will be depleted and this could spark off a confidence crisis which would lead residents of country X to rush to convert their holdings of national money into the commodity. By contrast, the surplus country can sterilise for longer and hence prevent a rise in its money supply. Such a strategy is clearly against the 'rules of the game' which state that there should be a fixed ratio between reserves of the commodity and the money supply. The system will remain credible only provided the 'rules' are adhered to by both countries.

## (N−1) System

In a world of N countries, one country – usually referred to as the Nth country – is at the heart of this system which in many ways can be seen as a development of the commodity standard outlined above. The Nth currency is convertible at a fixed price into a commodity such as gold.[18] All other currencies are fixed to the Nth currency. Thus in this system there are (N−1) exchange rates. Fixing each currency to the Nth currency ensures that all other currencies will be fixed to each other. As with the commodity standard, arbitrage ensures that all exchange rates are compatible. An example of how the arbitrage process works is given in Box 1.2.

Given that exchange rates are fixed in this system, it is interesting to ask how adjustment occurs. As with a commodity standard, certain 'rules of the game' have to be adhered to if the system is to operate credibly. However, here the rules are different since there is no automatic connection between the money supply in any one country and the commodity backing the Nth currency. Thus countries with balance of payments disequilibria must undertake policies to secure adjustment. For the deficit countries, the presumption is that they will instigate deflationary policies. The problem of course is that if prices and wages are sticky then the cost may be in terms of increased unemployment (something which could also be true under the gold standard). Similarly surplus countries are expected to reflate. The problem with such 'rules' is that whilst it is difficult for the deficit countries to avoid adjustment, the surplus ones feel much less pressure. Deficit countries could try to forestall adjustment by sterilising the impact of the fall in their foreign exchange reserves. Falling foreign exchange reserves automatically leads to a decline in the domestic money supply since the monetary base has both a domestic and a foreign component. Sterilisation involves the monetary authorities buying domestic bonds, so that the falling

[18] Usually only the monetary authorities have the right to convert their holding of the Nth currency into the commodity. In this way, the (N−1) system seeks to economise on holdings of the commodity and instead force private citizens to hold the Nth currency as international money. We can note here that the European Monetary System is often known as an (N−1) system although the DM (the Nth currency) is not convertible into any commodity.

---

## BOX 1.2. Arbitrage and Exchange Rates in the (N−1) System

Assume that the US dollar is the Nth currency and that both the UK and Germany fix their exchange rate to the dollar. This implies a level for the sterling–Deutschmark exchange rate. Take the following example: Germany maintains its exchange rate between $0.49 and $0.51 per DM; the UK maintains sterling between $1.98 and $2.02. This implies automatically that the DM/£ exchange rate should lie between £0.243 and £0.258 per DM. We derive this by asking what £/DM rate is consistent with the dollar parities when they are at their extremes.

For the lower bound:

$$£/DM = \$/DM.£/\$ = 0.49(1/2.02) = £0.243 \text{ per DM}$$

For the upper bound:

$$£/DM = \$/DM.£/\$ = 0.51(1/1.98) = £0.258 \text{ per DM}$$

To understand why this should be true, let us assume that the dollar is trading at $2.00 per pound and at $0.50 per DM (that is the official parities are at their central rate). Assume further that the £/DM exchange rate falls to £0.20 per DM (outside the limits derived above). In this case, there are opportunities for profitable arbitrage (assuming for simplicity in what follows no trading costs). If we take $100 and convert it to sterling, we receive £50 (100(1/2.00)). This can then be converted to Deutschmarks at the rate of £0.20 giving us 250DM. These DM can then be converted back to dollars at the official parity of $0.50 giving us $125 dollars and hence a profit of $25.

Thus commercial banks and other arbitrageurs in the currency markets would undertake exactly this transaction. The result, of course, is that the £/DM exchange rate would rise towards £0.25 as sterling is sold and Deutschmarks purchased. At this exchange rate, there are no arbitrage profits to be made. Thus in this way only two official parities (N−1 = 3−1 = 2) need be quoted officially. Arbitrage will ensure that the others are consistent.

---

foreign component of the monetary base is offset by a rising domestic component. However, sterilisation for deficit countries cannot continue indefinitely. Eventually their reserves will become very scarce as they continually finance their deficits whilst maintaining their exchange rate fixed to the Nth currency. At some point therefore adjustment will have to follow. Surplus countries, by contrast, can more easily build up their reserves and sterilise the impact (through selling domestic bonds) without being forced to adjust.[19] Thus an (N−1) system has a tendency to produce an adjustment asymmetry – it is the deficit countries that often bear the costs of adjustment disproportionately. It is here that the (N−1) system is slightly different from the gold standard. In the latter, adjustment in both countries was automatic, in theory, because of the fixed ratio between the money supply and reserves of the commodity. Under the (N−1) system, no such fixed ratio exists and the method through which deflation and reflation occur have, in practice (as we shall see), often been unspecified, leaving greater room for discretion.

---

[19] Sterilisation in surplus countries has to end when the government is unable to sell any more government bonds to the public.

The Nth country is in a special position and this creates a second asymmetry in the system. It should abstain from intervention in the foreign exchange markets – it is the responsibility of the $(N-1)$ countries to maintain their chosen exchange rate with the Nth country. This has important implications for the balance of payments of the Nth country. Since the balance of payments of the world as a whole must balance, the Nth country must accept whatever aggregate balance of payments position the other $(N-1)$ countries wish to have. This avoids the incompatibility between balance of payments targets which might otherwise arise. Thus if the rest of the world is running a surplus in aggregate, the Nth country must run a deficit. The deficit is financed by the accumulation of the Nth currency by central banks in the rest of the world. This occurs automatically as a result of intervention by the rest of the world to prevent their currencies from appreciating relative to the Nth currency. This second asymmetry, the so-called reserve currency centre asymmetry, effectively allows the Nth country to finance its balance of payments deficits by issuing liabilities on itself.[20]

This brings us to the issue of the provision of international money and liquidity and the special role that the Nth country plays here. The Nth currency is effectively the international means of exchange. It is the currency in which Central Banks in the $(N-1)$ countries are most likely to hold their reserves so as to facilitate intervention to keep their exchange rate fixed to the Nth currency at the agreed parity.

McKinnon (1979) notes that this implies that the Nth country should have certain desirable features. Firstly, the Nth country should be large. Given that the Nth country has to accept whatever balance of payments position is compatible with the other $(N-1)$ countries, largeness will prevent that balance of payments position from becoming overwhelming. Were the balance of payments disequilibrium of the Nth country too large, then it would have a greater impact on its economy and its willingness to remain passive might be called into question. Thus a large, fairly closed, economy is a good candidate for the Nth country.

A second important and related feature of the Nth currency is that it should be acceptable. As we noted above the Central Banks in the $(N-1)$ countries will prefer to hold their reserves in the Nth currency. Acceptability requires therefore that Central Banks be confident that the Nth currency will not lose its value. Should a confidence crisis arise then large conversions of the Nth currency into the commodity will ensue and this will lead to the collapse of the system if external holdings of the Nth currency exceed the value of the commodity held by the Nth country's monetary authorities. Acceptability will be promoted by the Nth country maintaining low inflation.

It is not only Central Banks which derive benefit from using the Nth currency to conduct international transactions. McKinnon (1979) also notes that commercial banks have a lot to gain from the existence of a vehicle currency. Commercial banks will conduct most foreign exchange transactions between the $(N-1)$ currencies through the Nth currency rather than directly. The reason for this is simple. The larger and thicker[21] are foreign exchange markets, the lower are transactions costs

---

[20] We should recall, however, that these liabilities can be exchanged into the commodity by Central Banks in the other (N–1) countries. Additionally, note that this buildup of the Nth currency with other central banks will need to be sterilised if it is not to be reflationary and hence relieve the deficit in the Nth country.

[21] A thick market is one where lots of transactions take place.

and hence the difference between the buy and sell rates. Thus the financing of trade between two of the (N−1) countries will be cheaper if conducted through the Nth currency. Only in a small number of cases will trade between two (N−1) countries be large enough to warrant a separate foreign exchange market (McKinnon gives the example of trade between France and Germany being large enough to support a Deutschmark–French franc foreign exchange market).

Thus to conclude, in the (N−1) system the Nth country is at the heart of the system. For this reason, the system is often referred to as a hegemonic system. But the crucial role played by the Nth country, or hegemonic leader, implies that its economic condition is paramount. In other words, if the Nth country does not remain economically strong, then this system will come under increasing pressure which may eventually lead to its collapse. We discuss this in more detail when we examine the Bretton Woods system.

*Policy co-ordination and multilateral mechanisms of exchange rate management*

The above systems are either highly structured (in the case of the commodity standard and the (N−1) system) or completely free (in the case of floating exchange rates). The third way of organising the international monetary system involves a more intermediate stance. Into this category fall various attempts that have been made internationally to co-ordinate policy and manage exchange rates. Indeed, such an approach to the international monetary system has to varying degrees been common in the post-1973 period.

Crucial to the operation of what we might call a 'managed international monetary system' is the choice of exchange rate regime. This has important implications for adjustment and ultimately the degree of policy co-ordination which will be required. To understand why the issues of exchange rate regime, adjustment and policy co-ordination are related, we have to examine the causes of balance of payments disequilibria.

Balance of payments disequilibria arise from two main sources: either exogenous shocks or incompatible policies pursued by individual countries. We can look at each of these in turn. Exogenous shocks may not lead to balance of payments disequilibria if they have a symmetric impact of all countries. However, more often than not, exogenous shocks are also asymmetric. That is, they have differing impacts on different countries. An obvious example of an exogenous shock which has an asymmetric impact is a rise in oil prices. Oil exporting countries experience a rise in income and usually a current account surplus; oil importing countries, by contrast, experience a decline in income and a current account deficit. Thus the impact of an exogenous and asymmetric shock is directly felt in large balance of payments imbalances which must be adjusted.

The second source of balance of payments disequilibria is incompatible national policies. If a number of countries are pursuing deflationary policies in order to reduce inflation, then a country which is unwilling, for whatever reason, to follow and which seeks instead to reflate its economy (in the face of a world-wide recession) will experience a worsening of its trade balance with the rest of the world. This comes about as the decline in income in the majority of countries tends to reduce their demand for imports, whereas the reflating country by expanding economic activity will increase its demand for imports.

In theory, the more flexible the exchange rate, the more easily countries can respond to asymmetric shocks and the greater is the opportunity for individual countries to pursue their own policies. Balance of payments disequilibria are eliminated through movements of the exchange rate (as we described when discussing fully floating exchange rates). However, for reasons which will be explored in depth in Chapters 2 to 4, flexible exchange rates frequently do not allow adjustment without cost and governments often wish to manage exchange rates. Under these circumstances, there is a need for some form of policy co-ordination. This can either take the form of a co-ordinated response to the various asymmetric shocks which hit the world economy or attempts to come to some agreement on the economic priorities to which policy should be directed.

The role of international liquidity (or financial flows) in a system of policy co-ordination is to help to smooth the adjustment process. It is inevitable that disequilibria will persist in the short run. Thus to ensure that individual countries are not forced to undertake corrective measures independently, liquidity must be available to finance these disequilibria. How exactly this is organised and the extent to which countries rely on private sources of liquidity (such as the international capital markets) are issues that must be addressed by participating countries.

Our discussion here has been rather brief. The intention has been to introduce some of the themes which will be recurring throughout this book. The question of exchange rate management is tackled more fully in Chapter 4 and the issue of policy co-ordination is taken up again in Chapters 5 and 7.

*Monetary union*

The final method of organising the international monetary system which we want to introduce here is that of a full-blown monetary union. The key feature of this system is that individual currencies are eliminated and a common currency is adopted. The implications of this are discussed in depth in Chapter 5, where we discuss the issue of European monetary union. Here, we can make two general points.

The first relates to the issue of international money and liquidity. With only one currency circulating within the union, clearly the problem of what should act as 'international money' is solved. The union currency will now have some legal status in the same way as national currencies have in individual countries. Thus the benefits of one currency which we discussed above will be realised.

The second point relates to the issue of adjustment. Within a monetary union, balance of payments disequilibria no longer exist, at least in their usual manifestation. Instead, balance of payments problems become regional problems, topics which fall outside the usual boundaries of international finance. However, we discuss these issues in greater depth in Chapter 5 where we consider European monetary co-operation.

**The systems in practice: a history of the international financial system**

A brief glance at the history of the international monetary system illustrates the operation of a number of the systems (or at least variants on the systems) which we identified before. There we presented some theoretical analysis of how different systems are supposed to work. In reality, of course, the practice of a system rarely followed its theory, illustrating the lesson that all systems rely on confidence, the rules of the game being adhered to and compromises being found. Thus, by examining the history of the international financial system we can assess the strengths and weaknesses of each type of system. The conclusion that emerges from such an examination is that the success of a particular system depends crucially on the international institutional structure designed to support the system and on the effectiveness of the various institutions in ensuring that countries stick to the 'rules of the game'.

*The gold standard*

The gold standard, which operated fully from 1870 to 1914 and then for a short period in the 1920s, is an example of one of the two automatic mechanisms we discussed above, namely the commodity standard (the other being flexible exchange rates). The pre-World War I era of the gold standard is referred to as the period of the 'classical gold standard',[22] when, it is frequently alleged, the gold standard was working in its textbook fashion. By contrast, the second phase of the gold standard, that in the inter-war period, is often called the 'managed gold standard', reflecting the fact that a number of the 'rules of the game' were being clearly flouted.

We raise here the question of whether the gold standard ever operated according to its textbook version. We begin therefore by outlining how the gold standard was supposed to operate. We then move on to examine its operation and breakdown. Finally, we end with an assessment of the calls for its return as a means of ensuring stability in the international monetary system.

As we noted above, the gold standard operated like a commodity standard where gold was the commodity which stood at the heart of the system. Each country fixed the price of gold. In the case where fiduciary money circulated, this was the price at which fiduciary currency was converted into gold.[23] In the UK the price of an ounce of gold was set at £3 17s 10½d.; in the US it was $20.67. Given these two national prices, arbitrage kept the dollar–sterling exchange rate at $4.867.[24] Thus, in this way, gold could be seen as the anchor of the system and convertibility ensured that exchange rates between countries remained fixed.

In theory, gold also had a central role as international money. In other words, all international payments were made in gold and balance of payments disequilibria were settled in gold. Given the fixed relationship between the national money supply and gold reserves held by the monetary authorities, adjustment was supposed to occur automatically.

For this automatic adjustment mechanism to operate two conditions were required.[25] Firstly, prices and wages had to be fully flexible. The automatic decline in the money supply following a current account deficit was intended to lower wages and prices, thus improving the competitiveness of the country. However, if wages and prices were sticky, then the result would merely be a decline in economic activity and unemployment. Secondly, the monetary authorities had to stick to the 'rules of the game' and not sterilise the effect of any balance of payments disequilibrium. The authorities can sterilise under the gold standard by merely failing to alter the money supply in circulation as gold reserves alter. To take the example of a balance of payments deficit, the outflow of gold from the deficit country should have led the monetary authorities to reduce the money supply. If they did not, then clearly the deficit continued.

---

[22] See, for example, Bordo (1981). The managed gold standard is often also called the gold bullion standard (see, for example, Cooper, 1982). The difference between the two is that in the gold standard proper, gold coins circulate nationally as a medium of exchange. In the gold bullion standard gold coins do not circulate, although the monetary authorities still stand ready to convert fiduciary money to gold at the fixed price.

[23] The case where notes and coins circulated instead of gold is often referred to as the Gold Bullion Standard.

[24] A description of the arbitrage mechanism and how it operated appears earlier.

[25] Triffin (1964) argues that both these conditions held much less after World War I. Firstly, wages and prices became increasingly sticky as a result of the growing strength of trade unions. Secondly, governments sterilised actively. The first of these points is debatable since unemployment did seem to move around a lot even in the pre-1914 period.

The benefit of adhering strictly to the 'rules of the game' was greater stability of the economy. In particular, it was argued that the gold standard prevented inflation because the money supply was controlled via the link with gold.[26] Moreover, there was little room for discretionary monetary policy, provided the monetary authorities did not sterilise. As Cooper (1982, p.4) argues the great benefit of the gold standard was supposed to be in terms of improved economic performance:

> The idealized gold standard as it appears in textbooks conveys a sense of automaticity and stability – a self-correcting mechanism with minimum human intervention, which assured rough stability of prices and balance in international payments.

It is by now largely recognised that the reality of the gold standard was somewhat different from this textbook story.[27] There are three main points which come out of the literature: firstly, did gold assume the role it was supposed to as an international means of payment; secondly, did the monetary authorities act as described by the theory; and, finally, were wages and prices flexible. We address each of these in turn.

Firstly, there is the question of how central a role gold played as an international means of payment. Both silver and fiduciary money circulated nationally even during the period of the classical gold standard. Triffin (1964) provides some estimates of the growth of credit money, which he argues was crucial in offsetting the fluctuations in the money supply had countries relied solely on gold. But it was not just at the national level that gold did not have its pivotal central role. At the international level, payments imbalances were increasingly settled through the use of reserve currencies (chiefly sterling, but also French francs and Deutschmarks). Triffin (1964, pp.43, 45) notes that capital flows played a large role in financing the current account deficit of the US, Australia, Canada and other 'developing countries'. These flows originated from the UK and, to a lesser extent, Germany and France. Moreover, these capital movements tended to be cyclical.[28] Capital importing countries tended to experience a drying up of capital inflows in bad times and this tended to contribute to economic instability.

Lindert (1969) has undertaken a major study of the composition of reserve holdings and capital flows in the period 1900–1913.[29] He argues that there are a number of reasons why currencies were more popular as a means of international payments even during the classical gold standard. Firstly, holdings of foreign currencies earn interest in contrast to gold. This makes foreign currencies more attractive to monetary authorities as a means of holding their reserves. Secondly, transport costs are lower if currencies are used to meet international obligations. Finally, it was thought to be more difficult to accumulate gold than it was to lose it. Hence if a country financed its deficit through foreign exchange holdings, then it could keep its gold reserves intact. For these reasons, currencies became increasingly important during the period of the classical gold standard.

[26] We can note that the theory of the gold standard has little to say about the implications of random increases in the gold supply as new discoveries are unearthed. Indeed, the implicit assumption of supporters is that the gold supply increase slowly allowing an accommodation of economic growth.
[27] Relatively recent studies of the gold standard include Triffin, 1964; Lindert, 1969; Bordo, 1981; Cooper, 1982 and Panic, 1992.
[28] We can note here that we shall see the same phenomenon of cyclicality of capital movements when we examine the large flows of private capital which occurred in the 1970s.
[29] See also Bordo (1981) and Panic (1992, pp. 69–80).

Sterling was the predominant currency (especially in Latin America and Asia), reflecting the dominant position of Britain in the world economy. However, on continental Europe the franc and the Mark were becoming increasingly important. Thus, although there were some fluctuations throughout the period (mainly associated with financial crises, which decreased the attractiveness of holding currencies), foreign currency holdings became more and more popular. Gold could hardly be said to have played its central role as international liquidity, even during the heyday of the gold standard (pre–World War I).

The second way in which the reality of the gold standard differed from the theory was with respect to the role of the monetary authorities (or central banks). The textbook story suggests that the monetary authorities should have acted passively, allowing the money supply to alter in response to the balance of payments situation. In other words, they were not supposed to undertake any sterilisation, but instead maintain the fixed ratio of money supply to gold. Panic (1992) notes, however, that several countries with current account deficits experienced persistent increases in their money supply and, more generally, money supply changes were unrelated to the balance of payments position. Triffin (1964) notes that sterilisation was common before 1914. Moreover, whilst the textbook story would suggest that interest rates should be negatively correlated,[30] in reality they were strongly positively correlated. This resulted partly from the tendency for central banks to manipulate interest rates to influence capital flows (in much the same way as they might nowadays). Triffin (1964) notes that the Bank of England were particularly adept at controlling international capital flows and generally had very little need for gold flows to finance any deficits. By contrast, the capital importing countries had much less ability to influence capital inflows and were highly dependent instead on the ease of monetary conditions in the international financial centres: when finance was easily available, deficits could be financed; when monetary conditions at the centre were tight, deficit countries were forced to adjust.

The third point about the operation of the gold standard relates to the issue of price and wage adjustment. We saw previously, the central role played by this means of adjustment in the textbook version of the gold standard. Triffin (1964) and Panic (1992, pp.62–3), however, argue that price levels in different countries tended to move in parallel. If the textbook version is correct, then we might expect them to be negatively correlated, since deficit countries should experience falling prices and surplus countries rising prices. Moreover, wage adjustments were also highly correlated and moreover tended to be small (Panic, 1992, p.55). Thus it is debatable as to whether competitiveness was restored in practice through changes in wages and prices.

Thus the gold standard of reality was rather different from that of the textbook. But what can we say about the supposed benefits of the gold standard. Were the benefits realised? This is important since many of those who wish to see a return to the gold standard argue that it will help to bring stability to the international economy. Stability is usually defined in terms of price and output stability. We can think of long-run stability (a flat trend for prices, for example) or short-run stability (which represents fluctuations around the trend). The gold standard was supposed to

---

[30] This arises from the fact that balance of payment disequilibria were supposed to lead to the money supply increasing (and hence interest rates decreasing) in surplus countries and vice versa in deficit countries. See also Panic (1992).

promote both types of stability. Bordo (1981) examines the record on price stability in the US and the UK. The UK was effectively on a gold standard (at a national level) from 1821. Bordo argues that if we plot the wholesale price index from 1821 to 1914 then it indicates that prices fell slightly by 0.4% per annum. Within the period, there were some large fluctuations, in response to changes in the supply of gold (new discoveries etc.). The US, which went on a gold standard in 1834, experienced a similar pattern. Bordo (1981) thus concludes that over the long-term the price level was largely stabilised during the gold standard – the trend was a flat one over a long period. Moreover, Bordo believes that agents at the time largely expected prices to be stable and hence would be more willing to enter into long-term contracts. Bordo cites additional evidence on output stability and unemployment and concludes that the gold standard also provided real stability (although he does concede that the Bretton Woods system which we discuss below has the best record on growth and unemployment).

Cooper's (1982, p.7) evidence contradicts these findings: 'price stability was not attained, either in the short run or in the long run, either during the period of the gold standard proper [1870–1914] or over a longer period during which gold held dominant influence [from early 19th century]'. In the long run, the argument that the period of the gold standard led to price stability depends crucially on the two years chosen for comparison. For example, Cooper notes that if the years 1822, 1856, 1877 and 1915 are chosen for the US, then the price level does indeed appear to be unchanged. Between those dates, however, large fluctuations are observed and one can construct long periods of either upward or downward price movements depending on the dates chosen. Furthermore, Cooper argues that it is short-run price instability which is the most costly, since this leads to people confusing relative price movements with absolute price movements. This can be better measured by looking at the variability of prices around their trend. Evidence from both the US and the UK suggests that the public did not expect prices to be stable. Cooper reaches this conclusion by examining the trend in long-term interest rates. If prices are expected to be stable, then long-term interest rates should be negatively correlated with the price level: a current price level higher than the 'norm' would lead to expectations of a fall in the price level and hence long-term interest rates should be falling. Instead, Cooper finds a positive correlation between long-term interest rates and prices (see Cooper, (1982) Fig. 2, p.12).

Triffin (1964) is likewise critical of the conclusion that the gold standard promoted price stability. He points out that fluctuations of between 30% and 50% were not uncommon. He also notes that the choice of start and end date is important and suggests that it is best to examine the price index from one peak to another *or* one trough to another. Employing this method he argues that the cumulative decline in prices over the whole century was 44% – in other words, a pronounced downward trend can be detected over the long term.

This lack of price stability either over the long term or the short term can perhaps be traced to fluctuations in the supply of gold. Cooper (1982), for example, provides evidence on the monetary gold supplies. He argues that the evidence suggests that supplies of monetary gold were partly influenced by the demand for nonmonetary gold and partly by changes in the supply of gold. For example, the gold discoveries in the 1850s in the US and Australia caused the gold stock to double. Table 1.1 indicates the variability of the stock of monetary gold.

*Table 1.1*    Percentage change in monetary gold stock

| Year | percentage change |
|------|-------------------|
| 1801–1839 | 18 |
| 1840–1849 | 13 |
| 1850–1859 | 88 |
| 1860–1869 | 30 |
| 1870–1879 | 17 |
| 1880–1889 | 11 |
| 1890–1899 | 35 |
| 1900–1909 | 46 |
| 1910–1919 | 37 |
| 1920–1929 | 22 |
| 1930–1939 | 37 |
| 1940–1949 | 30 |
| 1950–1959 | 17 |
| 1960–1969 | 3 |
| 1970–1979 | −4 |

*Source*: Cooper (1982, Table 3)

However, Cooper notes a very long lag between changes in the monetary gold stock and changes in the price level. He argues that this might be explained by a number of factors. First, the public might have been unaware of the magnitude of the increase in the gold supplies. Secondly, real output and trade might have increased thus breaking the quantity theory link between money and prices. Finally, the monetary stock was not just composed of gold, in particular, silver was also circulating as money. This last point brings us to Triffin's (1964) analysis. He argues that while gold discoveries played their part in explaining price movements, it is also necessary to examine the role of bank credit during the 19th century. At the beginning of the 19th century bank deposits accounted for about one third of the total money; by 1913, they were about nine tenths. Triffin gathers some tentative figures on monetary growth and the growth rates of its various components (gold, silver and bank credit). He argues that the evidence suggests that bank credit (and silver to some extent during the first half of the 19th century) helped to smooth monetary growth – had monetary growth been dependent solely on monetary gold stocks, then the fluctuations and hence the potential for instability would have been even greater.

Thus, what can we conclude about the success or otherwise of the gold standard and the pre-world war international monetary system? It certainly seems to be the case that the gold standard did not operate as the textbook theory suggested it would. Thus we have to be careful when assessing the reasons why it did not bring about the supposed benefits. This may have been because the textbook model was never imposed. However, it is perhaps more likely that outcomes would have been worse had the textbook model operated as theory suggests. Panic (1992), for example, argues that deficit countries did rather better under the actual gold standard than we might have expected precisely because practice departed from the theory. He argues that had the gold standard been run according to textbook principles, then deficit countries could easily have stagnated in the face of wage inflexibility. Instead, he argues, capital flows (especially in the form of long-term investment) as well as international migration, factors which do not figure in the theory, helped to prevent stagnation. In this respect banks in the City of London played a very important role. They essentially recycled the surpluses, from those countries such as the UK with surpluses on their current accounts, to deficit countries.[31] Triffin (1964) concurs and concludes that much of what occurred before 1913 was accidental rather than planned. The increases in gold production were completely random, relying as they did on new discoveries. The development of a large role for commercial banking and capital flows was also largely unplanned. Yet such institutional development had a crucial role to play in supporting much pre-1913 trade and development.

Our conclusion about the working of the gold standard is not only of historical interest, but also has some contemporary relevance. There are still now calls for a return to the gold standard, where the period is held up as something of a 'golden age' of the international monetary system.[32] The argument is that the gold standard brings discipline to monetary policy because of the need to back money creation by gold (or indeed some other commodity). We have shown here, however, that there never was a 'golden age' of the gold standard. Moreover, the role of international capital flows and the potential and active use of sterilisation indicate that the gold standard can be just as discretionary as monetary policy in our modern fiduciary system. The gold standard *per se* does not lead necessarily to the adoption of rules and hence for that reason a return to the gold standard will not necessarily bring greater credibility to the monetary authorities of any country. As Cooper (1982, p.45) concludes:

> these proposals [for a return to the gold standard or some form of commodity standard], taken together, raise the interesting philosophical question of why one should think that experts are more clever at devising operational, nondiscretional monetary regimes than they are at monetary management within a discretionary regime. If the desire for a nondiscretionary regime is really simply another way – misguided, as shown above, in the case of gold – of assigning priority above all others to the objective of price stability in the management of monetary policy, that can be done directly by instructing the Federal Reserve unambiguously to take whatever action is necessary to ensure price stability. If collectively we are ambivalent about that priority, that is the principal source of the problem, not the nature of the regime.

In other words, the gold standard as it operated in reality did not and does not provide any solution to the problem of monetary rules and credibility. If a government is not credible under the present regime, then it is unlikely that another regime such as the gold standard offers any panacea for immediate credibility.

Finally, we can note that the gold standard relied to a large extent on the hegemony of the British economy (see Brett, 1983, pp.29–39). The gold standard was suspended during World War I and attempts to return to it in the post-war period proved disastrous. This was partly the result of the fact that gold standard was restored with hugely misaligned exchange rates. But it was also the result of the related point, namely the decline in British hegemony. What the history of the gold standard teaches us is that even the supposed automatic methods of running the

---

[31] A point of interest which provides a parallel with the later period in the 1970s when banks were heavily involved in international lending is that many of the loans granted at the beginning of the century (especially to Latin America) were in default by the 1930s.

[32] See Cooper (1982) for a discussion of some of these proposals.

international financial system were crucially reliant on the strength of the institutions involved in their day-to-day running. In this respect the role played by the Bank of England and also private banks in the City of London were crucial to the reasonably smooth functioning of the gold standard as it was implemented in practice.[33] In particular, it was these institutions which provided much of the finance which allowed countries in the early stages of industrialisation to run continuous current account deficits without this being deflationary for their economies. Thus when the British economy began to decline and along with it the influence which the British had on the world economy and the role of sterling as an international currency, so the mechanisms that were designed to facilitate international transactions and a smooth functioning world economy tended to disintegrate.

*The inter-war period*     The lessons of the inter-war period are simple: the absence of co-operation and agreement about how the international monetary system should be organised has disastrous consequences for the economic health of individual countries. Whilst the causes of the 1930s depression are clearly complex and it is beyond the scope of analysis of this book to go into them, it is generally recognised that some form of international co-operation between the major players (UK, US and France) would have helped to bring a more speedy end to the depressed level of economic activity. Essentially we can identify three major attempts to restore order to the international monetary system during this period.[34] The first was the 1922 Conference at Genoa where the essential question dominating the discussion was whether a return to the gold standard was possible and indeed desirable. The second set of negotiations occurred in 1933 with the aim of determining whether there was a desire for international co-operation to stem the tide of competitive depreciations and rising tariffs. Finally, there was the so-called tripartite agreement between the UK, US and France in 1936 which laid down some general and rather vague principles regarding international co-operation but which nonetheless might be seen as the first tentative steps towards the new international monetary agreement of Bretton Woods which followed World War II.

At the 1922 conference in Genoa, the UK was keen to negotiate the restoration of the gold standard. The UK proposed a return to the gold exchange standard (at the pre-war parity of $4.86), albeit in a slightly different form – gold coins would no longer circulate and all UK gold would be centralised at the Bank of England. Internationally, it was proposed that only a few countries would maintain their reserves in gold – instead, the desire was that countries would keep their reserves in liquid claims on the reserve centres (UK, US, France and perhaps Germany). The aim of this proposal was to conserve gold stocks – trade would be financed by international capital flows. As we have seen, this was essentially how the pre-war gold standard had operated in practice.

The US, however, was highly sceptical about these proposals. It argued instead for a need to stabilise the European countries before any return to gold would be

---

[33] An interesting account of the power of the City of London and the rise of US finance during the inter-war period is given in Chernow (1990). Whilst this book is essentially a history of the Morgan Bank (and its various offshoots), it provides a fascinating account of the central role played by private bankers in controlling the international financial system at the turn of the century.

[34] The account which follows draws heavily from Clarke's two Princeton Studies which provide a comprehensive account of the monetary system in the inter-war period (see Clarke, 1973; 1977). Eichengreen (1990) also provides an interesting and detailed account of the period. See additionally Yeager (1966).

possible. Thus Norman Strong, head of the Federal Reserve Bank of New York, proposed an alternative stabilisation scheme which would manage gold flows and help to provide participating countries with access to international liquidity (see Clarke, 1973, p.16).

Neither of these plans were accepted and thus the international monetary system was left largely unregulated. The failure stemmed essentially from lack of agreement regarding German reparations and the repayment of the large amount of government debt that had accumulated during the war. It was hoped that a loan to Germany could be organised which would essentially allow Germany to meet its reparations payments. Disagreement over debts and reparations essentially hampered the stabilisation and reconstruction attempts of France and Germany. Germany was declared in default in 1922 and 1923 and as a result the Mark went into free fall. This led to the introduction of a stabilisation plan in Germany which was successful and this paved the way for a loan in 1924. The UK returned to the gold standard in 1925 at the pre-war parity. France finally completed its stabilisation programme (the Poincaré programme) in 1928 and returned to gold.[35]

Thus the gold standard was restored, albeit rather later than the UK had initially wanted. The lack of co-ordination in the return to gold, however, was to prove its undoing. The UK returned to gold at its pre-war parity. However, the continental European currencies were much depreciated following crisis and stabilisation. The result was that UK growth was severely curtailed by an overvalued exchange rate. Indeed Cooper (1982, p.20) concludes that the main lesson from the restoration of the gold standard was the strain that 'wrong' exchange rates can put on the international financial system, a lesson that has often been repeated in international monetary relations, not least most recently with the UK and the European Monetary System.

By 1933 the world economy was in severe depression and the UK had come off gold. Clearly all countries would have benefited again from some co-operation over economic policy, in particular to stem the competitive depreciations[36] and growth in protectionism, but again attempts at negotiating over restoring order to the international monetary system failed. Clarke (1973) identifies a number of causes for this failure to secure an agreement. Firstly, he argues that countries were acting in a highly short-termist and insular manner. They were unwilling to enter into an international agreement that might reduce their potential for manoeuvre with respect to domestic policies. Secondly, the war debt issue was still problematic. Whilst reparations had been stopped in 1931, the US was still reluctant to write off the war debts of European countries mainly because of opposition from the US public. European countries, however, saw this as a necessary step to help to promote recovery. Keynes (1931), for example, argued that reparations placed too great a burden on Germany and, given its low foreign exchange reserves, essentially forced it to run a current account surplus. Eventually the European countries defaulted, but the conflict over war debts tended to hamper attempts at co-operation over the international financial

---

[35] The US during the 1920s was on gold. However, the international economic environment did not play much of a role in determining the health of the US economy, which was more dependent on domestic conditions and policies. This allowed the US to take an essentially passive view of developments in the international monetary system during the 1920s.

[36] Competitive depreciation occurs when country X allows its currency to depreciate against country Y and then Y retaliates with depreciation against X. Of course, at the end neither X nor Y are any better off. Instead, it simply disrupts attention from better means of resolving the economic problems and conflict.

system in general. The final reason Clarke gives for the breakdown of the negotiations was the change in the US presidency from Hoover to Roosevelt in 1933. The latter was much more concerned about initiating a recovery using domestic policies. Thus the US interest in promoting international co-operation waned and with it any chance at securing an agreement.

The result of this second failure to secure a co-operative response to the world depression was that the three major powers (US, UK and France) went their own ways. The US, as we have already noted, retreated into domestic policy. France attempted to maintain a gold bloc. The UK formed the sterling bloc. The result was a number of competitive depreciations by the US and UK which eventually led to the currencies of the gold bloc becoming overvalued.

By 1936, it was clear that the French would have to devalue and a large amount of gold was flowing out of France into the UK and US due to heavy downward speculative pressure on the franc. The French, however, were reluctant to devalue unilaterally because they were concerned that this would simply lead to retaliation from the UK and US. The result was that they encouraged some negotiations between themselves and the UK and US. France wanted an agreement that following its devaluation, exchange rates would be stabilised between ±4.5% on either side of some agreed parity. However, this proposal had to be dropped because of strong opposition from the UK which was unwilling to commit itself in this way. An alternative proposal from the British which included reference to an eventual return to the gold standard had to be dropped because of opposition from the US. The final agreement, known as the tripartite agreement (concluded in September 1936), was couched in the vaguest of terms and involved separate statements made by the individual governments which discussed the desire for consultation and co-operation between them over the international monetary system.

Nonetheless, Clarke (1977) argues that the spirit of the agreement was stuck to by all three countries, even the UK which had in the first instance been the most reluctant to commit itself. The result was some bilateral co-operation between the US, UK and France on the issue of exchange rate management and convertibility of currencies into gold. France and the UK agreed that they would co-ordinate their interventions and that the UK would allow France to convert sterling accumulated as a result of intervention into gold, albeit at a variable price. A similar agreement was reached between the US and the UK where mutual convertibility was agreed although no exchange rate commitments were forthcoming. Thus the period before World War II ended with some attempts to restore order to the foreign exchange markets.

What can be said to have been learnt from this period? A lack of co-operation over economic policy can be very damaging for the world economy. There is no doubt that the depression could have been alleviated much more quickly had the major powers of the day been willing to commit themselves to some form of co-ordinated policy response. However, that would have required commitment to stabilising foreign exchange markets, something none of the countries were willing to contemplate, not least because it would shut the door on improving domestic economies through depreciation. So the fear that stabilisation of the international financial system might lead to a worsening of economic conditions in the short term were partly responsible for the unwillingness to co-operate.

However, this lack of willingness to co-operate was also related to the fact that the inter-war period was a time of great shift in world powers. The UK's role in the world economy was declining, not least because of its growing economic weakness. By contrast, the US was clearly emerging as the most powerful nation. Yet it was still unwilling to take on the role of hegemonic leader that its new economic power suggested for it and that the UK could no longer play. Instead, the US remained focused on its domestic economy and considered international developments as largely irrelevant.

Thus, in conclusion, we can argue that the lesson of the 1920s and 1930s is the importance of institutionalising the international financial system as a means of enhancing the potential for co-operation. Such co-operation need not have entailed a return to the gold standard but would have required some intervention to stabilise foreign exchange markets which witnessed frequent crises throughout the period. But the problems of the inter-war period were not just related to exchange rates. They were also connected with financial flows in the world economy and the issue of reparations. UK hegemony was declining and was accompanied by a decrease in its ability to finance industrialisation elsewhere. At the same time, the US as the emerging power were unwilling to take over the responsibilities which the UK had shouldered for some time. Various crises in financial markets also meant that private finance was not as forthcoming as it had been in the pre-war period. As a result, countries retreated into themselves and sought to ride out the depression alone. To some extent, the tripartite agreement started the process of reorganising the monetary system. But it was not until after World War II that the major powers were able to continue that process.

## The Bretton Woods system

Not surprisingly, World War II had a profound effect on the world economy. The US emerged from the war as by far the most powerful nation. Its industrial structure had been physically unaffected by the war and it now held 70% of the world's gold and foreign exchange reserves. Europe and Japan, by contrast, had been physically devastated by the war and needed financial and physical capital for reconstruction.[37] There was thus a huge recycling problem which needed to be met. The Bretton Woods agreement (July 1944) was negotiated between the strong (i.e. the US) and the weak (i.e. Europe, essentially represented by the UK) and not surprisingly the 'compromise' that resulted reflected mainly the proposals of the former.[38] On the one hand, the US, from its position of strength, was keen to ensure access to foreign markets for its goods. Europe, on the other hand, sought access to international credit in order to allow it to purchase the goods necessary for reconstruction. Although the resulting system that emerged, as Brett (1983) argues, placed rather more emphasis on a return to liberal trading arrangements, than it did on providing adequate resources to enable balance of payments deficits to be financed, it was nonetheless a step in the right direction.

The US were represented at the Bretton Woods conference by Harry Dexter White and the UK by John Maynard Keynes. Their two proposals formed the basis for the negotiations. Both agreed over the need for greater fixity of exchange rates. The disagreements arose over the question of financial flows and the problem of recycling in the world economy. White proposed that a fund would be created which would help to maintain balance of payments equilibria and encourage international

---

[37] We can note that the Third World was largely still colonised at this time and had very little influence in the design of the Bretton Woods system.

[38] See Brett (1983) for a discussion of the political compromise that was Bretton Woods.

trade. In particular, the aim was to eliminate controls on trade flows and restrictions on foreign exchange transactions. Keynes, by contrast, emphasised the need for a recycling mechanism to be found which would allow deficit countries to finance their development without the need to resort to trade restrictions. He was particularly concerned that without such a mechanism surplus countries would exert a deflationary impact on the world economy as a whole. These ideas are similar to his aggregate demand theory for the national economy. Permanent surpluses were equivalent to idle resources (or hoarding) which exert a deflationary influence on aggregate demand, without enabling deficit countries to have access to funds. Hence the latter would permanently have to adjust through deflation, thus exerting a deflationary influence over the world economy as a whole. Thus, Keynes proposed the establishment of an international Clearing Union which would receive funds from surplus countries and would lend them on to deficit countries. Recycling would be automatic and deflation avoided.

The actual outcome, as we shall see, conformed much more closely to White's proposals. The US were reluctant to support a proposal that, in their view, would lead to them having to provide a lot of finance (since immediately after the war they were major surplus country). Moreover, they were keen not to establish an institution which would simply allow countries to put off adjustment: by making liquidity more scarce, the incentive to adjust was large. Not surprisingly, given that the strength of the US and the fact that they contributed much of the finance for the new institutions, their views prevailed. The only concession to Keynes' ideas was, as we shall see, the so-called scarce currency clause which was intended to exert some influence on chronic surplus countries to force them to reflate their economies.

The Bretton Woods system was an $(N-1)$ system in which the US dollar acted as the Nth currency. De Grauwe (1989) argues that a return to the gold standard was impossible after World War II because the existing gold stock was thought to be too small to satisfy the world economy's liquidity needs. Moreover the existing stock of gold was very unevenly distributed (with, as we noted above, the US having the largest part of the stock). Thus the aim of the $(N-1)$ system was to conserve on gold stocks. The US maintained convertibility into gold at \$35 per ounce, but convertibility was restricted to foreign monetary authorities. All other countries (the $(N-1)$ countries) fixed their exchange rate to the dollar and maintained convertibility of their currencies into dollars. In other words, the world economy moved to a dollar–gold exchange standard.

The Bretton Woods agreement was built essentially on five main principles.[39] The first principle related to exchange rates. After the inter-war experience with floating exchange rates, competitive depreciations and increasing protectionism there was a clear preference for more fixed exchange rates. In the event the system that developed was one of exchange rates that could fluctuate up to ±1% on either side of their central parity (fixed in relation to the dollar). Changes in the exchange rate were to be allowed in the event of 'fundamental disequilibrium' (which we discuss later). In practice, only 10 major realignments took place during the Bretton Woods period (excluding 1949).

---

[39] See Scammell (1975), De Grauwe (1989), Brett (1983) and Tew (1982) for a discussion of the blueprint for the Bretton Woods system. We draw on their accounts in what follows.

The second principle addressed the question of international liquidity and reserves and their relationship to recycling. As we noted, Keynes' rather more ambitious plans for an international Clearing Union which would automatically take surpluses and recycle them to deficit countries were rejected. Nonetheless, given that exchange rates were fixed, it was recognised that countries needed to have access to international liquidity to allow them to finance *temporary* balance of payments disequilibria whilst adjustment was being undertaken. The result was a pool of currencies contributed by member countries according to a quota system (the size of the quota depending on the economic size of the country). This quota then represented a country's voting rights, drawing rights and its share in the government of the International Monetary Fund (IMF), the institution set up to administer the pool. Countries had the right to draw on other members' currencies up to a certain amount (determined by the size of the borrowing country's quota). These drawings or loans were only for short periods. Moreover the IMF attached certain conditions to borrowing which increased in their stringency the more a country borrowed.[40] The rationale for the limits on the amount that could be borrowed and the conditions attached to that borrowing was to ensure that countries did not put off adjustment.

The size of the pool of currencies held by the IMF has generally been recognised as being far too small. Whilst quotas have been revised periodically, the increases have only been to offset price increases – the real size of the pool of reserves has not increased. Moreover, holdings of individual currencies, particularly those of chronic surplus countries, have not been sufficient to meet the demand from deficit countries. In short, the provision of liquidity under the Bretton Woods agreement went a long way from meeting Keynes' idea that liquidity should be plentiful in order to prevent surplus countries from having a disinflationary effect on the world economy. Instead, liquidity was provided according to the White proposals.

The third principle was that the trading system should be open. In other words, the Bretton Woods agreements enshrined the principle of free trade. To this end, there was a desire to dismantle protectionism and restore convertibility for at least trade purposes. To help weaker countries a second institution, the International Bank for Reconstruction and Development (IBRD), was set up. It was charged with the role of promoting investment and development among the poorest countries of the world economy. In this way, they would be helped to meet international competition and be more willing to dismantle trade barriers. Trade issues themselves were to be overseen by a third new international organisation – the International Trade Organization (ITO). However, this was rejected by the US Congress because its charter took a far more interventionist stance than was acceptable to the US. Instead, the General Agreement on Trade and Tariffs (GATT), an agreement set up to organise the dismantling of tariffs, was adopted.

Fourthly, there was the issue of adjustment. We noted in our discussion of the $(N-1)$ system that such systems have a tendency to produce asymmetric pressures for adjustment (as between deficit and surplus countries). Under the Bretton Woods agreement, balance of payments disequilibria were intended to be the responsibility of *both* the deficit and the surplus countries. This was to be ensured through the operation of the scarce currency clause. The IMF could declare a currency scarce. Thus, for example, if a country went into persistent surplus with the result that its

---

[40] See Chapter 10 for a full discussion of the kind of conditions that are attached to IMF borrowing.

currency was in great demand from deficit countries, then the IMF could declare the currency scarce. In other words, the IMF could restrict access to that currency and hence make it very difficult for other countries to purchase exports from the surplus country.[41] The aim of this measure was to put pressure on surplus countries to adjust – otherwise, the 'scarcity' of their currency would make it very difficult for other countries to purchase their exports.

Williamson (1977, pp.113–25) argues that the need for symmetric adjustment is an important principle in a fixed exchange rate system. There are a two main reasons for this. Firstly, who should adjust depends crucially on the overall demand situation in the world economy. If there is generally an excess demand, then it is better if deficit countries adjust (so reducing the inflationary pressures resulting from the excess demand); if the world economy is in recession, then expansionary policies by surplus countries are the most obvious and best adjustment procedure. Secondly, if the balance of payments disequilibria is the result of a cost imbalance, then it is better that the country which is out of line with the majority be the one that adjusts. There is no presumption that this will necessarily be the deficit country. Thus it is important that the international monetary system have some method of forcing surplus countries to adjust.

The second asymmetry associated with the $(N-1)$ system was the special role played by the reserve centre: it could essentially finance any balance of payments disequilibria by issuing its own currency which would then accumulate in central banks of the other $(N-1)$ countries. The Bretton Woods system, as it was first set up, did nothing to deal with this asymmetry – the US could finance its deficit through increased foreign holdings of dollars. Only at a later stage with the introduction of the Special Drawing Right (SDR, which we discuss later) in the 1960s did the IMF provide the potential for removing this asymmetry. By using an artificially created asset, such as the SDR, and not a national currency, seigniorage does not accrue to one country and the reserve centre asymmetry is removed (see Williamson, 1977).

The issue of how adjustment was to be undertaken was left rather vague by the Bretton Woods agreement. As we noted above, exchange rate changes were allowed only in cases of 'fundamental disequilibrium'. However, this was never defined and in reality exchange rate changes played little useful role in promoting adjustment – exchange rate changes were only ever used in crisis circumstances. Additionally, protectionism could not be used to correct balance of payments disequilibria. Thus the presumption was that disequilibria would be corrected through deflation or reflation. The costs associated with such methods of adjustment, as we shall see, often led to adjustment being postponed with disastrous consequences for the Bretton Woods system.

The final principle of the Bretton Woods agreement related to the role of international institutions. It was clearly recognised that the system would be best implemented and operated through an institutional structure. As we have already noted, the IMF was set up to deal with the exchange-rate system and the provision of

---

[41] We can note that for this to work effectively, the IMF would have to be the major supplier of international liquidity. If international liquidity were available from elsewhere, then importers could simply turn to that source for currency. For example, suppose that the DM was declared a scarce currency, then if DMs were available only from the IMF, IMF action to declare the currency scarce could have a large impact on Germany's ability to export. But if importers of German goods can simply go to the international market to get DMs to pay for the goods, then the IMF's action will be largely useless – merely a gesture.

short-term liquidity to help with balance of payments disequilibria. The IBRD was designed to deal with longer-term financing of investment and the promotion of development. Finally the GATT was introduced to deal with trade issues. It can be argued that this desire to 'organise' the international financial system stemmed from the complete lack of organisation during the inter-war period. There was perhaps some belief that enshrining these principles within international organisations would ensure that the needs of the international financial system would not again be as neglected as they had been during the 1920s and 1930s. It is often argued (see, for example, Glyn *et al*, 1990) that the stability created by the Bretton Woods system contributed to the much better post-war economic performance of the industrial economies. And indeed that was what was intended after the instability of the 1920s and 1930s. But, whilst the creation of international organisations was a necessary condition to ensure that the system would not be neglected, history probably tells us that it was hardly a sufficient condition. The IMF and the IBRD have rarely been able to set their own agendas for the world financial system. Instead they have found it difficult to act independently from their major financiers, namely the major industrialised countries and particularly the US. Thus as private international capital markets grew in importance during the 1960s and 1970s, so the role played by these institutions declined significantly.[42]

The period following the negotiations of Bretton Woods until its demise in 1971 is usually divided into two distinct parts. The first period ran from 1945 to 1959: this was the period of reconstruction when the Bretton Woods system was essentially in mothballs. The second period, from 1959–1971, represents the time when the Bretton Woods system was seen in action. We discuss these two periods in turn.

The main obstacle to the introduction of the Bretton Woods system immediately after World War II was the absence of convertibility[43] in European countries. Britain had sought to restore the convertibility of sterling in 1947. However, there was a huge speculative crisis and within several weeks the UK lost two-thirds of its reserves. The failure of the UK to restore convertibility led other European countries, probably rightly, to believe that their currencies were not ready for convertibility either. The problem for European countries was a lack of foreign currency reserves with which to buy the much-needed goods that would aid reconstruction. Even intra-European trade was considerably hampered by this lack of foreign exchange. The US responded to these problems with the introduction of the Marshall Plan, which essentially gave between $4–$5 billion dollars to European countries per annum from 1948 to 1951. McKinnon (1979) notes that these sums were not in themselves that large (only about 4% of Europe's GNP) yet they were clearly very successful. McKinnon attributes this success to the fact that the Marshall Plan money was used partly to set up the European Payments Union (EPU). This was a means of organising trade within Europe in a way that would conserve scarce foreign exchange. The EPU was responsible for registering all intra-European trade. At the end of each month it would work out all the bilateral positions and these net positions would then be financed partly (40%) in gold or dollars and partly (60%) in credit granted by surplus countries (on which interest was paid). The result was a rapid growth in intra-European trade which was crucial to facilitating the reconstruction process.

---

[42] We discuss this in more detail in the second half of this book.
[43] We refer here to convertibility for trade transactions.

It was initially thought that a five year transition would be enough before the Bretton Woods system could come into full operation. However, by the end of 1952, there was no sign of a return to convertibility, exchange controls were still common and balance of payments were in disequilibrium. The IMF in this period could have played a critical role in establishing itself as the new 'keeper' of the international monetary system. However, as Scammell (1975) points out, the IMF did little to stamp its mark on the international financial scene. In particular, the IMF did little to establish equilibrium exchange rates and the rates proposed by individual countries were accepted (whether they were incompatible or not). The IMF's argument was that during the transition period exchange rates could be adjusted as required. However, Scammell argues that this rather passive role adopted by the IMF generally weakened its authority later on. Additionally, the IMF was generally unwilling to lend out its funds to those countries in need, for fear that it might run out of funds and when it did begin to lend after 1956, it quickly established a reputation for only lending short-term and with stringent conditions. Thus any hopes that the Fund would act in a Keynesian manner by acting as a source of plentiful liquidity to which members had automatic access rapidly faded.

In 1959 the EPU was disbanded and convertibility restored by European countries. This opened the way for the Bretton Woods system to come into full operation and the early 1960s represented the heyday of its achievements. McKinnon (1979) lists a number of achievements of the system: exchange rates were stable; foreign exchange was freely available for current transactions; trade grew very rapidly as did output per capita; and macroeconomic stability (with low inflation and unemployment) was achieved. However, it was not long before strains in the system began to show, strains that would eventually lead to the breakdown of the Bretton Woods system.

The first problem arose over the adjustment process. In particular, the issue of the speed of adjustment was a problem. We have already argued above that the only possible adjustment mechanism in the Bretton Woods system was that of deflation or reflation. Countries were reluctant to change their exchange rate and increased protectionism to help balance of payments deficits was outlawed. For some countries, however, adjustment through changes in aggregate demand was either difficult or costly (in terms of an increase in unemployment).

De Grauwe (1989) uses the familiar Swan diagram to illustrate some of the problems with slow adjustment under the Bretton Woods system. Figure 1.4 illustrates the Swan diagram. On the y-axis we have the real exchange rate, $R = SP^*/P$, where S is the spot exchange rate expressed as the domestic currency price of a unit of foreign currency; $P^*$ is the foreign price level; and P is the domestic price level. An increase in R implies a devaluation of the real exchange rate, thus making the economy more competitive. On the x-axis, we have absorption (A), which comprises consumption (C), investment (I) and government spending (G). From the national income identity we know that:

$$Y \equiv C + I + G + (X - M) \tag{1.5}$$

where $(X - M)$ is the current account. Using the definition of A given above, we can rewrite (1.5) as:

$$Y \equiv A + (X - M) \tag{1.6}$$

$$\Rightarrow \quad Y - A \equiv (X - M) \tag{1.7}$$

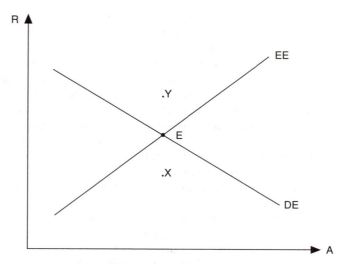

**Figure 1.4**  *The Swan diagram and the problem of adjustment under Bretton Woods*

In other words, if absorption exceeds income there will be a current account deficit (X < M).

The two schedules in the diagram represent two equilibrium conditions, domestic equilibrium (DE) and external equilibrium (EE). Domestic equilibrium is defined as full employment. If unemployment is above (below) its natural rate then the price level will begin to fall (rise). The schedule is negatively sloped for the following reason. An increase in R (an increase in the country's competitiveness) will cause the demand for exports and hence income to increase. Unemployment will fall below its natural rate and inflationary pressures will develop. To maintain equilibrium, therefore, a cut in absorption is required. Thus high levels of R are associated with low levels of A if the economy is in equilibrium. External equilibrium is defined as current account equilibrium. This schedule is positively sloped because as competitiveness increases (R increases), the balance of payments will move into surplus – to restore equilibrium, a rise in absorption is required.

De Grauwe (1989) uses this diagram to illustrate the problems of adjustment to a shock under the Bretton Woods regime. In particular he examines a domestic inflationary shock to mimic the conditions faced by deficit countries and a foreign inflationary shock to mimic the case of surplus countries. Taking the deficit country situation first, we find that a rise in wages will reduce competitiveness. In other words, the real exchange rate falls and the economy moves to a point like X in Figure 1.4. At X there is unemployment and a current account deficit. The critical question now is how does the economy adjust to this situation. There is clearly a need for a fall in domestic prices in order to restore competitiveness (in the face of a fixed exchange rate, S). If wages and prices are flexible then the rise in unemployment will reduce money wages causing domestic prices to decline. At the same time the current account deficit will lead the monetary authorities to purchase domestic currency (which is in excess supply on the foreign exchange market). Thus the domestic money supply will fall, further increasing the deflationary effect. The fall in the price level eventually restores the economy back to E. Thus with flexible wages and prices, adjustment will be automatic.

However, what happens if wages and prices are inflexible. De Grauwe argues that the economy is now stuck at X. In other words, disequilibria could persist for some time. Indeed, if prices are completely inflexible, then only a devaluation can restore equilibrium. Changes in absorption will only aggravate either the unemployment problem or the deficit problem. For example, an increase in absorption will cause the economy to move further to the right towards the DE schedule: unemployment will fall, but external equilibrium worsens. By contrast, a decline in absorption will help the current account but not domestic equilibrium (unemployment will increase further). Thus De Grauwe concludes that in a world of inflexible wages and prices devaluation becomes inevitable and the commitment to the fixed exchange rate quickly loses its credibility.

What about the situation in surplus countries? If a foreign inflationary shock makes a country more competitive, then it moves to a point such as Y in Figure 1.4. At Y there is a surplus on the current account and unemployment is below its natural rate (leading to inflationary pressures). Adjustment in this case is more easily engineered. Inflationary pressure arises both from the fall in unemployment and the authorities' interventions in the foreign exchange market. In this case, the monetary authorities will be selling domestic currency in the foreign exchange market to prevent the exchange rate from appreciating. This action automatically increases the money supply. Since wages and prices are rarely inflexible upwards, there is no reason why adjustment should not occur automatically. However, the authorities can resist the pressure for adjustment. If they are particularly concerned to contain inflationary pressures, then they can engage in sterilisation. In other words, at the same time as they intervene in the foreign exchange market thus increasing the domestic money supply, they can conduct open market operations (selling bonds) in order to reduce the money supply. Sterilisation will again delay the speed of adjustment and indeed was successfully undertaken by the German monetary authorities during the Bretton Woods period.

An alternative means of adjusting to the foreign inflationary shock would be through a revaluation of the exchange rate. This has the advantage that the surplus country need not accept an increase in the price level. Thus with downward wage-price inflexibility and with surplus countries being reluctant to accept price increases, the system becomes increasingly lacking in credibility. As De Grauwe (1989, p.39) concludes, 'a speculative crisis becomes inevitable' as it becomes clear to speculators that the only way equilibrium can be restored is via an exchange rate change.

How might this problem have been resolved? There are a number of possible options. First, what if Keynes' ideas had been adopted and surpluses had been automatically redistributed to deficit countries? This, in itself, would have been insufficient since the deficit needs to be eliminated, not simply financed. Thus it would be critical to use the recycled finance to improve competitiveness. For example, Pesaran (1986) has argued that supply side policies to direct resources toward investment and production of import substitute and exports can help to improve competitiveness rather than resorting to devaluation.[44] A second possible resolution to the adjustment problem might have been possible if the IMF had played a stronger role in the world economy and had it defined more clearly what 'fundamental disequilibrium' entailed. As we mentioned earlier, the IMF played only a small part both in fixing exchange rates at the outset and in helping to identify

---

[44] See also Thirlwall and Gibson (1992).

currencies which had become misaligned and would benefit from a change in their parity. In other words, a more flexible Bretton Woods might have avoided these contradictions which were to contribute to its downfall. Finally, we can note that there was little attention paid to the question of economic policy co-operation. As we shall argue later in this book, in an increasingly interdependent world, economic policy co-operation can be beneficial even with floating exchange rates. With managed or fixed exchange rates, the case for increased co-ordination of policies becomes even stronger.

In terms of the operation of the Bretton Woods system in the 1960s, Figure 1.5 illustrates the development of large balance of payments disequilibria at the end of the 1960s. The US, in particular, exhibited a large balance of payments deficit.

In addition to this problem of adjustment, there were also the problems of asymmetry between deficit and surplus countries and between the reserve centre and the rest of the world. We have already discussed above how these problems come about. We can simply note here that during the 1960s, the pressure on deficit countries was clear: France and the UK, both deficit countries, were both forced to adjust through devaluations in 1969 and 1967 respectively. By contrast, surplus countries such as Germany and Switzerland were able to continue with large surpluses throughout the period.

The US, the reserve centre, experienced an increasing deficit as can be seen from Figure 1.5. McKinnon (1979) argues that concern about the US balance of payments deficit was misplaced. He argues that the deficit was simply the residual outcome of the balance of payments positions of the other $(N-1)$ countries. As we argued above, the Nth country has to accept this if the $(N-1)$ system is to operate smoothly. Clearly this is not costless for the Nth country and McKinnon argues that the *quid*

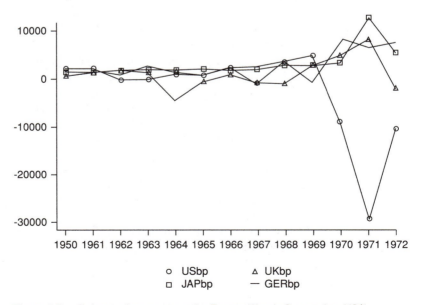

**Figure 1.5.** *Balance of payments under Bretton Woods System (mn US$)*

*Note*: USbp, GERbp, UKbp, JAPbp are the US, German, UK and Japanese balance of payments respectively

*pro quo* is that any resulting deficit can be financed simply by using the Nth currency, in this case US dollars. However, McKinnon's argument ignores the problems of confidence raised by the chronic US deficit. This issue of confidence in the US dollar takes us to problems of liquidity in the Bretton Woods system.

The liquidity problems of the Bretton Woods system can be stated quite succinctly: a dollar shortage in the 1950s gave way to a dollar glut in the 1960s. The problem of the dollar was neatly summed up by the 'Triffin Dilemma' (see Triffin, 1960). Essentially, the dilemma stated that:

> if the United States corrected its persistent balance-of-payments deficits, the growth of world reserves could not be fed adequately by gold production at $35 an ounce, but that if the United States continued to run deficits, its foreign liabilities would inevitably come to exceed by far its ability to convert dollars into gold upon demand and would bring about a "gold and dollar crisis".
>
> (Triffin, 1978, p. 2)

In other words, Triffin identified a technical dilemma at the heart of the Bretton Woods system. It was crucial that enough of the reserve currency (US dollars) be available to facilitate the rapid growth of trade that was witnessed in the post-war period. However, in order for US dollars to move into circulation overseas, it had to run a balance of payments deficit. Such a deficit would be bound eventually to undermine the credibility of the Bretton Woods system and hence lead to its demise.[45] In particular, the accumulation of dollars held by foreigners (essentially European central banks) would imply a rising dollar–gold ratio, eventually undermining confidence that the US could convert all dollars held overseas into gold. Thus Triffin concluded that, given that the US could not continue to run a balance of payments deficit indefinitely, it was of paramount importance to provide some other means of international liquidity. Triffin's solution was the introduction of a reserve asset, the SDR, whose creation would not be dependent on the balance of payments position of the reserve centre. Instead, SDRs could be created in line with demand for them to finance growing international trade (see Triffin, 1968).[46] If such a reserve asset was not created, then Triffin argued that the system would act in a deflationary manner.

The emphasis placed by Triffin on the possible deflationary effects of the Bretton Woods system has led to some criticism of his analysis. For example, Chrystal (1990) argues that Triffin was wrong for a number of reasons. First, the danger was not deflation but rather inflation. However, this criticism is a little unfair on Triffin. He thought that deflation was the most likely outcome because he assumed, on the basis of his analysis, that the US balance of payments deficit would have to be corrected, if the system were not to collapse. The fact that it was not corrected should merely lead us to conclude that the other aspect of Triffin's analysis was proved correct: namely that the system would collapse.

Chrystal's second criticism of Triffin is that the size of world reserves is irrelevant. This criticism stems from a monetarist view that the nominal size of the reserve stock should have no impact on real economic activity. In other words, this argument is

---

[45] We discuss later the origins of the US balance of payments deficit and its relationship with a weakening of the performance of the US economy.

[46] If SDRs were the solution to this dilemma at the heart of the Bretton Woods system, then they came along too late to be of any help in saving the system. Thus we do not discuss their role here in detail.

similar to the neutrality of money argument used at the national level and is hence subject to the same criticisms.

The final criticism made by Chrystal is that the problems of the 1950s and 1960s were treated as structural problems rather than simply the transitional problems that they were. Chrystal believes that the problem of the reserve shortage was merely transitional because once international capital markets developed, the need to provide official liquidity in the system would disappear. Such an argument, of course, presupposes that the outcome of relying on private international capital markets is a desirable one. This is clearly a big question which we address much later in the second part of this book.

De Grauwe (1989) is also rather critical of Triffin's analysis, suggesting that his analysis is incomplete. Triffin (1960) argued that if the US balance of payments deficit continued and the dollar–gold ratio continued to rise then the inevitable confidence crisis would be accompanied by huge scale conversions of dollars (held by European central banks) into gold. This would reduce the amount of dollars in the world economy and inevitably lead to deflation. It is the latter part of this argument that De Grauwe argues does not fit the facts. De Grauwe notes that whilst US gold stocks declined throughout the 1960s, there was no acceleration in the decline towards the end of the 1960s. Moreover, if Triffin's prediction was correct, then we would have expected to see a rise in the gold stocks of European central banks – however, their gold stocks also declined. Finally, deflation was not a problem following the collapse of Bretton Woods – instead precisely the opposite occurred – rapid inflation.

De Grauwe believes that the explanation of these facts lies in an examination of the relationship between the dollar and the price of gold. He applies Gresham's Law to the Bretton Woods liquidity problem. Gresham's Law argues that bad money will drive out good money as a means of exchange. Assume there are two currencies and the monetary authorities fix a price between them (call it the 'official price') and are willing to undertake transactions at that price. Assume furthermore that one of the currencies becomes more abundant. This will lead to a fall in its market price (the official price remaining the same). Agents will then face a profitable arbitrage opportunity. They can buy the abundant currency in the market (cheaply) and sell it to the authorities at the higher official price. Alternatively, looking at the problem from the point of view of the scarce currency, agents will buy it cheaply from the authorities and sell it in the market. The scarce money will therefore become even scarcer as it is taken out of circulation and hoarded. Alternatively, the abundant and 'bad' currency will circulate as the medium of exchange.

Applied to the Bretton Woods system, the two currencies are the dollar (the abundant currency) and gold (the scarce currency). The US monetary authorities quoted an official price between dollars and gold of $35 per ounce. As the volume of dollars increased relative to gold, so the market price of gold began to rise. At first the US and a number of European central banks managed to prevent the market price from rising above its official price by selling gold in the free market (hence the reason why European gold reserves were falling during this period).[47] By 1968, however, intervention in the free market had to be abandoned. The result was a sharp rise in the

---

[47] See Tew (1982, Ch. 9) for a comprehensive discussion of the various measures adopted by the US and European central banks to keep the official and free market prices of gold equal.

free market price of gold. In other words, the scenario in which Gresham's Law operates held and 'bad' money (the dollar) drove out 'good' money (gold).

De Grauwe concludes that whilst Triffin's dilemma was real, it was well on its way to being solved (through the introduction of SDRs from 1970) by the time that the system collapsed. Triffin's predictions were only correct up to a point – namely the collapse of the system if the US balance of payments deficit continued. The US did not lose all its gold reserves and central banks in Europe did not accumulate gold. However, this point of view seems a little harsh on Triffin. The reason why gold reserves remained with the US was simply because the US suspended the convertibility of the dollar into gold in 1971. Had it not have done this then there would have been a rush by European central banks to convert their dollars into gold before the inevitable dollar devaluation – indeed it was the threat of this that led to the suspension of dollar convertibility. Triffin thus has to be given credit for having got to the heart of this technical liquidity problem in the Bretton Woods system.

The growing loss of confidence in the dollar intensified the problems of Bretton Woods. It quickly became clear that the dollar was likely to be devalued and this led to large-scale speculation that largely became self-fulfilling. Sales of dollars were so large that eventually European central banks had to abandon intervention to support the dollar in May 1971. The Deutschmark and Dutch guilder floated and the Swiss franc and Austrian schilling revalued. Then on 15 August 1971 the US suspended the convertibility of the dollar into gold and a widespread unpegging of currencies from the dollar followed.

The liquidity and adjustment problems faced by the Bretton Woods system can be considered to be the immediate factors responsible for its downfall. Additionally, however, we can point to a number of more fundamental factors which played a role. McKinnon (1979) argues that a deeper reason for the collapse of Bretton Woods was the increased instability of the US economy in the 1960s. In particular, severe inflationary pressures developed due to an increase in the rate of growth of the money supply and an ever increasing fiscal deficit (mainly the result of financing the war in Vietnam). The fiscal deficit was transmitted into a current account deficit and because of the US's special reserve centre status, there was no pressure to adjust as there might have been in any other deficit country.

Brett (1983) points to an even more fundamental weakness in the US economy that began to manifest itself at this time, namely the growing weakness of the real productive capacity of the US economy. After World War II, as we noted previously, the US was by far the strongest country in the world economy. By the 1960s, however, technological innovation and productivity increases had slowed and countries such as Germany and Japan were catching up with the US very quickly. Brett relates this to a decline in the hegemony of the US in the world economy: it was no longer in a position to act as a strong leader and, moreover, to organise the international system as it preferred. Thus the crisis of confidence in Brett's view can be directly related to the decline of the US as the hegemonic power.

From a Keynesian point of view, the failure of Bretton Woods can be traced to the lack of an adequate recycling mechanism. As we have already noted, Keynes original proposals to the Bretton Woods conference were for an automatic recycling of funds from surplus countries to deficit countries. Crucial to the effectiveness of these funds is that they be used not just to finance consumption beyond a country's means, but that they be channelled into productive uses. Only in this way will the weaker, deficit countries increase their competitiveness, allowing them to compete more effectively with the stronger countries. Brett (1983) argues that this Keynesian view is perhaps a necessary condition for a more durable international monetary system, but it is by no means a sufficient condition. For Brett, there is an inherent tendency within the world economy for the weak to get weaker and the strong to get stronger.[48] If that tendency is not countered by 'effective policy interventions capable of offsetting these tendencies generated by free competition and intensified by orthodox policies [such as trade liberalisation]' (p.185), then disintegration of the international monetary system is inevitable.

Our analysis of the Bretton Woods system has highlighted the problems of managing the world economy even with the creation of international institutions charged with its organisation. The lessons of Bretton Woods are that for a system of fixed exchange rates to work the anchor country must be strong productively and have a stable macroeconomy. But additionally greater policy co-ordination is required to deal with the problems of adjustment more effectively and at lower cost in terms of employment. Adjustment is not something that will occur automatically and hence international institutions such as the IMF have a role to play here in promoting greater consultation and co-ordination between the major industrialised countries. During the period of Bretton Woods the IMF did not take an active role in promoting such negotiations[49] and hence it could be argued that the collapse of the system was inevitable.

*The Smithsonian agreement and the managed float (1971–present)*

Following the collapse of the Bretton Woods system, there was an attempt from December 1971 to March 1973 to move to a dollar standard.[50] This was known as the Smithsonian agreement where European currencies were to be pegged to the dollar, allowing a movement of $\pm 2\frac{1}{4}\%$ on either side of the central parity. European currencies were revalued and the price of gold was increased to $38 per ounce, but the dollar was no longer convertible into gold. Within this, a number of European countries introduced the 'snake in the tunnel' which was the first attempt by Common Market countries to minimise intra-European currency fluctuations.[51] Not surprisingly, given the lack of confidence in the dollar, the Smithsonian agreement lasted just over one year. Sterling was first to leave and float in June 1972 following another balance of payments crisis.[52] By the beginning of 1973, it was clear that further currency realignments would be necessary and downward speculative pressure on the dollar continued. The result was a move towards floating exchange rates from March 1973.

---

[48] Brett argues that this arises from the operation of cumulative causation ideas. See Brett, 1983, chapters 2–4 for a discussion of exactly how this process is supposed to operate.

[49] The problem for the IMF has always been its domination by the US. The US is a major provider of funds and hence has a substantial slice of the votes. This gives it an unduly large amount of influence within the institution. We discuss this further in Chapter 10.

[50] See Tew (1982) for a comprehensive account of the period immediately after the demise of Bretton Woods.

[51] The system was known as the 'snake in the tunnel' for the following reason. If each EU currency could move by $\pm 2\frac{1}{4}\%$ on either side of its dollar central parity, then this would allow for a fluctuation of $4\frac{1}{2}\%$ *vis-à-vis* the dollar. This implied that if one Common Market currency fell to its floor against the dollar whilst another moved to its ceiling, then the relative currency movement between these two EU currencies would be 9%. The European agreement sought to limit intra-Common Market fluctuations to only $4\frac{1}{2}\%$ and hence this effectively halved the size of the Smithsonian bands. The European currencies were confined to a 'snake' within the Smithsonian tunnel..

[52] Incidentally this marked the end of the sterling area which had been formed in the inter-war years. Only a few currencies continued to peg to sterling and most diversified their reserves (see Tew, 1982).

Table 1.2.    Exchange rate arrangements

(As of September 30, 1993)

| Currency pegged to | | | | | | Flexibility limited in terms of a single currency or group of currencies | | More flexible | | |
|---|---|---|---|---|---|---|---|---|---|---|
| US dollar | French franc | Russian ruble | Other currency | SDR | Other composite | Single currency | Cooperative arrangements | Adjusted according to a set of indicators | Other managed floating | Independently floating |
| Angola | Benin | Armenia | Bhutan (Indian rupee) | Libya | Algeria | Bahrain | Belgium | Chile | Cambodia | Afghanistan, Islamic State of |
| Antigua & Barbuda | Burkina Faso | Azerbaijan | Estonia (Deutschmark) | Myanmar | Austria | Qatar | Denmark | Colombia | China. P. R. | Albania |
| Argentina | Cameroon | Belarus | | Rwanda | Bangladesh | Saudi Arabia | France | Madagascar | Croatia | Australia |
| Bahamas. The | C. African Rep. | Kazakhstan | | Seychelles | Botswana | United Arab Emirates | Germany | Nicaragua | Ecuador | Bolivia |
| Barbados | Chad | Turkmenistan | | | Burundi | | Ireland | | Egypt | Brazil |
| | | | | | | | | | | Bulgaria |
| Belize | Comoros | | Kiribati (Australian dollar) | | Cape Verde | | Luxembourg | | Greece | Canada |
| Djibouti | Congo | | Lesotho (South African rand) | | Cyprus | | Netherlands | | Guinea | Costa Rica |
| Dominica | Côte d'Ivoire | | | | Fiji | | Portugal | | Guinea–Bissau | Dominican Rep. |
| Grenada | Equatorial Guinea | | | | Hungary | | Spain | | Indonesia | El Salvador |
| Iraq | Gabon | | | | Iceland | | | | Israel | Ethiopia |
| | | | | | | | | | | Finland |
| Liberia | Mali | | Namibia (South African rand) | | Jordan | | | | Korea | Gambia, The |
| Marshall Islands | Niger | | | | Kenya | | | | Lao P.D. Rep. | Georgia |
| Oman | Senegal | | | | Kuwait | | | | Malaysia | Ghana |
| Panama | Togo | | | | Malawi | | | | Maldives | Guatemala |
| St. Kitts & Nevis | | | | | Malta | | | | Mexico | Guyana |
| | | | | | | | | | | Haiti |
| St. Lucia | | | San Marino (Italian lira) | | Mauritania | | | | Pakistan | Honduras |
| St. Vincent and the Grenadines | | | Swaziland (South African rand) | | Mauritius | | | | Poland | India |
| Suriname | | | | | Morocco | | | | Sao Tome & Principe | Iran. I.R. of |
| Syrian Arab Rep. | | | | | Nepal | | | | Singapore | Italy |
| Yemen, Republic of | | | | | Papua New Guinea | | | | Slovenia | |

(Continued)

*Table 1.2.* (Continued)

(As of September 30, 1993)

| Currency pegged to | | | | Flexibility limited in terms of a single currency or group of currencies | | | | Adjusted according to a set of indicators | More flexible | |
|---|---|---|---|---|---|---|---|---|---|---|
| US dollar | French franc | Russian ruble | Other currency | SDR | Other composite | Single currency | Cooperative arrangements | | Other managed floating | Independently floating |
| | | | | | Solomon Islands | | | | Somalia | Jamaica |
| | | | | | Thailand | | | | Sri Lanka | Japan |
| | | | | | Tonga | | | | Tunisia | Kyrgyz Rep. |
| | | | | | Vanuatu | | | | Turkey | Latvia |
| | | | | | Western Samoa | | | | Uruguay | Lebanon |
| | | | | | | | | | | Lithuania |
| | | | | | Zimbabwe | | | | Venezuela | Moldova |
| | | | | | | | | | Viet Nam | Mongolia |
| | | | | | | | | | | Mozambique |
| | | | | | | | | | | New Zealand |
| | | | | | | | | | | Nigeria |
| | | | | | | | | | | Norway |
| | | | | | | | | | | Paraguay |
| | | | | | | | | | | Peru |
| | | | | | | | | | | Philippines |
| | | | | | | | | | | Romania |
| | | | | | | | | | | Russia |
| | | | | | | | | | | Sierra Leone |
| | | | | | | | | | | South Africa |
| | | | | | | | | | | Sudan |
| | | | | | | | | | | Sweden |
| | | | | | | | | | | Switzerland |
| | | | | | | | | | | Tanzania |
| | | | | | | | | | | Trinidad and Tobago |
| | | | | | | | | | | Uganda |
| | | | | | | | | | | Ukraine |
| | | | | | | | | | | United Kingdom |
| | | | | | | | | | | United States |
| | | | | | | | | | | Zaire |
| | | | | | | | | | | Zambia |

*Source:* IMF, International Financial Statistics, December 1993.

The period since 1973 can be characterised as a managed float, within which the European countries sought to move to closer monetary co-operation. The rest of the first part of this book essentially deals with this period. Thus we finish our account of the history of the international monetary system with some stylised facts of the period. It is these facts that we attempt to explain in Chapters 2–5.

There are essentially three points which can be made. First, although we have characterised the period as one of a managed float, this applies only to the major currencies such as sterling, the yen and the dollar. Table 1.2 provides a summary of the exchange-rate arrangements of IMF member countries as of 1993. A large number of developing countries peg their exchange rates to a particular currency or a composite group of currencies. The former practice often reflects former colonial links, an example of which is the group of African countries which peg to the French franc. Within the latter group, a number of developing countries peg their currencies to the SDR. The European countries have a co-operative arrangement, the Exchange Rate Mechanism of the European Monetary System (which we discuss in some detail in Chapter 5). Other countries have a managed float or are independently floating. These include a number of major world currencies (the dollar, yen and sterling) as well as some developing country currencies.

Secondly, what have been the characteristics of those currencies which have been floating? Figure 1.6 illustrates one of the main features of floating currencies: the exchange rate is highly volatile. We plot here the monthly average for the sterling–dollar exchange rate from 1968 to 1993 (dollars per pound). The increase in volatility post-1971 is clear. But it is not only the nominal exchange rate that is volatile. Figures 1.7 to 1.10 show movements in the real exchange rate of the dollar *vis-à-vis* the pound, Deutschmark and yen. The figures plot quarterly movements in real exchange rates defined using consumer price indices as follows:

$$R = SP^*/P \tag{1.8}$$

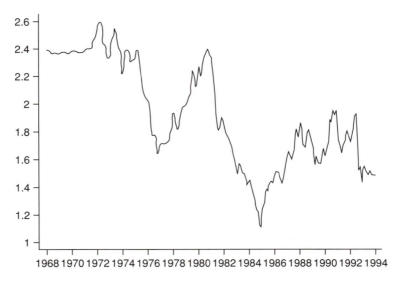

**Figure 1.6.**  *Dollar–pound exchange rate, 1968–94*

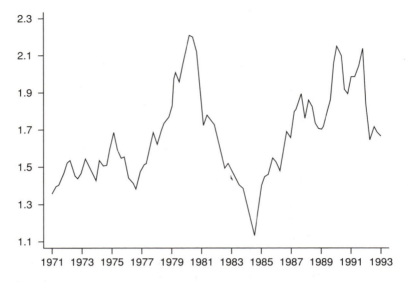

**Figure 1.7.** *Dollar–pound real exchange rate*

*Note*: an increase in the exchange rate is a dollar real depreciation.

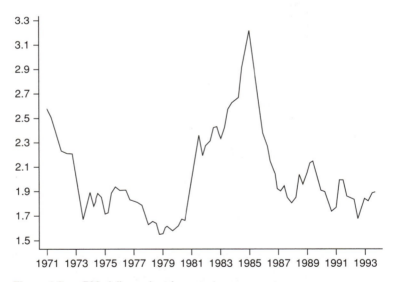

**Figure 1.8.** *DM–dollar real exchange rate*

*Note*: an increase in the exchange rate is a real Deutschmark depreciation.

where R is the real exchange rate, S is the nominal exchange rate (domestic currency price of a unit of foreign currency), $P^*$ is the foreign price level and P is the domestic price level. All four figures illustrate the point that bilateral real exchange rates have exhibited large swings. Figures 1.11 to 1.14 tell a similar story for the real effective exchange rates of the US, Japan, Germany and the UK (where a rise in the index implies a real appreciation of the currency). Figures 1.7 to 1.9, for example, illustrate

**Figure 1.9.**   *Yen–dollar real exchange rate*

*Note*: an increase in the exchange rate is a real yen depreciation.

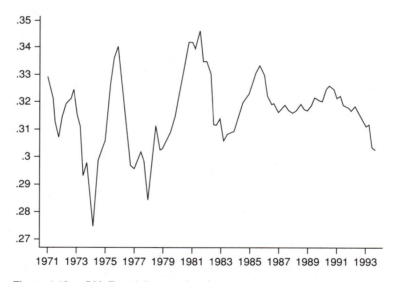

**Figure 1.10.**   *DM–French franc real exchange rate*

*Note*: an increase in the exchange rate indicates a real Deutschmark depreciation.

the large overvaluation of the dollar relative to the other major currencies in the early 1980s. This is confirmed in Figure 1.11 which illustrates the effective real exchange rate of the dollar. Both the yen and the Deutschmark show a strong trend appreciation in real terms over the period 1976 to 1994. It is interesting to note that in the case of the Deutschmark–French franc exchange rate (Figure 1.10), the swings in the real exchange rate have been less pronounced since 1983 when the French committed themselves wholeheartedly to the Exchange-Rate Mechanism of the European Monetary System.

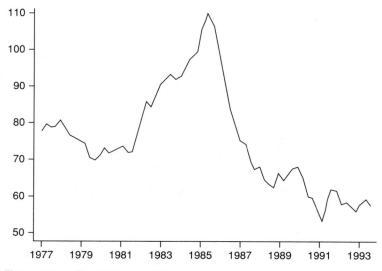

**Figure 1.11.**    *Real effective dollar exchange rate*

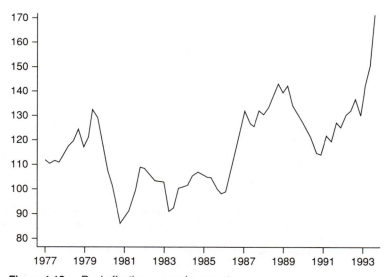

**Figure 1.12.**    *Real effective yen exchange rate*

**Figure 1.13.**    *Real effective DM exchange rate*

**Figure 1.14.**    *Real effective sterling exchange rate*

The final point which we can make relates to the role of floating exchange rates in helping the adjustment problem. In the later 1960s, there was a widespread feeling that the chronic balance of payments problems which emerged during the 1960s (see Figure 1.5) would be removed by the adoption of floating exchange rates. However, this does not appear to have occurred. Figure 1.15 indicates that the current account positions of the major industrial countries diverged significantly especially after 1980. This is particularly true of Japan and Germany which retain large surpluses on their current accounts in spite of the real appreciation which they have experienced since the advent of more flexible exchange rates.

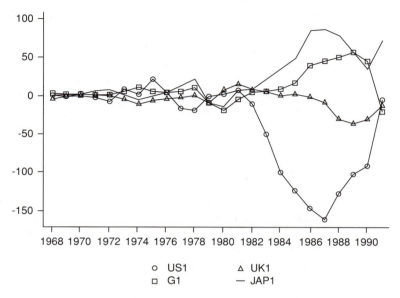

**Figure 1.15.** *Current accounts (bn US$)*

*Note*: US1, UK1, G1 and JAP1 are the US, UK, German and Japanese Current Accounts respectively.

## Conclusion

In this chapter, we have sought to introduce some of the concepts which we will be using throughout this book. We have also raised a number of questions which we examine in some detail in the following chapters. We began by outlining the main questions which have to be faced by any international financial system. In particular, we stressed the need for an adjustment mechanism and we discussed the role played by international money and financial flows in the world economy. Our argument throughout the chapter has been that each system requires a different set of institutions with their own 'rules of the game' to which member countries have to adhere if the system is to operate smoothly.

However, it is not the case that, provided each system is set up with its appropriate institutional structure, we are indifferent between these different systems. On the contrary, there exists a large debate within the international finance literature on the desirability or otherwise of different systems. As we saw in our discussion of the gold standard, a clear institutional structure prevailed with the 'rules of the game' defining how adjustment would be undertaken and what would be used as international money. However, we also argued that the gold standard did not bring the supposed benefits in terms of price and output stability in the countries which operated it. In other words, in adopting any particular form for the international financial system, we must pay attention not only to the institutional structure which will accompany our chosen system, but also to which system we think is desirable. In the remaining chapters of this book we attempt to examine exactly this question.

In Chapters 2 to 5, we focus on exchange rates and the role that they play in the world economy. In particular, in Chapters 2 and 3 we seek to understand what determines exchange rates and in this way we hope to shed some light on the stylised facts of the post-1973 period which we outlined above. This analysis allows us to move beyond the positive question of why exchange rates change to ask the normative question of what type of exchange system is most desirable. We address this in Chapter 4. Finally, in Chapter 5, we provide a case study of exchange rate co-operation by looking at the history of European monetary co-operation. This case study provides us with a rich catalogue of different types of exchange rate management, from the fairly loose version of the European Monetary System which operated in the early 1980s to the proposals for European Monetary Union.

In the second part of the book, we focus on the role of financial flows in the international financial system. In particular, we examine the implications of the increase in flows of private capital which have accompanied the massive growth in the international capital markets since the 1960s. We describe this phenomenon in Chapter 6, before going on to discuss its implications. We concentrate on two important consequences of the growth of private international flows for both macroeconomic policy (Chapter 7) and the stability of the international financial system (Chapters 8 and 9). Chapter 10 examines the role of the International Monetary Fund in the provision of finance and seeks to highlight some of the problems which exist currently with the official provision of finance to the world economy. Finally, Chapter 11 provides some conclusions and discusses the question of the reform of the international financial system.

## References

Abel, A.B. and Bernanke, B.S. (1992) *Macroeconomics*. Addison Wesley, New York.

Barro, R.J. and Gordon, D.B. (1983) 'Rules, discretion and reputation in a model of monetary policy', *Journal of Monetary Economics*, **12**.

Blanchard, O.J. and Fischer, S. (1989) *Lectures on Macroeconomics*. MIT Press, Cambridge, Mass.

Bordo, M. (1981) 'The classical gold standard: some lessons for today', *Federal Reserve Bank of St. Louis*, May.

Brett, E.A. (1983) *International Money and Capitalist Crisis: The anatomy of global disintegration*. Heinemann, London.

Chernow, R. (1990) *The House of Morgan*. Touchstone. Simon and Schuster, New York.

Chrystal, A.K. (1990) 'International reserves and international liquidity: a solution in search of a problem', in Bird, G. (ed.) (1990) *The International Finance Regime*. Surrey University Press in association with Academic Press, London. pp.9–28.

Clarke, S.V.O. (1973) 'The reconstruction of the international monetary system: the attempts of 1922 and 1933', *Princeton Studies in International Finance*, 33, November.

Clarke, S.V.O. (1977) 'Exchange-rate stabilization in the mid-1930s – negotiating the Tripartite Agreement', *Princeton Studies in International Finance*, 41, September.

Cooper, R.N. (1982) 'The gold standard: historical facts and failure prospects', *Brookings Papers on Economic Activity*, 1, 1–56.

Crockett, A. (1977) *International Money: Issues and Analysis*. Nelson, Sunbury-on-Thames.

De Grauwe, P. (1989) *International Money: post-war trends and theories*. Oxford University Press, Oxford.

Eichengreen, B. (1990) *Elusive Stability: essays in the history of international finance, 1919–39*. Cambridge University Press, Cambridge.

**Glyn, A., Hughes, A., Lipietz, A. and Singh, A.** (1990) 'The rise and fall of the golden age', in S. Marglin and J. Schor, *The Golden Age of Capitalism*. Oxford University Press, Oxford.

**IMF,** (1993) International Financial Statistics, December.

**Hirsch, F.** (1967) *International Money*. Penguin Books, Harmondsworth.

**Keynes, J.M.** (1931) *Essays in Persuasion*. Macmillan, London.

**Kindleburger, C.P.** (1984) *A Financial History of Western Europe*. George Allen and Unwin, London.

**Kydland, F.E. and Prescott, E.C.** (1977) 'Rules rather than discretion: the inconsistency of optimal plans', *Journal of Political Economy*, 85, 3. June.

**Laidler, D.** (1993) 'Why do people hold money and does it matter?' Bank of Scotland Lecture. Money, Macro and Finance Conference, St Andrews, September, 8–10.

**Lindert, P.H.** (1969) 'Key currencies and gold, 1900–13', *Princeton Studies in International Finance*, 24, August.

**Llewellyn, D.T.** (1990) The international monetary system', in Llewellyn, D.T. and Milner, C. (eds), *Current Issues in International Monetary Economics*, Macmillan, London.

**McKinnon, R.I.** (1979) *Money in International Exchange*. Oxford University Press, Oxford.

**Milner, C.** (ed.) (1987) *Political Economy and International Money: Selected Essays of John Williamson*. Harvester Wheatsheaf, Hemel Hempstead.

**Panic, M.** (1992) *European Monetary Union: Lessons from the Classical Gold Standard*. Macmillan, London.

**Peseran, H.M.** (1986) 'Structures in Keynsianism as an alternative to monetarism', in P. Nolan and S. Paine (eds.) *Rethinking Socialist Economics*. Polity Press, London.

**Sachs, J.D. and Larrain, F.** (1993) *Macroeconomics: The Global Economy*. Harvester Wheatsheaf, Hemel Hempstead.

**Scammell, W.M.** (1975) *International Monetary Policy: Bretton Woods and After*. Macmillan, London.

**Tew, B.** (1982) *The Evolution of the International Monetary System 1945–81*, 2nd edition. Hutchinson, London.

**Thirwall, A.P. and Gibson, H.D.** (1992) *Balance of Payments Theory and the United Kingdom Experience* (4th ed.). Macmillan, London.

**Triffin, R.** (1960) *Gold and the Dollar Crisis*. Yale University Press, New Haven.

**Triffin, R.** (1964) 'The evolution of the international monetary system', *Princeton Studies in International Finance*, 12.

**Triffin, R.** (1968) *Our International Monetary System: Yesterday, Today and Tomorrow*. Random House, New York.

**Williamson, J.** (1977) *The Failure of World Monetary Reform*. Nelson, Sunbury-on-Thames.

**Yeager, L.B.** (1966) *International Monetary Relations: Theory, History and Policy*, 2nd edition. Harper & Row, New York.

# 2 PURCHASING POWER AND INTEREST PARITY RELATIONS

At the end of the last chapter, we presented some evidence concerning the behaviour of exchange rates during the floating-rate period. We noted, in particular, that nominal exchange rates since 1973 have exhibited greater volatility and that real exchange rates have shown large swings. In this and the following chapter, we want to investigate some of the main theories of exchange rate determination. In doing so, we hope to shed some light on the pattern of exchange rate movements during the flexible exchange rate period.

We begin this chapter with two fairly basic theories relating to exchange rates. The first, purchasing power parity, emphasises the role of the prices of goods and services in determining exchange rates. The second – interest rate parity – focuses on the role of capital movements. We argue that, in and of themselves, both these two theories are insufficient to explain exchange rate changes. However, they are useful building blocks in a number of more complex theories of exchange rate determination which we consider later in the chapter. These include the monetary approach and portfolio models of exchange rate determination.

In examining the question of interest rate parity, the market for forward exchange and its relationship with the spot market have to be considered. It is often claimed that the forward exchange rate is an unbiased predictor of the future spot rate (that is, that the forward market is efficient). In this chapter, we consider the role that the forward market plays in the interest parity relations as well as surveying the empirical evidence relating to its efficiency.

The chapter is organised as follows. In the first section we examine purchasing power parity theory and try to provide a flavour of the numerous empirical studies which have been conducted to test this theory. We conclude that there are good theoretical reasons as well as a large amount of empirical material which both suggest that purchasing power parity does not hold. In the second section we outline two key interest parity relations: covered interest parity and uncovered interest parity. Whilst the evidence suggests that under certain circumstances covered interest parity holds, uncovered parity does not appear to have much support. We explore further the reasons for the breakdown of the uncovered parity relation in the third section where we discuss the forward market for foreign exchange and its link with the spot market. Real interest parity is considered in the fourth section. The final section offers some conclusions.

**Purchasing power parity**

One of the oldest models of exchange rate determination is that of purchasing power parity (hereafter PPP). It is often argued that it has its origins in sixteenth-century Spain (Einzig, 1970). It was popular in the eighteenth and nineteenth centuries among groups of Swedish, French and English bullionists.[1] In the twentieth century, it is associated mainly with the Swedish economist, Gustav Cassel. It was he who first used the term 'purchasing power parity' (Cassel, 1918), and he was interested not only in the theory of PPP but also undertook some empirical testing of the theory (1916; 1925).[2]

There are two main forms of PPP – absolute PPP and relative PPP. The absolute version is based on the 'law of one price' which is given as follows:

$$P_1 = SP_1^* \tag{2.1}$$

where $P_1$ is the price of good 1 in the domestic country, $P_1^*$ is the price of good 1 in the foreign country and S is the exchange rate (the domestic currency price of a unit of foreign currency). If the domestic country is the UK and the foreign country the US, then equation (2.1) states that the price of good 1 in sterling ($P_1$) must be equal to the sterling price of good 1 in the US ($SP_1^*$).

There are a number of rather strict assumptions which underlie this 'law'. First, it assumes no transport costs. Secondly, there is perfect information – individual agents know the prices of each good in both countries. Thirdly, it assumes there are no barriers to trade (either quantitative or price barriers such as tariffs). Finally, it assumes that the good in question is homogenous (otherwise, price differences may merely reflect differences in quality). These rather strong assumptions are required because the equality represented in equation (2.1) is brought about through arbitrage. For example, if $P_1 < SP_1^*$, that is, the sterling price of good 1 is less in the UK than in the US, then it will be profitable for arbitrageurs to purchase the good in the UK and ship it to the US. In this way, the increased demand for the good in the UK will cause $P_1$ to rise. $P_1^*$ will fall as the supply of good 1 increases in the US. Finally, the exchange rate will also alter. The increased demand for good 1 in the UK will lead to an increase in the demand for sterling (by US residents, to buy the good in the UK). Sterling will therefore appreciate, that is, S will fall. Various combinations of these changes will operate to restore the quality given in equation (2.1). It is now easy to see why the assumptions we mentioned earlier are required. The existence of transport costs would eat into the profitability of arbitrage such that arbitrage would cease to be profitable before equation (2.1) is restored. Lack of information or barriers to trade would actually prevent arbitrage from occurring and hence there would be no tendency for equation (2.1) to hold.

From the 'law of one price' we can derive the absolute (or strong) version of PPP. The law of one price refers only to one good. If we construct an index of the general price level in any two countries, where each good has an *equal* weight in both indices, then we can derive equation (2.2):

$$P = SP^* \tag{2.2}$$

where P and $P^*$ are the general price indices in the domestic and foreign countries

---

[1] Bullionists argued that gold (and/or silver) alone should act as money in any economy and, not surprisingly, they argued that the gold standard was the appropriate system for the international economy.

[2] We can note here that Holmes (1967) is unhappy to argue that Cassel believed exchange rates were determined solely with reference to relative price levels in different countries. He argues that a careful reading of Cassel suggests that he believed two main propositions regarding exchange rates. First, Cassel argued that under flexible exchange rates, monetary factors are the *main* determinants of exchange rates. Secondly, he believed the remaining determinants of exchange rates to include transport costs, tariffs, capital flows and, interestingly, expectations.

respectively. Equation (2.2) represents the absolute version of the PPP theory. If we arrange equation (2.2) we can derive:

$$S = P/P^*  \tag{2.3}$$

which states that the spot exchange rate between two currencies is equal to the ratio of the general price levels between two countries. Alternatively we can state that the price levels between the two countries, measured in the domestic currency, are equal, $P/SP^* = 1$.

In its relative (or weak) version, we replace equation (2.3) by equation (2.4):

$$S = bP/P^*  \tag{2.4}$$

where b is some constant which reflects factors preventing absolute PPP from holding (e.g. b could be a measure of transport costs, information costs etc.). The relative version of PPP can be interpreted as stating that, if b is constant, then the rate of change of the exchange rate between two currencies is equal to the difference between the rate of change of the price levels in each country. In other words:

$$dS/S = dP/P - dP^*/P^*  \tag{2.5}$$

The relative version of PPP thus focuses on movements in the exchange rate and the extent to which they reflect differential inflation. Equation (2.5) reflects the familiar proposition that, if the domestic price level is rising faster than the foreign price level, the exchange rate is depreciating (that is, S is rising) and vice versa. Whilst it is a weaker proposition than absolute PPP, in the sense that the price levels in the two countries can differ by some constant, it requires the additional assumption that in the base year absolute PPP held. If absolute PPP did not hold in the base year, then through time changes in the exchange rate may not reflect differential inflation in subsequent periods in the two countries, but instead may capture previous (i.e. pre-base year) influences on the exchange rate.

If PPP holds (in either form), then this also implies that the real exchange rate of a country should remain constant over time. The real exchange rate can be defined as:

$$R = SP^*/P  \tag{2.6}$$

That is, the nominal exchange rate multiplied by the ratio of foreign to domestic prices. The real exchange rate provides a measure of a country's competitiveness. An appreciation of the real exchange rate, a decrease in R (due either to an appreciation of the nominal exchange rate (a decrease in S), an increase in P or a fall in $P^*$) is associated with a decline in competitiveness and vice versa. If changes in the nominal exchange rate (S) over time offset any differential inflation, then clearly a country's competitiveness and its real exchange rate remain constant.

There are a number of questions which arise when interpreting PPP theory. First, as it stands, neither the absolute nor the relative version say anything about causation. Under floating exchange rates, the presumption is that PPP is a theory of exchange rate determination – S becomes the endogenous variable which responds to exogenous changes in P and $P^*$. In the absolute version, the exchange rate alters to ensure that domestic and foreign price levels are brought into equality. In the relative version, exchange rate changes will offset differences in the inflation rates across countries.

The second problem facing PPP is what goods are included in the general price level of a country. We have already noted the importance of ensuring that both the goods and the weights attached to each good in the index are identical. A more general problem relates to which goods should be included – in particular, should PPP apply to traded and nontraded goods or to only traded. Officer (1976) notes that Cassel argued that both should be included, since, as Keynes (1930) argues, if only traded goods are used, then PPP becomes very close to a tautology. (If we have no restrictions on trade or costs associated with arbitrage, then trade will ensure the equalisation of prices (expressed in a common currency) of homogenous tradeable goods.[3] If, however, PPP is to apply to both traded and nontraded goods prices combined, then we have to add two additional assumptions: that there is a high degree of substitutability between traded goods and nontraded goods (so that changes in the prices of the traded goods will cause changes in the prices of nontraded substitutes); and that there are no productivity differences between traded and nontraded goods sectors (we return to this latter point later).

The final problem is the question of whether PPP holds in the short run as well as the long run, or whether PPP can be considered only as a long-run theory of exchange rate determination. Others, however, argue that it holds only in the long run. In the short run, the exchange rate can move away from PPP, but PPP acts as a long-run anchor to which exchange rates will always return in the long run.

Some of these problems with interpreting PPP theory led to a number of proposals in favour of a cost parity theory (see Officer (1976) for a survey). Officer notes two arguments used to favour cost over price parity theories. First, costs of production are less influenced by exchange rate change than are prices. Hence it is likely to be more appropriate to assume costs are the exogenous variable and the exchange rate the endogenous one. Secondly, costs, because they exclude the volatile profit component, are more likely to represent long run prices or permanent levels of inflation than prices. However, cost parity also can be subject to a number of criticisms which make it unclear whether it is any better as a theory of exchange rate determination[4] and hence we do not pursue it further here.

Aside from problems of interpreting PPP, there have been a number of theoretical criticisms of it as a theory of exchange rate determination. We deal here with six criticisms which have often been cited in the literature.[5] First, it is argued, that the existence of information costs, transport costs and trade barriers which could change over time make it unlikely that PPP will ever hold. Information costs, which are usually incurred when discovering prices in different countries, are important because of the method through which PPP is supposed to be brought about, that is, via commodity arbitrage. Transport costs are incurred when goods are actually transferred from one country to another. Moreover, all this assumes that the goods can actually be transferred – quotas may prevent this. With tariffs, trade can take place, but there are costs involved in importing the good to the country where it is expensive, and

---

[3] We can note that Keynes used this argument to criticise the use of wholesale price indices in empirical investigation of PPP. Wholesale price indices were unsuitable because they tend to be dominated by traded goods (consumer price indices include services which are more likely to be nontraded).

[4] Officer (1976) notes a number of problems with cost parity theory: the same kind of index number problems exists – for example, costs vary between firms within industries (which firms should be used in the index?) and costs vary according to output levels; and, additionally there is a greater problem with empirical testing – data on costs is much more limited than that available for prices.

[5] The literature on PPP is enormous. On the criticisms of PPP, see, for example, De Grauwe (1989); Isard (1977, 1987); Katseli-Papaefstratiou (1979); Krueger (1983); MacDonald (1988); McKinnon (1979); and Officer (1976).

these costs could wipe out the arbitrageurs' profits. As we noted earlier, absolute PPP will not hold if costs of these kind exist (which clearly they do). Relative PPP will only hold if these costs remain constant over time. However, this too is unlikely: new forms of transportation alter prices; successive rounds of GATT agreements have altered tariffs; and information costs are probably lower as a result of new methods of communication (faxes, computers, etc). Thus whilst seemingly rather trivial, the invalidity of these assumptions could prevent PPP from being a good theory of exchange rate determination.

The second theoretical criticism of PPP is that the direction of causality is unclear. We interpreted it above as a theory of exchange rate determination – it is the exchange rate which changes in response to a disturbance to domestic or foreign prices. However, it could be argued that the exchange rate determines prices – since exchange rate changes can feed into price changes through the impact of the exchange rate on import prices and, if workers have a real wage target, these price changes can lead to wage changes and hence, via costs, to further price changes. Indeed some have argued that both exchange rates and prices are determined endogenously by variables unspecified by PPP theory (see, for example, Katseli-Papaefstratiou, 1979). Exchange rates and prices may be determined by income levels, production capacity, product quality, wages etc.

The third criticism relates to the implication of the theory that all disturbances are monetary, or at least that monetary disturbances are more important than real disturbances. Samuelson (1964) and Officer (1976) have argued that real disturbances – the result, for example, of the discovery of a natural resource or an innovation which changes productivity in one country – necessitate a change in relative prices and hence a change in the real equilibrium exchange rate of the country. For example, if a country discovers it has vast reserves of a natural resource, then this will necessitate an appreciation of the real exchange rate since the country has discovered additional wealth which can positively contribute to exports. There is therefore a departure from PPP.

A fourth and related criticism has been made by Balassa (1964) and concerns differential productivity growth in traded and nontraded goods sectors (in other words, a kind of real shock).[6] The argument runs as follows. It is usually the case that productivity is higher (or grows at a faster rate) in the tradeables sector in comparison to the nontradeable sector.[7] Assume we have two countries – Germany and the UK. Assume further that productivity in the tradeables sector in Germany is greater than productivity in the UK tradeables sector. Germany can afford larger increases in wages than the UK without losing competitiveness because of the greater productivity levels. However, the wage increase is likely to transmit itself to the nontradeables sectors in Germany. German prices thus increase faster than UK prices yet there is no loss in competitiveness and no need for the exchange rate to change. The result is that PPP does not hold.[8]

---

[6] See De Grauwe (1989) for a very good account of this problem and its impact on exchange rates in Japan, the US and Germany.

[7] We can note that differential productivity *levels* in different sectors affect *absolute* PPP. Differential productivity *growth* affects the relative version of PPP.

[8] De Grauwe (1989) provides some evidence on the importance of productivity differentials on PPP. He finds that if actual exchange rates are compared with PPP exchange rates uncorrected for productivity differentials, then there is little evidence for PPP. If, however, PPP exchange rates are corrected for productivity differentials then they follow actual exchange rates much more closely.

The fifth theoretical criticism which can be made of PPP is that it ignores the role of incomes in determining exchange rates. A role for income may arise from the effect of changes in income on demand for imports and the supply of exports. Presumably the extent to which income will affect the exchange rate will depend on whether one examines PPP as a short-run phenomenon (in which case the impact of the business cycle will be greatest) or a long-run phenomenon (in which case the effect of income will depend on whether we believe that the economy tends to full employment or not).

A final criticism of PPP theory is that it essentially views the demand for foreign exchange as a demand that derives from the desire to purchase goods and services in other countries. There is no role for capital flows. Indeed Cassel himself noted that both short-term and long-term capital movements could cause the exchange rate to deviate from PPP. Officer (1976) argues that this need not be the case – if capital flows are to cause long-run deviations then they must be persistently in one direction or the other, which he argues is unlikely. However, long-term capital flows such as foreign direct investment frequently last for a number of years in one direction. Moreover, even short-term capital flows could cause substantial deviations from PPP in the short run. Growing integration of capital markets since World War II has led to a large demand for foreign exchange to purchase foreign assets. Frenkel (1981) argues that the demand for foreign assets is determined by expectations of the future. Thus, 'exchange rates reflect expectations about *future* circumstances while prices reflect more *present* and *past* circumstances' (p.162). This implies that fluctuations in exchange rates will not follow fluctuations in price levels; in other words, that PPP will not hold.[9]

If there are good theoretical reasons for believing that PPP will not hold and thus is an inadequate theory of exchange rate determination, then it is perhaps not surprising that empirical studies have found little evidence in its favour. We can divide the evidence on PPP into tests of commodity arbitrage, tests of the absolute version and tests of the relative version. Within each group of tests, we are also interested in differences between long-run and short-run results.

Looking at the issue of commodity arbitrage first. Most authors conclude that commodity arbitrage appears not to maintain the law of one price. Isard (1977) examines manufactured goods from the US, Germany and Japan for the period 1970–75. He finds little evidence that the law of one price holds. These findings are confirmed by Kravis and Lipsey (1978). Fraser *et al.* (1990) investigate whether the law of one price holds in the long run. They use the econometric technique of cointegration. This essentially tests to determine whether two or more variables tend to move together over time. The advantage of this method is that it allows them to test specifically for a long-term relationship, abstracting from short-term consideration. They conclude that there is little evidence that the law of one price is valid, even in the long run. These results all focused on manufactured goods. It is interesting to see whether the law of one price holds for primary goods (which are more homogeneous). Isard (1977) on the whole finds that it does. By contrast, Michael *et al.* (1994), again using cointegration, find systematic deviations from PPP in wheat markets in the US, Rotterdam and Japan in the short run, although not in the long run.

---

[9] Katseli-Papaefstratiou (1979) notes that this was recognised as early as 1928 by Zolotas.

Frenkel (1981) conducts tests of the absolute version of PPP using regression analysis. He compares the floating exchange rate period of the 1920s with that of the 1970s. Evidence from the 1920s is supportive of PPP. With respect to the 1970s, however, he finds little evidence in favour of PPP. Frenkel suggests that this is a consequence of the fact that disturbances in the 1920s tended to be monetary in origin (in particular due to inappropriate monetary policy of the US Federal Reserve), whereas in the 1970s they tended to be real (for example, the oil price shock). As we explained previously, monetary disturbances do not necessitate a change in the real exchange rate, whereas real disturbances do. Frenkel's evidence for the 1920s is contradicted by Krugman (1978), who uses a longer sample period and finds results which are unfavourable to the PPP theory.

Tests of the relative PPP theory are far more numerous and generally take one of two forms – either regression analysis or a simple plot of the data concerned (nominal exchange rates, inflation or real exchange rates). Officer (1976) reviews a number of early tests of PPP. These focus on the floating period in the 1920s and give mixed results. Cassel (1916) found support for PPP using monthly data from 1915 on the Swedish krona and sterling. However, in his more extensive 1925 study which used monthly data from 1919–24 for the sterling–dollar exchange rate, he found deviations from PPP, which he explained largely through capital movements. Keynes (1923) and Graham (1930) using data from 12 European countries from 1919–23 found evidence in favour of PPP. By contrast, Angell (1926) and Heckscher (1930), who examined movements in the franc–dollar exchange rate and the Swedish krona respectively, did not find any support for PPP. Angell attributes deviations from PPP to changing degrees of confidence in the franc. Thus these early tests of PPP on data from the 1920s provide mixed results. One possible explanation is the problem of choosing a base year, and, probably more importantly, differences in the price indices used.[10]

Cumby and Obstfeld (1984) provide some graphical evidence for the 1960s and 1970s – they plot the real exchange rates for a number of major currencies (dollar, yen, Deutschmark (DM) etc.). They note that during the floating exchange rate period, deviations from PPP get larger and overall their results decisively reject PPP. De Grauwe (1989) plots percentage rates of change of the exchange rate and the inflation differentials for DM–dollar and yen–dollar. His results confirm those of Cumby and Obstfeld – the floating exchange rate period has been characterised by large deviations from PPP. Moreover often the exchange rate changes moved in different directions from the inflation differentials especially from 1974–84. MacDonald (1988) tests PPP by plotting nominal and real exchange rates together. Given PPP implies that the real exchange rate remain constant, a test of PPP is whether nominal and real rates move independently of one another. However, MacDonald finds considerable correlation between nominal and real rates for sterling and the Deutschmark relative to the dollar over the period 1975–85. Finally, Frenkel (1981) uses regression analysis to test the relative PPP theory in the 1970s. He finds little support.

More recent work which employs a rather different methodology has been carried out by Adler and Lehmann (1983) and MacDonald (1985). Adler and Lehmann argue that if PPP is valid, then changes in the real exchange rate should be serially

---

[10] The construction of price indices was still in its infancy at this time and it is not easy to find indices which are compatible across countries.

correlated and show a *cumulative* tendency to deviate from PPP (after some shock, say) followed by a *systematic* tendency to revert to it. Alternatively, if the real exchange rate follows a random walk where changes in the real exchange rate are serially uncorrelated, then this provides evidence against PPP.[11] They test these hypotheses by running the following regression:

$$Y_t = \sum_{i=1}^{n} b_i Y_{t-i} + V_t \tag{2.7}$$

where $y_t$ is the percentage change in the real exchange at time t. If the $b_i$ coefficients are jointly insignificantly different from zero, then changes in the real exchange rate follow a random walk. If, by contrast, some of the $b_i$s are significant then this is evidence in favour of PPP.

Adler and Lehmann test their hypothesis on annual data from 1900 to 1972 for exchange rates between the US dollar and eight other countries; and on annual data (1870–1975) for the US and Canada. Their results support the hypothesis that the $b_i$'s are jointly insignificantly different from zero and hence they reject PPP as a long-run theory of exchange rate determination. MacDonald (1985) runs a similar test on monthly data for the French franc, dollar and sterling bilateral exchange rates from January 1921 to May 1925. His results support the random walk hypothesis. In other words, there is no tendency for the real exchange rate during this period to revert to PPP and this result leads MacDonald to reject the validity of PPP during the 1920s.

A final group of papers use cointegration methods to test for PPP.[12] They use the equation: $s_t = \beta_t p_t - \beta^* p^*_t + \zeta_t$ where $s_t$ is the exchange rate and $p_t$ and $p^*_t$ are the domestic and foreign price indices respectively. If PPP holds, then the exchange rate, domestic and foreign prices should be cointegrated and $\beta = \beta^* = 1$. Taylor (1988) and Patel (1990) test for cointegration using the Engle–Granger two-step method. Having tested for the order of integration of prices and exchange rates, which they find to be I(1), they then test for cointegration, by examining whether the errors, $\zeta_t$, are stationary. Whilst Patel finds some evidence in favour of cointegration and hence PPP, Taylor does not.

MacDonald (1993) and Kugler and Lenz (1993) use multivariate cointegration techniques (Johansen procedure), which have the advantage of allowing a test of the hypothesis that $\beta = \beta^* = 1$ as well as testing for cointegration. Kugler and Lenz (1993) test for purchasing power parity for the Deutschmark *vis-à-vis* some fifteen other currencies using monthly data from 1973 to 1990. Their results are mixed: PPP is supported for some currencies but not for others. MacDonald (1993), using monthly data from January 1974 to June 1990 for the US dollar *vis-à-vis* the Canadian dollar, French franc, Deutschmark, yen and sterling, he finds some evidence of PPP: exchange rates appear to respond to relative prices, but the above restriction on the $\beta$'s is rejected.

In conclusion, therefore, our discussion of the theory and evidence concerning the PPP theory has shown that as a theory of exchange rate determination it is

---

[11] We can note that Adler and Lehmann derive some theoretical foundations which would be consistent with random walk behaviour. In particular, their model is based on efficient financial arbitrage leading to real interest rate equalisation.

[12] We assume here some working knowledge of cointegration techniques. For a comprehensive and very accessible discussion of these methods see Bhaskara Rao (1994).

inadequate. At best, it identifies only one of a number of factors which affect exchange rates. It is often employed as a long-run association in more complete models of exchange rate determination, as we shall see later in this chapter. This perhaps reflects its most useful role, namely as a benchmark as to where exchange rates *should* be. In other words, PPP (especially if corrected for productivity differentials) can give us a measure of what the equilibrium exchange rate is, based on the competitive position of a country.[13] Whether actual exchange rates converge on this equilibrium is, as we have seen, unlikely. We have to turn therefore to other theories of exchange rate determination which place greater emphasis on the financial factors if we are to go some way to explain actual exchange rate movements.

## Interest rate parity

One of the key weaknesses of the PPP theory of exchange rate determination, as we noted in the previous section, is its concentration on goods and services, to the exclusion of the importance of capital flows in the determination of exchange rates. To some extent the concept of interest parity allows us to remedy this omission, by providing some understanding of the way in which interest rates are linked between different countries through flows of capital. Unlike PPP, however, interest rate parity cannot be called a theory of exchange rate determination. Instead, it is often used as an association in newer theories of exchange rate determination which we will examine. Thus it is useful here to explain what is meant by interest rate parity and provide some discussion of empirical tests of the hypothesis.

There are three types of interest rate parity: covered interest rate parity; uncovered interest rate parity; and real interest rate parity. We examine here the first two. Real interest rate parity is considered later in the chapter.

### Covered interest rate parity

Covered interest rate parity (CIP) essentially states that returns between assets in different countries should be equalised. If they are not equalised, then there are opportunities for profitable arbitrage, the operation of which will bring the rates of return closer together.

There are a number of assumptions underlying this proposition. First the assets concerned must have the same degree of risk and the same maturity. Second there should be no transactions costs of information costs associated with finding out the rates of return on different assets in different countries. Finally, there should be no controls on capital flows. Under these conditions, we would expect the following equation to hold:

$$(1 + i_t^*)F_t / S_t = (1 + i_t) \qquad (2.8a)$$

where t is time; $i_t$ is the domestic nominal interest rate; $i_t^*$ is the foreign interest rate; $F_t$ is the forward exchange rate (that is, the price of foreign exchange quoted now, at time t, for settlement at a future date, t + 1); $S_t$ is the spot exchange rate at time t. The right-hand side of equation (2.8a) represents the return derived from investing one unit of the domestic currency in the domestic market (for example, through the purchase of a Treasury Bill or a deposit in a bank). The left-hand side represents the return from investing in the foreign market. The return in this latter case is more complex because of the existence of foreign exchange risk. If an investor takes one unit of the domestic currency, he/she has first to convert it into the foreign currency,

---

[13] See Officer (1976) for an extensive discussion of the role of PPP as a measure of the equilibrium exchange rate.

receiving $1/S_t$ units of the foreign currency. This amount is then invested, yielding (in foreign currency) $1/S_t(1 + i_t^*)$ at the end of the period. This amount of foreign exchange is sold in the forward market at the beginning of time, t, for domestic currency, at the forward exchange rate $F_t$.[14] This forward transaction is actually completed at the end of time, t, when the investment is realised. Overall, therefore, investment of one unit of domestic currency in the foreign market yields $(1 + i_t^*)F_t/S_t$ at the end of period t. We can note therefore that the transaction in the forward market ensures that the investor incurs no foreign exchange risk (i.e. the risk of the exchange rate changing while his/her investment is abroad).

Thus an investor has a choice – invest at home (with return $(1 + i_t)$) or invest abroad (with return $F_t(1 + i_t^*)/S_t$). The interest rate parity condition states that these returns will be equalised through arbitrage. To see how arbitrage works, it is useful to ask what happens if equation (2.8a) does not hold. Assume, for example, that:

$$(1 + i_t^*) \quad F_t/S_t > (1 + i_t) \tag{2.8b}$$

that is, the return abroad is greater than at home. In this case, domestic investors will seek to place funds abroad. They will purchase foreign exchange spot, causing the price of foreign exchange to rise (i.e. $S_t$ rises). At the same time, investors are selling foreign exchange forward (causing $F_t$ to fall). The foreign return thus gets smaller and smaller (as $F_t/S_t$ falls) restoring covered interest parity. Thus it is movements in capital induced by profitable arbitrage opportunities which cause interest rate parity to be restored. If arbitrage is efficient, then interest rate parity should hold continuously since any slight deviation from it will induce large capital movements.

The covered interest parity condition can be written in a more convenient, if slightly less accurate, form. If we take the natural logarithms of both sides of equation (2.8), then we derive.[15]

$$i^* - fp = i \tag{2.9}$$

where $i^*$ and $i$ are the foreign and domestic interest rates as before and fp is the forward premium (discount, if negative) on the domestic currency. If i is less than $i^*$, then the forward domestic currency must be at a premium (i.e. fp > 0).

There have been numerous tests of covered interest parity. There are three possible means of testing CIP. Firstly, we can simply plot the domestic return (i) and the foreign return ($i^*$ – fp) separately. If they move together, with no clear differences between them, then covered interest parity can be said to hold. The advantage of this method is that it is easy to do and can act as a first approximation. Its disadvantage, of course, is that it is not very accurate – small deviations might be undetectable yet may be significant. A second test is to calculate the deviations from interest rate parity and test whether they are insignificantly different from zero. Finally, we can use regression analysis:

---

[14] We discuss the determination of the forward exchange rate later in the chapter. For present purposes, it is enough to know that it exists.

[15] This is derived as follows:

$$(1 + i_t^*)F_t/S_t = (1 + i_t) \tag{2.8a}$$

Take the natural logarithms of both sides:

$$\text{In}(1 + i_t^*) + \text{In} F_t - \text{In} S_t = \text{In}(1 + i_t)$$

where ($\text{In} F_t - \text{In} S_t$) is the forward premium/discount on the domestic currency expressed as a percentage. If we assume, $\text{In}(1 + i_t^*) \approx i_t^*$ and $\text{In}(1 + i) \approx i$, then $i_t^* - fp = i$, where fp is the forward premium on the domestic currency.

$$fp = a + b(i^* - i) \qquad (2.10)$$

where, if $a = 0$ and $b = 1$, then CIP holds.

A number of earlier studies done in the 1960s and 1970s indicated that deviations from parity were not uncommon and, moreover, were sometimes quite persistent.[16] This was true across a wide range of currencies, and led inevitably to a number of papers which seek to explain these deviations.

Firstly, we can appeal to transactions costs. Frenkel and Levich (1975) note that if we consider the outward flow of arbitrage funds (from the domestic country) then there are four distinct costs which arbitrageurs will face: the sale of domestic securities (e.g. Treasury bills); the purchase of foreign currency (in the spot market); the purchase of foreign securities; and the sale of foreign currency (in the forward market). In other words, transactions costs arise from dealing in both the foreign exchange markets and the securities markets. Transactions costs are clearly significant in explaining departures from CIP, but the interesting question is *how* significant are they. Branson (1969) attempts to measure these costs by examining arbitrage between US/UK Treasury bills (January 1959–December 1964) and US/Canadian Treasury bills (January 1962–December 1964). He eliminates 'speculative' periods from the data and calculates the covered interest rate differential that existed during the remaining 'calm' periods.[17] For these 'calm' periods, two regressions as in equation (2.10) were run. In the case of the UK–US, the constant is insignificantly different from zero and the coefficient on the interest rate differential ($i^* - i$) is insignificantly different from 1. In the case of Canadian–US arbitrage, the constant 'is slightly positive and the slope slightly less than unity' (Branson, 1969, p.1033). These results confirm for Branson that deviations from CIP were small. He then uses the mean of these deviations as a measure of transactions costs, which he calculates as 0.18% in both cases.

The obvious problem with this approach is the assumption that all deviations from CIP are merely the result of transactions costs. This is particularly worrying for the UK–US case since at that time the UK had extensive controls on capital outflows. As we shall see later in Chapter 7, this led to large deviations from CIP right up until their removal in 1979.[18] This is not considered by Branson, yet if capital cannot flow out of a country because of controls then CIP may easily be broken.

Frenkel and Levich (1975) attempt to measure transactions costs in a different way. Transactions costs in foreign exchange markets are measured indirectly by determining the cost of triangular arbitrage (recall this was described in Chapter 1). They assume such arbitrage is efficient and hence use any deviations between what the exchange rate would be if arbitrage were efficient and what it actually is. With this method, they calculate transactions costs in the foreign exchange markets at around 0.12–0.13%. In securities markets there are two distinct costs: brokerage fees and the bid–ask spread. They then use Demsetz's (1968) formula which calculates total costs of transacting in securities markets as 2.5 times the bid–ask spread. This

---

[16] See Officer and Willet (1970) for a survey. See also Branson (1969), Aliber (1973) and Frenkel and Levich (1975).

[17] Branson (1969) defines speculative periods as those periods when the differential is high; for example, he eliminates June/July 1961 when a speculative crisis against sterling occurred.

[18] A potential reason why Branson does not find substantial deviations from parity is because he eliminates speculative periods. It was at those times that the capital controls were most biting (see Gibson, 1989 and Chapter 7).

yields an estimate of 0.019%. Hence they conclude that total transactions costs are between 0.14% and 0.15%.

As with Branson (1969), however, their estimates are based on certain strong assumptions – that triangular arbitrage is efficient. Clinton (1988) has criticised this assumption, arguing that it leads to an overestimation of transactions costs. He argues that transactions costs estimates should be based on the lowest possible costs faced by major arbitrageurs (e.g. banks), in which case, we have to estimate transactions costs in swap markets. The swap market that concerns him is that in which spot exchange is swapped for forward exchange. If, for example, a US bank wishes to invest in a covered Deutschmark asset, it can in *one* transaction swap into DMs at the spot rate and out of DMs at the forward rate. Thus instead of the two transactions identified by Frenkel and Levich (1975) and noted previously, arbitrageurs need only conduct one transaction. Clinton estimates transactions costs in this way by examining the bid–ask spread in the swap markets for US dollars into Canadian dollars, Deutschmarks, French francs, yen and sterling between November 1985 and May 1986. His results suggest transaction costs are only around 0.023–0.039%.[19] By adding this to the bid–ask spread in the euromarkets (as an estimate for dealing in securities markets), Clinton derives a total figure for transactions costs of around 0.06%. This is lower than Frenkel and Levich's (1975) estimates quoted above and is significantly lower than Frenkel and Levich's (1981) estimates of 0.50% for the floating exchange rate period.

Having derived estimates of transactions costs, we can now ask how far they go towards explaining deviations from interest rate parity. Frenkel and Levich (1975) examine two cases: firstly, arbitrage between the US and the UK using weekly data on 90-day Treasury Bills; and secondly, arbitrage in the euromarkets using eurodollar and eurosterling interest rates on 90-day deposits. They, like Branson, choose the 'calm' period from January 1962 to November 1967. They find that, in the first case, transactions costs account for around 85% of profitable arbitrage opportunities. In the second case, transactions costs account for almost all the deviations (greater than 99%). Clinton (1988) not surprisingly finds that less deviations from interest rate parity can be attributed to transaction costs. 15% of observations (in the case of dollar–sterling arbitrage) and 25% (in the case of arbitrage between the dollar and various other currencies) lie outside the neutral zone created by transactions costs. He thus concludes that transactions costs play a smaller role in explaining deviations from CIP than was originally thought.

A second reason why CIP might not hold is the existence of capital controls. These affect arbitrage between onshore markets, that is between two domestic markets. It does not affect arbitrage between euromarkets (or offshore markets), which are unaffected by capital controls.[20] This is confirmed by a number of studies. Looking first at arbitrage between different euromarkets, Marston (1976) regresses the non-dollar eurocurrency rate, $r_x$, on the eurodollar rate, $r_\$$, and the forward premium, fp (between x and the dollar):

$$r_x = a + b(r_\$) - c(fp) + u \qquad (2.11)$$

---

[19] The latter estimate was for the French franc where, Clinton argues, the swap market was constrained by capital controls, making the bid–ask spread rather high.

[20] This is an important distinction to make. The UK government, for example, can only impose capital controls on capital flows in and out of the UK. It therefore cannot prevent capital from flowing into or out of the eurosterling market in Paris. Indeed, capital controls are, as we shall see in the second half of this book, one of the main reasons for the growth of offshore markets.

If CIP holds then it is expected that a = 0 and b = c = 1. To allow for any influence of the forward premium on $r_x$, Marston estimates two set of equations.[21] The first, an ordinary least squares (OLS) regression, was estimated for the period 1965–70 using weekly data. In the case of the eurodollar and eurosterling markets (that is, $r_x = r_£$), the hypothesis that CIP help continuously could not be rejected. The second approach, an instrumental variables approach, confirmed this result. Thus Marston concludes that arbitrage between different euromarkets seems to be efficient. Gibson (1989) confirms this result for the period 1974–84.

By contrast, Llewellyn (1980) finds evidence of a persistent differential against sterling when considering CIP between the US and UK domestic (onshore) markets. In other words, the return from investing abroad was persistently greater than that from investing at home. Gibson (1989) tests this indirectly for the period 1974–84 and finds a similar result pre-1979.[22] After October 1979, CIP holds almost continuously. This finding can be attributed entirely to the removal of controls on capital outflows in October 1979. Similar results have been found for other European countries with capital controls (see EC (1988) on a variety of countries; and Johnston (1983) and Dooley and Isard (1980) on German controls on capital inflows).

A third explanation for deviations from interest rate parity is given by Aliber (1973). He argues that political risk may be important. He defines this as the risk that controls on capital movements or new taxes may be imposed before arbitrage funds are repatriated. He tests this hypothesis by considering eurosterling and eurodollar rates. He argues that as these markets come under the same legal jurisdictions they should have the same political risk.[23] Hence CIP should hold and the difference between the two rates can give us a measure of the forward premium and hence the forward exchange rate. He then notes that if this predicted forward rate is equal to the actual forward rate, then the hypothesis that these two assets have the same political risk is not incorrect. Any disparity between actual and predicted forward rates can then be attributed to political risk. He compares the results of this test with a similar test using UK and US Treasury bill rates – two assets which are quite definitely issued in two different political jurisdictions. If the difference between the actual and predicted forward rates using this measure is large then this can be attributed to political risk. He applies these tests to the period January 1968 to June 1970 and concludes that deviations from CIP are prevalent between the UK and US domestic markets because each country bears different political risk.

The problem with Aliber's analysis is that he makes no mention of actual capital controls, which, as we have already noted, affected the UK markets and the ability of arbitrageurs to take capital out of the UK. Hence the deviations from CIP which he uncovers may simply reflect *existing* capital controls rather than expectations of future controls. This point is made, more generally, by Dooley and Isard (1980). They argue that it is important to distinguish actual controls from the threat of future controls. Only the latter can be considered political risk. They seek to do this by examining the situation in Germany in the early 1970s (when capital controls on inflows were operational). They run a regression which hypothesises that the

---

[21] If fp affects $r_x$, then this could lead to biased coefficients.

[22] We discuss Gibson (1989) in more detail in Chapter 7, when we examine the impact of the euromarkets on monetary policy independence.

[23] We can note, however, that in the empirical part he takes the eurosterling rate from Paris and the eurodollar rate from London. This rather undermines the assumption of identical legal jurisdiction.

differential between the 3-month euroDM rate (in Zurich) and a domestic DM rate (3-month Frankfurt interbank rate) is a function of: existing capital controls (which they proxy by a dummy); German federal government debt (B); the wealth of the German private sector ($W_g$); and the wealth of nonresidents ($W_{NR}$). The last three factors are intended to capture political risk. Their idea of political risk seems closely related to portfolio risk – the idea that the more German assets held by non-residents, for example, the less willing they are to increase their holdings of German assets, unless compensated by a higher return.[24] Based on their results (which are rather poor), they argue that for an interest rate differential which reached a maximum of 10%, only a maximum of 2% could be attributed to the political risk premium.

The final explanation of deviations from CIP which we want to consider here is that of data imperfections. Taylor (1987) argues that profitable arbitrage opportunities occur at *one* point in time and hence when testing for CIP it is necessary to use *contemporaneously sampled* data. In other words, the interest rates and forward premium used must reflect those available in the market at any given time. He therefore collects data on 11, 12 and 13 November 1985 between 9a.m. and 4.50p.m. at 10 minute intervals. Figures were recorded (from a broker) for: spot and forward (1, 3, 6, and 12-month maturities) exchange rates for dollar *vis-à-vis* sterling; spot and forward (1, 3, 6, and 12-month maturities) exchange rates for Deutschmark *vis-à-vis* the dollar; and the eurosterling, eurodollar and euroDM interest rates (for the same maturities). He then conducts a test of CIP on these 144 observations.[25] His results indicate that at no time was there a profitable arbitrage opportunity between sterling and dollar assets. For arbitrage between dollar and DM assets, there was only one profitable opportunity – had someone invested $1 million, he/she could have made a profit of $200. He thus concludes that arbitrage is efficient and that CIP holds.[26] Taylor and Fraser (1990) undertake a similar task (for dollar–sterling arbitrage) over a longer period (7.8.87–1.9.87). They collect observations during this period 5 minutes before and after the release of any item of economic information on the UK or US economy. The aim here is to determine whether CIP holds continuously even when the market is being bombarded with 'news'. For a total number of observations of 6330, they find only 21 profitable arbitrage opportunities. In other words, the markets show very little evidence of inefficiency.

We can conclude therefore that CIP certainly seems to hold in offshore markets (once we make proper allowances for transactions costs and ensure that the data collected is contemporaneous). Evidence from arbitrage between domestic markets is

---

[24] We discuss portfolio models in more detail in Chapter 3.

[25] We can note that he is meticulous in taking the correct interest rates and exchange rate for each arbitrage opportunity. For example, for arbitrage from sterling to dollar, the operation goes as follows: (a) take a sterling deposit (attracted by a bank using the eurosterling *offer* rate); (b) exchange sterling for dollars at the spot *bid* rate; (c) lend these dollars in the eurodollar market receiving the eurodollar bid rate; (d) sell the dollars that the arbitrageur will receive on maturity of the eurodollar deposit for sterling using the forward *offer* rate. In other words, it is important to use the correct bid-offer rates because of the spread between them. In this way, Taylor controls for transactions costs (or at least those arising from bid-offer spreads).

[26] This result is perhaps not surprising since it is often argued (see Marston, 1976; Johnston, 1983; and Gibson, 1989) that non-dollar eurocurrency interest rates are institutionally determined in the sense that if asked for a quote for a euroDM or eurosterling interest rate, banks will often simply take the eurodollar rate and subtract the relevant forward premium. In other words, banks assume arbitrage is efficient and would not quote rates that would generate profitable opportunities.

64

more mixed, although it appears that in the absence of capital controls, deviations from CIP are few and small.

*Uncovered interest parity*

In the case of CIP, foreign exchange risk is removed by arbitrageurs entering into a forward contract. In the case that a forward contract is not entered into and hence the investor assumes the foreign exchange risk, then we can replace equation (2.9) by:

$$i^* + \Delta s^e = i \tag{2.12}$$

where $\Delta s^e$ is the expected change in the spot exchange rate. Equation (2.12) is known as uncovered interest parity (UIP) and we would expect it to hold if the path of the exchange rate is known with certainty or if arbitrageurs are risk neutral (in other words, they do not seek an extra return for taking on foreign exchange risk). From equations (2.12) and (2.9) we can see that $- fp = \Delta s^e$.

What equation (2.12) says is that if the foreign interest rate is higher than the domestic rate, then the domestic currency must be expected to appreciate (that is, $\Delta s^e < 0$, since $s^e_{t+1} < s_t$). If, however, there is uncertainty or if arbitrageurs are not risk neutral, then we would expect some deviation from UIP which would reflect a risk premium:

$$i^* + \Delta s^e - i = \rho \tag{2.13}$$

where $\rho$ is the risk premium. Alternatively one can note that, in the case of uncertainty or risk aversion, then $- fp$ and $\Delta s^e$ differ by the amount given by the risk premium, $\rho$.

MacDonald (1988) notes that these concepts allow us to distinguish between perfect capital mobility and imperfect capital mobility. Perfect capital mobility can be defined as involving assets which are identical in every respect except their currency of denomination (i.e. same maturity, risk etc.) and where arbitrage ensures that UIP holds continuously between them. If CIP holds, then this is not sufficient for perfect capital mobility, since the forward premium could include a risk premium. In this case where CIP holds but UIP does not, we have imperfect capital mobility.

Tests of UIP are more difficult to conduct than those for CIP because of the problem of getting data on the *expected* future spot rate. Often this is overcome by assuming rational expectations[27] which imply:

$$\Delta s^e = s_t^e - s_{t-1} = s_t - s_{t-1} + e_t \tag{2.14}$$

where $e_t$ is an error which is randomly distributed (i.e. not serially correlated) and with mean of zero. In other words, rational expectations says that the expected future spot rate, given the information available at time t, is equal to the actual future spot rate plus some random error. Hence a test of UIP is given by the following regression:

$$s_t = a_0 s_{t-1} + a_1 (i - i^*)_t + e_t \tag{2.15}$$

But this is not only a test of UIP, but also of the rational expectations assumption, $s_t^e = s_t + e_t$. If UIP and rational expectations hold then $a_0 = -1$, $a_1 = 1$ and $e_t$ should be serially uncorrelated with mean of zero (white noise).

---

[27] We explain the nature of this joint hypothesis when we discuss the question of the efficiency of the forward market for foreign exchange.

Tests of UIP (and rational expectations) have generally concluded that it does not hold, probably because of the existence of a risk premium. However, since we are testing a joint hypothesis, the failure to confirm UIP may equally stem from irrational behaviour by market participants due, for example, to the existence of limited information or due to bubble phenomena.

Hacche and Townend (1981) investigate UIP using the effective exchange rate of sterling from July 1972 to February 1980. Their results indicate that whilst $a_0$ and $a_1$ are correctly signed, and of the right magnitude, the residuals show evidence of serial correlation. This result is confirmed by the fact that the inclusion of lagged changes in domestic credit and the change in the exchange rate improves the equation.

Cumby and Obstfeld (1984) derive similar results from looking at the US *vis-à-vis* Germany, UK, Switzerland, Canada and Japan from 1976 to 1981. They find that for all countries except the US and Germany, the UIP relation has little support. In order to explore the reasons for the failure of UIP in more detail we have to turn to examine the efficiency of the forward market.

## The forward market for foreign exchange

In the previous section, we discussed the role of interest arbitrageurs in influencing the forward exchange rate. A second important group which operate in the forward markets are the speculators.[28] Speculators deliberately expose themselves to foreign exchange risk (in other words, they take an open position in the foreign exchange markets) and seek to make a profit by taking a view on what the future spot exchange rate might be. In order to understand the relationship between spot and forward exchange rates, we have to delve into the operations of the speculators more closely.

Speculators will trade currencies on the basis of the difference between the forward exchange rate now for three months hence, say,[29] f, and the expected spot exchange rate in three months time, $s^e$ (where for ease of exposition with empirical testing later, we use the logarithms of the relevant exchange rates). Assume that a speculator believes that the exchange rate in 3 months time will be more depreciated than the current forward rate (that is, $s^e > f$), then he/she will find it profitable to purchase foreign exchange in the forward market (at the exchange rate, f) and sell it back at a profit (provided his/her expectations are realised). We can illustrate this by means of a numerical example. Suppose that $s^e$ is £0.80 for $1 while f is £0.70 for $1. The speculator should buy a dollar now in the forward market (where the cost is £0.70). In three months time, the speculator will purchase the dollar for £0.70 which they can then convert back into sterling and receive £0.80 (assuming the actual spot rate in three months time is exactly what they expected). This is known as taking a 'long' position in the forward exchange market.

On the other hand, if the expected future spot exchange rate in 3 months time is appreciated relative to the forward rate ($s^e < f$), then the speculator will take a 'short' position. That is, he/she will sell the foreign currency forward in the anticipation

---

[28] A third group are the commercial traders who use the forward market to hedge against changes in the exchange rate. When importers and exporters undertake trade, payment for the goods received/sold is not usually settled immediately. Thus, for example, an importer will normally pay for the goods received some 3 months after taking delivery of the import. In this case, he/she may wish to cover the exchange rate risk which is assumed by buying the foreign exchange required now for delivery in three months time. In this case, the risk is covered in the forward exchange market. Exporters can similarly cover by selling the foreign exchange they expect to receive forward.

[29] Forward exchange markets exist for 1-month, 3-month, 6-month and sometimes up to 1-year ahead.

that when the forward contract is due, the foreign currency can be purchased in the spot market for a lower price.[30]

The process of taking long and short positions in the forward exchange market should ensure that the following is true:

$$s^e = f \tag{2.16}$$

In the first case, the act of buying dollars forward causes the sterling price of forward dollars to increase (that is, f increases). This will bring f closer to $s^e$. In the second case, where the speculator took a short position, the act of selling dollars forward causes the sterling price of forward dollars to fall. In both cases, the actions of speculators to bring $s^e$ into equality with f. Only when equation (2.16) holds will there be no incentive for speculators to enter into a long or a short position.

There are three rather strong assumptions required for the above analysis to be true. Firstly, we have to assume that speculators are risk neutral. If they were instead risk averse or risk loving, then speculative flows of funds would stop before $s^e$ was brought into equality with f. We explore the implications of risk averseness below. The second assumption is that speculators are not prevented from operating in the forward markets because of controls on capital movements. Finally, we have to assume there are no transactions costs. In the event that there were, then a wedge would be driven between the expected spot rate and the forward rate.

If equation (2.16) is a true representation of how the forward exchange rate is set by speculators and we add to that equation the assumption that agents are rational, then we can derive the efficient market condition which relates the actual spot exchange rate to the forward rate. If expectations are rational, then equation (2.17) will hold:

$$s_t = s^e_t + u_t \tag{2.17}$$

That is, the spot exchange rate at time t is equal to the expected spot rate at time t (given the information set available at time $t-1$, $\Omega_{t-1}$) plus some serially uncorrelated error which is randomly distributed with a mean of zero. To put it another way, this equation states that actual and expected spot exchange rates differ only by a random error. As with all rational expectations models, agents do not therefore make systematic errors.[31]

Substituting equation (2.17) into equation (2.16) we derive the efficient market condition for the forward exchange rate:

$$s_t = f_{t-1} + u_t \tag{2.18}$$

where $f_{t-1}$ is the forward exchange rate in period $t-1$ due for settlement in period t. Equation (2.18) states that the spot exchange rate should be equal to the forward rate plus some random error.

[30] A numerical example of when a speculator should take a short position is the following: assume that f is £0.70 for $1 and $s^e$ is £0.60 for $1. In this case, the speculator should sell $1 forward. In three months time, he/she will purchase a dollar in the spot market (at a cost of £0.60), use it to meet the forward contract and receive £0.70 in return. Again, provided the exchange rate is correctly anticipated, a profit will be made.

[31] We can note that this is what is often assumed when testing uncovered interest rate parity as we noted in section 2.2 above. We discuss the appropriateness of this assumption when we consider the evidence of survey data which gives us a series of *expected* spot exchange rates. These expected rates can be compared to actual rates and a test of equation (2.17) can be undertaken..

We can distinguish two different types of efficiency depending on the assumptions made about $\Omega$, the information set available to individual agents.[32] Firstly, there is weak form efficiency. A market is weakly efficient if a trader cannot make abnormal profits using past values of the price in that market. In other words, the information set in the case of the foreign exchange market is restricted to past values of the forward exchange rate. Secondly, a market is said to be semi-strong efficient if a trader cannot make abnormal profits by making use of past values of the variable in question (the forward exchange rate) or any publicly available information that might be of some use in predicting the future value of the variable. In the case of the foreign exchange market, such information could include past values of forward exchange rates in other foreign exchange markets for different currencies or information that might be expected to influence exchange rates such as interest rates, money supply figures, inflation rates etc.[33] Thus in the case of semi-strong efficiency, the information set is expanded to include all publicly available information. This is much closer to what is usually meant by assuming that agents form their expectations rationally – they use all publicly available information to do so.

It is important to note that the efficient market condition is a joint hypothesis. The first strand of that hypothesis is equation (2.16) which relates the expected spot exchange rate to the forward rate through speculators activities. The second strand is that agents are rational (equation (2.17)). If the market is thus found not to be efficient, we can come to one or both of two conclusions: our fundamental model of speculator behaviour is wrong and/or agents do not have rational expectations.

The model of speculator behaviour assumed that speculators were risk neutral. We can now ask what might happen to equation (2.16) if speculators are risk averse. In this case, the forward exchange rate and the expected spot rate can differ by an amount equal to the risk premium prevailing in $t-1$, $\rho_{t-1}$:

$$\rho_{t-1} + s^e_t = f_{t-1} \tag{2.19}$$

The simplest assumption which we can make regarding the risk premium is that it is some constant ($\alpha$) plus a random error ($e_{t-1}$), in which case after substitution of equation (2.17), equation (2.19) becomes:

$$s_t = -\alpha + f_{t-1} + (u_t - e_{t-1})$$
$$\Rightarrow s_t = -\alpha + f_{t-1} + \varepsilon_t \tag{2.20}$$

where $\varepsilon_t = (u_t - e_{t-1})$. Equation (2.20) states that, in the presence of risk aversion, the forward rate no longer predicts the spot rate.

The specification of the risk premium as a constant is an extremely simple one. It could be the case that the risk premium alters over time as investors' or speculators' perceptions of the riskiness of one currency relative to another changes. This is

---

[32] The key reference in this area is Fama (1970). His analysis relates mainly to the stock market, but the concepts used in foreign exchange markets are identical. We can note that where the stock market is concerned a third type of efficiency can be distinguished, namely strong form efficiency. A market is said to be strong form efficient if the price in that market reflects all available public and *private* information. In many cases, using private information to trade in shares may amount to insider trading. In the case of the foreign exchange markets what constitutes private information is less clear. Perhaps it could reflect government officials trading on the basis of official statistics before they were released.

[33] We discuss the possibility of using information other than exchange rates themselves in Chapter 3 where we examine the evidence that foreign exchange markets are strongly affected by 'news' relating to factors that might determine exchange rates.

known as a time-varying risk premium in the literature. As we shall see later on in this section, it is much easier to test empirically for a constant risk premium than it is for a time-varying one.

The efficiency of the forward market and the existence or otherwise of a risk premium is clearly related to our discussion of UIP. If we subtract $s_{t-1}$ from both sides of equations (2.16) and (2.17), then the connection with UIP is clear. Taking first equation (2.16):

$$s^e_t - s_{t-1} = f_{t-1} - s_{t-1}$$
$$\Rightarrow \Delta s^e_t = - fp_{t-1} \tag{2.21}$$

In the risk premium version of the model, equation (2.21) becomes:

$$\Delta s^e_t + \rho_{t-1} = - fp_{t-1} \tag{2.22}$$

Subtracting $s_{t-1}$ from both sides in equation (2.17), we derive:

$$s_t - s_{t-1} = s^e_t - s_{t-1} + u_t$$
$$\Rightarrow \Delta s_t = \Delta s^e_t + u_t \tag{2.23}$$

Using (2.23) in both (2.21) and (2.22) we can derive expressions for the expected change in the spot exchange rate which, assuming an efficient market, vary according to whether agents are risk neutral or risk averse.

$$\Delta s^e_t = - fp_{t-1} = \Delta s_t \qquad \text{risk neutral case} \tag{2.24}$$
$$\Delta s^e_t = \Delta s_t = - fp_{t-1} - \rho_{t-1} \qquad \text{risk averse case} \tag{2.25}$$

where we ignore the error terms for simplicity. In most tests of UIP equation (2.24) is assumed to hold. In other words, the forward market is assumed to be efficient and speculators to be risk neutral. Hence $\Delta s^e_t$ can be replaced either by the forward discount or by the actual change in the spot rate. It is for this reason that, as we have argued, tests of UIP represent a joint hypothesis, where we test whether agents are risk neutral, whether they have rational expectation, and whether they can arbitrage efficiently. In other words, rejection of UIP could be the result of a failure of any one of these factors. Hence in order to shed further light on the failure of UIP to hold, we need to look at tests of market efficiency.

The simplest test of market efficiency is to run a regression of the following type:

$$s_t = \alpha + \beta f_{t-1} + \varepsilon_t \tag{2.26}$$

The forward market is efficient and we have risk neutrality if $\alpha = 0$ and $\beta = 1$ and the residuals, $\varepsilon_t$, are white noise. If $\alpha = 0$ and $\beta = 1$, then the forward rate is an unbiased forecast of the future spot rate. A number of authors run this regression and use an F test to test the joint hypothesis just outlined. When conducting a test of this kind, it is necessary that the sampling period of the data be at least as great as the period over which the forward contract matures. Thus if $f_{t-1}$ is a 1-month forward rate, then it is necessary to use at least monthly data, that is, nonoverlapping data should be used. Using weekly data is likely to lead to a bias in the coefficients. We discuss this in more detail below.

MacDonald (1983a) examines the hypothesis of market efficiency by estimating equation (2.26) for the franc–dollar, dollar–pound and franc–pound exchange rates from February 1921 to May 1925. A simple OLS regression generates results which suggest that the null hypothesis of efficiency cannot be rejected at the 99% level of significance.

Most estimates of equation (2.26) relate to the post-1971 period of floating exchange rates. Frenkel (1981), for example, tests (2.26) using monthly data on Deutschmark, sterling and French franc *vis-à-vis* the dollar for June 1973 to June 1978). Using an F test to test the joint hypothesis that $\alpha = 0$ and $\beta = 1$, he cannot reject market efficiency for any currency. Longworth (1981) tests the above hypothesis for the Canadian dollar – dollar exchange rate for the period July 1970 to December 1978. The data used is monthly and the forward exchange rate is the 1-month rate. Similar F tests to Frenkel (1981) indicate that the null hypothesis cannot be rejected for the whole period, nor for any two-year subperiod within the whole period.

However, these results are not confirmed by other papers. Table 2.1 presents the results of similar tests for a variety of exchange rates taken from Baillie *et al.* (1983) and Bailey *et al.* (1984). On the whole these results suggest a rejection of the null hypothesis of market efficiency.

*Table 2.1.* Tests of Forward Market Efficiency

|  | $\alpha$ | $\beta$ | F test of $H_o$ | DW |
|---|---|---|---|---|
| £/$ | 0.0327 | 0.9560 | 2.12 | 1.33 |
|  | (.0159) | (.0219) |  |  |
| DM/$ | −0.0243 | −.9684 | 0.97 | 1.98 |
|  | (.0197) | (.0239) |  |  |
| Lira/$ | −.2345 | 0.9641 | 2.94 | 1.67 |
|  | (.1195) | (.0180) |  |  |
| Frfr/$ | -0.1736 | 0.8840 | 4.57 | 1.85 |
|  | (.0600) | (.0397) |  |  |
| Can $/$ | 0.0565 | 0.6418 | 5.72 | 1.96 |
|  | (.0172) | (.1143) |  |  |
| Swfr/$ | 0.1141 | 0.7974 | 1.57 | 1.55 |
|  | (.0656) | (.1204) |  |  |

*Note*: $H_o$: $\alpha = 0$ and $\beta = 1$
DW = Durbin Watson statistic which indicates whether there is serial correlation in the residuals.
Standard Errors are given in brackets.

*Source*: Baillie *et al.* (1983)

|  | Obs 1,5,9.. | Obs 2,6,10.. | Obs 3,7,11.. | Obs 4,8,12. |
|---|---|---|---|---|
| Lira/$ | 3.47[b] | 3.22[b] | 2.91[c] | 2.94[c] |
| £/$ | 1.97 | 2.56[c] | 2.28 | 2.12 |
| DM/$ | 1.06 | 0.73 | 0.95 | 0.97 |
| Frfr/$ | 4.06[b] | 3.88[b] | 5.65[a] | 4.57[b] |

These are the results of an F-test where the null hypothesis is that $\alpha = 0$ and $\beta = 1$.

*Note*: Obs x,y,z: refers to the observations taken for weeks x, y and z. Bailey *et al.* use weekly data. The forward exchange rate is for 1 month ahead. As indicated above it is important that the data used in each equation should not overlap. Hence they estimate four separate regressions for each currency using data at four-weekly intervals.

[a] = significant at 1% level
[b] = significant at 5% level
[c] = significant at 10% level

*Source*: Bailey *et al.* (1984)

Data Period (for both sets of results): for £, Dm, lira, Frfr – June 1 1973–April 8 1980; for Can$ and Swfr – Dec 1 1977–May 15 1980.

To be more specific, Baillie *et al.* (1983) reject the null hypothesis for the Canadian dollar, the French franc and the Italian lira. Moreover, in the case of sterling the Durbin–Watson statistic indicates autocorrelation in the residuals and hence we can again reject the null hypothesis. Similar results are presented in Bailey *et al.* (1984). These are reproduced in the second half of the table. As before, the null hypothesis is rejected for each regression in the case of the lira and the French franc. The null hypothesis cannot be rejected for the Deutschmark. In the case of sterling, the F-tests suggest non-rejection of the null, but again (and this is not shown in Table 2.1), the Durbin–Watson statistics indicate the presence of autocorrelation.[34]

Gregory and McCurdy (1986) criticise these rather simple tests. They note that there is little concern with the question of whether or not the regressions are correctly specified. In order to provide some indication of the validity of these tests, they undertake a variety of tests to determine whether there is serial autocorrelation in the residuals, whether the residuals are homoscedastic (using an ARCH test) and whether the parameters exhibit stability (using an information matrix test). They examine monthly data from January 1974 to December 1981 for the dollar *vis-à-vis* the French franc, the lira, the yen, sterling and the Deutschmark. First they determine whether the simple regression given in equation (2.26) is misspecified for the whole period. Their results indicate that for each currency there is severe misspecification of equation (2.26) over the whole period. Hence inferring anything from significance tests is incorrect. They then run the same regression over various sub-periods. Only from the results for those periods where the specification tests are passed do they draw any conclusion regarding the unbiasedness of the forward rate as a predictor of the spot rate. Only in the case of the Deutschmark can the null of unbiasedness not be rejected.

McFarland *et al.* (1994) also criticise the simple tests of forward market efficiency based on equations such as (2.26). In particular, they argue that, since the data is often nonstationary, hypothesis testing may not be valid. They therefore use cointegration techniques to examine efficiency for five currencies (Belgian franc, French franc, Deutschmark, sterling and lira) *vis-à-vis* the dollar. Their result reject the null hypothesis of efficiency in 3 out of 5 of the cases (sterling and lira exchange rates were efficient).

The need to use nonoverlapping data requires researchers to discard much information – weekly data, for example, could be used to test equation (2.26) and this would increase the sample size four-fold. However, as we have already indicated, it is not possible to use OLS estimates of (2.26) with data that is sampled more finely than the length of maturity of the forward contract. The reason is simple: if the data is overlapping, the error term $\varepsilon_t$ can no longer be expected to be white noise. The intuition behind this result is more complex. Let us assume that we are using weekly data with forward rates of 1-month maturity. Once the forward rate has been determined by market participants at time $t-1$, then 4 random shocks could occur before the spot rate is observed at time t (representing the four weeks between $t-1$ and t). These shocks will be influencing agent's determination of the forward rates that are observed *before* we get to the spot rate at time t. As a result, the errors $\varepsilon_t$ will follow a moving average process of order 3 (4–1), that is they will be serially correlated. With nonoverlapping data, however, random shocks which occur between $t-1$ and t

---

[34] Edwards (1983) also gets mixed results for £/$, DM/$, Frfr/$ and Lira/$ exchange rates for the 1970s.

cannot influence the determination of forward rates which we observe and hence there will be no autocorrelation as a result of *this* cause.[35]

Hakkio (1981) suggests a more efficient econometric technique which allows the use of overlapping observations without inducing serial correlation in the residuals. He uses a bivariate autoregression approach and notes that the efficient markets hypothesis implies certain nonlinear restrictions on the coefficients ($\alpha$, $\beta$, $\psi$ and $\delta$) in the two equations:

$$\Delta s_t = \sum_{i=1}^{4} \alpha_i \Delta s_{t-i} + \sum_{i=1}^{4} \beta_i \Delta f_{t-i}$$

$$\Delta f_t = \sum_{i=1}^{4} \gamma_i \Delta s_{t-i} + \sum_{i=1}^{4} \delta_i \Delta f_{t-i}$$

(2.27)

To test for the validity of the efficient market hypothesis using this methodology, Hakkio first estimates the two equations given in (2.27) separately without restrictions. He then imposes the restrictions and conducts a likelihood ratio test to determine whether or not the restrictions are accepted by the data. Using weekly data for 24 April 1973 to 5 May 1977 for the dollar relative to the Dutch guilder, the Deutschmark, the Canadian dollar, the Swiss franc and sterling, he concludes that the restrictions implied by the efficient market hypothesis are not accepted.

Baillie *et al.* (1983) also use the bivariate approach using the data noted in Table 2.1. They estimate equation (2.27) using OLS and then use a nonlinear Wald test to test the restrictions implied by the efficient markets hypothesis. Again the null hypothesis that the forward rate is an unbiased predictor of the future spot rate is rejected.

We noted in our theoretical discussion of market efficiency that we can distinguish two types of efficiency depending on the information set used: weak tests and semi-strong tests. Tests of this type use a regression of the following kind:

$$s_{t-1} - f_t = \pi x_t + \varepsilon_t$$

where $(s_{t-1} - f_t)$ is the forecast error and $x_t$ is some information set. If the forward market is efficient then we expect $\pi = 0$ and $\varepsilon_t$ to be white noise. In the case of weak tests, $x_t$ includes lagged values of the forward rate or the forecast error. Hansen and Hodrick (1980) conduct such a test using lagged values of the forecast error on data from the 1920s and the 1970s. The 1920s data relates to sterling exchange rates *vis-à-vis* the French franc, the Deutschmark and the dollar. Dollar exchange rates (*vis-à-vis* the Deutschmark, the French franc, sterling, the Swiss franc, the Canadian dollar, the yen and the lira) are used for the 1970s.[36]

The results for the 1920s indicate that efficiency can be rejected for the Deutschmark and French franc exchange rates. For the 1970s, evidence against the null hypothesis that $\pi = 0$ comes from the dollar/DM exchange rate and to some extent from the dollar/Swiss franc and dollar/lira exchange rates.[37]

---

[35] Of course, autocorrelation could result for other reasons, such as inefficiency. See Bailey *et al.* (1984) for a more formal statement of this problem..

[36] We can note that Hansen and Hodrick (1980) use data which is more finely sampled than the forecast interval (that is, overlapping data). To overcome the econometric problems which this causes (see discussion in text), they use OLS but with appropriate modifications to the covariance matrix.

[37] See also Edwards (1983), MacDonald (1983a) and Frenkel (1981) for other weak-form tests of market efficiency.

Semi-strong tests of market efficiency specify the information set, $x_t$, more broadly. Hansen and Hodrick (1980), for example, include the forecast errors from other foreign exchange markets in the information set. Market efficiency suggests that none of the coefficients on these forecasts errors should be significant. The results for their data from the 1970s indicate that the null hypothesis of market efficiency can be rejected in the case of the Canadian dollar–dollar, Swiss franc–dollar and DM–dollar exchange rates.

Longworth (1981) includes the lagged spot rate in a regression like equation (2.26). Market efficiency would imply that along with $\alpha = 0$ and $\beta = 1$, the coefficient on the lagged spot rate should equal zero. Longworth is unable to reject the null hypothesis for any currency,[38] probably because such a simple OLS regression is rather a weak test of efficiency. However, further investigation yields the interesting result that the lagged spot rate outperforms the forward rate at predicting the spot rate. In other words, during the period considered, profits could have been made by trading on the basis of the relationship between the spot rate and the forward rate at any given time. The opportunity for devising such trading rules is not supportive of market efficiency: speculators could have made abnormal profits.

An alternative method of testing for semi-strong efficiency, which has the advantage that a more efficient estimation technique can be used, is to take into account the fact that the error terms in OLS equations for different currencies *vis-à-vis* the dollar might be correlated at any one point in time. MacDonald (1983) notes that estimating equations such as (2.26) using OLS may be inefficient for the following reason. Usually a set of exchange rates relative to the dollar are used. However, given that we would expect that shocks emanating from the US would affect all exchange rates, the error terms will be correlated across equations. If only European exchange rates were used, then similar correlation could result from the operation of the European Monetary System which ties European currencies together.

Such contemporaneous correlation across regressions implies that the coefficients might not be efficient and that more efficient estimates could be derived by using Zellner's (1962) SURE method of estimation.[39] In this case the exchange rate regressions are estimated as a system of equations and the restrictions implied by efficiency can be tested using an F-test. Use of this method can be seen to be equivalent to a semi-strong test, since information from other exchange markets is incorporated into the regression for each country. MacDonald (1983) uses this method to test for efficiency using quarterly data from 1972 to 1979 for a variety of currencies relative to the US dollar. The SURE results indicate that the null of efficiency can be rejected for four out of the six currencies.[40]

Taylor (1988) also conducts tests using the SURE method for dollar–sterling, dollar–Swiss franc and dollar–yen exchange rates for the period March 1976 to July 1986. His results conclusively reject the hypothesis that the market is efficient for all three exchange rates.

[38] See above for a list of data used by Longworth (1981).
[39] SURE stands for Seemingly Unrelated Regression Estimator. SURE estimates are more efficient and hence the standard errors are usually lower than those obtained from using simple OLS. This makes hypothesis testing more reliable.
[40] The null is rejected in the cases of the Deutschmark, Swiss franc, French franc and Austrian schilling relative to the dollar. The null could not be rejected for sterling–dollar or Canadian dollar–dollar exchange rates. SURE results are also reported in Bailey *et al.* (1984).

The above semi-strong tests have concentrated on whether, along with the forward rate, information from other foreign exchange markets can be used to forecast the spot rate. However, it could equally well be true that other information that is relevant to exchange rate determination might be significant in predicting the future spot rate. MacDonald (1983) provides a semi-strong test of efficiency of the following type:

$$s_t - f_{t-1} = \alpha + \beta(Z_t - Z^e_t) + \varepsilon_t \tag{2.28}$$

where $Z_t$ is some vector of variables which might influence the exchange rate (in this case, this is restricted to the domestic and foreign money supplies). The left-hand side of the equation is the forecast error. The critical factor in this approach is the estimation of $Z^e_t$. MacDonald hypothesises that $Z_t$ is a function of the current account surplus, budget deficits, inflation rates and an interest rate variable. These are included with up to four lags. The fitted values of the regression are then used as the expected values of Z. The difference between the fitted values of the regression and the actual values of $Z_t$ represent the unanticipated part. Hence $(Z_t - Z^e_t)$, which is defined as unanticipated news about the money supply, is the residuals from the $Z_t$ equations.

If the market is efficient, then we should not expect either $\alpha$ or the $\beta$ coefficients on *lagged* news to be significant. Two sets of results are provided by MacDonald. Firstly (2.28) is estimated for each currency using OLS. The results indicate that news about the money supply is insignificant in the case of the UK, France and Germany. In the case of Switzerland, news about US money supply is significant and correctly signed. In the case of Austria, news about home money supply is significant but with the wrong sign. In the case of Canada, home news is again significant but this time with the correct sign. Where news is significant, it is unfortunately lagged news. If the market is efficient, then it should only be current news that is significant.

The second set of results are derived using the SURE method of estimation. The results of inefficiencies in the cases of Canada, Austria and Switzerland are strengthened. In addition, inefficiency is found for Germany and France. Only in the case of the sterling–dollar exchange rate was lagged news about the money supply not significant.

This representative sample of results from the large literature which tests for the unbiasedness of the forward rate as a predictor of the future rate tends to lead us to conclude that there is little evidence of market efficiency. What evidence there is tends to come from very simple econometric regressions whose results, for all the reasons we have mentioned above, are less than reliable. The question which now arises is why does there seem to be evidence of inefficiency. It is important to recall here that tests of market efficiency involve a joint test. Equation (2.26) and the restrictions placed on it by market efficiency is derived from two assumptions. Firstly, we assume that agents operating in the market are risk neutral. Secondly, we assume that they have rational expectations. Hence the results could stem from either the existence of a risk premium or the absence of rational expectations.

A number of articles seek to show that there is a risk premium. This has the attraction that we can still support the assumption of rational expectations and the market can be said to be efficient, albeit with risk averse speculators (in other words, equation (2.19) holds). As we indicated in the theoretical part of this section, the simplest assumption that can be made regarding the risk premium is that it is constant through time. Tests of this hypothesis are given by examining the results of estimating equation (2.26). A constant risk premium would be indicated by the significance of the constant term, $\alpha$.

Hansen and Hodrick (1980) note that for the 1920s their results give some support for the existence of a risk premium. The sign of the constant should be negative in their equations if it is considered that the Deutschmark and French franc were more risky than sterling (a not unreasonable assumption). However, the results show a positive constant and this causes them to add a note of caution to the conclusion that a constant risk premium was evident.

Table 2.1 shows that the constant is significant in the case of the sterling, lira, French franc and Canadian dollar equations (see top half, results from Baillie *et al.* 1983). MacDonald (1983) also finds some evidence of a significant constant in the case of the Swiss, German, French and Austrian equations. Thus there certainly seems to be some evidence of a constant risk premium.

It is much more difficult to determine whether there is any evidence of a time-varying risk premium. At a conceptual level it is to be expected that the risk premia on different currencies will change over time. There are several papers which seek to measure this risk premium.

Wolff (1987) uses a signal extraction approach to try to measure the size of the premium for sterling, the Deutschmark and the yen relative to the dollar. He uses 4-weekly data for the period 6 April 1973 to 13 July 1984. The signal extraction approach is often used in the engineering literature and its usefulness here lies in its ability to extract a series from a very noisy environment. This can be understood by examining equation (2.19):

$$\rho_{t-1} + s^e_t = f_{t-1} \qquad (2.19)$$

If we subtract $s_t$ from both sides and rearrange we can derive:

$$s^e_t - s_t + \rho_{t-1} = f_{t-1} - s_t$$
$$\Rightarrow v_t + \rho_{t-1} = f_{t-1} - s_t \qquad (2.29)$$

where $(s^e_t - s_t) = v_t$ which is a white noise term which arises due to the arrival of new information about the spot rate between $t-1$ and $t$.[41] On the right-hand side of equation (2.29) we have the forecast error. Essentially $\rho_{t-1}$ is the signal which we want to extract; $v_t$ is the noise around that signal.

The signal is extracted using Kalman filtering techniques, a time series analysis which allows simply the extraction of the signal. The results indicate that there is substantial variation in the premium for each currency over time: indeed over half the variance in the forecast error can be attributed, according to these results, to a time-varying risk premium.

It is interesting to note that Wolff is not concerned with trying to explain what causes the risk premium to change in his paper. He is merely attempting to determine the existence of such a premium. Domowitz and Hakkio (1985) and Taylor (1988) both seek to explain the risk premium in terms of measures of uncertainty. Domowitz and Hakkio (1985) model the risk premium as a function of the conditional variance of market forecast errors that arise when the forward rate is used to

---

[41] In other words, we are still assuming rational expectations here.

forecast the spot rate.[42] Using monthly data from June 1973 to September 1982 for sterling, French franc, Deutschmark, yen and Swiss franc relative to the dollar, they estimate a model of the following structure using maximum likelihood techniques:

$$\Delta s_t = \beta_0 + \beta_1[fp_{t-1}] + \theta h_{t-1} + \varepsilon_t$$
$$\text{where } h_{t-1}^2 = \alpha_0^2 + \alpha_1^2 \varepsilon_{t-2}^2 + \ldots + \alpha_4^2 \varepsilon_{t-5}^2 \tag{2.30}$$

If a risk premium is absent, then it is anticipated that $\beta_0 = \theta = 0$, $\beta_1 = 1$ and $\varepsilon_{t+1}$ should be white noise. Their results indicate little support for a risk premium.

Taylor (1988) models the risk premium as a function of stock market volatility in both the domestic and the foreign markets (see Figure 2.1). Intuitively his argument runs as follows. Assume that there has been recent high volatility of the returns on US shares. In this case, buying dollars forward (that is taking a long position in dollars) does not look attractive for the speculator. Hence the forward dollar exchange rate (defined as dollars per unit of sterling, yen or Swiss franc) will tend to rise as the forward dollar depreciates. This implies that $[s^e_t - f_{t-1}]$ falls and the risk premium on sterling (or whatever currency) vis-à-vis the dollar tend to fall. In other words, dollar assets become more risky. Alternatively an increase in UK share price volatility will lead to a rise in the riskiness of sterling assets and a rise in the risk premium.

Taylor captures this idea in the following model which is again estimated using a maximum likelihood Kalman filtering technique:

$$(s_t - f_{t-1}) = \rho_{t-1} + \varepsilon_{t-1}$$

$$\rho_{t-1} = \phi \rho_{t-2} + \theta_1 \pi_{t-1}^d + \theta_2 \pi_{t-1}^f \tag{2.31}$$

$\theta_1 \pi_{t-1}^d$ is the measure of domestic asset yield (i.e. sterling, yen or Swiss frances) volatility and $\theta_2 \pi_{t-1}^f$ is foreign asset yield (i.e. US) volatility. The first equation in (2.31) states that the forecast error is composed of a risk premium ($\rho$) and a white noise error term (this is the rational expectations error term which arises from the fact that news arrives between $t-1$ and $t$). The risk premium (given in the second part of equation (2.31)) is a function its own lagged value and domestic and foreign asset volatility. We expect $\phi$ to be positive if agents' behaviour exhibits inertia: that is, a positive risk premium in the last period tends to lead to a positive premium this period. $\theta_1$ is the coefficient on the domestic (that is sterling, yen or Swiss franc) asset volatility. An increase in domestic asset volatility is expected to lead to an increase in the risk premium. $\theta_2$ is the coefficient on foreign (that is US) asset volatility. An increase in foreign asset volatility reduces the risk premium on domestic currency.

The results indicate that $\phi$, $\theta_1$ and $\theta_2$ are correctly signed for each currency and are significant. Wald tests on the coefficients of the risk premium equation also indicate that there is strong support for a time-varying risk premium and that the risk premium depends on domestic and foreign asset volatility.

Using these results, Taylor derives estimates for the risk premia. Figure 2.1 reproduces the UK risk premium. Looking at the figure, a plausible story can be told. The premium rises towards the end of 1976 and peaks in early 1977 (the time of the sterling crisis). It then declines steadily up to the 1979 election (as markets start to anticipate a Conservative Party victory), although the period of the election results in

---

[42] We can note that the forecast errors are assumed to follow an ARCH process which implies that the conditional variance of the error is a function of the past forecast errors squared.

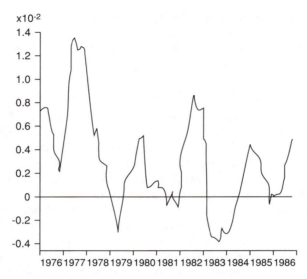

Source:    Taylor, 1988

**Figure 2.1.**    *The risk premium in the UK*

some uncertainty and a rise in the premium. It falls significantly on the announcement of the MTFS (in the March 1980 Budget). Two subsequent peaks within the
period considered represent the Falklands crisis and the final peak is the fall in oil
prices in 1985.

The problem with the above articles is that they all assume rational expectations
on the part of market participants. Thus in order to determine conclusively whether
or not the evidence of inefficiency found above is due to a risk premium or to a lack
of rational expectations, or to a combination of the two, we have to find some way of
testing the rational expectations assumption. The only method of doing this is to use
survey data.

Survey data refers to data which has been collected by asking individual agents in
the economy what expectations they have about the course of some variable. It thus
generates a series of expected values for the variable in question which can be compared with the actual values of the exchange rates. In this way the rational
expectations assumption given in equation (2.17) can be tested. Frankel and Froot
(1987), MacDonald and Torrance (1988), Taylor (1989) and Cavaglia *et al.* (1994),
among others, all examine the issue of market efficiency using survey data. A summary of the data used by each of these papers is presented in Table 2.2.

Frankel and Froot (1987) address two questions: are investors expectations
rational forecasts of actual spot exchange rates? (a test of equation (2.17)); and if not,
what method of expectations formation do agents tend to use? Overall they find that
the expected change in the spot rate is not an unbiased predictor of actual changes in
the exchange rate. For their data for the 1980s, they find that agents persistently
expected the dollar to depreciate when it did not. This could be interpreted as evidence that expectations are not formed rationally. However, unfortunately the
evidence is not conclusive. The results could simply reflect a peso problem, which
occurs when there is a small probability of a large change in the exchange rate. That

*Table 2.2.* Survey data used in testing for foreign exchange market efficiency

| Period | Currencies | Source | Length of expectations |
|---|---|---|---|
| **Frankel and Froot (1987)** | | | |
| 1976–85 | $ *vis-à-vis* DM, £, Frfr, Swfr and yen | American Express Banking Corporation: sample of 200–350 central bankers, private bankers, corporate treasurers and economists | 6, 12 months ahead |
| from 1981 | $ *vis-à-vis* DM, £, Frfr, Swfr and yen | *The Economist* Financial Report: sample of 14 international banks; at six week intervals | 3, 6, 12 months ahead |
| from 1983 | $ *vis-à-vis* DM, £, yen and Swfr | Money Market Services Inc; weekly and bi-weekly surveys | 3 months ahead |
| **MacDonald and Torrance (1988)** | | | |
| 1985 (second week) to final week January 1986 | DM/$ | Money Market Services UK; weekly and bi-weekly; survey of some 30 institutions in London and on the continent | 1 week, 1 month ahead |
| **Taylor (1989)** | | | |
| January 1981 July 1986 (monthly) | £/$ and effective sterling | survey of investment managers | 1 year ahead |
| **Cavaglia *et al.* (1994)** | | | |
| 1986–90 | various currencies relative to DM and £ | survey of banks and financial companies | 3, 6, 12 months ahead |

is, when the dollar was overvalued in the early 1980s, agents continually expected it to depreciate and hence they consistently overpredicted the value of other currencies against the dollar. However, it did not start to depreciate until 1985. This problem can lead to nonnormality and the standard errors of the test will be biased. Evidence from the AMEX data set for the period 1976–79 when there is no such peso problem also indicates bias and hence non-rational expectations.

A second interesting result generated by Frankel and Froot from the survey data relates to the second question. In particular, they seek to determine whether or not expectations have been stabilising or destabilising. If expectations are destabilising then the most recent trend in the market is simply extrapolated and hence band-wagon effects are possible. By contrast, if expectations are such that an appreciation in this period leads to expectations of future depreciation (at least partly back to its original level), then expectations can be said to be stabilising. The SURE method is used to pool the data from the various surveys and tests suggest that on the whole there is little evidence of destabilising expectation.

MacDonald and Torrance (1988) also find evidence of biased expectations using a simple test derived by using equation (2.17) in first differences. In addition, they also perform a weak efficiency test, by including past values of the spot rate and the expected spot rate (the forecast error). The results suggest that in the case of the weekly forecasts, the lagged forecast errors are not jointly significant; in the case of the 1-month forecasts (collected every two weeks) they find that the lagged forecast errors are strongly significant. Similar results are found for a semi-strong test which includes information from the forward market via the forward premium.

Attempts to model exchange rate expectations formation proved rather tricky and the results were not highly significant. Both adaptive and extrapolative methods of expectations formation were used. In the case of adaptive expectations the following model is used:

$$\Delta s^e_{t+i} = \alpha(s^e_t - s_t) \tag{2.32}$$

that is, the change in expectations this period is some function of last periods error. Estimates of the above equation indicate that the coefficient $\alpha$ is negative (for both the weekly and monthly horizons). In other words, behaviour is destabilising: an unanticipated appreciation ($s_t$ falls below $s^e_t$) causes $\Delta s^e_{t+i}$ to become negative: that is, further appreciation is expected. However, $\alpha$ is not significant in either of the equations.

In the case of extrapolative expectations, the expected change in the exchange rate is related to the most recent change:

$$\Delta s^e_{t+i} = -L(s_t - s_{t-i}) \tag{2.33}$$

If $L>0$, then speculation is stabilising because a depreciation last period (i.e. $s_t > s_{t+i}$), implies an expected appreciation this period ($\Delta s^e_{t+i} < 0$). If, on the other hand, speculation is destabilising, then $L < 0$: a depreciation this time implies an expected depreciation next time. The results indicate that L is negative for both cases. Again, however, the coefficients are not significant (although they are more significant than for the adaptive expectations equation). Overall, MacDonald and Torrance conclude that although it is difficult to model expectations, there is some evidence that expectations are destabilising.

Taylor (1989) concludes from his data set that both non-rational expectations and the existence of a risk premium seem to explain the fact that the forward premium is a biased forecast of the change in the spot rate. The novelty of Taylor's approach is that he uses the survey data to generate a series of the variance of expectations at any point in time. This is then used as a measure of uncertainty: the higher the standard deviation of expectations, the greater the level of uncertainty. He then uses this in order to model the risk premium. His results are strongly significant and indicate that as uncertainty increases, so does the risk premium on sterling.

Cavaglia et al. (1994) also find evidence of both irrationality and a risk premium. They use Froot and Frankel's (1989) method of decomposing the difference between the change in the spot rate and the forward premium using survey data. Take the following equation which tests for unbiasedness:

$$s_{t+k} - s_t = \alpha + \beta(_tf_{t+k} - s_t) + e_{t+k} \tag{2.34}$$

where $s_t$, $s_{t+k}$ is the spot exchange rate in periods t and t+k respectively; and $_tf_{t+k}$ is the forward exchange rate at time t for settlement at time t+k. Unbiasedness implies that $\alpha = 0$, $\beta = 1$ and $e_{t+k}$ is white noise. In estimating this equation, Cavaglia *et al.* find no evidence of efficiency. In order to decompose this lack of efficiency into that part due to non-rational expectations and that part due to the existence of a risk premium, they estimate the following two equations:

$$s_{t+k} - E_t s_{t+k} = \alpha_1 + \beta_1(_tf_{t+k} - s_t) + v_{t+k} \tag{2.35}$$

$$E_t s_{t+k} - s_t = \alpha_2 + \beta_2(_tf_{t+k} - s_t) + z_t \tag{2.36}$$

where $E_t s_{t+k}$ is the expected value at time t of the spot exchange rate at t+k. Equation (2.35) tests whether or not expectations are rational. It uses the forecast error $(s_{t+k} - E_t s_{t+k})$, calculated using the actual exchange rate and the expected exchange rate from the survey data, and determines whether or not it is a random error. In other words, with rational expectations, we would expect $\alpha_1$ and $\beta_1$ to the equal to zero since all agents use all available information to form their expectations. Their results indicate a rejection of this hypothesis and they conclude there is some evidence of irrationality.

Equation (2.36) allows us to test for the existence of a risk premium. On the left-hand side is the expected change in the exchange rate over the period t to t+k. On the right-hand side we have a constant and the forward premium. Recall that if there is no risk premium, then the expected change in the exchange rate should be equal to the forward premium and hence $\beta_2$ should be equal to 1 (with $\alpha_2$ equal to zero. If there is a constant risk premium, then $\alpha_2$ will be significant (with $\beta_2$ still being equal to one). If there is a time varying risk premium, then $\beta_2$ will be significantly different from 1. Cavaglia *et al.* (1994) find evidence of a time-varying risk premium. Thus they conclude that unbiasedness can be rejected for both reasons.

What therefore can we conclude about the efficiency of the forward market? Tests of efficiency which assume risk neutrality on the whole reject the hypothesis that the forward market is efficient. Further investigation into the reasons for such a rejection point to the fact that neither the assumption of rational expectations nor the assumption of risk neutrality appear to hold. Attempts to model the risk premium have, however, proved rather difficult and hence it is not possible to come with a clear answer as to why the risk premium might vary through time. Uncertainty certainly seems to play a part.

## Real interest rate parity

The final interest rate parity we want to consider here is that of the relationship between real interest rates across countries. In particular, it is interesting to address the question of whether capital flows ensure that real interest rates are equalised across countries. This is an interesting question because governments often seek to influence real interest rates in order to affect savings and investment decisions by individual agents.

Cumby and Obstfeld (1984) give a good account of the assumptions which lie behind the result of real interest rate equality across countries. We begin with the purchasing power parity condition, which recall states:

$$s_t - s_{t-1} = (p_t - p_{t-1}) - (p_t^* - p_{t-1}^*) \tag{2.37}$$

That is, the change in the spot rate from $t-1$ to $t$ will be equal to domestic inflation $(p_t - p_{t-1})$ minus foreign inflation $(p_t^* - p_{t-1}^*)$, where small letters represent logarithms. If (2.37) holds in every period, then we have *ex ante* PPP, that is, relative PPP is expected to hold in any period:

$$E_t(s_{t+i} - s_t) = E_t[(p_{t+i} - p_t) - (p_{t+i}^* - p_t^*)] \tag{2.38}$$

UIP states that:

$$i_{i,t} - i_{i,t}^* = E_t(s_{t+i} - s_t) \tag{2.39}$$

where $i_{i,t}$ is the i-period nominal interest rate. Combining equations (2.38) and (2.39), we derive:

$$i_{i,t} - i_{i,t}^* = E_t[(p_{t+i} - p_t) - (p_{t+i}^* - p_t^*)]$$

$$\Rightarrow i_{i,t} - E_t[p_{t+i} - p_t] = i_{i,t}^* - E_t(p_{t+i}^* - p_t^*) \tag{2.40}$$

which from the Fischer equation we know can be written as:

$$ir_{i,t} = ir_{i,t}^* \tag{2.41}$$

That is, the real interest rates ($ir_{i,t}$ and $ir_{i,t}^*$) are equalised over time and hence it is difficult for policy makers to influence them.

Cumby and Obstfeld (1984) test whether real interest rates are equal across countries by plotting 1-month real interest rate differentials from 1976–81 for the US *vis-à-vis* Germany, UK, France, Switzerland, Canada and Japan. Whilst the graphs show some evidence of serial correlation, real interest rates do not appear to be equal. They support this conclusion with regression analysis of the following type.[43]

$$(p_{t+i} - p_t) - (p_{t+i}^* - p_t^*) = a + b(i_{i,t} - i_{i,t}^*) + e_t \tag{2.42}$$

if $a = 0$ and $b = 1$, then the hypothesis of real interest rate equality cannot be rejected.

However, their evidence suggests a rejection of real interest rate parity (only in the case of the US *vis-à-vis* the UK is there evidence of a constant *differential* between real interest rates). Further investigation reveals that the reasons why real interest rate parity does not generally hold suggest it is because neither PPP nor UIP hold (assumptions required to generate the result of real interest rate equality across countries) – something which is not surprising given the extensive discussion of the empirical literature (that examines these two propositions) which we have just conducted. Mishkin (1984) using data on the US, Canada, the UK, France, Germany, the Netherlands and Switzerland for 1967–79 confirms these results.

## Conclusion

In this chapter we have investigated some simple relationships which might explain exchange rates. We examined first the theory of purchasing power parity. Our analysis led us to conclude that there are good theoretical reasons for thinking that PPP

[43] Equation (2.42) is derived from equations (2.38–2.41) above. If $ir_{i,t} = i_{i,t} - E_t(p_{t+i} - p_t)$ and $ir_{i,t}^* = i_{i,t}^* - E_t(p_{t+i}^* - p_t^*)$, the Fischer equations; if we assume rational expectations which implies that $E_t(p_{t+i} - p_t) = (p_{t+i} - p_t) + e_{1t}$ and $E_t(p_{t+i}^* - p_t^*) = (p_{t+i}^* - p_t^*) + e_{2t}$; then given real interest rate equality we can derive $(i_{i,t} - i_{i,t}^*) = (p_{t+i} - p_t) - (p_{t+i}^* - p_t^*) + e_t$, where $e_t = e_{1t} + e_{2t}$, which forms the basis for equation (2.42).

does not hold. Indeed such a conclusion was sustained by the evidence which did not provide much support for PPP.

This finding led us to look elsewhere for an explanation of exchange rate determination, particularly at interest parity conditions which reflect the role of increased capital mobility in determining exchange rates. We examined both covered and uncovered interest parity. Provided there are no controls on capital mobility, then CIP is brought about through arbitrage – there are few profitable opportunities which are not exploited. By contrast, the evidence suggests that UIP does not hold.

We explored the reasons for this further by looking at the relationship between the spot and forward exchange rate and asking whether the forward market is efficient. We concluded that the market is inefficient partly because of the existence of time-varying risk premium and partly because of irrationality on the part of market participants.

Both these findings have important policy implications. If participants are irrational, and, moreover, they tend to form expectations extrapolatively, then a policy of 'leaning against the wind' may be beneficial. A policy of 'leaning against the wind' refers to foreign exchange market intervention by the authorities which seeks to break a particular trend which is present in the market at any one time. Thus if private agents are causing sterling to appreciate, a policy of 'leaning against the wind' involves the authorities selling sterling.

If there is also a risk premium, then this implies that assets are not perfect substitutes. This implies that interest rates in any country may not be identical to those abroad even if there are no expectations of a change in the exchange rate. It also implies that sterilised intervention may work.

**References**

Adler, M and Lehmann, B. (1983) 'Deviations from PPP in the long run', *Journal of Finance*, XXXVIII: 5, 1471–87.

Aliber, R.Z. (1973) 'The interest rate parity theorem: a reinterpretation', *Journal of Political Economy*, 81: 6, 1451–9.

Angell, J.W. (1926) *The Theory of International Prices: History, Criticism and Restatement* Harvard University Press.

Bailey, R.W., Baillie, R.T. and McMahon, P.C. (1984) 'Interpreting economic evidence on efficiency in the foreign exchange market', *Oxford Economic Papers*, 36, 67–85.

Baillie, R.J., Lippens, R.E. and MacMahon, P.L. (1983) 'Testing rational expectations and efficiency in the foreign exchange market', *Econometrica*, 51, 553–63.

Balassa, B. (1964) 'The PPP doctrine: a reappraisal', *Journal of Political Economy*, 72: 584–96.

Bhaskara Rao, B. (ed.) (1994) *Cointegration for the Applied Economist*. St. Martin's Press, New York.

Branson, W.H. (1969) 'Minimum covered interest differential needed for interest arbitrage activity', *Journal of Political Economy*, 77: 6, 1028–35.

Cassel, G. (1916) 'The present situation of the foreign exchange', *Economic Journal*, 26, 62–65.

Cassel, G. (1918) 'Abnormal deviations in international exchanges', *Economic Journal*, 28 (December), 413–15.

Cavaglia, S.M.F.G., Vershoor, W.F.C. and Wolff, C.C.P. (1994) 'On the unbiasedness of foreign exchanges: irrationality or risk premium?', *Journal of Business*, 67: 3 (July) 321–43.

**Clinton, K.** (1988) 'Transactions costs and covered interest parity: theory and evidence', *Journal of Political Economy*, 96, 358–70.

**Cumby, R.E. and Obsfeld, M.** (1984) 'International interest rate and price level linkages under flexible exchange rates: a review of recent evidence', in J.F.O. Bilson and R.C. Marston (eds.) *Exchange Rate Theory and Practice*. NBER, Chicago University Press, Chicago.

**De Grauwe, P.** (1989) *International Money: post-war trends and theories*. Oxford University Press, Oxford.

**Demsetz, H.** (1968) 'The cost of transacting', *Quarterly Journal of Economics*, 82: 1 (February), 33–53.

**Domowitz, I. and Hakkio, C.** (1985) 'Conditional variance and the risk premium in the foreign exchange market', *Journal of International Economics*, 19, 47–66.

**Dooley, M.P. and Isard, P.** (1980) 'Capital controls, political risk and deviations from interest rate parity', *Journal of Political Economy*, 88: 2, 370–84.

**EC (1988)** 'Creation of a European financial area', *European Economy*, 36: (May).

**Edwards, S.** (1983) 'Floating exchange rates, expectations and new information', *Journal of Monetary Economics*, 11, 321–36.

**Einzig, P.** (1970) *The History of Foreign Exchange*. Macmillan, London.

**Fama, E.** (1984) 'Forward and spot exchange rates', *Journal of Monetary Economics*, 13: 3, 319–38.

**Frankel, J.A. and Froot, K.A.** (1987) 'Using survey data to test standard propositions regarding exchange rate expectations', *American Economic Review*, 77: 1, 133–53.

**Fraser, P., Taylor, M.P. and Webster, A.** (1990) 'An empirical analysis of long-run purchasing power parity as a theory of international arbitrage', University of Dundee, Discussion papers in Economics, 3.

**Frenkel, J.A.** (1981) 'Flexible exchange rates, prices and the role of news: lessons from the 1970s', *Journal of Political Economy*, 89: 4, 665–705.

**Frenkel, J.A. and Levich, R.M.** (1975) 'Covered interest arbitrage: unexploited profits', *Journal of Political Economy*, 83, 325–38.

**Frenkel, J.A. and Levich, R.M.** (1981) 'Covered interest arbitrage in the 1970s', *Economic Letters*, 8: 3, 267–74.

**Froot, K.A. and Frankel, J.A.** (1989) 'Forward discount bias: is it an exchange risk premium?', *Quarterly Journal of Economics*, February, 104: 416, 139–61.

**Gibson, H.D.** (1989) *The Eurocurrency Markets, Domestic Financial Policy and International Instability*. Macmillan, London.

**Graham, F.D.** (1930) *Exchange, Prices and Production in Hyperinflation Germany, 1920–23*. Princeton University Press.

**Gregory, A.W. and McCurdy, T.H.** (1986) 'The unbiasedness hypothesis in the forward exchange market', *European Economic Review*, 30, 365–81.

**Hacche, G. and Townend, J.** (1981) 'Exchange rates and monetary policy: modelling sterling's effective exchange rate', in W.A. Eltis and P.J.N. Sinclair (eds.) (1981) *The Money Supply and the Exchange Rate*. Oxford University Press, Oxford.

**Hakkio, C.S.** (1981) 'Expectations and the forward exchange rate', *International Economic Review*, 22, 663–78.

**Hansen, L.P. and Hodrick, J.R.** (1980) 'Forward exchange rates as optimal predictors of future spot rates: an economic analysis', *Journal of Political Economy*, 88, 829–53.

**Heckscher, E.F.** (1930) *Sweden, Norway, Denmark and Iceland in the World War*. Yale University Press.

**Holmes, J.** (1967) 'The purchasing power parity theory: in defence of Gustav Cassel as a modern theorist', *Journal of Political Economy*, 75: 5, 686–95.

**Isard, P.** (1977) 'How far can we push the law of one price?', *American Economic Review*, 67: 5, 942–48.

**Isard, P.** (1987) 'Lessons from empirical models of exchange rates', *IMF Staff Papers*, 34: 1, 1–28.

**Johnston, R.B.** (1983) *The Economics of the Euro-market: History, Theory, Policy*. Macmillan, London.

**Katseli-Papaefstratiou, L.T.** (1979) 'The reemergence of the purchasing power parity doctrine in the 1970s', *Princeton Special Papers in Economics*, 13. Princeton University Press.

**Keynes, J.M.** (1923) *A Tract on Monetary Reform*. Macmillan, London.

**Keynes, J.M.** (1930) *A Treatise on Money*. Macmillan, London.

**Kravis, I. and Lipsey, R.** (1978) 'Price behaviour in the light of balance of payments theories', *Journal of International Economics*, May.

**Kreuger, A.O.** (1983) *Exchange Rate Determination*. Cambridge University Press, Cambridge.

**Krugman, P.R.** (1978) 'Purchasing power parity and exchange rates', *Journal of International Economics*, 8: 3, 397–408.

**Kugler, P. and Lenz, C.** (1993) 'Multivariate cointegration analysis and the long-run validity of PPP', *Journal of Economics and Statistics*, LXXV: 1, 180–84.

**Llewellyn, D.T.** (1980) *International Financial Integration: the Limits of Sovereignty*. Macmillan, London.

**Longworth, D.** (1981) 'Testing the efficiency of the Canadian–US exchange market under the assumption of no risk premium', *Journal of Finance*, 36, 43–9.

**MacDonald, R.** (1983) 'Some tests of the rational expectations hypothesis in the foreign exchange market', *Scottish Journal of Political Economy*, 30: 3, 235–50.

**MacDonald, R.** (1983a) 'Tests of efficiency and the impact of news in three foreign exchange markets: the experience of the 1920s', *Bulletin of Economic Research*, 35: 2, 123–44.

**MacDonald, R.** (1985) 'Are deviations from purchasing power parity efficiency?', *Weltwirtschaftliches Archiv*, 121: 4, 638–45.

**MacDonald, R.** (1988) *Floating Exchange Rates: theories and evidence*. Allen and Unwin, London.

**MacDonald, R.** (1993) 'Long-run purchasing power parity: is it for real?', *Review of Economics and Statistics*, LXXV: 4, 690–95.

**MacDonald, R. and Torrance, T.S.** (1988) 'Exchange rates and the newa: some evidence using UK survey data', *The Manchester School*, LVI, 69–76.

**McFarland, J.W., McMahon, P.C. and Ngama, Y.** (1994) 'Forward exchange rates and expectations during the 1920s: a reexamination of the evidence', *Journal of International Money and Finance*, 13: 6, 627–36.

**McKinnon, R.I.** (1979) *Money in International Exchange*. Oxford University Press, Oxford.

**Marston, R.** (1976) 'Interest arbitrage in the euro-currency markets', *European Economic Review*, 7, 1–13.

**Michael, P., Nobay, A.R. and Peel, D.** (1994) 'PPP yet again: evidence from spatially separated commodity markets', *Journal of International Money and Finance*, 13: 6, 637–57.

**Mishkin, F.** (1984) 'Are real interest rates equal across countries?' An empirical investigation of international parity conditions', *Journal of Finance*, 1345–58.

**Officer, L.** (1976) 'The purchasing power parity theory of exchange rates: a review article', *IMF Staff Papers*, 23: 1, 1–60.

**Officer, L. and Willet, T.** (1970) 'The covered interest arbitrage schedule: a critical survey of recent developments', *Journal of Money, Credit and Banking*, 2: 2, 247–52.

**Patel, J.** (1990) 'PPP as a long run relation', *Journal of Applied Econometrics*, 367–79.

**Samuelson, P.A.** (1964) 'Theoretical notes on trade problems', Review of Economics and Statistics, May.

**Taylor, M.P.** (1987) 'Covered interest parity: a high-frequency, high-quality data set', *Economicia*, 54, 429–38.

**Taylor, M.P.** (1988) 'An empirical examination of long-run PPP using cointegration techniques', *Applied Economics*, 20, 1369–82.

**Taylor, M.P.** (1989) 'Expectations, risk and uncertainty in the foreign exchange market: some results based on survey data', *The Manchester School*, 57: 2, 142–53.

**Taylor, M.P. and Fraser, P.** (1990) 'Some "news" on covered interest parity', University of Dundee, Discussion paper in Economics, 6, January.

**Wolff, C.P.** (1987) 'Forward foreign exchange rates, expected spot rates and premia: a signal extraction approach', *Journal of Finance*, 42, 295–406.

**Zellner, A.** (1962) 'An efficient method of estimating seemingly unrelated regressions and tests of aggregation bias', *Journal of the American Statistical Association*, 57: 348–368.

# 3 EXCHANGE RATE DETERMINATION

After the move towards floating exchange rates around 1973, a large literature began to appear which sought to explain exchange rate movements. These newer theories challenged the older theories – the elasticities and absorption approaches – which, not surprisingly given they were popular during a period of fixed exchange rates, focused less on exchange rate determination and more on what determined the balance of payments position of any country.[1] The main building block of these models was concern with the trade account of the balance of payments. Exports and imports were assumed to depend upon domestic and foreign income (or aggregate demand), domestic and foreign price levels and the exchange rate. The key question which these models addressed was whether or not a change in the exchange rate could help to eliminate balance of payments disequilibria.

The capital account did not have any place in these models. However, growing capital mobility in the post-war period led to models which sought to incorporate both capital and current accounts. The most well-known of these models is the Mundell–Fleming model and its various extensions[2] (Fleming, 1962; Mundell, 1963). It essentially assumes that capital flows are a function of the difference between domestic and foreign interest rates. In equilibrium, the current account deficit or surplus would be exactly offset by a capital account surplus or deficit.

A distinguishing feature of both the elasticity and absorption models and the Mundell–Fleming model is that they are flow models. In other words, they focus on the flows of goods, services and capital between countries. By contrast, the newer theories of exchange rate determination which we examine here focus on a stock approach. In the Mundell–Fleming model, equilibrium can be achieved with a constant capital flow, responding to a constant interest rate differential. However, such flows have stock implications. For example, a capital outflow leads to domestic wealth-holders building up their stocks of foreign assets. Equivalently, a capital inflow leads to an increase in the stock of domestic assets held by foreigners. Additionally, the implications of current account imbalances are often incorporated into asset market models (particularly the portfolio models). A current account deficit implies that the country must either be running down its holdings of foreign assets or

---

[1] See Philbeam (1992), Hallwood and MacDonald (1986) and Thirlwall and Gibson (1992) for a good survey of these theories. It is assumed here that readers have some familiarity with these models from previous classes in international economics or open economy macroeconomics. We thus do not consider them further here.

[2] See Thirlwall and Gibson (1992) for a discussion of the Mundell–Fleming model as a theory of exchange rate determination. See also MacDonald (1988) for an extensive discussion of the extensions to the basic Mundell–Fleming model.

increasing its foreign indebtedness. A current account surplus implies an increase in domestic holdings of foreign assets or a reduction in the level of foreign indebtedness. In short, current account disequilibria have stock implications which have to be considered. Asset models incorporate these ideas (albeit to differing degrees) by ensuring that equilibrium is characterised by a *stock equilibrium*, where investors are happy with their portfolio of assets and have no desire to alter them – hence capital flows cease.

It is these various asset models which form the focus of this chapter. There are two main groups of asset market theories: monetary theories and portfolio theories. Of the former group, we examine here the flexible price monetary model (or the global monetarist model) and the sticky price monetary model, which is more commonly known as the overshooting model.

In addition to presenting these theoretical models, we also discuss the empirical evidence relating to them. As we shall see, the empirical performance of these models has been rather poor. Exchange rates are highly volatile and yet the factors which asset models identify as being important in determining them usually change only very slowly. Hence few of the models seem to explain exchange rate variation particularly well. Moreover, in terms of predicting exchange rates, it has often been found that asset models do not outperform a simple random walk model where the exchange rate this period is explained by last period's, although some recent research, as we shall see, overturns this result.

Disillusion with these asset models has led researchers to argue that exchange rates might be determined not only by a whole series of 'fundamental' factors, such as those suggested by the asset models, but also by the methods used by foreign exchange traders on a day-to-day basis. This has led to an interest in the role of noise traders and chartists and the possibility of speculative bubbles developing in foreign exchange markets. Thus in the final section of this chapter we examine some of these more recent ideas and ask whether they stand up to empirical investigation.

## Asset market approaches to exchange rate determination

As we noted in the introduction, modern theories of exchange rate determination focus on the role of assets in determining the exchange rate rather than the current account. Within the asset market approach to exchange rate determination there are two key groups of literature which can be distinguished by the assumption they make about asset substitutability. These are the monetary and portfolio theories. The monetary approach assumes that assets are perfectly substitutable, which, as we noted earlier, means that investors are indifferent between holding domestic and foreign assets, provided that the expected return on each asset is the same (hence uncovered interest rate parity (UIP) holds). The portfolio approach, by contrast, is distinguished by the fact that it does not assume perfect asset substitutability (and hence whilst covered interest parity (CIP) holds, UIP does not). Instead, wealth-holders are sensitive to the proportions of each asset they hold and even if it were the case that the expected return on one asset was larger than another, they would not hold all their wealth in the form of the asset with the higher return.

Frankel (1993, p.96) provides a useful and informative diagram which traces out the differences between these two branches. We reproduce a slightly modified version of that diagram in Figure 3.1. As the figure shows, the modern asset view of exchange rate determination assumes that capital is perfectly mobile. We do, however, examine what happens if capital is less than mobile as an extension to some of the models we will consider.

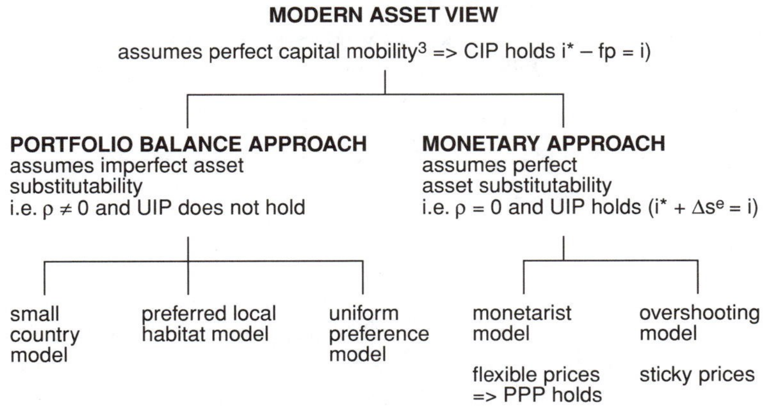

**MODERN ASSET VIEW**

assumes perfect capital mobility[3] => CIP holds $i^* - fp = i$)

**PORTFOLIO BALANCE APPROACH**
assumes imperfect asset
substitutability
i.e. $\rho \neq 0$ and UIP does not hold

**MONETARY APPROACH**
assumes perfect
asset substitutability
i.e. $\rho = 0$ and UIP holds ($i^* + \Delta s^e = i$)

small
country
model

preferred local
habitat model

uniform
preference
model

monetarist
model

overshooting
model

flexible prices
=> PPP holds

sticky prices

**Figure 3.1.** *Asset market models of exchange rate determination*

Within the monetary approach, there are essentially two main models which are distinguished according to the assumptions which are made about price flexibility. With perfectly flexible prices, purchasing power parity (PPP) is added to the assumption of UIP and this generates the monetarist version of the monetary approach. By contrast, if prices are sticky, then there is the possibility that the exchange rate overshoots its new long-run value, following a monetary shock. Hence these models are known as overshooting models.

Within the portfolio approach, models are distinguished according to the assumptions they make about asset-holding. In the small country model, it is assumed that whilst domestic residents can hold foreign bonds (as well as domestic bonds), foreigners cannot hold domestic bonds: the domestic country is so small that foreigners are uninterested in holding domestic assets. The uniform preference models by contrast assume that all wealth-holders have the same preferences, irrespective of their country of origin. Finally, the preferred local habit model makes the assumption that domestic residents prefer to hold a larger proportion of their portfolio in domestic assets and foreign residents prefer to hold more foreign assets. These different assumptions are discussed in more detail later.

## The monetary approach

The monetary approach to exchange rate determination focuses exclusively on the money market and it is the relationship between money demand and money supply which causes changes in the exchange rate. In particular, the exchange rate is seen as the equilibrium price between two stocks of money. Thus the monetary approach is an asset approach in which money is the only asset which is modelled explicitly.[4]

---

[3] If we add to perfect capital mobility, the assumption of rational expectations (such that $\Delta s^e = \Delta s + u$, where u is a randomly distributed error) then this implies that the foreign exchange market is efficient: $- fp = \Delta s^e + \rho$, which using the assumption of rational expectations can be rewritten as: $- fp = \Delta s + \rho + u => - fp - \Delta s = \rho + u$; that is, the market is efficient. Note that if there is also perfect asset substitutability, that is $\rho = 0$, then $- fp - \Delta s = u$ or $i - i^* - \Delta s = u$ which states that the forward exchange rate is an unbiased predictor of the future spot rate. We discussed these relationships in the previous chapter.

[4] Bonds exist in the background in some monetary models since there is an interest rate. However, since UIP holds continuously because of perfect asset substitutability, there is effectively only one bond in the world. Hence we can simply concentrate on the money market when discussing exchange rate determination.

*Flexible price monetary model*

One major strand of the monetary approach is the flexible price monetary approach, which we labelled the monetarist model above. A typical model of this kind is given by the following equations (which are in log-linear form).[5]

$$m - p = \phi y - \mu i \tag{3.1}$$

$$m^* - p^* = \phi y^* - \mu i^* \tag{3.2}$$

$$i = i^* + \Delta s^e \tag{3.3}$$

$$s = p - p^* \tag{3.4}$$

Equation (3.1) is a conventional money demand function. Real money supply $(m - p)$ is equal to real money demand (that is, money demand is homogeneous of degree 1 in prices). The money supply, m, is assumed to be exogenous. Money demand is a positive function of income, y, and a negative function of the domestic interest rate, i. Equation (3.2) is a similar money demand function for the foreign country. Notice that the parameters $\phi$ and $\mu$ are assumed to be identical for simplicity.[6] Equation (3.3) is UIP which we discussed in Chapter 2. Finally, equation (3.4) is PPP (again, see Chapter 2).

These equations embody the assumptions which underlie the monetarist model. Firstly, the money supply is assumed to be exogenous and stable.[7] Secondly, assets are perfectly substitutable and hence UIP holds continuously (there is no risk premium, $\rho$). Thirdly, the demand for money is a stable function of a few variables. Fourthly, income is assumed to be at its full employment level. Finally, PPP is assumed to hold continuously. These last two assumptions reflect the flexible price nature of the model.

We can solve equations (3.1) to (3.4) for the exchange rate. If we subtract equation (3.2) from (3.1) we derive an equation for relative money demands:

$$(m - m^*) - (p - p^*) = \phi(y - y^*) - \mu(i - i^*) \tag{3.5}$$

We know from equation (3.3) that $i - i^* = \Delta s^e$ and if we solve for the relative price level, we derive:

$$(m - m^*) - \phi(y - y^*) + \mu(\Delta s^e) = (p - p^*) \tag{3.6}$$

which from equation (3.4) gives us the equation for the exchange rate:

$$s = (m - m^*) - \phi(y - y^*) + \mu(\Delta s^e) \tag{3.7}$$

We can replace $\Delta s^e$ in this equation by noting from equation (3.4) that $\Delta s^e = \Delta p^e - \Delta p^{e*}$ and hence we can rewrite (3.7) as:

$$s = (m - m^*) - \phi(y - y^*) + \mu(\Delta p^e - \Delta p^{e*}) \tag{3.8}$$

---

[5] See, for example, Frankel (1993); Boughton (1988); Whitman (1975); Backus (1984); Frenkel (1976); Girton and Roper (1977); and Bilson (1978).

[6] This is just a simplifying assumption. Later in this chapter, when we discuss empirical applications of this model, we report some results where this assumption is relaxed.

[7] This implies that in the fixed exchange rate version of the monetarist model (the so-called global monetarist model) the government does not undertake any sterilisation of capital inflows or outflows. Recall that sterilisation refers to the activity of conducting open market operations in order to offset the impact of changes in foreign exchange reserves on the money supply. See Whitman (1975) for a comprehensive account of the global monetarist model.

This equation states that the exchange rate (the relative price of two currencies) is determined by relative money demands and money supplies. If domestic income increases relative to foreign income,[8] then this increases the demand for money (see equation (3.1)) relative to the supply. That is, there is an excess demand for domestic money and this causes the exchange rate to appreciate (that is, s falls). By contrast, an increase in the domestic money supply, m, causes s to rise. The excess supply of money causes the exchange rate to depreciate one-for-one. Similarly, if expected domestic inflation rises above that expected in the foreign country, then the demand for money falls and the exchange rate will depreciate. Thus the impact of exogenous shocks is always examined through its effect on the money market.

It is often the case that monetarist models specify what determines expected relative inflation. Frankel (1993, Ch. 4), for example, makes an extremely simple assumption: that expectations are formed rationally and expected inflation depends only on expected monetary growth.[9] This implies that we have to specify an equation for expected monetary growth. The usual assumption is that money supply growth follows a random walk:

$$\Delta m_t = \Delta m_{t-1} + u_1 \quad \text{and} \quad \Delta m^*_t = \Delta m^*_{t-1} + u_2 \tag{3.9}$$

where $u_1$ and $u_2$ are both random errors whose expected value is equal to zero. This implies that expected monetary growth is equal to actual monetary growth. Hence, the exchange rate equation becomes:

$$s = (m - m^*) - \phi(y - y^*) + \mu(\Delta m - \Delta m^*) \tag{3.10}$$

This states that if domestic monetary growth rises above foreign monetary growth, then the exchange rate will depreciate (that is, s will rise).[10]

Before examining the empirical evidence relating to monetarist models, we can make several remarks about these models from a theoretical standpoint. It is clear from the above that these models make rather strong assumptions. Firstly, there is the assumption that PPP holds continuously. In our discussion of PPP in the previous chapter, we listed a number of reasons why it may not always hold: transport and information costs; differential productivity growth effects and a prevalence of real shocks; the existence of trade barriers, etc. If purchasing power parity does not always hold, then the predictions of the monetarist model break down.[11] In particular, real exchange rate changes may occur. Secondly, the demand for money may not be a stable function of income and interest rates. In this case, changes in these variables may not lead to disequilibrium in the money market and hence may have no effect on the exchange rate. Finally, there is the assumption of perfectly flexible prices. This is not the place to discuss possible causes of price stickiness, but we can

---

[8] Note that the increase in income must be exogenous, since income is assumed to be a full employment and is therefore determined by factors outside the model such as labour supply, technology etc.

[9] This is the case because, assuming rational expectations implies that the expected variables in the model (in this case, expected inflation) are a function of all past and present variables in the model (these represent the information set from which expectations are formed rationally). If we further assume for simplicity that exogenous income growth is equal to zero, then expected inflation is equal to the rationally formed expectations regarding money supply growth. (For models where expected income growth is not assumed to be equal to zero and hence expected inflation depends on expected monetary growth and income growth, see Backus (1984) and Huang (1981).)

[10] See Barro (1978) for a more sophisticated specification of money supply growth where anticipated and unanticipated disturbances are considered.

[11] We discuss a monetarist model by Bomhoff and Kortweg (1983) which does not assume continuous PPP later.

certainly note that there is a large literature on this issue[12] If prices are not flexible, then we move to the sticky price version of the monetary approach.

*Empirical tests of the monetarist model*

Estimation of exchange rate determination models requires that they be solved for some kind of reduced form equation which expresses the exchange rate in terms of a number of exogenous factors which are observable. Tests of the monetary approach usually employ a reduced form equation of the following type:

$$s = (m - m^*) + a_1(y - y^*) + a_2(i - i^*) \qquad (3.11)$$

where, m is the logarithm of the money supply; y is income; and i is the interest rate. $A^*$ denotes foreign country variables. The unitary coefficient on relative money supplies in equation (3.11) reflects the neutrality of money which is a key component of the monetarist model. The coefficients $a_1$ and $a_2$ are hypothesised to be negative and positive respectively. An increase in domestic income relative to foreign income causes an increase in demand for money, a surplus on the balance of payments and hence s falls (that is the exchange rate appreciates). An increase in the domestic interest rate relative to the foreign rate causes the demand for money to fall, a deficit on the balance of payments and hence the exchange rate rises, that is depreciates.

Backus (1984) estimates equation (3.11) on quarterly data from 1971 until 1979 for the US dollar–Canadian dollar exchange rate. The results of his basic equation are reproduced below:

$$s = \underset{(3.26)}{1.124}(m - m^*) - \underset{(1.58)}{0.955}(y - y^*) - \underset{(1.33)}{0.012}(i - i^*)$$

$$DW = 0.30 \qquad R^2 = 0.264$$

This is a rather poor equation. Although the coefficient on relative money supplies is insignificantly different from 1 and the relative income term has the correct sign, the latter is not particularly significant and relative interest rates are insignificant with the wrong sign. More importantly, there is evidence of serial correlation of the residuals (as shown by the very low value of the Durbin–Watson (DW) statistic).

Dornbusch (1980) tests a similar monetary equation using quarterly data for the dollar–DM exchange rate over the period 1973(2)-1979(4). His results are similarly poor:

$$s = \underset{(2.81)}{5.76} - \underset{(0.07)}{0.03}(m - m^*) - \underset{(0.97)}{1.05}(y - y^*) + \underset{(1.90)}{0.01}(i - i^*)_s + \underset{(2.07)}{0.04}(i - i^*)_l$$

$$R^2 = 0.33; \quad DW = 1.83; \quad SE^{13} = 0.05 \text{ and } rho = 0.88$$

In this equation, Dornbusch includes both long- and short-term interest rate, on the assumption that long-term interest rates might reflect inflation differentials. The coefficient on the relative money supply term is very low, and both the money supply and income are insignificant. Furthermore, significant serial correlation in the

---

[12] See, for example, Mankiw and Romer (1991) for a comprehensive discussion of New Keynesian economics.

[13] SE is the standard error of the regression.

residuals led to the adoption of the Cochrane–Orcutt method of correcting the residuals[14] where the value of rho is 0.88. Dornbusch also reports that the equation is unstable in that if the lagged exchange rate is added, it is the only variable that remains significant.

Haache and Townend (1981) provide results for a monetarist model for sterling effective exchange rate from 1972 to 1980. Tests are conducted on both a restricted monetarist model (such as the one quoted earlier) as well as for a more general model which allows for lags in the adjustment process. Neither model performs well and provides any support for the monetarist model of exchange rate determination.

Backus (1984) attempts to improve on the above results by firstly allowing the coefficients on domestic and foreign money supplies, incomes and interest rates to differ. The reduced form given in equation (3.11) is derived from a model where the coefficients in the demand for money equation are assumed to be identical in both countries. Clearly this could be an unrealistic assumption. However, allowing the coefficients to differ does not improve the results. The second amendment which Backus (1984) makes is to endogenise the rate of interest. It is to be expected that the interest rate is endogenous in the equation (3.11) and hence that not only do changes in interest rates affect the exchange rate, but also that changes in the exchange rate influence the interest rate. If the interest differential is endogenised (through use of the interest parity relationship), then there is still no improvement in the performance of equation (3.11).

Huang (1981) offers a different approach to testing the monetary approach. The aim is to observe the volatility of the exchange rate and ask whether or not such volatility is consistent with an efficient market monetary approach to exchange rate determination.[15] Huang notes that the monetarist model states that the exchange rate at any given time is a function of both current and expected values of relative money supplies and relative incomes. Using data from March 1973 to March 1979 for the dollar–Deutschmark, dollar–sterling and sterling–Deutschmark exchange rates, he examines the variance of the exchange rate implied by the monetarist model and compares that to the variance of the actual exchange rate. If the monetarist approach has some validity, then the actual exchange rate should display a similar degree of volatility to the variance implied by the model itself. The results indicate that movements in the actual exchange are too volatile to be consistent with the monetarist model and an efficient market.

Two articles which do provide some support for the monetarist model are those of Frenkel (1976) and, more recently, MacDonald and Taylor (1994). Frenkel examines the validity of the model for a period of hyperinflation. He uses data from the German experience with hyperinflation in the 1920s (specifically, the data runs from February 1920 to November 1923). He first builds a simple model of the exchange rate under hyperinflation where the exchange rate is found to depend on both the

---

[14] This method of correcting for serial correlation is undesirable in that it assumes that the correlation takes a specific form. This should be borne in mind when examining a lot of the evidence on exchange rate determination – since much of the empirical work suffers from serial correlation which is corrected in this way. Serial correlation is often evidence of omitted variables and it would be better to search for those variables and eliminate it in that way.

[15] This approach obviously draws on Shiller's work on the volatility of stock prices and whether or not it can be explained by the efficient market approach to the stock market. See Shiller (1991) for a compendium of his work in this area.

money supply and inflation.[16] Estimates of this equation provide support for the monetarist approach. MacDonald and Taylor (1993; 1994) provide evidence in support of the monetary model as a long-run model of exchange rate determination for the dollar/sterling exchange rate over the period January 1976 to December 1990. In particular, they find evidence of cointegration between exchange rates, money, incomes and interest rates using Johansen techniques. However, the specific restrictions on the coefficients implied by the monetary model were rejected.

The general failure to find much support for the monetarist model has led some authors to attempt to develop a monetary model which allows departures from PPP. Dornbusch (1980) does this by incorporating the impact of current account effects which allows for the impact of real disturbances on the exchange rate rather than the exclusive concentration on monetary factors which is evident in the monetarist model. In the long run, equilibrium in this model is represented by full employment and current account equilibrium. He tests his ideas within a 'news' framework. The dependent variable is unanticipated depreciation (given by $\Delta s - i + i^*$) and this is hypothesised to be dependent on 'news' relating to the current account (that is, the actual current account minus what was expected), cyclical 'news' (that is expected minus actual output levels in both the domestic and foreign economies) and interest rate 'news'. He uses OECD 6-month forecasts for the major industrial countries as his expectations variables[17] and tests that model of the dollar effective exchange rate. His results are supportive of the model. There is no evidence of serial correlation and the coefficients have the anticipated signs. He thus concludes that this evidence provides some support for the view that unanticipated real as well as financial disturbances are important in determining exchange rates.

Bomhoff and Kortweg (1983) undertake a similar analysis to Dornbusch (1980). They derive an asset market model which allows for departures from PPP and estimate it in a 'news' framework for a number of industrialised country currencies *vis-à-vis* the dollar over the period 1973 to 1979.[18] The expected and unexpected variables are derived using Kalman filtering techniques.[19] They conclude that their results show limited support for the monetary approach even in this augmented version. In particular, they note that the lags in some of the equations between the impact of a change and its impact on the exchange rate are rather long, something which one would not anticipate in foreign exchange markets.

## Sticky price monetary (overshooting) models

Dornbusch (1976a) is perhaps the most well-known of the sticky price monetary models of exchange rate determination. One of the essential aims of the model is to develop a theory which might go some way to explaining the large fluctuations in exchange rates which, as we saw in Chapter 1, have been a feature of the floating

---

[16] The role for inflation essentially comes from his demand for money function which assumes that money demand under hyperinflation depends only on inflation. There is no role for interest rates or money supplies.

[17] Note that expected interest rates are not included in OECD forecasts. Unanticipated changes in relative exchange rates are thus calculated by using the residuals from an autoregression of short-term interest rate differentials.

[18] They use quarterly data. The industrialised countries include The Netherlands, France, Germany, Switzerland, Italy and the UK.

[19] Assume we have a series, $y_t = x_t + e_t$ where $e_t$ is white noise. Kalman filtering allows us to extract the $x_t$ series. Assuming we have data from period t, the filter works recursively: at t+1, it uses the information at t to make the best prediction of x; at t+2 it makes the best prediction of x using the information at t and t+1. In other words, it tries to extract a series $x_t$ which minimises the prediction errors based on the information available to it. See Harvey (1993) for a comprehensive discussion.

exchange rate period. Sticky price monetary models are often referred to as over-shooting models. Overshooting refers to the tendency for the exchange rate to overshoot its new equilibrium level following some exogenous shock to the system. Assume, for example, a shock which warrants depreciation of the exchange rate to a new long-run level. Overshooting implies that in the short run, the exchange rate will tend to over-depreciate, before appreciating towards its new long-run equilibrium value. The key result of overshooting arises in the model from differential speeds of adjustment in the goods and asset markets. In particular, it is assumed that following a disturbance, the asset market moves rapidly to its new equilibrium. The goods market, by contrast, is characterised by sticky prices and takes longer to adjust to a new equilibrium.

The model can be thought of as a branch of the monetary approach for a number of reasons. Firstly, it focuses on the money market and it is the relationship between money demand and money supply which determines the exchange rate. Secondly, it assumes perfect asset substitutability and hence UIP holds continuously. However, it departs from the monetarist model discussed above in that, because of price sticki-ness, the goods market has to be specified along with an equation for price adjustment.

We follow closely Dornbusch's (1976a) exposition of the model which is in log-linear form. We discuss other versions of the model below, when we relax some of the assumptions. As noted above, perfect asset substitutability along with perfect capital mobility ensures that UIP holds continuously:

$$i = i^* + \Delta s^e \qquad (3.12)$$

where it is assumed that the country under consideration is a small, open economy. This allows us to assume that it faces a given world interest rate ($i^*$). Expectations are given by:

$$\Delta s^e = \Theta(\bar{s} - s) \qquad (3.13)$$

where: $\Theta$ is the coefficient of adjustment ($\Theta > 0$); s = logarithm of the current exchange rate (the domestic currency price of a unit of foreign currency); and $\bar{s}$ is the logarithm of the long-run exchange rate. Equation (3.13) states that expectations are formed regressively. If the current exchange rate, s, is above its long-run rate, $\bar{s}$, then it will appreciate (that is, s will fall) towards its long-run level. We can note that the assumption of regressive expectations is not inconsistent with rational expectations. For a certain value of $\Theta$, it can been shown that (3.13) is consistent with rational expectations.[20] We present a rational expectations version of Dornbusch's model.

The long-run exchange rate is determined by monetary factors and real factors. If domestic prices increase at a faster rate than foreign prices, then the exchange rate will depreciate to maintain a constant real exchange rate. In this sense, the model embraces PPP and money is assumed to be neutral in the long run. However, the long-run exchange rate is also determined by real factors, which may warrant a change in the real exchange rate (for example, real, full-employment income may change due to a natural resource discovery, higher productivity, etc).

Money market equilibrium is given by the same equation used by the monetarist model already discussed. We replicate that equation here for convenience:

---

[20]  See Dornbusch (1976) for a proof of this.

$$m - p = \phi y - \mu i \tag{3.14}$$

We assume that the economy is at full employment,[21] so that real domestic income is exogenous and given.

Since prices are sticky, we have to specify the goods market. Equilibrium requires that aggregate demand equals aggregate supply. The demand for domestic output (d) is a function of the real exchange rate $(s + p^* - p)$, the domestic interest rate (i) and real domestic income (y). In its log-linear version, aggregate demand is given by:

$$d = \alpha(s + p^* - p) - \sigma i + \tau y \tag{3.15}$$

Aggregate supply is fixed at its full employment level, $\hat{y}$. If aggregate demand is greater than aggregate supply then prices will rise, and vice versa if aggregate demand is less than aggregate supply. This is reflected in the price adjustment equation:

$$\Delta p = \delta[\alpha(s + p^* - p) - \sigma i + \tau y - \hat{y}] \tag{3.16}$$

Equations (3.14) and (3.16), that is, the assets market equilibrium condition and the goods market equilibrium condition, form the heart of the Dornbusch model. Figure 3.2 shows a graphical representation of the model. The QQ schedule is derived from equation (3.14). If we substitute equations (3.12) and (3.13) into equation (3.14), we derive:

$$m - p = \phi y - \mu[i^* + \Theta(\bar{s} - s)]$$

$$\Rightarrow m - p = \phi y - \mu i^* - \mu\Theta\bar{s} + \mu\Theta s$$

$$\Rightarrow \mu\Theta s = m - p - \phi y + \mu i^* + \mu\Theta\bar{s}$$

$$\Rightarrow s = \bar{s} + (1/\mu\Theta)[m - p - \phi y + \mu i^*] \tag{3.17}$$

Equation (3.17) expresses the exchange rate and price level as a function of three exogenous variables: the real money supply, domestic real income and the foreign interest rate. For a given price level, the QQ curve tells us the exchange rate that generates money market equilibrium. It slopes downward for the following intuitive reason. If p falls below $\bar{p}$ (Figure 3.2), then the real supply of money rises. The domestic interest rate therefore falls to maintain money market equilibrium. However, if the domestic interest rate falls, then the interest parity condition (given by equation (3.12)) will be broken. The interest parity condition can be restored by creating an expected appreciation of the domestic currency, that is, a fall in $\Delta s^e$. This compensates investors for the fall in the domestic interest rate. Given regressive exchange rate expectations (see equation (3.13)), if s is above $\bar{s}$, then it is expected that s will appreciate (that is, that s falls), since when s is above $\bar{s}$, it is depreciated relative to its long-run value. Thus a relatively high level of s is required if p is low and the money market is to remain in equilibrium. To summarise, if p is low, this is associated with a lower domestic interest rate and therefore to restore interest parity, the exchange rate must be expected to appreciate. That is, a low p is associated with a high s (or an undervalued exchange rate). The negative slope of QQ is confirmed by equation (3.17) where s is a negative function of p. Thus point B in Figure 3.2 is

---

[21] Note that Dornbusch (1976a) relaxes this assumption in part V of the article. Departures from full employment can mean that overshooting is no longer a necessary outcome of the adjustment process.

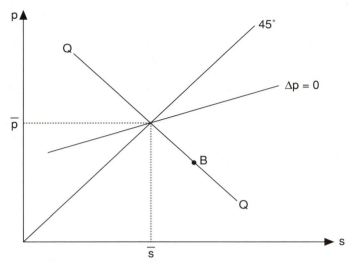

**Figure 3.2.** *Dornbusch's overshooting model*

associated with a price level below the long-run equilibrium level and an exchange rate above the long-run equilibrium level (i.e. undervalued).

The line $\Delta p = 0$ in Figure 3.2 represents combinations of s and p which ensure that excess demand is equal to zero, that is, the goods market is in equilibrium. We can derive the equation for $\Delta p = 0$ by substituting equations (3.12) and (3.13) into (3.16) and setting the result equal to zero:[22]

$$s = (1/(\alpha + \sigma\Theta)[\sigma(i^* + \Theta\bar{s}) - \alpha(p^* - p) - (\tau - 1)y] \tag{3.18}$$

The $\Delta p = 0$ curve is positively sloped, but is flatter than the 45° line. An increase in p above its equilibrium level has two effects on aggregate demand. Firstly, it reduces the real value of the money supply leading to an increase in interest rates. This reduces investment and thus aggregate demand (the Keynes effect). The second effect of the rise in the price level is on competitiveness. A rise in domestic prices reduces competitiveness and thus the demand for domestic net exports falls. For both reasons, aggregate demand falls below aggregate supply. In order to eliminate the excess supply in the goods market resulting from the price increase, the exchange rate, s, has to increase (that is, depreciate) more than proportionately to the price increase. Not only does the change in the exchange rate have to counteract the decline in competitiveness, but it also has to compensate for the Keynes effect. Thus the slope of the curve is less than that of the 45° line. This analysis also explains why above $\Delta p = 0$, there is an excess supply of goods and below an excess demand.

---

[22] This is derived as follows:

$$0 = \delta[(\alpha(s + p^* - p) - \sigma i + \tau y - \hat{y}]$$
$$=> 0 = \delta[(\alpha(s + p^* - p) - \sigma(i^* + \Theta(\bar{s} - s)) + \tau y - \hat{y}]$$
$$=> 0 = \delta[(\alpha s + \alpha(p^* - p) - \sigma i^* - \sigma\Theta\bar{s} + \sigma\Theta s + \tau y - \hat{y}]$$
$$=> 0 = \delta\alpha s + \delta\sigma\Theta s + \delta[\alpha(p^* - p) - \sigma i^* - \sigma\Theta\bar{s} + (\tau - 1)y]$$
since $y = \hat{y}$ because we assume full employment
$$=> \delta\alpha s + \delta\sigma\Theta s = -\delta[\alpha(p^* - p) - \sigma i^* - \sigma\Theta\bar{s} + (\tau - 1)y]$$
$$=> [\delta(\alpha + \sigma\Theta]s = \delta[\sigma i^* + \sigma\Theta\bar{s} - \alpha(p^* - p) - (\tau - 1)y]$$
$$=> s = (1/(\alpha + \sigma\Theta)[\sigma(i^* + \Theta\bar{s}) - \alpha(p^* - p) - (\tau - 1)y]$$ which is equation (3.18).

Having described the various components of the model, we can now turn to the impact of various shocks. The key assumption in this model which explains how the exchange rate responds to a shock is that of differential market adjustment. On the one hand, it is assumed that the goods market adjusts only slowly towards its new equilibrium. In terms of Figure 3.2, this implies that we can be off the $\Delta p = 0$ schedule. On the other hand, asset markets are assumed to clear continuously and hence we are always on the QQ schedule. The rationale for this assumption is that asset markets are usually seen as markets where prices (interest rates, exchange rates, etc.) move quickly towards their equilibrium levels following some exogenous shock. On the other hand, goods markets are characterised by price stickiness and thus move more slowly towards equilibrium. It is notable in this model that goods markets do actually reach equilibrium, at full employment output in the long run. This is something which more Keynesian models might deny.

Take the example of a contraction in the domestic money supply. This example is represented in Figure 3.3. The 45° line reflects the assumption that money is neutral in the long run. That is, changes in the supply of money have no long-run effect on the real economy. A given percentage increase (decrease) in the money supply will lead to the same percentage increase (decrease) in p and s. This can be seen to result from the fact that there is no money illusion or price stickiness in the long run. Thus relative prices are unchanged by changes in the money supply.

Assume initially that the economy is in equilibrium at point A, with the exchange rate equal to $\bar{s}$ and the price level, $\bar{p}$. The decrease in the money supply causes the asset market equilibrium schedule to shift to the left (to $Q'Q'$). The decline in the money supply causes the domestic interest rate to increase, disturbing the interest parity condition (equation (3.12)). Asset markets are now in disequilibrium. To restore equilibrium, an expected depreciation (i.e. a rise in s) is required. Thus for a given p, s has to be low (i.e. appreciated relative to its long-run value), for example at $s''$. At the old equilibrium point, A, there is also an excess supply of goods, because

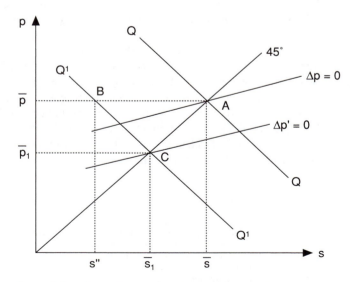

**Figure 3.3.**    *A monetary contraction in the Dornbusch model*

the contraction of the money supply has reduced aggregate demand. Thus for a given exchange rate, the price level must be lower to eliminate that excess supply, by increasing competitiveness and real money balances. The $\Delta p = 0$ function thus shifts downwards to $\Delta p' = 0$. A useful help to understanding Dornbusch's model is that it is easier first to locate the new long-run equilibrium and then analyse how the economy moves there. The new long-run equilibrium is given by point C, where the $Q'Q'$ schedule crosses the 45° line. Given that money is homogeneous of degree one (i.e. neutral), as argued above, in the long run a decrease in the money supply must lead to a proportional fall in the domestic price level and the long-run exchange rate (i.e. an appreciation). Thus the new equilibrium exchange rate is given by $\bar{s}_1$ and the price level by $\bar{p}_1$.

The long-run result is not the most interesting aspect of the model. Rather it is the short-run adjustment process by which the economy moves from point A to point C. The reduction in the money supply raises the domestic rate of interest for a given money demand in the short run. This arises because the reduction in the nominal money supply reduces the real money supply, since in the short run the price level is sticky. The rise in the domestic interest rate disturbs the interest rate parity condition (given by equation (3.12)). In particular, there is now an incipient capital inflow. This causes the exchange rate to appreciate. However, the exchange rate must appreciate beyond its new long-run equilibrium level, $\bar{s}_1$, so as to generate expectations of depreciation. Thus the exchange rate overshoots and this overshooting is necessary if asset market equilibrium is to hold continuously. If domestic interest rates have risen, then to restore interest rate parity, we must have expectations of a depreciation of the exchange rate back to its new long-run equilibrium level. Thus the economy moves from A to B in the short-run: with prices fixed, only the exchange rate can adjust to maintain asset market equilibrium.

How then does the economy move from B to C? At B, there is an excess supply of goods, since for the given price level, $\bar{p}$, the exchange rate has appreciated reducing the demand for net exports. This leads to price adjustment via equation (3.16). In particular, prices will fall in the long run. This increases the real money supply and causes interest rates to fall. As interest rates fall, an incipient capital outflow develops, causing the exchange rate to depreciate to its new long-run level. The economy therefore moves down $Q'Q'$ from B to C.

Thus in Dornbusch's overshooting model the exchange rate reacts to ensure asset market equilibrium. Moreover, when the continuous clearing asset market is combined with slow adjustment in the goods market, the exchange rate can overshoot. In this way, Dornbusch's model can provide an explanation for the large fluctuations in exchange rates which have been observed in recent times.

The Dornbusch model has served as the basis for a number of other models of the overshooting type. In many cases, these later models are extensions of the Dornbusch story which sometimes (but not always) arise from criticisms of the original version of the model. We can highlight a number of extensions which have been made.

Firstly, this model assumes output is constant at full employment. Dornbusch (1976a) relaxes this assumption to allow for short-run output adjustments. The impact of this is that exchange rates no longer necessarily exhibit overshooting. For example, with a fall in the money supply and therefore income, money demand is also reduced and interest rates may remain unchanged, or even fall. In other words, there is no rise in the domestic interest rate which causes the incipient capital inflow and appreciation of the exchange rate. However, even with this modification, the supply side of the model is rather simplistic (MacDonald, 1988). In particular, MacDonald argues that there is no attempt to model wage-price interactions.

Secondly, residents are not allowed to hold foreign money, they can only hold domestic money. This nonsubstitutability between monies in the model is in sharp contrast to the assumption that domestic and foreign bonds are perfectly substitutable (Ingram, 1978). However, the implications of the lack of substitutability between monies are important. In our example, when the economy moves from B to C, the exchange rate is expected to depreciate. If domestic and foreign money were perfect substitutes for each other, then holders of domestic currency would sell the currency and the exchange rate would depreciate to its new level immediately. Models in the monetary approach vein which allow domestic residents to hold foreign money are known as currency substitution models. In these models the idea is that residents seek to diversify their currency holdings. The problem which arises, however, is that very few individuals will actually hold foreign *currencies* as a means of diversification: instead, holding foreign bonds provides a similar service (albeit without the liquidity of holding foreign money) yet includes interest. Hence it is not clear that these models are any more realistic than those models where domestic residents are unable to hold foreign money.[23]

Thirdly, a number of authors have asked what happens in the Dornbusch model if we relax the assumption of perfect capital mobility and assume instead imperfect capital mobility (Frenkel and Rodriguez, 1982; Bhandari, Driskill and Frenkel, 1984). In this case, the exchange rate may undershoot. In other words, following a money supply decrease, for example, the exchange rate will appreciate only slightly in the first instance.

Frenkel and Rodriguez (1982) extend Dornbusch's model to incorporate a low degree of capital mobility.[24] This requires a replacement of UIP by a balance of payments equation which specifies both current and capital account parts. The capital flow equation is given by:

$$C = \eta[i - i^* - \theta(\bar{s} - s)] \tag{3.19}$$

where $\eta$ represents the degree of capital mobility. If $\eta = \infty$, then capital is perfectly mobile and UIP must hold continuously (otherwise, capital flows become infinite). The trade balance equation is given by:

$$\dot{T} = \varepsilon(s - p - \bar{s}) \tag{3.20}$$

where $(s - p)$ is the actual real exchange rate and $\bar{s}$ is the long-run equilibrium exchange rate. Adding these two equations together and setting the result equal to zero gives us an expression for balance of payments equilibrium:

$$\varepsilon(s - p - \bar{s}) + \eta[i - i^* - \theta(\bar{s} - s)] = 0 \tag{3.21}$$

Replacing the domestic interest rate by equation (3.14) solved for i ($i = 1/\mu[\phi y - m + p]$ $= 1/\mu(\phi y) - 1/\mu(m - p)$):

---

[23] Currency substitution models have been applied frequently to developing countries, where a foreign currency (such as the dollar) is often in circulation within the country alongside the domestic currency. See MacDonald (1988, Chapter 7) for a discussion of currency substitution models.

[24] We can note that Bhandari, Driskill and Frenkel (1984) present a similar model to that of Frenkel and Rodriguez (1982). The key difference is that the former examine the relationship between capital mobility and overshooting in a *stock* formulation of the capital account. As we shall see, the latter use a flow representation..

$$\epsilon(s - p - \bar{s}) + \eta[1/\mu(\phi y) - 1/\mu(m - p) - i^* - \theta(\bar{s} - s)] = 0 \qquad (3.22)$$

Equation (3.22) shows equilibrium combinations of s and p which generate balance of payments equilibrium. It is now the QQ schedule of Dornbusch's original model.[25]

We represent these new equations diagrammatically in Figure 3.4. Equation (3.19) generates a C = 0 schedule along which the capital account is in equilibrium. The schedule has a negative slope. A fall in the price level causes the real money supply to increase and hence the domestic interest rate to fall. Capital therefore flows out of the country and to restore equilibrium we require expectations of an exchange rate appreciation: the exchange rate must be depreciated relative to its long-run value. A low p is thus associated with a high s. Equation (3.22) generates the QQ schedule showing balance of payments equilibrium. If capital is highly mobile then QQ is negatively sloped, but steeper than C = 0. The rationale for this is as follows. Assume the price level falls from $\bar{p}$ to $p_1$. There are two effects. Firstly, the capital account effect arises from the increase in the real money supply and the fall in the domestic interest rate. This causes a capital account deficit. Hence, we require expectations of an appreciation of an amount $s_1\bar{s}$ if we were only interested in restoring capital account balance. However, the second effect is on the current account. The fall in the domestic price level causes the current account to improve and this offsets the capital account deficit to some extent. Hence to restore overall balance of payments equilibrium, the depreciation of the exchange rate need not be so great (only to $s_2$). At $p_1, s_2$ we have balance of payments equilibrium with a capital account deficit (because the expectations of an appreciation, $s_2\bar{s}$, are not large enough to restore capital account equilibrium) offset by a current account surplus (resulting from the fall in p).

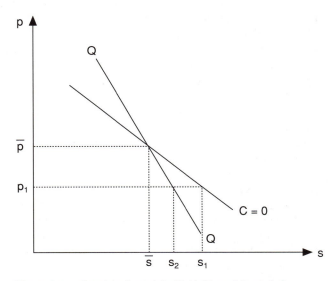

**Figure 3.4.** *Dornbusch model with highly mobile capital*

---

[25] Recall that in Dornbusch's original model, the QQ schedule was essentially composed only of the capital account (given by the UIP equation).

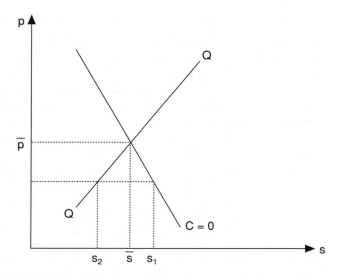

**Figure 3.5.** *Dornbusch model with immobile capital*

If capital is fairly immobile, then the QQ schedule is actually positively sloped (see Figure 3.5). If the domestic price level falls, then the capital account story is the same: there is a need for expectations of an appreciation to restore capital account equilibrium. However, note that the expectations need to be so great as in the previous case (in other words, the C = 0 schedule is much steeper). The current account story is also similar: the fall the p causes a current account surplus. Where the story differs from the highly mobile capital case is in the fact that the current account surplus outweighs the capital account deficit. Hence to restore balance of payments equilibrium an appreciation of the exchange rate is required (not a depreciation as occurred in the previous case). The appreciation reduces the trade surplus until it exactly offsets the small capital account deficit[26] and hence balance of payments equilibrium is restored.

What is the impact of an exogenous shock when the degree of capital mobility is less than perfect? Assume as before that there is an exogenous decrease in the money supply. If capital is mobile enough that the QQ schedule is downward sloping, then the overshooting result holds. If, on the other hand, the degree of capital mobility is low and the QQ schedule is positively sloped, then the exchange rate no longer overshoots. This case is illustrated in Figure 3.6. Assume the economy is initially at point A (note that we have not drawn in the three schedules which go through point A in order to make the diagram less cluttered). The 45° line shows us where the new long-run equilibrium is following the exogenous shock: a fall in the domestic money supply implies that the price level and the exchange rate must fall by the same proportion. Thus the new equilibrium is at point D.

As before, it is how the economy moves from A to D that is the interesting question. Initially prices are fixed. Hence the fall in the money supply causes the capital account to go into surplus, as the real money supply falls and domestic interest rates

---

[26] Note that the capital account deficit actually worsens following the appreciation, because the appreciation generates expectations of a depreciation which lead to further capital outflows.

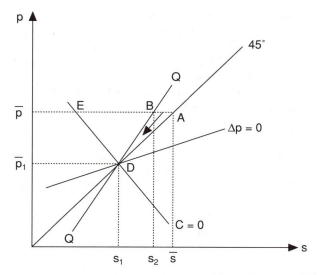

**Figure 3.6.** *Dornbusch model with immobile capital: an exogenous shock*

rise. However, the surplus is very small since capital is not very mobile. The exchange rate appreciates, but only to $s_2$.[27] This capital account surplus is exactly offset by a current account deficit (which results from the appreciation of the exchange rate with prices fixed at their original level). As prices start to fall, the domestic interest rate falls reducing the capital account surplus. Meanwhile, the current account deficit declines as competitiveness increases. If the exchange rate remained at $s_2$, then eventually the balance of payments would go into overall surplus. To prevent this, and maintain balance of payments equilibrium, the exchange rate has to appreciate further until the new price-exchange rate equilibrium is reached at D. Thus the impact of a low degree of capital mobility in the Dornbusch model is that the exchange rate undershoots its new equilibrium.[28]

It is interesting to mention that there are several other modifications to the Dornbusch model that generate similar results, that is undershooting. Niehans (1977), for example, assumes that portfolio adjustment (that is, the adjustment of actual financial assets held to those that investors desire to hold) is slow and this is enough to eliminate the overshooting result. Driskill (1980) generates undershooting by including wealth effects in the asset demand functions.

A fourth extension of the Dornbusch model is to examine the impact of imposing rational expectations on the model.[29] Given that the model is a deterministic one,

---

[27] Note that at B the capital account is not in equilibrium, since the domestic interest rate is still high and there are expectations of an appreciation ($= s_2\bar{s}_1$). For the capital account to be in equilibrium again, the exchange rate would have to appreciate by much more to move the economy to point E on the $C = 0$ schedule.

[28] Note that Frenkel and Rodriguez derive the border condition, where the QQ schedule is vertical and the exchange rate jumps to its new equilibrium immediately following a shock. This condition is given by $\eta = \varepsilon\mu$. When $\eta < \varepsilon\mu$ and capital is fairly immobile, the QQ schedule is positively sloped (and vice versa).

[29] It is useful to read the Appendix to this chapter which outlines the basic structure of rational expectations models. The appendix lays out some basic principles which are used in the text.

rational expectations is equivalent to perfect foresight. The advantage of extending the model in this direction is that we can then examine the difference between anticipated and unanticipated exogenous shocks. It is also useful to prepare the ground for an examination of a more dynamic version of the Dornbusch model, presented by Buiter and Miller (1981), which we discuss later.

The model presented follows MacDonald (1988). Assuming perfect foresight in Dornbusch's model implies replacing equation (3.12) for UIP by:

$$i = i^* + \Delta s \tag{3.23}$$

since $\Delta s^e = \Delta s$ ( $= ds/dt$). If we substitute this equation into the rest of the Dornbusch model discussed above (ignoring equation (3.13)), then we can derive a model which is represented by two dynamic equations for $\Delta s$ and $\Delta p$ (3.24 and 3.25):

$$\Delta s = i - i^*$$

substituting in from equation (3.14):[30]

$$\Delta s = (\phi/\mu)y + (1/\mu)p - (1/\mu)m - i^* \tag{3.24}$$

Finally, we take the equation for $\Delta p$ ( $= dp/dt$), that is equation (3.16), which we reproduce below:

$$\Delta p = \delta[\alpha(s + p^* - p) - \sigma i + y(\tau - 1)] \tag{3.16}$$

We can solve this model using a phase diagram by plotting these two schedules in s, p space (see Figure 3.7).

The $\Delta p = 0$ schedule is the same as in the simple Dornbusch model we considered. It has a positive slope but is flatter than the 45° line. The $\Delta s = 0$ schedule did not exist in the simple Dornbusch model. To understand why it is horizontal, we have to take equation (3.24) and set it equal to zero and solve for p:

$$\Delta s = 0 = (\phi/\mu)y + (1/\mu)p - (1/\mu)m - i^*$$

$$=> i^* - (\phi/\mu)y + (1/\mu)m = (1/\mu)p$$

$$=> \mu i^* - \phi y + m = p \tag{3.25}$$

Equation (3.25) shows that the schedule $\Delta s = 0$ does not depend on s and hence there is only one p which ensures that the exchange rate is stable, namely $p_1$. Thus $\Delta s = 0$ is represented by a horizontal line at $p_1$.

The arrows in Figure 3.7 illustrate what happens to the system if it moves away from either of these two schedules. Firstly, we examine what happens if the economy moves away from $\Delta p = 0$ schedule. To the left of $\Delta p = 0$, s is too low for each given level of p (that is, the exchange rate is too appreciated to generate $\Delta p = 0$). There must therefore be an excess supply of goods and thus the price level is falling. By contrast, to the right of $\Delta p = 0$, the exchange rate is too high (that is, too depreciated) for each given price level and hence there is an excess demand for goods. This causes prices to rise. The vertical arrows in Figure 3.7 indicate these movements in the domestic price level and we can see from these movements that $\Delta p = 0$ is a stable relationship. That is, if the economy moves off the $\Delta p = 0$ schedule, there is a tendency for it to move back towards it.

---

[30] From equation (3.14) we know that $i = (\phi/\mu)y + (1/\mu)p - (1/\mu)m$, which we can substitute for i and hence derive equation (3.24).

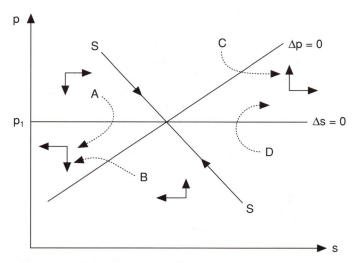

**Figure 3.7.** *Dornbusch overshooting model with perfect foresight*

Secondly, we can examine the case of deviations from $\Delta s = 0$. For points below $\Delta s = 0$, the price level is too low relative to that required for equilibrium. Hence real money balances are high and the domestic interest rate is low. To maintain UIP with perfect foresight (that is, equation (3.23)), we need expectations of an appreciation and hence the actual exchange rate has to be appreciating (since $\Delta s^e = \Delta s$). Thus s is falling as represented by the horizontal arrows. By contrast, above $\Delta s = 0$, the price level is too high for equilibrium. This implies a low real money supply and a higher domestic interest rate. To maintain UIP, we require expectations of a depreciation of the exchange rate and given perfect foresight, this means that the actual exchange rate is depreciating. In other words, s is rising. Thus we can see that this relationship is unstable.

We are now in a position to ask what happens to the economy if it is at a point such as A. At point A, there is an excess supply of goods and the domestic interest rate is 'too high'. Thus prices are falling and the exchange rate is depreciating. The economy is therefore moving in a south-easterly direction towards equilibrium. However, before reaching equilibrium, it crosses the $\Delta s = 0$ line. Now, interest rates are 'too low' and hence the exchange rate must be appreciating. The system therefore moves off on an unstable path. The exact opposite occurs if we are at point D. If the economy is at point B, then there is excess demand for goods hence p is rising and the domestic interest rate is 'too low' and hence s is falling. The economy thus moves in a north-westerly direction until it crosses the $\Delta p = 0$ schedule where there is excess supply in the goods market and hence prices start to fall. The system again shows instability. The exact opposite occurs if we begin at a point such as C.

This indicates that the system is saddlepoint unstable. In other words, there exists a unique saddlepoint path exactly where the unstable tendencies are offset by its stable tendencies. That saddlepoint path is shown as SS in Figure 3.7.[31] If the

---

[31] Note that we can find the saddlepoint path by observing the arrows of motion. It must lie in the regions where there is a tendency for the system to move towards equilibrium and it must lie in between points A and C and B and D since we know that if the economy is on either of those points, it will start out towards equilibrium, but then be deflected once it crosses either of the two schedules.

economy is in disequilibrium, then saddlepoint stability states that with perfect fore-sight, the economy will jump onto SS and hence move towards equilibrium, E, without ever crossing either of the two schedules.

What happens in this economy if there is an exogenous unanticipated monetary contraction? This is illustrated in Figure 3.8. Assume initially that the economy was in equilibrium at point A. The monetary contraction implies that the economy will move to a new long-run equilibrium at point C (on the 45° line, because of long-run money neutrality). Notice that the Δs = 0 curve shifts downwards following the con-traction of the money supply because at each s, the price level is now lower to maintain money market equilibrium. At the same time, the Δp = 0 schedule shifts downwards since at each exchange rate, the price level is now too high, creating an excess supply of goods which lowers the price level (at each exchange rate).

The economy moves from A to C via a point such as B. Prices are sticky in the short run and hence real money balances fall and the interest rate rises to equilibriate the money market. To maintain interest parity, expectations of a depreciation are required. These come about via a jump appreciation of the exchange rate from A to B. At B, the exchange rate is now overappreciated relative to its new long-run equi-librium value and hence we have expectation of depreciation combined with actual depreciation. Thus the system moves directly to its new saddlepoint path. It then fol-lows that path, $S_1S_1$, to its new equilibrium at C. In other words, as prices start to fall (because there is an excess supply of goods are point B) and the real money supply slowly rises, the domestic interest rate falls again. Thus to maintain interest parity, expectations of depreciation also have to fall and hence this implies in a rational expectations model that the actual exchange rate depreciates. A unanticipated fall in the money supply thus generates the same overshooting result in a rational expecta-tions framework as it did in the regressive expectations model discussed.

The advantage of a rational expectations framework is that we can also examine the impact of an anticipated exogenous shock. Assume for example that the

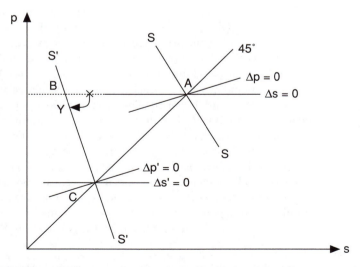

**Figure 3.8.**  *A monetary contraction in the rational expectations version of the Dornbusch overshooting model*

government announces a once-for-all monetary contraction.[32] The new equilibrium must again be at C. However, the economy will move from A to C in a different way from adjustment following an unanticipated monetary contraction. When the policy change is announced, the exchange rate moves immediately to point X, that is, it jump appreciates before the actual change in the money supply. If the exchange rate did not appreciate on the announcement, then there will be capital gains. In other words, agents know that when the money supply change does come, appreciation will occur and hence are expecting capital gains. Given rational expectations, agents choose point X so that p and s follow their trajectory to the new saddlepoint path, $S_1S_1$. To understand this, we have to ask ourselves what happens to the economy at point X. The appreciation has caused an excess supply of goods in the goods market and hence prices will begin to fall slowly. This causes real money balances to rise (recall that the money supply has still not changed, that is the policy has not been implemented) and hence the interest rate falls. To maintain interest parity, we require expectations of an appreciation at X, which, given rational expectations, implies that the actual exchange rate is still appreciating (that is, s is falling). Hence the fall in p and s from point X takes the economy to the saddlepoint path at Y. Once the money supply change is actually implemented, the economy is already on the new saddlepoint path and moves towards equilibrium as before. Thus the key difference between unanticipated and anticipated monetary contractions is that in the latter case the exchange rate jumps even before the money supply change is implemented. There is still overshooting.

The above versions of the Dornbusch model have all concentrated on once-for-all monetary shocks. Yet in reality, it is more common for governments to undertake monetary contraction by reducing the rate of growth of the money supply. This occurs because economies rarely experience zero inflation. Yet this is an assumption which has been explicit in our discussion up until now. Thus the final modification to the Dornbusch model which we want to undertake is that of making it more dynamic and introducing a non-zero secular rate of inflation.

Buiter and Miller (1981) developed a model which enables us to consider the impact of monetary policy designed at reducing the *rate of growth* of the money supply. The model is in the same spirit as Dornbusch in that it assumes that money is neutral in the long run, but that in the short run the goods market adjusts much more slowly than asset markets. The model has the familiar uncovered interest parity condition and money market equilibrium given by equations (3.26) and (3.27):

$$i = i^* + \Delta s^e = i^* + \Delta s, \text{ since } \Delta s = \Delta s^e \tag{3.26}$$

$$m - p = \phi y - \mu i \tag{3.27}$$

where in the above and what follows, $\Delta x = dx/dt$, since Buiter and Miller's model is in continuous time – we use this abbreviation for simplicity of notation. Aggregate demand depends negatively on the real interest rate $(i - \Delta p)$ and positively on the real exchange rate $(s - p)$.[33] The latter results from the fact that an increase in the real exchange rate represents a depreciation and hence an improvement in competitiveness.

---

[32] We examine the more realistic case of a programme of monetary growth contraction later on when we discuss the Buiter and Miller (1981) model.

[33] Foreign prices are set equal to 1 so that $p^*$ (the logarithm of foreign prices) is zero.

$$d = \alpha(s - p) - \xi(i - \Delta p) \tag{3.28}$$

The price equation relates the change in prices not only to the excess of aggregate demand over full employment income, but also to the core or trend rate of inflation, $\pi$:

$$\Delta p = \delta(d - \hat{y}) + \pi \tag{3.29}$$

If we set full employment output to 1 (and hence the logarithm of output, $\hat{y}$, is equal to zero), then equation (3.29) can be rewritten as:

$$\Delta p = \delta d + \pi \tag{3.30}$$

Finally, we assume that core inflation is equal to the rate of monetary growth ($\Delta m$):

$$\pi = \Delta m \tag{3.31}$$

These equations form the heart of the Buiter and Miller model.[34] Before going on to examine how the model works and, in particular, its dynamic properties, it is useful to outline the main conclusions and give some intuition for them. Essentially Buiter and Miller show that a monetary growth contraction can be associated with a large appreciation of the exchange rate (which overshoots its new long-run equilibrium value) and as a result leads to output costs and unemployment. This is true even if the policy is announced in advance and is believed by agents in the economy. In this sense, it strikes a blow at monetarist models which claim that credible monetary contractions will be associated with less, if not zero, cost. The driving force behind this result is that, even although money is neutral in the long run, short-run output effects occur because of sluggish adjustment of prices.

We can understand the story behind this result by taking an example. Assume that the economy is in long-run equilibrium with inflation equal to monetary growth equal to 10%. Assume that the authorities then announce and implement a policy which cuts monetary growth to zero. From equation (3.31), we can see that inflation immediately falls to zero.[35] The key to understanding how the economy reacts is to ask what happens to the real interest rate. If monetary growth has been cut to zero and inflation has fallen to zero, then clearly real money balances ($m - p$) must be unaltered. Hence to maintain money market equilibrium (equation (3.27)), the nominal interest rate will have to remain the same. This, however, implies that the real interest rate ($i - \Delta p$) has increased. This causes an incipient capital inflow and the exchange rate appreciates resulting in output costs as the tradeables sector is squeezed. This effect will be even greater if inflation enters directly into the money demand function. The fall in inflation causes real money demand to rise and hence, with real money supply fixed, this requires a rise in the nominal interest rate in order to maintain money market equilibrium. In this case, the real interest rate rises by even more and there is a larger output effect.

---

[34] We can note that we have removed a number of the factors which Buiter and Miller use in their model, such as North Sea oil effects, taxes on capital flows, indirect taxes, etc. These make the model more complex and are not required here where we consider mainly the impact of monetary policy within the model. Similar simplifications are undertaken by both Artis (1981) and MacDonald (1988).

[35] Buiter and Miller make this rather strong assumption since they believe it fits in rather well with monetarist views of how the economy works. It has the additional advantage of making the model more simple. As we see later, the model as it stands can be described by two differential equations. If inflation adjusts only slowly to changes in money growth, then this would require a third differential equation for inflation which would only make the model more complex. Buiter and Miller (1981) do discuss what happens if this assumption is relaxed (see pp.156–9).

We can illustrate this story more formally by examining the dynamic properties of the Buiter and Miller model. Define l as liquidity or real balances (that is, $l = m - p$) and q as the real exchange rate $(s - p)$ or competitiveness. From equations (3.26) to (3.31), we can derive two differential equations which describe the motion of the system (see Appendix 2). Firstly, there is the equation for the growth of liquidity. Substituting equation (3.31) into (3.30) and then using (3.27) and (3.28) to eliminate i and d we can derive:

$$\Delta l = [(1/\Xi)\delta\xi]l + [(1/\Xi)\delta\mu\alpha]q + (1/\Xi)\,\pi \qquad (3.32)$$

where $\Xi = \xi(\delta\mu - \phi) - \mu$. Secondly, there is the equation for the change in competitiveness, $\Delta q$. Taking (3.26) and (3.30) and adding them together and then substituting as before for i and d using (3.27) and (3.28), we derive:

$$\Delta q = (1/\Xi)l + [(1/\Xi)\alpha(\delta\mu - \phi)]q + [(1/\Xi)\mu]\pi - i^* \qquad (3.33)$$

These two equations can be plotted in $l - q$ space where along the schedule there are combinations of l and q such that $\Delta p = \Delta l = 0$ (that is, liquidity and competitiveness are constant). This is illustrated in Figure 3.9. The $\Delta l = 0$ schedule is negatively sloped because as liquidity increases, so interest rates are lower. To maintain interest rate parity, there has to be expectations of appreciation and given rational expectations, this implies that the actual exchange rate is appreciating (that is, s and hence q is falling). Another way of thinking about this is that low interest rates are associated with countries which have appreciating currencies in a world of high capital mobility. To the left of $\Delta l = 0$, liquidity and competitiveness are too low for equilibrium. Low liquidity tends to generate higher nominal interest rates and thus leads to an excess supply of goods which is compounded by low competitiveness. Thus prices fall and liquidity $(m - p)$ increases. This is represented by the horizontal arrows to the left of $\Delta l = 0$, which point rightwards. To the right of $\Delta l = 0$ the opposite is occurring. In other words, liquidity and competitiveness are at a very high level which creates an excess demand for goods. Hence prices rise and liquidity falls, generating the horizontal arrows which point leftwards.

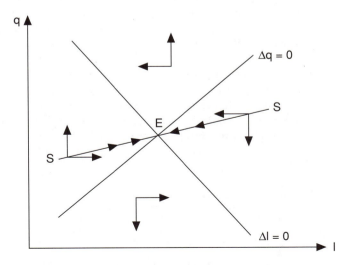

**Figure 3.9.**   *The Buiter and Miller model*

The $\Delta q = 0$ schedule can either be positively or negatively sloped, depending on the value of $\delta$, that is the speed of adjustment in the goods market. We assume here that the goods market is slow to adjust (that is, $\delta$ is low) and this ensures that $\Delta q = 0$ is positively sloped.[36] To the right of $\Delta q = 0$, liquidity is too high for equilibrium. This implies that the nominal interest rate is low and the exchange rate is appreciating (recall that if the interest rate is low, then the model requires expectations of appreciation to maintain UIP). Competitiveness thus gets worse and this is represented by the arrows pointing south in Figure 3.9. By contrast, to the left of $\Delta q = 0$, the exchange rate is depreciating and competitiveness is improving, generating northward pointing arrows.

The description of the workings of the system indicate that whilst the relationship $\Delta l = 0$ is stable (that is, away from $\Delta l = 0$ the system automatically moves towards it), the relationship $\Delta q = 0$ is unstable. This generates a saddlepoint equilibrium where the saddlepath is given by SS. If the economy suffers a shock, then the assumption of rational expectations ensures that the exchange rate jumps putting the economy on the new saddlepath which will take it safely to the new equilibrium. It is the exchange rate which jumps because the asset market adjusts quickly whereas the goods market (and hence the price level) does not.

Let us now examine a number of policy options within this model. Assume firstly that the government decreases the rate of monetary growth. This case is illustrated in Figure 3.10 where we assume that the economy is initially at point A. The new long-run equilibrium is at C since money is neutral. This is represented in Figure 3.10 by the fact that competitiveness is unchanged at q. The contraction in monetary growth causes both $\Delta l = 0$ and $\Delta q = 0$ to move to the right. $\Delta l = 0$ moves to the right because at each level of competitiveness, the monetary contraction causes an excess supply of goods. Liquidity must therefore rise (and indeed does, through the induced fall in p) to restore equilibrium. $\Delta q = 0$ moves to the right because at each level of liquidity, the monetary contraction causes the nominal interest rate to fall which implies that the currency must be appreciating (that is, q is falling).

The form taken by the move from A to C depends on whether or not the monetary contraction was anticipated or not as well as the lag between the announcement and its implementation. Assume initially that the monetary contraction was unanticipated and implemented immediately. In this case, the economy moves from A to C via a point such as B. The explanation for this is as follows. Initially liquidity $(m - p)$ is unchanged following the contraction. This occurs because inflation responds to the cut in monetary growth immediately. Hence if we have a contraction of monetary growth from say 10% to 5%, then m increases at only 5% in the following period, but so does p: that is, $(\dot{m} - p)$ remains unchanged. This implies that the nominal interest rate remains unchanged (to preserve money market equilibrium).[37] An unchanged nominal interest rate along with lower inflation causes the real interest rate to rise and attracts an incipient capital inflow. The exchange rate thus

---

[36] See Buiter and Miller (1981, pp.150–52) for an in-depth discussion of the slope of $\Delta q = 0$ and its implications. The slope of $\Delta q = 0$ is given by $1/[\alpha(\phi - \delta\mu)]$. For small values of $\delta$, this becomes positive. A positive slope for $\Delta q = 0$ ensures that the system has a saddlepoint equilibrium. Indeed, even if $\Delta q = 0$ is negatively sloped the system has a saddlepoint equilibrium, provided that it is steeper than the $\Delta I = 0$ schedule. In the case that $\Delta q = 0$ is negatively sloped and flatter than $\Delta I = 0$, then the system is globally unstable.

[37] We ignore the impact of inflation on the demand for money (which we have discussed briefly) for simplicity here.

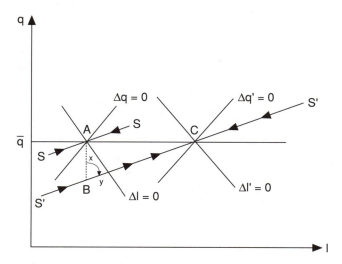

**Figure 3.10.**  *A monetary contraction in the Buiter–Miller model*

appreciates in a single jump to point B. This takes the economy to the new saddle-path from which it moves slowly to equilibrium.

If the policy is unanticipated but there is a delay between the announcement and its implementation, then the economy will only initially move to point X (Figure 3.10). The appreciation of the exchange rate associated with the move to X causes an excess supply of goods and prices start to fall (even before the monetary policy contraction is implemented). Hence liquidity rises and the nominal interest rate falls. This requires that the exchange rate continues to appreciate after reaching X. The economy thus moves towards Y (q is falling and l is rising) on the saddlepath. Y is reached when the policy is implemented and the economy simply moves along the new saddlepath S′S′ until C is reached.

Thus, whilst the extent of the appreciation may differ depending on whether the policy is anticipated/unanticipated and announced and implemented immediately or the implementation is delayed, the impact of a monetary contraction is to cause over-shooting of the exchange rate.[38] In particular, the exchange rate overappreciates causing output effects. Disinflation is thus costly.

A second interesting policy question which we can ask is what happens if the government announces a programme of monetary contraction over a number of periods. This is the kind of policy which was pursued in the UK in the early 1980s as part of the Medium Term Financial Strategy (MTFS). Initially this policy involved a reduction of the rate of monetary growth each year over four years. The cuts in monetary growth were announced at the beginning of the policy (that is, in year 1). The arguments in favour of such a strategy are that the government gains some credibility and that agents are able to adjust their expectations accordingly. Hence the output costs should be lower. Such a strategy is illustrated in Figure 3.11.

---

[38] Note that we did not examine the impact of anticipated policy which is subsequently announced and implemented at the same time. The impact of such a policy is identical to the case where there is a delay between announcement and implementation.

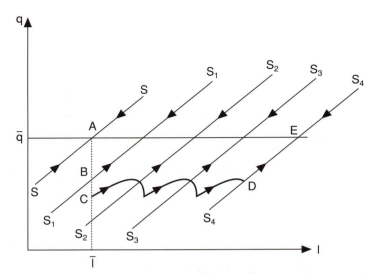

**Figure 3.11**    *The medium term financial strategy in the Buiter–Miller model*

Assume the economy is at A, we know that the four years of monetary contraction will eventually take the economy to a point such as E once it reaches its new long-run equilibrium. Notice that in Figure 3.11 we have drawn only the saddlepaths since the figure would become too cluttered if the $\Delta q = 0$ and $\Delta l = 0$ schedules were included (they exist going through points such as A and E). The interesting question is how the economy moves from A to E. If the policy had simply a one-year effect then the economy would move to B (as described above in relation to Figure 3.10). However, in the case of a policy spread over a number of years, we have to take into account the fact that the further cuts in monetary growth have already been announced in year 1. $S_1S_1$ to $S_4^iS_4$ are the new saddle paths associated with each yearly cut. The key factor to understanding what happens is that whilst the policy in year 1 is unanticipated, years 2 to 4 are anticipated. This implies that exchange rates will jump such that competitiveness falls to a point such as C which is below B. If the level of competitiveness jumps only to B, then there would be expectations of future capital gains (when the policy for years 2–4 is implemented) which is inconsistent with rational expectations. If future capital gains are anticipated, then they are fully incorporated into the exchange rate now (that is, in year 1). Hence competitiveness must jump beyond B if future jumps are to be avoided. From point C, it takes the rather strange path denoted by the heavy line to point D and hence upwards to point E. This strange path reflects the fact that the policy of monetary contraction is not continuous – instead, monetary growth is cut in discrete steps every year.

The implications of this policy are clear. The exchange rate remains over appreciated for some time. This squeezes the tradeables sector and reduces output and increases unemployment. The policy is far from costless.

Finally, we can ask what happens if agents do not fully believe the announced policy change. This situation is illustrated in Figure 3.12. The simplest way to examine this situation is to assume that agents attach a probability to each outcome, where the possible outcomes are that the policy is undertaken and that the policy is reneged

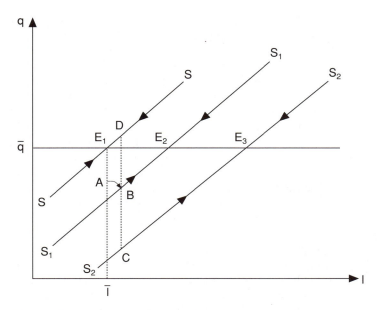

**Figure 3.12.** *A less than wholly credible policy announcement in the Buiter–Miller model*

on. Assume the economy is initially at $E_1$ and that the government announces a monetary contraction. In the event that the policy is implemented, the new saddle-path is given by $S_2S_2$ with the equilibrium at $E_3$. If the policy is not implemented, then the new long-run equilibrium will remain at A. $S_1S_1$ represents the expected saddlepath which is a weighted average of current policy and announced policy (where the weights are probabilities attached to each outcome). Initially the economy will move to A and then to B since the policy has been announced but not implemented. Once at B, the policy is either implemented or not. If the policy is implemented, then there will be a jump in the exchange rate causing competitiveness to fall to C and the economy will follow the saddlepath to $E_3$. On the other hand, if the government reneges on its policy, competitiveness will move to D and the economy will move along the original saddlepath, SS, back to $E_1$.

What are the policy implications of overshooting models in general and the Buiter–Miller version in particular? Clearly if the government can avoid the over-shooting behaviour of the exchange rate following a monetary contraction, then disinflation will be a much less costly affair. The Buiter–Miller model points to three possible policies which might help. Firstly, the government could impose a real interest rate equalisation tax. This would prevent the post-tax real interest rate from rising, prevent appreciation and hence reduce the costs. Buiter and Miller do indeed suggest this as an attractive policy to accompany any attempt at contraction of the monetary growth rate.

A second possible option is to have a one-off increase in the *level* of the money supply at the same time as the contraction of the monetary *growth rate* is announced. Recall that the reason for the rise in the real interest rate is that the nominal interest rate remains fixed since liquidity, $m - p$, is initially frozen at its pre-stabilisation programme level. A one-off increase in m would allow the nominal interest rate to fall thus preventing the real interest rate from rising. Again the costs of disinflation could be mitigated if not avoided. The obvious problem with such a policy (as Buiter and Miller, p.173 point out) is that it might jeopardise the government's credibility. Starting a contractionary monetary policy by increasing the money supply hardly instills confidence into economic agents.[39]

A final possibility is to disinflate by pegging the exchange rate. Cassola e Barata (1992) extends the Buiter–Miller model to examine what effect this has. He shows that the effect of fixing the nominal exchange rate prevents the real exchange rate from appreciating. Instead of a jump in the exchange rate following the announcement of a monetary contraction, there is a large capital inflow.[40] Interestingly, this capital inflow does exactly what the increase in the *level* of the money supply would do as we have suggested. It prevents the real interest rate from being high for too long and again reduces the costs of disinflation. We consider the pros and cons of fixing the nominal exchange rate later in Chapter 5 when we discuss the experience European countries have had within the European Monetary System.

*Empirical tests of the overshooting model*

How does the overshooting model stand up to empirical tests? At the level of providing a possible explanation for specific instances of exchange rate overshooting, the model appears useful. Indeed, Dornbusch (1981) in evidence to the Treasury and Civil Service Committee attributed the sharp appreciation of sterling in 1980–81 to overshooting following the slowdown in the growth of the money supply. We noted that indeed this was the case that the Buiter and Miller (1981) dynamic version of the Dornbusch model did predict that the Medium Term Financial Strategy would lead to overshooting. A rather interesting paradox arises, however, with respect to the MTFS. Whilst the exchange rate appeared to behave according to what the overshooting model would predict, actual monetary growth persistently overshot its target growth rates. Currie (1984) provides a possible explanation for this. He argues that overshooting of targets led to expectations that the authorities would correct the overshoot. The result was that the exchange rate appreciated. Clearly this explanation only holds provided the government has credibility that it will implement the policy and stick to it. The more monetary targets are missed without correction, the less credible the government will become and hence the exchange rate will no longer act as if policy were being carried out as announced.

An alternative explanation of the appreciation of sterling from 1979 to 1981 is the role of North Sea oil. The UK became self-sufficient in 1980 and hence the oil price rise in 1979 had a significant wealth effect for the UK economy. This effect would be expected to lead to pressure for the exchange rate to appreciate.[41]

To examine more accurately the role that monetary policy played in the appreciation of sterling in the early 1980s, we must clearly turn to regression analysis to allow us to control for other possible effects. The reduced form equation which can be derived from the Dornbusch model usually includes the domestic (and foreign) money supplies, price levels and incomes.

Driskill (1981) estimates a reduced form equation for the dollar–Swiss franc exchange rate over the period 1973 to 1977 (quarterly data). He is explicitly seeking

[39] Presumably, though, if the agents are rational then they will understand the rationale for the policy.
[40] Cassola e Barata (1992) also assumes that there are some capital controls making capital mobility less than perfect. This ensures that the capital inflow is not infinite.
[41] MacDonald (1988) provides an interesting discussion of these two alternative hypotheses. In particular, he examines the impact of a resource discovery in the overshooting model.

to test whether the Dornbusch simple overshooting story performs better or worse than a modified Dornbusch story which allows for imperfect capital mobility. The equation results support PPP in the long run. In the short-run there is some evidence of overshooting as indeed some simulations show. However, there is also evidence which supports the imperfect capital mobility version of the model. Driskill clearly favours the modified Dornbusch equation, but it is not obvious that his results support such a conclusion: his equation provides evidence for and against both models.

Haache and Townend (1981) estimate a version of Dornbusch in a dynamic framework, where lags of these variables are also included:

$$\Delta s_t = -0.472 + 0.146\Delta p_t - 0.466\Delta p_{t-1} - 0.858\Delta p^*_t + 0.027\Delta p^*_{t-1}\ 0.148\Delta y_t$$
$$\quad (2.46)\quad (0.71)\qquad (2.21)\qquad\quad (1.22)\qquad\quad (0.04)\qquad\quad (1.5)$$

$$- 0.023\Delta y_{t-1} + 0.477\Delta y^*_t - 0.600\Delta y^*_{t-1} - 0.384\Delta m_t - 0.311\Delta m_{t-1}$$
$$\quad (0.26)\qquad\quad (2.31)\qquad\quad (2.86)\qquad\quad (2.20)\qquad\quad (1.69)$$

$$+ 0.008\Delta i^*_t - 0.005\Delta i^*_{t-1} + 0.036\Delta PFO_t - 0.041\Delta PFO_{t-1} - 0.872\Delta s_{t-1}$$
$$\quad (0.77)\qquad (0.41)\qquad\quad (2.01)\qquad\qquad (2.14)\qquad\qquad (6.13)$$

$$- 0.667\Delta s_{t-2} + 0.187\Delta s_{t-3} - 0.004(s + m - p^*)_{t-1} + 0.160y_{t-1}$$
$$\quad (4.30)\qquad\quad (1.59)\qquad\quad (0.25)\qquad\qquad\qquad (2.35)$$

$$- 0.000i^*_{t-1} - 0.050y^*_{t-1} - 0.541U_{t-1}$$
$$\quad (0.08)\qquad\quad (0.95)\qquad\quad (3.82)$$

$$SE = 0.013 \quad R^2 = 0.44 \quad DW = 2.129$$

where U is the unemployment rate, PFO is the oil price, S is the effective exchange rate (where a rise is an appreciation) and i is a long-term interest rate on bonds. The equation is estimated using monthly data for the period 1972 to 1980. We can note that this equation models both the short-term determinants of the sterling effective exchange rate (represented by the first differenced variables) and the long run determinants (represented by levels of the variables). The long-run solution can be found by setting $t = t - 1$ and solving for s. Haache and Townend note that their results suggest that a change in the money supply causes a more than proportionate change in the exchange rate in the next period with further overshooting in the period after that. In the long run, money neutrality has been imposed. North Sea oil has a short-run impact, although the effect in period t is offset in period $t-1$. The other variables in the equation either have the wrong sign or are insignificant. In particular, the long-run equation is poor.

Finally, MacDonald and Taylor (1994) also test a monetary model where liquidity effects are present in the short run. They employ a dynamic error correction model, whose long-run equilibrium is given by the familiar flexible-price monetary model:

$$s_t = \beta_1 m_t + \beta_2 m^*_t + \beta_3 y_t + \beta_4 y^*_t + \beta_5 i_t^L + \beta_6 i_t^{L*} + \gamma_t$$

where $i_t^L$ is a long-term interest rate. The residuals from this cointegrating regression are used in the short-run dynamic model as the error correction mechanism (ecm). Additionally, short-run interest rates are included reflecting the potential for real interest rate effects from a monetary policy change. Their preferred equation is given by:

$$\Delta s_t = -0.017\Delta i^{L^*}_{t-3} + 0.008\Delta i^s_t + 0.006\Delta^2 i^{s^*}_t - 0.026\text{ecm}_{t-1} - 0.052$$
$$\phantom{\Delta s_t = } (0.005) \qquad\qquad (0.003) \qquad (0.003) \qquad\quad (0.008) \qquad\qquad (0.017)$$

$R^2 = 0.14$ SE of the regression = 3% and a variety of tests were passed. The results from this equation are particularly encouraging in that they represent one of the few models to be found in the empirical literature on exchange rate determination which manages to outperform a random walk in forecasting tests.

Overall, the evidence for Dornbusch's overshooting model (or at least modified versions of it) is mixed. In general, the earlier work was characterised by equations which did not perform well and this made it rather difficult to come to any strong conclusions. The more recent work of MacDonald and Taylor, however, suggests that if the dynamics are correctly specified and distinguished from the long-run equilibrium, then some support for monetary models can be found.

## Portfolio models of exchange rate determination

In the monetary models of exchange rate determination the exchange rate was seen as the relative price of domestic and foreign assets, where the emphasis is on money. Portfolio models incorporate specifically a greater number of assets: money as well as domestic and foreign bonds. In this sense, portfolio models can be seen as broader than the monetary models (either the overshooting or the monetarist version). Portfolio models have a number of key distinguishing features.

Firstly, it is assumed that UIP does not hold. In other words, assets are not assumed to be perfectly substitutable. This could be for any number of reasons: differential political risk; differences in the liquidity characteristics of assets; different currencies of denomination leading to foreign exchange risk; default risk; differences in the tax treatment of assets, etc. Whatever the cause, the fact that UIP does not hold implies that there exist well-defined asset-demand functions. Wealth-holders are assumed to hold a diversified portfolio of assets. The demand for an asset is hypothesised to be a function of expected rates of return (on both the asset itself and various substitutes) as well as of wealth. The expected rate of return on foreign assets is defined as the foreign interest rate plus the expected rate of depreciation of the domestic currency. Thus expectations of exchange rate movements are also important in portfolio models. Many models assume that exchange rate expectations are static,[42] since this simplifies the model considerably. However, Dornbusch and Fischer (1980), Allen and Kenen (1980) and Branson and Henderson (1985) introduce a variety of possible methods of expectations formation, including rational expectations. Exchange rate expectations influence the demand for domestic and foreign bonds. For example, if the domestic exchange rate is expected to depreciate, then this will tend to increase the demand for foreign bonds and reduce the demand for domestic bonds. This is the result of the fact that a depreciation of the domestic exchange rate increases the domestic currency value of foreign assets. In this section, we assume static expectations throughout.

The role of wealth in affecting asset demands implies that changes in the prices of the assets, as well as actual exchange rate changes, lead to further effects on asset

---

[42] See, for example, MacDonald (1988), Allen and Kenen (1976), Bisignano and Hoover (1982), and Genberg and Kierzkowski (1979).

demands. These effects occur because of the impact of asset price changes and exchange rate changes on wealth. For example, an increase in the price of foreign assets will increase wealth leading to an excess demand for all assets and vice versa. An appreciation of the domestic exchange rate reduces the domestic currency value of foreign assets, thereby reducing wealth and with it the demand for each asset. A depreciation of the domestic exchange rate increases wealth.

A second feature of portfolio models is that they often model the exchange rate in a macroeconomic model of an open economy. Along with asset markets (the markets for money and bonds), the real sector can be modelled. One of the implications of this is that portfolio models can produce a variety of different results depending on the way in which the real economy is modelled. For example, some models assume price flexibility and full employment,[43] whereas others are more Keynesian in their conception.[44] Here we do not intend to present a full macroeconomic model, but rather concentrate on the asset side of the models and their integration with the current account.

Thirdly, portfolio models distinguish between short-run and long-run exchange rate determination. Usually, the exchange rate in the short-run is determined solely by wealth-holders preferences for foreign and domestic assets. The exchange rate alters so as to ensure that asset markets are in equilibrium. In the long run, there is a role for the real sector of the economy and in particular the current account. The short-run equilibrium exchange rate determines the current account which, in turn represents net foreign asset accumulation. This accumulation again causes exchange rate changes. Long-run equilibrium is reached only once the current account is in equilibrium.

The final feature of portfolio models is their emphasis on the distinction between stocks and flows. The relevance of this distinction for portfolio theories in international finance was first noted by Allen (1973). In that paper, she assumed that exchange rates were fixed and thus the model concentrates on the determinants of capital flows. Her criticism of traditional capital flow equations is that they assume capital flows are a function of differences in the *levels* of interest rates. The Mundell–Fleming model is a good example: if the domestic interest rate is lower than the foreign interest rate, then we expect a continuous capital outflow until the differential is eliminated. Allen (1973) hypothesises that capital flows are reactions to portfolio disequilibria, resulting from, among other things, *changes* in differential interest rates. As capital flows out of the domestic economy, because, say, of an interest rate differential against domestic assets, so the proportion of residents wealth held in foreign assets increases. In other words, the capital outflow has a stock implication – the domestic currency value of the stock of foreign assets will be increasing. The implications of this are that the capital outflow will cease eventually, even if the interest rate differential persists. This occurs because the assumption that domestic and foreign assets are not perfect substitutes implies that wealth-holders desire a diversified portfolio. If the capital outflow continues for long enough, then eventually almost all wealth would be held in foreign assets. This cannot happen in portfolio models because the benefits of diversification would then be lost. Capital flows cease even if interest rate differentials persist because assets are perceived to have different

---

[43] See, for example, Dornbusch and Fischer (1980).
[44] See, for example, Allen and Kenen (1980), who develop a comprehensive portfolio model of exchange rate determination.

risks. Thus in portfolio models, capital flows are dependent not on the level of the interest rate differential, as in Mundell–Fleming, but rather on changes in the differential.

The second stock-flow distinction in portfolio models relates to the implications of current account imbalance for asset accumulation. Current account deficits and surpluses are flow concepts. However, they have stock implications. In particular, in portfolio theory, current account surpluses (deficits) imply an increase (decrease) in domestic holdings of overseas assets. If exchange rates are floating, then a current account surplus must accompany a capital account deficit (so that the balance of payments sum to zero). A capital account deficit (or a capital outflow) increases wealth-holders holdings of foreign assets. If the long-run equilibrium of portfolio models is to be characterised as a *stock* equilibrium, then this implies that the exchange rate in the long run must ensure that the current account is in balance and hence that the stock of foreign assets held by residents is unchanging.

The model we present here is that of Branson (1977). We examine first the role of asset markets in determining the short-run exchange rate, before going on to discuss the role of the current account and the long-run equilibrium exchange rate.

Branson (1977) (Figure 3.13) assumes that the country is small, implying that the world interest rate is exogenous and that foreigners (that is, residents of the rest of the world) do not hold domestic assets. There are three assets in the model. B represents *net* holdings of domestically issued bonds and hence is essentially private sector holdings of government debt.[45] Changes in the supply of B arise from sales of newly issued government debt to the private sector (the result, perhaps, of a budget deficit). F is *net* holdings of foreign-issued bonds which are denominated in foreign currency. If F is positive, then an increase in the current account surplus will cause F to rise further. If F is negative (that is, the country is a net debtor), then current account deficits will cause F to become more negative. Finally, non-interest bearing domestic money, M, exists and its supply changes as a result of open market operations conducted by the domestic central bank. For the moment, we assume that the supply of each of these assets is fixed.

Equations (3.34) to (3.36) represent the equilibrium conditions for each asset, that is supply equals demand:

$$M = M(i, i^* + \Delta s^e)W, \qquad \partial M/\partial i, \partial M/\partial(i^* + \Delta s^e) < 0 \qquad (3.34)$$

$$B = B(i, i^* + \Delta s^e)W, \qquad \partial B/\partial i > 0, \partial B/\partial(i^* + \Delta s^e) < 0 \qquad (3.35)$$

$$SF = F(i, i^* + \Delta s^e)W, \qquad \partial F/\partial i < 0, F/\partial(i^* + \Delta s^e) > 0 \qquad (3.36)$$

$$W \equiv M + B + SF \qquad (3.37)$$

where i is the rate of return on domestic assets; $i^* + \Delta s^e$ is the expected rate of return on foreign assets and W is wealth. Equation (3.37) is the wealth constraint. An increase in wealth increases the demand for all three assets. We assume here that exchange rate expectations are static, that is, $\Delta s^e = 0$.

The equations can be solved to determine the domestic interest rate and the exchange rate. Note that one of the three asset equilibrium equations is redundant: given the wealth constraint, if the foreign and domestic bond markets, say, are in

---

[45] We are interested here in *net* asset holdings. These can be represented by domestic government debt held by the private sector, since all other intra-private sector credits and debits will cancel each other out.

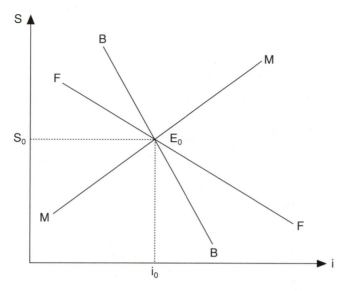

**Figure 3.13.** *Branson (1977) portfolio model of exchange rate determination*

equilibrium, then the money market must be also. Branson represents each of these equilibrium conditions in interest rate–exchange rate space, thus allowing us to discuss the solution to the model diagrammatically.

MM, which represents equilibrium in the money market, is positively sloped because an increase in S (that is, a depreciation of the exchange rate) causes wealth to rise (since SF increases). The rise in wealth increases the demand for money and hence, given a fixed money supply, necessitates a rise in the interest rate to restore equilibrium. The BB shows points of equilibrium in the domestic bond market. It is negatively sloped, because the rise in wealth, consequent on the increase in S, generates an excess demand for domestic bonds which raises their price and causes the interest rate to fall. Finally, FF is also negatively sloped. A rise in the domestic interest rate, i, reduces the demand for foreign assets. As holders of foreign assets sell F, so S falls (that is, the domestic exchange rate appreciates).

If domestic and foreign bonds are gross substitutes, then this implies that BB will be steeper than FF. Gross substitutability means that $\partial B/\partial i > \partial F/\partial i$ and that $\partial B/\partial i^* < \partial F/\partial i^*$. In other words, an increase in the domestic interest rate causes the demand for domestic assets to rise more than it causes the demand for foreign assets to fall. Similarly a rise in the foreign interest rate causes the demand for foreign bonds to rise by more than it causes the demand for domestic bonds to fall. Thus an increase in the domestic interest rate causes the demand for domestic bonds to rise by a given amount: the fall in the demand for foreign bonds is much lower. Hence the exchange rate has to fall by more to restore equilibrium in the domestic bond market than it has to fall to restore equilibrium in the foreign bond market. In other words, BB is steeper than FF. Equilibrium is given at $E_0$ where the three schedules cross.

We are now in a position to examine the implications of some exogenous shocks for the short-run equilibrium exchange rate. We examine first shocks to asset supplies (or asset accumulation, as Branson calls it) before going on to look at the impact

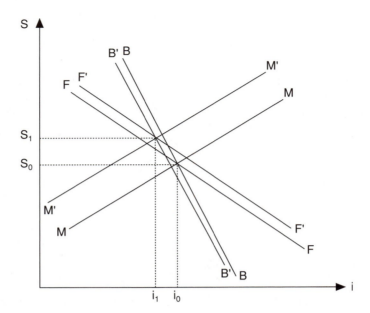

**Figure 3.14.** *A rise in the money supply in the Branson portfolio model*

of monetary policy. Assume that the government increases its spending and finances the increase by a rise in the money supply. This scenario is shown in Figure 3.14. The rise in the money supply causes MM to shift up and to the left: at each exchange rate, the domestic interest rate must have fallen to maintain money market equilibrium. The resulting portfolio disequilibrium (an excess supply of M and an excess demand for B and F) causes investors to purchase domestic and foreign bonds. With fixed supply, the rise in demand for B causes the price of domestic bonds to rise and the interest rate to fall. In other words, with a given exchange rate, the interest rate must fall, causing BB to move to the left. Finally, FF must move to the right. At each domestic interest rate, the excess demand for foreign bonds will only be eliminated through a rise in the exchange rate (that is, a depreciation) which increases SF and hence W. Strictly speaking we need only analyse the impact of the exogenous shock using two out of the three schedules, since given the wealth constraint, if two of the markets are in equilibrium, then the third one must be also. However, we include all three schedules here for completeness.

The impact of a bond-financed increase in government spending (that is, an increase in the supply of B) is analysed in Figure 3.15. The BB schedule moves to the right since at each exchange rate, the interest rate that now clears the bond market must be higher. Portfolio disequilibrium takes the form of an excess demand for money and foreign bonds and an excess supply of domestic bonds. The excess demand for money causes MM to shift down and to the right: at each exchange rate, the interest rate that clears the money market must be higher. This implies the FF must move up and to the right to intersect B′B′ and M′M′ at the new equilibrium $E_1$ (if two markets are in equilibrium, the third must also be). FF indeed does move up because at each interest rate, the exchange rate must be higher to increase the domestic currency amount of foreign bonds held in each portfolio.

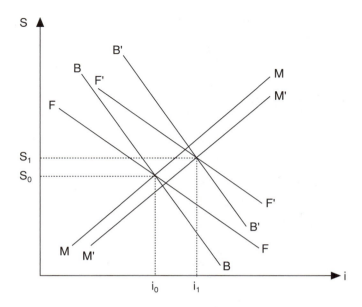

**Figure 3.15.** *A rise in the supply of bonds in the Branson portfolio model*

The impact on the domestic interest rate is clear: it rises. However, the impact on the exchange rate is ambiguous. In Figure 3.15 it is drawn such that the new equilibrium exchange rate is higher. The increased supply of domestic bonds creates not only a substitution effect (via the rise in the domestic interest rate) but also has a wealth effect: a larger supply of domestic bonds in circulation increases investor wealth.[46] The rise in wealth increases the demand for foreign bonds, but this is offset by the rise in the domestic interest rate (which tends to reduce demand for foreign bonds). If F and B are close substitutes (and closer than B and M), then the effect on the exchange rate will be negative. That is, the substitution effect resulting from the rise in i will outweigh the income effect resulting from the rise in W and hence overall the demand for foreign bonds will fall. This causes the domestic currency to appreciate (as residents switch out of foreign bonds). On the other hand if M and B are closer substitutes, then the rise in the domestic interest rate will be less and hence the wealth effect on foreign bonds will outweigh the substitution effect causing an excess demand for F. Overall, therefore, the exchange rate will rise (that is, depreciate). This latter case is illustrated in Figure 3.15.

We could also examine the impact of an increase in F in the same way. The results of all these changes in asset supplies are presented in Table 3.1.

We can now turn to the impact of open market operations. Let us assume that the government undertakes open market operations to increase the money supply. That is, money is exchanged for bonds. A critical difference between this policy and those discussed above is that here there is only a substitution effect (wealth is unchanged and hence there is no income effect). This case is illustrated in Figure 3.16. The policy creates an excess supply of money and an excess demand for domestic bonds.

---

[46] In spite of the rise in wealth, there is still an excess supply of domestic bonds, since because investors want to diversify, they do not want to hold all of the increase in wealth in the form of domestic bonds.

*Table 3.1.* Exogenous Shocks in Branson's Portfolio Model

| Effect on: | ΔM | ΔB | ΔF | ΔB = −ΔM | SΔF = −ΔM |
|---|---|---|---|---|---|
| | Effects of Asset Accumulation | | | Effects of Open Market Operations | |
| domestic interest rate, i | − | + | 0 | − | − |
| exchange rate, s | + | ? | − | + | + |

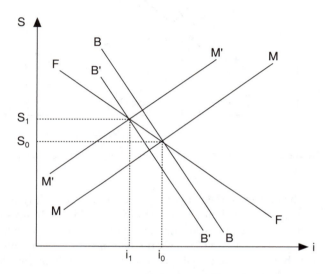

**Figure 3.16.**  *Open market operations in the Branson portfolio model*

MM shifts up and to the left, since at each exchange rate, the interest rate required to clear the money market has fallen. As bonds are bought, so the price rises and the domestic interest rate falls: BB moves left to B'B'. The fall in i causes an excess demand for foreign bonds and the economy moves up the original FF schedule as the exchange rate depreciates. In the new equilibrium, the exchange rate is higher and the domestic interest rate lower.

The government could undertake open market operations in foreign assets and exchange M for F. In this case the government would buy foreign bonds from domestic residents in exchange for money. The results of this scenario are identical to the more usual swap of money for domestic bonds. Both results are summarised in Table 3.1.

The above analysis has concentrated on the short-run impact of exogenous shocks to asset supplies on the exchange rate and the domestic interest rate. In order to examine the effect of these changes in the long run, it is necessary to introduce the real side of the economy. The exchange rate generated above could easily lead to a non-zero current account. However, this has longer-term implications. A surplus on the current account, for example, must, with flexible exchange rates, be offset by a deficit on the capital account. In other words, capital is flowing out of the country and domestic residents are accumulating foreign assets. If the current account is in deficit, then this implies that residents are running down their holdings of foreign assets (or increasing their foreign debt, $F < 0$). The changes examined above are thus likely to create only a temporary equilibrium. For long-run equilibrium, the current account must be in balance so that the stock of foreign assets is constant.

Let us assume that the current account ($Z$) measured in domestic currency is composed of net exports (NX) and net income on foreign assets ($i^*SF$). The current account is equivalent to the net accumulation of foreign assets, $\Delta F$:

$$X(SP^*/P) + i^*SF = Z = \Delta F \tag{3.38}$$

An important question which arises when discussing the long-run equilibrium of a portfolio model is whether or not it is stable. Assume that asset market equilibrium generates an exchange rate of $S_1$ which leads to a current account surplus. This implies that $F$ is rising. The key question is whether or not this rise in $F$ tends to reduce the current account surplus and hence the accumulation of $F$. If it does, then the system can be said to be stable and a long-run equilibrium where foreign asset accumulation has ceased exists. A rise in $F$ has two effects on the current account. Firstly, as $F$ increases, the exchange rate tends to fall (that is $S$ rises) as investors seek to maintain portfolio diversification in the face of an increase in wealth (the rise in wealth causes investors to repatriate some of their funds, resulting in a rise in $S$). Appreciation reduces competitiveness and hence net exports fall reducing the current account surplus. However, the second effect is destabilising in that it works to increase the surplus still further. The rise in holdings of $F$ increases net income from abroad thus increasing the current account surplus. The system is stable only if the former effect via net exports outweighs the latter.

If we assume that the system is stable,[47] then how exactly is adjustment to the long-term equilibrium brought about? We can answer this question by going back to examine the longer-term impact of an open market operation which exchanges money for domestic bonds. We can show that the rise in the money supply in the long run will increase prices, but the increase will be less than proportionate for reasons which become clear below. That is, money is not neutral in this model. Figure 3.17 illustrates the path taken by the exchange rate and prices following the shock.

Assume that the economy was in long-run equilibrium before the shock with the price level equal to $P_0$ and the exchange rate at $S_0$. Recall that the short-run impact of the shock was to increase the exchange rate to restore asset market equilibrium. Let us assume, for simplicity, that the exchange rate adjusts instantaneously at $t_0$ when the open market operations are conducted. Thus the exchange rate at $t_0$ adjusts immediately to its new short-run level at $S_2$. $S_2$ may either be above or below the new long-run equilibrium exchange rate given by $S_1$. That is, the exchange rate may initially overshoot or undershoot depending on the substitutability of assets.[48] Figure 3.17 is drawn assuming the exchange rate has overshot. The price level adjusts only slowly to its new equilibrium and this causes further changes in the exchange rate. At $S_2$, the relative price ratio $SP^*/P$ has risen above the value required to generate current account equilibrium ($S$ has increased, and $P$ has not changed). This leads to a

---

[47] This requires that the trade elasticities are rather large, so that the effect of the appreciation on net exports is big.

[48] More specifically, if the demand for foreign assets is more responsive to changes in the domestic interest rate than the demand for money, then the exchange rate will overshoot. That is, if $\partial F/\partial i > \partial M/\partial i$ then there is overshooting. On the other hand, if $\partial F/\partial i < \partial M/\partial i$, there is undershooting.

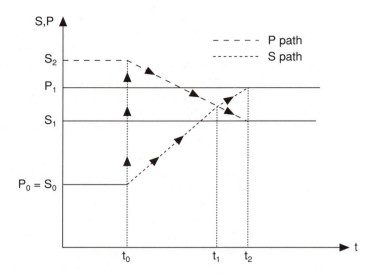

**Figure 3.17.**  *The paths of the exchange rate and the price level following an expansionary monetary policy*

current account surplus and F starts to rise. The rise in F causes the exchange rate to appreciate (that is, S falls) as investors seek to diversify the resulting increase in wealth. Assuming stability, the fall in S reduces the surplus. As we can see in Figure 3.17, after $t_0$, P is now rising and S is falling. At the point where the two paths cross, the relative price ratio is identical to what it was before the disturbance. But because net income from assets abroad has now risen, the current account is still in surplus and therefore F is still rising and S falling. S will continue to fall until the price ratio is such as to generate net exports equal to the new level of net income from foreign assets. Only at that level of the exchange rate will the current account be zero and the economy in long-term equilibrium. Note that in the new equilibrium relative prices have changed: money is not neutral in this model.

In the above example, we assumed that the exchange rate adjusted monotonically from its temporary equilibrium at $S_2$ to its new long-run equilibrium at $S_1$. However, this need not be the case. If the exchange rate starts to fall rapidly at $S_2$, then it could fall below its new long-run equilibrium before turning back and converging towards it. This scenario, what Branson (1984) terms 'multiple overshooting', is illustrated in Figure 3.18. The exchange rate falls faster than in the first case. This causes the current account to reach zero before domestic prices have stopped rising (at $t_1$). Hence F is constant for an instant. However, the continued rise in P is detrimental to competitiveness with the result that the current account starts to deteriorate. F thus begins to decline (to finance the deficit) and S begins to rise. Only when domestic prices have stopped rising, will long-term equilibrium be restored.

Branson (1984) extends this model to include rational expectations. The results of monetary policy are identical. Multiple overshooting is still as likely as in the model with static expectations. The only real difference which results from adding rational expectations is that the exchange rate *always* jumps following a disturbance to take the economy on to its new saddlepath which it then follows to the new equilibrium. Recall that we assumed that the exchange rate jumped to its initial short-run

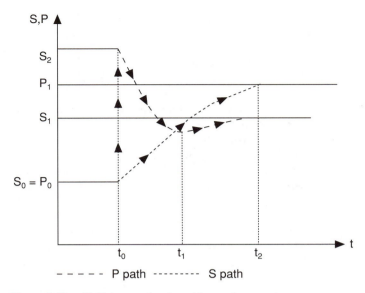

**Figure 3.18.**   *Multiple overshooting of the exchange rate*

equilibrium following a shock merely as a simplification so that we could examine the long-term effects more closely. Rational expectations generate a rationale for the jump.

Branson's model is a small country model which assumes that foreigners do not hold domestic assets (neither money nor bonds). However, whilst this assumption is convenient, it is perhaps not very realistic. Two other possible assumptions which have been made are those of uniform asset preferences and preferred local habitat. The former assumes that residents and foreigners have identical portfolio preferences. In the latter, asset preferences are asymmetric. Residents have a preference for domestic assets over foreign assets, whilst foreigners have a preference for foreign assets over domestic. The rationale for such an assumption is that investors prefer to have a larger proportion of their portfolio in assets denominated in the currency of their country of residence.

The impact of these different assumptions on exchange rate determination is neatly outlined by Frankel (1983). He starts with the uniform preferences model which generates an equation such as (3.39):

$$B/SF = \beta(i - i^* - \Delta S^e) \qquad (3.39)$$

This states that the ratio of domestic bonds to foreign bonds in an investor's portfolio depends on the relative return $(i - i^* - \Delta S^e)$.[49] $\beta$ reflects the fact that investor's have uniform preferences. It is important to define B and F carefully, since it is this aspect which alters according to the assumptions made about asset preferences. When we assume uniform asset preferences, B is the *net* supply of domestic currency denominated bonds and F is the *net* supply for foreign currency denominated bonds. Given that we are interested in *net* asset supplies, B and F represent the supply of outside

---

[49] Note that we ignore the money market here on the grounds that if the markets for domestic and foreign bonds are in equilibrium, then the money market must be also because of the wealth constraint.

assets. If governments issue debt denominated only in their own currency, then B is equivalent to domestic net government debt and F to foreign net government debt. Assuming static expectations, we can rearrange equation (3.39) to give us a reduced form equation for the exchange rate:

$$s = \alpha + \beta(i - i^*) + b - f \tag{3.40}$$

where the lower case letters represent logarithms of the variables. Note that this equation states that a rise in b and a fall in f will cause the exchange rate to increase, that is appreciate (effects which are the same as in the Branson (1977) model).

If we move to a small country model and assume that foreigners can no longer hold domestic assets, then the equation showing the determinants of the balance in portfolios between domestic and foreign assets alters to become:

$$B_h/SF_h = \beta_h(i - i^* - \Delta S^e) \tag{3.41}$$

$B_h$ and $F_h$ are domestic and foreign bond holdings by residents only. In other words, in this model we ignore the impact of foreign holdings of either B or F.[50] Again we can derive a reduced form equation for the exchange rate:

$$s = \alpha + \beta_h(i - i^*) + b_h - f_h \tag{3.42}$$

Finally, if we move to the preferred local habitat assumption regarding preferences then we have two equations, one for residents and the other for foreigners:

$$B_h/SF_h = \beta_h(i - i^* - \Delta S^e) \tag{3.43}$$

$$B_f/SF_f = \beta_f(i - i^* - \Delta S^e) \tag{3.44}$$

$B_f$ and $F_f$ are domestic and foreign bond holdings by foreigners. Frankel (1983) notes that the data required to estimate this model is rarely available: it is usual to find only data on B ($\equiv B_h + B_f$) and F ($\equiv F_h + F_f$) along with resident wealth ($W_h \equiv B_h + SF_h$) and foreigner wealth ($W_f \equiv B_f + SF_f$). Substituting these into identities into equations (3.43) and (3.44) allows the derivation of a rather complex reduced form for the exchange rate, where S is a function of B, F, $W_h$, $W_f$. Again an increase in B and a fall in F cause S to rise.

Thus different assumptions regarding portfolio preferences generally imply the need to be very careful about how B and F are defined. This is something to which we return below when we discuss empirical tests of the portfolio model.

In conclusion, it is clear from our brief account of portfolio models, that they can generate similar results to the sticky price monetary models. In other words, they can account for exchange rate volatility or misalignment since it is possible for the exchange rate to overshoot its new equilibrium following some exogenous disturbance. But portfolio models do not simply have this advantage. Theoretically, they are perhaps more satisfying than monetary models. They allow a wider range of assumptions to be made about asset substitutability – indeed the monetary model can be seen as a special case within the portfolio model where assets are assumed to be perfect substitutes. Moreover, their incorporation of current account factors leads to a more sophisticated view of the impact of monetary shocks. Monetary models assume that in the long run PPP holds so that monetary policy is neutral. By

---

[50] Note that $B_h$ is essentially identical to B given that by assumption only domestic residents hold domestic assets. We retain the subscript here merely for emphasis.

contrast, portfolio models suggest that such an assumption is misplaced, because since the exchange rate changes which result from exogenous shocks have implications for the current account, this implies that the net foreign asset position of the country will change. This in turn has implications for the net income earned from net foreign assets. Thus in so far as monetary shocks lead to changes in the net asset position of a country, their effects are not neutral, even although we assume that prices are flexible in the long run.[51]

*Tests of portfolio models of exchange rate determination*

There are major data problems associated with attempts to test portfolio models of exchange rate determination. Data on resident and nonresident holdings of bonds, securities and other assets are not normally available. Instead it is only usually possible to find aggregate data. Nonetheless there have been a number of studies which seek to determine the empirical validity of the portfolio model.

One of the first studies conducted was that of Branson *et al.* (1977; 1979). They test a reduced form portfolio model equation of the following type:

$$S = f(M, M^*, F, F^*)  \tag{3.45}$$

where $F$ and $F^*$ are domestic holdings of foreign bonds and foreign holdings of domestic bonds, respectively. Equation (3.45) is estimated using monthly data from August 1971 to December 1976 for dollar–DM exchange rate. They endogenise money via a money multiplier equation:

$$M = q(HG + S.FG)  \tag{3.46}$$

where HG is the domestic component of the monetary base and FG is the foreign component (S.FG measures foreign reserves in domestic currency). If governments do not intervene in the foreign exchange market, then M must be exogenous and hence we need not endogenise money in equation (3.45). However, if government do intervene and undertake complete sterilisation, then we must estimate equation (3.45) and endogenise M using the reaction function which specifies exactly how the government reacts to meet their target values for money, the exchange rate and foreign reserves. They indeed find that Germany conducted a lot of sterilisation and hence the better results are derived from the second method of estimation.

The results are reproduced below:

$$s = -4.85 - 0.06M1_g + 0.09M1_{us} + 0.68F_g - 0.40F_{us}$$
$$(-0.1)\ (-1.7)\quad (2.8)\qquad (1.7)\qquad (-1.9)$$

$$R^2 = 0.937 \quad DW = 1.35 \quad \rho = 0.87$$

where the subscripts g and us indicate Germany and the US respectively and M1 is used as the monetary stock variable. Net foreign assets (F) are estimated by taking cumulative current accounts, because of the unavailability of a direct measure. As MacDonald (1988) points out, this is unsatisfactory, because the cumulative current account surpluses include foreign assets held by residents of the US or Germany in third countries, which are largely irrelevant to the determination of the bilateral

[51] Branson and Henderson (1985) note that with fixed prices, the exchange rate returns to its original level following an open market operation. All the brunt of adjustment is borne by the interest rate which falls or rises to restore money market equilibrium depending on whether the open market operation is expansionary or contractionary.

Deutschmark–dollar exchange rate. Although the results are supportive of the portfolio model, there are a number of econometric problems (in particular auto-correlation).

Branson *et al.* (1979) update the results to March 1978. There is now some evidence of instability in the equation and $F_g$ becomes insignificant. They account for this by noting that German net foreign assets were initially positive; they then turn negative in the period January 1973 through to March 1975; thereafter they are again positive. This raises a problem for estimation since the portfolio model predicts that the sign of the coefficients on F change according to whether F is positive or negative. Branson *et al.* explore this by estimating two equations over each sub-sample. They do indeed find that the equations are much improved and the coefficient on $F_g$ reverses from one subperiod to the next.

Backus (1984) tries to estimate a similar equation for the US dollar–Canadian dollar exchange rate on quarterly data from 1971 to 1979. He finds little support for the model – the signs of the variables are all wrong and very little is significant.

Bisignano and Hoover (1982) are fairly critical of Branson *et al.* (1977; 1979). They note that the reduced form of Branson *et al.* depends heavily on the small country assumption which is never actually tested. Bisignano and Hoover specifically test the small country assumption by using Granger causality tests on Canadian and US interest rate. If Canadian assets do not Granger-cause US interest rates, but US asset Granger-cause Canadian interest rates, then Canada can be described as a small country. Their tests show that Canada is not a small country. Hence they develop a two country model, which has the small country model as a special case. This model has a reduced form of the following type:

$$s = s(M, B, F, G, M^*, B^*, F^*, G^*) \tag{3.47}$$

where B and $B^*$ represent domestic and foreign bonds and G and $G^*$ are domestic assets issued in foreign currency and held by foreigners and foreign assets issued in domestic currency and held by residents respectively. The problem with their more general model is that the signs of each variable cannot be determined *a priori* – the model is too complex to determine them. Their results are more successful than a Branson *et al.* type equation and are again broadly supportive of the portfolio model.

Kearney and MacDonald (1985; 1986) attempt to estimate the portfolio model using a structural model rather than the usual reduced forms. In addition, they specify bank loans as a fourth possible asset. Essentially, this entails estimating asset demand functions. Their results provide some support for the portfolio model.[52]

With respect to forecasting, however, the portfolio models seem to perform very badly. Meese and Rogoff (1983, 1984) test the forecasting power of a modified version of the portfolio model which includes real interest rate differentials.[53] However, success is limited, and the modified portfolio model does very badly at forecasting future exchange rates: in particular, it does not outperform a random walk.

---

[52] We can note that the main differences between the two papers are that: the 1985 paper uses SURE (Seemingly Unrelated Regression Equation) estimates and models the real sector along side the asset demand functions. This allows some simulations to be carried out. The 1986 paper uses the Theil–Goldberger procedure.

[53] See Frankel (1979) for a discussion of the real interest rate differential model of exchange rate determination. This is a modified version of the monetary theory and it argues that exchange rate changes are a function of differential inflation rates in addition to differential income, wealth, money supplies and nominal interest rates.

One can point to a number of problems which could explain this failure. Most are of an econometric nature – for example, poor data and poorly specified dynamics. As we noted in our discussion of overshooting models, the more clearly specified are the short-run dynamics of exchange rate determination, the more support there is for the model. In addition, however, MacDonald (1988) points to the unstable environment of the 1970s and 1980s. For example, exchange rates have been affected significantly by the two oil price shocks and the international debt crisis. Such shocks are difficult to incorporate easily into econometric models yet are clearly very important. On the whole, therefore, it is difficult to come to any firm conclusion about the validity of the portfolio approach. Its contribution, however, has been to highlight the importance of asset demands and supplies as determinants of the exchange rate.

## 'News' approach to testing models of exchange rate determination

If there is one conclusion to emerge from the account of theories of exchange rate determination, it is that the balance of the evidence suggests that the theories do not appear to perform particularly well empirically. We have already pointed out that exchange rates are highly volatile. By contrast, those factors which are used to explain the exchange rate in these theories are much less volatile. Hence it is perhaps not surprising that exchange rate determination models seem empirically to explain only a small proportion of exchange rate movements.

The 'news' approach to exchange rate determination begins with this observation. It then goes on to argue that exchange rate volatility might be explained by the fact that new information is constantly becoming available in the foreign exchange markets. Hence any change in the exchange rate from one period to the next (or alternatively any difference between the forward rate and the future spot rate) might simply reflect unanticipated changes in the fundamental factors explaining exchange rates. Thus the concern in this literature is to disaggregate the various determinants of the exchange rate into expected and unexpected components. From there we can determine whether 'news' plays a large role in determining spot exchange rates.

Such 'news' items affect the expectations of dealers in the foreign exchange markets. As a result, the implications of any piece of news should be quickly and efficiently incorporated into the spot or forward exchange rates. This occurs as dealers buy and sell currencies on the basis of their altered expectations. In this way, the new literature is closely related to the literature on the efficiency of the forward exchange rate market which we discussed in Chapter 2. In particular, if any news becomes available between the setting of the forward rate and the associated spot rate, then this might account for some of the biasedness of the forward rate in predicting the future spot rate. Thus, for example, with one-month forward exchange rates, it might be the case that during the month relevant new information becomes available which causes traders to revise their expectations about the spot rate. If this is the case, then the forward premium (the logarithm of the forward rate minus the spot rate) will explain very little of the change in the spot rate.

If new information is important, then tests of forward market efficiency should incorporate unexpected changes in variables influencing the exchange and then conduct the usual efficiency tests. This, as we shall see, is indeed what a number of authors do. In particular the following regression (or a variation on it) is common:

$$s_t - f_{t-1} = \beta(X_t - X_{t-1}^e) + u_t \tag{3.48}$$

where $X_t$ is a vector of relevant news variables and $X_{t-1}^e$ is the expected value of X formed at time $t-1$ for time t. $u_t$ is the usual error term. If news is important then it is to be expected that $\beta$ will differ from zero.

If new information is important, then it is crucial to decide what information is relevant. In other words, what is contained in vector X? Not surprisingly this depends on the model of exchange rate determination which is chosen. Table 3.2 is compiled from Hoffman and Schlagenhauf (1985). They provide a number of alternative variables for inclusion in X along with the expected signs. These signs follow from the various assumptions which each model makes and the rationale for the signs should be clear from our discussion of each model. In the case of the portfolio model, an increase in the current account surplus represents an increase in the supply of foreign bonds and an increase in the budget surplus represents a reduction in the supply of domestic bonds.

We can divide this literature into three groups, according to the way they estimate an equation like (3.48) and the kind of data which they use. The first group estimates either (3.48) or a variant using either OLS or two-stage least squares (2SLS). Hoffman and Schlagenhauf (1985) estimate all three models given in Table 3.2 using OLS. They examine monthly and quarterly data (1973–81) for the dollar *vis-à-vis* the French franc, sterling, Deutschmark and yen. Money supply, real income, inflation and interest rate variables are all expressed as domestic relative to foreign: for example, news about the domestic money supply relative to the foreign money supply.[54] Only the current accounts and budget deficits of the portfolio equation are entered separately. Expected variables are constructed by running a fourth-order autoregressive process:

*Table 3.2.*   Exchange rate Determination in a 'news' framework

| domestic variables | money supply | real income | inflation | nominal interest rate | current account surplus | budget surplus |
|---|---|---|---|---|---|---|
| monetarist model | | + | − | + | | |
| overshooting model (Dornbusch)[a] | + | − | | − | | |
| Frankel's Real Interest Differential model | + | − | + | − | | |
| portfolio model | | | | − | − | − |

*Note*: The spot exchange rate is defined as the domestic currency price of a unit of foreign currency.

[a]   Dornbusch's original overshooting model does not include the inflation term.

+ implies that an unexpected increase in, say, the domestic money supply causes the spot exchange rate to increase, that is depreciate.

− implies that an unexpected increase in, say, domestic real income causes the spot exchange rate to decrease, that is to appreciate.

News equations often include the above variables for the foreign country, where the signs expected on foreign money supply, real income, etc. are the opposite of those above.

---

[54]   In other words, foreign variables are not entered separately.

$$X_t = \alpha X_{t-1} + \beta X_{t-2} + \gamma X_{t-3} + \delta X_{t-4} + \varepsilon_t \tag{3.49}$$

$\varepsilon_t$, the equation residuals, are then used as the unexpected change in X at time t or news. Their results are mixed. We discuss here only the quarterly results; the monthly ones are poorer. In the case of the monetarist model, 9 out of the 12 signs (across all four currencies) are correct, but only 3 are significant. Moreover, none of the countries produces a reasonable monetarist equation. The RID model equations have 14 out of 16 correct signs, but only 7 of those are significant. For the overshooting model, 7 out of 12 signs are correct and only 6 significant. The money supply coefficients are particular poorly specified. Finally, for the portfolio model equations 19 out of 20 signs are correct, but only 9 of those are significant. Overall, the French and UK equations are reasonable for the portfolio model.

Overall, the results are very mixed and it is not possible to come out very strongly in favour of any of the models. All equations are poor with wrong signs and insignificant variables. Moreover, the explanatory power of these equations is very low (as measured by the $R^2$).[55]

Frenkel (1981) tests a variant of equation (3.48) where the dependent variable is simply the spot rate and the forward rate appears as an explanatory variable. He uses 2SLS and considers news concerning only relative interest rates. He tests this equation on data for the dollar *vis-à-vis* sterling, the Deutschmark and the French franc over the period 1973 to 1979. Only in the case of the dollar–sterling exchange rate is the news element significant.[56]

The second group of articles which we can identify employ the SURE (Seemingly Unrelated Regression Estimator) method for testing the impact of news on the spot exchange rate. The rationale for using this method is that, since most work looks at various exchange rates relative to the dollar, the foreign news elements in each equation are the US money supply, interest rate, etc. Hence the errors of the equations for each currency are likely to exhibit contemporaneous correlation and thus the SURE method is a more efficient method of estimating the coefficients.

MacDonald (1983a; 1985a) examines the influence of domestic and foreign news in the following regression:

$$\text{forecast error} = s_t - f_t = \alpha + \beta(\text{domestic news}) + \gamma(\text{foreign news}) \tag{3.50}$$

News is generated using two methods. Firstly he uses a variation on the autoregressive process outlined above in equation (3.49) to generate news regarding both interest rate and money supplies. Secondly, for the money supply news alone, he uses a multivariate time series approach which hypothesises that the money supply is influenced by lagged values of the money supply, lagged interest rates, lagged

[55] We can note that Hoffman and Schlagenhauf prefer the monetarist model. However, this decision is based on the size of the $R^2$s. Unfortunately there is very little information on tests for autocorrelation, heteroscedasticity etc. which might allow us to choose between the equations on better grounds. Given that the explanatory variables in the monetarist equations are rarely significant, it is not really valid to conclude as they do.

[56] Other papers which test an equation similar to (3.48) include Copeland (1984) and Doukas and Melham (1986). Copeland (1984) tests for the importance of news concerning money supplies, interest rates and income. However, his results are again very poor. Only news about the money supply seems to be significant. Doukas and Melham (1986) examine the impact of money supply announcements in Canada and the US on the weekly spot Canadian dollar–US dollar exchange rate. Their results provide some evidence for the importance of news.

inflation and lagged income. He uses data from the 1920s.[57] The equations with news about domestic and foreign interest rates perform much better than the money supply equations. The variables are correctly signed and a number are significant. Moreover, the addition of some lagged news regarding interest rates improves the equation.[58] The money supply equations (whichever method of estimating the news is used) are much poorer: neither domestic nor foreign news seems to be significant.

Edwards (1982; 1983) also uses the SURE method of estimation. He focuses not only on the importance of news in affecting the spot exchange rate, but also on whether the incorporation of news removes the biasedness of the forward rate as a predictor of the spot rate. News about real money supplies, real incomes and the real interest rate are all included in his model. He uses dollar exchange rates *vis-à-vis* sterling, the Deutschmark, the French franc and the lira for various periods during the 1970s. News variables are extracted from an autoregressive equation such as (3.49). The results are mixed: there are a number of wrong signs and many of the news terms are insignificant. However, a test of market efficiency on these results suggests that the null hypothesis of efficiency cannot be rejected for the Deutschmark, sterling and lira markets. The French franc–dollar market still exhibits inefficiencies.

An obvious problem with these tests is that they are highly dependent on the method by which news is extracted from actual observations of the variables. The final group of literature differs from the above in that they use different means of deriving expected and unexpected variables. Dornbusch (1980) uses OECD forecasts of major macroeconomic variables for the large industrial countries. In particular, forecasts of the current account and cyclical factors are compared with actual data: the difference between the two represents the news. He runs the following regression using the effective dollar exchange rate:

$$\Delta s - (i - i^*) = \alpha_0 + \alpha_1 CAE \ \alpha_2 CYC - \alpha_3 CYC^* + \alpha_4 INN \tag{3.51}$$

The left-hand side of equation (3.51) is equivalent to the forecast error between the actual change in the spot exchange rate ($\Delta s$) and that suggested by the forward premium ($i - i^* = - fp$, if covered interest parity holds). CAE is news about the current account; CYC is domestic cyclical news; $CYC^*$ is foreign cyclical news and INN is interest rate differential news.[59] The results lead Dornbusch to conclude that unanticipated real and financial disturbances do have some role to play in determining exchange rates.

MacDonald and Torrance (1988) examine the role of news regarding changes in money supplies by using survey data on the expected change in the money supply. This gets around the problem of having to construct a series of the expected money supply. They use data for sterling *vis-à-vis* a variety of currencies (both monthly and quarterly) to run the following regression:

$$\Delta s_t = \alpha_1 + \alpha_2 \Delta MR_t + \alpha_3 \Delta ME_t + u_t \tag{3.52}$$

[57] As we noted earlier, he looks at the dollar–franc, pound–franc and dollar–pound exchange rates over the period February 1921 to May 1925.

[58] It might be thought that the inclusion of lagged news goes against the efficient market hypothesis: since news should be incorporated quickly into the spot exchange rate. However, MacDonald (1983a) argues that if there is a publication lag, then lagged news could be significant and market efficiency still hold.

[59] Note that to generate news about interest rate differentials, Dornbusch (1980) uses an autoregression like (3.48).

where $\Delta MR$ is the unexpected change in the money supply and $\Delta ME$ is the expected change. If the market uses information efficiently, then $\alpha_3$ should be equal to zero, whereas $\alpha_2$ will be significant. The results are very poor: neither coefficients are significant and hence it is difficult to judge the role of unanticipated monetary shocks.

In conclusion, the results of the news equations are rather poor. There is only scant support for the idea that the particular items of news used here are relevant to exchange rate determination. This may result from the difficulty of extracting the news element from actual data, although even with survey data, the results are no better. Alternatively it may simply be that these models look at the wrong kinds of news. The majority of the articles take a monetary view of exchange rate determination and hence examine factors such as unexpected money supply changes, interest rate changes and so on. Perhaps, however, it is other items of news which are important. Thus, whilst news ideas are theoretically interesting in that they might well account for exchange rate volatility, a lot more research needs to be done to determine exactly what items of news are relevant to exchange rate determination.

## Recent attempts at explaining exchange rate misalignment

The news approach we have discussed focuses mainly on the issue of exchange rate volatility. However, we noted in Chapter 1, that the floating exchange rate period has been characterised by a tendency for exchange rates to become misaligned, that is, to move away from their long-run fundamental equilibrium value for an extended period. Two very recent theories have focused on this issue. The first is the literature on rational speculative bubbles; the second is the work of Frankel and Froot on heterogeneous expectations (chartists and fundamentalists).

The rational bubble literature seeks to explain persistent departures of asset prices from their fundamental determinants whilst still assuming rational behaviour on the part of market participants.[60] This is possible if one notes that the price of an asset today ($P_t$) is a function not only of the return one expects whilst holding the asset (the dividend) but also of its expected resale value (and hence the expected price in the future). This is represented in equation (3.52):

$$P_t = [E(D_{t+1}|I_t) + E(P_{t+1}|I_t)]/(1+r) \tag{3.52}$$

$D_{t+1}$ is the dividend in period t+1; $I_t$ is the information set available at time t; $P_{t+1}$ is the price of the asset in period t+1 (its resale value); and r is the discount rate. If we assume that investors have rational expectations, then equation (3.52) can be solved to generate:

$$P_t = \sum_{i=1}^{\infty} E(D_{t+i}|I_t)/(1+r)^i + B_t \tag{3.53}$$

$B_t$ can be interpreted at the bubble component[61] and could take the following form:

$$B_t = E(B_{t+1})/(1+r) \tag{3.54}$$

that is, the bubble this period is equal to the discounted value of the expected bubble next period. Rearranging equation (3.54) and given rational expectations, we get:

[60] See Camerer (1989) for a survey. See also Flood and Garber (1982), Blanchard and Fischer (1989, Chapter 5) and the *Journal of Economic Perspectives*, Symposium on Bubbles, Spring 1990, 4: 2.

[61] Essentially $B_t$ arises from the solution to the model: it is equivalent to the arbitrary constant that appears when solving differential equations.

$$B_{t+1} = (1 + r)B_t + z_t \tag{3.55}$$

where $z_t$ is a random error serially uncorrelated with a mean of zero. Equation (3.55) states that the bubble grows in each period at the discount rate, r. Only if this is true can those participating in the bubble be considered rational: in each period, holding on to the asset yields a rate of return commensurate with investors' discount rate. If, as is likely, the bubble has a probability of bursting in each period, then provided investors are risk neutral, the bubble must grow at an expected rate equal to r. If investors are risk averse and the probability of the bubble bursting increases the further away the price of the asset moves from its fundamentals, then the bubble must grow exponentially: that is, the expected return in each period must be greater than the period before to compensate investors for holding on to the asset.

This account was not specifically related to exchange rates. However, it is easy to see how the bubble story can apply in foreign exchange markets. The price of the asset becomes the spot and the expected spot rates. The market fundamentals chosen depend on the model of exchange rate determination. For example, with a monetary model, market fundamentals would be represented by relative money supplies and incomes. Alternatively a portfolio model of fundamentals would include the supplies of various assets (domestic and foreign). This illustrates an important point: when it comes to testing for evidence of a bubble, a joint hypothesis is being tested. Not only are we testing for the presence of a bubble but also the model of fundamental exchange rate determination. In view of the difficulties which we discussed above in trying to estimate fundamental models, empirical tests of bubbles should perhaps carry a health warning.

Evidence on the existence of bubbles is mixed. It has often been claimed that the appreciation of the dollar in the period June 1984 to February 1985 can be explained by the existence of a bubble. Frankel and Froot (1990) note that following a large appreciation in the early 1980s the dollar appreciated some 20% further. This, they argue does not appear to be explained easily by fundamentals. The initial appreciation pre-June 1984 can be explained by a large interest differential consequent on the tight monetary policy being pursued alongside a loose fiscal policy. However, after 1984, when the fundamental indicators began to suggest that a dollar depreciation should occur, the dollar continued to rise until February 1985. Such behaviour could therefore be explained by the presence of a rational speculative bubble.

More formal tests of the presence of bubbles have been conducted by Meese (1986) and Pittas (1989) among others. Meese (1986) tests for the presence of a bubble in monthly data from 1973–82 for the dollar *vis-à-vis* the Deutschmark, yen and sterling. He uses a monetary model to represent exchange rate fundamentals: relative money supplies and incomes are included. He tests for cointegration between the exchange rate and these fundamental determinants. The hypothesis is that lack of cointegration could imply the presence of a bubble. This indeed is what he finds and hence he has to conclude that bubbles could have existed for these dollar exchange rates.

Pittas (1989) tests for speculative bubbles using more recent data from January 1975 to December 1986 for the dollar *vis-à-vis* sterling, the Deutschmark and the yen. The fundamental model of the exchange rate is a modified monetary approach which allows for overshooting. Hence the real exchange rate is included in the cointegrating regression. The results suggest an inability to reject the null hypothesis of no cointegration thus indicating an absence of bubbles. This result is confirmed by a second test conducted by Pittas on the period 1981 to 1985. This involves adding a dummy variable which takes the value of one during the period when a bubble is hypothesised to exist.

The mixed results at the empirical level are not the only problem faced by the bubble literature. There are in addition several theoretical problems (Camerer, 1989). Firstly, there can never be a negative bubble. Since the price of an asset has a lower bound of zero, a negative bubble could never start. We can understand this conclusion by asking what the path of the asset price would be if a negative bubble were to start. It would have to have expected negative growth in each period equal to the discount rate. However, this implies that eventually the price would have to become negative. Since this cannot happen, a negative bubble cannot start if investors are rational.

A second problem is that bubbles must begin at the start of the assets life. The bubble cannot start in the middle of the life of the asset, since in this case rational agents would anticipate it and hence it would have to start the period before and so on until the logical conclusion is that rational bubbles must start immediately an asset comes into existence. Finally, an asset with a finite life and a fixed redemption value cannot become the object of a rational bubble: the bubble will not start since rational traders will know that it has to end at some fixed known point.

The first two problems rule out the idea that bubbles can arise, burst, arise again, etc. The third problem rules out bubbles in a large number of assets (although it would not apply to exchange rates). Hence it appears that strictly rational bubbles are a very limited concept. This leads Camerer (1989) to conclude that it may be more fruitful to look at 'near rational' bubbles. These bubbles rely on the idea that some traders believe that there is always a greater fool out there who will be willing to purchase the asset at a higher price than it was bought for. In others words, even if it is the case that traders will lose (it is a negative sum game), traders may be unduly optimistic about the profits they could receive because they believe that they can sell out before the price collapses. One could appeal to Kindleberger's (1978) argument that in any market there are the inside traders (the professionals) who may very well start a bubble and the outsiders (the amateur traders) who come into the market late (just before the bubble bursts) and who act as the 'greater fools' by purchasing the asset when the insiders start to sell out.

The second group of papers which seek to explain exchange rate misalignment are the work of Frankel and Froot (1987; 1990). They focus on the role played by heterogeneous expectations. Frankel and Froot (1990) argue that there are a number of pieces of evidence which support the idea that expectations in foreign exchange markets are not homogeneous. First, survey forecasts show a wide dispersion of opinion, especially for the longer maturities. Secondly, the large volume of trade which takes place could only result from heterogeneous expectations (transactions take place because agents have different views about the price being offered).

When it comes to modelling these heterogeneous expectations, Frankel and Froot (1987) make the following simplification. They assume that there are two types of forecasters: fundamentalists who use Dornbusch's overshooting model; and chartists who extrapolate past experience to arrive at their forecasts. Essentially the fundamentalists can be thought of as taking a long-term view, whereas the chartists take a short-term view. Portfolio managers trading in the market use a weighted average of these two forecasts. The key feature of portfolio managers is that they update the weights used according to who is doing better. So, for example, if the fundamentalists prove to be correct, then they will take on more weight in the portfolio managers portfolio and vice versa.

Their model explains the rise in the dollar in the early 1980s by the rising importance of chartists in the forecasts of portfolio managers. Assume that the exchange rate is initially in equilibrium (that is, approximately equal to its fundamental value), that portfolio managers are giving 100% weight to the fundamentalists and that both the exchange rate and the weight are constant. Assume now that there is a shock to the system which persists for slightly longer than was expected. In terms of the dollar, this could be represented by the real interest differential in favour of the US in the early 1980s. Over time, the weight given to fundamentalists in the portfolio managers' forecast will begin to fall. This occurs because the fundamentalists continue to get their forecast wrong and hence portfolio managers pay less and less attention to it.

As a result, the dollar exchange rate appreciates relative to other currencies and it moves away from its fundamental value. Eventually the weight given by portfolio managers to the fundamentalist forecasts falls to zero and the exchange rate stops appreciating and remains at its over-appreciated level. The results is a sustained appreciation of the dollar even although fundamentalists were predicting a depreciation.

This model can explain the dollar rise in the early 1980s. In order to explain its subsequent fall, Frankel and Froot have to include the cumulated current account in the equation for the actual exchange rate. As the current account deficits get larger and larger (due to the appreciation), this causes the net stock of US foreign assets to decline. Increased borrowing abroad by the US will eventually be seen to be unsustainable and hence dollar assets become less and less attractive. As the current account plays an increasing role in determining the actual exchange rate, so the dollar begins to depreciate. As a result, portfolio managers increase the weight given to fundamentalists in their forecasts and the depreciation accelerates.

Simulations of the model indicate that the exchange rate can follow a path of appreciation followed by depreciation, that is prolonged periods away from fundamentals can be explained. Frankel and Froot (1990) quote the results of a questionnaire conducted by Euromoney of a number of forecasting services over the 1970s and 1980s. The results indicate broad support for Frankel and Froot's model. In 1978, the vast majority of the forecasting services used a fundamentalist model to predict the future exchange rate. By 1985, however, the pattern had altered completely with much more weight being placed on technical analysis (that is, a chartist approach).

The models examined in this section are still rather in their infancy. What is clear from our brief examination of them is that they attempt to explain why the actual exchange rate moves in the way it does rather than seeking to determine how it should move were agents always to focus on fundamentals. It is in this way that these models represent a departure from the traditional monetary or portfolio approaches to exchange rate determination with which we began this chapter. Perhaps in that departure, it will be possible to build more accurate models of actual exchange rate movement than has been done so far.

**APPENDIX 1: Solutions to Rational Expectations Models**

This appendix, which draws extensively on Begg (1982), is designed to explain the structure of rational expectations (or, in our case, perfect foresight) models and show how the solution can be represented diagrammatically.

Assume we have a model which can be described by two differential equations:

$$\Delta x = \alpha x + \beta y + \eta \tag{A1}$$

$$\Delta y = \gamma x + \delta y + \kappa \tag{A2}$$

where x and y are two variables, $\Delta x$ and $\Delta y$ are dx/dt and dy/dt respectively and the greek letters (with the exception of $\Delta$) denote the model's parameters, which are assumed to be constant. Equations (A1) and (A2) state that the rate of change of x and y depend on the levels of x and y.

We can derive the equilibrium values of x and y, say $x^*$ and $y^*$, by setting equations (A1) and (A2) equal to zero and then solving them simultaneously:[62]

$$0 = \Delta x = \alpha x + \beta y + \eta \tag{A3}$$

$$0 = \Delta y = \gamma x + \delta y + \kappa \tag{A4}$$

$$=> \quad x^* = (\beta\kappa - \eta\delta)/(\alpha\delta - \beta\gamma) \tag{A5}$$

$$\text{and} \quad y^* = (\gamma\eta - \alpha\kappa)/(\alpha\delta - \beta\gamma) \tag{A6}$$

In order to examine how the model behaves when it is not in equilibrium, we can use equations (A1) and (A2) and plot them on a phase diagram in (x, y) space. Each schedule shows combinations of x and y such that $\Delta x = 0$ and $\Delta y = 0$. From equation (A1), we derive the equation for the $\Delta x = 0$ schedule and from equation (A2) we derive the $\Delta y = 0$ schedule (by setting both equations equal to zero and solving for x and y respectively):

$$x = -(1/\alpha)(\beta y + \eta) \tag{A7}$$

$$y = -(1/\delta)(\gamma x + \kappa) \tag{A8}$$

Equations (A7) and (A8) illustrate three potential cases. Firstly, the system could be globally stable which implies that if actual x and y are off the $\Delta x = 0$ and $\Delta y = 0$ schedules, then the system will move back to equilibrium automatically. This case is illustrated in Figure 3.A1. Here we assume that $\alpha$, $\gamma$, $\delta < 0$ and $\beta$, $\eta > 0$. These restrictions imply that $\Delta x = 0$ is positively sloped and $\Delta y = 0$ is negatively sloped. What happens if the system is in disequilibrium? Take for example point A. At point

---

[62] To derive $x^*$ we need to eliminate y. Multiply equation (A3) by $\delta$ and equation (A4) by $-\beta$:

$$0 = \alpha\delta x + \beta\delta y + \eta\delta$$
$$0 = -\beta\gamma x - \beta\delta y - \beta\kappa$$

Add the two equations together:

$$0 = (\alpha\delta x - \beta\gamma x) + (\beta\delta y - \beta\delta y) + (\eta\delta - \beta\kappa)$$
$$=> \quad \beta\kappa - \eta\delta = (\alpha\delta - \beta\gamma)x$$
$$=> \quad x = x^* = (\beta\kappa - \eta\delta)/(\alpha\delta - \beta\gamma) \text{ which is equation (A5).}$$

To derive $y^*$ we eliminate x. Multiply equation (A3) by $\gamma$ and (A4) by $\alpha$:

$$0 = \alpha\gamma x + \beta\gamma y + \gamma\eta$$
$$0 = -\alpha\gamma x - \alpha\delta y - \alpha\kappa$$

Add the two equations together:

$$0 = (\alpha\gamma x - \alpha\gamma x) + (\beta\gamma y - \alpha\delta y) + (\gamma\eta - \alpha\kappa)$$
$$=> \quad 0 = (\beta\gamma - \alpha\delta)y + (\gamma\eta - \alpha\kappa)$$
$$=> \quad (\alpha\delta - \beta\gamma)y = (\gamma\eta - \alpha\kappa)$$
$$=> \quad y = y^* = (\gamma\eta - \alpha\kappa)/(\alpha\delta - \beta\gamma) \text{ which is equation (A6).}$$

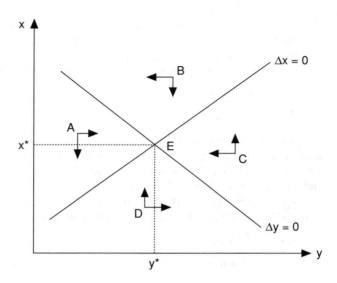

**Figure 3.A1.**   *CASE I – globally stable solution*

A, we are to the left of the $\Delta x = 0$ schedule, implying that y is too low for each x to generate a constant x. From equation (A1) we can see that if y is too low, then $\Delta x$ must be negative, in other words, x is decreasing (this is represented by the downward arrow at A). At the same time, we are also to the left of the $\Delta y = 0$ schedule, that is, x is too low for each y. From equation (A2) we can see that with $\gamma < 0$, $\Delta y$ must be positive (since $\gamma x$ is a smaller negative number relative to the value required to generate $\Delta y = 0$). That is, y is increasing and moving back towards $\Delta y = 0$. Thus if the economy is in disequilibrium at a point such as A, then this implies that x is decreasing and y is increasing, moving the system back towards E. A similar exercise can be done for the other points, B, C or D (the arrows in the diagram illustrate the movement of x and y).

In conclusion, therefore, if the parameters of the system are such as to generate a globally stable solution, then this implies that if the economy moves away from E, then forces within the system will move it back automatically.

The second case we can examine is that of global instability. If we assume that $\alpha, \gamma, \delta > 0$ and $\beta < 0$ then although $\Delta x = 0$ and $\Delta y = 0$ are both the same slopes as before, we now get very different arrows of motion. In other words, the system now behaves very differently when it is not in equilibrium. This case is illustrated in Figure 3.A2. Assume the system has moved to point A. Here we are to the left of $\Delta x = 0$ schedule and y is too low for each given x. From equation (A1) this implies that $\Delta x > 0$ (since $\beta < 0$, $\beta y$ is a smaller negative number). In other words, x is increasing, moving the system away from the $\Delta x = 0$ line. At the same time, we are also to the left of $\Delta y = 0$ schedule. This means that for each y, x is too low to generate equilibrium. From equation (A2) we can see that y must be decreasing moving us away from equilibrium. Similar analysis again yields the same results for points B, C or D, that is, the system is globally unstable and it if moves away from its equilibrium at point E, it will not return.

The final and most important case to consider is a system which displays a saddle-point equilibrium. This is what characterises the Dornbusch model with rational expectations which we have already considered. The case of a saddlepoint equilibrium is one where the dynamics of the system exhibit aspects of both cases I and II previously considered. Assume that the parameters of our system are α > 0 and β, γ, δ < 0. In this case, the equation for Δx = 0 is the same as in case II: that is, if the economy is not on the Δx = 0 schedule, the dynamics of the system will move x and y further from Δx = 0. The equation for Δy = 0 is identical to case I: that is, if the economy is not on the Δy = 0 schedule, the dynamics of the system will move x and y further towards Δy = 0. This case is illustrated in Figure 3.A3.

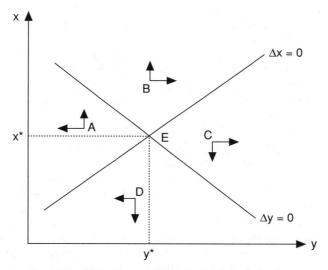

**Figure 3.A2.** *CASE II – globally unstable solution*

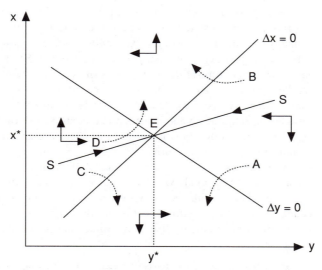

**Figure 3.A3.** *CASE III – saddlepoint equilibrium*

In order to understand the saddlepoint equilibrium property more clearly, it is useful to examine what happens to the system when it is out of equilibrium. Let us assume we are at point B. Here we are to the right of $\Delta x = 0$: for each level of x, y is too high to generate equilibrium. From equation (A1), this implies that $\Delta x < 0$ (recall that $\beta < 0$ and hence $\beta y$ is a larger negative number). That is, x is decreasing and this represents the unstable part of the system: we are moving away from the $\Delta x = 0$ schedule. At the same time, at B, we are to the right of the $\Delta y = 0$ schedule: x is too high for each given level of y. From equation (A2) this implies that with $\gamma < 0$, $\Delta y < 0$ (since $\gamma x$ is now a larger negative number). In other words, y is decreasing and this represents the stable part of the system. Thus from B, the system starts moving towards the south-west as the dotted arrow shows (note that at the moment it is moving towards E). However, once it crosses the $\Delta x = 0$ schedule we are now to the left of $\Delta x = 0$ and thus x begins to increase[63] moving the system further away from equilibrium in a north-west fashion.

If we start at point A, the system again moves in a south-westerly direction towards E until it hits the $\Delta y = 0$ schedule. After crossing the $\Delta y = 0$ schedule, the system is now to the left of the $\Delta y = 0$ schedule, and hence y starts increasing. Since x is still declining the system moves off away from equilibrium in a south-easterly direction.

We can relate similar stories for points C and D: once the system crosses either the $\Delta x = 0$ or the $\Delta y = 0$ schedules, it diverges from its equilibrium point, E. Notice, however, that Figure A3 has an additional schedule drawn, SS. The key characteristic of a saddlepoint solution to a rational expectations model is that there is one line along which the system will converge. This is represented in Figure A3 by schedule SS. SS represents all points of disequilibrium from which it is possible to start and reach equilibrium. The schedule is found by taking all points where the system begins to move towards equilibrium and arrives before crossing either of the two schedules, $\Delta x = 0$ or $\Delta y = 0$. Intuitively speaking the saddlepoint path is a unique path along which the equilibriating tendencies of the system (represented by the $\Delta y = 0$ schedule) outweigh the disequilibriating tendencies (represented by the $\Delta x = 0$ schedule).

The implication of the saddlepoint property is that only if the economy happens to be on SS, will it move towards equilibrium. This may cause some concern, since presumably only by chance will the exogenous shock that moves the economy away from E be such that the economy happens to find itself on SS. However, rational expectations (or perfect foresight) imply that if the steady state of the economic system is a saddlepoint, the economy will succeed in locating SS since rational expectations says that is where the economy should go. Indeed those who favour the assumption of rational expectations in macroeconomic models believe that a globally stable equilibrium is undesirable. This is because, as there are an infinite number of paths to equilibrium, expectations formation will be very difficult (agents will not know which of the infinite paths the economy will take). To look at it another way, forward looking agents with rational expectations essentially solve the model which determines the path taken by the economy over all time. Hence convergence is no longer a chance event. If agents do not act to put the economy on SS, then the economy will shoot off in an unstable direction. Since agents know this, they will form their

---

[63] To the left of $\Delta x = 0$, y is now too low for each given x. This implies from equation (A1) that $\Delta x > 0$, that is, x is increasing.

expectations such that the economy does move to SS and they will then act accordingly, thus returning the system to its saddlepoint path.

## APPENDIX 2: Derivation of Key Buiter–Miller Equations

Equation (3.32) for $\Delta$ is derived as follows. Take equation (3.30) and substitute for $\pi$ using equation (3.31):

$$\Delta p = \delta d + \pi \tag{3.30}$$

$$\Rightarrow \Delta p = \delta d + \Delta m, \text{ since } \pi = \Delta m$$

$$\Rightarrow 0 = \delta d + \Delta m - \Delta p$$

$$\Rightarrow 0 = \delta d + \Delta l, \text{ since } \Delta m - \Delta p = \Delta l \tag{A1}$$

We then use equations (3.27) and (3.28) to substitute in for i and d and we solve for $\Delta l$. Starting with equation (3.27) we can solve for i:

$$i = (\phi/\mu)y - (1/\mu)m + (1/\mu)p$$

$$\Rightarrow i = (\phi/\mu)y - (1/\mu)l, \text{ since } -[(1/\mu)m - (1/\mu)p] = -(1/\mu)l \tag{A2}$$

We can substitute this into equation (3.28) to derive an expression for d:

$$d = \alpha(s - p) - \xi\{[(\phi/\mu)y - (1/\mu)l] - \Delta p\}$$

$$\Rightarrow d = \alpha q - (\xi\phi/\mu)y + (\xi/\mu)l + \xi\Delta p, \text{ since } (s-p) = q$$

substitute from equation (3.30) for $\Delta p = \delta d + \pi$:

$$d = \alpha q - (\xi\phi/\mu)y + (\xi/\mu)l + \xi(\delta d + \pi)$$

which after some rearranging and noting that y is equal to d in equilibrium (since output is demand determined) gives us:

$$d = \{(\alpha\mu)/[(1-\xi\delta)\mu + \xi\phi]\}q + \{\xi/[(1-\xi\delta)\mu + \xi\phi]\}l + \{(\xi\mu)/[(1-\xi\delta)\mu + \xi\phi]\}\pi \tag{A3}$$

If we then substitute this expression for d into equation (A1) and then rearrange, we derive equation (3.32) in the main text:

$$\Delta l = [(1/\Xi)\delta\xi]l + [(1/\Xi)\delta\mu\alpha]q + (1/\Xi)\pi \tag{3.32}$$

where $\Xi = \xi(\delta\mu - \phi) - \mu$.

Equation (3.33) is derived as follows. Take equations (3.26) and (3.30):

$$i = i^* + \Delta s \tag{3.26}$$

$$\Delta p = \delta d + \pi \tag{3.30}$$

Given that (3.26) is an equation, we can add its left-hand side to the left-hand side of equation (3.30) and its right-hand side to the right-hand side of equation (3.30) without destroying the equality of equation (3.30). This manipulation generates the following:

$$i + \Delta p = i^* + \Delta s + \delta d + \pi$$

$$\Rightarrow \Delta s - \Delta p = i - i^* - \delta d - \pi$$

$$\Rightarrow \Delta q = \Delta s - \Delta p = i - i^* - \delta d - \pi$$

We can then substitute for i and d using equations (A2) and (A3) already derived.

Note that again y = d. After much algebraic manipulation we arrive at equation (3.33) in the main text:

$$\Delta q = (1/\Xi)l + [(1/\Xi)\alpha(\delta\mu - \phi)]q + [(1/\Xi)\,\mu]\pi - i^*  \qquad (3.33)$$

where $\Xi = \xi(\delta\mu - \phi) - \mu$ as before.

## References

Allen, P.R. (1973) 'A portfolio approach to international capital flows', *Journal of International Economics*, 3: 2, 135–60.

Allen, P.R. and Kenen, P. (1976) 'Portfolio adjustment in open economics: a comparison of alternative specifications', *Weltwirtschaftliches Archiv*, 112: 1.

Allen, P.R. and Kenen, P. (1980) *Asset Markets, Exchange Rates and Economic Integration*. Cambridge University Press, Cambridge.

Artis, M.J. (1981) 'From monetary to exchange-rate targets', *Banca Nazionale del Lavoro Quarterly Review*, 138 (September).

Backus, D. (1984) 'Empirical models of the exchange rate: separating the wheat from the chaff', *Canadian Journal of Economics*, XVII: 4, 824–46.

Barro, R.J. (1978) 'A stockastic equilibrium model of an open economy under flexible exchange rates', *Quarterly Journal of Economics*, 92: 149–64.

Begg, D.H.K. (1982) *The Rational Expectations Revolution in Macroeconomics*. Philip Allan, Oxford.

Bhandari, J.S., Driskill, R. and Frenkel, J.A. (1984) 'Capital Mobility and exchange rate overshooting', *European Economic Review*, 24: 309–20.

Bilson, J.F.O. (1978) 'The monetary approach to the exchange rate – some empirical evidence', *IMF Staff Papers*, 25: 48–75.

Bisignano, J. and Hoover, K. (1982) 'Some suggested improvements to a simple portfolio balance model of exchange rate determination with special reference to the US dollar–Canadian dollar rate', *Weltwirtschaftliches Archiv*, 19: 19–37.

Blanchard, O.J. and Fischer, S. (1989) *Lectures on Macroeconomics*, MIT Press, Cambridge, Mass.

Bomhoff, E.S. and Kortweg, P. (1983) 'Exchange-rate variability and monetary policy under rational expectations: some Euro-American experience 1973–79', *Journal of MonetaryEconomics*, 11: 2, 169–206.

Boughton, J.M. (1988) 'The monetary approach to exchange rates: what now remains?', *Princeton Essays in International Finance*, 171, (October).

Branson, W.H. (1977) 'Asset markets and relative prices in exchange rate determination', *Sozialwissenschaftliche Annalen*, 1: 69–89.

Branson, W.H. (1984) 'Exchange rate policy after a decade of "floating"', in J.F.O. Bilson and R.C. Marston (eds.) *Exchange Rate Theory and Practice*. National Bureau of Economic Research, The University of Chicago Press, Chicago.

Branson, W.H., Halttunen, H. and Masson, P. (1977) 'Exchange rates in the short run: the dollar–Deutschmark rate', *European Economic Review*, 10: 303–324.

Branson, W.H., Halttunen, H. and Masson, P. (1979) 'Exchange rates in the short run', *European Economic Review*, 12: 395–402.

Branson, W.H. and Henderson, D.W. (1985) 'The specification and influence of asset markets', in B.P. Kenen and R.W. Jones (eds.) *Handbook of International Economics*, Vol. 2. North Holland, Amsterdam.

Buiter, W.H. and Miller, M. (1981) 'Monetary policy and international competitiveness: the problem of adjustment', in W.A. Eltis and P.J. Sinclair (eds.) *The Money Supply and the Exchange Rate*. Oxford University Press, Oxford.

Camerer, E. (1989) 'Bubble and fads in asset prices', *Journal of Economic Surveys*, 3: 1, 3–41.

Cassola e Barata, N. (1992) *Portugal and the European Monetary System*. PhD thesis presented to the University of Kent, Canterbury.

Copeland, L. (1984) 'The pound sterling/US dollar exchange rate and the "news"', *Economic Letters*, 15: 109–113.

Currie, D.A. (1984) 'Monetary overshooting and the exchange rate', *The Manchester School*, 28–48.

Dornbusch, R. (1976a) 'Expectations and exchange rate dynamics', *Journal of Political Economy*, 84: 6, 1161–76.

Dornbusch, R. (1980) 'Exchange rate economics: where do we stand?', *Brookings Papers on Economic Activity*, 1: 143–85.

Dornbusch, R. (1981) 'Evidence to the Treasury and Civil Service Committee', Memoranda on Monetary Policy, HC 770, HMSO, London.

Dornbusch, R. and Fischer, S. (1980) 'Exchange rates and the current account', *American Economic Review*, (December), 70: 5, 960–71.

Doukas, J. and Melham, M. (1986) 'The reaction of spot and forward rates to new information', *European Economic Review*, 30: 305–24.

Driskill, R.A. (1980) 'Exchange rate dynamics, portfolio balance and relative prices', *American Economic Review*, 70: 776–83.

Driskill, R.A. (1981) 'Exchange rate dynamics: an empirical investigation', *Journal of Political Economy*, 89: 2, 357–71.

Edwards, S. (1982) 'Exchange rate market efficiency and new information', *Economic Letters*, 9: 377–82.

Edwards, S. (1983) 'Floating exchange rates, expectations and new information', *Journal of Monetary Economics*, 11: 321–36.

Fleming, M. (1962) 'Domestic financial policies under fixed and under floating exchange rates', *IMF Staff Papers*, 9: 369–79.

Flood, R.P. and Garber, P.M. (1982) 'Bubbles, runs and gold monetarization', In P. Watchel (ed) *Crises in the Economic and Financial Structure*. Lexington Books, Cambridge, Mass.

Frankel, J.A. (1979) 'On the mark: a theory of floating exchange rates based on real interest differentials', *American Economic Review*, 69: 4, 610–22.

Frankel, J.A. (1983) 'Monetary and portfolio balance models of exchange rate determination', in J.S. Bhandari and B.H. Putnam (eds.) *Economic Independence and Flexible Exchange Rates*. MIT Press, Cambridge, Mass.

Frankel, J.A. (1993) *On Exchange Rates*. MIT Press, Cambridge, Mass.

Frankel, J.A. and Froot, K.A. (1987) 'Using survey data to test standard propositions regarding exchange rate expectations', *American Economic Review*, 77: 1, 133–53.

Frankel, J.A. and Froot, K.A. (1990) 'Chartists, fundamentalists and trading in the foreign exchange market', *American Economic Review*, 80: 2 (May), 181–85.

Frenkel, J.A. (1976) 'Monetary approach to the exchange rate: doctrinal aspects and empirical evidence', *Scandinavian Journal of Economics*, 78: 2, 200–24.

Frenkel, J.A. (1981) 'Flexible exchange rates, prices and the role of news: lessons from the 1970s', *Journal of Political Economy*, 89: 4, 665–705.

Frenkel, J.A. and Rodriguez, C.A. (1982) 'Exchange rate dynamics and the overshooting hypothesis', *IMF Staff Papers*, 29: 1–30.

**Genberg, H. and Kierzkowski, H.** (1979) 'Impact and long run effects of economic disturbances in a dynamic model of exchange rate determination', *Weltwirtschaftliches Archiv*, 451–76.

**Girton, L. and Roper, D.** (1977) 'A monetary model of exchange market pressure applied to the post-war Canadian experience', *American Economic Review*, 67: 4, 537–48.

**Hacche, G. and Townend, J.** (1981) 'Exchange rates and monetary policy: modelling sterling's effective exchange rate', in W.A. Eltis and P.J.N. Stirling (eds.) *The Money Supply and the Exchange Rate*. Oxford University Press, Oxford.

**Hallwood, P. and MacDonald, R.** (1986) *International Money: theories, evidence and institutions*. Basil Blackwell, Oxford.

**Harvey, A.C.** (1993) *Time Series Models*, 2nd ed. Harvester Wheatsheaf, Hemel Hempstead.

**Hoffman, D.L. and Schlagenhauf, D.** (1985) 'The impact of news and alternative theories of exchange rate determination', *Journal of Money, Credit and Banking*, 17: 3, 328–46.

**Huang, R.D.** (1981) 'The monetary approach to exchange rates in an efficient foreign exchange market: tests based on volatility', *Journal of Finance*, 36: 1, 31–41.

**Ingram, J.C.** (1978) 'Expectations and floating exchange rates', *Weltwirtschaftliches Archiv*, CXIV: 422–447.

*Journal of Economic Perspectives* (1990) 'Symposium on bubbles', 4: 2.

**Kearney, C. and MacDonald, R.** (1985) 'Asset markets and the exchange rate: a structural model of the sterling–dollar rate, 1972–82', *Journal of Economic Studies*, 12: 3, 3–20.

**Kearney, C. and MacDonald, R.** (1986) 'A structural portfolio balance model of the sterling–dollar exchange rate', *Weltwirtschaftliches Archiv* 122: 3, 478–96.

**MacDonald, R.** (1983a) 'Tests of efficiency and the impact of news in three foreign exchange markets: the experiences of the 1920s', *Bulletin of Economic Research*, 35: 2, 123–44.

**MacDonald, R.** (1985a) 'News and the 1920s experience of floating exchange rates', *Economic Letters*, 17: 379–83.

**MacDonald, R.** (1988) *Floating Exchange Rates: Theories and Evidence*. Allen and Unwin, London.

**MacDonald, R. and Taylor, M.P.** (1993) 'The monetary approach to the exchange rate' *IMF Staff Papers*, 40: 1, 89–107.

**MacDonald, R. and Taylor, M.P.** (1994) 'The monetary model of the exchange rate: long-run relationships, short-run dynamics and how to beat a random walk', *Journal of International Money and Finance*, 13: 3, 276–90.

**MacDonald, R. and Torrance, T.S.** (1988) 'Exchange rates and the news: some evidence using UK survey data', *The Manchester School*, LVI: 69–76.

**Mankiw, N.G. and Romer, D.** (eds.) (1991) *New Keynesian Economics, vols. 1 and 2*. MIT Press, Cambridge, Mass.

**Meese, R.A.** (1986) 'Testing for bubbles in exchange markets: a case of sparkling bubbles', *Journal of Political Economy*, 94: 2, 345–73.

**Meese, R.A. and Rogoff, K.** (1983) 'Empirical exchange rate models of the seventies: do they fit our sample?', *Journal of International Economics*, 14: 3–24.

**Meese, R.A. and Rogoff, K.** (1984) 'The out of sample failure of empirical exchange rate models: sampling error or misspecification?', in J.A. Frenkel (ed.)

*Exchange Rates and International Macroeconomics.* NBER, Chicago University Press, Chicago.

**Mundell, R.** (1963) 'Capital mobility and stabilisation policy under fixed and flexible exchange rates', *Canadian Journal of Economics*, 29: 4, 475–85.

**Niehans, J.** (1977) 'Exchange rate dynamics with stock/flow interaction', *Journal of Political Economy*, 85: 1245–57.

**Philbeam, K.** (1992) International Finance. Macmillan, London.

**Pittas, N.** (1989) 'On the exchange rate of the dollar: market fundamentals versus speculative bubbles', Birkbeck College, Discussion Paper, 2/90 (October); *The Manchester School*, 61: 2, 167–84.

**Shiller, R.** (1991) *Market Volatility*. MIT Press, Cambridge, Mass.

**Thirlwall, A.P. and Gibson, H.D.** (1992) *Balance of Payments Theory and the United Kingdom Experience, (4th ed.)* Macmillan, London.

**Whitman, M.V.N.** (1975) Global monetarism and the monetary approach to the balance of payments', *Brookings Papers on Economic Activity*, 3, 491–555.

# 4 EXCHANGE RATE MANAGEMENT, TARGET ZONES AND FIXED EXCHANGE RATES

In the last two chapters we have been considering how flexible exchange rates work and what factors are important in their determination. The focus was on the positive economics question: how do flexible exchange rates behave? We concluded that theories of exchange rate determination still appear to have a lot to explain. That is, much of the movement in exchange rates cannot be accounted for. In this chapter, we move more into the realm of normative economics. In particular, we want to ask whether a flexible exchange rate system is desirable. What advantages can it confer on an economy? This inevitably leads us into a discussion of greater management of exchange rates. We discuss how fixed exchange rate systems work as well as looking at some of the arguments that have been put forward in favour of fixed, or more fixed, exchange rates.

This debate between greater flexibility and greater management of exchange rates witnessed a revival during the 1980s. The various disappointments associated with flexible exchange rates led to a number of attempts at exchange rate management. Probably the most well-known of these is the European Monetary System and this is the subject of the next chapter. But in addition there were also the Plaza and Louvre agreements between the Group of Seven (G7) industrial countries.[1] These agreements aimed to manage the dollar and in particular to control its depreciation after 1985 (Box 4.1).

This chapter is organised as follows. In the first section, we review some of the arguments which favour flexible exchange rates. These arguments stem from the debate initiated by Friedman in 1953 with his seminal article on the case for flexible exchange rates. We also review the evidence concerning the operation of flexible exchange rates since 1973. Flexible exchange rates are most like the general equilibrium paradigm outlined in Chapter 1. In a flexible exchange rate system there is a minimum of institutional baggage and optimal solutions are reached simply by market actors trading in their own interests.

Four issues arise associated in some way with weaknesses of such a minimal institutional framework and all are related to the problem of uncertainty which, as we argued in Chapter 1, is one of the main reasons for taking the institutional framework of the international financial system more seriously. These include the lack of discipline under flexible exchange rates, the problems of volatility and misalignment and finally the foregone benefits of a single currency. In the second section, we discuss these four arguments that favour more exchange rate management or indeed even complete exchange rate fixity, while in the third section we examine how exchange

---

[1] The group of seven include US, UK, Japan, Germany, France, Canada and Italy.

---

> ## BOX 4.1.   The Plaza and Louvre Agreements
>
> During the early 1980s, the dollar appreciated substantially in spite of a growing trade deficit and persistent expectations that it would devalue. The reasons behind this huge appreciation can be usefully explained within the Mundell–Fleming framework.
>
> The US was following a policy of very tight money (via monetary base control) alongside a loose fiscal policy. Both these policies caused a large rise in interest rates. With perfectly mobile capital, the resulting large capital inflows caused exchange rate appreciation.
>
> The appreciation led to a large overvaluation of the dollar and in September 1985 the G5 met and agreed on joint intervention to bring the dollar down. This was known as the Plaza Agreement and it represented a large change in the attitude of the major industrial countries towards exchange rate management.
>
> The dollar peaked in February 1985 and by February 1987 had fallen by 35%, using a trade-weighted effective exchange rate. Against the Deutschmark and the yen, it had fallen by 48% and 42% respectively. In spite of this, the US balance of payments deficit was still large. Thus in February 1987, James Baker (the US Secretary of State) offered West Germany and Japan a new deal whereby the US would agree to a 'reference zone' for the dollar, Deutschmark and yen if Germany and Japan would take steps to boost growth.
>
> The Louvre Agreement, concluded towards the end of February, agreed to just that. Intervention was sanctioned to prevent further depreciation of the dollar. At the same time, it was agreed that Germany and Japan would take measures to reflate whilst the US would attempt to cut the budget deficit. In the months after Louvre, the dollar was indeed stabilised through intervention.
>
> *References*: *The Economist*, 5.10.85 (pp.68–9); 14.2.87 (p.71); 28.2.87 (p.13); and 11.7.87 (p.83).

rate management might actually work. In particular we focus on the problems of speculative attacks within managed systems as well as considering the literature on target zones. These latter sections provide the background for our discussion of European monetary integration in the next chapter.

The issues discussed in the second and third sections favour to a greater or lesser extent different degrees of exchange rate management, from a loose target zone system as envisaged by Williamson (1983) to full monetary union. Different institutional frameworks (with their different degrees of exchange rate management) maximise the ability of the system to cope with certain of these problems, but are not themselves without their costs. Thus, for example, the worst effects of misalignment can be successfully eliminated merely through some loose form of exchange rate management. But the benefits of a single currency can only be fully realised by complete monetary union, which itself has costs. Hence there are inevitable trade-offs involved in the design of any institutional setting and we need to balance these trade-offs in deciding which institutional structure we wish to adopt.

## The case for flexible exchange rates

The case for flexible exchange rates was originally, and most forcibly, put forward (at least in the post-war period) by Friedman (1953), mainly in response to dissatisfaction with the workings of the Bretton Woods system. Flexible exchange rates can be defined as 'rates of foreign exchange that are determined daily in the markets for foreign exchange by forces of demand and supply, without restrictions on the extent to which rates can move imposed by the government' (Johnson, 1970, p.198). In this sense, they attempt to make practice as close as possible to the general equilibrium paradigm discussed in Chapter 1.

In principle, allowing the exchange rate to float avoids all the difficulties involved in fixing the price of foreign exchange (Johnson, 1970). This can be explained with the help of a simple diagram which shows the demand and supply of foreign exchange (Figure 4.1). If the government, or monetary authorities, fix the exchange rate at $S_1$, then the domestic currency price of foreign exchange is too high (that is, the exchange rate is undervalued) relative to its equilibrium level. As a consequence, there is an excess supply of foreign exchange in the market. If the government wants to maintain the price at $S_1$, then it will have to step in and purchase the excess, thus adding to its foreign exchange reserves. Alternatively it could impose controls on capital inflows. By contrast, if the price is set too low (e.g. at $S_2$), then there is an excess demand for foreign exchange. The government has either to supply the excess demand from its own reserves or to impose quantitative controls on the use of foreign exchange (through controls on capital outflows). In other words, if the government chooses to fix the exchange rate at a rate other than the equilibrium rate (S in Figure 4.1), then it has to intervene in the foreign exchange market to eliminate excess demands and supplies.

Moreover, a second and related problem with fixed exchange rates was raised by the proponents of flexible exchange rates. If underlying competitive conditions change necessitating a change in the exchange rate, then in a floating exchange rate system the exchange rate will automatically change. Often those espousing flexible exchange rates have in mind purchasing power parity theory (Dunn, 1983, p.2). Hence should domestic prices be rising faster than foreign prices, the exchange rate will be expected to depreciate. By contrast, in a fixed exchange rate system, if, for example, the competitive position deteriorates intervention will be required if the

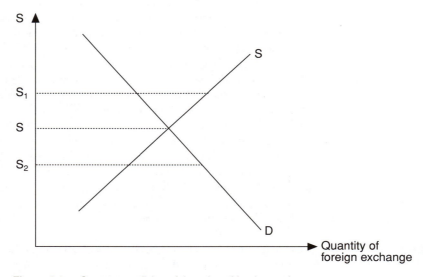

**Figure 4.1.**  *Government fixing of the price of foreign exchange*

*status quo* is to be maintained, and that intervention may become unsustainable as foreign exchange reserves are run down.[2] Were flexible exchange rates adopted, none of these problems would be encountered and the market mechanism would adequately deal with the question of adjustment.

How do speculators fit into the above scenario? Johnson (1970) argues that speculators would facilitate and smooth the adjustment of the exchange rate. We can look again at the example of deteriorating competitiveness warranting a depreciation of the exchange rate. Speculators, it is argued, see that the underlying conditions in the economy necessitate a depreciation. They would therefore sell the currency, causing it to depreciate. This argument builds on Friedman's (1953) claim that speculation would only be profitable if it were stabilising. Say, for example, the exchange rate appreciates above its long-run level, then the only way speculators can make a profit is for them to step in and sell the domestic currency causing the exchange rate to depreciate back towards its equilibrium level. In this way, floating exchange rates should not exhibit instability: on the contrary speculation should be stabilising.

This view that speculation is stabilising is part of the more general argument put forward by proponents of flexible exchange rates that complicated institutional controls on exchange rates are unnecessary. There are no information problems in this world and hence no reason to think that the government, for example, is any better informed about where the long-run equilibrium exchange rate is than the private sector. Indeed private agents have an incentive to use all available information in forming their views of the correct level of the long-run exchange rate since otherwise they will lose money.

This view of flexible exchange rates has been seriously challenged by the operation of the floating rate system since 1973. As we saw in Chapter 1, exchange rates have exhibited much volatility and in addition have frequently spent long periods away from their long-run fundamental equilibrium level (misaligned). Moreover, our analysis in Chapter 3 suggested that models of exchange rate determination perform very poorly empirically. In other words, it does not seem to be the case that fundamentals always drive exchange rates. Moreover, models of speculative bubbles suggest that speculators can make profits by buying and selling currencies in such a way as to take the current market rate away from its fundamental rate. Thus problems may arise with respect to information and co-ordination if private agents operate alone without any stronger institutional setting.

In addition to the view that floating exchange rates work better than fixed exchange rates, proponents of floating rates argue that they confer three advantages on an economy which adopts them: they allow easy adjustment to external disequilibria; they confer monetary autonomy on a country; and they provide insulation from external shocks.

The first advantage is that they provide a method of adjustment to external disequilibria in the way we have described. Johnson (1970) argues that a serious defect of the Bretton Woods system in the 1950s and 1960s was the lack of an adequate adjustment mechanism. This allowed external imbalances to persist over a long period. If the exchange rate is flexible, then external imbalances are taken care of and the government can use monetary and fiscal policy to meet internal goals such as

---

[2] Of course, if the competitive position of the country improves, then the exchange rate will now be undervalued relative to its new equilibrium. In this case the government accumulates reserves, something which is sustainable for a much longer period than the example given in the main text.

stable prices, full employment, growth, etc. In addition, flexible rates are supposed to reduce the pressure on the government to impose controls on either the movement of goods and services or capital. That is, flexible exchange rates should help to minimise the amount of protectionism in the world economy.

These claims have both been challenged by the experience with floating rates in the 1970s and 1980s. Artus and Young (1979) note that the same current account imbalances persisted after the widespread adoption of floating exchange rates in spite of exchange rate changes in the 'correct' direction. They argue that this cannot simply be put down to the large exogenous shocks which the world economy experienced in the 1970s. Instead, it must be the case that exchange rate changes have to be accompanied by other supporting factors. In particular, demand management policies must also be compatible with current account adjustment. In this respect, Artus and Young (1979, pp.662–3) argue that demand management policies in the period after 1973 were not generally directed towards improvements in the current account. This is not surprising given that one of the claims for floating exchange rates is that demand management policies can be directed towards internal goals. Moreover, exchange rate changes in themselves may no longer be very effective. Artus and Young (1979) argue that the reduction in money illusion has reduced the ability of exchange rate depreciations to alter relative prices. Depreciations may simply lead to further rounds of wage increases as workers are fully aware of the impact of depreciation on the domestic price level. Furthermore, changes in prices caused by exchange rate depreciations may not alter demand for the product. Artus and Young (1979, pp.665–6) give the example of Switzerland where the exchange rate by 1978 had appreciated by some 30–50% (since 1973). In spite of this, export volumes were still rising and demand for Swiss products was strong. They attribute this to the high quality goods produced which, because they have few substitutes, have very low price elasticities of demand. In other words, Swiss competitiveness is a consequence mainly of non-price factors. Similar arguments could be applied to German and Japanese exporters and may account for the persistent surpluses in those countries in spite of sustained exchange rate appreciation over the floating rate period (see Chapter 1).[3]

Dunn (1983, pp.12–13) argues that the evidence is not supportive of the claim that there is less pressure for protectionism in a floating regime. Whilst tariffs were lowered in the 1970s and 1980s through the various GATT rounds, this was also true in the 1950s and 1960s when exchange rates were fixed. Moreover, non-tariff barriers have tended to increase since the 1970s (Greenaway, 1983).

The second advantage which a country has if it adopts a floating exchange rate is monetary autonomy[4] and this can be seen using the Mundell–Fleming framework. With flexible exchange rates, monetary policy becomes more effective than fiscal policy. With a high degree of capital mobility, a fiscal expansion results in an exchange rate appreciation (because the domestic interest rate rises and capital flows in). This chokes off the expansionary impact of the fiscal policy on demand. By contrast, a monetary expansion is associated with a falling interest rate and hence a capital outflow. The ensuing exchange rate depreciation gives an added boost to

---

[3] See also Thirlwall and Gibson (1992) on why exchange rate changes may not always bring about an improvement in competitiveness. For an alternative view, see Krugman (1991a).
[4] See Friedman (1953), Johnson (1970) and Goldstein (1980).

aggregate demand thus ensuring that the monetary expansion is more effective than the fiscal expansion.

Thus flexible exchange rates allow a government to have an independent monetary policy. Not surprisingly for monetarists such as Friedman and Johnson, this is important, since it allows a country to adopt a constant growth monetary rule as a means of stabilising the economy. Under fixed exchange rates, the money supply becomes endogenous and hence beyond the control of the monetary authorities. We can see this by recalling the familiar identity:

$$HPM \equiv D + F \tag{4.1}$$

where HPM is high powered money; D is the domestic component (notes, coins and reserves held at the central bank by commercial banks); and F is the foreign component of the money supply. The latter alters every time the government intervenes in the foreign exchange markets. That is, F is changes in the level of foreign exchange reserves held at the central bank.

In order to see the intuition behind the identity given in (4.1), we can use the following example. Assume that we have a German exporter who is paid in dollars for his/her export. Assume further that the exporter wishes to exchange the dollars for Deutschmarks. This represents an additional demand for DMs and would cause the exchange rate to appreciate (*ceteris paribus*) if the exchange rate were floating. If the Deutschmark is fixed, then the Bundesbank has to step in and buy up the dollars, supplying Deutschmarks in their place. In this way, the domestic money supply has increased by an amount equal to the change in foreign exchange reserves (measured in DMs) held by the Bundesbank.

Thus whenever the central bank undertakes intervention in the foreign exchange market in order to maintain its exchange rate at parity, the domestic money supply is automatically altered. One way of delinking the total money supply from its foreign component is through sterilisation. In this example, as F is rising, the Bundesbank could at the same time sell bonds to the non–bank public thus reducing D. Overall, therefore, the money supply would remain the same. However, so the argument goes, sterilisation cannot continue for ever and hence an independent monetary policy is inconsistent with a fixed exchange rate. By contrast, with flexible exchange rates, foreign exchange reserves do not change (the central bank does not intervene) and hence the country can pursue a completely independent monetary policy.

The above arguments hold only if the government is willing to allow the exchange rate to move to whatever level is compatible with its monetary policy. The impact of capital flows on exchange rates is very powerful and this can lead to large effects on the real economy. The example of the UK during the period of monetary tightness from 1979–81 is instructive in this respect. In an attempt to reduce inflation, the UK government adopted monetary targets. The resulting large rise in the real interest rate caused a huge capital inflow. The impact was a sustained appreciation of the real exchange rate (the government at this time had completely abandoned any form of exchange rate management in keeping with their monetarist policies). The real effects of the exchange rate appreciation were large. The tradeables sector was badly affected by the fall in competitiveness and many manufacturing companies went bankrupt. By the time that monetary policy had eased and the exchange rate returned to a more 'normal' level, a significant part of the tradeables sector had disappeared. Thus conducting a monetary policy without regard for its impact on the exchange rate can have real effects by altering significantly the relative price of tradeables and nontradeables[5] Such arguments that monetary autonomy is limited even under flexible exchange rates because the government cannot be completely indifferent to the level of the exchange rate have been powerful in supporting the case of those in favour of the old-style European Monetary System. This is something to which we return in the following chapter.

The final advantage which flexible exchange rates are supposed to confer is insulation from external shocks. At its simplest, this argument states that the domestic economy is insulated from changes in demand for domestic exports because of foreign business cycles. A rise in foreign demand for domestic exports causes the exchange rate to appreciate and vice versa, thus ensuring no change in the domestic economy's income level. Similarly the domestic economy is protected from foreign inflation (or more generally a foreign monetary shock), which simply results in an exchange rate appreciation (recall the monetarist model of the balance of payments in Chapter 3).

At a theoretical level, these results have been challenged: the claims that floating exchange rates completely insulate the domestic economy have largely been abandoned. For example, in the two-country Mundell–Fleming model, a monetary expansion in one country leading to a rise in its income will cause a contraction of income in the other country. Thus the question now is whether flexible exchange rates are more or less successful at providing insulation for the domestic economy. The results are mixed and are highly dependent on whether the domestic economy is assumed to be a small economy; whether expectations are rational or adaptive; how the supply-side of the economy is modelled; and whether prices are flexible or sticky.[6] Not surprisingly models which are more monetarist in spirit still have the result that more insulation is provided by flexible exchange rate in the long run.[7] This result that even flexible exchange rates do not provide complete insulation is backed up by simulation results from global macroeconometric models. Bryant *et al.* (1989), for example, show that a contraction in the US in the late 1980s to reduce the fiscal and external deficits would have caused a fall in output in other industrialised countries. Moreover, Darby (1983) shows that pegged exchange rates do not necessarily imply that shocks are transmitted rapidly from one country to another, because countries manage to sterilise the impact of foreign monetary shocks fairly successfully.

Thus the claims for flexible exchange rates have proved to be exaggerated. The idea that flexible exchange rates would provide freedom for governments to pursue internal goals, monetary autonomy and act as an insulation mechanism against foreign shocks now appears rather optimistic. Neither governments nor private agents in the economy can be indifferent about what value the exchange rate assumes at any particular time. And this generates an uncertainty which is absent from the general equilibrium view – the level of the exchange rate in the future will be unknown. Such uncertainty generates a case for institutional arrangements which

---

[5] See Eltis and Sinclair (1981) for a number of articles which explore the impact of monetary policy on the exchange rate and the real sector.

[6] See, for example, Hool and Richardson (1983), Witte (1983), Taylor (1989) and various articles in Bryant *et al.* (1989) which consider the insulating properties of flexible versus fixed exchange rates, *inter alia*.

[7] Witte (1983), for example, provides a two-country model where a change in the rate of foreign monetary expansion will be transmitted to the domestic economy in the short run. In the long run, however, domestic inflation is returned to its original level, that is the domestic economy is insulted.

favour more exchange rate management. But, in addition, those who favour more intervention in foreign exchange markets point to other advantages to having more stable exchange rates. It is to these arguments that we now turn.

## The benefits of greater exchange rate fixity

Much of the early debate over the type of exchange rate system a country should adopt was rather polarised. That is, completely fixed exchange rates were contrasted with fully flexible rates (see, for example, Johnson, 1970; Friedman, 1953). However, some of the arguments which have been put forward are just as applicable to the case for greater exchange rate management. In the more recent literature, there are two distinct strands: the first polarises the debate even further by considering the case for moving beyond fixed exchange rates towards monetary union (De Grauwe, 1992; Torres and Giavazzi, 1993); the second concentrates on the benefits of having a target zone for the exchange rate (Williamson, 1983; Williamson and Miller, 1987). In this section we consider four arguments which have been put forward in favour of some degree of exchange rate intervention: the discipline argument; the need to reduce exchange rate volatility; the desire to eliminate misalignments; and, finally, the benefits of a single currency. All four of these arguments to a greater or lesser degree favour more or less management of the exchange rate. In the previous section, the favoured institutional arrangements were clear – a fully flexible exchange rate system. In this section, the arguments are more complex and encompass a wide variety of institutional arrangements from a loose target zone system to full monetary union. Each arrangement involves not only its own benefits, but also certain costs. In order to shed some light on the trade-offs involved in different types of system, we have to examine these costs and benefits in some detail. Many of the arguments we explore here are useful for our analysis of the experience of European monetary integration in the next chapter.

### The discipline hypothesis

The discipline hypothesis has two aspects which both suggest that greater exchange rate fixity helps to promote lower inflation. The first aspect is that flexible exchange rates tend to promote inflation, although the evidence for this is rather mixed as we shall see. The second aspect is that fixed exchange rates force countries to contain inflation and hence a credible disinflation strategy might involve a country fixing its exchange rate to a low inflation neighbour.

Flexible exchange rates are said to promote inflation because of downward price inflexibility (see Goldstein, 1980; Artus and Young, 1979; and Dunn, 1983). Depreciations of the exchange rate cause the domestic price level to increase as the price of imported consumer products and inputs rise. With fully flexible prices, appreciations should cause domestic prices to fall. However, in practice, domestic importers may simply prefer to keep the domestic price the same and reap the extra profit. This asymmetry, often called the 'ratchet effect' (Goldstein, 1980), will result in a net price increase which if it feeds through to wages can lead to an inflationary spiral.

Crockett and Goldstein (1976) have considered the validity of this hypothesis. At the theoretical level, they argue that a ratchet effect is unlikely. Exchange rate depreciations and appreciations tend to occur over the short run under flexible exchange rates. Hence for the inflationary effect to occur, it is necessary that short-run changes in the exchange rate have an immediate effect on real variables in the economy. They argue that this is highly unlikely: exchange rate changes are slow to operate on real economic activity. Their empirical evidence confirms this view. They find no evidence of any inflationary bias under flexible exchange rates.

The second aspect of the discipline hypothesis carries much more weight and indeed, as we shall see in the next chapter, forms one of the core arguments in favour of a country joining the exchange rate mechanism of the European Monetary System. A country which wishes to disinflate can choose to do so by fixing its exchange rate to a currency with a proven record of low inflation. Moreover, for reasons that we shall see, disinflation through fixing the exchange rate is sometimes thought to lower the costs (in terms of unemployment) which any disinflation strategy usually faces.

In order to understand how the disinflation strategy works, we can take the example of two countries (Germany and the UK, say). Assume that the UK is a high inflation country with a deficit on its currency account whereas Germany is a low inflation country with a surplus. Assume further that the two countries decide to fix their exchange rates against each other (and that realignments are impossible).

The German surplus will cause an incipient appreciation of the exchange rate implying that the German authorities have to intervene to sell Deutschmarks. In exchange for the Deutschmarks, they receive foreign currency. From the identity given in equation (4.1) this increases the foreign component of the money supply and hence the monetary base, leading to a multiple increase in Germany's broad money supply. This process would keep the exchange rate stable and help to reduce pressure on the exchange rate by expanding the economy. In the case of the UK, the reverse occurs. The deficit causes an incipient decrease in sterling. The UK authorities therefore have to buy pounds, foreign exchange reserves decline and with them the domestic money supply. As a result the UK economy disinflates and this also helps to restore equilibrium between the two countries.

This description suggests that the process is automatic (everything follows naturally from the exchange rate target) and symmetric (both countries have adjusted to restore equilibrium). However, this need not be the case. What happens if the German monetary authorities seek to sterilise the impact of the reserve change on their domestic money supply? In other words, at the point when the monetary authorities are selling Deutschmarks (and hence increasing the foreign component of the money supply), they intervene through, say, open market operations to sell bonds and reduce the money supply. Overall, therefore, the German money supply is unchanged.

What about the UK? The British monetary authorities could also sterilise to prevent their money supply from decreasing and the deflationary impact of the fixed exchange rate. To do this, they would have to buy back government bonds. However in the case of the UK (a deficit country) there are clear limits to sterilisation. For as long as the UK sterilises, its current account deficit persists and the authorities have to intervene in the foreign exchange markets. In other words, foreign exchange reserves are continuously being run down. Foreign exchange reserves are an exhaustible resource and hence sterilisation cannot occur indefinitely.

Such a constraint does not apply to the surplus country. Germany simply accumulates foreign exchange reserves.[8] The consequence is an inherent asymmetry within the system. The surplus country can retain a tight monetary policy while the deficit country is forced to adjust to the level of inflation in the surplus country. If it does

---

[8] Or, at least, the constraint is not as binding. In the long run, the government will be unwilling and possibly unable to sell bonds continually at the given price to its citizens, since the latter may not wish to save indefinitely.

not adjust, then the UK will face deteriorating competitiveness and eventually find it impossible to maintain the fixed exchange rate. This inherent asymmetry in fixed exchange rate systems takes the form of a disinflationary bias.

What about the costs of this route to disinflation? It is frequently argued that because an exchange rate target is more credible, disinflation will reap a credibility bonus which reduces the costs in terms of unemployment. This argument has been developed from work on credibility and monetary targets within a rational expectations Lucas surprise supply function framework (see, for example, Kydland and Prescott, 1977; Barro and Gordon, 1983). De Grauwe (1992) provides a graphical representation of Barro and Gordon's model and additionally modifies their analysis to examine the role of credibility and the costs of disinflation through a nominal exchange rate target. We follow this analysis closely here.

The analysis is conducted within an expectations-augmented Phillips curve diagram and it assumes two countries with identical Phillips curves. Government preferences about inflation and unemployment are represented through indifference curves. In general the indifference curves are concave to the origin: that is, as inflation declines, the authorities become less and less willing to accept higher unemployment to reduce inflation further. Additionally, indifference curves nearer to the origin have both less inflation and less unemployment and hence are preferred.

The shape of the indifference curves allows us to distinguish two kinds of governments. Firstly, there are hard-nosed governments who are tough on inflation and allow unemployment to increase substantially in order to reduce inflation. In Figure 4.2, the hard-nosed government's indifference curves are fairly flat: that is, in order to reduce inflation (by an amount, ab, say) the government is willing to accept a large

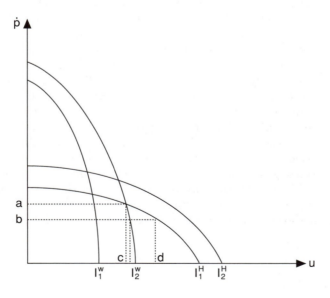

**Figure 4.2.** *Hard-nosed and wet-nosed governments*

increase in unemployment (from c to d).[9] Secondly, there are wet-nosed governments which are much softer on inflation and hence willing to accept quite a large increase in inflation in order to reduce unemployment. Wet-nosed governments have much steeper indifferent curves.[10]

Given these two sets of preferences, we can establish equilibrium in these two economies: hard-nosed and wet-nosed. This is shown in Figure 4.3 which includes, in addition to the indifference curves, short-run Phillips curves ($PC_1$ etc) and a long-run vertical Phillips curve (LRPC). Since the structures of the economies are the same, the only thing which differs between the two countries in Figure 4.3 are the indifference curves. We show that the wet-nosed government equilibrium (point W) has a higher level of inflation than the hard-nosed equilibrium (point H).

In Figure 4.3, both governments have an incentive to cheat on the zero-inflation natural rate of unemployment outcome given at point A. Point A is on indifference curve $I_2$ for both governments ($I^H_2$ for the hard-nosed government and $I^W_2$ for the wet-nosed government). $PC_1$ shows the short-run trade-off which is available to each government. Point A, however, is not an equilibrium. Both governments have an incentive to cheat and hence a policy rule (say a monetary growth rule) which maintains the economy at point A cannot be considered credible. The wet-nosed government can reach a higher indifference curve ($I^W_1$) by inflating the economy and moving to point C.[11] The hard-nosed government will have an incentive to move to point B (on indifference curve, $I^H_1$). Not surprisingly, the government which cares about unemployment more is willing to move to a higher level of inflation to get the benefits in terms of lower unemployment.

The two economies will not stay at points B and C. Inflationary expectations are still zero yet inflation in both countries has increased. In the next period, agents in the economies realise that inflation has increased and hence adjust their expectations accordingly. In other words, the benefits from cheating will be offset by costs as both governments end up back on the long-run Phillips curve (LRPC) at the natural rate of unemployment but with a higher level of inflation. It is easy to show that the hard-nosed government will end up at H, whilst the wet-nosed government will end up at W. Points W and H are both equilibria for each government for the following reasons. Firstly, as they are on the long-run Phillips curve, actual inflation is equal to expected inflation. Secondly, the indifference curves ($I^H_3$ and $I^W_3$) are both tangential to the short-run Phillips curves $PC_2$ and $PC_3$ at points H and W and hence there is no incentive for further cheating by either government.

We can use this analysis to examine what happens when the two governments decide to fix their exchange rate. In particular, De Grauwe asks whether a nominal exchange rate target is any more credible than the monetary growth rule we have considered. He concludes that it may not be since fixing the exchange rate may not lead to the wet-nosed government gaining credibility because it always has the incentive to engineer a surprise devaluation. We illustrate this result in Figure 4.4.

---

[9]  We can note that in the extreme, a government which cares only about inflation will have a horizontal indifference curve.

[10]  If we take the extreme position, then a government which cares only about unemployment will have vertical indifference curves.

[11]  This expansion would have to take the form of a surprise monetary expansion: recall that in a Lucas surprise supply framework, output can only exceed its natural rate if prices are higher than expected.

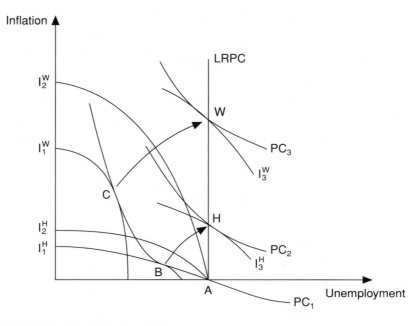

**Figure 4.3.** *The incentive to cheat*

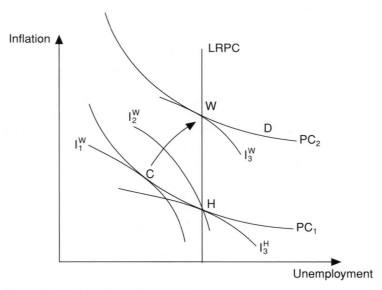

**Figure 4.4.** *Fixing the exchange rate*

We represent the hard-nosed government by Germany and the wet-nosed one by the UK. Germany has a lower level of inflation and its economy is at H. By contrast, the UK economy is located at W. If the UK government fixes its exchange rate to the German one, then as we argued above its inflation rate will converge on that of Germany's. That is, the economy will move towards H (which is on a higher indifference curve, $I^W_2$ instead of $I^W_3$).

Is this credible? Can the UK government convince agents in the economy that it can stay at point H? De Grauwe argues that there is an incentive for the UK government to cheat at H by engineering a surprise devaluation. The surprise devaluation increases inflation unexpectedly and hence the UK economy moves to C, on a higher indifference schedule still. Of course, in the long run there are costs as the economy ends up back at W once expectations have adjusted. De Grauwe concludes that the fixed exchange rate rule is no more credible than a monetary growth rule.[12] This has strong implications for the costs of disinflation within this framework. A credible policy can imply that the high inflation country move from W to H without much increase in unemployment. This occurs because inflationary expectations adjust immediately to those given by $PC_2$: workers thus reduce their nominal wage claims immediately the economy moves to H. By contrast, if the disinflating government does not have credibility, then disinflation will be costly. Agents will not believe that inflation is going to fall and hence they will not alter their wage bargaining behaviour. The result can be a large increase in unemployment as the economy moves from W to H via a point such as D.

De Grauwe's conclusion that a nominal exchange rate target is no more credible than a monetary target is rather a strong one. As De Grauwe himself recognises, it can be argued that there are good reasons why an exchange rate target might more easily gain credibility than a monetary target. If this is so, then disinflation through a nominal exchange rate target may result in lower costs. Exchange rate targets are more visible and hence politicians tend to lose face if they either devalue their exchange rate or leave a fixed exchange rate system altogether. Missing monetary targets, by contrast, is much more opaque. The political cost of devaluation has long been recognised. Goldstein (1980), for example, quotes some evidence from Cooper who conducted a study of devaluations in 36 developing countries. He found that 30% of governments fell within a year of devaluation compared with 14% in the control group (where no devaluation occurred). Finance ministers fared even worse: 60% resigned or were sacked compared with 18% in the control group. Whilst this study examined developing countries, anecdotal evidence suggests that devaluation can often have political costs in industrial countries: the UK experience in 1992 is a good case in point. For this reason, it is often argued that disinflating through a nominal exchange rate target can be more credible and hence the costs of disinflation will be less.

We examine the empirical validity of this conclusion in the next chapter. What is important for our purposes here is that greater exchange rate management might allow these benefits of greater discipline to be realised. Note, however, that the institutional arrangements which generate these benefits must be strong enough to give the country credibility. A very loose form of exchange rate management is unlikely to confer the benefits discussed here.

## Volatility and uncertainty

It is often argued that flexible exchange rates, because they are more volatile, generate more uncertainty and hence can reduce the volume of trade. In Chapter 1, we noted that exchange rate volatility had been a prominent feature of the floating period and each of the theories of exchange rate determination discussed in Chapter 3 provide their own rationale for the phenomenon.

---

[12] We can note that De Grauwe (1992) notes that only through giving up its currency can the UK's policy become fully credible. That is, the UK has to enter a monetary union with Germany.

The point made by those who favour more intervention in foreign exchange markets is that exchange rate volatility results in costs. Artus and Young (1979) point to three costs. Firstly, exchange rate instability means that exporters and importers become uncertain about the price at which their goods will sell. Hence it becomes more difficult to plan output and firms will be more reluctant to engage in foreign trade. Secondly, foreign direct or long-term foreign investment might also decline. Companies are reluctant to undertake foreign direct investment which happens to be profitable at the current exchange rate if they cannot be certain that the exchange rate will remain there. Finally, sudden changes in the value of reserve currencies can be problematic. Artus and Young (1979, pp.683–4) point to the weakness of the dollar in 1978. This resulted in every country experiencing a change in an important bilateral exchange rate. Moreover, it gave an incentive for those holding dollars as a reserve currency to diversify their holdings and leave themselves less open to movements in the value of one currency.

It is usually argued by supporters of flexible exchange rates (Johnson, 1970) that the first source of uncertainty can be eliminated, or at least significantly reduced, through use of the forward market. Indeed empirical studies which seek to determine the impact of exchange rate uncertainty on international trade have not found any effect.[13] However, the forward market is developed only for certain foreign exchange markets. Smaller developed countries or developing countries might be more severely affected because their forward markets are thin and thus forward cover can often be expensive.[14] The costs of forward cover can also be expensive for small/-medium firms; larger firms, by contrast, are better able to manage the currency composition of their assets and liabilities. The effects on long-term foreign investment are even more difficult to measure. However, it might be expected *a priori* that, since such long-term projects cannot be covered in the forward market, uncertainty due to exchange rate instability might well be a problem.

Volatility might be a particular problem if it results in the exchange rate becoming misaligned (that is, moving away from its fundamental long-run equilibrium level for a period). If Frankel and Froot's (1987; 1990) model of noise trading and the role of chartists versus fundamentalists has some validity,[15] then excessive volatility of exchange rates could lead to them moving away from their equilibrium level. The costs of this are considered in the next section.

Clearly volatility can be substantially reduced even by a loose form of exchange rate management. It will obviously be completely eliminated if monetary union is adopted. Thus the problem of volatility and the uncertainty it generates provides a case for all degrees of foreign exchange market intervention.

*Exchange rate misalignments and the case for exchange rate management*

In Chapter 1 we noted that exchange rates in the floating period have not only been volatile, but have also exhibited a tendency to large swings. Williamson (1983) argues that this is because floating exchange rates have a tendency to persistent departures from long-run equilibrium (what he terms, misalignments).

To substantiate his claim, Williamson calculates the fundamental equilibrium exchange rate (FEER). The FEER is that exchange rate which would have been

---

[13] See, for example, Hooper and Kohlhagen (1978) and McCulloch (1983).

[14] Williamson (1983) for example quotes some evidence that suggest that volatility has much larger negative effects on developing countries international trade.

[15] We discussed their model in Chapter 3.

required to ensure that at any point in time the current account imbalance equals the underlying capital account, where the latter is determined by examining the savings investment relationship within the domestic economy. If savings are greater than investment, then a country will export capital (that is have a capital account surplus). By contrast a country will import capital if it has a high rate of investment relative to domestic savings. Given the figures for the capital account, the IMF multilateral exchange rate model is then used to calculate an appropriate exchange rate which generates a current account position of equal and opposite sign to the capital account. That is, if the country has a capital account deficit, then the FEER must be such that a current account surplus is generated (see Box 4.2).

---

### Box 4.2.    The Calculation of FEERs

Williamson (1983) calculates the FEERs which he uses to argue that misalignments were large in the 1980s in the following way. He initially derives a FEER for 1976–77, by asking what exchange rate was required to ensure that at the time the current account imbalance of any country was equal to its underlying capital account. The latter is dependent on the relationship between domestic savings and domestic investment. Take the case where investment exceeds domestic savings. This implies that the country will require capital inflows (an underlying capital account surplus). The capital account surplus generates the need for a current account deficit for equilibrium on the balance of payments and this suggests an appropriate exchange rate, the FEER.

In practice, therefore, Williamson estimates target values for the current account by examining the relationship between domestic savings and domestic investment in any particular country. The FEER, the exchange rate which will generate the currency account position, is then derived from the IMF's multilateral exchange rate model. In this model, the current balance is assumed to be a function of not only the real effective exchange rate (the FEER), but also the terms of trade and the relative pressure of demand. Hence we can solve for the real effective exchange rate needed to produce a given current account balance under the assumption that demand pressures were normal (that is, the country was neither in a boom nor a recession). For most countries 1976–77 represent a period of normal demand levels and hence provide a good base.

Having derived a FEER for 1976–77, figures for 1983 are calculated by extrapolation taking into account what exogenous shocks would have implied for each exchange rate in the intervening period. Williamson argues that there are potentially several developments which would have affected the FEERs between 1976–77 and 1983: the second oil price rise; the UK becoming self-sufficient in oil; the emergence of the US as a large capital importer; and, more generally, differential productivity growth. For example, the effects of the second oil price rise on the UK was to cause the sterling FEER to appreciate since the UK became a major oil exporter in the early 1980s. The effect of differential productivity growth causes Williamson to allow the FEER for Japan to appreciate by 1% per year.

The results, as we note in the main text, suggest that in 1983 the US dollar was 18% overvalued relative to its FEER; sterling was 11% overvalued and the yen and the Deutschmark were undervalued by 6% and 4% respectively.

Using this methodology, Williamson calculates that in 1983 misalignments were rather large: the dollar was 18% overvalued relative to its FEER; the UK was 11% overvalued; and the yen and the Deutschmark were undervalued by 6% and 4% respectively. Clearly the measurement of misalignment is crucially dependent on the assumptions required to generate estimates of the FEER. However, the size of the misalignments in the case of the dollar and sterling indicate that there could be quite a bit of measurement error in deriving the FEER, yet these currencies could still be misaligned.

If we accept that exchange rates can become misaligned, then what are the costs? Williamson (1983) argues that long periods of overvaluation or undervaluation cause changes in the price of tradeables relative to nontradeables. Take, for example, a period of extended overvaluation. Export industries become uncompetitive and labour and capital are released from those uses. If capital is malleable and labour homogeneous, then these resources could simply be employed in the nontradeables sector. However, in reality, labour cannot be redeployed easily without training; and capital is often scrapped. Overvaluation thus usually implies unemployment and underutilisation of capital resources. In severe cases, such as occurred in the UK and US in the early 1980s, it can lead to the phenomenon of deindustrialisation. That is, overvaluation actually drives firms out of business and, when the exchange rate misalignment is reduced, the company no longer exists to take advantage of the increased competitiveness.

If misalignment persists and periods of overvaluation are followed by undervaluation, then misalignment can also increase uncertainty. Investment in export industries becomes increasingly risky, since it may be the case that exchange rate changes will make the investment uncompetitive for long periods.

Dunn (1983, p.10) also points to the effect of misalignment on long-term debt accumulated in foreign currencies. He gives the example of a Canadian company which has borrowed in US dollars to finance a long-term project. If the real exchange rate remains constant, then the capital gain on the asset (purchased by the loan) will be exactly offset by any change in the domestic currency value of the foreign liability (the dollar debt). Assume, for example, that prices in Canada increase by 10% relative to US prices (which are constant) over the period of the loan. This means that the Canadian company experiences a capital gain of 10% on the assets purchased. If the real exchange rate is to remain constant, then the nominal exchange rate must depreciate by 10% relative to the US dollar. Hence the Canadian dollar value of the companies debt will rise by 10%. In other words, the Canadian company has experienced a rise in both its liabilities and assets by 10%. The increased debt burden can be offset by the rise in its assets. By contrast, if real exchange rates change a lot, then foreign borrowing to finance domestic investment can be risky. Indeed, a real depreciation of the exchange rate will cause the domestic value of foreign liabilities to increase without a corresponding increase in the domestic value of assets. In this case, heavy losses will ensue.

Thus the costs of misalignment lead Williamson (1983) and Williamson and Miller (1987) to argue that case for managed exchange rates where the monetary authorities seek to keep the nominal exchange rate within a target zone, defined as 10% on either side of the FEER. The 10% banks allow for possible errors in calculating the FEER. If the FEER proves difficult to estimate and large errors are made, then more tightly defined target zones may not reduce the degree of misalignment. Hence the exact institutional arrangements suggested by this problem depend on the empirical issue of our ability to measure the FEER.

*The advantages of a single currency: the optimal currency area literature and economic and monetary union*

The benefits of a single currency within any country are that (Johnson, 1970, p.201):

> it simplifies the profit-maximizing computations of producers and traders, facilitates competition among producers located in different parts of the country, and promotes the integration of the economy into a connected series of markets, these markets including both the markets for products and the markets for the factors of production (capital and labour).

It is therefore tempting to argue that if fixed exchange rates were adopted between nations, all these benefits would follow. Even with some form of exchange rate management, some of these benefits might be realised if the system is associated with the emergence of one currency in which trade is conducted (as we noted in Chapter 1). If a single currency is issued in the place of national currencies, there will be the additional welfare gains associated with a reduction in transactions costs associated with having to exchange one currency for another. These benefits would be greater the larger the amount of intra-monetary union trade. However, there are costs to having a single currency, not least the loss of exchange rate and monetary policy. The optimal currency area literature[16] seeks to balance these benefits and costs and examines the conditions under which countries are more likely to experience a net benefit from having a single currency. In particular, this literature addresses the question of what sort of countries should join together to form a single currency area. In this section, we want to consider some of the theoretical arguments within this literature. In this way we can highlight some of the trade-offs that are involved in choosing the exact form which institutionalised exchange rate management could take.

The adoption of a single currency clearly eliminates the possibility of using the exchange rate as a policy instrument to rectify external disequilibria. We can illustrate the implications of this by means of the following example. Take a country such as Scotland, which is an important oil producer and assume that there is a shock which takes the form of a fall in the price of oil. If Scotland were not part of a monetary union, then the shock would lead to a deficit on its current account. There are two ways in which it could attempt to restore equilibrium. It could deflate and the resulting reduction in domestic prices and wages would make it more competitive in other tradeable goods areas and restore equilibrium. Alternatively, it could devalue or allow its exchange rate to depreciate. This also reduces real wages but this method is attractive because it spreads adjustment more evenly (all workers experience a reduction in their real wage). And it copes with the co-ordination problems which might arise in actually engineering an across-the-board reduction – workers individually may be unable to signal their willingness to accept lower real wages. Moreover, deflation will create unemployment if wages and prices are sticky. What happens if Scotland is part of a monetary union? A devaluation or depreciation of the exchange rate is no longer an option and hence the economy will go into recession. Scotland may no longer have a balance of payments problem, but instead has a regional problem within the UK monetary union.

The optimal currency area literature points to three factors which might mitigate the cost of losing exchange rate policy. These are a high degree of factor mobility, openness and product diversification. Firstly, with respect to factor mobility,

---

[16] See, for example, Fleming (1971), Corden (1972), Mundell (1961), Kenen (1969) and McKinnon (1963). Ishiyama (1975) provides a useful survey. For a more up-to-date survey of the literature see De Grauwe (1992).

Mundell (1961) argues that the greater the mobility of capital and labour the lower the costs joining a monetary union. He considers an asymmetric microeconomic demand disturbance which increases demand for the products of, say, region A and decreases demand for the products of region B. If wages and prices are sticky in a downwards direction, the reduction in demand in region B causes unemployment. In region A, by contrast, there is an excess demand for labour and the potential for inflation. One solution to the problem is simply for the unemployed workers to move to region B in the monetary union where labour is wanted. This eliminates both the unemployment problem in region B and the inflationary pressure in region A. Hence the more mobile are factors of production, the smaller the costs of joining a monetary union.

McKinnon (1963) suggests that the loss of the exchange rate is less costly, the more open an economy is. The argument is simple. In an economy which is very open, exchange rate changes are less effective at improving competitiveness because money illusion is low. As we argued earlier, exchange rate devaluations improve competitiveness because the real wage falls (due to the increase in the price of imported goods which feeds into the domestic price level). However, in an open economy, workers are more aware that devaluations increase the domestic price level and hence they demand nominal wage increases to offset the effect. Thus the gain in competitiveness induced by the exchange rate change is quickly eroded. McKinnon concludes that highly open economies have only low costs to joining a monetary union.[17]

The third mitigating factor is the degree of product diversification. Consider a microeconomic demand disturbance caused by a decrease in demand for one product which the country exports (Kenen, 1969). If product diversification is high, then this decline in demand affects only one product amongst many and the consequences for the economy, even although it has no ability to change the exchange rate, are rather insignificant.

The second major cost of monetary union is that the ability to conduct an individual monetary policy is lost because monetary policy is directed from the centre rather than by individual member countries. This has led a number of economists to argue that the more similar inflation rates are between potential members of the monetary union, the more appropriate the adoption of a single currency will be (Haberler, 1964; Fleming, 1971). Indeed more generally Ingram (1973) argues that the closer the degree of policy integration generally at the macroeconomic level, the more easy it is to form a monetary union. In other words, the more countries want to reduce inflation differentials *as their own objective* and the more willing they are to co-ordinate policy, the less is given up when independent monetary policy is relinquished.

In conclusion, the optimal currency area literature takes a relatively sophisticated view of deciding the area in which a single currency should circulate. If the net benefits are to be maximised, then the countries which join together should have similar policy goals and macroeconomic performance and should conduct a lot of trade with each other. Our discussion here has illustrated that the choice of institutional

---

[17] Such an argument assumes workers are never willing to accept a real wage cut. If they are, then devaluation might be a way of bringing that about without encountering the co-ordination problems which might arise if the real wage cut had to be engineered in each specific bargaining agreement. Moreover, devaluation has the added attraction that relativities are unaltered and hence may make real wage cuts more acceptable.

arrangements for exchange rate management affects not only the degree to which the benefits of management/fixity can be realised but also that different systems may have different costs. Having highlighted the costs associated with full monetary union, we now turn to look at problems which might arise from looser forms of exchange rate management.

**Exchange rate management: operation and problems**

The experience with floating exchange rates and, in particular, their failure to deliver all the benefits promised led many industrial countries to adopt increasing intervention to manage their exchange rates. The European Monetary System set up in 1979 represents one of the more formal attempts at monetary integration. Less formal arrangements involve the Group of Seven countries and their management of the dollar *vis-à-vis* the Deutschmark and the yen in the later 1980s (after the so-called Plaza and Louvre agreements – see Box 4.1). These experiences with exchange rate management have led to various models about how managed exchange rates behave and the problems which the authorities might face in maintaining an exchange rate within a band or zone.

In this section, we want to review some of this literature. We begin with the issue of target zones and how an exchange rate within a target zone is supposed to behave. We then go on to discuss the problem of speculative attacks in fixed or managed exchange rate regimes.

*Exchange rate target zones*

Flood and Garber (1991) describe a target zone as a compromise between fixed and floating exchange rates. Explicit margins are set for exchange rate fluctuations and while the exchange rate is within the bands, policy can be directed at the domestic economy;[18] when the exchange rate reaches the outer limits of the band, then intervention and policy changes are required to keep it within the bands.

The motivation for the growing literature on target zones reflects the increased importance of exchange rate management in the international monetary system. Williamson's (1983) influential work on exchange rate misalignments and volatility (which we have already discussed) argued in favour of setting target zones for the major international currencies. The theoretical literature which we are about to examine has therefore grown out of the policy proposals which surrounded disillusionment with floating exchange rates.

The main concern of the literature on target zones[19] is how the exchange rate might be expected to behave when agents know that it is being kept within bands. The key result of the literature is that the existence of a target zone will alter expectations within the zone. In particular, a change in fundamentals which might normally have led to a 10% change in the exchange rate will now have a smaller effect on the exchange rate. Hence an exchange rate operating within a target zone is expected to exhibit less volatility than a freely floating exchange rate. And exchange rate expectations, if the zone is fully credible, lie within the target zone bands.

Krugman (1991a) provides the basic model of exchange rate behaviour within a target zone. The actual exchange rate is a linear function of fundamentals and the expected future exchange rate. In Krugman's model, the fundamentals included the money supply and velocity:

---

[18] This implies that there is some monetary independence within a target zone, something which can make it rather attractive to governments who want to maintain some control over monetary policy.

[19] See Krugman (1991a); Flood *et al.* (1991); Frankel and Phillips (1991) and the various articles in Krugman and Miller (1992). Svensson (1992) provides a very clear and interesting survey.

$$s = m + v + \gamma E(ds)/dt \qquad\qquad (4.2)$$

where s is the spot exchange rate; m is the domestic money supply; v represents shocks arising from changes in velocity; and E(ds)/dt is the expected rate of depreciation. All variables are in logarithms. Equation (4.2) states the familiar flexible-price monetary model propositions that: (a) if the money supply rises, then the excess supply of money will generate a balance of payments deficit and hence the exchange rate will depreciate (s will rise); (b) if money demand rises, velocity falls, then an excess demand for money will ensue leading to a balance of payments surplus and an exchange rate appreciation (s will fall). In addition to these fundamentals, the expected change in the exchange rate will also affect that actual exchange rate by an amount determined by $\gamma$. We can note that fundamentals could easily be expanded to include variables such as relative outputs, relative money supplies, domestic and foreign interest rates, etc.

Krugman makes two key assumptions. Firstly, the target zone is assumed to be completely credible. That is agents do not believe that the exchange rate will ever move outside its bands. Secondly, the central bank intervenes only at the margins (that is, when the exchange rate reaches its outer limits). We examine the implications of relaxing those assumptions later on.

The money supply is assumed to be under the control of the central bank and they change m in order to keep the exchange rate within its bands. Thus m is increased when the exchange rate reaches the lower limit and decreased when it reach its upper limit. In other words, the central bank does not sterilise the automatic change in the money supply that results from its intervention in the foreign exchange market. When the exchange rate is within the band, the money supply is constant (this follows from our assumption about central bank intervention). Velocity, v, by contrast, is an exogenous stochastic variable which cannot be controlled by the central bank. It is assumed to follow a continuous time random walk (Brownian motion without drift).

Figure 4.5 illustrates the relationship between the exchange rate and the fundamentals under floating exchange rates (FF) and when the exchange rate is within a target zone (TT). Under floating exchange rates, the money supply is constant, and

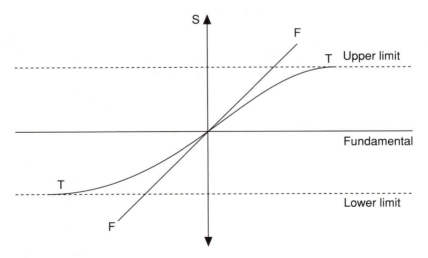

**Figure 4.5.** *Exchange rate behaviour in a target zone model*

hence the exchange rate will only change with shocks to velocity. This is represented by the schedule FF in Figure 4.5. FF is a 45° line: a 10% increase in the fundamentals (velocity) leads to a 10% increase in the spot exchange rate (a 10% depreciation). Since velocity follows a continuous time random walk, so also will the exchange rate.[20] To put it another way, the exchange rate will always be equal to the fundamental. The intuition for this is as follows. If the exchange rate follows a continuous time random walk without drift, then the expected rate of depreciation will be equal to zero. We can see this from the following equations. If the exchange rate follows a random walk, then:

$$s_t = s_{t-1} + e_t$$
$$=> \Delta s_t = e_t \tag{4.3}$$

Hence the expected change in the exchange rate is given by:

$$E(\Delta s_t) = E(e_t) \tag{4.4}$$

where $e_t$ is a serially uncorrelated error with zero mean. Thus with the money supply constant and the last term in equation (4.2) equal to zero, s will depend linearly on v alone. Hence the exchange rate will depend linearly on velocity alone.

The TT schedule represents the relationship between the exchange rate and the fundamentals under a target zone. The relationship has two characteristics. Firstly, the slope of the TT schedule is always less than 1, implying that a 1% change in fundamentals leads to a less than 1% change in the spot exchange rate. To understand the intuition, assume that the exchange rate is close to its upper band (that is, it is weak). The exchange rate is more likely to appreciate (recall that the system is credible). In this case, the domestic currency will be at a forward premium reflecting expectations of an appreciation. Expectations of an appreciation cause the actual exchange rate to appreciate (from equation (4.2)). Hence for a given increase in velocity when the exchange rate is close to its upper limit, the actual exchange rate change will be less. In other words, s rises but by less than the rise in v because of the offsetting effect of exchange rate expectations (see equation (4.2)). Thus the spot exchange rate departs from its fundamental determinant because the expected depreciation of the exchange rate becomes non-zero.

An exactly symmetric situation exists at the lower band. As the exchange rate approaches its lower band, exchange rate expectations will become positive (that is a depreciation is expected). Thus a 1% decline in fundamentals will lead to a less than 1% change in the spot exchange rate. This effect is known in the literature as the 'honeymoon effect' since it implies that in a credible target zone exchange rate expectations will act as a stabilising influence and keep the exchange rate within its bands without the need for intervention. This accounts for the result that the exchange rate is less volatile in a target zone.

The second characteristic of the TT schedule is that its slope tends to zero at the edges of the band. This is known as the 'smooth-pasting' result and it implies complete independence between the exchange rate and its fundamentals at the limits of the target zone. Taking the example of the upper band we can provide the intuition for this as follows. First, we can note that at the edges of the bands the expected

---

[20] Svensson (1992) notes that this is an attractive assumption since it is compatible with the empirical work of Meese and Rogoff (1983) which suggests that the exchange rate follows a random walk.

change in the fundamental must become suddenly non-zero. In other words, there is a jump in the expected change in the fundamental. Recall that within the band, the fundamental follows a continuous time random walk and the expected change in the fundamental is zero. At the upper limit, however, the expected change in the fundamental suddenly becomes negative, because the fundamental can either remain at the edge or decrease (as the government intervenes to reduce the money supply). We can see this by noting that the expected change in the fundamentals is given by:

$$E\Delta(m + v) = E(\Delta m) + E(\Delta v) \tag{4.5}$$

$E(\Delta v)$ is zero since if $v_t$ is a continuous time random walk, then:

$$v_t = v_{t-1} + e_t$$
$$=> \Delta v_t = e_t$$
$$=> E(\Delta v_t) = 0 \text{ since } E(e_t) = 0 \tag{4.6}$$

Thus the expected change in the fundamentals at the limit is equal to the expected change in the money supply which becomes negative because of government intervention in the foreign exchange market. Hence we get a jump in expectations regarding the fundamentals: before we reach the upper limit, the expected change is zero (since m is constant and $E(\Delta v)$ is zero); at the limit the expected change become negative.

Secondly, there can be no jump in the expected change in the exchange rate, because the actual exchange rate cannot jump. The actual exchange rate is a linear function of two continuous variables: the fundamental and the expected rate of depreciation of the spot exchange rate. If the actual exchange rate is a continuous variable, then the expected change in the exchange rate must also be a continuous variable. Thus the jump in the expected change in the fundamentals can have no effect on the actual exchange rate since the latter is a function only of continuous variables. It would be inconsistent with our theory if the actual exchange rate jumped and hence it cannot. In this way, the exchange rate must become insensitive to the fundamental at the upper limit (that is, TT has a zero slope) – the exchange rate and the fundamental become delinked.

One can incorporate some interesting extensions to the model. Firstly, Krugman (1991a), in his original paper, considers what happens if the target zone is less than fully credible. This extension requires the inclusion of a time-varying risk of realignment in the model. The expected rate of depreciation of the exchange rate (in equation (4.2)) now becomes a weighted average of the expected rate of realignment (that is, the change in the central parity) and the expected change in the exchange rate relative to its central parity (that is, the expected rate of depreciation within the band). Figure 4.6 illustrates what happens. With less than full credibility Krugman (1991a) shows that the TT schedule still has a slope of less than one, but it is steeper than the full credibility TT schedule. Thus as the exchange rate reaches the upper limit at $f^*$, one of two things can happen. Either the government defends the exchange rate and hence the exchange rate will jump back into the band onto the full credibility TT schedule (to A). Or the zone is not defended and the exchange rate will jump onto the free floating FF schedule (to B). Thus less than full credibility regimes still offer greater exchange rate stability (that is, the honeymoon characteristic is still present), but at the limits, the exchange rate can jump (that is, the smooth pasting condition no longer holds).

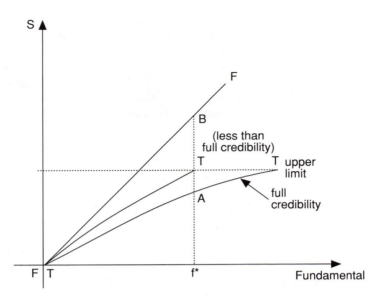

**Figure 4.6.**  *A less than credible target zone*

A second possible extension is to consider what happens if intramarginal interventions are allowed. That is, the central bank can intervene when the exchange rate is within the band, not just at the limits. The result of this modification is that the relationship between the exchange rate and the fundamentals within the bands becomes less S-shaped than the TT schedule in Figure 4.5.[21] This occurs because intervention is occurring even in the middle of the bands, and hence the exchange rate behaves less like a free float even within the bands (not just at the edges).

A final extension is to ask whether the width of the bands is important. Delgado and Dumas (1992) show that changing the width of the bands has implications for the degree of interest rate volatility which we might expect to see accompanying a target zone. The general result is that a target zone increases the extent to which interest rate volatility will occur: instead of allowing the exchange rate to move outside certain limits, the government alters the money supply and hence the interest rate. Delgado and Dumas show, not surprisingly, that the wider the bands, the lower the amount of interest rate instability. Symmetrically, a narrowing of the bands ensures that volatility in the fundamentals will translate into greater interest rate volatility provided the exchange rate remains within the bands.

Empirical tests of the basic Krugman model have not tended to be supportive. The target zone model suggests that exchange rates should be nonlinearly related to fundamentals. Flood *et al.* (1991) plot EMS exchange rates against a derived fundamental.[22] The graphs show that the relationships appear to be linear, not what one would expect if one accepts that the ERM is close to a target zone system. One possible explanation is that the target zone is less than credible and that the degree of

---

[21]  In particular, it becomes more linear with nonlinearities only at the edges.

[22]  The fundamental is estimated as the actual spot rate minus the expected rate of depreciation (given by the interest rate differential). In other words, uncovered interest parity is assumed to hold.

credibility changed over time. Frankel and Phillips (1991) argue that the ERM of the later 1980s conformed more closely to Krugman's model than that of the early 1980s. They suggest that this is evidence of greater credibility.[23] One problem with testing the target zone model is that any test involves a joint hypothesis. Rejection can result either because the basic target zone idea is wrong or because the fundamental model chosen is inappropriate.

If target zones are not credible, then they face a major problem which all fixed (or semi-fixed) exchange rate systems face, namely the potential for speculative attacks. Indeed Flood and Garber (1991) examine the relationship between speculative attacks and target zone models. Their paper is essentially a technical contribution in that they seek to show that target zone models are the mirror image of speculative attack models. In doing so, they also discuss how a target zone could suffer from a speculative attack. We now turn to the literature which discusses this problem.

*Speculative attacks*

The speculative crisis literature owes its roots, like the target zone literature, to Paul Krugman. Krugman (1979) presents a deterministic model of balance of payments crises under fixed exchange rates.[24] The central result of the model is that in a situation where the central bank has finite reserves and it is creating domestic credit at a constant rate, the fixed exchange rate regime will break down following a speculative run. Flood and Garber (1984) and Obstfeld (1986) both extended the basic Krugman model to the stochastic case where there is uncertainty about the rate at which credit is expanding. Whilst the timing of the speculative run now becomes uncertain, the central result that the regime will break down still holds.

Blackburn and Sola (1993) use the following equations to illustrate the structure of these models. We start with the deterministic case, where speculators have perfect foresight.

$$M_t/P_t = \alpha_0 - \alpha_1 i_t \qquad \alpha_0, \alpha_1 > 0 \tag{4.3}$$

Equation (4.3) represents money market equilibrium. It states that the real money supply (M/P) is equal to real money demand (which depends only on interest rates, i). The t-subscripts refer to time.

$$P_t = S_t P^* \tag{4.4}$$

that is, purchasing power parity holds. P and $P^*$ are the domestic and foreign price level respectively; S is the exchange rate.

$$i_t = i^* + \dot{S}_t/S_t \tag{4.5}$$

Equation (4.5) is uncovered interest parity (UIP) where $i^*$ is the foreign interest rate (assumed constant) and $\dot{S}_t/S_t$ is the expected rate of domestic currency depreciation.

$$M_t \equiv D_t + F_t \tag{4.6}$$

The money supply is defined as domestic credit (D) and the value of foreign currency reserves (F).

$$D_t = \mu \qquad \mu > 0 \tag{4.7}$$

[23] We can note that Flood *et al.* (1991) would probably disagree with Frankel and Phillips (1991). The former note that from their results, there is not even any support for the target zone model from the DM–Guilder exchange rate. They argue that this exchange rate target zone did not lack credibility and that it should have behaved as the Krugman model suggests.

[24] By deterministic, we imply there is no uncertainty. Speculators therefore have perfect foresight and hence we can pinpoint the timing of the attack precisely.

Domestic credit is assumed to be growing at a constant exogenous rate equal to $\mu$. Partner domestic credit, by contrast, we will assume to be constant.

Using these, we can show that excessive domestic credit creation will be reflected in a loss of reserves. If we take equation (4.3) and substitute in from equation (4.4) for $P_t$ and then substitute in for $i$ from equation (4.5) we can derive:

$$M_t / P_t = \alpha_0 - \alpha_1 i \tag{4.3}$$

$$\Rightarrow M_t / S_t P^* = \alpha_0 - \alpha_1 (i^* + \dot{S}_t / S_t)$$

Multiplying through by $S_t P^*$ and rearranging gives us equation (4.8):

$$\Rightarrow M_t = \alpha_0 S_t P^* - \alpha_1 i^* S_t P^* - \alpha_1 \dot{S}_t P^*$$

$$\Rightarrow M_t = \beta_0 S_t - \beta_1 \dot{S}_t \tag{4.8}$$

$$\text{where } \beta_0 = (\alpha_0 - \alpha_1 i^*) P^* \text{ and } \beta_1 = \alpha_1 P^*$$

If the exchange rate is fixed, $S_t = \hat{S}$ and $\dot{S}_t = 0$, and hence equation (4.8) becomes:

$$M_t = \beta_0 \hat{S} \tag{4.9}$$

From equation (4.6) we know that $M_t = D_t + F_t$ and hence we can rewrite equation (4.9) as:

$$F_t = \beta_0 \hat{S} - D_t \tag{4.10}$$

Since $\hat{S}$ is constant because we are assuming a fixed exchange rate regime, equation (4.10) implies that the rate of change of F must be equal to minus the rate of change of D. So if domestic credit is *increasing* at the rate $\mu$, then F must be *falling* at the same rate.

We noted that in these models the stock of reserves held by the central bank is assumed to be finite. This implies that if domestic credit creation continues at a rate $\mu$, then at some point in the future, the stock of foreign exchange reserves will be exhausted and the exchange rate regime will collapse.

If we introduce speculators with perfect foresight into the model, then this simply hastens the collapse of the regime. Forward looking speculators will realise that the regime is unsustainable and hence they will sell domestic currency now in order to avoid later losses. The act of selling forces a collapse in the regime *now* as reserves are exhausted. Figure 4.7, which is taken from Flood and Garber (1984), illustrates what happens.

Before time $t_0$, D is rising at a rate $\mu$ and F is falling at a rate $\mu$ (refer to the upper part of Figure 4.7). Hence the total money supply ($M_t$) is unchanged. If no attack occurred, then the central bank would eventually run out of reserves at time $t_1$. However, before this, rational agents anticipating a collapse of the regime sell domestic currency and this causes a discrete fall in foreign exchange reserves (F) and hence also a discrete fall in the total money supply at time $t_0$. After $t_0$, the exchange rate floats and the money supply continues to grow at a rate equal to $\mu$ (D is still growing at $\mu$ and F is now constant and equal to zero). The lower section of Figure 4.7 shows the time path of the exchange rate. It is initially fixed at $\hat{S}$. But in the post-speculative attack regime, we assume that the currency floats,[25] and hence after $t_0$, it depreciates at the same rate $\mu$.

[25] If the post-speculative attack regime is not a floating one, then the timing of the attack can change. Assume, for example, that the exchange rate is allowed to float for a period before it is repegged at a higher level than it was before (that is, it is allowed to depreciate). In this case, the timing of the speculative attack will depend on the amount of depreciation allowed and the duration of the floating period. For example, the larger the depreciation, the quicker the speculative attack will occur. However, this can be offset by the length of the temporary floating period (see Blackburn and Sola, 1993).

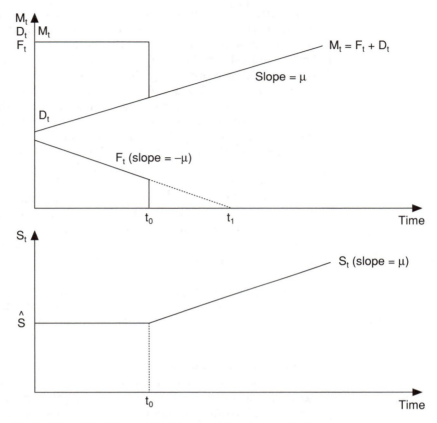

**Figure 4.7.**  *A speculative attack in a fixed exchange rate regime*

An obvious extension to the model is to consider what happens if we drop the deterministic aspect of the model and assume some kind of uncertainty. In this case, speculators no longer have perfect foresight, but we assume that they have rational expectations. There are two kinds of uncertainty which can be introduced to the model: uncertainty about the path of domestic credit expansion and uncertainty about the volume of reserves the central bank is willing to use to defend the fixed regime.

The case of uncertainty about the path of domestic credit creation is examined by Flood and Garber (1984) and Obstfeld (1986).[26] In the perfect foresight case, the timing of the collapse is known with certainty and the exchange rate cannot jump (this is the case, because if we knew the exchange rate was going to jump depreciate at some time in the future, we would sell domestic currency now). Under the fixed exchange rate regime, therefore, the forward discount (which given our assumption of UIP is identical to the expected rate of depreciation) never deviates from zero. If there is uncertainty about domestic credit expansion, then the expected rate of depreciation (or the forward discount) becomes non-zero. In particular, the expected rate of depreciation becomes a function of the probability that the fixed exchange rate regime will collapse and the expected exchange rate should the regime collapse.

---

[26] See also Dornbusch (1987) for a comparison between the two cases.

The effect of introducing this kind of uncertainty into the model is to make the date of collapse uncertain. Moreover, as the expected rate of depreciation becomes very large prior to the collapse, the domestic interest rate will rise (given that UIP holds). Obstfeld (1986) shows that it is possible for self-fulfilling crises to occur, that is, the regime can collapse simply because agents think it is going to.

The second possible source of uncertainty is over reserves. Krugman (1979) in his original article notes that if the market is uncertain about the amount of reserves the government will commit itself to defending the fixed rate, then periods of alternating crises and recoveries can occur. The intuition is fairly simple. If speculators are uncertain about the amount of reserves the central bank is willing to commit, then tests of their commitment may occur. Speculators have nothing to lose, even if they are proved wrong. Cumby and van Wijnbergen (1989) formalise Krugman's ideas. In the basic model that we have discussed, we assumed that the fixed regime was abandoned when reserves fell to zero. Cumby and van Wijnbergen argue that this is not very realistic. Instead, the central bank is assumed by agents to abandon the fixed regime when reserves reach a level, $F^*$, but $F^*$ is not known to agents with certainty. The results are similar to the case of domestic credit uncertainty in that speculative attacks can become self-fulfilling.

A second possible extension to the basic model is to abandon the assumption of perfect price flexibility. This allows for speculative attacks to have real effects. An obvious real effect from a fixed exchange rate regime where domestic credit is expanding at a rate incompatible with the fixed exchange rate is that the real appreciation (due to the rise in prices) causes a loss of output as competitiveness declines. If the monetary authorities persist with the exchange rate target, then the cumulative overappreciation will erode the credibility of the target (Dornbusch, 1982). Rational agents may question the authorities commitment to the target in the face of output losses and this could bring forward the timing of the run.

Changing the degree of capital mobility can also change the timing of attacks (Blackburn and Sola, 1993). For example, if capital is not perfectly mobile yet goods prices continue to adjust instantaneously, then the timing of the attack will be delayed because reserves fall at a slower rate. When there is both imperfect capital mobility and goods prices are sticky, then the effect on the timing of the collapse are ambiguous.

A final set of extensions to the basic model seek to incorporate some means of defense against the attack. A rather obvious defense would be to change the policy which is triggering the collapse in the first place.[27] That is, the central bank could reduce domestic credit expansion once an attack is imminent. If agents are sure that this will occur, then the attack will be postponed indefinitely (see Blackburn and Sola, 1993).

Alternatively, the central bank could borrow. Buiter (1987) considers the case where the government conducts a one-off open market sale of interest-bearing bonds.[28] This leads to an increase in reserves as the level of domestic credit falls.

---

[27] Although note that Obstfeld (1986) shows that this may not be enough: even if domestic credit expansion is consistent with continuing the fixed exchange rate regime. If speculators are uncertain about the path of the money supply then they could still trigger a self-fulfilling attack.

[28] Note that the borrowing considered here is domestic borrowing and that there is no fundamental fiscal correction. Hence the impact of the borrowing is to increase domestic credit expansion in the future to meet interest payments.

However, since the central bank raises only a one-off loan from the domestic markets[29] and no fundamental fiscal correction occurs, the impact of the borrowing is to increase interest payments in the following period. Hence after borrowing domestic credit expansion increases (to allow interest payments to be met). The impact of borrowing is either to delay the attack or to bring it forward. If the borrowing occurs early (relative to when the collapse would have occurred without borrowing) then the collapse is brought forward, because domestic credit will increase faster in subsequent periods because of the interest payments. Hence reserves fall faster and the collapse comes about sooner. By contrast, if the borrowing occurs later (that is, just before the collapse would have occurred), then the increase in reserves more than compensates for the fact that following the borrowing reserves will fall quicker.

A final defence is capital controls. Wyplosz (1986) shows that if there are controls on capital outflows, a speculative attack can be prevented. The intuition is simple. If controls on capital outflows prevent residents from converting their domestic currency into foreign exchange, then the reserves of the central bank are safe. This case is particularly relevant to the European situation in the early 1980s and we discuss this in the next chapter.

There has been some empirical work done on balance of payments crisis models. We discuss these further in the next chapter when we consider the EMS. Here we can note two pieces of empirical work on Latin American countries. Cumby and van Wijnbergen (1989) apply their model to the speculative runs experienced by Argentina between 1979 and 1981, when a preannounced crawling peg was followed. They use their model to estimate the probability of collapse of the regime. Their results indicate that the probability of collapse rises to 77% in December 1980, just prior to the actual collapse in 1981. Blanch and Garber (1986) use the Mexican experience between 1973 and 1982. They also find that their model predicts devaluations well.

In conclusion, the models of balance of payments crises essentially offer us a different way of showing that the monetary authorities cannot follow a monetary policy which is inconsistent with the fixed exchange rate target. If they do, then a speculative attack and the abandonment of the exchange rate target is inevitable. From an empirical point of view, speculative attacks in fixed exchange rate systems are a common occurrence and thus the story which these models tell has a lot of intuitive appeal. Indeed we return to the question of the relevance of these models for the EMS story in the following chapter.

## Conclusion

In this chapter, we have sought to explore some of the issues which are relevant to differing exchange rate systems. We began by outlining the reasons why exchange rate management became more popular during the 1980s. We argued that the experience with floating exchange rates did not live up to expectations. Instead, problems of volatility and misalignment have led a number of economists to argue in favour of intervention by the monetary authorities in the foreign exchange market.

However, opting for some form of exchange rate management still leaves us with a whole set of possible institutional arrangements depending on the degree of management undertaken. Unfortunately, the choice of institutional arrangements is unlike

---

[29] One might defend this rather simplistic assumption by appealing to the fact that the central bank will at some point after repeated borrowing face a situation that it cannot borrow more (unless it changes its policy). The sequence of events following this last approach to the market will be identical to the case considered by Buiter here.

the choices we face on visiting the supermarket – we cannot pick the best of everything. Instead, as we have emphasised throughout this chapter, different institutional arrangements encompass different trade-offs. For example, target zones reduce uncertainty associated with volatility and misalignment but may increase uncertainty with respect to the likelihood of a speculative attack. Hence the design of a target zone system may not simply require margins for the exchange rate. In addition, institutional arrangements to promote more extensive policy coordination or to introduce a Tobin-style tax to reduce the worst excesses of speculative capital movements may be required. Alternatively, if we feel the risk of speculative attack is too great and, moreover, we wish to derive all the benefits of a single currency and this inflation discipline, then we may opt for monetary union. But again this arrangement is not without its costs and may require further institutional change to mitigate the regional problems which may manifest themselves. In the following chapter, we discuss some of these trade-offs in more detail with reference to European monetary co-operation.

## References

**Artus, J.R. and Young, J.H.** (1979) 'Fixed and flexible exchange rates: a renewal of the debate', *IMF Staff Papers*, 26: 654–98.

**Barro, R.J. and Gordon, D.B.** (1983) 'Rules of discretion and reputation in a model of monetary policy', *Journal of Monetary Economics*, 12.

**Blackburn, K. and Sola, M.** (1993) 'Speculative currency attacks and balance of payments crises', *Journal of Economic Surveys*, 7: 2, 119–44.

**Blanch, H. and Garber, P.M.** (1986) 'Recurrent devaluations and speculative attacks on the Mexican peso', *Journal of Political Economy*, 94: 148–66.

**Bryant, R.C., Helliwell, J.F. and Hooper, P.** (1986) 'Domestic and cross-border consequences of US macroeconomics policies', in R.C. Bryant, D.A. Currie, J.A. Frenkel, P.R. Masson and R. Portes (1989) Macroeconomic Policies in an Interdependent World. The Brookings Institution/CEPR/IMF, Washington, D.C.

**Buiter, W.H.** (1987) 'Borrowing to defend the exchange rate and the timing of and magnitude of speculative attacks', *Journal of International Economics*, 23: 221–39.

**Corden, W.M.** (1972) 'Monetary Integration', *Princeton Essays in International Finance*, 93.

**Crockett, A.D. and Goldstein, M.** (1976) 'Inflation under fixed and flexible exchange rates', *IMF Staff Papers*, 23: 509–44.

**Cumby, R.E. and van Wijnbergen, S.** (1989) 'Financial policy and speculative runs with a crawling peg: Argentina, 1979–81', *Journal of International Economics*, 27: 111–27.

**Darby, M.R.** (1983) 'International transmission under pegged and floating exchange rates: an empirical comparison', in J.S. Bhandari and B.H. Putnam (eds.) *Economic Interdependence and Flexible Exchange Rates*. MIT Press, Cambridge, Mass. 427–71.

**De Grauwe, P.** (1992) *The Economics of Monetary Integration*. Oxford University Press, Oxford.

**Delgado, F. and Dumas, B.** (1992) 'Target zones, broad and narrow', in P.R. Krugman and M. Miller (eds.) *Exchange Rate Targets and Currency Bands*. CEPR, NBER, Cambridge University Press, Cambridge.

**Dornbusch, R.** (1982) 'Stabilisation policies in developing countries: what have we learned?', *World Development*, 10: 9, 701–8.

**Dornbusch, R.** (1987) 'Collapsing exchange rate regimes', *Journal of Development Economics*, 27: 71–83.

**Dunn, R.M.** (1983) 'The many disappointments of flexible exchange rates', *Princeton Essays in International Finance*, 54: (December).

**Eltis, W.A. and Sinclair, P.J.N.** (eds.) (1981) *The Money Supply and The Exchange Rate*. Oxford University Press, Oxford.

**Fleming, M.** (1971) 'On exchange rate unification', *Economic Journal*, 81: 467–88.

**Flood, R.P. and Garber, P.M.** (1984) 'Collapsing exchange rate regimes: some linear examples', *Journal of International Economics*, 17: 1–13.

**Flood, R.P. and Garber, P.M.** (1991) 'The linkage between speculative attack and target zone models of exchange rates', *Quarterly Journal of Economics* (November) 1367–72.

**Flood, R.P., Rose, A.K. and Mathieson, K.** (1991) 'An empirical exploration of exchange rate target zones', *IMF Working Paper*, WP/91/15, February.

**Frankel, J.A. and Froot, K.A.** (1987) 'Using survey data to test standard propositions regarding exchange rate expectations', *American Economic Review*, 77: 1, 133–53.

**Frankel, J.A. and Froot, K.A.** (1990) 'Chartists, fundamentalists and trading in the foreign exchange market', *American Economic Review*, 80: 2 (May), 181–85.

**Frankel, J.A. and Phillips, S.** (1991) 'The EMS: credible at last?', NBER Working Paper, 3819: also in Frankel, 1993.

**Friedman, M.** (1953) *Essays in Positive Economics*. Chicago University Press, Chicago.

**Goldstein, M.** (1980) 'Have flexible exchange rates handicapped macroeconomic policy?', *Special Papers in International Economics*. 14.

**Greenaway, D.** (1983) *International Trade Policy: from tariffs to the new protectionism*. Macmillan, London.

**Habeler, G.** (1964) 'Integration and growth in the world economy in historical perspective', *American Economic Review*, 54: 1–22.

**Hool, B. and Richardson, J.D.** (1983) 'International Trade, indebtedness and welfare repercussions among supply constrained economies under floating exchange rates', in J.S. Bhandari and B.H. Putnam (1983) (eds) *Economic Interdependence and Flexible Exchange Rates*. MIT Press, Cambridge, Mass.

**Hooper, P. and Kohlhagen, S.W.** (1978) 'The effect of exchange rate uncertainty on the prices and volumes of international trade', *Journal of International Economics*, 8: 483–511.

**Ingram, J.C.** (1973) 'The case for European monetary integration', *Princeton Essays in International Finance*, 98 (April).

**Ishiyama, Y.** (1975) 'The theory of optimum currency areas: a survey', *IMF Staff Papers*, 22 (July).

**Johnston, H.G.** (1970) 'The case for flexible exchange rates, 1969', Federal Reserve Bank of St. Louis, 52: 12–24.

**Kenen, P.** (1969) 'The theory of optimum currency area', in R.A. Mundell and A.K. Swoboda (eds) *Monetary Problems of the International Economy*. University of Chicago Press, Chicago. 41–60.

**Krugman, P.R.** (1979) 'A model of balance payments crises', *Journal of Money, Credit and Banking*, 11: 311–25.

**Krugman, P.R.** (1991a) 'Target zones and exchange rate dynamics', *Quarterly Journal of Economics*, CVI: 3, 669–84.

**Krugman, P.R. and Miller, M.** (1992) *Exchange Rate Targets and Currency Bands*. CPER, NBER, Cambridge University Press, Cambridge.

**Kydland, F.E. and Prescott, E.C.** (1977) 'Rules rather than discretion: the inconsistency of optimal plans', *Journal of Political Economy*, 85: 3 (June).

**McCulloch, R.** (1983) 'Unexpected real consequences of floating exchange rates', *Princeton Essays in International Finance*, 153 (August).

**McKinnon, R.I.** (1963) 'Optimal Currency Areas', *American Economic Review*, 53 (September).

**Meese, R.A. and Rogoff, K.** (1983) 'Empirical exchange rate models of the seventies: do they fit out of sample?', *Journal of International Economics*, 14: 3–24.

**Mundell, R.A.** (1961) 'A theory of optimum currency area', *American Economic Review*, 51: 657–65.

**Obstfeld, M.** (1986) 'Rational and self-fulfilling balance of payments crises', *American Economic Review*, 76: 1, 72–81.

**Svensson, L.E.O.** (1992) 'An interpretation of recent research on exchange rate target zones', *Journal of Economic Perspectives*, 6: 4, 119–44.

**Taylor, M.P.** (1989) 'Expectations, risk and uncertainty in the foreign exchange market: some results based on survey data', *The Manchester School*, 57: 2, 142–53.

**Thirlwall, A.P. and Gibson, H.D.** (1992) *Balance of Payments Theory and the United Kingdom Experience*, 4th ed. Macmillan, London.

**Torres, R. and Giavazzi, F.** (1993) *Adjustment and Growth in the Economic and Monetary Union*. CEPR, Cambridge University Press, Cambridge.

**Williamson, J.** (1983) *The Exchange Rate System*. Institute for International Economics, Washington, D.C.

**Williamson, J.** (1993) 'On designing an international monetary system', *Journal of Post-Keynesian Economics*, 15: 2, 181–92.

**Williamson, J. and Miller, M.H.** (1987) 'Targets and indicators: a blueprint for the international co-ordination of economic policy', *Policy Analyses in International Economics*, 22. Institute for International Economics, Washington, D.C.

**Witte, W.E.** (1983) 'Policy interdependence under flexible exchange rates: a dynamic analysis of price interactions', in J.S. Bhandari and B.H. Putnam (eds) *Cointegration for the Applied Economist*. St. Martins Press, New York.

**Wypolsz, C.** (1986) 'Capital control and balance of payments crises', *Journal of International Money and Finance*, 5: 167–79.

# 5 MONETARY INTEGRATION IN THE EUROPEAN UNION

## with Euclid Tsakalotos

The history of European monetary co-operation is a fairly short one. But, since the experience is a rich one, it is instructive to use it as a case study of monetary co-operation in general and exchange rate management in particular. The European Monetary System (hereafter EMS), the most concrete manifestation of European monetary co-operation, began as a relatively flexible target zone system in 1979, became progressively more rigid especially after 1987 and finally, since 1993, has been more loose than at any time during its history. These developments in the EMS have prompted a growing debate regarding the method by which Europe should adopt a single currency. For example, should European countries jump directly to a single currency without a period of more fixed exchange rates or should they first adopt more fixed exchange rates? These debates about the form which European monetary co-operation should take can be understood in the light of our conclusions at the end of Chapter 4. Different institutional structures of exchange rate management not only have different benefits but also different costs. Changes in the perceived balance of costs and benefits can lead to changes in the favoured institutional structure. In this sense, European monetary integration provides us with a rich catalogue of lessons which can be learnt about the advantages and disadvantages of different institutional structures. Thus, in this chapter, we investigate some of the theoretical ideas we discussed in Chapter 4. Using the ideas developed there we hope to shed some light on the process of European monetary integration.

The Treaty of Rome which established the European Common Market made no mention of monetary integration and the related issues of monetary and fiscal policy co-operation. It was not until the Werner report (in 1970) that monetary co-operation was first discussed. It argued that Europe should aim to achieve monetary union by 1980. However, the subsequent breakdown of the Bretton Woods system and the rise in oil prices (and the consequences for balance of payments disequilibria) led to an abandonment of the plan. Instead, the breakdown of Bretton Woods led to more modest attempts at exchange rate co-operation among Common Market countries, the so-called 'snake' arrangement. The snake involved European countries fixing their exchange rates and allowing up to 2.5% movement on each side of the central rate. By the end of 1978, Germany, Belgium, Luxembourg, The Netherlands and Denmark continued to adhere to the system. The UK, France and Ireland had originally been members but subsequently left at various points (the UK, for example, was a member for only 6 weeks).

Plans for the EMS were adopted in July 1978 and the system came into existence in 1979. In the first section of this chapter we want to examine how the system has operated and its various successes and failures. In doing so, we will draw on some of the theoretical ideas developed in Chapter 4. In particular, we focus on the extent to which the EMS has helped with disinflation within the European Union (EU). We also discuss the question of the stability of the system and provide an analysis of why it (partially) broke down in July 1993.

The goal of the EU countries is to move towards closer monetary integration by the end of the decade. The second section focuses on Economic and Monetary Union (EMU). We discuss plans to move towards monetary union by focusing on various stages outlined in the Delors report and the Maastricht Treaty. A particularly important question in this respect is the extent to which the EU can be considered an optimal currency area. By addressing this question, we can shed some light on the problems which the EU might face and the policies which might have to accompany monetary union if any costs are to be mitigated.

## The European Monetary System (EMS)

The main objective of the EMS is the promotion of monetary stability within Europe. To this end, the system had three immediate aims when it was established in 1979. The first was the reduction of inflation in EU countries. Stabilisation of prices requires not only domestic price stability, but also foreign price stability and exchange rate stability.[1] In the late 1970s and early 1980s, a number of European countries suffered from high levels of inflation (see Figure 5.1). Through the EMS, countries sought to lower inflation permanently.[2]

A second aim of the EMS was the promotion of exchange rate stability. The problems of volatility and misalignment associated with floating exchange rates (which we discussed in Chapter 4) are thought to hamper trade flows and investment. In this respect the EMS can be seen as an attempt to increase trade between EU countries and to promote investment and hence growth.

A final aim of the system was the *gradual* convergence of economic policy. Initially exchange rates were not rigidly fixed and realignments were possible. This was seen as crucial to the success of the system. Too little flexibility when economic policies had not yet converged was seen as damaging to the prospects for greater integration: the system would quickly break down as policy divergence undermined its viability. Instead it was argued that as economic policy converged, so exchange rates could become more fixed, operating with smaller bands and fewer realignments.

## The features of the EMS

The EMS consists of three main elements: the European Currency Unit (the ECU), the Exchange Rate Mechanism (ERM) and the European Monetary Cooperation Fund (EMCF).

The ECU is a weighted average of all EU currencies where the weights depend on the size of each country and its importance in intra-EU trade. Thus, not surprisingly, the most important currencies in the ECU are the Deutschmark, the French franc and sterling. It functions largely as a unit of account and also as a means of settlement between central banks.

The ERM is the heart of the EMS. Each member of the ERM has a central rate quoted against the ECU. This in turn sets central rates against all other ERM currencies. The exchange rate, up until July 1993, was allowed to fluctuate either up to

---

[1] Recall that changes in the exchange rate can lead to changes in the price of imported goods and hence this feeds into overall domestic prices. Stabilising the exchange rate can therefore prevent this source of inflation in the domestic economy.

[2] The method by which fixed exchange rates might help to reduce inflation was discussed in Chapter 4. We examine the success of the EMS in meeting this goal in more detail below.

2.25% or 6% on either side of the central rate. In July 1993, the fluctuation bands were increased to 15% on either side of the central rate. Not all EU countries are members of the ERM. At its inception, Germany, France, Belgium, Denmark, Italy, The Netherlands, Luxembourg and Ireland joined. The UK, which has been a member of the Common Market since 1973, did not join the ERM until October 1990. It subsequently left in September 1992 along with Italy. Spain and Portugal joined the EC in 1986 and the ERM in June 1989 and April 1992 respectively and have remained in the system. Greece, which joined the EU in 1981, has never been a member of the ERM.

Currencies are maintained within the bands through compulsory intervention by the monetary authorities in the foreign exchange markets. If two currencies reach one of their bilateral exchange rate margins, then the monetary authorities of the weaker currency must intervene to purchase their currency preventing further depreciation. By contrast, the monetary authorities of the stronger currency will be intervening to sell their currency to prevent further appreciation. In this way, currencies are kept within their bands of fluctuation.

In its original conception, an important part of the ERM is the divergence indicator. This is supposed to act as a warning device, indicating which country is diverging from its central rate. It should give a clear indication of the country on which the burden of adjustment should fall. The value of the divergence indicator for each currency, i, is given by the weighted sum of the divergence of currency i from each of the other currencies:

$$a^i_t = \Sigma_j \, w^j_t \, d_t^{j,i} \tag{5.1}$$

where $w^j_t$ is the weight of currency j in the ECU basket and $d_t^{j,i}$ is the deviation of currency j from its central parity *vis-à-vis* currency i.[3] The threshold for the indicator is 75% of the divergence which would have occurred had currency i deviated by the full 2.25% from all other currencies (assuming the fluctuations bands to be ±2.25%). If the actual indicator, $a^i_t$, is above the threshold, then country i is supposed to take action by adjusting macroeconomic policy to bring it into line with its exchange rate commitment. Giavazzi and Giovannini (1989) show that the indicator discriminates against smaller countries. That is, because of the weighting system, it is much easier for a small country to find its currency passing the critical level than a larger country. In practice, the divergence indicator has not been used: countries are not required to take action if their currency passes the threshold. As we shall see later, this has tended to increase the asymmetry of the system.

It is possible for a central rate to be realigned. Table 5.1 shows the history of realignments in the ERM since its inception. The table illustrates three key points about the operation of the ERM. First, in the early years of the ERM there were many realignments, reflecting the flexibility of the system. There were 7 realignments in the period up to the end of 1983. Secondly, certain countries have always tended to realign in a certain direction. For example, the Deutschmark and Dutch guilder have always revalued their central parity whereas the lira and French franc (with the exception of the July 1985 realignment) have always devalued. We return to the implications of this pattern of realignments later in the chapter. Finally, the period 1987 to September 1992 was a very stable period for the system, but since

---

[3] See Giavazzi and Giovannini (1989, Ch. 2).

*Table 5.1.* ERM realignments

| Date | DM | Ff | Dg | Il | Bf | Dk | Lf | Ip | Sp | Pe |
|---|---|---|---|---|---|---|---|---|---|---|
| 9/79 | +2.0 | | | | | −3.0 | | | | |
| 11/80 | | | | | | | −5.0 | | | |
| 3/81 | | | | -6.0 | | | | | | |
| 10/81 | | +5.5 | −3.0 | +5.5 | −3.0 | | | | | |
| 2/82 | | | | | −8.5 | −3.0 | −8.5 | | | |
| 6/82 | +4.3 | −5.8 | +4.3 | −2.8 | | | | | | |
| 3/83 | +5.5 | −2.5 | +3.5 | −2.5 | +1.5 | +2.5 | +1.5 | −3.5 | | |
| 7/85 | +2.0 | +2.0 | +2.0 | −6.0 | +2.0 | +2.0 | +2.0 | +2.0 | | |
| 4/86 | | −3.0 | +3.0 | | +1.0 | +1.0 | +1.0 | -8.0 | | |
| 1/87 | +3.0 | | +3.0 | | +2.0 | | +2.0 | | | |
| 1/90 | | | | −3.7 | | | | | | |
| 14/9/92 | +3.5 | +3.5 | | −3.5 | +3.5 | +3.5 | +3.5 | +3.5 | +3.5 | +3.5 |
| 17/9/92 | | | | | | | | | −5.0 | |
| 11/92 | | | | | | | | | −6.0 | −6.0 |
| 1/93 | | | | | | | | −10.0 | | |
| 5/93 | | | | | | | | | −8.0 | −6.5 |
| 3/95 | | | | | | | | | −7.0 | −3.5 |

*Notes*: DM = Deutschmark, FF = French franc, DG = Dutch guilder, IL = Italian lira, BF = Belgian franc, DK = Danish kroner, LF = Luxembourg franc, IP = Irish punt, SP = Spanish peseta and PE = Portuguese escudo.

then several periods of crisis have been apparent. It is in this sense that the ERM constitutes an interesting catalogue of different regimes and institutions.

The final feature of the EMS is the EMCF. This provides credit for members to help in adjusting balance of payments problems. Each EU country deposits 20% of its foreign exchange reserves and gold with the EMCF which can then be lent out to countries in need of foreign exchange. There are a variety of facilities with different time periods. The very short-term financing facility is available only to ERM countries and provides finance for 45 days or less. The short-term facility provides finance for less than 9 months and is intended to help with short-run balance of payments problems. Finally, the medium-term financing facility provides finance for 2–5 years and is intended to help solve balance of payments problems of a structural nature. Conditions are usually attached by the EU to this finance.

*The achievements of the ERM*

One of the main aims of the ERM was to reduce exchange rate volatility. Studies which examine this question compare the variability of ERM currencies with both the 1973–79 period and with other non-ERM currencies post 1979 (sterling, yen and dollar).[4] In spite of realignments, exchange rate stability has been achieved. This conclusion is also clear from an examination of the figures in Chapter 1. A cost to this increased stability could be increased variability of interest rates. The rationale is simple. As countries seek to stabilise their exchange rates, domestic interest rates may have to be altered frequently to reduce pressure on the exchange rate. For example, if there is strong

[4] See, for example, Artis and Taylor (1988); Giavazzi and Giovannini (1989). Artis and Taylor (1994) conduct some non-parametric tests on the volatility of both ERM and non-ERM exchange rates. These tests avoid the problem of assuming that exchange rates follow a normal distribution (something which is implicitly assumed if variances are used as a measure of volatility). Their results confirm the view that the volatility of intra-ERM exchange rates fell after 1979. By contrast, the volatility of non-ERM currencies increased.

pressure for the exchange rate to appreciate, then interest rates may have to be lowered and vice versa. However, Artis and Taylor (1988) note that the improved exchange rate stability has not been at the cost of higher domestic interest-rate volatility and this is confirmed by their 1994 study. This is probably related to the important role that capital controls played in the ERM in the 1980s and we will discuss this further.

An important question is whether increased exchange rate stability actually has any benefits for real economic variables. Has it promoted greater trade between EU countries, for example? Tests of this hypothesis have proved rather less successful at finding a link. Studies by Cushman (1983) and Kenen and Rodrick (1986) show that increased variability is detrimental to trade. Gotur (1985), by contrast, does not find a link. Sapir and Sekkat (1990) examine the impact of exchange rate volatility on the price of tradeables. They find little evidence that exchange rate changes are passed through to price changes and hence conclude that volatility has little effect on international trade. However, presumably if the prices of tradeables are not changing, yet exchange rates are, firms are absorbing the effect of the changes through increased profit variability. This may act to hamper firm planning and, to the extent that firms are risk averse, may lead to reduced investment in tradeables production. Indeed, anecdotal evidence suggests that there is some benefit to small to medium-sized firms in a reduction in exchange rate volatility, perhaps because they find it more costly and difficult to hedge in futures markets.

The second main aim of the ERM was to reduce inflation in EU countries. We noted in Chapter 4 how we might expect a fixed exchange rate system to help in reducing inflation and we recap that argument briefly here. If a country with a high inflation rate fixes its exchange rate to a country with a low inflation rate, then the high inflation country will have to disinflate if it does not want to suffer a loss of competitiveness (via a real exchange rate appreciation). This arises because of the important asymmetry which operates within a fixed exchange rate system. Low inflation countries, which are more likely to experience pressure for their currency to appreciate, have to intervene to sell their currency. However, they can sterilise the impact of the rise in foreign exchange reserves on their domestic money supply and hence their foreign exchange market intervention is not reflationary. By contrast, the high inflation, deficit country experiences a decline in reserves (as it intervenes to buy its currency) and sterilisation is more difficult because ultimately it will face a constraint in the form of a shortage of foreign exchange reserves.

This basic asymmetry lies at the heart of the ERM. Germany is the low inflation centre country and it has, throughout the operation of the ERM, been very reluctant to ease its monetary policy. Thus it has often resorted to sterilisation. Other members of the ERM have used exchange rate fixity with Germany as a means to reduce inflation: tying the exchange rate has forced these weaker countries to disinflate by maintaining high interest rates (as a means of keeping their exchange rates within the band).

A number of studies have examined the contention that the ERM has effectively worked as a Deutschmark zone.[5] There are a number of pieces of evidence which suggest that the ERM has worked asymmetrically. First, the Divergence Indicator has not operated in practice. As we noted earlier, the Divergence Indicator is supposed to identify the currency which is out of line. In theory, it should have been able to identify the Deutschmark as a currency which was frequently diverging from all the other currencies and hence brought about the appropriate response (reflation)

[5] See, for example, Giavazzi and Giovannini (1989, Chapter 4); Fratianni and von Hagen (1990); and Melitz (1988; 1990).

from the German monetary authorities. However, as we have already noted, the Divergence Indicator always allowed larger countries more leeway. Moreover, since the Indicator did not bind countries to take any action, Germany could ignore any calls for reflation from other countries.

Secondly, Giavazzi and Giovannini (1989) point to evidence on intervention within the system to support their view that Germany was the leader. By and large the evidence on intervention indicates that the burden of intervention fell on non-DM currencies. This is true both with respect to intervention at the margin as well as intra-marginal interventions.[6] Thirdly, Giavazzi and Giovannini also point to interest-rate evidence in support of their claim. At times of expected realignments, German interest rates were unaffected: that is, they did not tend to decrease to offset the expected appreciation of the Deutschmark. By contrast, Italian and French off-shore interest rates increased,[7] indicating that they felt the effect of the expected realignment and were it not for the existence of capital controls, their domestic economies would have been badly affected as we show later.

The final piece of evidence which supports the claim that the ERM operates asymmetrically is that inflation in initially higher inflation countries did converge on German levels. From Figure 5.1, it is clear that German inflation did not increase throughout the period. Instead, inflation in the other countries shows a distinct tendency to converge on German levels. Some argue that, given inflation also declined in other OECD countries, the ERM experience was by no means unique. Figure 5.2, which compares ERM countries (excluding Germany) with other OECD countries, indeed confirms that inflation fell elsewhere. However, this merely suggests that there are alternative methods of disinflating (via monetary or fiscal policy, for example). It does not suggest that the ERM did not contribute to inflation reduction among its member countries.[8]

Fratianni and von Hagen (1990) challenge the view that the ERM has operated asymmetrically. They estimate reaction functions for ERM countries. These show the extent to which countries sterilise and react to changes in monetary policy in other countries. They argue that German dominance of the system implies that:

(i)    Germany should not react to other ERM members' monetary policy
(ii)   other ERM countries should not react to changes in monetary policy in either other ERM countries or the rest of the world
(iii)  each ERM country reacts only to German monetary policy changes.

Their results do not support any of these hypotheses. In particular, they show that German monetary policy reacted to changes in France and Italy. They therefore conclude that German dominance of the system is a myth. However, these results are not conclusive. Melitz (1990) in his comment on their paper argues that Fratianni and von Hagen take a very extreme view. He argues that a leader (Germany) can respond to the

---

[6]  Intra-marginal intervention refers to central bank intervention when the exchange rate is not at either of the limits. Technically, central banks within the ERM are obliged to intervene only when the exchange rate reaches the outer bands. However, central banks often intervene when the exchange rate is within its band in order to prevent it reaching the outer limits. Intervention at the margins refers to central bank intervention at the outer limits of the exchange rate bands.

[7]  Offshore interest rates are used because they are unaffected by capital controls. We discuss the impact of capital controls on the relationship between offshore and onshore (domestic) interest rates later in the chapter.

[8]  Fratianni and von Hagen (1990) are among those who suggest that the ERM experience is not different from the rest of the OECD. This might be true in terms of outcome, but is not necessarily true in terms of the method used to disinflate.

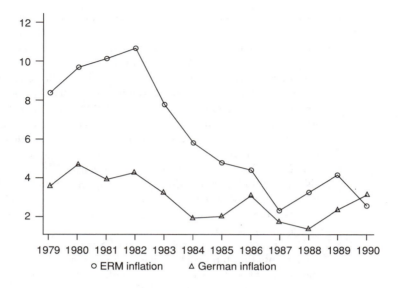

**Figure 5.1.** *Inflation in ERM countries*

*Note*: ERM inflation is average inflation in the 7 original ERM countries (excluding Germany).

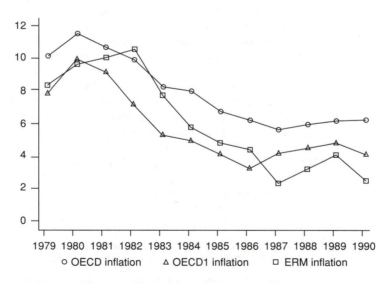

**Figure 5.2.** *Inflation in ERM and OECD countries*

*Note*: OECD inflation is inflation in a wide sample of OECD countries (Australia, Austria, Canada, Finland, Greece, Japan, Norway, Portugal, Spain, Sweden, UK and US). OECD1 excludes the three southern European economies (Greece, Portugal and Spain) since it is well-known that their disinflation programmes began later in the 1980s. ERM inflation is inflation in the ERM original seven members excluding Germany.

followers (non-German ERM countries) whilst still being the leader and directing the general orientation of policy. In other words, it might still be the case that in spite of their findings, Germany can be considered to be the lead country within the ERM.[9]

In our analysis, we have treated the ERM largely as if it is a fixed exchange rate system. However, even in its pre-1993 version it allowed exchange rates to vary. The bands (which in some cases allowed for up to 12% movements in the exchange rate) provided some flexibility – indeed the ERM was similar to a target zone with published bands.[10] In addition, realignments were possible and, as we have noted, there were a number of realignments especially in the early 1980s. The evidence suggests that realignments only partially offset inflation differentials between countries like France and Italy, and Germany. In other words, France and Italy experienced a persistent anti–inflation bias through a real appreciation of their currencies in spite of a number of devaluations and this undoubtedly accounts for the decline in inflation over the 1980s. Such evidence provides further support for the view that the ERM operated asymmetrically.

We argued in Chapter 4 that fixed exchange rate systems not only can help to reduce inflation but also that they can do so with reduced costs in terms of unemployment. This results from the credibility bonus derived from pegging a currency to another currency with a low inflation reputation. As we showed in Chapter 4, within an expectations-augmented Phillips curve framework, the credibility bonus reduces the costs of disinflation because expectations adjust quickly to the change of regime.

This argument was used by a number of ERM countries as a benefit of joining the system. The reputation of the Bundesbank in fighting inflation would, it was argued, be transferred to the high inflation country. However, the evidence in favour of the proposition is mixed. Figure 5.3 illustrates the unemployment experience of ERM countries alongside that of the two groups of OECD countries already considered. This Figure illustrates the rather poor employment experience of the ERM countries compared to OECD countries in general.

Such graphical evidence on unemployment is by no means conclusive in rejecting the credibility bonus hypothesis for there is always the problem in such analysis of the counterfactual. Unemployment in ERM countries might have been even higher were it not for the credibility bonus. Hence we have to delve deeper into the issue of credibility if we are to assess the contribution of the ERM.

A number of authors calculate the so-called misery index for ERM and non-ERM countries (De Grauwe, 1990; Davies, 1989). This is combined inflation and unemployment in each country. The evidence from this measure is not supportive of the enhanced credibility view. This test of the credibility hypothesis suffers from the same problems as the graphical evidence. Indeed, De Grauwe (1990) argues that the costs of disinflation were high in ERM countries because of the nature of their labour markets.[11] They are much less able to respond to shocks because of inflexibilities

---

[9]  We can also note that Giavazzi and Giovannini (1989) argue that estimation of reaction functions is a difficult task. In particular, it is very easy to misspecify the function and hence derive results that overestimate the degree of monetary independence which countries enjoyed.

[10]  Publication of the bans within a target zone is a matter of some debate. The argument against publication is that it gives speculators something to aim at. By contrast, Williamson (1983, p.68) argues that 'publication encourages honesty and improves the information available to the market, which will be beneficial so long as the policy is sensibly conducted'. On balance, therefore, he prefers publication.

[11]  Calmfors and Driffill (1988) argue that flexibility in labour markets can result from either a highly centralised system of wage bargaining or a highly decentralised system. Intermediate degrees of centralisation offer the worst possible scenario for the unemployment costs of reducing inflation. Henley and Tsakalotos (1992) note that France and Italy both suffer from intermediate degrees of wage bargaining with the result that a large increase in unemployment is required to lower wage and hence price inflation.

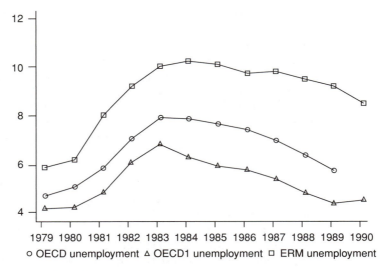

**Figure 5.3.** *Unemployment in ERM and OECD countries*

*Note*: OECD unemployment is unemployment in a wide sample of OECD countries (Australia, Austria, Canada, Finland, Greece, Japan, Norway, Portugal, Spain, Sweden, UK and US). OECD1 excludes the three southern European economies (Greece, Portugal and Spain) since it is well-known that their disinflation programmes began later in the 1980s. ERM is unemployment in the ERM original seven members excluding Germany.

compared to other OECD countries. Hence it is not possible to reach a conclusion on the relative costs of disinflation in the two groups of counties.

An alternative method of testing the credibility hypothesis, which overcomes some of the above problems, is to examine wage-price dynamics in different countries. Giavazzi and Giovannini (1989), for example, estimate wage and price equations for individual ERM countries over the pre-1979 period and then use the estimated equation to forecast over the ERM period. The hypothesis is that a credibility bonus will show up in a significant (downward) shift in the parameters of the equations in the post-1979 period. In the case of France there is a significant downward shift, although actual inflation diverges from that predicted by the pre-1979 equation only in 1982. In the case of Denmark and Italy there is no evidence of a downward shift in 1979. However, for Italy it is possible that a shift occurred later, in 1985. Giavazzi and Giovannini attribute this lack of success in identifying a structural break in 1979 to the idea that agents in the economy need to go through a learning process. Credibility is not gained immediately a country joins the ERM, but has to be earned through its experience within the system.

Finally, Fitoussi *et al.* (1993) examine the French experience in some depth since 1983 when commitment to exchange rate stability in France is widely held to have begun. They use a NAIRU (non-accelerating inflation rate of unemployment) framework to consider the question of the costs of disinflation within the ERM. They argue that the costs of disinflation might be high because labour markets are slow to adjust. They provide estimates of two specific speeds of adjustment which are crucial in determining the costs of disinflation. First, how quickly does rising unemployment exert a downward pressure on wage demands? Secondly, once wage inflation is moderated, does this improve competitiveness thus potentially translating itself into lower employment? Their results suggest that in the long run a 1% increase in unemployment decreases the real wage by 6.5%. This is quite a large effect, but the coefficient representing speed of adjustment of wages to unemployment suggests that they adjust by only 10% per annum. Once wage inflation is reduced, they find that the benefit is quickly felt in prices which for each 1% fall in wages decline by 0.53%.[12] Thus Fitoussi *et al.* argue that these results account for why unemployment in France remained so high for such a long period of time. Whilst the process of adjustment appears to be working in France, it is a slow process and problems of hysteresis in labour markets tend to outweigh any possible gains from a credibility bonus.

Thus the question of the output costs of disinflation within the ERM remains a tricky one. At best it now appears that the credibility bonus has to be earned over a period of operating within the system. But if credibility is low on entering the system, then presumably the costs of disinflation cannot be avoided. We can perhaps argue only that once inflation is reduced within the ERM it is less likely to rise again since credibility has been established and is easier to retain. The rationale for this is put forward by, among others, Davies (1989).[13] He argues that within the ERM it is more costly to relax a counter-inflation strategy since this would lead to greater losses in competitiveness and hence output than for countries outside the system.[14] Hence inflation might be more easily maintained at a low level within the system. Such an argument certainly finds some support in the experience of the later 1980s. ERM countries successfully maintained low inflation whilst the UK, for example, which remained outside the ERM experienced a mini-boom and a subsequent reversal of the reduction in inflation.

We have been discussing at length the achievements of the ERM. However, it should be clear that much of the achievement has been for countries other than Germany. An important question which therefore arises if we view the ERM as an asymmetric system is: what has Germany gained from participating? The arguments relating to reputation and credibility are clearly not relevant for the centre country, since it is the one which already has a reputation which the others are seeking to benefit from. Melitz (1988) argues that Germany gains from the co-operative nature of the ERM. In particular, it tends to reduce the tendency for the Deutschmark to appreciate and hence stabilises the real effective Deutschmark exchange rate. Indeed, since countries like France and Italy experience a real appreciation, Germany must during the 1980s have benefited from a real depreciation, at least relative to other ERM countries. Hence Germany perhaps gains more in terms of improved competitiveness than she loses in terms of upsets to monetary policy. Giavazzi and Giovannini (1989) provide evidence in support of this argument. They note that in spite of the large current account surpluses, Germany has managed to minimise fluctuations in her real effective exchange rate. Indeed such gains could be more secure than the supposed gains for the other ERM members in terms of reputation and the reduced costs of disinflation.

---

[12] The remaining effect of the decline in wages shows up as an increase in profits which, in turn, increases investment.

[13] See also Backus and Driffill (1985) on the importance of gaining a reputation for establishing credibility.

[14] Perhaps it would be more accurate to say that it *was* more costly. With the 15% bands on either side of the central parity, there is quite a bit of room for relaxing the policy stance without losing competitiveness.

*The stability of the ERM*

We argued in Chapter 4 that fixed exchange rate regimes or target zone regimes are prone to speculative attacks which often makes their survival precarious. An interesting question which arises therefore in connection with the ERM is why it was so successful for such a long period. In this section we examine the durability of the ERM at least until September 1992. Our answer to this question is important not only in and of itself. It also enables us to understand better the ERM's (partial) breakdown in the early 1990s. There are five factors which have been identified in the literature as being important in explaining the durability of the ERM.

Firstly, there is the issue of co-operation among ERM countries and the existence of the various financing facilities. The ERM is part of a wider scale of co-operation among EU countries. Since a number of other EU policies rely to some extent on exchange rate stability, the 1992 Single Economic Market and agricultural policy for example, there has been a greater willingness among EU countries to accept the discipline imposed by exchange rate co-operation. Moreover, the framework of co-operation between ERM members is institutionalised through meetings of the Finance Ministers and the existence of the various credit facilities organised by the EMCF. Thus any changes within the ERM, realignments, changes in the bands, etc, are discussed collectively and agreed upon before any announcement is made. As we have argued elsewhere in this book, such arrangements can be considered useful in general for the international financial system as a whole.

At the Basle–Nyborg meeting in 1987 the amount of money available for supporting the ERM was increased and access to the very short-term financing facility was permitted for intra-marginal interventions. The ability to use the ECU for settlements between EU Central Banks was also increased. The importance of these institutional developments lies in the fact that they allow Central Banks to have access to a large amount of funds to enable them to protect their central parities against speculative attacks. In addition, co-operation through Finance Minster meetings has helped at times to enable more orderly realignments, although, as we will argue, co-operation between Finance Ministers has sometimes been more the result of fortuitous factors rather than by design.

A second reason for the durability of the ERM is that as a system it incorporates some clever operational features. A good example in this respect is the existence of the bands within which exchange rates can fluctuate. In its pre-1993 version, the ERM had two fluctuation bands: narrow bands ($\pm 2.25\%$) and wider bands ($\pm 6\%$). This allowed countries with a greater inflation problem, such as Italy and eventually Spain and Portugal, more flexibility and autonomy to converge gradually on other ERM countries.

In addition, the wider bands of fluctuation can help in realignments. This is illustrated in Figure 5.4. Assume we have two currencies, say the French franc and the Italian lira. The top half of the diagram illustrates the case of narrow bands, that is the case of the French franc. The bottom half illustrates the case of Italy with wider bands. Assume that both currencies depreciate their central parity rate by 5% from $s_1$ to $s_2$. In the case of France this implies that at time $t_1$ the exchange rate will have to take a discrete jump if it is to move into the new fluctuation bands. By contrast, the lira does not have to jump on the day of realignment: with its wider fluctuation bands, the new bands overlap the old ones. Of course, a similar result could also be achieved if the size of realignments are limited – the new bands would then again be more likely to overlap the old.

The importance of the width of the bands at times of realignments lies in the role

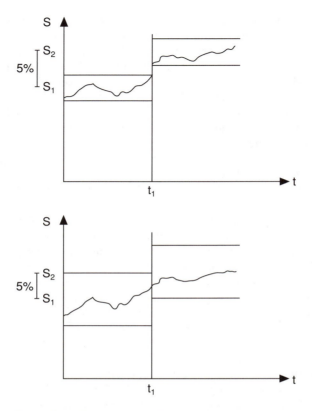

**Figure 5.4.**    *Realignments with narrow and wide bands*

of speculators. In the case of the French franc, speculators have almost a one-way bet. As Table 5.1 illustrates, it is not difficult to guess before a realignment which way a currency is likely to move. A 5% devaluation in the case of the French Franc presents speculators with a large gain if they sell francs before the realignment and buy back afterwards. By contrast, in the case of Italy, the exchange rate need not depreciate on the day of the realignment: it may even appreciate and still remain within the new bands. Thus speculators face greater uncertainty in speculating against the lira compared to the French franc. They are therefore likely to engage in less speculation and this makes realignments more orderly.

Furthermore, ERM countries, at least until September 1992, took care over the timing of realignments. Under the Bretton Woods system, countries often took a long time to decide on devaluation (the most well-known example being the UK before its devaluation in 1967 – see Chapter 1). This increased the speculative pressure against the potentially devaluing currency and made it rather easy for speculators to make profits. In the ERM the realignments of the early 1980s were decided upon quickly and the decision was always announced on a Saturday. In this way, when the markets opened on Monday morning, traders were aware of the new bands and trading could continue in an orderly fashion.

A third factor accounting for the success of the ERM is luck. During the 1980s there were a number of fortuitous circumstances which helped to promote stability within the ERM. The fact that the UK was not a member was fortuitous in that it implied that there was only one large reserve currency in the system, the Deutschmark. This limited the amount of speculative capital moving around the system and potentially putting pressure on various parities. Moreover, given the ambivalence of the UK in general to its role in Europe, its nonmembership in the 1980s probably also limited the number of policy disagreements.

In the early 1980s the dollar's strength also reduced the amount of pressure on the system. Normally when the dollar is weak, international capital flows into the Deutschmark and this causes pressure for it to appreciate relative to the other ERM currencies. Other ERM currencies either have to raise interest rates to protect their central parity or undertake a realignment. When the dollar is strong, however, the pressure on the Deutschmark and hence the ERM is much less. In the later 1980s, when the dollar started to depreciate, the Plaza and Louvre agreements between the Group of Seven helped to lessen pressure on the Deutschmark by managing the dollar's decline. This relationship between dollar and Deutschmark exchange rates prompts Thygesen (1990) to call for the new European Central Bank to take over in Stage II (of the Delors Plan) some of the intervention with respect to third currencies which is currently undertaken by individual European Central Banks. The experience in the 1980s also emphasises the important of a stable and co-operative environment in helping to promote ERM stability.

Probably the most important fortuitous factor of the 1980s relates to the policy goals of various ERM governments. By and large, the aim of all ERM governments was disinflation. In this sense policy co-operation followed naturally and most ERM countries were willing to accept the discipline implied by membership of the system. Indeed, as we shall see later in this section, the co-operative nature of policy in the 1980s was absent in the 1990s. It can be argued that the fact that co-operation between ERM governments came fairly easily in the 1980s prevented a build-up of experience in mediating disputes and highlighted the weakness of the institutions to promote co-operation when policy disagreements surfaced.

A fourth factor which was responsible for the durability of the ERM was the existence of capital controls. We can best appreciate the role played by capital controls by using the covered interest parity condition introduced in Chapter 2:

$$i_d = i_f - fp_d \tag{5.2}$$

where $i_d$ and $i_f$ are the domestic and foreign interest rates respectively and $fp_d$ is the forward premium on the domestic currency. The effect of controls on capital movements is to drive a wedge between domestic and foreign returns:

$$w = i_d - (i_f - fp_d) \tag{5.3}$$

If the wedge is positive then this indicates that controls on capital inflows are binding, since the domestic return is above the foreign return. By contrast, if the wedge is negative, then controls on capital outflows are binding.

The importance of capital controls in the ERM is two-fold. Firstly, they allowed countries some monetary independence at least in the short run.[15] We can illustrate

---

[15] There is some disagreement about the effectiveness of capital controls over the long run. Many argue that the impact of the controls is gradually eroded as agents find ways of getting around them (see EC, 1988). However, the experience of the UK which had controls on capital movements from 1948 to 1979 suggests otherwise (see Gibson, 1989). We discuss the UK case later in this book.

this by taking two examples (Gibson and Tsakalotos, 1991). In the case of Spain, controls on capital inflows in the last years of the 1980s, after Spain had joined the ERM, allowed her to maintain a tighter monetary policy than would otherwise have been possible. Domestic interest rates were above German interest rates, but the peseta was not expected to depreciate since Spain was credibly committed to its exchange rate target within the ERM. This implied that the forward discount on the peseta was either small or nonexistent. Large capital inflows ensued, the peseta moved to the top of its band and the government was under pressure to reduce interest rates. The latter would, of course, have undermined Spain's disinflationary stance. Hence instead the Spanish authorities introduced controls on capital inflows. w in equation (5.3) became positive and allowed the authorities to maintain their disinflation programme.[16]

The second example of the role which capital controls can play in giving a country some monetary independence is closer to the cases of France and Italy during the 1980s. They wished to maintain domestic interest rates at a lower level than that implied by interest parity (the wedge in equation (5.3) was often negative). Controls on capital outflows prevented capital leaving the country and precipitating a realignment. Thus capital controls, by allowing countries some leeway in conducting their monetary policy enhanced the stability of the ERM. Any short-term policy disagreements could, to some extent, be accommodated.

In addition to granting some policy independence, capital controls also helped to stave off speculative attacks. As we argued in Chapter 4, one of the main problems associated with fixed (or semi-fixed) exchange rate systems is the potential for self-fulfilling speculative attacks. We also noted that capital controls can act as a means of forestalling a speculative attack since they limit the extent to which agents can move out of the currency (Wyplosz, 1986). In the simple speculative attack model, inflation differentials can spark of a speculative attack when reserves fall to a critical level. When countries like Italy and France joined the ERM their inflation rates were quite a bit above that of Germany. Hence speculative attacks could easily have been triggered. However, capital controls helped ERM countries to maintain their parities and to delay realignments. The delaying of realignments was critical in their anti-inflation strategy. If high inflation countries had to realign as soon as higher than average inflation began to affect their competitiveness adversely, then the ERM could have been no different from a crawling peg and any discipline could have been lost.

Evidence that speculative capital outflows could have undermined ERM countries in the 1980s is given by Gibson and Tsakalotos (1993). They examine the determinants of speculative capital outflows (capital flight) from Italy, France, Greece, Spain and Portugal. Their results indicate that capital flight from France increased when expectations of devaluation increased. Capital controls limited the extent of that speculation and hence enabled realignments of the French franc to occur successfully. In the case of Italy, capital controls were tightened whenever expectations of devaluation increased, with the consequence that capital flight was contained.

---

[16] This, in essence, was the heart of the Walters critique against the UK joining the ERM (see Walters, 1990). He argued that joining the ERM would be inflationary since we would have to cut interest rates to prevent appreciation of the exchange rate. Of course, this was not what happened when the UK joined, because of a lack of credibility. On the whole domestic interest rates had to be maintained above German ones because expectations of depreciation kept the forward premium on sterling negative.

Additional evidence that capital controls have been important at times of realign-ments can be gleaned from examining onshore–offshore interest rate differentials around the times of realignments between 1981 and 1983.[17] France again provides a useful example. Offshore interest rates are unaffected by the existence of capital con-trols. The EuroFrench franc interest rate is a rate on time deposits in French francs held outside of France and hence the French authorities have no control over this rate – it is unaffected by capital controls. The onshore interest rate is simply the domestic interest rate. Figure 5.5 plots these two rates.[18] It is clear that prior to realignments interest rates in the offshore market (ffrlibor) rose to very high levels. Domestic interest rates (ffr), however, were relatively unaffected falling throughout the period 1981 to 1983. Had capital controls not been operating, then domestic interest rates would have had to rise to similarly high levels, with detrimental effects on the domestic economy.[19]

Capital controls within ERM countries were slowly eliminated towards the end of the 1980s (for example, France and Italy had removed capital controls almost com-pletely by 1987).[20] If they were so crucial to the durability of the system, as we have argued, then this suggests that their removal would create problems for stability. However, not all authors agree and this brings us to the final factor which is stressed by some economists to explain why the system survived so long: growing credibility of the exchange rate parities.

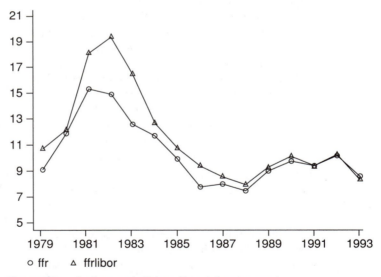

o ffr    △ ffrlibor

**Figure 5.5.**    *Onshore and offshore French Interest rates*

[17] See the studies by Basevi on Italy and Wyplosz on France in EC (1988).
[18] We can note that the interest rates used here were quarterly and hence they include a lot of smoothing. With monthly interest rates, the impact of realignments is even more striking.
[19] Note the removal of capital controls after 1986 accounts for the convergence of both interest rates thereafter.
[20] Technically, EU countries were supposed to remove all controls on capital movements by 1 July 1990. Spain and Ireland were given an extension until the end of 1992 and Greece and Portugal until the end of 1995.

A number of authors argued that the ERM without capital controls would be stable because the absence of controls on capital movements would lend a new credibility to the system. The experience of the ERM between 1987 and 1992 is usually quoted in support of this argument. Giavazzi and Spaventa (1990) argue that the removal of capital controls indicated a regime shift: countries, rather than borrowing German credibility, were themselves now committed to low inflation and fixed exchange rates. This acted as a signal that central parities would no longer be altered for the simple reason that orderly realignments would become much more difficult without capital controls. Hence rational forward-looking agents would not expect realignments.[21]

We can think of this argument in relation to the literature we discussed in Chapter 4 on target zones. There we noted that the existence of a target zone would alter expectations. If the target zone is fully credible then the expected future exchange rate should lie within the target zone. Svensson (1990) examines this argument for ERM countries. He assumes uncovered interest parity and uses the forward exchange rate as a proxy for the expected future spot rate. His results for the period 1979–90 suggest that the expected future rate of ERM currencies continually lay outside the ERM target zone. This, he concludes, suggests that realignments were always expected and the zone was not credible.

Frankel and Phillips (1991) undertake a similar analysis for the period 1987–91 using monthly data. Instead of using the forward rate as a measure of exchange rate expectations, they use survey data. Their results indicate that the ERM gained a significant increase in credibility after 1990. They also note that the expected future rate for the Dutch guilder *vis-à-vis* the Deutschmark has always been within the ERM bands, suggesting, not surprisingly (given the information in Table 5.1), that the guilder bands have always been credible.

What can we make of these arguments regarding the stability of the ERM? The first two factors, the existence of credit facilities and the nature of realignments, were undoubtedly helpful in maintaining stability. However, it cannot be said that on their own they would have been enough. Had speculative flows of capital been larger in the early 1980s, then the system would probably have broken down sooner. Hence we are left with the element of luck which the system had (particularly in terms of the common policy goal of fighting inflation which all ERM countries shared in the 1980s), the role that capital controls played and perhaps the idea that the system had slowly built up some credibility during the 1980s thus allowing it a period of calm in the late 1980s and early 1990s, although the evidence for this has always been weak. In assessing the importance of each of these factors, it is necessary to delve into the reasons for the crises within the system in September 1992 and again in July 1993.

The September 1992 crisis witnessed the departure of Italy and the UK from the ERM.[22] As Table 5.1 shows, the peseta was devalued by 5% and additionally Ireland, Portugal and Spain all tightened their capital controls. Problems continued into 1993, with Ireland, Portugal and Spain all experiencing downward speculative pressure. This led to several realignments of those currencies. In June 1993, the French franc also started to experience strong downward speculative pressure and it

---

[21] A similar argument is put forward by Bini Smaghi and Micossi (1990).

[22] In addition to the problems of ERM currencies proper, the Scandinavian countries which had been pegging to the ECU abandoned their exchange-rate commitment. Finland abandoned the peg on 8 September 1992; Sweden on 19 November 1992 and Norway on 10 December 1992.

was agreed on 2 August to widen the fluctuation bands to ±15%. This effectively signalled the breakdown of the system since such wide fluctuation bands require little intervention to maintain – the system can hardly even now be described as a loose target zone. How can we account for this reversal of fortune?

An important factor relates to the reversal of the fortuitous circumstances which had existed in the early 1980s. The most important of these was the breakdown in agreement on the goals of policy. Countries like France were of the opinion that they had deflated enough and that the EU should now turn to addressing the problem of growth and unemployment. This desire to loosen policy became particularly acute when industrial countries entered a major recession. At the same time, German monetary union provided a large shock to the German economy. The financing of monetary union led to large increases in interest rates. Hence the policy convergence which had characterised the 1980s was under threat. And if policy convergence was under threat, then whatever increase in credibility which the ERM might have enjoyed in 1990 rapidly fell.

De Grauwe (1994) argues that the ERM has always suffered from declines in credibility during periods of recession, precisely because policy conflicts can easily arise. Using interest rate differentials as a measure of credibility,[23] he finds a negative correlation between credibility and unemployment. Simple regressions also provide support for his view.

But at the same time as policy divergence was manifesting itself, there was growing impetus for monetary union. In particular, the Delors plan had mapped out a route to monetary union that involved a 'harder' ERM as its second stage. There were to be fewer realignments; controls on capital movements were to be completely eliminated; and all countries were to join the system with the ±2.25% fluctuation margins. With the removal of capital controls, the system was undermined by the policy disagreements which emerged. And, of course, when the speculative attacks followed, it proved very difficult for the monetary authorities to defend their central parities or to instigate orderly realignments.

The experience of the early 1990s once again highlights to so-called 'impossibility triangle'. A country cannot have a fixed exchange rate, free capital mobility and pursue an autonomous monetary policy at the same time. What happened to the ERM within this context was that whilst exchange rates were becoming more fixed and capital more free to move around, so countries were more keen to pursue their own domestic policy goals. The collapse of 1992/93 can thus hardly been seen as surprising when viewed with hindsight. However, it has left analysts with different proposals about how Europe can get back on the road to further monetary co-operation and, in particular, different ideas about how the impossibility triangle can be resolved. The problem, once more, is finding the best institutional structure which can help Europe to realise the most favourable benefits of managing exchange rates, such as reducing misalignments and instability as well as increasing credibility. A full answer to the question of what measure Europe should take at present requires not only an analysis of what Europe needs now but also an idea of where it wants to go. Hence we suspend judgement on what should be done now until after we have examined in more detail the goals of EMU.

---

[23] This follows the approach of Svensson (1990) which we have discussed. A higher interest rate differential indicates greater expected devaluation (given uncovered interest parity) and hence lower credibility.

**Economic and Monetary Union**

Monetary co-operation in the EU has the ultimate aim of proceeding to a full monetary union. In December 1991 in Maastricht, the European Council of Ministers agreed a revision to the Treaty of Rome which makes monetary union a goal of the EU and which sets out a strategy by which that goal might be achieved.

The Maastricht Treaty grew out of the Delors Report which was published in 1989. The Delors Report argued that EMU was best achieved via a gradualist and parallel approach (Fratianni et al., 1992). The concept of parallelism relates to the fact that economic union and monetary union were seen as two separate parts of a single whole and hence the aim was to move towards both in parallel, the rationale being that monetary union itself would require a high degree of economic convergence if it were to be successful. The gradualist aspect of the Delors Report was reflected in the stages by which monetary union was to be achieved. This gradualist approach reflected the view that economic integration was a slow process.

Much of the debate surrounding EMU centred around the Delors report and its various stages. It is therefore useful for us to outline them here. In Stage 1 all countries were to join the ERM with 2.25% intervention bands, capital controls were to be removed and a single financial area created. At the same time, EU countries were to co-operate more on monetary policy and engage in some mutual surveillance of economic developments and budgetary policies of member states. Finally, at the end of Stage 1, the Delors Report stated that a new treaty be agreed for Stages 2 and 3.

In Stage 2, the exchange rate commitment via the ERM was to become more stringent. Realignments were not to be ruled out, but were expected to become more and more infrequent. Additionally, a central European body (the European System of Central Banks, ESCB) was to take more responsibility for monetary policy to prepare the way for the conduct of a future common monetary policy.

Finally, Stage 3 involved the irrevocable fixing of exchange rates with a view to the eventual replacement of national currencies by a single European currency. Monetary Policy within Europe is transferred fully to the European Central Bank.

The timing of these stages was not fully specified within the Delors Report. It insisted only that Stage 1 begin on 1 July 1990. To this end, capital controls were eliminated in all EU countries by that date, with the exception of Ireland, Spain, Portugal and Greece. These countries all had extensions: in the cases of Spain and Ireland until the end of 1992; in the cases of Greece and Portugal to the end of 1995. Up until the first crisis in the ERM in September 1992, all countries except Greece had joined the ERM and Italy had moved to the narrower bands. Hence Stage 1 was well under way. The crisis in the ERM was a set-back for the process and we discuss the implications of this for the transition to EMU later in this chapter.

The Maastricht Treaty signed in December 1991 set out a clearer timetable for EMU and also laid down conditions which have to be met by member countries to be eligible for proceeding towards a single currency. Stage 1 was to be completed by the end of 1993. From 1 January 1994, Stage 2 of EMU began. The European Monetary Institute (EMI) was created to begin the process of co-ordinating monetary policy. By 31 December 1996, the European Commission and the EMI will report to the European Council of Ministers on progress by member states with the conditions. From 1 January 1997, the way is open for those who meet the criteria to decide a date for movement to a single currency and the creation of a European Central Bank (ECB, the EMI exists only in the transition period). The UK can exercise the right to opt out of a single currency if it wishes.

The conditions which countries have to meet to be eligible for membership of EMU relate to macroeconomic and institutional factors. First, inflation must not exceed the average of inflation in the 3 lowest inflation countries by more than 1.5%. Secondly, the interest rate on long-term government bonds must not exceed by 2% average interest rates in the 3 countries with the lowest inflation rates. Thirdly, the government deficit must not be more than 3% of GDP. Fourthly, the government debt to GDP ratio must not exceed 60%. Fifthly, the exchange rate must have been fixed within its ERM narrow bands without a realignment for at least 2 years. Finally, the statutes of the central bank must be compatible with those of the proposed ECB.

Clearly the process by which EMU is achieved is an interesting and important issue for the EU and we discuss the transitional aspects of monetary union at the end of this section. We begin, instead, with an analysis of the problems which have to be faced at the end-point of the process, monetary union itself. In Chapter 4 we discussed the theoretical literature on optimal currency areas which focuses on the costs and benefits of monetary union. We argued that the costs involve essentially giving up both the exchange rate as a policy tool and the ability to have an independent monetary policy. The benefits arise from the reduced uncertainty generated by having a single currency, the potential for increased credibility in fighting inflation as well as a reduction in the problems of exchange rate volatility and misalignments. Our first task in this section is to quantify some of these costs and benefits within the context of the EU.

If EMU does proceed in Europe, then it is important to discuss the way in which monetary and fiscal policy is to be conducted. With respect to monetary policy, much of the literature has focused on the question of the constitution of the ECB. With respect to fiscal policy, issues are more complex. There are two central questions which we focus on here. First, will individual countries have autonomy to carry out fiscal policy within EMU? Secondly, is there a need for some larger role for centralised fiscal policy?

*The costs and benefits of EMU*

The EU has estimated the economic benefits from a single currency to be around 10% of EU GNP.[24] The most obvious benefit is the elimination of transaction costs associated with the exchange of currencies. However, this amounts to a gain of on average only 0.5%.[25] The rest of the benefits come from greater monetary stability and the elimination of exchange rate risk.

Emerson (1990) argues that a single currency will promote efficiency, stability and equity within the EU. With respect to efficiency, resource allocation will improve as prices more accurately signal where resources should flow within the EU. The argument here is that at present, with 12 different currencies, the law of one price does not operate and hence efficient resource allocation is impaired. Stability comes from reduced exchange rate variability and uncertainty as well as greater price stability that is supposed to follow from the adoption of an independent status for the central bank. As we have noted before, the econometric evidence on the effect of exchange rate variability on trade and investment is rather weak. However, the EU calculates that the impact is large from information drawn from survey data. Finally, the

[24] See the Commission of the European Communities (1990).
[25] Smaller countries are expected to gain more here, because the transactions costs associated with exchange are greater. Larger countries with highly traded international currencies will gain less.

dynamic effects of EMU on growth should help to make the EU more equitable. New endogenous growth theories[26] stress the fact that an increase in productivity and investment can lead to a virtuous circle. Emerson notes that if EMU reduces the risk premium between EU countries by around 0.5% only, something which would lead to greater investment, then growth could increase leading to a cumulative gain of around 5% of European GNP over the long run.

Eichengreen (1993) is sceptical of these large gains. In particular, he questions the argument which states that in order to reap the benefits of the Single Economic Market (SEM), Europe has to adopt a single currency. His view stems from a belief that the costs of exchange rate instability are minimal, something which could be concluded from the inability of econometric work to find a link between instability and trade/investment. In addition, the EU's arguments can be criticised for being rather vague: quantifying the effects of exchange rate stability on resource allocation are inevitably rather speculative.

In Chapter 4, we noted that the costs of adopting a single currency depend on the extent to which the area in question suffers from asymmetric shocks which are normally best dealt with through exchange rate changes. The Commission, among others, has argued that the process of economic integration within the EU has made, and will make, asymmetric shocks less likely (Emerson, 1990). However, this may be too sanguine a view. Bayoumi and Eichengreen (1993) argue that asymmetric shocks (both demand and supply shocks) are quite prevalent in the EU. An examination of the period 1962–88 shows that the peripheral EU countries experienced more asymmetric shocks than the core EU countries (the latter being Germany, France, Belgium, Luxembourg, The Netherlands and Denmark). This suggests that the newer and poorer member of the EU will have greater problems with monetary union than the older members of the EU. In addition, they show that the EU as a whole experienced more asymmetric shocks over the period than did the US regions.

These arguments suggest that the costs of a single currency could be high. However, a possible criticism of Bayoumi and Eichengreen's conclusions is that they show only that asymmetric shocks have been more prevalent in the past – they tell us nothing about the likelihood of asymmetric shocks in the future. Indeed, as we have noted, the Commission's argument is that asymmetric shocks are likely to decline in importance as European integration proceeds. However, Krugman (1991b; 1992a) argues that an examination of the historical pattern of regional development in the US suggests that the process of European integration will possibly lead to a greater prevalence of asymmetric shocks. Krugman (1991b) notes that the location of industry in US regions is much more concentrated than that in EC countries at present. The removal of all barriers to trade with the creation of the SEM is likely to result in EU industry becoming more concentrated as in the US. But greater regional concentration of industry will also tend to enhance the probability of asymmetric shocks. Moreover, Krugman argues that capital mobility will tend to magnify the impact of such shocks since capital frequently flows to the more prosperous regions. Thus, Krugman concludes that asymmetric shocks are likely to become more frequent after 1992 not less and hence the costs of losing the exchange rate as a policy instrument will be greater.

---

[26] See, for example, Romer (1994) for a general review of endogenous growth theories. For an application to the EU, see Baldwin (1989).

Up till now, we have focused on asymmetric shocks and their implications for monetary union. However, it is not only asymmetric shocks which might have adverse effects on regions within a monetary union. Business cycles can be considered to be the outcome of three interacting factors: shocks (either asymmetric or symmetric); propagation mechanisms (the consumption function, investment function etc.); and policy responses. Symmetric shocks followed by different propagation mechanisms throughout different EU regions could lead to different cyclical patterns and hence varying optimal policy responses across different EU regions. Dickerson *et al.* (1995) examine business cycles within the EU as a whole over the period 1960 to 1990 and show that there is little correspondence. This is true both with respect to the timing of cycles and their magnitude (that is the distance from trough to peak). Only for a core group of countries is a greater degree of similarity in business cycle behaviour found. Thus both symmetric and asymmetric shocks could prove costly within European monetary union.

We noted in Chapter 4 that the above costs can be mitigated if the countries adopting a single currency have highly mobile capital and labour, if they are open and if they have a diversified export product base. The European Commission argues that the EU is already at, or at least progressing towards, something like an optimal currency area – EU economies are becoming more open and more closely linked by intra-EU trade, controls on capital movements are being eliminated and labour mobility is being enhanced.

Labour mobility is thought to be crucial to lowering the costs of asymmetric shocks. In the absence of downward wage flexibility, unemployment would normally result in the region affected negatively by an asymmetric shock. If labour is mobile, then the unemployed can move out of the badly affected region (reducing unemployment) to the positively affected region (which, if it is to avoid inflationary pressure, will benefit from the influx of labour). Indeed, within the US, Eichengreen (1993) notes that mobility of labour plays a large part in helping states adjust to asymmetric shocks. However, in Europe, labour mobility is much more limited. In part, this is a consequence of language and cultural barriers (Goodhart, 1990). But, in addition, labour mobility *within* individual European countries is less than in the US (Eichengreen, 1993). That is, the Europeans seem much more unwilling to move around even within their own countries than the Americans, far less to move between European countries. Faini and Venturini (1994) argue that low labour mobility can be attributed to the complex relationship between migration and income. At very low levels of income, an increase in income can result in a rise in migration since potential migrants now have the monetary means to engage in migration. As incomes rise, however, a home-bias effect takes over and migration is reduced. In particular, citizens prefer to remain in their own countries for social, cultural and psychological reasons. As a result, income differentials do not encourage people to migrate. Faini and Venturini find that even the poorer southern European countries have already passed the point at which citizens prefer to stay at home. The obvious implication is the labour mobility in the EU as a whole is unlikely to be very large and hence unlikely to contribute to mitigating the costs of EMU.

By its very nature, it is difficult to estimate the costs and benefits to Europe of adopting a single currency. However, the above analysis suggests that the costs will not be insubstantial. Hence the design of policy at EU level might prove critical in helping to mitigate these costs and it is to this issue which we now turn.

*Monetary policy at
the European level
and the European
Central Bank (ECB)*

We argued earlier in this chapter that one of the main benefits of the ERM was the role it has played in reducing inflation and promoting price stability within Europe. The main concern of the Commission with respect to monetary policy at the European level has been to ensure that the institutional structure within monetary union will continue to promote this goal of low inflation.

In particular, we have already noted in this chapter that countries like Italy and France borrowed Bundesbank credibility. The question which arises now is how will this credibility be affected by monetary union? In order to provide an answer to this question, it is useful to begin by analysing the problem within a 'monetary union' without a single currency but with more or less irrevocably fixed exchange rates, that is, something like Stage 2 of the Delors plan.

In such a system, a European central bank is not strictly necessary: and that there are in fact two ways in a fixed exchange rate system we can have an anti-inflationary anchor: ceding all monetary authority to the leading central bank in the group; creating a new institution in charge of a co-ordinated monetary policy. The former represents a continuation of the practice that has characterised the ERM (while it still had the narrow bands). In other words, the Bundesbank targeted its own price level using monetary policy and all other European central banks operated their monetary policy in a reactive way to achieve currency stability. Germany thus would continue to operate as the asymmetric leader. The advantage of such an approach is that any credibility which non-German European countries had would continue. The disadvantage is that other countries may be unwilling to allow Germany to continue to play such an important role. As we have seen, the tensions within the ERM in the 1990s have resulted partly from a divergence over policy. One advantage of monetary union for countries other than Germany has always been that this would give them a greater say in Community-wide monetary policy than they have within the exchange rate arrangements which exist at present.

For this reason, the Delors Report and the Maastricht Treaty emphasise the need to create an appropriate institutional structure at EU level not only to enable monetary policy to be conducted centrally, but also to increase the amount of co-operation between different European countries. As we have already noted, the Maastricht Treaty set up the European Monetary Institute (EMI) at Stage 2 which will be replaced by the European Central Bank (ECB) at Stage 3 when the single currency is adopted.

The literature on the creation of an ECB has emphasised the institutional structure required to generate a Europe with low inflation.[27] To that end, the ECB has been designed to be completely independent of political institutions within the EU and is to devote itself exclusively to price stability. The economic rationale for this stems from the literature on credibility.[28] The concern was that the ECB would reflect the interests not only of Germany (the low inflation country) but also of other EU countries, some of whom are likely to be more tolerant of inflation. If the inflation rate in the EU was some weighted average of each country's interests, then it might have implied an ECB which was 'softer' on inflation than the arrangements within the ERM of the 1980s. Hence the credibility of the new ECB would have been undermined. The implications of this are that the agents would have expected the

---

[27] See the Commission of the European Communities (1990), Eichengreen (1993), Goodhart (1992) and Fratianni *et al.* (1992) among others.
[28] See, for example, Barro and Gordon (1983); Backus and Driffill (1985).

ECB to engineer a surprise inflation, hence making it more difficult for the new institution to maintain low inflation. Thus the fear is that the new institution, in order to gain a reputation, may have to conduct a period of tight monetary policy which could lead to Europe having high real interest rates for quite some time after monetary union. If, on the other hand, the ECB is set up independently, then such problems may be avoided or at least lessened.

However, under the terms negotiated in the Maastricht Treaty, whilst the new institution is to be independent from the political authorities, the Council of Ministers is still responsible for exchange rate policy. Hence it is still possible for the Council of Ministers to set an exchange rate target for the ECB which is incompatible with its goal of low inflation. So the extent to which the ECB will succeed in being a completely independent organisation devoted only to the task of stabilising prices must be called into question.[29]

Whether this will be costly for the EU depends in large part on the extent to which independence for the Central Bank is important in ensuring low inflation. The credibility argument is derived from a new classical framework in which there is little role for stabilisation policy since all markets clear – inflation in this framework is simply a monetary phenomenon which requires strong monetary policy to eliminate. However, there are good theoretical reasons for thinking that inflation depends on the overall institutional framework in an economy, not just the relationship between the Central Bank and the government. Henley and Tsakalotos (1993a) argue that it is the design of institutions which mediate conflict, and particularly labour market institutions, which is crucial in determining whether inflation can be successfully eliminated without the cost of rising unemployment. They argue that if inflation is seen as the outcome of conflict over income distribution in any economy, then a tight monetary policy simply succeeds in reducing inflationary pressures *because* it increases unemployment. The rise in unemployment is crucial since it is that which moderates wage demands and lessens the distributional conflict by weakening labour. Thus they conclude that it should come as no surprise that disinflation experiments (either through monetary or through exchange rate targeting) have been associated with high unemployment as we noted was the case for France and Italy above. By contrast, the design of appropriate labour market institutions can allow a government to lower inflation without the need to raise unemployment.

Such theoretical arguments against the simple credibility view can be backed up by empirical evidence on this issue. Mayer (1993), himself a monetarist, argues that new classical economists have not show that credibility is the critical issue in the fight against inflation. Krugman (1990) also points to evidence of long periods in countries of low inflation which have not relied on independent central banks For example, whilst there are economies such as Germany which have had a low inflation record and an independent central bank, there are also other low inflation countries, such as Japan, where the central bank has no independence. In other words, there is evidence which suggests that there is no simple relationship between central bank independence and low inflation records. Instead inflation performance depends less on the institutional framework in which the central bank and more on how the central bank fits in with other institutional arrangements in the economy[30] Thus is seems safe to

---

[29] Of course, if the ECU floats against the other major currencies, then there will be no conflict between exchange rate and monetary policy.

[30] It is beyond the scope of this book to examine this argument in detail. The reader is referred to Henley and Tsakalotos (1993) for a comprehensive discussion.

conclude that the debate on the institutional structure of the new European Central bank and the appropriate anti-inflation strategy which should be pursued needs to be widened beyond simple discussions regarding its independence.

In this respect, there is the question of the democratic accountability of the new institution. Eichengreen (1993) notes that the ECB will have to publish a quarterly report and submit an annual report to the European Parliament. But, at present, the European Parliament is a much weaker body relative to, say, US Congress or Senate. In the US, the Federal Reserve is independent of political institutions. However, both Congress and Senate have much greater powers than the European Parliament to call witnesses from the Federal Reserve Board to account for their actions in front of various committees. In Europe, the European Parliament has no such powers. As a result, Eichengreen argues that the institutional structure for the ECB envisaged within the Maastricht Treaty will worsen the 'democratic deficit' which is already perceived to exist with respect to other EU institutions.

Nonetheless, if monetary policy in the EU is to be restricted to the control of inflation, then this raises the potential for fiscal policy to play a stabilising role. It is to this question which we now turn.

## Fiscal policy and EMU

There is a large debate within the literature on monetary union on the role for fiscal policy both at individual country level and at a centralised EU level. Two key questions arise. First, will individual countries have the ability to conduct independent fiscal policies within EMU? Second, should the EU itself have a much larger budget which could enable it to conduct fiscal policy at the European level? Obviously these two questions are linked, for, if individual countries still retain fiscal independence, then there might be less of an argument for fiscal policy at the European level. In this section we want to examine these two questions. We argue that irrespective of whether individual countries continue to have the ability to conduct an independent fiscal policy, there is still a good case for expanding the EU budget to allow for more centrally directed fiscal policies. Such a case rests on the fact that a larger central budget can provide the benefits of both automatic stabilisers and an active fiscal stabilisation policy.

Fiscal autonomy is useful to individual European countries if they are affected by asymmetric shocks. Take, for example, an asymmetric demand shock which causes one EU country to go into recession. Within a monetary union, the interest rate is no longer available as a policy instrument which can be used to offset this negative shock (monetary policy is now conducted at the EU level). This observation leads Allsopp (1994) to argue that fiscal policy will have to take its place. Demand shocks can be countered by loosening or tightening fiscal policy as is appropriate. Moreover, using fiscal policy in this manner may even be more desirable than relying on monetary policy, since it allows the latter to be used solely to achieve *medium-term* monetary stability.

Masson and Melitz (1990) also argue for the importance of fiscal autonomy after examining simulations using the IMF's MULTIMOD world model. They look at the impact of a shock to a monetary union comprising of only Germany and France. They assume that France has a balanced current account position whereas Germany has a 4% surplus. Following monetary union, the union has a current account surplus of 2% and hence the ECU (the union currency) appreciates to restore current account balance. The deflationary impact on France of this shock can be mitigated if France is able to pursue an independent fiscal policy. Overall, they conclude that the ability to continue having an independent fiscal policy is useful within a monetary union to offset the impact of such asymmetric shocks. Bean (1992) argues along similar lines: 'Active national fiscal policies will be needed more than ever after monetary union, and imposing unnecessary constraints [the Maastricht criteria] is a major error, especially in the absence of a Community-wide fiscal system' (p.51). Thus the case for fiscal autonomy seems rather strong.

However, for one group of economists, the neo-Ricardians, the question of fiscal autonomy is largely irrelevant. They argue that fiscal policy is useless for stabilisation of individual economies. Assume, for example, that a country suffers a negative shock which reduces national income. If fiscal policy is to play a stabilising role, then this necessitates an increase in aggregate demand by the government and hence a rise in the government budget deficit. Let us assume that the government finances this deficit by borrowing from the private sector. Neo-Ricardians argue that this will have no effect on the overall level of aggregate demand in the economy. The reason is simple. Rational, forward-looking agents know that the debt accumulated will have to be repaid at some point in the future and that this will entail higher taxes. Agents will therefore increase their savings now in anticipation of higher taxes in the future. Overall, therefore, aggregate demand in the economy will remain unchanged. Fiscal policy has no ability to offset the negative effects of the shock. Whether individual European countries have the autonomy to respond to shocks is thus presumably irrelevant for neo-Ricardians.

There are a number of reasons why such a position is untenable.[31] Not least of these is the fact that neo-Ricardians have to assume that agents do not suffer liquidity constraints.[32] If agents would like to borrow more than they are able to and hence are not consuming optimally, then they may not save more when the government borrows to finance its deficit. Instead, they will take advantage of the government's ability to borrow to raise their consumption closer to its optimal level. In this case, fiscal policy will have some impact on aggregate demand and hence whether a country has fiscal autonomy within EMU is not an irrelevant question. But, even if the Ricardian argument is true, then the problems for EMU do not disappear. If there is no opportunity for using fiscal policy to replace the role of monetary policy as a means of short-term demand management in individual EU countries, then the move towards monetary union will lack credibility. Countries will have incentives in the face of asymmetric shocks to opt out of the monetary union.

A useful way of looking at the question of fiscal autonomy is to use the debt-dynamics equation (which highlights the governments intertemporal budget constraint):

$$db/dt = (r-g)b + d - s \tag{5.4}$$

where $db/dt$ is the rate of change of the debt/income ratio (b); r is the real interest rate; g is the real growth rate; d is the primary (that is, non-interest) government deficit; and s is seigniorage revenues. Equation (5.4) illustrates why individual EU countries might not have much fiscal autonomy within EMU by highlighting the link between fiscal and monetary policy.

---

[31] See Buiter (1985) and Seater (1993) for good surveys of the theoretical debate about Ricardian equivalence as well as the empirical evidence.

[32] Others include the assumptions that people have to care about their children as much as they do about themselves and that there has to be full employment.

If monetary policy is geared towards low inflation, then EMU might entail a loss of seigniorage revenues, s. Seigniorage arises partly from the supply of notes and coins in the economy.[33] If inflation is kept low, then revenues from seigniorage will also be low (arising only from the growth of money demand associated with higher income levels). For most European countries, this loss of seigniorage revenue is not that important. The amount of revenue raised in this way is small. For some countries, the southern European economies in particular, the loss of seigniorage revenues is more important. These countries have traditionally relied on this source of revenue because of underdeveloped tax systems.[34] Thus for this group, EMU will compromise their fiscal autonomy, if reforms of the tax system are not undertaken.

A second factor limiting fiscal autonomy is the need to maintain debt/income ratios within sustainable limits. If the debt/income ratio rises to the point where borrowing is made more difficult, then clearly fiscal independence is compromised. The question therefore which arises is what level of debt/income ratio has to be reached before further borrowing becomes impossible. This is a tricky question and there are likely to be several factors associated with EMU which work both to raise the debt/income ratio and perhaps to lower it.

There are two factors which work to raise the critical debt/income ratio beyond which countries will find it difficult to raise money in the international capital markets. Firstly, the move towards greater fixity of exchange rates removes the risk of devaluation and hence savers in other countries will be more willing to hold assets denominated in individual European currencies. Of course, within full monetary union, devaluation of individual currencies is eliminated completely. Moreover, if the ECU is a low inflation currency, it will be attractive to non-EU residents and hence European countries may be able to borrow more from outside the EU and at a lower interest rate (reflecting the lower risk premia).

Secondly, international capital markets may believe that individual EC countries have an implicit guarantee against default. If we examine the history of international lending to Eastern European countries before the 1980s, we can find some support for this idea. The 'umbrella' theory stated that lending to Eastern European countries was low-risk because their debts were implicitly guaranteed by the Soviet Union, which, it was argued, would be unwilling to allow one of the Warsaw pact countries to default.

There is also a factor which might work to strengthen the constraint on debt/income ratios. The removal of capital controls implies that governments no longer have a captive pool of domestic savings to finance public deficits. Hence they will have to remain creditworthy with international capital markets in order to compete for funds successfully. However, the empirical evidence that international capital markets do severely credit ration economies with large debts is limited. Lending to developing countries, which we discuss in Chapter 9 of this book, indicates that countries can borrow large amounts without coming up against a credit limit. Eichengreen (1990a, b) argues that countries such as France, Germany and the UK (which as Table 5.2 indicates have relatively low debt/income ratios) may find it rather easy to get access to the international pool of savings and may thus have much

---

[33] The other source is reserves held at the central bank by commercial banks. But the ability to raise seigniorage revenues from this source is being squeeze by the Second Banking Directive (see Gibson and Tsakalotos, 1992).

[34] See Giavazzi and Giovannini (1989) and Gibson and Tsakalotos (1992).

more fiscal autonomy than countries such as Greece, Italy, Denmark and Ireland whose debt/income ratios are much higher.

The balance of these arguments on the scope for fiscal autonomy is rather tricky and it is difficult to determine *a priori* whether EU countries will have more or less fiscal autonomy within monetary union.[35] What is important, however, is that the EU Commission itself clearly appears to be worried about the potential for a loosening of the fiscal constraint which individual EU countries face. As a result, it itself has sought to tighten the limits which countries face through the conditions included in the Maastricht agreement.[36] As we have noted, this limits both the size of government budget deficits and the level of the debt/income ratio. The figure for the budget deficit is particularly tough: the 3% figure is a maximum and not an average over the cycle. In this way, it severely limits the scope for automatic stabilisers to play a role when a region has gone into recession. The scope for active fiscal policy is, of course, even more severely curtailed by such limits. Table 5.2 shows only 2 countries in 1993 (Ireland and Luxembourg) met the deficit condition; five countries (France, Luxembourg, the UK, Germany and Spain) met the debt/income condition. Hence the ability of individual countries to have fiscal autonomy may be limited simply by the Maastricht conditions.

If fiscal autonomy of individual countries within monetary union is limited, then this perhaps suggests the need for a greater role for a central EU budget to enable the EU to play a greater role in conducting fiscal policy.[37] But the argument for extending the role for the EU budget does not rest on the question of whether individual countries will have fiscal autonomy alone. Eichengreen (1993) argues that centralised fiscal policy within a federal system (such as the EU might become) can play three roles (see also Bean, 1992). Firstly, it can have an equalising effect on different regions. With a progressive tax structure, poorer regions will pay less into the central budget and richer regions more. In this way, transfers from the central fiscal authorities work to raise the amount of assistance given to poorer regions. The CEPR (1993) argue that there are two fundamental problems with the establishment of a fiscal authority which aims at redistribution. The first is that only poor countries would want to join an EMU with such features. The second is the fact that joining such an EMU may be time inconsistent for some states. The time inconsistency results from the fact that if some regions are hit by a permanent and large shock, then it may be optimal for unaffected regions to opt out of the federal fiscal agreement. Such arguments may point to the need for political commitment to a federal Europe before EMU goes ahead – there is no point in EMU going ahead unless individual European countries are committed to the project beyond simply the narrow net economic

---

[35] An argument which is sometimes put forward suggesting that fiscal autonomy will be limited is the problem of imposing differential income tax rates within a monetary union. This argument states that if labour is mobile then it will tend to move to areas where taxes are low. This thus limits the ability of some regions to impose higher tax rates. Given the low mobility of labour within Europe, relative, say, to the US, this argument is probably less relevant. However, as we shall see later, low labour mobility actually increases the case for needing more fiscal autonomy or greater central fiscal policy. If labour is immobile, then a negative asymmetric shock will lead to unemployment in the affected region, increasing the benefits of automatic stabilisers or a more active central fiscal policy.

[36] In addition, there have been suggestions to include a no bailout clause in the Maastricht Treaty. This would state that the EU would not be responsible for rescuing any individual member which found itself unable to meet its international obligations. See Eichengreen (1990a, b).

[37] For two very different views on the role of a centralised fiscal policy in the European Union after EMU, see CEPR (1993) and Fitoussi *et al.* (1993).

*Table 5.2.*   The Maastricht Conditions and EU Countries in 1993

| Target | FR | IR | LX | NE | UK | BE | DN | GE | SP | GR | IT | PG |
|---|---|---|---|---|---|---|---|---|---|---|---|---|
| Inflation | 2.1 | 1.4 | 9.6 | 2.1 | 1.6 | 2.8 | 1.3 | 4.2 | 4.6 | 14.4 | 4.5 | 6.5 |
| Interest Rates | 6.8 | 7.7 | 6.9 | 5.3 | 7.5 | 7.2 | 7.2 | 6.5 | 10.2 | 21.2 | 11.4 | 12.5 |
| Budget Deficits | 5.9 | 3.0 | 2.5 | 4.0 | 7.6 | 7.4 | 4.4 | 8.3 | 7.2 | 15.4 | 10.0 | 8.9 |
| Debt | 44.9 | 92.9 | 10.0 | 83.1 | 53.2 | 198.4 | 78.5 | 48.9 | 55.6 | 113.6 | 115.8 | 69.5 |

*Note*: FR = France, IR = Ireland, LX = Luxembourg, NE = Netherlands, UK = United Kingdom, BE = Belgium, DN = Denmark, GE = Germany, SP = Spain, GR = Greece, IT = Italy, PG = Portugal. Figures which are underlined meet the criteria.
*Source*: *The Financial Times*, 12.5.94, p.2.

benefits they think they might derive from it. It does not, however, seem to provide any case against the setting up of a fiscal authority for redistributive purposes within EMU if that is what European countries want.

Estimates show that the redistributive role of a federal fiscal system can be large. Atkesen *et al.* (1992) estimate the redistributive impact of the US and Canadian federal fiscal systems. They run the following regression:

$$(Y - tax + transfers)_i / (Y - tax + transfers)_{us} = \alpha + \beta Y_i / Y_{us} + \varepsilon_i \qquad (5.5)$$

where Y is *per capita* personal income; tax and transfer are *per capita* federal taxes and transfers respectively and the subscripts i and us refer to individual states and the US (or Canada for the Canadian regression) as a whole. The coefficient $\beta$ measures the extent to which a rise in gross relative incomes is reflected in a rise in net relative incomes. Using data on US regions between 1969 and 1986, $\beta$ was found to be 0.774 across all regions. This implies that 77.4% of the original regional differences in income remain after the federal fiscal system is taken into account. Alternatively, some 22.6% of the original differences are eliminated through fiscal transfers. For Canada the results indicate that the federal system eliminates some 39% of the initial regional differences. This higher figure reflects the constitutional obligation of the Canadian federal government to redistribute via the federal system. Hence federal fiscal systems can have an important equalising effect on different regions.

A second role for central fiscal policy is its coinsurance function. A centralised fiscal structure provides automatic stabilisation for regions which suffer a temporary loss of income. Take the following example. Imagine there is a shock to the north-east region of England, due say to a decline in demand for the goods it produces. This would lead to a fall in income in the north-east and a rise in unemployment (assuming wages and prices are not perfectly flexible). However, with the UK centralised fiscal system, automatic changes to the amount of tax paid by the north-east and to the amount of government spending they receive will help to offset the fall in income. As income falls, the amount of taxes paid to the centre will also fall. Similarly the amount of unemployment benefits and other social spending will rise. The fiscal deficit of the north-east (that is, central government spending in the north-east minus central government income raised there) will increase. This transfer to the region is automatic, that is, it does not require any change in central government policy on taxation or spending. And it will help to limit the fall in the region's income and hence the rise in unemployment. If, by contrast, taxation and spending in the region were a purely local affair, then the local government would automatically go into deficit. Thus a local fiscal system can also act as an automatic stabiliser. However, the cost of this would be borne entirely by the people of the north-east. The usefulness of national fiscal stabilisers is that the costs are spread over the entire nation.

The CEPR (1993) again argue against this role for a centralised fiscal authority. In particular, they note that there is a moral hazard problem. Regions may inflict shocks on themselves (for example, through excessive wage claims) if they know that the shock will be offset by the central budget. Moreover, even if the shock is a 'genuine' one, adjustment may be delayed if federal transfers are available. In response to these points, we can note there is no evidence that suggests that regions within existing monetary unions act in this way. Moreover, again these arguments simply point to the need for commitment to the process of European integration. Indeed, it could be argued that such commitment will be more easily achieved if individual regions are confident that when they are hit by negative shocks, they will not simply be left by the rest of the union to deal with the consequences alone.

Atkesen *et al.* (1992) also provide results on the extent to which US and Canadian federal systems provide a stabilisation function using the following regression:

$$\Delta\{(Y - \text{tax} + \text{transfers})_i/(Y - \text{tax} + \text{transfers})_{us}\} = \alpha + \beta\Delta(Y_i/Y_{us}) + \varepsilon_i \qquad (5.6)$$

The coefficient $\beta$ can be interpreted in a similar way as before, with stabilisation being the aim rather than redistribution. $(1-\beta)$ represents the extent to which the budget stabilises income in the short run in any particular region. The results indicate that the total stabilisation effect for the US is around 30% and for Canada around 17%.

It is easy to see how this argument can be used at EU level to generate a case for an enlarged EU budget. As asymmetric shocks affect different regions within Europe, so an enlarged budget would transfer funds from areas where the shock has increased economic activity to areas where activity has fallen. At present, however, the EU budget is only around 1% of GNP. If the EU were to replicate the US's federal system, for example, then a much larger EU budget would be required and the tax and benefit system would have to be made much more sensitive to regional income. Eichengreen (1990a, b) provides some useful back-of-the-envelope calculations which indicate the task required. If for example half of the EU were hit by a 10% reduction in income, then the transfers which would be required to meet US levels of automatic stabilisation would be 1.5% of GNP. To match this, the EU budget would have to increase by 50%, assuming that all the revenue was directed towards the regions affected. Given that the EU at present has commitments in other areas (for example, agriculture), a large expansion of the EU budget would be necessary if the coinsurance role were to be adopted.

The final role that a centralised fiscal system plays is a stabilisation function. Goodhart (1990) argues that there is a case for an active fiscal policy at the EU level, because of the danger that fiscal policy will be too conservative if left to individual

European nations. This argument relies on the importance of spillover effects.[38] A fiscal expansion within one country in a monetary union will lead to a large spillover into other regions because of the large marginal propensity to import. This raises income in other regions within the union. However, the costs of the fiscal policy are borne only by the region undertaking the initial expansion. In other words, a fiscal expansion will create large social benefits to the wider monetary union which exceed the private benefits to the individual country. As with any situation where there is a positive externality, the producer of the good (in this case fiscal expansion) tends to underproduce it. That is, there will be a tendency for fiscal conservatism because individual EU regions cannot internalise the externality. The EU as a whole, by contrast, could internalise the externality if fiscal policy were more centralised.

The importance of this clearly depends on the extent to which spillovers are important. Eichengreen (1993) argues that the above effect is offset by the fact that higher domestic interest rates abroad caused by the fiscal expansion in the home country tend to operate to dampen the expansionary effect on other regions. For this reason, studies of spillover effects have tended to find that they are small (see Bryant *et al.*, 1989). However, such studies have tended to look at the extent to which US policies affect those in other industrial countries and vice versa. The degree of integration between industrial countries in general might be rather lower than the degree of integration between EU countries. Hence for the latter, the positive effects of the spillover might be much greater. Moreover, as EU countries become even more integrated and their marginal propensities to import from each other increase further, Goodhart's argument might become more relevant, thus creating a case for a greater degree of fiscal stabilisation at EU level.

In conclusion, there are therefore good reasons to think that the EU may have to play a larger role in fiscal policy than it does at present if monetary union is to be successful. Not only would a larger EU budget more effectively operate as an automatic stabiliser to mitigate the impact of asymmetric shocks, but it might also have to play a larger discretionary role in stabilising the EU economy. This will be particularly true if, as we have argued, the spillover effects of fiscal policy conducted at the regional level increase and if individual regions within the monetary union have less fiscal independence to respond to shocks. It is important to note, finally, that an enhanced role for fiscal policy at the European level does not imply that individual regions or states within EMU would not be able to have considerable control over a large proportion of the budget spent locally. The federal fiscal systems of the US, Canada and Germany provide clear evidence that fiscal federalism need not lead to greater centralisation. Indeed, for countries such as the UK, which have always had greater centralisation of budgetary decisions and which have perhaps experienced growing centralisation over recent years, a move towards fiscal federalism at the EU level could actually imply a greater devolution of budgetary responsibility to the regions not less. In this sense, a more centralised fiscal budget at the EU level may prove to be politically attractive to regions within existing states.

## The transition to EMU

We have already outlined the proposed path by which European countries intend to proceed towards economic and monetary union. Its most obvious problem is the

---

[38] Fitoussi *et al.* (1993) also argue that the spillover effects arising from the effect of one country's fiscal policy on another's generate a case either for more co-ordinated fiscal policy or a more centralised fiscal budget.

central place given to the ERM following the crisis in July 1993 when the bands of fluctuation were increased to ±15%. This jeopardised the completion of Stage 2 of the Maastricht Treaty with its emphasis on exchange rate stability in the run up to monetary union in Stage 3.[39] The critical question that therefore arises is what the EU can do to get progress to MU back on track.

We argued in the first section of this chapter that fixed exchange rates without capital controls are highly unstable if policy disagreements between countries surface as indeed they did in the early 1990s. We noted that the crises within the ERM could be explained by the fact that at the same time as there was pressure to make the ERM a harder system, the policy consensus between EU countries which had existed in the 1980s broke down: there was little agreement on the policies that should be adopted in response to the unemployment problem in Europe and this was exacerbated by the deepening recession. Here we want to argue that there is a need to strengthen the institutional structure at Stage 2 in order to promote closer policy co-operation between EU member states. As we shall see, the role of the European Monetary Institute (EMI), the body set up to oversee some of the aspects of the transition to EMU, is crucial in this respect.

The need to strengthen the institutional structure is also crucial if a two-speed Europe is to be avoided. The term two-speed Europe is used to refer to the situation where a core group of countries (Germany, France, the Netherlands, and possibly Belgium and Luxembourg) move to a single currency alone. Such a provision is allowed for in the Maastricht Treaty and could begin in 1999. A two-speed Europe is probably to the disadvantage of the EU in general and peripheral countries in particular. Continuing integration of the EU may be weakened by such a move. Peripheral countries will be disadvantaged in that they will have little input to the form which EMU will take, the structure of the ECB and the choices which are made regarding fiscal policy. Instead they will only be able to join the system as it exists at a later stage. Thus ways of avoiding such an outcome may be considered to be desirable.

There have been a number of suggestions regarding possible routes to EMU following the problems faced by the ERM. A first option is to reimpose controls on capital movements which would facilitate a return to narrower bands. Controls could be maintained until a single currency was adopted. This approach has been suggested by Eichengreen and Wyplosz (1993). They argue for the imposition of (non-interest bearing) reserve requirements on open positions in foreign exchange taken by banks.

---

[39] Fratianni *et al.* (1992) provided an interesting assessment of the Maastricht Treaty prior to the disruptions in the ERM. They argued that the transition process is flawed. The problem arises because the Delors plan and the Maastricht Treaty argue for a gradual approach to monetary union to allow for greater economic convergence between the potential members. The problem with gradual strategies, however, is that they often suffer a lack of credibility in that the public does not believe that monetary union will ever be completed. This implies that risk premia continue to be included in national interest rates and higher expected inflation rates continue to be built into wage claims in individual countries. Withdrawal from the monetary union process thus becomes ever more likely as the prospects for meeting the Maastricht conditions recede. The Maastricht Treaty seeks to overcome this lack of credibility by giving a prominent role to exchange-rate fixity in the transition. Fratianni *et al.* argued that exchange-rate fixity in Stage 2 is designed to signal commitment to the monetary union process – only if EU countries' economic policies converge will the maintenance of fixed exchange rates be possible. Such a strategy might be perfectly acceptable were exchange-rate flexibility in the transition to monetary union not so useful, particularly to mitigate some of the transitional costs associated with the completion of the Single Economic Market with its emphasis on industrial restructuring. Hence they conclude that the emphasis given in the Maastricht Treaty to the exchange rate is too great.

This is equivalent to a tax on capital movements where a speculative position is taken and in this respect is close to the proposal made by Tobin (1978). Artis (1994) notes that such a tax would be possible under the Maastricht Treaty even although it is generally opposed to controls on capital movements. The Treaty itself mentions only administrative quantitative controls and hence does not technically preclude the use of controls engineered through the imposition of reserve requirements.

Controls of this type are certainly an attractive proposition. The experience of the 1980s suggests that controlling capital movements was effective at preventing speculative crises and allowing relatively smooth realignments.[40] The usual argument against capital controls is that they distort the international allocation of resources. However, it is difficult to believe that allowing financial institutions to take short-term speculative positions in currencies is crucial to resource allocation. This is surely more dependent on long-term capital flows and allowing capital to move to countries where the long-term real return is higher. In spite of this, it is unlikely that a return to controlling capital movements is something to which EU countries will agree. The removal of such controls was central to the Single Economic Market programme and the creation of a single European financial area.

A second possible option is for the EU to move rapidly towards monetary union, forgetting about the need for a transitional period. Indeed, this is a view taken by a number of authors who argued that the intermediate stage of the hard ERM might well be unstable (see Giovannini, 1991; Padoa Schioppa, 1992). However, the need for rapid adjustment in individual economies would likely mean that this strategy would involve large costs, especially for the weaker European economies.[41] Moreover, it is not clear that this option commands much political support, with the Germans, in particular, being opposed to it following their experience with the joining of East and West Germany.

A third option is for a softer, more flexible ERM to be reintroduced. Artis (1994) notes that this might involve regular reviews of parities and a changing of parities in line with relative inflation rates in EU countries. But, as Currie and Whitley (1994) point out, whilst such flexibility might appear attractive, it is not clear how such an option would cope with realignments. The opportunity for speculative attacks would still be there.

A final option is for greater emphasis to be given to policy co-ordination. Artis (1994) argues that at present the move from Stage 2 to Stage 3, as envisaged in the Maastricht Treaty, is rather abrupt in the sense that monetary policy at Stage 2 is still the responsibility of member states. This essentially implies that the Bundesbank could continue setting German monetary policy with reference to German economic conditions and leaving the other countries to follow their lead. The EMI has only an advisory role. At Stage 3, there is then a rather sudden transfer of monetary policy to the European Central Bank.

Artis (1994) and Currie and Whitley (1994) argue that a better transition would entail an enhanced role for the EMI. In particular, this would imply first a move away from policy directed at achieving German objectives to European objectives; and secondly a move away from policy based on a diagnosis of purely German problems to one based on a diagnosis of European problems (Artis, 1994, p.199). The

---

[40] See Gibson and Tsakalotos (1991) on why reimposition of capital controls may help to avoid a two-speed Europe.

[41] See Gibson and Tsakalotos (1991) for a discussion of the problems which the southern European economies may face with such a strategy.

obvious institutional mechanism through which such co-operation could be mediated is the EMI. A possible problem with this strategy is opposition from the Germans. However, Currie and Whitley argue that such a strategy is probably in the interests of Germany. Given that spillovers between EU countries are not insignificant and may be expected to increase as integration proceeds, the formulation of policy based on European rather than simply national needs will actually be more efficient. Moreover, a key advantage of this strategy is that it will allow some experience of co-ordinating policy at the EU level to be gained and this, of course, will prove vital at Stage 3.[42] For surely the success of EMU depends crucially on Europe being better able to mediate different policy objectives and diagnoses and Stage 2 of the transition process does not seem too early to begin this process.

Moreover, co-operation, if it is to be effective, needs to move beyond simply co-operation regarding monetary affairs strictly defined. Our discussion of fiscal policy and the need for a larger budget has important implications here. If it is the case that economies within the EU fear that monetary union will imply more regional problems, then this will weaken their resolve to make the necessary commitment to EMU and also increase speculation that they will drop out of the process. A discussion of measures to mitigate these regional problems can, therefore, also increase the credibility of such potential co-operation in the second stage on the path to EMU. Other issues which could also usefully figure in co-operative discussions could include unemployment and growth. As we noted earlier in this chapter, increased unemployment can lead to increased policy disagreements and a reduction in credibility. Thus, it is hard not to conclude that the move towards EMU is not just a question of weighing a set of isolated economic costs and benefits, it must also include some institutions for economic policy making which mimic policy-making forums in other monetary unions.

## The lessons of European monetary integration

Our study of the history of European monetary co-operation as well as our discussion of the possible future for such co-operation has provided an interesting case study of some of the issues of exchange rate management which we raised in Chapter 4. In particular, the history of the ERM, the Delors plan and the Maastricht Treaty all highlight the costs and benefits associated with different types of exchange rate system. The ERM began as a flexible target zone system of exchange rate management. Realignments prevented the build-up of unsustainable real exchange rate changes with their associated implications for competitiveness and capital controls provided some defence against speculative attacks. Throughout the 1980s, however, the system became more rigid. Capital controls were removed and realignments became less frequent. The costs of this did not manifest themselves until disagreements over policy direction surfaced in the early 1990s. And the result was the move towards a system of exchange rate management which can barely be characterised as a loose target zone.

The question which Europe now faces is where it should go from here. And, here one of the main themes of this book again becomes important, namely the importance of developing a framework for co-operation if any international financial system is going to be successful. To see this, we can return to the impossibility triangle which we raised at the end of the first section of this chapter. It is not possible for a

---

[42] We can note that Artis (1994) favours a move towards narrower bands as policy co-ordination proceeds. Currie and Whitley (1994) do not emphasise this as part of their proposals for a modified Stage 2.

system of exchange rate management to have fixed exchange rates and no controls on capital movements with, concurrently, its members pursuing different policies. If, in the transition to EMU, a hard ERM or even a not so hard ERM is not bolstered by other institutions (such as discussion about a larger federal budget or policies to promote growth and regional convergence), then once again disagreement about policy goals, with some countries emphasising employment more than inflation, will surface. If the market see this occurring in any intermediate stage before EMU is adopted, then destabilising forces will once again come to the fore as they did in 1992 and 1993. But the need for co-operation is equally, if not more, important even if a fast track to EMU is adopted. For high unemployment, regional disparities and so on may severely undermine the political will for continuing with monetary union with perhaps irreversible consequences for monetary co-operation within Europe.

## References

Allsopp, C.J. (1994) 'Discussion', of R. Barrell, A. Britton and N. Pain 'When the time was right', in D. Cobham (ed.) *European Monetary Upheavals*. Manchester University Press, Manchester. 141–5.

Artis, M.J. and Taylor, M.P. (1988) 'Exchange rates, interest rates, capital controls and the EMS', in F. Giavazzi, S. Micossi and M. Miller (eds) *The European Monetary System*. CEPR, Cambridge University Press, Cambridge.

Artis, M.J. (1994) 'Stage Two: feasible transitions to EMU', in D. Cobham (ed.) *European Monetary Upheavals*. Manchester University Press, Manchester. 188–225.

Artis, M.J. and Taylor, M.P. (1994) 'The stabilising effect of the ERM on exchange rates and interest rates', *IMF Staff Papers*, 41: 1, 123–48.

Atkesen, A., Bayoumi, R. and Masson, P. (1992) 'Private capital flows, federal fiscal systems and EMU: evidence from existing monetary unions', in C.A.E. Goodhart (ed.) *EMU and the European System of Central Banks after Maastricht*. Financial Markets Group, LSE, London.

Backus, D. and Driffill, J. (1985) 'Inflation and reputation', *American Economic Review*, 75: 3.

Baldwin, R. (1989) 'On the growth effects of 1992', NBER Working Paper 3119. NBER, Cambridge, Mass.

Barro, R.J. and Gordon, D.B. (1983) 'Rules, discretion and reputation in a model of monetary policy', *Journal of Monetary Economics*, 12.

Bayoumi, R. and Eichengreen, B. (1993) 'Shocking aspects of European monetary integration', in F. Torres and F. Giavazzi (eds) *Adjustments and Growth in the European Monetary Union*. CEPR, Cambridge University Press, Cambridge.

Bean, C.R. (1992) 'Economic and monetary union in Europe', *Journal of Economic Perspectives*, 6: 4, 31–52.

Bini Smaghi, L. and Micossi, S. (1990) 'Monetary and exchange rate policy in the EMS with free capital mobility', in P. De Grauwe and L. Papademos (eds) *The European Monetary System in the 1990s*. Longman, London, 120–154.

Bryant, R.C., Currie, D.A., Frenkel, J.A., Masson, P.R. and Portes, R. *Macroeconomic Policies in an Interdependent World*. The Brookings Institution/CEPR/IMF, Washington, D.C.

Buiter, W.H. (1985) 'Government deficits reinterpreted', *Economic Policy*, 1 (November), 13–79.

**Calmfors, L. and Driffill, J.** (1988) 'Bargaining structure, corporatism and macro-economic performance', *Economic Policy*, 6 (April).

**CEPR** (1993) Making Sense of Subsidiarity: how much centralisation for Europe? Monitoring European Integration, 4, Centre for European Policy Research, London.

**Currie, D.A. and Whitley, J.** (1994) 'What route to European monetary integration', in D. Cobham (ed.) *European Monetary Upheavals*. Manchester University Press, Manchester. 167–83.

**Cushman, D.O.** (1983) 'The effects of real exchange rate risk on international trade', *Journal of International Economics*, 15: 45–63.

**Davies, G.** (1989) Britain and the EMS. Economic Study, 1, Institute for Public Policy Research, London.

**De Grauwe, P.** (1990) 'The cost of disinflation and the European Monetary System', *Open Economics Review*, 1: 2, 147–74.

**De Grauwe. P.** (1994) 'Toward EMU without the EMS', *Economic Policy*, 18 (April), 147–85.

**Dickerson, A.P., Gibson, H.D. and Taskalotos, E.** (1995) 'Comparisons of EU business cycles revisited', *Studies in Economics*, University of Kent, 95/1.

**EC** (1988) 'Creation of a European financial area', *European Economy*, 36 (May).

**EC** (1990) 'One market, one money', *European Economy*, 44 (October).

**Eichengreen, B.** (1990a) 'The costs and benefits of european monetary unification', CEPR discussion paper, 453 (September).

**Eichengreen, B.** (1990b) 'Currency union', *Economic Policy*, 10 (April), 118–187.

**Eichengreen, B.** (1993) 'European Monetary Unification', *Journal of Economic Literature*, 31: 1321–57.

**Eichengreen, B. and Wyplosz, C.** (1993) 'The unstable EMS', *Brookings Papers on Economic Activity*, 1.

**Emerson, M.** (1990) 'The economics of EMU', in K.O. Pöhl *Britain and EMU*. Centre for Economic Performance, London School of Economics, London.

**Faini, R. and Venturini, A.** (1994) 'Migration and growth: the experience of southern Europe', CEPR Discussion paper, 964 (May).

**Fitoussi, J-P., Atkinson, A.B., Blanchard, O.E., Flemming, J.S., Malinvaud, E., Phelps, E.S. and Solow, R.M.** (1993) *Competitive Disinflation: the Mark and Budgetary Policy in Europe*. Oxford University Press, Oxford.

**Frankel, J.A. and Phillips, S.** (1991) 'The EMS: credible at last?', NBER Working Paper, 3819; also in J.A. Frankel (eds.) *On Exchange Rates*. MIT Press, Cambridge, Mass.

**Fratianni, M. and von Hagen, J.** (1990) 'Asymmetries and realignments in the EMS', in P. De Grauwe and L. Papademos (1990) *The European Monetary System in the 1990s*. Longman, London. 86–113.

**Fratianni, M., von Hagen, J. and Waller, C.** (1992) 'The Maastricht way to EMU', *Princeton Essays in International Finance*, 187 (June).

**Giavazzi, F. and Giovannini, A.** (1989) *Limiting Exchange Rate Flexibility*. MIT Press, Cambridge, Mass.

**Giavazzi, F. and Spaventa, L.** (1990) 'The new "new" EMS', in P. De Grauwe and L. Papademos (eds) *The European Monetary System in the 1990s*. Longman, London. 65–84.

**Gibson, H.D.** (1989) *The Eurocurrency Markets, Domestic Financial Policy and International Instability*. Macmillan, London.

Gibson, H.D. and Tsakalotos, E. (1991) 'European Monetary Union and macro-economic policy in Southern Europe: the case for positive integration', *Journal of Public Policy*, 11: 3, 249–273.

Gibson, H.D. and Tsakalotos, E. (1992) *Economic Integration and Financial Liberalisation: prospects for southern Europe*. Macmillan, London.

Gibson, H.D. and Tsakalotos, E. (1993) 'Testing a flow model of capital flight in five European countries', *The Manchester School*, 61: 2, 144–6.

Giovannini, A. (1991) 'Is European economic and monetary union falling apart?', *International Economic Outlook*, 1: 1, 36–41.

Goodhart, C.A.E. (1990) 'Fiscal policy and EMU', in K.O. Pöhl *et al.* (eds) *Britain and EMU*. Centre for Economic Performance, London School of Economics, London.

Goodhart, C.A.E. (1992) (ed.) *EMU and the European System of Central Banks after Maastricht*. Financial Markets Group, London School of Economics, London.

Gotur, P. (1985) 'Effects of exchange rate volatility on trade', *IMF Staff Papers*, 32: 475–512.

Henley, A. and Tsakalotos, E. (1993) 'Corporatism and the European labour market after 1992', *British Journal of Industrial Relations*, 30: 4. (December).

Henley, A. and Tsakalotos, E. (1993) *Corporatism and Economic Performance*. Edward Elgar, Aldershot.

Henley, A. and Tsakalotos, E. (1993a) 'Monetary rules versus consensual discretion: corporatism and the future of Keynesian policy-making', in D. Crabtree and A.P. Thirlwall (eds) *Keynes and the Role of the State*. Macmillan, London.

Kenen, P. and Rodrick, D. (1986) 'Measuring and analysing the effects of short-term volatility in real exchange rates', *Review of Economics and Statistics*, 68: 311–15.

Krugman, P.R. (1990) *The Age of Diminished Expectations*. MIT Press, Cambridge, Mass.

Krugman, P.R. (1991b) *Geography and Trade*. MIT Press, Cambridge, Mass.

Krugman, P.R. (1992a) 'Lessons of Massachusetts for EMU' in *A Single Currency for Europe*. CEPR, London.

Masson, P. and Melitz, J. (1990) 'Fiscal policy independence in a European Monetary Union', CEPR Discussion paper, 414 (April).

Mayer, T. (1993) *Truth versus Precision in Economics*. Edward Elgar, Aldershot.

Melitz, J. (1988) 'Monetary discipline and cooperation in the EMS', in F. Glavazzi, S. Micossi and M. Miller (eds) *The European Money System*. CEPR, Cambridge University Press, Cambridge.

Melitz, J. (1990) 'Comment on Fratianni and von Hagen', in P. De Grauwe and L. Papademos (eds) (1990) *The European Monetary System in the 1990s*. Longman, London.

Padoa-Schioppa, T. (1992) 'The September storm: EMS and the future of EMU', *International Economic Outlook*, 2: 2, 4–8.

Romer, P.M. (1994) 'The origins of endogenous growth', *Journal of Economic Perspectives*, 8: 1, 3–22.

Sapir, A. and Sekkat, K. (1990) 'Exchange rate volatility and international trade', in P. De Grauwe and L. Papademos (eds) *The European Monetary System in the 1990s*. Longman, London. 182–93.

Seater, J.J. (1993) 'Ricardian equivalence', Journal of Economic Literature, 31: 1, 105–41. Thygesen, N. (1990) 'Benefits and costs of an economic and monetary union relative to EMS', in P. De Grauwe and L. Papademos (eds) *The European Monetary System in the 1990s*. Longman, London.

Svensson, L.E.O. (1991) 'The simplest test of target zone credibility', CEPR Discussion Paper, January, 495.

Tobin, J. (1978) 'A proposal for international monetary reform', *Eastern Economic Journal*, 4: 153–9.

Walters, A. (1990) *Sterling in Danger*. Fontana, London.

Williamson, J. (1983) The Exchange Rate System. *Institute for International Economics*, Washington, D.C.

Wyplosz, C. (1986) 'Capital controls and balance of payments crises', *Journal of International Money and Finance*, 5: 167–79.

# 6 INTERNATIONAL LIQUIDITY AND THE GROWTH OF INTERNATIONAL FINANCIAL MARKETS

In Chapter 1, we provided a schematic representation of the types and sources of liquidity in the international financial system. We argued that international liquidity could be held either officially (by monetary authorities and international institutions) as well as privately (by multinational companies, domestic firms and private individuals). In addition to this distinction between holders of international liquidity, we also noted that it was useful to think of two main sources for this liquidity. The first is official sources. These include the various international monetary institutions, and in particular the IMF. The second is private sources, which are the international financial markets. In this chapter we want to focus on the holders and sources in more detail. Such an analysis is crucial to understanding the sources of the rapid growth in international financial flows which has been a feature of the world economy since the late 1960s.

The chapter is divided into three main sections. The first two sections focus on the holders of international liquidity. In the first section, we briefly examine the private use of international liquidity. We address the question of what determines whether a currency becomes a vehicle currency, that is a currency used in international exchange. The second section focuses on official holders of international liquidity and examines the role of international reserves in the international monetary system. The aim is to examine the demand for reserves by the monetary authorities. In particular, we ask what the optimal holdings of reserves are and what their composition should be. We argue that the importance of reserve holdings for monetary authorities stems from their usefulness in managing or indeed fixing exchange rates.

The third section turns to the question of the sources of international liquidity. We focus here on the role of the international financial markets as providers of international liquidity, both to private agents and institutions as well as monetary authorities. A significant development since the beginning of the 1970s has been the growth of international financial markets, particularly offshore markets such as the Eurocurrency markets. As we shall see in later chapters of this part of the book, this growth has had a number of implications for the international financial system. For the more developed countries, the growth of international financial markets has important consequences for the conduct of domestic macroeconomic policy in general and monetary policy in particular. We investigate this further in Chapter 7. For developing countries, the international financial markets played a significant role in financing balance of payments imbalances in the 1970s. The legacy of this has been the international debt crisis. An analysis of this crisis forms the heart of Chapters 8 and 9 where we investigate the role of international banks in lending to developing countries. In this chapter, we set the scene for these subsequent chapters by examining closely the reasons for the growth of international financial markets. To this end, we focus on both theoretical and historical reasons for their growth.

## The demand for privately held international liquidity

When examining the demand for liquidity by private agents in the international financial system, it is useful to think in terms of the functions that money plays in an economy. A necessary attribute of money is that it is a store of value. However, there are a number of assets which might be considered good stores of value. Hence we have to distinguish money from these assets by appealing to two important reasons why private agents may wish to hold money: it is an efficient medium of exchange and it can be held for speculative purposes.

The literature on the vehicle currency hypothesis examines the role of international money as a medium of exchange.[1] This literature draws on developments in the theory of the transactions demand for money. Baumol (1952) develops a model of the transactions demand for money which assumes that an individual receives a certain flow of income in each period from which he or she makes a steady stream of payments. The income is held in the form of both bonds (which receive a certain interest rate) and money (which earns no interest). Each time bonds are converted to money a fixed brokerage fee is payable and hence conversions are made in discrete lumps. From these assumptions, the model generates two main conclusions. First, average transactions balances are positive. Secondly, an increase in the real volume of transactions made causes average cash balances to increase but by less than the increase in transactions. In other words, there are economies of scale involved in cash holdings.

We can apply this model to international transactions. As trade in goods, services and assets increases, we might expect that the average money balances required to finance this trade increase but less than proportionately to the increase in transactions. However, as we noted in Chapter 1, currency plurality is a feature at the international level. There is no custom or law which determines which currency is used to make international payments. Swoboda (1969) examines the implications of this. He argues that in the international sphere there will be significant economies to be gained from conducting international transactions in a few currencies.

There are two parts to this argument. First, Swoboda notes that not only are there economies of scale to be gained from pooling resources (Baumol's argument), but there are also economies to be gained from holding only one currency for international transactions. These economies derive from the fact that the cost of acquiring information (which might be important to determining which currency should be held) declines as the use of a particular currency increases. That is, there are information economies. This suggests that only one currency will emerge for use in international transactions. The second part of Swoboda's argument notes that there is a further consideration, that of the presence of risk. If exchange rates are flexible or can be realigned, then there is a risk involved in holding a particular currency, namely that its value relative to other currencies might change. This leads to gains from diversification. The risk can be reduced if private agents hold several currencies. These holdings may take the form of currency substitution where agents hold non-interest bearing currencies in their portfolios.[2] Alternatively interest bearing assets such as bonds could be held. Whatever the form in which different currencies

[1] See, for example, Halm (1968), McKinnon (1969), Swoboda (1969) and Chrystal (1978; 1990).
[2] See MacDonald (1988) for a good survey of currency substitution models.

are held, Swoboda's two arguments together suggest that several currencies will emerge in the international system rather than simply one currency.

The second reason why there might be a demand for holding international liquidity is a speculative motive. At the level of the domestic economy, Keynes argued that money might be held for speculative purposes by those who wish to take a view of the movement of bond prices. If interest rates are expected to rise and hence bond prices to fall, then agents may wish to hold money in order to avoid the capital loss that would result from holding bonds. We can identify a similar speculative motive for holding money at the international level. Here speculation takes the form of taking a view on changes in the value of currencies relative to each other. This motive for holding currencies suggests that the demand for international currencies might be quite unstable. If speculation has a significant role to play in the international monetary system (and our analysis in Chapters 3 and 4, in particular, suggests that it does), then there might be rather large and abrupt changes in the composition of international currencies held by private individuals.

## Officially held liquidity and the role of international reserves

Liquidity is held at the international level not only by private agents, but also by official institutions and, in particular, domestic monetary authorities. Their motives for holding currencies are rather different from the ones outlined in the previous section. International reserves are held for two related reasons. First, they allow the monetary authorities to intervene to influence the value of their currency against other currencies. If the authorities are managing the exchange rate or fixing the exchange rate, then a stock of international reserves is crucial to their success. Secondly, reserves are held as a buffer stock against undesirable and immediate adjustment of the balance of payments. As we shall see in Chapter 9, in the period immediately after the oil price shocks of 1973–4, oil importing countries used their reserves to finance the resulting current account deficits, thus eliminating the need for either large exchange rate changes or adjustment of the domestic economy (– through, say, deflation).

The optimal reserves holdings for these purposes are dependent on the costs and benefits of holding reserves. Presumably, monetary authorities will seek to hold reserves up to the point where the marginal benefits of the reserves held is exactly equal to the marginal costs.[3] The benefits of holding reserves are clearly the costs of balance of payments adjustment through demand manipulation and the costs of not being able to intervene and influence the path of the exchange rate. Bird (1982) argues that the costs of adjustment will depend on the size and frequency of balance of payments deficits. The larger and more frequent deficits are, the larger the costs of adjustment and hence the greater the benefits from holding a stock of reserves which allows adjustment to be optimally spread across a number of periods.

The role for reserves in mitigating the costs of adjustment might be thought to depend on the exchange rate regime. If flexible exchange rates can help to eliminate balance of payments disequilibria, then the need for reserves might be less. By contrast, in a fixed exchange rate system where balance of payments disequilibria have to be eliminated through changes in domestic monetary and fiscal policy, the role for reserves in mitigating the costs of adjustment might be considered to be greater.

The costs of holding reserves are obviously an opportunity cost. Reserves may earn a rate of interest, but a higher return might have been possible if the reserves

---

[3] See Bird (1982).

were invested elsewhere (in, say, more productive longer-term investments). This factor might be particularly relevant for developing countries where holding scarce foreign currency in the form of reserves might have large costs in terms of the returns on projects foregone.

Balancing these costs and benefits essentially comes down to choosing between the level of income in a particular country and its stability. A high level of reserves will have large costs in terms of investments foregone and hence income might be lower than it otherwise would be. However, large reserves allow income to be less variable in that they allow slower adjustment to shocks than would occur if reserves were insufficient to cover any balance of payments adjustment problems.

Heller and Khan (1978) seek to model the demand for reserves for different country groupings under different exchange rate regimes. They estimate the following regression:

$$\log FR_t = \alpha + \beta \log(M/Y)_t + \gamma \log M_t + \delta \log \sigma^2_t + u_t \qquad (6.1)$$

where $FR_t$ is the level of foreign exchange reserves at time t, M/Y is the import to income ratio, M is the level of imports and $\sigma^2$ is a measure of the variability of the balance of payments.[4] An increase in M/Y reflects an increase in the openness of the economy and hence one might anticipate a positive sign on $\beta$: the more open the economy, the greater the need for reserves. However, if M/Y is simply a proxy for the marginal propensity to import, then it reflects the costs of adjustment. The higher the marginal propensity to import, the lower the costs of adjustment (a given change in the balance of payments can be achieved by a small change in income) and hence the expected sign of $\beta$ is negative. Thus the effect of M/Y is ambiguous. The level of imports is simply a scale variable and hence we expect $\gamma$ to be positive. If there are economies of scale along the lines discussed in the first section of this chapter, then $\gamma$ will also be less than one. Variability of the balance of payments is expected to influence the demand for reserves positively. In other words, $\sigma^2$ captures a risk element: greater variability creates greater uncertainty and hence more reserves are held.[5]

Their results provide strong support for equation (6.1) across a broad range of country groupings. In addition, they show that there was a structural break in the demand for reserves function in the 1971–2 period. This they argue reflects the move from fixed to floating exchange rates. In the case of industrial countries, the reserve function shifted downwards, confirming the idea that under a regime of floating exchange rates, less reserves are needed. By contrast, developing countries experienced an upward shift in their demand for reserves. Heller and Khan suggest that this reflects the increased uncertainty and variability in the balance of payments which is associated with pegging their currencies to a floating currency.

Up till now we have been considering the demand for reserves in total. However, in a world of numerous currencies, there is also the issue of the composition of reserves held to be considered. The key point to make regarding reserve composition is that countries choose to hold reserves in a variety of different currencies and

---

[4]  $\sigma^2$ is defined as the variability of reserves. For each country grouping an autoregressive integrated moving average (ARIMA) model for reserves is estimated. The residuals from this equation are then squared and used as a measure of variability. Note that this is a measure of *unexpected* variability since the residuals of the ARIMA equation are used.

[5]  We can note that Heller and Khan do not consider the costs of holding reserves. They argue that previous studies have showed the insignificance of this variable, something which might reflect the difficulty of finding a good proxy for the opportunity cost of holding reserves.

assets. One of the broad trends which we can identify in reserve composition is that the importance of gold has declined since the 1960s. In 1969, gold accounted for 49.5% of reserves; by 1982 that had declined to 9% (if gold is valued at its official Bretton Woods price).[6] By contrast, holdings of foreign currencies as reserves increased from 42% in 1969 to 80.2% in 1982.

Table 6.1 provides a breakdown of the currency composition of reserves over the 1960s to the 1980s. It illustrates the dominant role of the US dollar throughout the period. Even though holdings of dollars have declined, they still account for over half of all reserve holdings. Concurrent with the fall in the importance of the dollar, there has been a rise in the importance of other currencies, particularly the Deutschmark and the Japanese yen.

Table 6.1 also provides for a comparison between reserve holdings of industrial countries and developing countries. This shows that developing countries tend to hold more sterling and less Deutschmarks than industrial countries. This results from the fact that many developing countries still peg their exchange rates to sterling, reflecting their former colonial ties with the UK. One might have expected a similar argument to apply to the French franc. However, developing countries do not appear to hold more French francs than the industrial countries.

The advantage of using foreign currencies as reserves is their lower production costs compared to gold. As we noted in Chapter 1, a country whose currency is a reserve currency has the benefit that it derives seigniorage from the supply of its currency as an international reserve. This allows countries to finance their current account deficits by increasing the holdings of their currency by other monetary authorities (something which, as we saw in Chapter 1, the US did in the 1960s). However, there are costs to being a reserve currency and these have often been emphasised by both Japan and Germany. In particular, Germany argues that flows into and out of Deutschmarks causes excessive exchange rate fluctuations and, as we saw in Chapter 5, can put pressure on the EMS. Flows of capital into Deutschmarks cause the exchange rate to appreciate and this can be detrimental to the competitiveness of domestic industry. Furthermore, Germany argues that the benefits in terms of financing current account deficits are zero, since it has consistently had a surplus on its current account.[7]

More generally, we can note that the growth in importance of other currencies since the breakdown of the Bretton Woods has led to the existence of what might be called a multiple reserve system. This is often thought to have increased instability of exchange rates as a result of switching between reserve assets as monetary authorities take speculative positions on the major reserve currencies. However, whilst there is evidence that the composition of reserves does change from year to year, this is more a consequence of changing values of currencies when they are measured in a common unit (usually the SDR). Monetary authorities do not tend to change their reserve holdings for speculative reasons. Instead, the increased volatility of exchange rates is more likely to be the result of private agents speculating in the international currencies.

In conclusion, we can say that monetary authorities tend to hold reserves in order to enable them to intervene in the foreign exchange markets to manage their

---

[6] We can note that if gold is valued at its market price, it formed 55.4% of reserves in 1982. This reflects the increased price of gold since the breakdown of Bretton Woods system rather than an increase in the quantity of gold held by monetary authorities. For this reason, we usually use its official price when discussing its importance as a reserve asset.

[7] See Monthly Report of the Deutsche Bundesbank, 1979.

*Table 6.1.* The currency composition of international reserves (%)

| All Countries | 1973 | 1975 | 1980 | 1985 | 1990 | 1992 |
|---|---|---|---|---|---|---|
| US dollar | 84.5 | 85.2 | 73.1 | 64.8 | 57.5 | 64.4 |
| Pound sterling | 5.9 | 4.1 | 3.0 | 3.0 | 3.4 | 3.2 |
| Deutschmark | 6.7 | 6.6 | 14.0 | 15.1 | 18.6 | 13.0 |
| French franc | 1.2 | 1.3 | 1.3 | 0.9 | 2.3 | 2.5 |
| Swiss franc | 1.4 | 1.7 | 4.1 | 2.3 | 1.4 | 1.3 |
| Netherlands guilder | 0.4 | 0.6 | 0.9 | 1.0 | 1.1 | 0.7 |
| Japanese yen | .. | 0.6 | 3.7 | 8.0 | 8.8 | 8.1 |
| Others | .. | .. | .. | 4.9 | 6.9 | 9.8 |
| *Industrial Countries* | | | | | | |
| US dollar | | | | 65.2 | 56.0 | 64.9 |
| Pound sterling | | | | 1.8 | 1.9 | 2.3 |
| Deutschmark | | | | 19.5 | 21.9 | 14.4 |
| French franc | | | | 0.1 | 2.5 | 3.0 |
| Swiss franc | | | | 2.1 | 1.1 | 0.6 |
| Netherlands guilder | | | | 1.0 | 1.3 | 0.5 |
| Japanese yen | | | | 8.9 | 9.6 | 7.4 |
| Others | | | | 1.4 | 5.9 | 6.9 |
| *Developing Countries* | | | | | | |
| US dollar | | | | 64.5 | 60.7 | 63.6 |
| Pound sterling | | | | 4.3 | 6.4 | 4.6 |
| Deutschmark | | | | 10.0 | 11.6 | 10.9 |
| French franc | | | | 1.9 | 2.0 | 1.9 |
| Swiss franc | | | | 2.6 | 2.1 | 2.5 |
| Netherlands guilder | | | | 0.9 | 0.7 | 0.9 |
| Japanese yen | | | | 6.9 | 7.3 | 9.0 |
| Others | | | | 9.0 | 9.0 | 6.7 |

*Source*: IMF World Economic Outlook, Annual Report – various years. Washington, D.C.

*Notes*: ECUs issued against dollars are included in dollar holdings. ECUs issued against gold are excluded. We can note that in 1992, the share of reserves held in ECUs by industrial countries was 17% and by all countries was 9.4%. Only countries which actually provide a currency breakdown of their reserves are included in the table.

exchange rates. The rising importance of currencies in the composition of international reserves reflects this need (gold is not a useful way to hold reserves which are to be used for intervention). In addition, we can argue that the growing diversification of reserve holdings reflects a desire by monetary authorities to reduce the risk of holding all their reserves in one currency.

**The growth of international financial markets and international financial flows**

Our focus up till now has been on the holders of international liquidity. In this section, we turn to consider the question of the provision of international liquidity. To this end, we want to examine the role of the international financial markets, which, since the 1970s have been major providers of liquidity in the international financial system. As such they also account for the large growth in international financial flows in the world economy. We examine first some figures which describe the nature of international financial markets, looking both at international banking markets as well as bond markets. We then go on to look at two main theories which seek to explain the growth of such markets. The first focuses purely on transactions costs and regulation avoidance. The second takes more of a portfolio perspective on the growth of financial markets, stressing factors such as differential risk. Finally, in this section, we provide a small case study of the growth of a market which has been very influential, the Eurodollar market. We show how various aspects of both theories can be applied to Eurodollar market growth.

## The nature and growth of international financial markets

The growth of international banking markets has been very rapid since the late 1950s, in part due to the development of the Eurocurrency markets. International banking before the eurocurrency markets took the form of banks conducting business in their domestic currency with nonresidents. Banks located in London, for example, borrowed and lent to non-residents in sterling. The Eurocurrency markets were a new innovation: banks began to deal in foreign currencies (that is, currencies other than that of the country in which the bank was located). Thus banks in London, for example, began to deal in dollars. More generally, international banking nowadays refers to banking activities with non-residents in both domestic and foreign currencies.

Tables 6.2 and 6.3 provide some indication of the size and growth of international banking since the early 1960s. We measure size by the foreign currency assets of banks which report to the BIS, since this captures well the concept of Eurobanking,[8] namely banks dealing in currencies which are different from their country of origin. It is clear that it grew very quickly throughout the 1960s. Growth rates of over 20% per annum were the norm. On average, growth in the 1970s was a little lower. Overall, however, these growth rates were higher than the growth of national banking. During the 1980s growth slowed significantly and was more variable. The initial slowdown in 1983 was mainly as a result of the international debt crisis. The market then bounced back in the mid-1980s as lending to higher quality borrowers (mainly industrial countries) increased. However, performance thereafter was more patchy and 1991 and 1992 witnessed the first decline in the size of the markets (mainly as a consequence of the recession in industrialised countries).

A feature of the markets from their inception is the prominence of the US dollar. As can be seen from Table 6.4, the dollar consistently accounted for over 70% of total assets up until the mid-1980s. Over the whole period, the Deutschmark has grown in importance as has the yen. This reflects their increasing attractiveness both for private agents and as reserves with the central banks. Sterling's importance decreased rapidly in the 1960s, steadying at around 1–2 per cent in the 1970s and early 1980s. Since the mid-1980s, it has enjoyed some revival.

In addition to the traditional major international currencies, the 1980s saw an increase in the number of smaller or newer currencies used in international banking markets. The ECU, which came into existence in 1979 with the setting up of the EMS, witnessed rapid growth. As a basket of currencies, the ECU has a more stable value than individual currencies within it. As a result, it is an attractive currency in which to hold assets, in essence providing a ready-made diversified portfolio. Alongside the ECU, although to a much smaller extent, other European currencies have begun to feature on the international markets.

---

[8] Using foreign currency liabilities gives us similar results.

*Table 6.2.*  Growth of international banking: foreign currency assets of reporting banks (in billions of US dollars)

| Year | Europe | Japan & Canada | US | Other countries[f] | TOTAL |
|---|---|---|---|---|---|
| 1963 | 10.49 | 1.89 | .. | .. | 12.38 |
| 1964 | 12.24 | 2.42 | .. | .. | 14.85 |
| 1965 | 15.33 | 3.00 | .. | .. | 18.33 |
| 1966 | 20.25 | 6.22 | .. | .. | 26.47 |
| 1967 | 24.85 | 7.26 | .. | .. | 32.11 |
| 1968 | 37.70 | 8.68 | .. | .. | 46.38 |
| 1969 | 58.17 | 12.14 | .. | .. | 70.31 |
| 1970 | 78.25 | 14.92 | .. | .. | 93.17 |
| 1971 | 101.13 | 13.81 | .. | .. | 114.94 |
| 1972[a] | 131.84 | 18.09 | .. | .. | 149.93 |
| 1973 | 187.62 | 28.24 | .. | .. | 215.86 |
| 1974 | 215.17 | 32.78 | .. | .. | 247.95 |
| 1975 | 257.73 | 32.22 | .. | .. | 289.95 |
| 1976[b] | 305.32 | 36.39 | .. | .. | 341.71 |
| 1977 | 384.84 | 35.86 | .. | .. | 420.70 |
| 1978 | 501.97 | 47.61 | .. | .. | 549.58 |
| 1979 | 639.94 | 59.10 | 136.4 | .. | 835.44 |
| 1980 | 751.24 | 83.55 | 176.9 | .. | 1011.69 |
| 1981 | 840.05 | 100.41 | 256.3 | .. | 1196.76 |
| 1982[c] | 1023.60 | 129.70 | 361.4 | .. | 1514.70 |
| 1983 | 1027.20 | 150.90 | 396.0 | .. | 1574.10 |
| 1984[d] | 1061.10 | 170.20 | 409.6 | 512.3 | 2153.20 |
| 1985 | 1292.40 | 240.70 | 424.4 | 555.2 | 2512.70 |
| 1986 | 1676.80 | 398.30 | 468.7 | 677.3 | 3221.10 |
| 1987 | 2140.00 | 629.80 | 508.9 | 878.5 | 4157.20 |
| 1988 | 2128.00 | 781.70 | 555.8 | 1045.8 | 4511.30 |
| 1989 | 2409.00 | 892.20 | 600.8 | 1238.5 | 5140.50 |
| 1990 | 3224.00 | 1004.30 | 578.4 | 1447.1 | 6253.80 |
| 1991 | 3208.80 | 990.20 | 587.0 | 1455.6 | 6241.60 |
| 1992[e] | 3270.50 | 879.20 | 558.2 | 1489.8 | 6197.70 |

[a] excludes the BIS deposits from 1973 onwards.

[b] includes Austria, Denmark and Ireland from 1977.

[c] now includes external lending by banks in their domestic currency to non-residents under a wider concept of international banking.

[d] European countries include Finland and Norway from 1984.

[e] figure for Japan and Canada includes Japan only for 1992.

[f] data on other countries is rather patchy and disconnected pre-1984. Its exclusion implies that the total figure jumps in 1984.

*Source*: Bank for International Settlements (BIS) Annual Report, various years. Basle.

*Table 6.3.* Percentage growth rates of total international banking assets, 1963–92

| Year | % | Year | % |
|------|------|------|------|
| 1963 | ... | 1977 | 20.80 |
| 1964 | 18.19 | 1978 | 26.72 |
| 1965 | 21.05 | 1979 | 24.06 |
| 1966 | 36.75 | 1980 | 19.14 |
| 1967 | 19.32 | 1981 | 16.80 |
| 1968 | 36.77 | 1982 | 23.56 |
| 1969 | 41.60 | 1983 | 3.88 |
| 1970 | 28.15 | 1984 | 31.33 |
| 1971 | 21.00 | 1985 | ... |
| 1972 | 26.58 | 1986 | 24.84 |
| 1973 | 36.44 | 1987 | 25.51 |
| 1974 | 13.86 | 1988 | 8.17 |
| 1975 | 15.65 | 1989 | 13.06 |
| 1976 | 16.43 | 1990 | 19.60 |
|      |       | 1991 | −0.002 |
|      |       | 1992 | −0.007 |

... Not available or negligible.
Growth Rates are calculated by subtracting the natural logarithms.
*Source*: Calculated from Table 6.2.

*Table 6.4.* Currency breakdown of external assets in foreign currency of BIS reporting banks (in Europe)

| Year | $ | £ | Sfr | DM | Yen | DG | Ffr | ECU | Bfr | IL | Other[a] |
|------|------|------|------|------|------|------|------|------|------|------|------|
| 1964 | 75 | 8 | 6 | 9 | ... | ... | ... | ... | ... | ... | |
| 1965 | 77 | 6 | 5 | 9 | ... | ... | ... | ... | ... | ... | |
| 1966 | 80 | 4 | 5 | 7 | ... | ... | ... | ... | ... | ... | |
| 1967 | 81 | 4 | 4 | 8 | ... | ... | ... | ... | ... | ... | |
| 1968 | 81 | 2 | 5 | 10 | ... | ... | ... | ... | ... | ... | |
| 1969 | 81 | 1 | 5 | 11 | ... | ... | ... | ... | ... | ... | |
| 1970 | 77 | 1 | 5 | 13 | ... | ... | ... | ... | ... | ... | |
| 1971 | 71 | 2 | 8 | 16 | ... | ... | ... | ... | ... | ... | |
| 1972 | 76 | 2 | 6 | 16 | ... | ... | ... | ... | ... | ... | |
| 1973 | 72 | 2 | 8 | 17 | ... | ... | ... | ... | ... | ... | |
| 1974 | 74 | 1 | 7 | 16 | ... | ... | ... | ... | ... | ... | |
| 1975 | 72 | 1 | 6 | 16 | ... | ... | ... | ... | ... | ... | |
| 1976 | 75 | 1 | 6 | 16 | ... | ... | ... | ... | ... | ... | |
| 1977 | 72 | 1 | 6 | 18 | ... | ... | ... | ... | ... | ... | |
| 1978 | 71 | 2 | 6 | 20 | 1 | ... | ... | ... | ... | ... | |
| 1979 | 70 | 2 | 6 | 20 | 1 | ... | ... | ... | ... | ... | |
| 1980 | 73 | 2 | 7 | 17 | 1 | ... | ... | ... | ... | ... | |
| 1981 | 74 | 2 | 7 | 15 | 2 | ... | ... | ... | ... | ... | |
| 1982 | 75 | 1 | 5 | 11 | 1 | 0.8 | 0.7 | 0.5 | 0.6 | 0.2 | 3 |
| 1983 | 76 | 1 | 5 | 10 | 1 | 0.9 | 0.8 | 1.0 | 0.6 | 0.3 | 3 |
| 1984 | 73 | 1 | 6 | 12 | 3 | 1.0 | 1.1 | 2.3 | 0.7 | 0.3 | ... |
| 1985 | 68 | 2 | 7 | 13 | 4 | ... | ... | 3.1 | ... | ... | 3 |
| 1986 | 65 | 2 | 7 | 13 | 5 | ... | ... | 3.3 | ... | ... | 4 |
| 1987 | 58 | 2 | 7 | 14 | 7 | 0.8 | 1.2 | 3.6 | 0.6 | 0.5 | 5 |
| 1988 | 59 | 3 | 5 | 13 | 7 | 0.7 | 1.2 | 3.8 | 0.6 | 0.6 | 6 |
| 1989 | 58 | 3 | 4 | 13 | 7 | 0.8 | 1.6 | 4.3 | 0.6 | 0.9 | 6 |
| 1990 | 53 | 4 | 4 | 14 | 7 | 1.0 | 2.6 | 4.7 | 0.7 | 1.8 | 7 |
| 1991 | 52 | 4 | 4 | 14 | 6 | 1.0 | 3.1 | 5.4 | 0.6 | 2.5 | 8 |

Where Sfr = Swiss francs; DG = Dutch guilders; Ffr = French francs; Bfr = Belgian francs; and IL = Italian lire.
[a] includes foreign currency positions of banks in the US.
... not available or negligible

*Source*: BIS Annual Reports, various years.

The figures used in Table 6.2 are gross estimates of the markets' size. That is, they include interbank deposits between countries.[9] Thus if we are measuring the size of the markets using an asset measure, the figure will include not only nonbank non-resident assets, but also bank non-resident assets. It is customary when considering the size of national banking markets to net out interbank positions. The rationale is simple: including interbank positions leads to double-counting of the flow of funds from the original nonbank depositor to the final nonbank lender.

The principle of double-counting can be illustrated by the following example: assume that a flow of funds is occurring from a bank or non-bank in country A to a bank or non-bank in country D. Furthermore, assume that the flow passes through banks in countries B and C, which are both in the reporting area. The flow will be double-counted because of the interbank transaction which occurs between countries B and C. This flow should be netted out if we are interested in the intermediation role played by international markets.[10]

Ellis (1981) shows that between 1973 and 1980 the size of the interbank market remained remarkably stable at around 70%. This implies that for the purposes of analysing the growth of these markets, gross estimates are sufficient. If, however, we were interested in the intermediation role or liquidity-creating effects of the markets, then net estimates would give a more accurate picture.

A final important development in international banking which we can mention here is the expansion of the markets beyond the European area, mainly as a result of the growth of offshore banking markets. Banks in these offshore markets are often able to take advantage of more favourable tax treatment and fewer regulations on their activities than exist in the 12 European Reporting countries used by the BIS to define the Eurocurrency markets. Table 6.5 shows the importance of assets held in Europe for selected dates after 1973. The role of the strictly defined Eurocurrency markets has declined from well over half of international bank lending in 1973. Nonetheless, European assets still account for half of total international bank lending today.

The second major group of international financial markets are the international bond markets.[11] Like international banking, the international bond markets comprise two major parts. Firstly, there are the foreign bond markets, which consist of bonds issued on various domestic bond markets by nonresidents. Secondly, there are the Eurobond markets – markets where bonds are issued in currencies other than the currency of the country where the market is located. The Eurobond markets, like the Eurocurrency markets, emerged in the 1960s. Eurobonds are typically medium-term, fixed-rate, coupon-paying bonds issued publicly by major corporations or sovereign borrowers. They differ significantly from bank credit in that they are tradeable in secondary markets.

Like the Eurocurrency markets, the dollar is the major currency of denomination for Eurobonds. If we look at new Eurobond issues in 1990, the US dollar accounted for some 40%; sterling and the yen followed with 12% each; the ECU had 10% and the Deutschmark 9%.

---

[9] We can note that they do not include interbank deposits within each country.

[10] We should note that the BIS does not remove all interbank transactions from its net measures of international banking markets. See Gibson (1989, pp.6–7) for a more extensive discussion of gross and net figures.

[11] See Davis (1992a) for a good discussion of international bond markets especially in London.

*Table 6.5.*   The volume of international bank lending conducted in the Euromarkets

| Year | European Assets | Total Assets | % |
|------|------|------|------|
| 1973 | 188 | 292 | 64.4 |
| 1976 | 305 | 584 | 55.7 |
| 1980 | 751 | 1322 | 56.8 |
| 1983 | 880 | 1754 | 50.1 |
| 1985 | 1292 | 2513 | 51.4 |
| 1988 | 2128 | 4485 | 47.4 |
| 1991 | 3207 | 6240 | 51.4 |
| 1992 | 3271 | 6197 | 52.8 |

(billions of US dollars)

*Source*: BIS Annual Reports, various years.

*Table 6.6.*   International bond markets – gross new issues per annum (bn $US)

| Year | bonds[a] | note issuance facilities (NIFs)[b] |
|------|------|------|
| 1979 | 38.9 | |
| 1980 | 39.4 | |
| 1981 | 48.8 | 1.0 |
| 1982 | 71.7 | 2.4 |
| 1983 | 73.6 | 3.3 |
| 1984 | 107.7 | 18.8 |
| 1985 | 163.6 | 50.3 |
| 1986 | 221.5 | 71.1 |
| 1987 | 181.2 | 72.9 |
| 1988 | 220.1 | 79.0 |
| 1989 | 264.6 | 66.4 |
| 1990 | 239.8 | |
| 1991 | 318.9 | |
| 1992 | 341.9 | |

[a]  including Eurobonds (Floating Rate Notes (FRNs) etc and foreign bond issues.
[b]  NIFs allow borrowers to raise funds over the medium-term through the issuance of a stream of short-term notes. In the mid 1980s, some medium-term notes also appeared. A large component of this market is the Euro-commercial paper market.

*Source*: BIS Annual Reports, various years

International bond markets grew particularly strongly in the 1980s following bank problems with the international debt crisis. Indeed, the greater variance in the growth of international banking markets since the 1980s can in part be attributed to this new rival. Table 6.6, which provides information on new issues, indicates their rapid growth in the 1980s.

The boom in Euro-bond markets in the mid-1980s not only reflected problems in international banking markets, but was also the result of the highly innovative nature of the bond markets and the associated growth of derivatives. Floating Rate Notes (FRNs), for example, comprised a large part of growth of Euro-bond markets at least until the late 1980s. These were a new innovation in that they were bonds with interest rates which altered every 3, 6 or 9 months. They were therefore highly popular at times of interest rate uncertainty. However, by 1987, the market was in trouble and issues declined dramatically. The perpetual FRN market (that is, FRNs which are never redeemed) collapsed and problems in other FRN markets with mispricing of issues led to many institutions scaling down their involvement in bond markets. This accounts for the decline in new issues in the bond markets in 1987 (Table 6.6). Other innovations were the asset-backed bond which were bonds backed by usually illiquid assets and the equity warrant bonds which gave investors the option of purchasing the issuer's equity at some specified price and date.

The later 1980s saw a rapid growth in derivatives. For example, interest rate and currency swaps began to be popular. These essentially allow a borrower to raise funds in the market where he/she has a comparative advantage (that is, the market in which funds can be raised at the lowest possible cost). The loan raised can then be swapped in the bond markets for the type of interest payments required (floating or fixed) or the currency wanted.

In addition to the innovative nature of these markets, regulatory changes were also important. For example, the BIS (in its Annual Report, 1985/86) notes that changes in Japanese regulations in 1985 led to a large increase in the number of yen bonds that could be issued either in the Euromarkets or in Japan (to non-residents). Aside from granting permission for yen bond issues, the Japanese authorities also allowed foreign institutions to lead manage[12] issues and removed a withholding tax which had existed on non-resident holdings of yen bonds. As we shall see later in this section, when we examine in detail the growth of the Eurodollar market as an example of the growing importance of international financial markets, changes in domestic regulations are often crucial to explaining the emergence of new markets.

Aside from the growth in long-term bond markets, short-term note issues grew rapidly after 1985 (see Table 6.6). A major component of these markets is the Euro-commercial paper market which has the advantage that the notes issued do not need to be underwritten. This reduces the costs of raising money in these markets and like the long-term Eurobond markets, they are often used for interest rate and currency swaps.

Thus a major feature of the 1980s was a growing securitisation of international financial markets. In other words, there was a move from bank-based intermediation to market-based intermediation. Bonds came to be seen as better investments than traditional bank lending, not least because they are marketable and hence do not tie a financial institution permanently to a particular borrower in the way that traditional bank lending does. Hence a number of countries (particularly the industrial countries) were able to raise funds on the bond markets at a much lower cost than they could from banks. Additionally, the 1980s was a period of low inflation and falling interest rates, conditions in which bond issuing flourishes. From the point of view of banks, the Euro-bond markets were more attractive since they allowed greater scope for gaining income from off balance sheet items. Off balance sheet items are assets which banks do not actually hold. Instead, they gain income from selling these assets to other institutions or private agents. They arrange the issue and perhaps underwrite the issue. Increased participation by banks in such items has been a major feature since the 1980s.

---

[12] Bond issues are often managed by what is known as a lead financial institution. It organises the bond issue and brings in other institutions to help with the underwriting and placement of the issue.

Towards the end of the 1980s, however, international bank lending again became popular to the detriment of the bond markets. Traditional bank lending played a major role in financing some of the balance of payments imbalances in industrial countries.[13] Bonds were less attractive because of a rise in long-term interest rates and the fact that the stock market crash in October 1987 reduced the liquidity of Eurobonds. By the early 1990s, the situation had again changed in favour of bond markets as interest rates began to fall and most industrial countries went into recession.

Overall, it now appears that both bond and banking markets are crucial elements to international financial markets. Growing securitisation in the 1980s may have slowed growth in international banking, but it certainly did not result in its eclipse. Instead, borrowers use both markets, choosing between them on the basis of the cheapest and most appropriate source of funds at any one time.

## Theories of the growth of international financial markets

There are three main theories which seek to explain the rapid growth of international financial markets witnessed since the 1960s. Some have applied traditional bank multiplier models to argue that the markets can grow endogenously. We discuss these models in Chapter 7 when we examine the possible inflationary effects of international markets. Here we consider the other two theories. The first emphasises the transactions costs and regulation advantages which international markets enjoy over their domestic counterparts. The second places more emphasis on portfolio reasons why investors may wish to hold assets in international rather than domestic markets. We examine each of these theories in turn before going on to look at a case study in international financial market development, namely the growth of the Eurodollar market.

The transactions costs and regulation theory argues that the existence of international banking markets can be explained in terms of disintermediation. In other words, borrowers and lenders use the markets which give them the lowest transactions costs or the best return. Johnston (1983, p.82 and the annex to Ch. 4) shows that a necessary condition for the development of new international markets is that the *sum* of transactions costs which borrowers, investors and financial institutions incur should be lower than those in domestic markets. As Johnston notes, an international bank may still find it worthwhile to set up in London rather than the home city of New York, even if both borrowers and investors found that their transactions costs were higher with the bank located in London rather than New York. All that would be required is that the cost to the intermediary of setting up in London is substantially lower than the cost of setting up in New York – low enough to offset the larger costs to depositors and investors.[14]

If this theory is to explain the development of international markets, then there must be good reasons why international markets have lower transactions costs. We can point to several general factors here. First, transactions costs might be lower because of differential regulations between domestic and international markets. Traditionally domestic financial markets have been highly regulated by the relevant central bank. For example, in the case of banking, reserve requirements or interest

---

[13]  See BIS Annual Reports, 1987/88.

[14]  We can note that Niehans and Hewson (1976) develop a more detailed model reflecting this idea which shows that the costs incurred by the three parties will determine the amount of funds which flow through any particular international centre.

rate ceilings on deposits can increase the cost of intermediation and hence make domestic markets less competitive. Similarly in the case of bond markets, differential tax treatment of domestic and international bonds can confer an advantage on international markets.

A second reason why transactions costs may be lower in international markets is related to the wholesale nature of these markets. The main operators in international markets include countries, multi-national companies and financial institutions themselves. Deposits and loans are for large denominations (usually a minimum of a million currency units) and this tends to reduce the transactions costs because of economies of scale. In particular, the smaller number of depositors and lenders helps to reduce information costs and improvements in global telecommunications have decreased the advantages to a bank of being located close to its customers, something which is usually thought of as crucial to the gathering of information.

A third factor which can explain lower transactions costs is the competitive nature of international financial markets. We can take international banking markets as an example. It is widely acknowledged that these markets are highly competitive.[15] However, an analysis of the level of competition within the banking industry does not fit easily into any of the standard theories of market structure and competition. Competition can be defined as rivalry between producers. In this sense, it is clear that the perfectly competitive equilibrium represents no competition. Producers are not seeking to compete actively with one another and the behaviour of one producer will have no effect on other producers. At the other extreme the textbook case of pure monopoly is not a competitive situation, since one producer controls total production within that industry.

In reality these two extremes are rarely witnessed and most industries can be classified as competitive, albeit to varying degrees. We can offer two pieces of evidence which suggest that international banking markets are highly competitive. First, the world economy has experienced increasing financial integration since the 1950s and there has been an increase in the number of banks competing with each other for international business. If we take the example of London, the world's largest international banking centre, then the number of banks represented there increased steeply in the late 1960s and early 1970s (Table 6.7). Whilst increasing bank numbers is not conclusive evidence of increased competition (the banks could be colluding), it is difficult not to conclude that the magnitude of banks in London makes the market there highly competitive and, as we shall see in Chapter 9, declining costs of intermediation were a feature of the late 1970s in these markets.[16]

Furthermore, there is a second piece of evidence which supports this view. For the highly innovative nature of these markets is also suggestive of a competitive environment. We noted earlier that the development of the international bond markets in the 1980s was in part due to new innovative instruments which reduced the transactions costs for borrowers raising funds on the international markets.

Increased competition and the new innovations that often follow essentially reduce interest rate spreads (that is the difference between borrowing and lending rates) in financial markets. Borrowers thus find the markets attractive because the costs of borrowing are reduced. Depositors are attracted by higher deposit rates. There is no

---

[15] See, for example, McMahon (1985), Kettell and Magnus (1986) and Johnston (1983).
[16] See Gibson (1989, Ch. 1.4) for further evidence that these banks compete in the international markets for business.

*Table 6.7.*    Foreign banks in London

| Year | Direct[a] | Indirect[b] | Total | growth |
|------|--------|----------|-------|--------|
| 1967 | 114 | ... | 114 | ... |
| 1968 | 135 | ... | 135 | 15.5 |
| 1969 | 138 | ... | 138 | 2.2 |
| 1970 | 163 | ... | 163 | 15.3 |
| 1971 | 176 | 25 | 201 | 18.9 |
| 1972 | 215 | 28 | 243 | 17.3 |
| 1973 | 232 | 35 | 267 | 9.0 |
| 1974 | 264 | 72 | 336 | 20.5 |
| 1975 | 263 | 72 | 335 | −2.9 |
| 1976 | 265 | 78 | 343 | 2.3 |
| 1977 | 300 | 55 | 355 | 3.4 |
| 1978 | 313 | 69 | 382 | 7.1 |
| 1979 | 330 | 59 | 389 | 1.8 |
| 1980 | 353 | 50 | 403 | 3.5 |
| 1981 | 353 | 65 | 418 | 3.6 |
| 1982 | 379 | 70 | 449 | 6.9 |
| 1983 | 391 | 69 | 460 | 2.4 |
| 1984 | 403 | 67 | 470 | 2.1 |
| 1985 | 399 | 64 | 463 | −1.5 |
| 1986 | 400 | 47 | 447 | −3.6 |
| 1987 | ... | ... | 453 | 1.3 |
| 1988 | ... | ... | 448 | −1.1 |
| 1989 | ... | ... | 451 | 0.7 |
| 1990 | ... | ... | 451 | 0.0 |

... not available
[a] representation through a branch, representative office or subsidiary.
[b] representation through a stake in a joint venture or a consortium.

*Source*: *The Banker*, various issues

doubt that competition is greater in international markets than in domestic markets. The latter tend to be more oligopolistic: there are far fewer participants and collusion is often apparent. Thus for these reasons, competition in international financial markets can make transactions costs much lower than in domestic markets and hence can account for the growth of international markets over the last decades.

The theory of international financial market growth which we have been considering above assumes that assets and liabilities within the two markets (international and domestic) are perfect substitutes for each other. The second theory seeking to explain the growth of international markets drops this assumption and instead views the decision to operate in one market rather than the other as the outcome of a more general portfolio decision (Johnston, 1983, pp.87–98; see also Chapter 3 where we discuss the general idea of portfolio models).

Domestic and international assets might not be perfect substitutes because of differential exchange risk, sovereign risk, political risk or regulatory risk. In this case the supply of funds to or the demand for funds from international markets will be a function not only of the prospective return which these markets offer but also the level of perceived risk relative to holding domestic assets. In addition, wealth will be important: an increase in wealth will result in an expansion of both the international and domestic markets.

An appealing feature of the portfolio model is that it can more easily explain why rates of return in the domestic and international markets might differ without a large flow of funds between the two. Interest rate differentials can persist in portfolio models because of differential risk: the investor or borrower is no longer interested simply in the return net of transactions costs, but in the risk-adjusted return. Studies which examined the initial growth of the Eurodollar market suggest that capital flow adjustments to changes in interest rates or wealth are speedy.[17]

*The Eurodollar market*

The Eurodollar market is one of the largest single international financial markets and moreover it was one of the first to emerge in the post-war period. The Bank for International Settlements (BIS Annual Report, 1963/64, p.127) has defined a Eurodollar as:

> a dollar that has been acquired by a bank outside the US and used directly or after conversion into another currency for lending to a nonbank customer, perhaps after one or more redeposits from one bank to another.

The initial location of the Eurodollar market was in London. But as with other international markets, the geographical location of these offshore dollars has subsequently spread beyond Europe to Asia and various offshore markets.

Given the now well-established role of the Eurodollar market, it is interesting to use its development as a case study which might shed some light on the two theories of international banking market growth. There are a number of historical factors which can account for the growing importance of Eurodollars, some of which directly relate back to the transactions costs/regulation avoidance and portfolio theories.[18]

The market first emerged in the late 1950s. An initial triggering factor was clearly related to changes in regulations. Following the sterling crisis in 1957, the Bank of England imposed restrictions on the use of sterling to finance non-UK trade as a means of limiting speculative pressure on sterling. Before the imposition of these restrictions, banks in London had offered sterling facilities to exporters and importers from all over the world. With the change in regulations, banks in London began to offer their customers dollar facilities. The general return to convertibility in 1957 reinforced this new line of business, by permitting an increase in the supply of privately held dollars. As a result, between 1957 and 1963, Eurodollar holdings in London banks increase by around $4 billion.[19]

A second historical factor accounting for the emergence of these markets was the US balance of payments position. In the late 1950s, the US balance of payments (excluding official financing) turned from an overall surplus to a deficit. Between 1959 and 1963, there was a large net capital outflow of around $2 to $2.5 billion dollars per annum. Friedman (1969) argues that the deficit was neither a necessary nor a sufficient condition for the establishment of a Eurodollar market. It was not necessary, because the EuroDeutschmark market had become established in spite of persistent surpluses on the German balance of payments. It was not sufficient because, although the deficit provided dollars for foreigners, it could not be presumed that they would want to hold them in the form of Eurodollar deposits (as

---

[17] See, for example, Hendershott (1967) and Knight (1977).
[18] This section draws on Gibson (1989, Ch. 1).
[19] These figures are based on Bank of England data on the foreign currency liabilities and claims on nonresidents of banks in London.

opposed, say, to deposits held in the US). Klopstock (1968), however, suggests that the deficit was an important source of funds to the market in the early stages of its development. Major holders of dollars (largely European central banks, who accumulated dollars as part of their obligation to intervene to maintain their Bretton Woods exchange rate parities) preferred to place their dollars in the Euro-markets rather than in the US. Such preferences might simply have reflected the better return (net of transactions costs) offered in the Euromarkets compared to domestic US markets. However, it has also been argued that there were portfolio reasons. The ability of the US to freeze dollar assets held in the Eurodollar market is much more limited than for dollars held in the US. This factor has been emphasised in relation to the depositing of dollars by the Soviet Union at the height of the Cold War in the Euro-markets rather than in the US. This illustrates that portfolio factors were also important in determining where dollars were deposited.

During the 1960s, the main development affecting the growth of the Eurodollar market was the various regulations and controls on capital movements which were introduced by the US. The worsening US balance of payments position led to the imposition of a variety of controls on capital outflows. In 1963, the Interest Equalisation tax made it more expensive for nonresidents to issue bonds in New York. A tax was imposed on US residents who purchased these bonds and hence for the bonds to be attractive and offer competitive returns relative to domestic bond issues, a higher interest rate had to be offered. The result was a dramatic decline in the number of bond issues in New York and a corresponding rise in the use made by non-US companies of the Eurodollar market as a source of funds. In 1964 the Voluntary Foreign Credit Restraint Programme was introduced. This limited the quantity of loans which banks based in the US could make to nonresidents. In 1965 legislation on Foreign Direct Investment limited the ability of US companies to set up overseas subsidiaries. The impact of these various controls on capital movements halted capital outflows from the US. To avoid the new regulations, US banks set up subsidiaries in London. There, they took in dollar deposits and lent out dollars to those who would formerly have raised money in the US domestic markets. Johnston (1983) quotes evidence from Brimmer and Dahl (1975) on the resulting growth of overseas branches of US banks. In 1964, the number of US banks with branches overseas was 11; this increased to 79 in 1970. Over the same period, the assets of overseas branches increased from $6.9 billion to $42.6 billion and the number of overseas branches from 181 to 536. Thus the effect of US regulations on capital flows was to shift the emphasis of international banking away from national banking systems to the Euro-banks.

Controls on US banks for monetary policy purposes strengthened this disinter-mediation process still further. Two regulations are of particular importance here. First, Regulation Q limited the payment of interest on demand deposits and allowed the Federal Reserve to set a ceiling on time deposits rates. Normally, this ceiling was inoperative: market rates were below the ceiling and hence US banks had no trouble attracting funds. Between 1966 and 1969 the ceiling became operable. In other words, the market interest rate in the US rose above the ceiling rate as a result of tight US monetary policy. Banks, of course, were unable to raise their deposit rates and hence the volume of funds available to banks fell as other investment opportunities became more attractive. Being short of funds, US banks turned to the Eurodollar market. They borrowed dollars from their branches abroad which were unaffected by the interest rate ceiling and could therefore continue to offer competitive rates. Thus Regulation Q stimulated the growth of the Eurodollar market in two ways, as the BIS recognised in their Annual Report (1964/65). First, it reinforced the market's ability to offer interest rates on deposits – even deposits at call (demand deposits) – which were higher than domestic dollar rates. Second it increased the demand for dollars as US banks sought to circumvent domestic credit restraint policies.

The second regulation which affected Eurodollar market growth in the 1960s was Regulation D. At a general level, the fact that Eurobanks were exempt from reserve requirements (at least up until 1969) reinforced their ability to offer more competitive interest rates. Reserve requirements are costly in that they tie up funds which could otherwise be lent out to profitable investment projects. Hence they reduce the overall return received by a bank and lower deposit rates. At a more specific level, in 1969 a 10% reserve requirement was imposed on marginal borrowings by US banks from the Eurodollar markets. The reason for this was the US authorities' desire to reduce the volume of repayments of loans which US banks had accumulated whilst the interest rate ceiling was operable. US banks were keen to repay their loans because as monetary policy in the US eased in 1969, so interest rates fell below the Regulation Q ceiling. However, repayments would have further increased the volume of capital outflows and hence in order to limit repayments, the Federal Reserve made it more expensive for US banks to reborrow. In November 1970, the marginal reserve requirement was increased to 20%. However, the measures proved to be ineffective since US interest rates continued to fall, causing the cost of maintaining Eurodollar borrowings to become too expensive.

In January 1974, the US removed the capital controls it had introduced in the 1960s. Paradoxically, this also enhanced the role of the Eurodollar market. After the removal of the controls, US banks could freely arbitrage between the US domestic market and the Eurodollar market.[20] This led to a greater integration of the national and Eurocurrency segments of the dollar market. Thus the impact of controls and regulations in the 1960s and their subsequent removal in the early 1970s were critical factors accounting for the growth of the Eurodollar market at that time.

By the beginning of the 1970s, the Eurodollar market was well established. Bell (1973) argues that the events of the early 1970s with the breakdown of the Bretton Woods system and the floating of exchange rates provided a further boost to the markets. The inflows of dollars into Europe in 1970 and 1971 led to increases in European central banks' holdings of dollars. The Bundesbank was particularly affected as speculators moved out of dollars and into Deutschmarks. Given that the dollar inflows from the underlying US balance of payments deficit were perhaps only a quarter of total dollar flows in Western Europe and Japan over the year to August 1971, the Eurodollar market may have greatly enhanced the problem of the dollar's weakness (Bell, 1973, p.91). Bell concludes that the existence of the Eurodollar market probably caused the realignments and the subsequent breakdown of the Bretton Woods system to occur sooner than it would have done in the absence of a Eurodollar market. Central banks in Europe tended to prefer to deposit their dollar foreign reserves in the Euromarkets and this enabled speculators to borrow dollars which they subsequently sold for other European currencies, further weakening the dollar.

It is difficult to determine whether the increase in Eurodollar business was the result of portfolio factors (Central Banks and speculators preferred to operate in the

[20] See Chapter 7 on arbitrage between domestic dollar and Eurodollar markets.

offshore markets because of lower regulatory risk) or whether it was simply a question of lower transactions costs, allowing speculators to borrow dollars at lower rates than they could in the US and enabling European Central banks to derive a higher rate of return on their dollar holdings.

Shortly after the breakdown of the Bretton Woods, the quadrupling of oil prices created both a demand and a supply stimulus to the Euromarket. The IMF's oil fund facility and its borrowing facilities in general were inadequate to meet the resulting demand for balance of payments deficit financing especially by the non-oil developing countries. OPEC surpluses in 1974 amounted to some $58 billion and much of this was placed in the Eurodollar market, both because of the higher return which could be earned there and for political reasons. OPEC countries were reluctant to place their wealth in US domestic markets where there was the risk that restrictions might have been imposed on its use. Thus the Eurodollar market provided an obvious and convenient channel for capital to be moved from surplus to deficit countries and Eurobanks became inextricably linked with the recycling role in the face of continued balance of payments disequilibrium in the international monetary system. We explore this role and its implications for the stability of the international financial system in some detail in Chapters 8 and 9 when we examine the origins of the international debt crisis.

The final factors which account for the growth of the Eurodollar market are the role of the interbank market and the innovative nature of the Eurodollar market (particularly the medium-term syndicated credit market). Domestic and international financial markets have two major components: firstly, the interbank mechanism, and secondly, the channelling of funds from initial depositors to ultimate borrowers. In the Euromarkets, the former plays a far more important role. In the Eurodollar market, the interbank market, as we have noted, accounts for some 70% of the banks' aggregate liabilities. This contrasts with the situation in the US domestic market, where the Federal Funds interbank market accounts for only 12.5% aggregate liabilities (Ellis, 1981, p.353). The existence of such a large interbank market allows banks to match the inflow and outflow of funds from deposits and loans by lending excess funds or borrowing to meet lending commitments. This reduces the need to maintain a stock of liquidity assets which would act as a safety margin (precautionary reserves). Ellis (1981) finds that there is much variety in the reliance on interbank funds between different banks. The larger, better known banks tend to have a smaller percentage of their foreign currency liabilities in the interbank market. For example, for American banks over the period 1978–81, the percentage varied between 42% and 54%. This is in contrast with consortium banks whose reliance on the interbank market over the same period was about 80%.[21] The general efficiency of the interbank mechanism helps to reduce the transactions and information costs in the Eurodollar market and thus allows them to operate on smaller margins.

Two innovations, associated with end-uses of funds, which substantially contributed to the expansion of the Eurodollar medium-term credit market in the 1970s are roll-over credits and the syndicated loan system. The main feature of roll-over credits is that the interest rate changes every so often and hence they reduce the risk

---

[21] Consortium banks are banks which are owned by a number of major banks. They were very popular in the 1970s and were set up by larger banks to specialise in lending to specific areas (either geographical or sectors). This reliance on lending to specific sectors (e.g. sovereign lending to Latin America) created great difficulties for them in the 1980s following the emergence of the international debt crisis.

of interest rates moving against a bank when it borrows short and lends long. By reducing the risk of making losses if deposit rates should rise, it enables banks to offer higher interest rates on short-term deposits whilst at the same time being able to commit these funds long-term. From the borrower's point of view, roll-over credits imply that interest rates at the time of borrowing are less important, because if they should fall over the course of the loan, the borrower will reap the benefits. Naturally, the borrower will also have to pay the cost if interest rates rise.

The second innovation was the syndicated loan system. Syndicated loans are loans put together by a group of banks. They allow borrowers to borrow much larger sums at lower transactions costs (the borrower has only to approach one bank, the lead bank, to arrange the loan). Additionally they allow banks to diversify their risk more easily. As a result of these benefits, it was the syndicated loan market which was largely responsible for organising sovereign loans to developing countries in the 1970s to cover their current account deficits. Both innovations have their associated problems, as was to become clear in the early 1980s, and we discuss these further in Chapter 9.

This brief account of the development of the Eurodollar market has illustrated how both transactions costs and regulation reasons as well as portfolio factors can account for the development of international banking markets in the post-war period. A similar account can be compiled to explain the development of other Eurocurrency markets such as the EuroDeutschmark and Eurosterling markets as well as offshore banking markets in general.[22] The same is true of international bond markets as we saw briefly at the beginning of this section.

## Conclusion

In this chapter we have discussed questions relating to the holdings of liquidity in the international financial system as well as examining the sources of that liquidity. We argued that with respect to privately-held liquidity the vehicle currency hypothesis tells us that, because of economies of scale, only a few currencies are likely to be important in international transactions in goods, services and assets. This has indeed been confirmed by our examination of the international financial markets, a major source of liquidity in the international system. These markets are still dominated by the dollar which accounts for over 50% of total assets. The yen and the Deutschmark increased in importance since the 1960s and 1970s partly as a consequence of the move towards floating exchange rates. This move increased the risks of holding assets denominated in just one currency, the dollar, and hence the desire for diversification by international investors can explain Deutschmark and yen growth. In the 1980s, a number of markets in other European currencies emerged, but their overall importance is still small.

The trend towards currency diversification in private holdings of international liquidity has also been witnessed by official holders. In the second section of this chapter we examined why countries hold foreign exchange reserves. We argued that principally they allow governments to finance balance of payments deficits and to manage their exchange rate against the major currencies. Not surprisingly, therefore, dollars, Deutschmarks and yen form the vast majority of currencies held by central banks.

---

[22] See Gibson (1989, Ch. 1) for a brief account of the development of the Eurosterling and EuroDM markets. The BIS in its Annual Reports also provides in depth accounts of the role of regulations in explaining the development of other international financial markets.

The final conclusion we can draw from this chapter relates to the growing importance of international markets as providers of international liquidity. In the third section we provided some descriptive data on the growth of both international banking markets and international bond markets. We argued that the growth of these markets can be explained in two ways. First, financial institutions since the 1960s have been much more aggressive in trying to avoid domestic regulations which affect their activities. Hence many of the new markets result from the ability of banks in different locations to reduce the transactions costs associated with intermediation. The second reason for the growth of the markets is a portfolio one: a number of investors and borrowers preferred to deal with international markets rather than domestic markets. The reason is simple: international markets have a lower level of regulatory risk than domestic markets. Moreover, it has often been more convenient for countries to deposit dollar holdings outside of the US to avoid their assets being seized should their relationship with the US deteriorate. The experience of Iran in 1979 which suffered large losses following the freezing of assets held in the US is particularly pertinent here.

Overall, the growth of international sources of liquidity changed the structure of liquidity provision and financial flows in the international financial system. In particular, the various international institutions set up under the Bretton Woods system (the IMF and World Bank) played an ever more limited role as providers of liquidity. As we shall see in the following chapters, these developments were to have a profound influence on the operation of the international financial system in general and its stability in particular.

## References

Bank for International Settlements, *Annual Report*, various years, Basle.

Baumol, W.J. (1952) 'The transactions demand for cash: an inventory theoretic approach', *Quarterly Journal of Economics*, 66: 554–6.

Bell, G. (1973) *The Eurodollar Market and the International Financial System*. Macmillan, London.

Bird, G. (1982) *The International Monetary System and Less Developed Countries*. Macmillan, London.

Chrystal, A.K. (1978) 'International money and the future of the SDR', *Princeton Essays in International Finance*, 128 (June).

Chrystal, A.K. (1990) 'International reserves and international liquidity: a solution in search of a problem', in G. Bird (ed.) (1990) *The International Financial Regime*. Surrey University Press in association with Academic Press, London, 9–28.

Davis, E.P. (1992a) 'The Eurobond market', in D. Cobham (ed.) *Markets and Dealers: the economics of the London financial markets*. Longman, Harlow.

Ellis, J.C. (1981) 'Eurobanks and the interbank market', *Bank of England Quarterly Bulletin*, 21: 3, 351–64.

Friedman, M. (1969) 'The Eurodollar market: some first principles', *Morgan Guaranty Survey*, October, 4–14.

Gibson, H.D. (1989) *The Eurocurrency Markets, Domestic Financial Policy and International Instability*. Macmillan, London.

Halm, G. (1968) 'International financial intermediation: deficits malignant and benign', *Princeton Essays in International Finance*, 68.

Heller, H.R. and Khan, M.S. (1978) 'The demand for international reserves under fixed and flexible exchange rates', *IMF Staff Papers*, December, 623–49.

Hendershott, P. (1967) 'The structure of international interest rates', *Journal of Finance*, 22, 455–65.

**IMF**, *World Economic Outlook*, Annual Report, various years. Washington, D.C.

**Johnston, R.B.** (1983) *The Economics of the Euro-Market: History, Theory, Policy.* Macmillan, London.

**Kettell, B. and Magnus, G.** (1986) *The International Debt Game.* Graham and Trotman, London.

**Klopstock, F.** (1968) 'The Euro-dollar market: some unresolved issues', *Princeton Essays in International Finance*, 65.

**Knight, M.** (1977) 'Eurodollars, capital mobility and forward exchange markets', *Economica*, 44: 173: 1–21.

**MacDonald, R.** (1988) *Floating Exchange Rates: Theories and Evidence.* Allen and Unwin, London.

**McKinnon, R.I.** (1969) 'Private and official international money: the case for the dollar', *Princeton Essays in International Finance*, 74.

**McMahon, C.** (1985) 'Change and development in international financial markets', *Competition and Co-operation in International Banking.* The Institute of Bankers, London.

**Niehans, J. and Hewson, J.** (1976) 'The Eurodollar market and monetary theory', *Journal of Money, Credit and Banking*, February, 1–28.

**Swoboda, A.** (1969) 'Vehicle currencies and the foreign exchange market: the case of the dollar', in R.Z. Aliber (ed.) *The International Market for Foreign Exchange.* Praeger, London.

# 7 INTERNATIONAL FINANCIAL MARKETS, INFLATION AND INTERDEPENDENCE

The growing size and importance of the international financial markets have brought the issue of their impact on monetary aggregates and monetary policy to the fore. In this chapter, we examine the implications of growing international capital flows both for the global economy as well as for individual countries. To this end, we ask two important questions.

First, are international financial markets a potential source of inflationary pressure within the international system? This question reflects one of the early worries which economists had about the rapid growth of the Euromarkets in particular. The fear was that if the Euromarkets could grow endogenously without any control from individual national monetary authorities, then they might lead to large global inflationary pressure. In the first section, we review the literature on credit creation in the euromarkets. We outline the various theoretical models which have been used to address the question of their inflationary potential. In addition, we provide some analysis of the empirical work. We show that the literature by and large suggests that the influence of the growth of international financial markets on world inflationary pressure is minimal.

The general failure to find any evidence that the international financial markets have led to large inflationary pressures caused attention to turn to a second way in which their growth might affect monetary policy. The question here is whether the international financial markets operate as an international transmission mechanism by which countries have become more interdependent. In other words, do international markets act as a channel through which monetary policy changes in one country transmit themselves to other countries? In the second section, we focus on this issue and examine the case of the UK and the transmission of monetary policy effects from the US. Overall, we conclude that the growth of international financial markets has led to increased financial integration in the world economy.

Finally, in the concluding section, we address some of the implications of the above. In particular, we look at the gains from international economic policy co-operation. The gains from such co-operation are larger the greater the spillover effects from policy changes within individual countries. If the growing internationalisation of finance has increased these spillover effects, then the case for co-operation is strengthened.

## The Eurocurrency markets and inflation

As we saw in Chapter 6, much of the growth of the international financial markets in the 1960s and 1970s was due to the increased importance of the Eurocurrency markets, particularly the Eurodollar market. A number of authors (see, for example, Bell (1973) and Friedman (1969)) argued that these markets had a large endogenous capacity for growth. As a consequence, they could cause world monetary growth to accelerate and with it world inflation. At a theoretical level, there are three main approaches to this issue which are evident from the literature. First, the simplest and earliest models employed a fixed coefficient approach. This essentially views credit creation in the Euromarkets in the same way as multiplier models view credit creation domestically. Dissatisfaction with this approach led to some work which applied Tobin's 'new' view of money to Euromarket growth.[1] Finally, a more radical view of the issue was taken by Niehans and Hewson (1976) which concluded that the main role played by the Eurocurrency markets is liquidity or credit distribution rather than creation. We address each of these three approaches in turn.

*Fixed coefficient or multiplier models of credit creation*

Multiplier models of credit creation in the Euromarkets apply traditional multiplier theory used to measure the credit creating potential of the domestic banking system. The rationale is simple. First, Eurocurrency deposits are often held as an international means of payment (for the financing of flows of goods and services and the purchase of international assets) in the same way that domestic bank accounts are. Secondly, Eurobanks hold precautionary reserves which might be thought of as their reserve base in the same way as domestic banks' reserve base comprises those assets which are held with the Central bank. On the basis of these two observations, Friedman (1969) argues that the Eurocurrency markets should be treated identically to domestic banking markets and hence the tools used to analyse the latter are equally good at analysing the former.[2]

It is generally agreed that banks can create credit through adding to their assets and liabilities. As Johnston (1983, p.217) notes, this is true provided that banks add to net income and wealth in an economy and provided that some of the additional wealth is redeposited within the banking system. Multiplier theory takes that view one step further by arguing that the amount of credit created can be accurately estimated by using fixed, or at least predictable, ratios.

Two critical assumptions are employed in these models. First, the reserve base is assumed to be exogenous. That is, banks cannot manipulate their reserve base or create reserves to allow them to finance more loans. Secondly, banks must be fully loaned up: if they receive additional deposits, they relend as much as they can. This is equivalent to assuming that there is a demand for all the loans which a bank wishes to supply.

Given these two assumptions, the multiplier model is easy to derive. We assume that there are two groups of agents in the process: banks and private agents (both depositors and borrowers). An initial stock of deposits, $D_p$, is provided by private agents in the economy. Banks use these deposits to make loans only after a proportion of the deposits has been kept as reserves. If we call that proportion r, then banks make $(1-r)D_p$ loans. The act of making a loan adds to the volume of private sector liquidity, some or all of which finds its way back to the banking system as further deposits. This then allows banks to make additional loans and so the process continues.

The final stock of deposits will depend critically on the assumption made regarding how much of the loans to the private sector make their way back into the banking

---

[1] See, for example, Hewson and Sakakibara (1975; 1976) and Hewson (1975).
[2] See also Fratianni and Savona (1971); Makin (1972; 1973); Lee (1973) and Willms (1976) for examples of this approach.

system. Let us assume at present that there are no leakages from the private sector. In other words, all loans made eventually find their way back into the banking system. In this case, the bank receives $(1-r)D_p$ new deposits and again makes further loans after retaining a proportion r for reserves. These loans $(1-r)^2D_p$ are again redeposited and so the process continues with the volume of new deposits at each stage tending towards zero. The total stock of deposits once the multiplier process has ended will therefore be given by:

$$D = D_p + (1-r)D_p + (1-r)^2D_p + (1-r)^3D_p + \ldots\ldots \tag{7.1}$$

$$=> D = (1/r)D_p \tag{7.2}$$

where $(1/r)$ can be considered to be the multiplier. Equation (7.2) states that the total stock of deposits will be a stable multiple of the initial volume of funds deposits in the banking system. Since r is less than one (not all deposits are held as precautionary reserves), the multiplier will be greater than 1.

This model where all loans are redeposited within the banking system is usually considered to be too simplistic. In the domestic banking system, leakages can occur as individuals move into cash. Since cash holdings are usually quite small (especially in more developed banking systems), redepositing in the domestic system is high. By contrast, leakages from the Euromarkets are likely to be much higher. Dollar loans, for example, made by Eurobanks could find their way into the domestic US money market or could be exchanged for other currencies and be redeposited in other countries' banking systems or nondollar Euromarkets. We can modify the multiplier to take this potential for leakages into account. Assume that from each loan made by the Euromarket from the initial deposit only $(1-c)$ is redeposited within the Euromarkets; the proportion c therefore leaks out to other markets. In this case (using the same reasoning), the final stock of deposits will be:

$$D = D_p + (1-r)(1-c)D_p + \ldots \tag{7.3}$$

$$=> D = \{1/[1-(1-r)(1-c)]\}D_p \tag{7.4}$$

Equation (7.4) indicates that the new multiplier is smaller (although still greater than 1) than the simple one given in equation (7.2). Intuitively the rationale for this result is that the Eurobanks create fewer deposits from an initial injection into the markets because fewer loans find their way back into the Euromarket system.

*A priori*, the multiplier given in equation (7.4) for the Euromarkets could either be larger than that for the domestic banking system or smaller. The factor which works to make it smaller is the large leakages we might expect from the Euromarkets (that is c is high). On the other hand, however, Eurobanks are not required to hold compulsory reserve requirements as domestic banks are. Instead, they hold only precautionary reserves. Willms (1976) has argued that since Eurobanks match the maturity of their assets and liabilities quite closely,[3] the amount of precautionary reserves held is rather small, that is, r is small. This works to increase the multiplier. Willms provides an interesting table of potential multipliers given different estimates for r and c. This is reproduced as Table 7.1. As is clear from the table, if we believe

---

[3] The matching of maturities of assets and liabilities is important if precautionary reserves are to be minimised. Bank runs can cause even solvent institutions to fail if they are unable to repay all their deposits when they are due because their loans are for a longer time period. We discuss the question of maturity mismatching in the Euromarkets later in this section.

*Table 7.1.*  Potential values of the Eurocurrency multiplier

| Leakage Coefficient, c | Reserve ratio, r | | | |
|---|---|---|---|---|
| | 0.2 | 0.1 | 0.05 | 0.0 |
| 1.0 | 1.0 | 1.0 | 1.0 | 1.0 |
| 0.8 | 1.19 | 1.22 | 1.23 | 1.25 |
| 0.6 | 1.47 | 1.56 | 1.61 | 1.67 |
| 0.4 | 1.92 | 2.17 | 2.33 | 2.50 |
| 0.2 | 2.78 | 3.57 | 4.17 | 5.00 |
| 0.0 | 5 | 10 | 20 | ∞ |

*Source*: Willms (1976, p.206, Table 1)

that leakages from the Euromarket system are large (greater than 40%), then the multiplier is likely to lie somewhere between 1 and 2.

There have been a number of attempts to estimate the size of the above two multipliers empirically. The first approach is simply to estimate the multiplier *ex post*. From equation (7.2) we know that the multiplier is given by:

$$1/r = D/D_p \tag{7.5}$$

D is the total stock of deposits in the Eurocurrency market. $D_p$ is the initial stock or the given reserve base. This effectively assumes that the only constraint on the stock of deposits held by Eurobanks is the reserves that they manage to accumulate. Causality therefore runs from reserves to the final stock of deposits. As Johnston (1979, p.224) points out, this is a rather strange assumption. It might seem more sense to assume that Eurobanks accumulate deposits and then hold reserves accordingly.

Estimates using this method range quite widely. Fratianni and Savona (1971) estimate the multiplier using this approach to have been 7 in 1964, falling to 3 in 1967. Makin (1972) estimates a long-run multiplier of 18.5 and a short-run one of 10.3 using quarterly data from 1964 to 1970.

One of the major problems with this approach, which in part explains the divergent estimates derived using it, is the problem of defining the reserve base. In general some measure of indebtedness of US banks to their foreign branches or foreign banks is used, the idea being that Eurobanks hold reserves against their dollar deposits in the US. Fratianni and Savona (1971), for example, use the foreign indebtedness of US banks to their foreign branches. However, as they themselves recognise this is a problematic measure. In addition to representing precautionary reserves, deposits of foreign branches of US banks with their parent banks could represent the parent borrowing from its branch to meet its obligations rather than having to go to the Federal Funds market where funds are perhaps more expensive. Alternatively, the Eurobank could simply have chosen to lend to its parent on the basis of sound commercial sense. Neither of these two deposits could be considered precautionary reserves which could be called upon to finance a shortage of liquidity in the Eurobank. This suggests that the measure used by Fratianni and Savona tends to overestimate the volume of reserves held by Eurobanks. However, by including only reserves held by US banks' branches abroad, the precautionary reserves of the Euromarkets may be underestimated.

Willms (1976) raises even more problems with the measurement of reserves. Should our measure of reserves include all liquid assets held in the US or only demand deposits? Clearly the former is much larger than the latter and hence will generate a lower multiplier. Additionally, should we include all foreign banks or just foreign branches of US banks and within the latter should we include the deposits of foreign branches of US banks on their parent banks? In order to test the sensitivity of the results to different choices with respect to what should be included in reserves, Willms provides estimates for a number of possible definitions of reserves for each quarterly from 1964 to 1974. We report the mean values here to give some flavour of the differences. If we define reserves as demand deposits of all foreign commercial banks with large US banks (that is, excluding foreign branches of US banks) we get a figure for the multiplier of 14.2. If we include foreign branches of US banks, then the multiplier drops to 6.1. If we widen the assets included as reserves to be all short-term assets held by foreign commercial banks and US foreign branches in US banks, then the multiplier falls further to 2.5. Various other definitions provide different results. Moreover, Willms finds not only a high variance between multipliers depending on which measure is used, he also finds that over time all the multipliers have tended to increase and that there is a large variance. Willms concludes, not surprisingly, that this method of calculating the size of the multiplier is less than satisfactory.

The alternative approach to estimating the multiplier using the fixed coefficient approach is to try to derive estimates for the leakage coefficients in equation (7.4). With this approach smaller multipliers have been derived. Mayer (1971) calculates a multiplier of between 1.05 and 1.09. Swoboda (1970) estimates it to be between 1.25 and 1.75, but further work in his 1980 paper suggest it is smaller at between 1.02 to 1.09. Finally, Lee (1973) estimates the multiplier at 1.3 in March 1963 and 1.92 in December 1969.

Clearly these estimates appear less variable. However, this approach to measuring the multiplier is not without its own set of problems. Often guesses are simply made as to the size of the reserve ratio, $r$. But the real problem is the measurement of $c$, the ratio of leakages from the Euromarkets either to national markets in the same currency or to other currencies. Lee (1973) provides a fairly comprehensive account of possible estimates of $c$. He uses measures of the short-term liabilities of US banks to various groups of investors: foreign central banks, foreign commercial banks, foreign private nonbanks and international organisations. The assumption behind his work is that estimates of the average holdings of assets in the US by these various groups represent a good estimate of the marginal holdings. Thus the ratio of foreign central bank deposits in the US banking system to their total holdings of deposits is taken as an estimate of the leakage which might ensue if a Eurobank were to make a loan to that central bank. The former ratio is an average concept, whereas the leakage co-efficient is strictly a marginal phenomenon.

Central banks have been interesting operators in the Eurocurrency markets. Clendenning (1970) suggested that the size of the Eurocurrency multiplier in the 1960s and early 1970s might have been crucially dependent on the extent to which central banks (and European central banks in particular) redeposited in the market. If we assume that leakages from the Eurodollar market ($c$) are mainly to national markets other than the US (that is the dollars are converted into other currencies) and that central banks are fixing their exchange rates to the dollar, then the multiplier will depend on the extent to which central banks redeposit the dollar proceeds of their foreign exchange market intervention in the Eurodollar market. As private agents convert their dollar loans into other currencies, this puts downward pressure on the dollar exchange rate. Non–US central banks then have to intervene in order to prevent their exchange rates from appreciating. As a result they accumulate dollars, which, if they deposit them in the Eurodollar market significantly reduces the amount of leakages. As a consequence the multiplier will be higher. Of course this scenario only applies when the exchange rate is being fixed. If exchange rates are left to float, then central banks conduct no foreign exchange market intervention (or, at least, significantly less), with the result that Eurodollar loans are not redeposited in the Eurodollar market. In the 1960s and early 1970s when European central banks were accumulating large amounts of dollars and tended to redeposit them in the Eurodollar market, the multiplier may well have been high.

Willms (1976) criticises the above models in that they view the Euromarkets as separate entities from the domestic markets, whereas in fact they are linked. He develops a three-stage banking system model which incorporates the idea that a switch of deposits from the domestic markets to the Euromarkets affects credit creation not only in the latter but also in the former. The three-stage approach involves Eurobanks, domestic banks and domestic central banks as well as the nonbank public. He argues that two key relationships are relevant:

$$D_d = (1/r_d)R_d \tag{7.6}$$

$$D_e = [1/(r_e r_E)]R_e \tag{7.7}$$

Equation (7.6) relates domestic deposits ($D_d$) to the reserve money base of domestic banks ($R_d$), where $r_d$ is the reserve requirements held at the central bank. Equation (7.7) states that Eurocurrency deposits ($D_e$) are related to the reserves which Eurobanks hold with domestic commercial banks ($R_e$) via the term $1/(r_e r_E)$. $r_e$ is the ratio of reserves held by domestic banks on Eurobank reserves held with them; $r_E$ is the ratio of deposits held by Eurobanks at domestic banks.

The idea behind this approach can be illustrated by a simple example. Assume that the domestic reserve requirement $r_d$ is 0.10; that domestic banks hold 20% of Eurobank reserves deposits as reserves (that is $r_e$ is 0.20); and finally that Eurobanks hold 10% of their total deposits as reserves with domestic banks ($r_E$ is 0.10). Using equation (7.6) we can see that for each unit of reserves, the system can create either 10 units of domestic deposits (1/0.1) or 50 units of eurodeposits (1/(0.2 × 0.1)). If the commercial banking sector has 100 units of reserves of which 95 are devoted to domestic deposits and 5 to eurodeposits, then domestic deposits can increase to 950 units and eurodeposits to 250 units. The total volume of deposits created by the whole system is then 1200 units. If there had been no Euromarket, the total volume of deposits created could only have been 1000 units. Thus the Euromarket enables the system to expand the total volume of deposits by 20%.

Willms (1976) provides empirical estimates using the above model for both the Eurodollar and EuroDeutschmarks markets. He finds that 80% of Eurodollar deposits are additional dollar created whereas only 35% of EuroDeutschmarks deposits are additional Deutschmark creation. He concludes therefore that even if the multiplier estimates are small, the impact of the Eurocurrency markets on the total money stock for any currency may still be large.

Willms' estimates might be intellectually more satisfying in that they view the Euromarkets as an extension of domestic banking activity, but they suffer from the problem that they are still within the tradition of the fixed coefficient models. Fixed relationships are hypothesised between the holding of reserves and the ability to create deposits from them. However, this approach has been criticised strongly by models which take a portfolio approach to the question of Eurodollar deposit creation.

**Tobin's 'New' view of money and the Euromarkets' ability to create credit**

Hewson and Sakakibara (1975; 1976) argue that the fixed coefficient approach to estimating multipliers is fundamentally flawed. They draw on Tobin's insights for the domestic banking system (Tobin, 1963) and apply them to the Euromarkets. In general, Tobin's arguments suggest that the scale of bank deposits within the banking system will be affected by depositor preferences and the investment opportunities available to banks. The emphasis here is on relative risks and returns in different markets. These insights lead to a number of criticisms which can be made of the fixed coefficient approach.

Firstly, the various ratios (c and r) are assumed to be stable or predictable. Makin (1972; 1973) shows that the precautionary reserves held by Eurobanks is stable and predictable. He hypothesises that the stock of reserves held depends on the Eurodollar rate (which represents the opportunity cost of holding reserves), the CD rate (which is a proxy for the cost of running out of reserves), the variance of assets over the previous four quarters (a measure of uncertainty and hence the need to hold reserves) and, finally, the equilibrium stock of deposits supplied. The equations are generally well-specified providing some support for the multiplier view of the Euromarkets. However, redepositing in the Euromarkets as we indicated above is less likely to be stable. Thus the benefit of the multiplier approach in terms of its simplicity and the ease with which the credit creating potential can be calculated is lost.

A second criticism of the multiplier approach is that it assumes that there is sufficient demand for loans from the banking system. In other words, banks can lend out as much as they want to at the going interest rate. If, on the other hand, loan demand is weak, then the multiplier process will be thwarted – if new additional loans are made, then deposits cannot further expand. Up till now we have been assuming that banks themselves are willing to supply all the loans they can, given the precautionary reserves they wish to hold. The third criticism questions this assumption. It implies that banks are willing to take on the new risks associated with the increased loans. However, if banks prefer not to take on such risks then again the multiplier model will be inappropriate.

Fourthly, the multiplier model assumes that the reserve base of banks is exogenous and that banks are unable to create reserves themselves. In the domestic banking system, where reserve requirements are set by the monetary authorities, this might be an appropriate assumption. However, in the Euromarkets where precautionary reserves are held with domestic banks, this is less appropriate. Mayer (1979) argues that Eurobanks can acquire or dispose of excess reserves in the interbank market. Hence the ratio of total liabilities to reserves, which as we saw above is often used as a measure of the multiplier, is 'almost entirely devoid of causal significance' (p.20). We cannot simply view the reserve base of Eurobanks as exogenous deposits from which they can create new deposits.

The final criticism of the multiplier approach is that it ignores the impact of interest rate movements on the size of the Euromarkets. Hewson and Sakakibara (1975) illustrate the impact of interest rate changes on the multiplier using the following diagram (Figure 7.1).

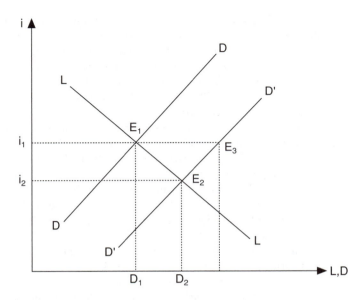

**Figure 7.1.** *Interest rate movements in the Euromarkets and the impact on deposit creation*

Figure 7.1 illustrates the demand for loans from the Euromarkets (LL) and the supply of deposits (DD). The former is assumed to be a negative function of the interest rate (i) and the latter a positive function. Equilibrium is initially at $E_1$. Assume that there is a change in depositor preferences which makes the Euromarkets more attractive. The supply of deposits shifts to the right (to $D'D'$) and the initial inflow of deposits is given by $E_1E_3$. At $E_3$, there is an excess supply of deposits which will cause interest rates to fall[4] from $i_1$ to $i_2$. The new equilibrium is at $E_2$. However, the fall in interest rates, causes some marginal deposits to be withdrawn from the Euromarkets. Overall in the new equilibrium, deposits have risen only from $D_1$ to $D_2$. The 'multiplier', which equals the final change in deposits over the initial inflows, is thus given by $D_1D_2/E_1E_3$ which is less than one. In other words, the '-multiplier' may actually be a divisor. The actual value of the multiplier will depend on the slopes of LL and DD. Hewson and Sakakibara estimate the demand for loans and supply of deposits functions and this allows them to calculate a multiplier of 1.05 for the period January 1968 to December 1972.[5]

*Gross liquidity creation versus net liquidity creation in the Euromarkets*

Niehans and Hewson (1976) offer a more radical departure from the multiplier model than even that provided by Hewson and Sakakibara's analysis. They argue that the multiplier estimates (even taking interest rate changes into account) represent *gross* liquidity creation in the Euromarkets. The asset side of the balance sheet is ignored, with a measure of the liquidity created by the Euromarkets being taken as some measure of the liabilities of banks (deposits). They argue that what is relevant

---

[4] Note that we assume that deposit and lending rates are identical for simplicity.
[5] Johnston (1983) expands these ideas to develop a general equilibrium portfolio model for the Euromarkets. He concludes similarly that the size of the multiplier is likely to be very small once the interconnections between the domestic and Eurocurrency markets are taken into account.

for spending decisions of agents in the economy is *net* liquidity creation, which depends not only on banks' gross liabilities, but also their gross assets. In particular, the extent to which net liquidity is created through maturity transformation.

Maturity transformation occurs when the maturity structure of assets and liabilities differs. Positive maturity transformation requires banks to borrow short-term and lend long-term. That is, they take in deposits which are for say three months and lend out those deposits for several years. Niehans and Hewson term this net liquidity creation. Negative maturity transformation implies that loans made by Eurobanks are for a shorter time period than their deposits. Eurobanks in this case destroy net liquidity. Finally, if the maturities of assets and liabilities are matched, then we have zero net liquidity creation.

Hewson (1975) provides some calculations of maturity transformation in the Euro-markets, using Bank of England data for September 1973 on the maturity structure of assets and liabilities in foreign currencies of banks located in the UK. Given London's major role as a Euromarket centre, this should provide some guide to maturity transformation in the markets as a whole. His results indicate that maturity transformation is limited in the Euromarkets: he finds only a very small tendency for Eurobanks to borrow short and lend long. Moreover, he notes that the extent of mismatching in the Euromarkets is much less than is found in the US domestic banking system.

Hewson (1975) concludes that this seems to be a sensible result. In particular, it explains why Eurobanks hold low levels of reserves: precautionary reserves are required exactly because of maturity mismatching and hence if little occurs, there is less need to hold them. But if Eurobanks do not create net liquidity, what is their *raison d'être*? Hewson argues that their main function is liquidity distribution. Since Eurobank centres have low transactions costs, it is often less costly to distribute liquidity indirectly from one country to another by going through a Euromarket centre. Eurobanks thus specialise in distributing liquidity globally rather than actually creating it.

The implications of this for the multiplier are clear. Using the gross change in deposits resulting from some initial deposit flow into the system is only useful as an indicator of liquidity creation in the market if the liquidity of those deposits is greater than the liquidity of the loans created from them. In the conventional money multiplier model for the domestic banking system, this is a valid assumption. Deposits are withdrawable on demand whereas loans are much more illiquid. Hence the gross change in deposits provides some indication of liquidity created by the banking system. However, since Eurobanks match the maturities of their assets and liabilities, gross deposit creation is little guide to net liquidity creation which must be extremely low.

These conclusions are based on data for only one point in time. Gibson (1989) provides an analysis of maturity transformation using Bank of England data from 1973 to 1985. The data is classified into the maturity structure of assets and liabilities for both banks and nonbanks. This allows an analysis of maturity mismatching in the interbank market as well as in the system as a whole by looking at end-sources and end-uses of funds. Additionally the data is divided into five sections based on the nationality of London-based banks. These sections are British banks, American banks, Japanese banks, consortium banks and foreign banks (includes banks from Commonwealth countries as well as other nationalities excluding Japan and America).

The degree of maturity mismatching can be analysed using a Lorenz curve which is commonly used in measuring income inequality. This method is also employed by Hewson (1975). Whilst this does not allow us to measure the exact quantity of maturity transformation that has taken place, it does make for easy quantitative and visual comparisons through time. The first step is to calculate the percentage of total liabilities and total assets in each maturity class.[6] These percentages are then cumulated and the Lorenz curve plots the cumulated percentage of liabilities in the various maturity classes against the cumulated percentage of claims. If there is a perfect matching of maturities, then the plot follows the 45° line. To the extent that it deviates from the 45° line, the banks are engaging in maturity transformation and the further the curve from the 45° line, the greater the degree of mismatching. If the plotted curve is below the 45° line, there is positive maturity transformation; if above, negative.

We reproduce some of the Lorenz curves from Gibson (1989) in Figures 7.2–7.6. Figure 7.2 shows the extent to which general maturity transformation occurred in all London Eurobanks. Over the whole period maturity transformation increased. This increase was not continuous but occurred in two particular phases. During the first period, 1973–75, the mismatch curve moved out substantially in each year. There was then a period from 1975 to 1982 with little change. This was followed by another increase. Figure 7.3 indicates that the mismatch found in the aggregate data presented in Figure 7.2 was largely due to mismatching of nonbank liabilities and claims. Mismatching in the interbank market (not shown here) was very small. In terms, therefore, of Hewson's net liquidity creation, there is some evidence that banks were creating net liquidity at least in their dealings with nonbank customers.

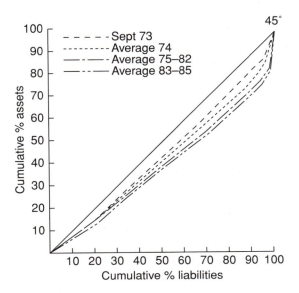

**Figure 7.2.** *Maturity transformation – all banks*

---

[6] There are 7 categories in the Bank of England data: less than eight days; eight days to less than one month; one month to less than three months; three months to less than six months; six months to less than one year; one year to less than three years; and three years or more.

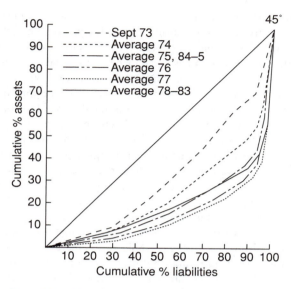

**Figure 7.3.** *Maturity transformation – nonbank claims and liabilities*

Figures 7.4 to 7.6 provide evidence on mismatching by different groups of banks in the London markets. These figures include both interbank and nonbank liabilities and claims. They indicate that there is some difference in behaviour between these different groups. Japanese banks engage in the least maturity mismatching. This reflects regulations imposed by the Japanese Ministry of Finance in the early period which prohibited medium- or long-term overseas loans by branches of Japanese banks abroad. Only when these regulations were lifted in 1978 did the amount of mismatching by the Japanese banks increase. Consortium banks lie at the other end, having engaged in much positive maturity mismatching and hence net liquidity creation. This reflects the fact that consortium banks rely on short-term funds raised in the interbank market which they then lend out for much longer periods.

The data suggests that London-based Eurobanks have almost always engaged in positive maturity transformation. Gibson (1989) attributes these findings both to exogenous influences operating on the Euromarkets as well as to the internal dynamics of the markets. The two main exogenous effects were the 1973 oil price rise and the subsequent recycling role of the Euromarkets and the 1982 debt crisis and subsequent reschedulings. The oil price rise of 1973 increased positive maturity transformation as Eurobanks took in short-term deposits from OPEC countries which they lent out in the medium-term syndicated credit market to developing countries to cover the current account deficits induced by the oil price rise. This accounts for the continuous increase in mismatching between 1973 and 1977. It is interesting to note that the oil price rise of 1979 did not have the same effect on mismatching which remained fairly stable between 1978 and 1982. This might reflect the greater maturity of the Euromarket: there was much less of an increase in competition after 1979. The second period of increased mismatching occurred between 1983 and 1985. This might reflect the involuntary increases in loan maturities which were associated with rescheduling of developing country debt. We discuss these two influences in greater detail in Chapter 9.

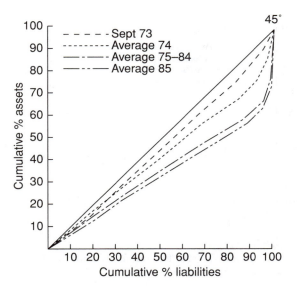

**Figure 7.4.** *Maturity transformation – British banks*

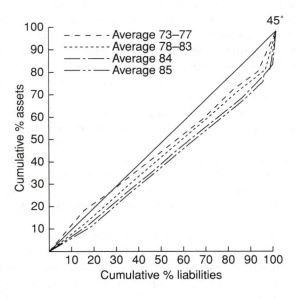

**Figure 7.5.** *Maturity transformation – Japanese banks*

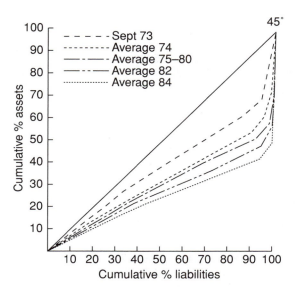

**Figure 7.6.** *Maturity transformation – consortium banks*

Aside from the exogenous influences on the Euromarkets, Gibson also attributes the rise in mismatching to the internal dynamics of the markets. The new recycling opportunities after the first oil price shock attracted many banks into the markets especially since at that time domestic loan demand was rather slack. As we saw in Chapter 6, the number of foreign banks in London increased rapidly and this was associated with growing competition. Banks essentially faced a borrowers' market, something which is often associated with a rise in the maturity of loans.

What do these results suggest for net liquidity creation in the Euromarkets. The figures for 1973 confirm Hewson's (1975) findings. However, the evidence of positive maturity mismatching in later periods conflict with Hewson's conclusion that Euro-banks engage mainly in a liquidity distribution function. The large size of the interbank market and the lack of mismatching there certainly confirms that liquidity distribution is an important function of the Euromarkets. However, in addition, it appears that Eurobanks increasingly played a role as creators of net liquidity. This suggests, contrary to Hewson's conclusion, that they have had an important impact on economic activity on a global level at various points during the 1970s and 1980s.

*Transmission effects of international financial markets*[7]    Interdependence between national economies occurs because of economic integration through flows of goods, services and capital. In this section, we concentrate on financial integration and its relationship with monetary policy interdependence. In particular, we examine the role of the international financial markets in increasing capital flows and hence financial integration. One way of specifying the degree of financial integration between different countries is through the covered interest rate parity condition which we discussed in some detail in Chapter 2. It is also worth recalling this condition is the mechanism through which capital flows link national economies in most of the theories of exchange rate determination which we examined

---

[7] This section draws heavily on Gibson (1989, Chapters 2–4).

in Chapter 3. Here we want initially to recap on the arguments put forward in Chapter 2 about interest parity before going on to examine the role that the Eurocurrency markets play in arbitrage relations between countries and examining some of the empirical evidence on interdependence.

*Financial integration and the interest rate parity condition*

The covered interest parity condition is given by:

$$i_d = i_f - fp_d \tag{7.8}$$

where $i_d$ is the domestic interest rate; $i_f$ is the foreign interest rate; and $fp_d$ is the forward premium on the domestic currency *vis-à-vis* the foreign currency. The interest rate parity condition is a necessary condition for complete financial integration. [8] In itself, however, it tests only the efficiency of arbitrage between two financial centres. If we wish to reach a conclusion about the degree of interdependence between the domestic and foreign countries, then we also have to consider insulation mechanisms and sterilisation mechanisms which might be at work.

Insulation mechanisms 'refer to certain features of the system (such as movements in the forward exchange rate in response to changes in interest rates), which automatically insulate either domestic interest rates or money supplies from monetary developments in other countries' (Llewellyn, 1980, p.170). Consider the case where the foreign interest rate rises. In this case, interest parity is broken and there is an incentive for arbitrageurs to place funds in the foreign market, where the return is higher. However, this entails buying and selling in the foreign exchange market. The arbitrageur will sell domestic currency in the spot market, whilst at the same time selling foreign currency forward (the amount of foreign currency sold forward will be the amount he/she expects to receive at the end of the period of investment in the foreign country). This causes the spot domestic currency exchange rate to depreciate and the forward exchange rate on the domestic currency to appreciate. In other words, the forward premium on the domestic currency (which is the difference between the spot and forward rate) will rise. This could completely restore interest parity, without necessitating a change in the domestic interest rate. That is, some or all of the adjustment to the rise in the foreign interest rate may be absorbed by the change in the forward premium and the domestic interest rate may not move in line with the foreign one despite a high degree of financial integration between the two countries. A key insulation mechanism which may preserve some independence of monetary policy despite financial integration is therefore flexible exchange rates.

Sterilisation mechanisms, which operate in the same way as insulation mechanisms, are deliberate policy measures introduced to offset any external influence on the domestic money supply when there are fixed exchange rates. The authorities may engage in open market operations, for example, in response to a change in the external component of high powered money, thus neutralising the effect of the change on the domestic money supply. The cost of such action is higher volatility of exchange reserves. It does, however, provide some monetary independence in a financially integrated world. The extent to which such sterilisation can be carried out when the domestic country seeks to maintain a covered interest rate differential against

---

[8] Van Gemert and Gruijters (1994) also use the covered interest parity condition to measure the degree of financial integration between countries. In addition, they consider asset substitutability which they measure by uncovered interest parity (see Chapter 3) and monetary integration which they denote by the nominal interest rate differential.

domestic assets is limited in practice by the stock of reserves which the central bank holds. Monetary independence can therefore usually only be maintained in the short run.

*The influence of the Eurocurrency markets*

The introduction of the Euromarkets adds to the number of arbitrage channels through which policy effects can be transmitted. Along with the channel considered in equation (7.8), two new ones are added. Firstly, there is the opportunity for arbitrage between the Euromarkets and their corresponding national market (for example, between the Eurosterling and the domestic sterling markets). This arbitrage differs from that considered above in that here no exchange risk (or currency risk) is involved. Secondly, there is arbitrage between the markets in the different Euro-currencies, which does involve exchange risk and therefore the foreign exchange market, but in a very different way from the traditional arbitrage considered above.

Arbitrage between national and Eurocurrency markets is determined by the nature of banking controls on domestic deposits and loans, and the different transactions costs in the two markets. The supply of funds to the Eurosterling market, for example, by both banks and nonbanks (S) can be represented by the following function:

$$S = f(r_{d\pounds} - i_{d\pounds}, i_e, i_b, P) \tag{7.9}$$

where $r_{d\pounds}$ and $i_{d\pounds}$ are the Eurosterling deposit rate and the domestic sterling deposit rate respectively;[9] $i_e$ is the effective cost of raising funds domestically; $i_b$ is the return on lending money in the domestic interbank market; and P are portfolio considerations. Following Van Gemert and Gruijters (1994) we can distinguish portfolio factors which influence an investor's optimal portfolio and those which affect his/her ability to achieve it. The former include political risk and country risk; the latter include factors such as quantitative capital controls (direct controls) and reserve requirements on capital outflows and withholding taxes on interest received from abroad (indirect controls).

The supply function represented in equation (7.9) captures the supply of funds both from banks and non-banks. UK banks' supply of funds to the Eurosterling market will depend on the return offered in the Eurosterling market (that is, the Eurosterling deposit rate) relative to the domestic cost to banks of raising funds ($i_e$). We might also expect the supply to depend on the domestic interbank rate – the return which UK domestic banks could get on lending the money in the sterling interbank market ($i_b$).

The effective cost of raising funds domestically ($i_e$) is not just the domestic deposit rate. Reserve requirements involve further costs since the reserves that must be held against these deposits have a lower return. If the return on reserves is zero, then the effective cost per unit is:

$$i_e = \frac{i_d + x_d}{1 - R_d} \tag{7.10}$$

where $i_d$ is the domestic deposit rate; $x_d$ is other costs per unit; and $R_d$ are domestic reserve requirements. The term $x_d$ captures the effect of any other costs incurred because of regulation, such as Federal Deposit Insurance in the US.

[9] Note that we adopt the following notation in this section: r refers to Eurocurrency market interest rates; i to domestic market interest rates.

Non-banks will similarly be influenced by the interest rate differential – the return on Eurosterling deposits relative to those in the domestic market $(r_{d\pounds} - i_{d\pounds})$. The greater this differential, the greater the supply of non-bank funds to the market. The supply will eventually be limited by the portfolio considerations of investors (P) which we have already discussed. Such considerations may prevent domestic investors from placing further funds in the Eurosterling market, even if the return is greater.

On the demand side, banks and non-banks are again involved. We can write the demand for funds from the Eurosterling market (D) as follows:

$$D = g(r_{1\pounds} - i_{1\pounds}, i_e) \qquad (7.11)$$

where $r_{1\pounds}$ and $i_{1\pounds}$ are the Eurosterling and domestic sterling lending rates. Domestic banks will demand loans from the Euromarket only when the rate they pay is less than the effective cost of raising funds at home $(i_e)$. Non-banks' demand for loans will depend on the relative costs of raising funds in the Eurosterling market and in the domestic sterling market.

Given the demand and supply functions for the Eurosterling market, we can now determine the impact of efficient arbitrage on the relationship between interest rates in the two markets. The Eurosterling rate should stay within a band. The upper limit of this bank is the effective cost of raising funds domestically, $i_e$. If the Eurosterling rate rises above this, then UK banks will borrow funds domestically at a cost $i_e$ and place them in the Eurosterling market. The lower band is the rate at which it becomes profitable for domestic banks to borrow in the Eurosterling market. If the Eurosterling rate falls below this then the demand for funds by banks from the Eurosterling market would be large, the actual amount of funds borrowed being dependent on the opportunity for profitable relending domestically.

Up till now we have been considering arbitrage between the same currency. If we consider arbitrage between a national market and a Eurocurrency market of different currencies, then the forward exchange market plays a role. In particular, exchange rates now enter the supply and demand functions. The supply of funds, for example, will be positively related to the covered Eurodollar rate and the expected appreciation of the dollar. Efficient arbitrage between say the UK domestic and Eurodollar markets will imply that the following interest parity condition holds:

$$i_\pounds = r_\$ - fp_\pounds \qquad (7.12)$$

where $i_\pounds$ is the UK domestic interest rate; $r_\$$ is the Eurodollar rate and $fp_\pounds$ is the forward premium on sterling per unit of dollar (expressed as a percentage).

The forward exchange rate also plays a key role in the other set of arbitrage conditions – those between different Eurocurrencies. However, the process is different from that envisaged by traditional analysis. Institutionally, all non-dollar Eurocurrency interest rates are determined by the subtraction of the appropriate currency's forward premium on the dollar from the Eurodollar rate. For instance, in the case of the Eurosterling market:

$$r_\pounds = r_\$ - fp_\pounds \qquad (7.13)$$

where $r_\pounds$ is the Eurosterling rate.

This essentially stems from the efficient interbank mechanism which is integral to the Eurocurrency system. Arbitrage is assumed to be efficient and therefore if interest rates were quoted which led to the inequality of equation (7.13), then an infinite volume of funds would flow from the low return market to the high return market. The important point about the relationship in this case is that an increase in the Eurodollar rate will automatically lead to an adjustment of the Eurosterling rate. Funds need not flow to cause this to happen: adjustment occurs in anticipation of such movement. If the forward premium is also allowed to vary, then some adjustment may be borne by it, as it rises in anticipation of excess demand for forward sterling. As the forward premium rises, this reduces the increase in the Eurosterling rate.

Thus the existence of the Eurocurrency markets greatly increases the channels through which arbitrage can be conducted. What effect does this have on interdependence? Traditional arbitrage took place between national markets with the interest parity condition given in equation (7.8) being relevant. Interdependence would result here from capital mobility, fixed exchange rates and the dominating influence of large countries. We noted in Chapter 2, however, that evidence that interest parity holds between national markets tends to be mixed. We argued that these mixed results might be a consequence of the existence of transactions costs, controls on capital movements as well as different political risks.

The Eurocurrency markets might actually increase interdependence without arbitrage necessarily taking place directly between the two national markets. Let us assume that there is perfect arbitrage between different Eurocurrency markets; good arbitrage between national and Eurocurrency markets of the same currency; and, for the sake of simplicity, no arbitrage directly between national markets. Consider now the effect of an increase in the US domestic interest rate. This causes investors to think that they have invested too little in the US and too much in the UK. Those who want to borrow funds turn to the Eurodollar market, increasing the demand for funds which they then onlend to the US domestic market. There is also a decrease in the supply of funds to the Euromarkets as greater returns can be earned in the US domestic market. Thus there will be an excess demand for Eurodollars and this puts upward pressure on the Eurodollar rate.

The change in the Eurodollar rate will cause a readjustment of other Eurocurrency rates as well as some adjustment through the forward premium. It is likely that the Eurosterling rate will increase and arbitrage will then transmit this to the UK domestic market. Thus the results of this 'chain-arbitrage' mechanism indicate that there is potential for greater interdependence through greater capital mobility because of the extra channels through which monetary policy effects can be transmitted. The fact that these markets are outside the control of the domestic government (or at least subject to fewer controls) enhances the finding.

*A case study of the relationship between the US and the UK*

Earlier, we argued that the increased number of potential arbitrage channels consequent on the growth of the Eurocurrency markets could increase interdependence between national economies. Here we want to examine the case of the relationship between the US and the UK and ask whether UK monetary policy has been increasingly influenced by US policy changes. To this end, we want to examine the empirical evidence on the arbitrage channels, discussed above, which involve the Eurocurrency markets. We also consider UK monetary policy both pre-1979 and post-1979 to determine whether or not the removal of capital controls in the UK enhanced interdependence.

In Chapter 2, we provided some discussion of tests of the hypothesis that arbitrage

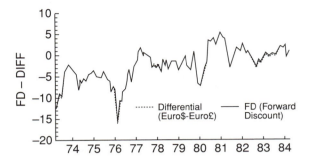

**Figure 7.7.**  *Eurodollar–Eurosterling arbitrage, 1974–84*

between different Eurocurrency markets is efficient.[10] The results indicate very little deviation from interest rate parity especially if we include transaction costs, which create a tunnel within which arbitrage is not profitable. These results are confirmed by Figure 7.7 which plots the difference between the Eurodollar and Eurosterling interest rates and the forward discount on sterling. Here we are interested also in whether the Eurosterling rate is determined by the Eurodollar rate and the forward premium on sterling *vis-à-vis* the dollar – the alternative hypothesis being that the Eurosterling rate is determined by conditions in the UK money markets.

Efficient arbitrage is certainly consistent with the view that non-dollar Eurocurrency interest rates are determined institutionally. However, this finding does not tell us anything about the direction of causation. Figure 7.8 plots the relationship between the Eurosterling rate and the Local Authority loan rate (LA rate, hereafter).[11] The differential between these two rates is far greater than any differential between the Eurodollar and Eurosterling interest rates (adjusted for the forward premium). This confirms the idea that the Eurosterling rate is institutionally determined by the Eurodollar rate with little influence exerted by the UK money markets.

There are several studies which examine the efficiency of arbitrage between the Eurodollar and the US domestic markets and the related question of the determination of the Eurodollar interest rate. Rich (1972) finds that the US Treasury bill rate is important in determining the Eurodollar rate over the period March 1959 to December 1964. Johnston (1983) and Argy and Hodjera (1973) find that arbitrage between the Eurodollar and US domestic markets is very near perfect. Argy and Hodjera also test for the influence of regulation Q on the Eurodollar market. They find that when Regulation Q was effective, additional demand for Eurodollars tended to raise the Eurodollar interest rate: for every 1 per cent the market rate was above the ceiling rate, the Eurodollar rate would rise by 0.4 per cent. Herring and Marston (1977) similarly find that Regulation Q affected the Eurodollar interest rate.

Gibson (1989) tests the efficiency of outward arbitrage between the US domestic market and the Eurodollar market for the period 1979–84.[12] Figure 7.9 plots the

---

[10]  See, for example, Marston 1976) and Gibson (1989, Chapter 4).

[11]  We return to an analysis of the relationship between the Eurosterling and domestic sterling interest rates later in this section.

[12]  A test of outward efficiency only can be undertaken because during this time, US banks were net suppliers to the Eurodollar market (see Gibson, 1989, pp.76–7).

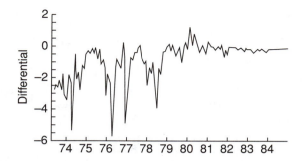

**Figure 7.8.**   *Differential between Eurosterling and domestic sterling interest rates, 1974–84*

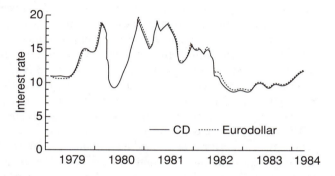

**Figure 7.9.**   *Eurodollar–domestic dollar arbitrage*

Eurodollar interest rate along with the Certificate of Deposit rate (CD rate) adjusted for federal deposit insurance and reserve requirements.[13] In spite of the very high variability of interest rates especially during the period 1979–81, the relationship is very close. Only during 1981 and 1982 was the Eurodollar rate consistently higher than the adjusted CD rate suggesting that banks were not engaging in outward arbitrage to the extent required to eliminate the differential in favour of the Eurodollar market. This can partly be explained by the increase in perceived riskiness of the Eurodollar market because of the debt servicing difficulties of Eastern European countries which emerged in 1980–81 only to be followed in 1982 by the start of the international debt crisis. The fact that Eurodollar interest rates were above domestic US interest rates at this time, perhaps suggests that US banks required a risk premium to place additional funds in the Eurodollar market.

With respect to the question of the direction of causality between the Eurodollar and domestic dollar interest rates, we can argue that it is the latter that tends to determine the former. That is, US domestic monetary policy is a major determinant of Eurodollar interest rates. The high degree of variability of interest rates from 1979–81 can be explained entirely in terms of the adoption of monetary base control by the US Federal Reserve. Moreover, during 1979 and 1980, the Eurodollar interest

[13] The CD rate is the secondary CD rate. This is used because US banks tend to use it when calculating the cost of funds (rather than the primary CD rate). See Kreicher (1982) and Johnston (1983).

rate followed the rise in the domestic dollar interest rate in spite of the fact that conditions in the Eurodollar market suggested an interest rate fall. The second oil price shock brought about a major rise in the supply of deposits to the market. New deposits from oil exporting countries which had been $6 billion in 1978 totalled $38 billion in 1979 (BIS Annual Report, 1980, pp.106–10). Whilst credit demand from deficit countries also rose, the BIS concludes that supply was probably greater than demand from 1979–81 as indicated by the continuing borrower's market. Yet the Eurodollar rate rose during 1979, as Figure 7.9 shows, in response to the tightening of monetary policy in the US and the introduction of monetary base control.

Thus we can conclude that the relationship between the Eurodollar rate and the domestic US dollar rate is a close one. Moreover, throughout the market's history, US monetary policy has tended to exert an important influence on the Eurodollar rate. This suggests that US monetary policy has been more easily transmitted to the rest of the world through the Eurodollar market, something we will consider more explicitly.

The final arbitrage channel which we wish to consider is the relationship between the Eurosterling and domestic sterling interest rates. Figure 7.8 plots the Eurosterling rate and the domestic sterling rate. The latter is represented by the LA loan rate which is a parallel money market rate. Since a high proportion of interbank deposits are deposited in the LA market, this suggests that the LA market is a good substitute for the Eurosterling market (Einzig, 1974). The Figure indicates that there was a persistent interest differential against domestic sterling assets up until 1979.

We can easily account for this interest rate differential. The reason for this was the existence of controls which prevented UK residents taking capital out of the country and hence taking advantage of the higher interest rate available in the Eurosterling market. If capital controls had not existed, then UK residents would have moved funds into the Eurosterling market. The resultant capital outflow and deterioration in the balance of payments would have put upward pressure on domestic interest rates. After October 1979 when capital controls were removed, arbitrage seems to have been efficient.

It is interesting to note that the differential against domestic sterling assets was far from constant in the pre-1979 period. Indeed, changes in the differential appear to have been related to sharp movements in the forward discount on sterling *vis-à-vis* the dollar. Although the forward discount does not enter into the interest parity condition for arbitrage between the Eurosterling and LA markets, its influence is nonetheless felt indirectly. The theoretical reason for this apparent role for the forward discount is seen by recalling the method by which the Eurosterling interest rate is determined. The arbitrage condition is given by:

$$r_{\pounds} = r_{\$} - fp_{\pounds} \tag{7.14}$$

If the forward premium on sterling is negative and getting larger (that is, the forward discount on sterling widens), then the Eurosterling rate will increase for a given Eurodollar rate. Hence if the LA rate remains unaltered (something which was possible only because of controls on capital outflows), then the differential against domestic sterling assets widens. Indeed Gibson (1989, pp.87–9) confirms this with an examination of the factors which determined the forward discount on sterling over the whole period.

Having analysed the empirical evidence on the various arbitrage channels between the UK and US markets, we are now in a position to examine the impact of the

Eurocurrency markets on interdependence between the US and the UK in both the pre-1979 period and the post-1979 period. Our analysis shows that a rise in the US domestic interest rate will transmit itself to the Eurodollar market. Arbitrage between the Eurodollar and Eurosterling markets will then cause the Eurosterling interest rate to rise and this will transmit itself to the UK domestic market. In other words, efficient arbitrage has increased interdependence.

But of course this conclusion in part depends on the extent to which insulation mechanisms can operate to shield the UK market from monetary policy changes in the US. Gibson (1989, Chapter 4.6) undertakes a detailed study of the movements in US and UK interest rates over the period 1974 to 1984. Her analysis suggests that three main factors determined the degree of influence which US monetary policy exerted on UK policy over the period 1974–84.

Firstly, before 1977, exchange rate policy was important and frequently tended to dominate domestic monetary policy concerns. Attempts to halt a falling pound would frequently lead to rises in interest rate whether domestic monetary conditions warranted them or not. Capital controls helped to allow domestic interest rates to remain to some extent below those abroad (or at least below what they would otherwise have been) and enabled exchange rate policy to be more easily implemented. This is not a surprising result. Interdependence tends to be greater when a country is seeking to pursue an exchange rate target as we saw in Chapter 5. This occurs because the insulation mechanism provided by movements in the forward premium is more limited if exchange rate targets are adopted.

The second conclusion is that the removal of capital controls greatly enhanced the interdependent environment in which UK monetary policy was conducted. Expectations of changes in UK interest rates were frequently generated by changes in US interest rates. Such expectations were less evident (although not wholly absent) before 1979, because arbitrageurs and speculators felt that the authorities could choose between several responses to such a disturbance.

The final conclusion which we can draw from the UK experience is that the stability of financial markets is an important factor in determining the insulation offered to a country from interest rate changes abroad through movements in the forward premium. By contrast, when there was speculative pressure on sterling, and the forward discount widened, interest rates in the UK generally responded to a change in US interest rates (even when the government did not have an explicit exchange rate target as it had in the pre-1977 period). The efficiency of arbitrage via the Eurocurrency markets made it very difficult at certain times for the UK authorities to resist monetary policy pressures from the US.

In conclusion, therefore, we have argued that there exists a highly efficient arbitrage network between domestic and Eurocurrency markets. We have argued that arbitrage between different Eurocurrency markets seems to be institutionally determined and is highly efficient. Similarly, arbitrage between domestic and Eurocurrency markets, in the absence of capital controls, is very efficient. In the case of the UK, the existence of capital controls significantly affected arbitrage efficiency with large differentials against sterling being maintained. Capital controls therefore appeared to offer some degree of insulation and, therefore, some freedom of policy choices. After the removal of capital controls in October 1979, interdependence between the UK and the US increased. This caused increased difficulties in controlling monetary conditions when the authorities wished to pursue a policy which was different from that followed in other countries.

But such a conclusion is not only confined to the British case. Van Gemert and Gruijters (1994) examine the degree of financial integration among some 11 OECD countries (Belgium, Denmark, France, Germany, Italy, the Netherlands, Australia, Canada, Japan, the UK and the US). Average mean absolute deviations from covered interest parity are then calculated for the period 1973 to 1993. The findings indicate that financial integration increased throughout the 1980s. For the seven countries which were following a flexible exchange rate policy (Germany is included since it represents the ERM's float against the rest of the world), financial integration increased after 1974 and then again after the early 1980s. Both these dates coincide with the removal of capital controls in these countries. For the 6 countries who had experience with the ERM, financial integration increased only towards the end of the 1980s, reflecting their continued use of capital controls.

Thus evidence for increased financial integration is not only confined to the case study countries examined here. With ERM countries, it is likely that German monetary policy was the dominating force in the determination of their national monetary policies rather than the US. And, of course, their pursuing of fixed exchange rates when capital controls were no longer in place can only enhance such a conclusion.

## Conclusions: the implications of increased financial integration and interdependence

We have argued that increasing capital flows associated with the chain arbitrage mechanism has resulted in a growing interdependence in the world economy. In particular, monetary policy is often unable to respond to domestic economic conditions when capital mobility is high and if governments are managing the exchange rate. We argued in Chapters 4 and 5 that there are good reasons for the monetary authorities to care about the level of the exchange rate. Moreover, some form of exchange rate management is likely to remain the policy choice of most industrial countries. Under such circumstances, changes in interest rates, especially in larger countries such as Germany and the US, will necessitate responses from the monetary authorities of smaller countries, responses that might not always be in the interests of their domestic economies.

In essence, the existence of high capital mobility can lead to a divergence between social and private gain. For arbitrageurs, the private benefits of capital flows is clear: they are able to place their funds where they will earn the highest returns. But the social effect (that is, the impact on the wider economy) may be negative: in our specific case, interest rates are altered when there was no real economic reason to do so. More generally the divergence between social and private gain was arguably witnessed during the ERM crisis in the UK in September 1992. There again the private gain was large: speculating on a devaluation of sterling within the ERM was a fairly safe bet. The social cost, however, was the government's abandonment of its exchange rate target and its suspension of ERM membership. This had implications not only for the UK's relationship with its European partners, but also for the government's monetary policy and exchange rate strategy.

What might be the policy response to such divergences between private and social benefits? A first possibility is to introduce new controls over capital movements. This has received renewed attention in the 1990s. As we saw in Chapter 5, the crisis in the ERM has led some commentators to suggest that controls on capital movements might provide a solution to the problem of the path to EMU. More recently, and in a wider context, the issue of slowing capital movements has received attention in the '-Policy Forum' section of the *Economic Journal*.[14] Entitled 'Sand in the wheels of

---

[14] See Eichengreen, Tobin and Wyplosz (1995), Garber and Taylor (1995) and Kenen (1995).

international finance', it considers, among other things, the case for a Tobin-style tax on international capital movements (see Tobin, 1978). Eichengreen, Tobin and Wyplosz (1995) argue that a half per cent tax on global transactions, which translates into an annual rate of 4% on a three-month arbitrage deal where money leaves a country and is then repatriated, would help to increase monetary autonomy. They contend that such a tax would be invaluable because 'central banks and governments cannot always create exchange rate expectations consistent with the domestic interest rates they desire' (p.164). More generally they note that whereas global financial markets are nowadays highly efficient and speedily adjust to any change in circumstances, the real economy is still slow to adjust because the costs are high, information imperfect and expectations fuzzy. In these circumstances, welfare can be improved by intervening in financial markets to slow their adjustment capacity.

Garber and Taylor (1995) are critical of this proposal. In particular, they argue that a tax on capital movements will result in disintermediation to other centres (where the tax does not apply) and a disintermediation to other financial instruments which are not subject to the tax. However, Eichengreen, Tobin and Wyplosz are keen to note that their proposal would only work if it were uniformly and universally applied. This, they argue, would require surveillance for an international institution such as the International Monetary Fund or the Bank for International Settlements. They rightly point out that similar surveillance is already conducted by other multilateral institutions such as GATT (The General Agreement on Trade and Tariffs) and hence should not be dismissed as unrealistic or unworkable.

A second but not necessarily incompatible response to increased interdependence and the possible divergence of social and private benefits is to increase policy co-ordination between industrial countries. It is well-known that the benefits from policy co-ordination are greater, the greater the spillovers from one country to another.[15] Currie (1990) notes that the Group of Thirty have defined international economic policy co-ordination as a process where 'countries modify their economic policies in what is intended to be a mutually beneficial manner, taking account of international economic linkages' (quoted in Currie, 1990, p.125). Whilst there have been some attempts at international discussions on co-ordination (notably by the Group of Seven countries at their various economic summits), frequently these discussions simply entail a statement of the aims of individual countries without any real attempt at assessing the impact of one country's policies on the ability of another to succeed. In other words, there has been very little evidence of true policy co-ordination.

Both these proposals require a strengthening of international institutions if they are to have any chance of successful implementation. Only such institutions could become well-equipped to provide the information required to formulate, implement and monitor proposals of this kind. Inevitably disagreements would occur and the process might require some time before the benefits are realised. But, in the face of growing globalisation of financial markets, the benefits could be substantial.

## References

**Argy, V. and Hodjera, Z.** (1973) 'Financial integration and interest rate linkages in industrial countries', *IMF Staff Papers*, 20: 1, 1–77.

**Bell, G.** (1973) *The Eurodollar Market and the International Financial System*. Macmillan, London.

**Clendenning, W.** (1970) *The Eurodollar Market*. Clarendon Press, Oxford.

---

[15] See Currie (1990) for a good review of the policy co-ordination literature.

**Currie, D.** (1990) International policy co-ordination', in D.T. Llewellyn and C. Milner (eds) *Current Issues in International Monetary Economics*. Macmillan, London.

**Eichengreen, B., Tobin, J. and Wyplosz, C.** (1995) 'Two cases for sand in the wheels of international finance', *Economic Journal*, 105: 1, 162–72.

**Einzig, P.** (1974) *Parallel Money Markets: Volume I: the new money markets in London*. Macmillan, London.

**Fratianni, M. and Savona, P.** (1971) 'Eurodollar creation: comments on Prof. Machlup's propositions and developments', *Banca Nacionale del Lavoro Quarterly Review*, 24: 97, 110–28.

**Friedman, M.** (1969) 'The Eurodollar market: some first principles', *Morgan Guaranty Survey*, 4–14.

**Garber, P. and Taylor, M.P.** (1995) 'Sand in the wheels of foreign exchange markets: a sceptical note', *Economic Journal*, 105: 1, 173–80.

**Gemert, H. van and Gruijters, N.** (1994) 'Patterns of financial change in the OECD area', *Banca Nazionale del Lavoro Quarterly Review*, 190: 271–94.

**Gibson, H.D.** (1989) *The Eurocurrency Markets, Domestic Financial Policy and International Instability*. Macmillan, London.

**Herring, R. and Marston, R.** (1977) *National Monetary Policies and International Financial Markets*. North-Holland, Amsterdam.

**Hewson, J.** (1975) *Liquidity Creation and Distribution in the Eurocurrency Markets*. Lexington Books, Lexington, Mass.

**Hewson, J. and Sakakibara, E.** (1975) *The Eurocurrency Markets and their Implications*. Lexington Books, Cambridge, Mass.

**Hewson, J. and Sakakibara, E.** (1976) 'A general equilibrium approach to the eurodollar market', *Journal of Money, Credit and Banking*, 8: 3, 297–323.

**Johnston, R.B.** (1983) *The Economics of the Euro-Market: History, Theory, Policy*. Macmillan, London.

**Kenen, P.** (1995) 'Capital controls, the EMS and EMU', *Economic Journal*, 105: 1, 181–92.

**Kreicher, L.L.** (1982) 'Eurodollar arbitrage', *Federal Reserve Bank of New York Quarterly Review*, Summer, 10–21.

**Lee, B.E.** (1973) 'The Eurodollar multiplier', *Journal of Finance*, 28: 4.

**Llewellyn, D.T.** (1980) *International Financial Integration: the limits of sovereignty*. Macmillan, London.

**Makin, J.H.** (1972) 'Demand and supply functions for stocks of Eurodollar deposits: an empirical study', *Review of Economics and Statistics*, 54: 2, 381–91.

**Makin, J.H.** (1973) 'Identifying a reserve base for the Eurodollar multiplier', *Journal of Finance*, 28: 3, 609–17.

**Marston, R.** (1976) 'Interest arbitrage in the Euro-currency markets', *European Economic Review*, 7: 1–13.

**Mayer, H.W.** (1971) 'Multiplier effects and credit creation on the Eurodollar market', *Banca Nazionale del Lavoro Quarterly Review*, 24: 98, 233–62.

**Mayer, H.W.** (1979) 'Credit and liquidity creation in the international banking sector', *BIS Economic Papers*, November, 1.

**Niehans, J. and Hewson, J.** (1976) 'The eurodollar market and monetary theory', *Journal of Money, Credit and Banking*, February, 1–28.

**Rich, G.** (1972) 'A theoretical and empirical analysis of the eurodollar market', *Journal of Money, Credit and Banking*, 4: 3, 616–35.

**Swoboda, A.** (1970) 'The eurodollar market: an economist's point of view', *The Eurodollar*. The Graduate School of Banking, University of Wisconsin, Chicago.

**Tobin, J.** (1963) 'Commercial banks as creators of money', in D. Carson (ed.) *Banking and Monetary Studies*. Irwin, Homewood, Illinois.

**Tobin, J.** (1978) 'A proposal for international monetary reform', *Eastern Economic Journal*, 4: 153–9.

**Willms, M.** (1976) 'Money creation in the eurocurrency market', *Weltwirtschaftliches Archiv*, 112: 2, 201–30.

# 8 INTERNATIONAL BANK LENDING: A THEORETICAL FRAMEWORK

The large growth in international banking activity in the 1960s and 1970s was associated with a much greater role for private capital in the world economy. Private sources of finance became increasingly important in dealing with the problems of international adjustment and financing which we discussed at some length in Chapter 1. The purpose here is to introduce some theoretical issues relevant to bank lending. The analysis is of relevance both to domestic and international bank lending, although our concern in this book is more obviously with the latter. The framework outlined can be applied generally to the problems which might arise from the private provision of finance and, in particular, can be used to analyse many of the frequent financial disturbances which have recently characterised international financial markets. Here we use the framework, by way of illustration, to examine the role of private capital in the recycling of funds from surplus to deficit countries following the oil price shocks of 1974–5 and 1979. This culminated in what has come to be known as the debt crisis which broke in August 1982 when Mexico announced that it was unable to meet repayments on its foreign debt. In this chapter we focus on some theoretical ideas before going on to examine the debt crisis in some detail in the following chapter.

International banking involves a number of risks additional to those which banks face in normal commercial lending. The way in which banks deal with these risks and the uncertainty associated with lending to sovereign entities in particular is crucial to the stability not only of individual financial institutions but also of the whole international financial system. The argument in this chapter is that there are good theoretical reasons for thinking that financial markets have a tendency towards overlending which can cause crisis only to be followed by a period of underlending and a shortage of liquidity in the international financial system. An examination of bank behaviour in the face of international lending risks is important for understanding how this overlending might come about.

The chapter is organised into three main sections. In the first section, we discuss the efficient market view of the way in which banks operate. It argues that lenders will ensure adequate compensation for the risks which they undertake. The consequence is that private banking markets will efficiently allocate capital internationally by taking finance from surplus units (individuals, companies or countries) and distributing it to deficit units. Whilst mistakes may be made and defaults might occur, there should be no tendency to financial crises.

In the second section we go on to discuss a variety of market failures which affect international lending. The focus is on information deficiencies and asymmetries which are prevalent in credit markets. We examine the appropriate response of banks to those failures and assess the extent to which this literature is correct to argue that the existence of both risk premia and credit rationing ensures the stability of the international financial system. Finally, in the third section we turn to the question of the causes of financial crises. We discuss the idea that competitive pressures combined with these failures identified in section two are likely to lead to banks taking on too many risks without adequate compensation. The result is that credit markets have a propensity to generate financial crises. Defaults can threaten the solvency of individual institutions and additionally have negative consequences for those countries which find themselves starved of funds. In general, the stability of the system as a whole comes into question. This has profound implications for the method by which the issues of adjustment and liquidity are dealt with by the international financial system. In particular, it cautions strongly against relying solely on private sources of liquidity to finance balance of payments deficits.

## The efficient market view of bank lending

International capital markets play an important role in intermediating between savers and borrowers from different countries. They shift savings from areas where they are abundant and hence cheap to those where they are scarce and hence expensive. Global welfare is thus improved by a reallocation of capital to those areas where it can be used most productively. The efficient market view of bank lending argues that private unregulated international capital markets can conduct this intermediation efficiently and hence will promote the optimal allocation of resources. Devlin (1989) argues that in the early 1970s international banks were seen as representing a non-political and efficient source of development finance. Moreover, through their lending, they would actively promote efficient development policies by making loans only to countries which were following good investment policies. In short, the discipline of the market was applied to international capital flows.

Intermediation, in addition to transferring funds between surplus and deficit units, also involves the banks in reconciling the different preferences of borrowers and lenders. Lenders usually require access to their funds at fairly short notice. Borrowers, by contrast, prefer repayment to occur over a longer period. This is particularly true in the case of the financing of development projects whose gestation period can be very long. Llewellyn (1990a) argues that these considerations imply that the mechanism by which finance is transferred between surplus and deficit units should satisfy a number of criteria. The range of instruments offered should be large in order to give both borrowers and lenders more choice as well as promoting an optimal sharing of the risks involved. The supply of finance should be stable and not subject to large discontinuities which make investment planning more difficult. Contracts should ensure that debt-servicing obligations do not exceed the ability to repay, thus helping to reduce incentives to default. The lending institution should be careful to include an efficient pricing of risk and investments should be monitored to guarantee that the funds are being used for the purposes specified. Finally, it is important that the mechanisms of intermediation limit the systemic hazards to the international financial system.

The efficient market view argues, on the basis of standard general equilibrium theory, that competitive markets are the best framework in which to achieve these objectives. In order to understand why, we have to examine the concepts of competition and efficiency and their relationship to each other. Efficiency is usually defined in allocative terms. Markets are allocatively efficient if they establish prices which encourage savings to flow to the most promising investment opportunities. Tinic and

West (1979) argue that allocative efficiency has two aspects in the financial sector. First, operational efficiency ensures that buyers and sellers of the product can purchase transaction services at prices that are as low as possible given the costs involved: in other words, those providing the services of an intermediary between end-users and end-depositors do not earn abnormal profits. Secondly, pricing efficiency means that the prices of loans and deposits should reflect the value of the investment to society. This requires that all information of relevance to the investment be included in the price.

The market structure that guarantees that resources are allocated efficiently in the manner we have described is that of perfect competition. Profit maximising producers and utility maximising consumers ensure an efficient allocation of resources. First, the price of the financial services (represented by the spread between the deposit and loan rates as well as any fees associated with transactions) is equal to the marginal cost of providing them. This implies that the market will be operationally efficient. Secondly, the interest paid on the loan, or the inducement offered for the deposit is only the expected yield plus a risk premium (that is, pricing efficiency). These two conditions together ensure an efficient allocation of resources, given allocative efficiency in all other (non-credit) markets.

Should a new profitable lending opportunity become available, such as the recycling of oil surpluses, the excess profits accruing to existing lenders will attract new entrants. Individual lenders' profits will fall as supply of the product and demand for the factors of production increase. The former reduces the price of the product; the latter increases the cost of producing it.

Our discussion of the efficient market view has made only brief mention of uncertainty and risk. Given that, as we have noted, an important function of banks is to assume the risk inherent in financing investment, we need to discuss the efficient market approach to this issue. Tinic and West (1979, p.156) define any investment as risky if it has more than one possible real return. The measurement of risk involves a determination of the dispersion (or the probability distribution) of these possible returns. It is usual to divide the risk of an investment into two sections. First, systematic risk is the portion of the variability in returns associated with movements in general economic activity and therefore affects the capital market as a whole. Secondly, there is unsystematic risk, which is associated specifically with individual investments.

All loans which a bank undertakes will contain elements of both risks. However, a bank is able to diversify away the unsystematic component of risk. To understand this, we can look at the 'market model' (Bernoulli, 1954; Blume, 1971). This relates the return on any asset i at time t ($R_{it}$) to the return on the market (that is, all banks' financial assets) as a whole ($R_{mt}$):

$$R_{it} = a_i + b_i(R_{mt}) + e_{it} \qquad (8.1)$$

where $a_i = r_f(1 - b_i)$ ($r_f$ is the risk-free interest rate). $e_{it}$ is a random error which embodies elements of unsystematic return on asset i, that part which cannot be explained by the change in the return on banks' assets in general; $b_i$ measures the systematic volatility of asset i which is dependent on the degree to which the return on asset i is correlated with the return to banks as a whole. A $b_i$ of less than one implies that asset i is less risky than the market as a whole; a $b_i$ of greater than one implies that it is more risky.

The variance of the return on the ith asset, $s^2(R_i)$, which can be thought of as a measure of the total riskiness of assets i, can be represented as the sum of two components:

$$s^2(R_i) = b_i^2 s^2(R_m) + s^2(e_i) \tag{8.2}$$

where the first term on the right hand side is the systematic risk element $(b_i^2 s^2(R_m))$ and the second term the unsystematic risk element $(s^2(e_i))$. If a bank holds a portfolio of assets, then we can calculate the variance of returns on the portfolio, $s^2(R_p)$ which tends to:

$$1/n^2(b_1 + b_2 + b_3 + \ldots + b_n)^2 s^2(R_m) \to b_a^2 s^2(R_m) \text{ as } n \to \infty$$

where $b_a$ is the average b for all assets in the portfolio. As n, the number of randomly selected assets, increases, $b_a$ tends towards 1 (that is, towards the risk of all assets in the market combined) and hence the variance of the portfolio tends to approach the variance of all assets in the market. Thus the risk on the whole portfolio converges on the value of the systematic risk of that portfolio and unsystematic risk has been successfully eliminated.

Nonetheless, the banks' portfolio will contain a systematic component or risk and, if the bank is risk averse, the expected return will have to compensate the bank for the degree of systematic risk which each loan or portfolio of loans entails. Which portfolio is chosen, will depend on the bank's attitude to risk.[1] We can represent this using indifference curves as shown in Figure 8.1. $U_0$, $U_1$ and $U_2$ are indifference curves for a risk averse bank. They are positively sloped because as risk increases, the expected return on the bank's portfolio must also increase as compensation, so that the overall level of utility remains unchanged. The higher the indifference curve, the greater the level of utility (since a higher indifference curve is associated with a higher expected return for a given level of risk).

The portfolio opportunities available to a bank are represented by the schedule AB in Figure 8.2. The riskiness of the portfolio is measured by the variance of returns. As the riskiness of a portfolio increases, so the expected return on that portfolio rises, but at a decreasing rate. The point at which AB is tangential to the highest indifference curve is the optimal portfolio for the bank, given its preferences regarding the relationship between risk and return. In Figure 8.2 this is at point E. The risk of the optimal portfolio is given by $s^{2*}$ and this consists of systematic risk only. The expected return on this optimal portfolio $(E(R^*))$ is enough to compensate the bank for the risk involved. How does this come about? The bank must distinguish between loans on the basis of the price charged: any borrower will have to pay a risk premium on top of the basic interest rate, where the risk premium represents the amount of systematic risk involved in the investment. If the borrower is unwilling to pay the risk premium, then the bank will not make the loan.

As McKenzie and Thomas (1992) note, the efficient market view we have outlined makes two key assumptions. The first relates to the information available to banks. Banks are able to assign probabilities to the possible outcomes of any lending. That is, they can objectively calculate the expected return on any project as well as the dispersion of returns. This allows them to calculate the expected return on any portfolio (simply the weighted average of the expected returns on each individual loan) as well as its riskiness (measured by the variance of returns). The second key assumption

---

[1]  This draws on McKenzie and Thomas (1992).

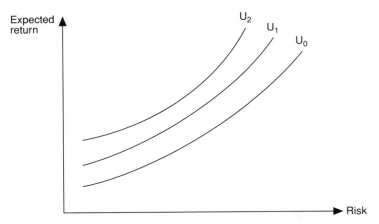

**Figure 8.1.** *A risk averse bank*

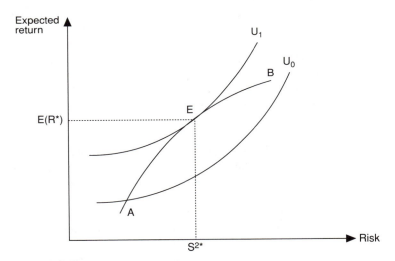

**Figure 8.2.** *The optimal portfolio*

relates to the behaviour of banks. Whilst the bank might make mistakes, the critical point is that these mistakes are not systematic. If the bank makes systematic errors, then corrective action will be taken to avoid them. The result is that this model generates stable behaviour on the part of lenders. On average, they can assess the risks involved in any lending objectively and can hence charge higher interest rates to compensate for any additional risk undertaken.

**Market failures and the behaviour of international banks**

Market failures have no place in the efficient market view of intermediation. However, a significant market failure which has important implications for credit markets is the problem of information deficiency.[2] Information is costly to gather and is often

---

[2] There is a large volume of work on the implications of information failures in economics in general and finance in particular. See, for example, Akerlof (1970), Spence (1973), Stiglitz and Weiss (1981), Grossman and Hart (1983) and Greenwald and Stiglitz (1986).

imperfect with one party in a transaction knowing more than the other. Before we examine the implications of this for bank behaviour, we need to examine why banks need to gather information in the first place.

*The risks involved in international banking and the need for information*

Essentially, the need for information arises because the products of the banking industry are non-homogeneous. The degree to which a product is homogeneous depends on the extent to which buyers regard the products of all sellers as identical and on the extent to which sellers have no preferences as to the buyer to whom they sell. With respect to one of the products of the banking system, deposits, depositors have definite preferences for certain banks, based on political as well as economic decisions. With regard to the other banking product, loans, banks also have definite preferences about whom they wish to lend to. Because there are different risk categories of borrower, the construction of an efficient portfolio requires a bank to distinguish between different borrowers. Information therefore needs to be gathered to enable a bank to do this.

Bank lending, both domestic and international, involves a number of different risks and control of these risks relies crucially on information. Firstly, there are two risks associated with maturity transformation – interest rate risk and funding risk. As we noted in Chapter 7, maturity transformation or mismatching occurs when the maturity structure of assets and liabilities differ. Financial intermediaries usually engage in positive maturity transformation; they borrow short and lend long. This exposes them to funding risk. There is a danger that the bank will not be able to fund the loans that it is making for longer periods than the deposits have been placed for. That is, they may be unable to refinance a loan (that is, attract new deposits) whatever interest rate they are offering. The second risk associated with maturity mismatching is the interest rate risk. Interest rates may alter. In this case a bank can refinance loans but at an interest rate which may be greater than that on the previous financing of the loans. If the interest rate on the loan is fixed over its lifetime, then the bank may make a loss. Recognition of this risk led to the development of roll-over loans. However, even if the banks eliminate this risk through perfect matching of the roll-over periods of loans and deposits, the interest rate risk associated with mismatching is passed on to the borrower. If interest rates rise sufficiently, this may increase the probability that the borrower defaults. Thus the development of roll-over loans may only have changed the risk from interest rate risk to an increased risk of default. Dealing with these risks requires that banks closely monitor the amount of mismatching they are undertaking. Given that, interest rate forecasting is also useful as an indication of the amount of risk they face if the maturity structure of their assets and liabilities do differ.

The second main risk category is credit risk. This refers to the creditworthiness of borrowers and their potential for default. In domestic banking, this risk is often termed commercial risk and is assessed by examining company performance. Banks have a lot of experience of dealing with these risks.

International lending, however, introduces a greater number of risks which are not present in domestic lending: country risk, sovereign risk, foreign exchange risk, transfer risk and currency risk. We deal with each of these in turn in order to highlight some of the aspects of risk which are specific to international bank lending.

Country risk arises when a borrower in a country other than the one in which the bank is located is unable or unwilling to service its foreign currency loans. In other words, it arises from cross-border lending and is caused by circumstances in the country to which the loan has been granted. The events which generate country risk can be of a political, social or economic nature and in the event that they cause debt servicing problems, these problems will be experienced typically by all borrowers in that country.

Economic factors which contribute to country risk might include a slowdown in economic growth in the country concerned, a rapid rise in input costs, a fall in export demand, inappropriate government policy and, in general, any economic change which places debt servicing in jeopardy. Social factors which contribute to country risk include the potential for social unrest due to factors such as unequal income distribution, poor labour–capital relations, etc. If social division becomes particularly acute, then it can, at worst, lead to civil war, something which clearly increases country risk enormously. Finally, political factors are critical in determining the risk of making loans to a particular country. Here an important issue for banks is the political stability of the country. We discuss this in more detail when we consider sovereign risk.

What should be clear is that in assessing country risk a whole number of factors must be considered. Expertise is required not only in aspects of a country's economic performance, but also social and political conditions. If a bank specialises in cross-border lending to only one country or a small selected group of countries, then information on these risks can be sought from contacts within the countries concerned and, of course, through time, from experience. But the more countries a bank lends to, the more difficult or costly it will be to gather the requisite information. Dealing with country risk in this latter case may be difficult unless large amounts of resources are committed to the task.

Where the borrower in cross-border lending is the government of a sovereign nation, country risk also involves sovereign risk. Sovereign risk arises because of the existence of nation states and is defined as the risk that debt servicing might be suspended because of government policies or political events within the country concerned. Again, therefore, there are both political, social and economic aspects of sovereign risk. From the economic point of view, government policy is clearly important in influencing the returns which might be expected from any project. But political issues can be just as decisive in determining sovereign risk. For example, the takeover by a military government can frequently lead to sudden and dramatic changes in government policy with severe consequences for the repayment of debt contracted under the old regime. Such considerations bring us to a critical issue associated with sovereign risk: there is the possibility that the borrower is able to repay its obligations but is unwilling to do so.[3] In other words, because the borrower is a nation state, it has the option to renege on its debts. Such a course of action is not available to domestic borrowers: their assets would be seized in lieu of repayment. However, with sovereign borrowers, there are no international courts which have the right to seize the country's assets. Thus in assessing the risks of cross-border lending, a bank has also to consider the question of a country's willingness to pay.

Most international lending is done in a currency other than that of the borrower (usually US dollars, as we saw in Chapter 6). Loans therefore have to be repaid in dollars and the country needs to have access to foreign exchange to meet its repayment commitments. The risk that a country will not have the foreign exchange to

---

[3] See Eaton and Gersovitz (1983) for a discussion of some of the strategic issues involved in dealing with sovereign risk. We discuss these issues later in Chapter 9.

repay its debt obligations is known as foreign exchange risk. Foreign exchange is most obviously gained from exporting and hence the export performance of a country will be important to determining the extent of the risk involved in any loan. But even if the foreign exchange is available, individual borrowers within the country may experience difficulties in getting access to it if the government imposes exchange controls. This risk is known as transfer risk.

The final risk which we identified as being important in *international* banking is currency risk. Cross-border lending exposes banks to currency risk in that their assets and liabilities may be not denominated in the same currencies. In assessing the importance of currency risk a bank has to consider the currency composition of its assets relative to its liabilities. To the extent that a bank's assets and liabilities are perfectly matched then no currency risk is present. However, this is rarely the case and hence it is important to look at the two components of currency risk: inflation risk and exchange risk (Philbeam, 1992). Inflation risk refers to the fact that inflation is uncertain and hence the real return (the nominal return minus expected inflation) from a project is uncertain. The real return on a domestic loan is the nominal interest rate minus the expected domestic inflation rate. If purchasing power parity holds, then the return from a foreign loan is the nominal interest rate minus expected foreign inflation. Thus the variance of inflation will determine the extent of inflation risk. Exchange risk refers to the risk associated with movements in exchange rates which represent departures from purchasing power parity. A real exchange rate appreciation of the foreign currency will increase the expected from a foreign currency loan and vice versa. This could lead to large gains or, more importantly, losses to a bank making a foreign currency loan.

What should be a bank's response to these risks associated with international lending? To take the case of country risk, for example, there is some debate about whether banks should spend the resources required to assess it. The resources required are not inconsiderable: Nagy (1984) estimates that the annual cost at mid-1983 of conducting a brief evaluation 100 countries and an in-depth evaluation of 20 was $850,000. Haegele (1980) argues that if the international financial market for cross-border loans is nearly perfect, then information will be efficiently and quickly reflected in interest rate spreads (the premium paid over base rate, usually London Interbank Offered Rate (LIBOR) in international lending). Any individual bank can use the spread to gauge the risk involved in lending to a particular country, so there is no need to engage in costly country analysis. Nagy (1984), by contrast, argues that the market is not so perfect and thus an individual bank can ensure better performance by investing in country risk analysis.

Nagy's argument relies on the existence of imperfections in financial markets. There is, however, a more powerful argument for engaging in country risk analysis. Grossman and Stiglitz (1980) examine the problems posed by the cost of gathering information for pricing in financial markets. They argue that if the price of a stock supposedly reflects the aggregation of information which differs across individuals, then a paradox will arise. If the market aggregates information perfectly, then the market price, acting as a signal, would convey all the information investors require to know and thus there would be no incentive to gather information (Haegele's argument). But if there is no incentive to gather information, there is no market and therefore the price cannot aggregate all the different information in an efficient way. In other words, if banks rely on the market spread to determine the risk involved, the market spread would not reflect the risks, because no bank would have engaged in gathering the information.

These arguments relate to problems of gathering information when it is costly to do so. However, in addition to the costs, there is also the question of the availability of information at any price. Banks generally find up-to-date published information on countries difficult to come by. The main sources are the IMF, the World Bank, OECD, BIS and UN. These institutions only began to collect information on foreign debt after lending had begun, primarily because they are not designed specifically for the banks but rather for the use of the international agency which produces them. The World Bank, for example, in its debt tables published only government or government guaranteed loans until 1982–3 when it included private debt; the IMF concentrates on its own members and their drawing and borrowings; the BIS includes private as well as government debt, but only that which is reported by banks in the Group of Ten plus Switzerland and some offshore banking centres.

Information is not only important for a bank when it is making its decision about whom to lend to. It is also important for a bank to monitor the actions of borrowers. The nature of financial intermediation differs from normal exchange transactions in an economy. The latter usually involve the exchange of goods for money (or some means of payment) now. Financial intermediation involves banks lending now for repayment in the future. The contract which specifies how much is to be lent and at what price is agreed before the loan is made. The price reflects therefore the *ex ante* risk of the project.[4] The borrower's return is the returns yielded by the project over and above the given debt service. As such, it can often be in the interests of the borrower to increase the riskiness of the project after the loan contract has been signed, since this might allow a higher expected return to be gained in the future. Hence the lender must control the borrower's use of the money and this involves the gathering of information which will allow monitoring to take place effectively (Devlin, 1989).

*The implications of imperfect information for bank lending*

In the efficient market view of bank intermediation, the risks inherent in banking lending must be compensated for by price variations. Loans of higher risk should have risk premia attached so that the expected return to the bank compensates it for the risk it undertakes. Many authors have claimed that in practice the variation in price between loans does not properly reflect the variation in risk. Instead, there is a role for credit rationing in the determination of loan portfolios.

Credit rationing is defined as the situation which occurs when banks are unable or unwilling to allocate funds between borrowers purely on the basis of price: instead they ration the quantity available to each borrower. Much of the early literature on credit rationing attributed it to sticky interest rates associated with oligopolistic conditions in credit markets and to interest rate ceilings imposed by usury laws. Such a view denies credit rationing any rationale, independent of market structure or social pressures.

Later work has sought to explain how credit rationing can arise endogenously as a result of optimising behaviour on the part of banks.[5] A particularly interesting and

---

[4] See Stiglitz (1989) for a good discussion of the nature of financial intermediation.

[5] The phenomenon of credit rationing has been discussed by, among others, Hodgman (1960), Freimer and Gordon (1965), Jaffee and Modigliani (1969), Kindleberger (1975), Kapur (1977), Eaton and Gersovitz (1981a,and b), Stiglitz and Weiss (1981).

seminal work in this area is that of Stiglitz and Weiss (1981). Their explanation for credit rationing derives from recognition of information imperfections within credit markets. Credit rationing occurs because higher interest rates will have an unfavourable impact on the riskiness (or quality) of the loan through two distinct effects.

The first is an adverse selection effect. The borrower is likely to have more information about the prospective investment than the lender (that is, the bank) and thus we have a situation of asymmetric information. The lender is aware that the quality of potential borrowers differs: in other words, that different borrowers have different probabilities of repaying the loan. Given that the expected return to the bank is dependent on the probability of repayment, the bank would prefer to identify borrowers who are more likely to repay. Various screening devices are therefore used. If the interest rate is used, then those who offer to pay a higher interest rate are likely on average to be worse risks. They are willing to pay such an interest rate because they are unworried by the prospect of being unable to repay. Thus as the interest rate offered by the borrower rises, so will the average riskiness of the loan, possibly resulting in a lowering of expected bank profits.

Secondly, the incentive effect means that as the interest rate rises, firms are likely to switch to more risky projects, because higher rates lower the return on all successful projects, so that the least risky projects cease to be profitable at high rates.

As Stiglitz and Weiss argue, if information were perfect and costless, then the bank would be able to control all the actions of the borrower which might affect the return on the investment project. The adverse selection effect and the incentive effect arise in the case of costly and imperfect information, because the bank is unable to assess and monitor borrowers in sufficient depth. Hence it is in the interest of a profit maximising bank to practice credit rationing.

We illustrate this situation in Figure 8.3. If the demand for loans is $L_1$, then the bank will be willing to supply this amount at an interest rate of $r_1$. If, however, the demand for loans rises to $L_2$ and borrowers are willing to offer a higher interest rate to try to attract loans to meet their demand, the bank will be unwilling to supply such an amount. The supply of loans schedule is backward bending because as interest rates rise beyond $r^*$, the incentive and adverse selection effects imply that the expected return to the bank falls: although the bank is receiving a higher interest rate

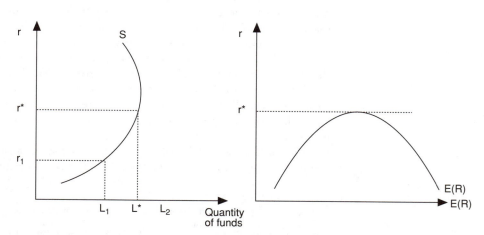

**Figure 8.3.**   *Credit rationing*

on lending, the probability of default increases. Overall, as shown in the right-hand part of Figure 8.3, the expected return (E(R)) to the bank begins to fall. Credit is rationed to $L^*$ even although demand is potentially higher. In traditional demand and supply analysis, the existence of excess demand would cause potential borrowers, who had not received loans, to increase the interest rate they were willing to pay. However, this would simply produce a worse risk and hence in the presence of information asymmetries those borrowers do not receive loans.

Stiglitz and Weiss' argument shows that it is likely that there will be some combination of credit rationing and a spread of interest rates which will compensate for risk within credit markets. Some borrowers will face both risk premia and exposure limits, because of the banks' inability to ensure that the expected return reflects risks fully.

The question which now arises is how banks choose the exposure limit for each borrower. Stiglitz and Weiss say nothing about this problem, although when there is imperfect information regarding the use to which the borrower will put the funds, then it is not clear how much should be lent. This problem is all the more pressing if a bank is incurring sovereign risk. Enforcement of contract is a problem when dealing in international markets and when the borrower is a sovereign entity. Sovereign borrowers have the option of repudiating their debts. Eaton and Gersovitz (1981a, 1981b) suggest that the amount lent should be such that the costs of default to the borrower are exactly equal to the benefits of default to the borrower. If there were no costs to defaulting, then it would not be in the bank's interests to lend at all to the prospective borrower. However, it is possible to identify some costs. Exclusion from future borrowing is probably the most serious. But additionally there may be costs in terms of a withdrawal of trade credit and attempts to sequestrate assets belonging to the country concerned. The benefits of default are more obvious: they are equal to the savings made on the repayments that would have been due. A lender should therefore always ensure that the amount lent is not enough to cause the benefits of default to outweigh the costs.

In conclusion, therefore, the implications of imperfect information for bank lending are clear: banks should practice credit rationing. In this way banks avoid the build-up of excessive risks.

## The potential for crisis[6]

The problem of providing a general definition applicable to the wide range of financial disturbances which might be labelled financial crises is a tricky one. A useful starting point is the definition given by Eichengreen and Portes (1987):

> A financial crisis is a disturbance to financial markets, associated typically with falling asset prices and insolvency among debtors and intermediaries, which ramifies through the system, disrupting the market's capacity to allocate capital within an economy. In an international financial crisis, disturbances spill over national borders, disrupting the market's capacity to allocate capital internationally.
>
> (Eichengreen and Portes, 1987, p.10)

This definition can be considered a useful starting point, but a number of points can be made which help to bring out some of its weaknesses (Gibson and Oppenheimer, 1992). First, it links without qualification falling asset prices and insolvency among debtors and intermediaries. This confines the cause of financial crises to a sharp

---

[6] This section draws heavily on Gibson and Oppenheimer (1992) and Gibson (1989).

decline in the value of *marketable* financial assets, that is assets which have prices. However, in many cases the assets of financial intermediaries are nonmarketable and do not have prices. This is particularly true in the case of banks, which are our particular interest here. Whilst their assets do not have prices, it is conceivable that there might be a sudden drop in the *value* of the assets, which could have a similar impact to falling asset prices. To cover the case of non-marketable claims, or of asset prices which are implicit or unidentifiable, the definition could be modified to refer to 'falling asset values' or to specify 'and/or insolvency . . .'.

The second point put forward by Gibson and Oppenheimer about this definition relates to the reference to 'ramification through the system'. They argue that this points to the difference between a crisis and an ordinary commercial failure in the financial sector. A financial crisis requires that a number of institutions are affected and their solvency threatened. However, this can occur through the failure of only one institution in the first instance. There are two reasons for this. Firstly, lack of information can imply that unexpected failure of a single prominent institution raises doubts about the soundness of others. Depositors question the ability of the typical bank to differentiate its loans from those of competitors in terms of borrower-quality. If, for example, a large vehicle manufacturer or an ice-cream company fails, the usual assumption would be that its products were insufficiently attractive relative to those of competitors. There is no doubt an element of systematic risk in every case (a bad summer affects all ice cream sales) but it is still the least competitive producers who go out of business. In banking, analogous considerations *may* apply, i.e. a bank may be seen as having made unique errors in its lending business or in its internal safeguard mechanisms against fraud; but the likelihood of errors being non-unique, and other banks therefore being equally vulnerable, is far greater than in manufacturing or commerce. Thus the failure of one institution can lead to other institutions experiencing a crisis of confidence.

The second factor which can cause failure of one institution to affect others is the interlocking debt structures which are the essence of any banking system. Three such elements can be identified. Firstly, the bank may be unable to pay back all its depositors' money, so that depositors lose and not just the bank's shareholders. Secondly, a failed or failing bank will be unable to roll-over some loans which the borrowers, under normal conditions might have expected to be renewed. Those in debt to the bank, who expected their overdrafts, for example, to be renewed, will have to repay sooner than expected and may have to realise some of their assets to do so. If the numbers affected are large, then this may result in the quantity of assets for sale being sufficient to cause a fall in their price thus making it more difficult for those in debt to the bank to acquire the money to repay. Bankruptcy of either corporate or individual debtors could result. A final factor is that other banks may be affected either if they had deposits with the failed bank or if the failed bank had deposits with them through a loss of confidence leading to a run on banks unconnected with the failed bank. These other banks will experience a liquidity crisis. Thus financial crises are characterised by strong systemic effects but it is important to remember that there is the potential for these effects to arise simply from the failure of one institution.

A third point relating to the definition which Gibson and Oppenheimer make is that a crisis may be more than a matter of 'disrupting the allocation of capital' (by which is presumably meant a short-lived failure of the capital market; longer-term or structural failure could hardly be subsumed under the term 'crisis'). Banks are also responsible for administering the economy's payments system and for meeting businesses' working capital requirements. A breakdown here can have widespread repercussions on the level of economic activity.

Such repercussions are a form of negative externality. Solow (1982) points out that any business failure has some external impact – for example, through regional multiplier effects. Normally such externalities will be narrowly limited by the convergence process of the multiplier mechanism. The difference in the case of banking is that debt linkages and the spread of a pessimistic psychology may outweigh the convergence process, so that the impact on the business climate of a single failure is magnified rather than dampened.

The final point which Gibson and Oppenheimer make is that the macro-economic dimension and systemic nature of a financial crisis suggests the desirability of official intervention, both to contain the crisis itself and to limit its consequences for economic activity. This is strongly emphasised by Eichengreen and Portes in their historical comparison of the 1930s with the 1980s.

A quite different viewpoint on the question of financial crisis is given by Schwartz (1986). She asserts that a *real* as opposed to 'pseudo-financial crisis' occurs only when official intervention is absent or incompetent. A real crisis, in Schwartz's view, is characterised by a sudden increase in the public's demand for high powered money, by a squeezing of the reserves of the banking system and by attempts by banks to restore their reserve position either through calling in loans or through selling assets. In other words, Schwartz tends to associate a real financial crisis with all the characteristics of a bank run. She insists that a real crisis of this nature has not occurred in Britain since 1866 or in the United States since 1933.

Schwartz's definition is inadequate. By attributing the onset of a crisis exclusively to shortcomings of official policy, it sidesteps the question of why markets should behave in a way that makes official intervention appropriate. A crisis contained *ex post* may still have been a serious threat to the financial system *ex ante*. Schwartz argues that the authorities have only to secure the provision of a system of deposit insurance in order to forestall any possible crisis. However, deposit insurance cannot provide a straightforward or complete solution because of the problem of moral hazard. This problem arises again because of information deficiencies in financial markets. The principle is most clearly visible in insurance markets. The probability of having your car stolen, for example, is dependent on the care taken to prevent theft: for example, in locking it securely, etc. If the insurance company could observe the care taken, then each premium would be determined by the risk of the insured contingency and the insurance company could break even. However, often the insurance company cannot observe the level of care taken. Premiums are set on the basis of historical information regarding how many times the event insured against occurred in the past. If the car owner is fully insured, there is no incentive to take care: there will be no personal loss if the car is stolen. A similar dilemma applies to the provision of deposit insurance or lender-of-last-resort facilities. There is little incentive for the bank to take care over the risks it incurs if it is insured. This generates a case for prudential supervision of banks and the need to leave scope for discretionary intervention by the central bank.

Furthermore, Schwartz focuses exclusively on the acute phase of a financial crisis. She denies any link between this phase and subsequent longer-term reactions of deflation. As she expresses it, a deflation is a consequence of restricted growth of bank reserves but it is not pre-cipitated by the public's behaviour. The essence of a financial crisis is that it is short-lived, ending with a slackening of the public's demand for additional cur-rency. A disinflation or a deflation may be long drawn out. Nominal wealth may decline, real debt may rise, but these are not financial crises.

(Schwartz, 1986, pp.11–12)

This argument fails to distinguish between steady-state deflation and adjustment to a crisis. It is perfectly possible to envisage steady-state price deflation as an equilibrium process, in the manner of Friedman's (1969a) 'Optimum Quantity of Money'. But this is quite different from prolonged dislocation and underutilisation of resources in the aftermath of a financial crisis.

If financial crises do exist and cannot simply be dealt with through the existence of deposit insurance, then the question which arises is what causes them. The answer to such a question is clearly crucial to understanding what measures need to be taken to prevent crises from occurring. We can point here to three general approaches to financial crisis. The first is that offered by Minsky and Kindleberger.[7] They take a broad institutional approach to financial crises, drawing heavily on historical experi-ence. A second approach is the rather narrowly focused, rigorous models of speculative bubbles and their collapse (which we discussed in Chapter 3).[8] A final approach is the view that financial crises are a failure to optimise, resulting from the interaction of market structure and bank behaviour under conditions of extreme uncertainty. There are a number of strands to this approach. There are those who emphasise the role of market structure (Gibson, 1989; Davis, 1992). Other place greater emphasis on uncertainty (Guttentag and Herring, 1986; McKenzie and Thomas, 1992). We attempt to discuss here these various strands in a way which brings them together to generate one theory of financial crises based on the impor-tance of bank responses to market failures within a highly competitive environment.

## The Minsky–Kindleberger approach to financial crisis

The Minsky–Kindleberger story of financial crisis starts with a situation of some modest spare capacity in the economic system. An exogenous disturbance creates a new investment opportunity. Economic agents respond. Investment and production increase. A boom develops, fuelled by expansion of bank credit. As part of the pro-cess it is natural that asset prices rise while output prices initially remain stable. Eventually spare capacity is absorbed and output prices do rise. When higher output prices lead in turn to a further increase in asset prices and thence to additional planned investment, the system enters a speculative phase. Speculators (who pur-chase an asset for resale rather than for use or for the income stream to be derived from it) become an increasing proportion of those acquiring financial assets. At the same time, the profitability of underlying investments tends to be overestimated. Confidence may reach what Minsky (1982a, p.121) calls 'conditions of euphoria'. We move into a 'mania' or 'bubble' (Kindleberger 1978, p.17).

The bubble may burst in several ways. Speculators may start selling to realise profits. Fraudulent activities may be uncovered. Whatever the trigger, confidence can be lost rapidly, leading to asset price falls, debt defaults and potential runs on banks. Recession in economic activity may then follow.

[7] See Kindleberger (1978); Minsky (1982a, 1982b); Kindleberger and Laffargue (1982).
[8] See, for example, Batchelor (1986); Flood and Garber (1980; 1982); and, for a good survey of the litera-ture, the *Journal of Economic Perspectives*, 1990.

An important question in the Minsky–Kindleberger story is the extent to which the behaviour of agents can be described as rational. Minsky is more inclined to consider that agents act irrationally. Kindleberger (1978), by contrast, regards irrationality as unusual, and a reflection of market failure rather than aberrant individual conduct:

> I conclude that despite the general usefulness of the assumption of rationality, markets can on occasions – infrequent occasions, let me emphasize – act in destabilizing ways that are irrational overall, even when each participant in the market is acting rationally.
>
> (Kindleberger, 1978, p.41).

Kindleberger offers several distinct (but not mutually exclusive) explanations for these occasional departures from rationality. First, markets may exhibit a mob psychology (positive or negative). This is similar to Minsky's 'euphoria'. Secondly, a speculative boom may begin with rational behaviour on the part of individuals in the sense that they invest in an asset because they expect to receive a good income from it. Only later are assets traded on the basis of capital gains resulting from price rises (this, as we shall see later, is close to rational speculative bubble models). This may be rational from individual investors' point of view, but will drive the price of the asset further and further away from its fundamental value[9] – a case of 'market irrationality'.

A third explanation is that the market may be composed of two groups of speculators: those who act in a stabilizing manner, buying when the price is low and selling when it is high ('insiders' or 'professionals'), and those who act in a destabilizing manner. The latter buy when the price is high and sell when it is low, because they become infected by the euphoria associated with initial price movements which have been instigated by the professional 'insiders'.

*Rational speculative bubbles and financial crises*

By contrast with the Minsky–Kindleberger approach to financial crises, the rational speculative bubble literature specifically rejects the notion that financial crises are the outcome of irrational behaviour.[10] To some extent, it can be argued that the difference is a matter of vocabulary and analytical style rather than substance. Flood and Garber (1980; 1982) and Blanchard and Watson (1982) formalise Kindleberger's notion of trading in assets on the basis of expected capital gains rather than on the basis of the income which the asset is expected to yield. Thus the market price of an asset no longer depends on market fundamentals alone but is also a positive function of its own expected rate of change. In addition, rational expectations are assumed, i.e. agents make no systematic prediction errors. Hence the price of an asset depends not only on its expected rate of change but on its actual rate of change. This means that

---

[9] The value of an asset is defined as the discounted present value of the stream of income the asset is expected to yield. Hence 'market irrationality' could be said to imply either extravagant and implausible revisions of the expected income stream or equally extravagant adjustments to the subjective rate of discount (or both). A strong defender of efficient markets would claim that asset price movements reflect legitimate market revisions of an asset's prospects. A critic would reply that volatility of asset prices is greater than can be satisfactorily explained by new information about fundamentals becoming available (see, for example, Shiller, 1981).

[10] We can note that there seems to be some debate over whether speculative bubbles can actually occur with rational expectations. Tirole (1982) suggests that bubbles are not possible within a dynamic rational expectations equilibrium framework and that explanations of bubbles should focus on non-rational behaviour.

asset prices are delinked from economic fundamentals and can be described in terms of bootstraps equilibria and self-fulfilling mechanisms, similar to Kindleberger's 'market irrationality'.

We do not go into the mechanisms of the models *per se* here. We have already discussed them in Chapter 3. Our interest instead lies with the implications of these models for financial crises. Financial crises could result from bursting speculative bubbles where financial institutions have large holdings of the asset concerned. If the bubble is present in a large number of assets (for example a general stock market bubble), then the price fall could severely undermine the value of assets held by financial institutions.

One problem with these models is their emphasis on asset prices. As we have noted, not all assets have prices. This makes it more difficult to apply these models to nonmarketable bank assets. In the rational bubble models, it is the ability of speculators to realise short-term price gains (capital gains) by selling the asset before the crash which allows us to describe their behaviour as rational, even when they bought the asset at a price above its fundamental value. For them, the intrinsic long-term value of the investment is irrelevant. But if the asset is nonmarketable, then realising any short-term gains is not possible. Banks are locked in to their investments and hence the long-term fundamental value of those investments must be of paramount importance in deciding whether or not to lend to a given borrower.

Thus financial crises in banking markets in general may result from rational bubbles, in so far as banks invest in marketable assets, such as bonds, foreign exchange, shares, etc. Banks may, for example, take positions in foreign currency or engage in speculative maturity mismatching (i.e. taking a view on interest rates). In the case of banks' more usual business of general commercial lending, however, any short-term gains are non-realisable, so the case for describing over-lending on the part of banks as rational is weaker. Banks have to weigh the short-term gains against the possibility of long-term losses if the assets become non-performing with the banks still locked in.

## Financial crises as a failure to optimise

We argued in the second section that banks should, in the face of the information deficiencies prevalent in credit markets, practice credit rationing to limit the amount of risk taken on. In this way rational behaviour should imply that crises will be avoided. To the extent that crises do occur in practice, this is perhaps better normative than positive economics. Crises can be accounted for by a failure of banks to act optimally. The question that then arises is why banks might act suboptimally in a way which increases the potential for instability in the financial system. We want to argue here that their failure to optimise arises from the interaction between bank behaviour under conditions of uncertainty and the role of market structure.

Knight (1921) distinguishes between risk and uncertainty. An uncertain situation can be described as one where creditors are unable to estimate the probability of loss (or alternatively the probable gain). By contrast, in the presence of risk, we can use information on past events to estimate the objective probability of a particular future contingency occurring. Under uncertainty, estimates of probabilities can only be subjective and are liable to fluctuate with the state of confidence in the market. Uncertainty can be transformed into risk by gathering information, but only to a limited extent. Not all uncertainty can be removed. First, events may not be experienced often enough to allow adequate data to be collected. Secondly, the causal structure of a frequently experienced event may change each time, thus preventing information being used to calculate objectives probabilities.

McKenzie and Thomas (1992) note that the efficient market view of financial intermediation implicitly assumes that measures of risk and expected return can be derived objectively by the bank. This is also true of the literature which focuses on a credit rationing framework to explain international bank lending. Eaton, Gersovitz and Stiglitz (1986), for example, portray 'uncertainty' in terms of a probability distribution which they appear to regard as objective. In the Stiglitz and Weiss (1981) model the probability distribution is a subjective one.[11] But in neither model are the implications of subjectivity adequately discussed.

How do banks behave in the face of uncertainty? A number of authors have considered this question. Gibson (1989) and McKenzie and Thomas (1992) suggest that the herd instinct becomes important. That is, a bank which is considering lending to a particular borrower observes whether other institutions are also lending. If they are, then this is taken as a sign of credit-worthiness of the borrower and so the loan is more likely to be given. The herd instinct is a form of free-riding in the presence of costs involved in information gathering. In effect, a bank takes advantage of the fact that other banks may have invested in information on a potential borrower and decided that the borrower is credit-worthy and how much should be lent (the exposure limit). In a situation where credit rationing should be used to limit the risk of borrower default, free-riding can potentially be dangerous. The free-riding bank has no idea of the exposure limit which the banks undertaking the analysis have placed on the borrower. It is easy to see how over-lending can occur. Moreover, if other banks are involved in similar lending, then the costs to banks of having lent incorrectly to a particular borrower are often less than if one bank alone has overlent. In the latter case, the central bank may allow an organised failure of the institution concerned. By contrast, in the former case, the central bank cannot let all banks fail in an organised fashion – the problem becomes one which affects all institutions in general and no one institution in particular.

Guttentag and Herring (1986) argue that the existence of uncertainty may lead to disaster myopia. The argument is that banks tend to ignore the potential impact of events which have a low probability of occurring, especially if such events have not occurred for some time. The result is that the financial system becomes 'increasingly vulnerable to major shocks during long periods when no such shocks occur' (Guttentag and Herring, 1986, p.1).

A final consequence of uncertainty which is noted by McKenzie and Thomas (1992) is that of cognitive dissonance. Errors obviously result in the real world as a consequence, at least in part, of imperfect information. However, if uncertainty is high, then if new information becomes available which points to errors in past decisions, management is often slow to react. This is termed cognitive dissonance. New information is often selectively used to justify past decisions in order to prevent a loss of self-esteem. Such behaviour is likely to exacerbate the potential for crisis since it tends to prolong erroneous lending.

These factors become even more important if banking markets are highly competitive. The argument is that competition combined with information failures and uncertainty can generate an increasingly fragile financial system. Exposure limits become too loose and the risk premia too small, thus weakening banks' ability to deal with the risks inherent in international lending. Heightened competition can often result from new entrants into a particular line of business. This can be encouraged

---

[11] See Stiglitz and Weiss (1981), p.395, footnote 4.

either by the existence of a new profitable lending opportunity (for example, the recycling opportunity presented to international banks as a result of the oil price rises of the 1970s) or by deregulation which allows banks to move into areas they were previously prevented from operating in.

There are two main views in the literature on the consequences of heightened competition. The first view states that the impact is temporary. Llewellyn (1990a) takes the example of the build-up of lending to developing countries to explain this view. He argues that the role of banks can be considered as one of stock adjustment to two simultaneous shocks combined with some overshooting. The shocks were the demand for debt by developing countries (as a result of the investment opportunities available to them) and the sharp rise in banks' international lending (which he attributes in part to the relaxation of regulations). These two shocks caused portfolio disequilibrium. The new desired equilibrium entailed an increase in the ratio of external assets to total assets for banks and increased debt to income ratios for developing countries. We illustrate the process of portfolio adjustment in Figure 8.4. The top half of the figure represents the situation for the borrowers and the bottom half shows lender behaviour.

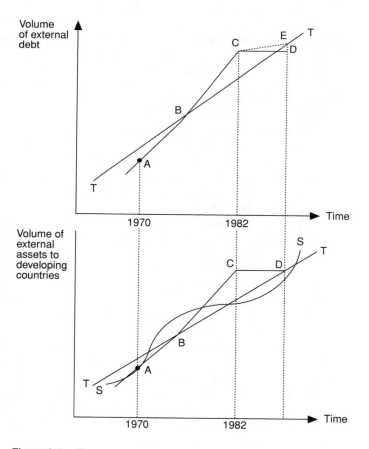

**Figure 8.4.**  *Temporary overshooting on the way to a new stock equilibrium*

With respect to borrowers, TT represents the desired long-term trend and expected sustainable level of debt. In 1970, the actual volume of external debt was below that desired. Developing countries had not had access to the international markets to the extent that they would have wished. AB thus represents the stock adjustment. However, the easy availability of credit led developing countries to borrow more than they would overwise have wanted. The build-up of external debt thus overshot the long-run desired level and by 1982 developing countries found themselves at a point such as C (above the TT line).

For the lenders (the banks) there is a similar story. TT is the trend desired volume of external assets to developing countries. The schedule SS is a more accurate representation of how we might expect the volume of external assets to vary through time. The cyclical nature of SS depicts the fact that, in practice, the desired level will be above or below the trend dependent on cycles in preferences for domestic versus external lending. At A, in 1970, the actual stock is below that desired. AB again represents the stock adjustment and BC the overshoot.

By 1982, the exposure of banks to developing countries was too high relative to their capital base. Both banks and borrowers were above their long-term desired or sustainable positions. Banks subsequently kept external assets at the level indicated by C, with the result that at some time in the future, as their total balance sheets grew, this would become the optimal amount (at point D). For debtors, however, this strategy has been less than optimal. They have faced large negative net transfers.[12] A better way of adjusting back to a sustainable level of debt would have been via CE. Instead, banks have forced them to follow the path CD.

The conclusion of this analysis is that crises can arise as a consequence of adjustment to the new long-run equilibrium following a disturbance. The crisis is the consequence of overshooting as a result of heightened competition in the new markets. Once banks and borrowers are more acquainted with the new type of lending, sustainable positions (along TT) are maintained. Overshooting is thus just temporary.

The alternative view is that the tendency for fragility and crisis is a more permanent feature of financial markets. Booms in lending are followed by periods where credit is scarce. This is the approach adopted by Gibson (1989). She outlines a theory of crisis for application to the international credit markets which draws on some of the literature which we have already discussed. Four phases are identified. Phase I begins with a situation where a new profit opportunity has appeared for banks in the international sphere as the result of an exogenous change in the macroeconomic environment (the increase in oil prices in 1973–4 being an obvious potential trigger). The extent to which banks move into this new area depends on the level of confidence in the banking sector and on the intensity with which banks are looking for new ways to expand their balance sheets. The level of bankers' confidence is a key variable throughout this analysis and is essentially dependent on the stage of the financial cycle in which we find ourselves. Confidence is important initially, because it determines how risky the new profit opportunity is viewed as being. Where the banks' management is confident about the prospect for growth, the riskiness of the new investment will seem less and banks are more likely to view the new investment opportunity as a profitable one in which they should get involved. Let us

---

[12] That is, they have been on balance transferring funds to the industrial countries. We discuss this concept in more depth in Chapter 9.

assume that this is the case here. Banks looking for new avenues to expand their balance sheets feel confident enough to move into the new area produced by the exogenous shock to the world monetary system.

However, the new business may still be considered more risky than traditional banking pursuits (for example, domestic retail banking). New borrowers therefore face both a risk premium and some credit rationing (as a result of the information asymmetries). As more banks move into the area, confidence increases and the opportunity begins to be viewed by banks still outside the new area as one which should not be missed. Competition intensifies as the number of banks chasing the new profit opportunities expands. This is especially so if there is an increasing internationalisation of banking and the number of banks based in the major financial centres is increasing. This produces a greater incentive for banks to be seen in the new and fashionable area.[13] Devlin (1989) argues that international lending in the 1970s began initially with large US banks. However, they were soon challenged by US regional banks and European and Japanese banks.[14] He argues that in effect the supply of loans schedule, as a result of these new entrants, became horizontal rather than the backward bending supply schedule that should occur if banks behave optimal in the presence of information deficiencies (see Figure 8.3).

We now enter Phase II, where balance sheets are validated. Profits are being made and reinforce the banks' decision that this area was and is a good profit opportunity. Confidence increases further. So does competition as more banks get involved in the new lending.

Four consequences follow from this increased confidence and competition. First, as Barclay (1978) argues, there is a tendency for too many new entrants to be attracted to the market, because not all entrants know about the existence of other entrants (an information problem) and because it is not clear now many new entrants the market will support. This problem was discussed by Richardson (1960) in the general context of investment decision. He argues that without information regarding the investment plans of their competitors, entrepreneurs cannot formulate their own investment plans – because they do not know by how much total supply is liable to increase unless they know their competitors investment plans. The competitors face the same problem. The result is that the adjustment mechanism under perfect competition is an illusion and the optimal number of entrants is unlikely to materialise.

Although supply is increasing, demand will probably be increasing for some time, as borrowers learn of the existence of the new market. If demand does not increase as fast as supply, profits will fall, causing an important margin of safety to come under pressure. Profits can be described as a margin of safety because they bolster reserves,

---

[13] Davis (1992) attributes new entry to declining sunk costs of entry. Sunk costs are costs that cannot be recovered on leaving the market and hence usually act as a barrier to entry. Sunk costs may decline as a result of product innovation, the establishment of new markets, technical advances or reduced regulation. The establishment and importance of the interbank market in international lending markets, for example, meant that incumbent banks lost much of their advantages (namely the ability to collect deposits through their retail outlets) and allowed greater ease of entry by new smaller banks who could rely on the interbank market as a source of funds. Technological advances reduced the need for a physical presence in the market and hence also reduced the costs of entry. The implications of a decline in sunk costs are that competition is likely to be enhanced by new entry or the threat of entry. Davis (1992) then argues that certain consequences – in terms of increased financial fragility which we outline below – can follow.

[14] The latter entered later once regulations limiting their involvement in international lending were removed.

which combined with capital cover any bad debts and defaults that the bank may have to face (see Minsky, 1982a, p.74). Given the attraction of too many entrants because of increasing confidence under conditions of imperfect information, there is a tendency to overproduction. Too many suppliers are chasing too little demand. Is the resulting profits squeeze a short-run phenomenon or something more fundamental? There are three reasons why it should be considered more fundamental.

Firstly, as Pitman (1985) argues, there may have been a need for a large investment in expertise, which has to be maintained at a certain level to reap economies of scale in banking information. Although we argued earlier that the herd instinct in financial markets is to some extent a substitute for genuine information, there will be some attempt on the part of banks to set up a department dealing with the new lending market, even if its effectiveness, in the initial stages, is to be doubted. Given possible economies of scale, it may be cheaper to have a large proportion of assets in the area, and withdrawal may be difficult and protracted.

Secondly, if prospects worsen, many banks may not consider withdrawal appropriate in the first instance. They may even engage in an aggressive pricing strategy to enlarge their share of the business (see Group of Thirty, 1982b), taking losses in the short run in order to obtain the profit available from opportunities when competitors have withdrawn. Price warfare will, of course, reduce profits further.

Thirdly, supply may increase further as new nationalities of banks join the market, who were previously prevented through regulations within their respective countries of origin. Llewellyn (1982), for example, points to the case of the American banks in 1974 and Japanese in 1977 whose entrance into the market, after regulations preventing entry were removed caused a once-for-all stock increase in international lending and put downward pressure on profits.

The second consequence of increased competition is that the risk–return relationship deteriorates and credit exposure limits are increased. The impact of increasing competition on risk premia is two-fold: first, it decreases them; secondly, it decreases the spread of premia (that is the difference between the highest and lowest premia) as banks compete amongst one another to try to maintain, if not increase, their individual market shares.[15] Many have argued that, with greater competition and the need for banks to maintain their market share, individual lenders cannot stop the erosion of risk premia, if their competitors are not making sufficient provision for risk.[16] Methods that usually prevent this erosion in the quality of banks' assets may be rendered ineffective (Barclay, 1978). Shareholders are not in a position to judge the soundness of loans made and face the general problem of shareholder authority. Borrowers are unlikely to complain, because they are benefiting from the reduced prices and increased amount of credit available and, in some cases, probably believe that they will repay the money. Finally, depositors are interested only in their deposits, not in the general prosperity of the bank. This leads to a discontinuity in attitude such that in normal circumstances depositors do not bother, but when the risk becomes great they are inclined to withdraw their deposits, causing a run on the bank, by which time it is too late to improve loan quality and the bank is liable to fail.[17]

---

[15] Devlin (1989) and McKenzie and Thomas (1992) also argue that banks were not interested solely in profit maximisation. The desire to maintain or increase market share leads to the idea of the bank as a salesperson seeking actively to sell loans to customers.

[16] See, for example, Revell (1980), Pitman (1985), Group of Thirty (1982b).

[17] Deposit insurance might also make depositors unworried about the safety of the bank.

A loosening of credit limits is also likely to arise as a result of increased competition and confidence. This leads to a greater concentration of loans within a particular risk class than might be advisable for diversification reasons. Innovations may have the effect or the intention of decreasing the apparent concentration for individual banks. Syndication is the mechanism through which individual banks reduce their risk in the medium–term Euromarket: each bank finances only a small part of each loan. This, however, ignores the fact that concentration of borrowers for the system as a whole may increase. In conjunction with the increased interdependence that results from such an innovation, this means that systematic risk has probably not decreased.

Thirdly, increased competition results in an increase in the maturity of loans. This is part of the package of better terms available to borrowers which include lower risk premia and higher credit limits.

Fourthly, the increased confidence and competition, combined with the decrease in profits, causes the banks to move into greater risk areas in order to try to maintain or increase earnings. Revell (1980) suggests that speculative maturity mismatching will increase, with an associated increase in interest rate and funding risks. Minsky (1982b) describes this as a feature of what he terms a speculative finance unit. Long positions in assets are financed by short–run liabilities which implies interest rate risk. Together with greater maturity mismatching, banks also speculate on interest rate changes and foreign exchange rate changes. However, where exchange rates and interest rates are very volatile, it is difficult to guess the correct movements and very costly to guess wrong. The effect of such behaviour is thus to increase the volatility of profits.

Gibson and Oppenheimer (1992) argue that these four consequences of increased confidence and competition imply increased risk both to individual banks and to the system as a whole. Some brief comments are in order before we move on to consider what happens when the crisis occurs. First, why are banks able and willing to sacrifice short–run profits considerations? A partial answer is presumably that they are interested not so much in immediate profit maximisation, as in increasing market share and the size of their balance sheets (Devlin, 1989). If their competitors move into the new area, there is strong motivation for them to follow, otherwise they will lose their relative position. Moreover, each bank hopes that if it can become well–established in a market and force out some of its rivals, greater long–term profits will be possible.

Secondly, why is the deterioration in the risk–return relationship allowed to happen and why do banks not realise that this will be damaging in the future? Firstly, growing confidence will result in banks assessing risk on the basis of a more optimistic view of the investment: recall that banks are operating in an uncertain environment where the objective assessment of risk is not possible. Secondly, retribution for bad banking seldom occurs immediately (Revell, 1980; Barclay, 1978). The banker who underprovides for risk and engages in speculative activities will probably earn greater profits in the short–term than a prudent rival. In many cases, the new entrants were the first to involve themselves in such activities; but as confidence increases, the more established become involved.

These various elements combine to produce a situation of overlending and increasing fragility. We enter Phase III of the cycle. Risks have not been properly assessed or provided for, speculative activity may be playing a prominent role and declining profits may have affected the degree to which banks have provided reserves against bad debts. A crisis is increasingly possible. We can identify several factors that might act as the trigger. As Fisher (1932) recognised, investments made for speculative purposes are a likely cause of a crisis. A default or need for rescheduling on the part of a major borrower can spark off a crisis because it raises doubts about the quality of some of the banks' assets. Moreover, because competition and aggressive pricing has reduced banks' reserves, the ability to deal with possible loan losses is reduced. Defaults or reschedulings may occur because of actors exogenous to the banking system, for example, a decline in economic activity or the collapse in the price of an important export commodity, but may also be encouraged by factors endogenous to the banking system. For example, the roll-over loan is thought to reduce interest rate risk inherent in maturity mismatching. However, the risk of an increase in the interest rate is passed on to the borrower and it is possible to conceive of a situation where an increase in the interest rate in the Eurodollar market causes the borrower severe repayment problems.

The sequence of events during the crisis period, Phase IV, is dependent on the initial trigger but even if only one bank is affected initially, interdependence within the system as a result of the interbank market and syndication is liable to generate a domino effect and many banks may subsequently get into difficulties. As McMahon (1985) argues, the interbank market is more fragile and susceptible to shocks than other forms of funding and could cause a failure of the system. In the event of rescheduling or default, many banks will be affected because of the process of syndication, Moreover, reschedulings or defaults may be bunched, as Revell (1980) and Barclay (1978) argue is likely, because of the economic problems that affect one borrower have a high probability of affecting many; this is the systemic risk element which cannot be diversified away.

There are several characteristics of the crisis period. Liquidity in the market, in this case mainly the interbank market, dries up so that banks are unable to refund their loans. Other assets which the banks consider to be liquid under normal conditions either become illiquid or must be sold at well below their non-crisis value, resulting in losses for the banks. Confidence gives way to pessimism and banks as yet unaffected will try to move out of the lending area affected. Such a process increases the fragility of the situation by adding to domino effects. Rescheduling forces banks into involuntary lending and greater maturity mismatching. They may be unable to write of the losses without severely weakening or exhausting their reserves. Finally, the decline in confidence may not be confined to the wholesale market and may reach the general public, sparking off a run on banks. The potential for social costs can be enormous if government intervention to halt the crisis does not occur.

## Conclusion

We have sought in this chapter to outline some of the theoretical issues relevant to international bank lending. The efficient market view of bank lending argues that banks will adequately compensate themselves for the risk they undertake when lending by building a diversified portfolio where the risk of the portfolio is compensated for through the existence of risk premia. Through optimising behaviour banks allocate capital internationally in an efficient way. We have argued that this view of banking was inadequate. In particular, it ignores the problems that arise as a result of information deficiencies which are prevalent in financial markets. Optimising behaviour in the presence of risk entails that banks should practice credit rationing. In this way financial fragility is prevented and crises are avoided. Whilst this is good normative economics (banks *should* act in this way), it does not appear to be good *positive* economics. Crises do occur and therefore have to be explained.

We sought the explanation for crises by examining the role of competition in the presence of these market failures. We argued that the lack of information in credit markets leads not just to risky outcomes but to a situation that can be better characterised as uncertain. Calculation of objective probabilities associated with the returns from investments is not possible. Instead, the probability distribution of returns is likely to be subjective and as such can change as the degree of confidence in financial markets alters. When combined with excessive competition, banks can behave in ways which increase the fragility of the financial system. They no longer compensate themselves for the risk of default by setting appropriate risk premia and credit limits. Crises can therefore result.

Such crises have important social costs in that they severely undermine the ability of banks to allocate capital efficiently. This creates a case for some form of intervention both to prevent crises from occurring and to limit the impact of any financial crises which do happen to occur. Such arguments have important implications for the design of any international financial system. If the provision of finance, particularly for recycling, is left to private institutions, then optimal outcomes may not be forthcoming. The availability of finance may become procyclical – being abundant when the world economy is doing well and scarce when it is doing badly. In this way private finance provision may become destabilising, because of the inherent nature of financial markets. Hence the considerations discussed in this chapter call into question the appropriateness of assigning the problems of international liquidity and adjustment to private financial institutions. Instead there is a strong case for the design of institutions which are better able to control the behaviour of private financial institutions and also better equipped to cope with the recycling problem.

## References

Akerof, G. (1970) 'The market for lemons', *Quarterly Journal of Economics*, 84: 3, 485–500.

Barclay, C.R. (1978) 'Competition and financial crises – past and present', in C.R. Barclay, E.P.M. Gardener and J. Revell, *Competition and Regulation of Banks*. Bangor Occasional Papers in Economics, 14. University of Wales Press, Bangor.

Batchelor, R.A. (1986) 'The avoidance of catastrophe: two nineteenth century banking crises', in F. Capie and G.E. Woods (eds) *Financial Crises and the World Banking System*. Macmillan, London.

Bernoulli, D. (1954) 'Exposition of a new theory on the measurement of risk', *Econometrica*, 22: 23–6.

Blanchard, O.J. and Watson, M.W. (1982) 'Bubbles, rational expectations and financial markets', in P. Watchel (ed.) *Crises in the Economic and Financial Structure*. Lexington Books, Cambridge, Mass.

Blume, M.E. (1971) 'On the assessment of risk', *Journal of Finance*, 26: 1, 1–10.

Davis, E.P. (1992) *Debt, Financial Fragility and Systematic Risk*. Oxford University Press, Oxford.

Devlin, R. (1989) *Debt and Crisis in Latin America: the supply side of the story*. Princeton University Press, Princeton.

Eaton, J. and Gersovitz, M. (1981a) 'Debt with potential repudiation: theoretical and empirical analysis', *Review of Economic Studies*, 48: 289–309.

Eaton, J. and Gersovitz, M. (1981b) 'Poor country borrowing in private financial markets and the repudiation issue', *Princeton Studies in International Finance*, 47, June.

Eaton, J. and Gersovitz, M. (1983) 'Country risk: economic aspects', in R.J. Herring (ed.) *Managing International Risk*. Cambridge University Press, Cambridge.

Eaton, J., Gersovitz, M. and Stiglitz, J.E. (1986) 'The pure theory of country risk', *European Economic Review*, 30: 481–513.

Eichengreen, B. and Portes, R. (1987) 'The anatomy of a financial crisis', in R. Portes and A.K. Swoboda (eds) *Threats to International Financial Stability*. Cambridge University Press, Cambridge.

Fischer, I. (1932) *Booms and Depressions*. Adelphi Co., New York.

Flood, R.P. and Garber, P.M. (1980) 'Market fundamentals versus price-level bubbles: the first tests', *Journal of Public Economy*, 88: 745–70.

Flood, R.P. and Garber, P.M. (1982) 'Bubbles, runs and gold monetarization', in P. Watchel (ed.) *Crises in the Economic and Financial Structure*. Lexington Books, Cambridge, Mass. 275–93.

Freimer, M. and Gordon, M.J. (1965) 'Why bankers ration credit', *Quarterly Journal of Economics*, August, 397–416.

Friedman, M. (1969a) *The Optimum Quantity of Money and other Essays*. Chicago University Press, Chicago.

Gibson, H.D. (1989) *The Eurocurrency Markets, Domestic Financial Policy and International Instability*. Macmillan, London.

Gibson, H.D. and Oppenheimer, P.M. (1992) 'Financial crises and the international debt problem', Applied Economics Discussion Paper, 135, April. Institute of Economics and Statistics, Oxford.

Greenwald, B. and Stiglitz, J.E. (1986) 'Externalities in economies with imperfect information and incomplete markets', *Quarterly Journal of Economics*, 101: 4, 229–64.

Grossman, S.I. and Hart, O. (1983) 'An analysis of the principle–agent problem', *Econometrica*, 51: 1, 7–45.

Grossman, S.I. and Stiglitz, J.E. (1980) 'On the impossibility of informationally efficient markets', *American Economic Review*, 70: 3, 393–407.

Group of Thirty (1982b) *Risk in International Bank Lending*. Group of Thirty, New York.

Guttentag, J.M. and Herring, R.J. (1986) 'Disaster myopia in international finance', *Princeton Essays in International Finance*, 164, September.

Haegele, M.J. (1980) 'The market still knows best', *Euromoney*, May, 121.

Hodgeman, D.R. (1960) 'Credit risk and credit rationing', *Quarterly Journal of Economics*, May, 258–78.

Jaffee, D.M. and Modigliani, F. (1969) 'A theory and test of credit rationing', *American Economic Review*, 59: 850–72.

Kapur, I. (1977) 'An analysis of the supply of Euro-currency finance to developing countries', *Oxford Bulletin of Economics and Statistics*, 39: 3, 171–81.

Kindleberger, C.P. (1975) 'Quantity and price, especially in financial markets', in C.P. Kindleberger, *International Money*. Allen and Unwin, London.

Kindleberger, C.P. (1978) *Manias, Panics and Crashes*. Macmillan, London.

Kindleberger, C.P. and Laffargue, J.P. (1982) *Financial Crises: Theory, History and Policy*. Cambridge University Press, Cambridge.

Knight, F.H. (1921) *Risk, Uncertainty and Profit*. Houghton Mifflin, Boston.

Llewellyn, D.R. (1990a) 'The international capital transfer mechanism of the 1970s:

a critique', in G. Bird (ed.) *The International Financial Regime*. Surrey University Press in association with Academic Press, London. 29–66.

**McKenzie, G. and Thomas, S.** (1992) *Financial Instability and the International Debt Problem*. Macmillan, London.

**McMahon, C.** (1985) 'Change and development in international financial markets', *Competition and Co-operation in International Banking*. The Institute of Bankers, London.

**Minsky, H.P.** (1982a) *Inflation, Recession and Economic Policy*. Wheatsheaf Books, Brighton.

**Minsky, H.P.** (1982b) 'The financial instability hypothesis: capital processes and the behaviour of the economy', in C.P. Kindleberger and J.P. Laffargue (eds), *Financial Crisis: Theory, History and Policy*. Cambridge University Press, Cambridge.

**Nagy, P.** (1984) *Country Risk*. Euromoney Publications, London.

**Philbeam, K.** (1992) *International Finance*. Macmillan, London.

**Pitman, B.** (1985) 'Organising for the future', in *Competition and Co-operation in World Banking*. Institute of Bankers, London.

**Revell, J.** (1980) *Costs and Margins in International Banking: An International Survey*. OECD, Paris.

**Richardson, G.B.** (1960) *Information and Investment: a study in the working of the competitive economy*. Oxford University Press, Oxford.

**Schwartz, A.** (1986) 'Real and pseudo-financial crises', in F. Capie and G.E. Woods (eds) *Financial Crises and the World Banking System*. Macmillan, London.

**Shiller, R.** (1981) 'Do stock prices move too much to be justified by subsequent changes to dividends?', *American Economic Review*, 71: 421–36.

**Solow, R.M.** (1982) 'On the lender of last resort', in C.P. Kindleberger and J.P. Lafargue (eds) (1982) *Financial Crisis: Theory History and Policy*. Cambridge University Press, Cambridge.

**Spence, M.** (1973) 'Job market signalling', *Quarterly Journal of Economics*, 87: 3, 355–74.

**Stiglitz, J.E.** (1989) 'Financial markets and development', *Oxford Review of Economic Policy*, 5: 4, 55–68.

**Stiglitz, J.E. and Weiss, A.** (1981) 'Credit rationing in markets with imperfect information', *American Economic Review*, 71: 3, 393–410.

**Tinic, S. and West, R.** (1979) *Investing in Securities: an efficient markets approach*. Addison–Wesley, Cambridge, Mass.

**Tirole, J.** (1982) 'On the possibility of speculation under rational expectations', *Econometrica*, 50: 5, 1163–81.

# 9 THE INTERNATIONAL DEBT CRISIS

On 15 August 1982, Mexico declared that it was no longer able to service its large foreign currency debt owed to private international commercial banks. Numerous other countries followed and by the end of the 1980s, some forty countries were involved in annual rescheduling negotiations with commercial banks. The consequences of these widespread debt servicing problems have been severe, not only for the parties most directly involved (middle-income developing countries and international banks), but also for the functioning of the international financial system. Only through a careful management of the debt crisis has stability of the financial system been preserved. But this has usually been at the cost of great hardship in developing countries whose economies have, by and large, stagnated over the last decade. In this chapter we want to examine the debt crisis as a case study in the role of financial flows within the international financial system. We contend that the experience of the 1970s and 1980s suggests that banks are not well-suited to the role of major lenders to developing countries and argue for a much greater role for international institutions in the supervision of international financial flows.

The first section begins with an account of the build-up of debt to developing countries. In particular, we discuss the characteristics of the debt and the burden which it has placed on developing countries. In the second section, we examine the underlying causes of the debt build-up. We focus on several issues. First, the abrupt change in the financing of current account deficits in the early 1970s from official flows to private flows directed mainly through the medium-term syndicated Euro-credit markets. Secondly, we consider the role of the banks. In Chapter 8, we discussed some of the risks inherent in international bank lending. Here we examine how banks dealt with these risks in their lending to developing countries and ask whether the methods used were adequate. Thirdly, we investigate the policies of developing countries themselves to determine whether they can be seen as responsible for their inability to repay. Finally, we look at the role of the various shocks to the international monetary system in the late 1970s and early 1980s. These factors, which include the major world recession, are often considered to be the triggering factors in the debt crisis.

The third section provides an examination of the post-1982 management of the debt crisis. By and large, the approach adopted has been a case-by-case one where individual countries have sought to negotiate rescheduling agreements with their creditors. Various initiatives such as the Baker and Brady plans are also discussed. In the final section of this chapter, we conclude with a discussion of some of the more recent proposals to reduce the debt overhang which continues to hamper growth in developing countries. We also discuss the question of future financial flows to developing countries in the light of the lessons which the debt crisis has taught us.

## Characteristics of the debt build-up

The rapid increase in the total value of external debt of developing countries throughout the 1970s and 1980s is illustrated in Figure 9.1. The debt burden grew from just over $50 billion to over $1,600 billion, an increase of some thirty-two fold. A critical factor to remember is that this debt is external debt, owed to foreign governments, international institutions or foreign private banks. Moreover, it is foreign currency debt (mainly denominated in dollars) and hence has to be repaid in foreign currency.

A major feature of the debt build-up in the 1970s was the rising amounts borrowed from private creditors. Figure 9.2 illustrates the path of debt owed to private creditors as a percentage of total debt (in this case, long-term public or publicly guaranteed debt). In the case of Latin America and the Caribbean countries, the rise in debt from private creditors is very pronounced up until 1982. This is a consequence of the rapid growth in the medium-term syndicated Eurocredit market during the 1970s. After 1982, the effect of the debt crisis was to increase these countries' dependence on official creditors.[1] The figure also indicates that Sub-Saharan African countries have always relied more heavily on official creditors. Borrowing from private creditors reached a peak of only 40% in the early 1980s. A similar trend can be detected in lending to African countries: a rise up until 1982, followed by a fall.

One feature of the debt build-up which is indirectly shown in Figure 9.2 is the fact that debt owed to private creditors tends to be quite highly concentrated among a small number of countries. Many low income countries (which tend to be concentrated in Sub-Saharan Africa) did not have access to the private international capital

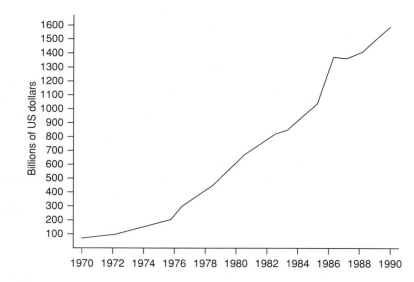

**Figure 9.1.**  *Total debt in developing countries*

[1] Official creditors include industrial country governments as well as the major international institutions.

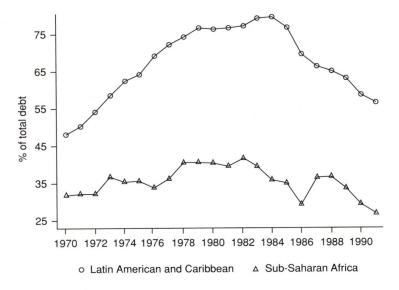

**Figure 9.2.**   *Debt to private creditors*

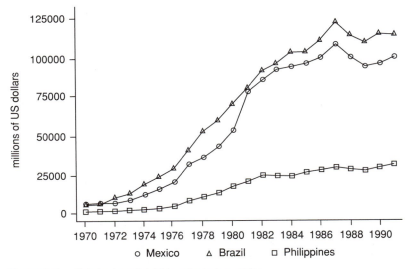

**Figure 9.3.**   *Total external debt in selected countries*

markets. By contrast, Latin American countries borrowed quite freely with the result that banks now have large concentrations of nonperforming debt from only a few countries.

Figure 9.3 illustrates the build-up of debt to three of the major debtors to private creditors: Brazil, Mexico and the Philippines. The debt accumulation of the two Latin American countries tends to follow a similar pattern to the build-up of external debt in developing countries generally. The Philippines, by contrast, had a slower accumulation of external debt. In spite of this, the Philippines, like the other two countries, has debt servicing problems.

It is often the case the total debt figures give a poor indication of the debt burden of a particular country. Clearly the burden of debt is related to the country's size and ability to generate foreign exchange. For this reason, other measures of debt burden are often employed. Debt to GNP ratios for Brazil, Mexico and the Philippines are shown in Figure 9.4. This indicates that the Philippines has the highest debt/GNP ratio of all three countries, in spite of the fact that its total debt is lower.

Since the debt has to be serviced using foreign currency, the debt service ratio (which is interest and principal repayments over exports) is often used as a measure of the ability of a country to service its foreign currency debt. Figure 9.5 plots this ratio for the three countries. This illustrates the large rise in debt servicing burden which all three countries experienced as a result of the debt build-up of the 1970s. In

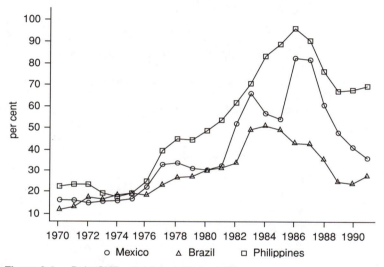

**Figure 9.4.**   *Debt/GNP ratios in selected countries*

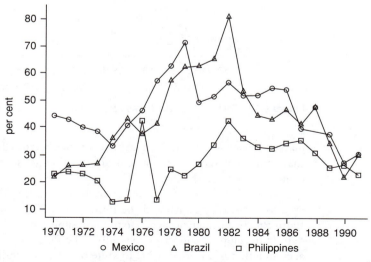

**Figure 9.5.**   *Debt service ratios in selected countries*

the cases of Brazil and Mexico, over 50% of export earnings had to be used to servicing debt for a substantial period during the 1970s and 1980s. The fall in the debt service ratio after 1986 in part reflects the fact that these countries failed to meet their debt servicing obligations,[2] rather than indicating that debt servicing commitments fell.

As we noted in the introduction to this chapter, the debt crisis became apparent in August 1982. One of the immediate problems raised by developing countries' debt servicing problems was the risk to bank stability. Cline (1984) provides some indication of bank exposure to developing countries. Table 9.1 illustrates the size of the problem and the potential for international financial instability.

Bank capital represents the last line of defence to allow it to absorb losses before depositors can no longer be repaid. What Table 9.1 illustrates is the fact that US banks would have had severe problems had these developing countries defaulted. European banks were less highly exposed, but the situation was still severe. Cline notes that the 9 largest US banks had even greater exposures: their exposure to non-oil developing countries plus eastern Europe was 188.2% of their capital base in 1977 and 235.2% in 1982. The above figures exclude oil-exporting developing countries which have also suffered debt servicing problems.

It might be argued that it was unlikely that all developing countries would default. Cline therefore calculates the impact on US banks of selective defaults or simply nonrepayment of debt due for a certain period. If Argentina, Brazil and Mexico had declared a 1 year moratorium on their debt (that is, they missed 1 year's interest and principal repayments), then the 9 largest US banks would have lost 28% of their capital base. Such a reduction in banks' capital base causes them to cut back on lending and hence can have a severe contractionary effect on the world economy.

Thus, the large build-up of debt which occurred in the 1970s and early 1980s undermined the stability of the international financial system. In order to understand why such large amounts of debt were accumulated, we need to delve deeper into the fundamental causes of the debt build-up.

*Table 9.1.* US bank exposure as a percentage of banks' capital base

|  | 1977 | 1978 | 1979 | 1980 | 1981 | 1982 |
|---|---|---|---|---|---|---|
| Non-oil Developing Countries | 115 | 114 | 124 | 132 | 148 | 146 |
| Non-oil Developing Countries plus Eastern Europe | 132 | 130 | 140 | 146 | 164 | 155 |

*Source*: Cline (1984).

[2] The debt service used to calculate this ratio is the actual debt service made by the country in any one year. Hence the ratio can fall simply because the country fails to meet its debt servicing obligations.

## The underlying causes of the debt build-up

In this section we want to examine the factors which can be said to have caused the debt build-up and subsequent crisis. An understanding of these factors is crucial to assigning responsibility for the debt crisis and perhaps more importantly to ensure that it does not happen again. This latter goal requires us to question the form of financial flows within the international monetary system in the 1970s and 1980s. Were they appropriate and how was the burden of risks shared out between the various participants?

In order to allow us to draw some conclusions on this issue we focus here on four aspects of the debt build-up. We examine first the origins of the debt crisis in the large shift in financial flows subsequent to the first oil price rise. We note the large increase in the role of private international capital markets as recyclers of the OPEC surpluses.

Secondly, we investigate the behaviour of banks with respect to the risks inherent in international lending which we identified in Chapter 8. We argue that international banks were ineffective at dealing with the risks mainly as a result of the influence of competition on their perceptions of the risk involved in lending to developing countries.

The third factor we look at is the role of developing country policies. Our investigation here is rather incomplete. A full analysis of the role of developing countries would require in-depth case studies, something which is beyond the scope of this book. Nonetheless we conclude tentatively that the majority of developing countries did seek to use the borrowed funds for investment. Explanations for their inability to meet repayments must therefore lie elsewhere.

The final set of factors which we examine is the role of the macroeconomic shocks which affected the world economy in the early 1980s. In particular, the world recession significantly reduced the export revenues of developing countries. This group of factors might be considered systematic risk which banks could not easily diversify away: all developing countries are affected in the same way by world recession and hence all can get into repayment difficulties at the same time. It is often argued that these factors triggered the debt crisis (Allsopp and Joshi, 1986).

### Financial flows in the international financial system

As we argued in Chapter 1, one of the main roles of the international financial system is to ensure that mechanisms are in place to facilitate the transfer of funds from countries where capital is abundant to those where it is scarce. Developing countries as a group tend to be characterised by capital scarcity. This scarcity results from both a potential abundance of investment opportunities as well as a shortage of finance to undertake such projects.

The shortage of finance takes two forms. First, there is a lack of domestic savings. This results in part from the low levels of income in developing countries which implies that a large part is absorbed simply by expenditure on necessities. Low savings might also be related to the underdeveloped nature of financial systems in developing countries. The absence of a developed financial system implies that savers find it difficult to place their funds directly into investment opportunities.

In addition to the domestic savings shortage, there is also a foreign exchange shortage. Development projects usually require the import of goods (particularly physical capital) and services which cannot be provided by the domestic economy. Although foreign exchange can be accumulated through exports, this is rarely enough and developing countries normally have a current account deficit (a development deficit). The consequence is that they have to attract capital inflows from abroad. These flows can take a variety of forms: aid, foreign direct investment, borrowing from industrial country governments or borrowing from the international capital markets. Clearly each type of inflow has different implications for repayments.

In 1973–74, the price of oil increased dramatically. Thus as well as the normal development need for foreign exchange, developing countries experienced a sharp increase in the cost of their imports. Indeed, as Table 9.2 indicates, the oil price rise generated a large recycling problem for the international monetary system. Overall, current account imbalances (regardless of sign) doubled from 1–1.5% of GNP during the 1950s and 1960s to 2–3% in the 1970s (Stanyer and Whitley, 1981). The oil price rise caused industrial countries in 1974 to move into a large deficit of around 20 billion SDRs. Oil importing developing countries, which had been running an overall deficit in 1972 and 1973 saw it increase sharply to around 18.5 billion SDRs. Balancing these deficits was the huge surplus of oil exporting developing countries of 40 billion SDRs.

It is important to note that these figures give us a picture only of the *ex post* financing problem resulting from the oil price rise (Stanyer and Whitley, 1981). These deficits had to be financed by capital flows or changes in reserves. However, they underestimate the *ex ante* nature of the problem because they give no indication of the amount of adjustment which countries undertook to reduce the *ex post* financing problem.[3] Nonetheless, as our concern here lies mainly with the financing of imbalances which did occur, the figures in Table 9.2 give a good indication of the scale of the problem.

It is clear from Table 9.2 that some adjustment did occur during the 1970s. This is particularly true of the industrial countries who actually achieved a surplus of 12 billion SDRs by 1978. Oil exporting developing countries also experienced a dramatic fall in their surplus so that by 1978 they had a small deficit. Oil importing developing countries, however, continued to run large deficits throughout the 1970s. The 1979 oil price rise returned imbalances to their 1974 pattern. Industrial countries as a whole went back into deficit in 1979 and 1980. Oil importing developing countries again experienced a large rise in their deficit. Oil exporting developing countries experienced a large surplus.

Thus the pattern of current account deficits throughout the 1970s and early 1980s

*Table 9.2.*  Current account imbalances (mn SDRs)

|  | 1972 | 1973 | 1974 | 1975 | 1976 | 1977 | 1978 | 1979 | 1980 | 1981 |
|---|---|---|---|---|---|---|---|---|---|---|
| Industrial Countries | 7954 | 9531 | −20820 | 4091 | −11740 | −15396 | 12140 | −20474 | −47724 | −16480 |
| Oil Exporting Developing Countries | 373 | 1967 | 40381 | 14771 | 16606 | 12244 | −2546 | 43125 | 79155 | 38531 |
| Oil Importing Developing Countries | −5791 | −5276 | −18482 | −25676 | −16386 | −10205 | −25301 | −37638 | −58120 | −80571 |

*Note*: Oil importing and exporting countries are as defined by the IMF.

*Source*: IMF Balance of Payments Yearbooks.

[3] To get some indication of the *ex ante* nature of the problem, we would have to take into account the monetary and fiscal deflationary packages introduced by oil importing countries as well as exchange-rate changes. Only in this way would the true impact of the oil price rise on balance of payments imbalances be identified.

was subject to large swings. This clearly posed an important recycling problem for the international financial system. In the early 1970s, the OPEC surpluses had to be recycled to finance industrial country and oil importing developing country deficits. Just before the second oil price rise in 1979, it was the industrial countries' surplus which had to be recycled to finance developing countries continued deficits. Finally, post-1979, the financing requirements returned to their early 1970s pattern once more.

In order to understand how recycling took place it is instructive to examine the various methods through which current account deficits can be financed and the changing importance of financing methods in the post-1973 period as compared to pre-1973. Stanyer and Whitley (1981) provide a major study of this issue. They conclude that in the 1950s and 1960s, developing countries' current account deficits were financed in the main through official aid flows and foreign direct investment. Post-1973, however, there was a rapid increase in the importance of international capital markets in recycling.

Stanyer and Whitley (1981) examine the contribution made by different forms of capital inflows to developing countries to financing their current account deficits. The first source of foreign exchange available to developing countries is aid. Aid flows in the period 1960 to 1973 accounted for around 0.30% of developing countries GNP. Between 1974 and 1979, they increased slightly to 0.34%. Such a small increase implies that aid made little contribution to the growing imbalances.

The introduction of measures to attract foreign direct investment is another possible means of financing a current account deficit. However, foreign direct investment is dependent on the long-term investment strategies of multi-national companies. Moreover, policies to encourage foreign direct investment cannot easily be implemented overnight. This form of finance is therefore little suited to responding to short-term financing needs. Not surprisingly, therefore, although the amount of foreign direct investment increased as a percentage of developing countries' GNP, it had only a slight impact on reducing the financing needs of oil importing developing countries.

A third way in which deficits can be financed is through medium-term or long-term borrowing. This takes two main forms. First, developing countries often borrow from industrial country governments, usually on concessionary terms. Stanyer and Whitley note that this made a substantial contribution in absolute terms to recycling, increasing from $5.5 billion dollars in 1973 to $19.1 billion in 1980. Its relative importance, however, declined slightly. The second form of borrowing is from the private international capital markets. This form of finance made a substantial and increasingly important contribution to deficit financing throughout the period. In Table 9.3, we divide flows to developing countries into private and official flows. This clearly indicates the rising importance of private sources, most of the increase in which can be traced to increased bank lending to developing countries.

The final source of finance for developing countries is loans from the official international institutions such as the IMF and World Bank. They contributed only to a small proportion of the financing. This was partly a consequence of the fact that their funds were completely inadequate to the task. Moreover, there was a lack of political will among industrial countries to launch an international initiative with respect to the recycling problem raised by the oil price rises. It is important to recall that the oil price rise occurred at a time when international monetary co-operation had completely broken down (with the failure of Bretton Woods). There was also a

*Table 9.3.*   Official and private flows to developing countries (percentages)

|          | 1970 | 1973 | 1979 |
|----------|------|------|------|
| Official | 46.4 | 30.9 | 28.1 |
| Private  | 53.6 | 69.1 | 71.9 |

*Source*: Bird, G. (1982)

widespread belief that floating exchange rates would solve the balance of payments problems that emerged. But in addition to these problems, it has to be noted that developing countries themselves were rather more keen to borrow from the international capital markets rather than the international institutions because of their desire to avoid the conditionality which the latter imposed.[4]

Thus, in conclusion, the mechanics of recycling changed enormously during the 1970s. Before 1973, responsibility for recycling was in the main in the hands of industrial country governments, either through aid or direct lending to developing countries or through the major international institutions set up by the Bretton Woods system to deal with imbalances. Since 1973, private financial institutions have played an increasingly important role in recycling. Since 1982, developing countries have been in arrears on the repayment of this private debt accumulated during the 1970s. We therefore have to question whether the form that recycling took after the oil price rise was appropriate to the needs of developing countries.

**The international banking system**

The large growth in the role of international banks as major recyclers of funds in the international monetary system raises the question of the suitability of banks for this type of lending. In Chapter 8, we discussed some of the risks inherent in international lending and developed some ideas about the potential for financial crisis in the presence of information deficiencies. Our examination of the role of the banks in international lending in the 1970s and 1980s can provide an interesting case study of the way in which banks dealt with these risks and how the crisis came about.

The first two risks we identified are those associated with maturity transformation: interest rate risk and funding risk. We showed in Chapter 7 that maturity transformation increased in two distinct phases throughout the 1970s and 1980s. The first phase was in 1973–5 and the second in 1982–3. The increase in the first phase can be attributed in part to the recycling boom. Oil exporting countries tended to deposit their oil revenues in the international markets in short-term deposits.[5] Developing countries who borrowed from the market desired medium-term loans (of around 8 years). In this way the amount of maturity transformation undertaken by banks increased. The recycling opportunity also attracted a number of banks into the market and the consequent increase in competition led to the emergence of a borrowers market in the mid-1970s. That is, borrowers were able to negotiate loans with attractive maturities and interest rates. Although borrowers negotiated increases in the maturity of their loans, there was no corresponding increase in the maturity of deposits and hence mismatching increased. The second phase of increased maturity

---

[4] We discuss the question of conditionality associated with lending by international institutions in Chapter 10.
[5] The rationale for maintaining the revenues in short-term liquid deposits was simple. It would allow access to the money when more long-term investments became available.

mismatching can perhaps be attributed to the debt crisis. Maturity mismatching increased because of the need for rescheduling, often with longer maturities, again without an increase in deposit maturity.

The increased maturity mismatching throughout the 1970s and 1980s led to banks taking on extra risk. Two innovations, however, led banks to believe that they were minimising that risk. First, there was the development of roll-over loans, whose interest rate altered in line with market rates every three or six months. This innovation clearly reduces the interest rate risk faced by a bank – if a bank has to raise deposit rates to attract new money to finance the loan, then the increased cost will be passed on to the borrower. From the borrower's point of view, the development of roll-over loans has the advantage that borrowing no longer needs to be confined to periods when interest rates are low. If the loan is negotiated during a period of high interest rates, the borrower knows that he or she will benefit should interest rates fall. However, the weakness of roll-over loans is that, although the bank reduces one type of risk it faces, it may be the case that it does not reduce another, namely default risk. If interest rates rise substantially during the period of the loan, then the consequent increase in the debt servicing burden may be too great and the borrower may be unable to meet the repayments. Thus roll-over loans might successfully reduce interest rate risk, but only at the cost of passing that risk on to the borrower with the subsequent potential for servicing difficulties.

The second innovation in the Euromarkets, a large interbank market, reduced the potential for funding risk associated with maturity mismatching. Funding risk is the risk that the bank will be unable to refinance the loan at any price. The development of a large interbank market offers banks access to liquid funds which can be attracted at short notice. Any bank thus experiencing difficulties with refinancing a loan can simply approach the interbank market and bring in some deposits.

There are, however, two problems with the interbank market as it has developed in the Euromarkets. First, it tends to increase interdependence within the system which could affect its stability. The size of the interbank market (which we noted in Chapter 6 was some 70% of assets and liabilities) significantly increases the interlocking debt structure between banks. Thus if bank A gets into difficulties and has to withdraw deposits it holds with bank B, then this could cause liquidity problems for bank B and lead to knock-on effects on other banks. A second problem with the interbank market is its operation during crises. Interbank funds tend to be much more volatile than nonbank deposits. Rumours move around international banking centres very quickly and deposits can be withdrawn quickly should rumours persist for more than 24 hours. Thus the interbank market can precipitate liquidity crises which can be quickly transmitted through the system at times of crisis.

The second main group of risks which are particularly pertinent to bank operations in the medium-term syndicated credit market are credit risks in general and sovereign risk in particular. Syndicated loans were one way in which the banks sought to diversify their holdings of external assets to developing countries. A syndicated loan occurs where a group of banks get together to provide a loan to a borrower. One bank is usually responsible for negotiating the loan and it effectively sell participations in the loan to other banks. There are a number of advantages to syndication. First, it allows lenders to diversify risk. They can participate in many loan deals rather than simply a few. This spreads the risk associated with dealing with only a small set of borrowers. To put it another way, unsystematic risk is reduced.

A second advantage of syndicated loans is that they allow larger amounts to be put together in one single loan. This saves the borrower engaging in lengthy and costly negotiations with a number of banks to enter into several contracts for smaller amounts. Instead the borrower can simply negotiate with the lead bank the total amount which it wishes to borrow.

The final advantage is that banks have often argued that if many of them are involved in loans to a particular country then this will reduce the risk of default. This is true because in the event of default, political pressure will be brought to bear on the borrower from a number of countries whose banks are involved rather than just one.

The problem with syndication is that it tends to magnify the effects of a default on the system as a whole, especially since it has usually been associated with cross-default clauses. Cross-default clauses state that if a country defaults on one loan, it has to default on all of them.[6] Hence whenever a country has repayment problems, the number of banks which are affected is large. As with the interbank market, syndication tends, therefore, to increase interdependence within the system. Moreover, syndication reduces system risk only in so far as it reduces individual bank risk. It does not reduce concentration within the system to particular areas *per se*.

The second means of dealing with credit risk is through interest rate variation. Loans granted for more risky projects or to more risky borrowers carry a higher interest rate so that the expected return compensates the bank for the risk undertaken. The cost of a loan in the medium-term credit market is composed of several parts:

$$\text{cost of the loan} = \text{interest rate} + \text{spread} + \text{fees} \tag{9.1}$$

The interest rate is often LIBOR, the London Interbank Offered Rate quoted on Eurodollars. The fees largely cover administrative costs[7] and hence the spread can be taken as an indication of the return to the bank (see Gibson, 1989, Chapter 6).

It is interesting to examine what happened to spreads in the syndicated medium-term credit market in the period up to and after the debt crisis. Gibson (1989) examines movements in spreads for a number of country groups as well as individual countries for the period 1977 to 1986. The trend in quarterly average spreads for all countries (developing and industrial) is shown in Figure 9.6a and Figure 9.6b shows quarterly average maturities. Generally over the whole period, spreads fell, with the trend being most pronounced from 1977 until the middle of 1980. Spreads then stabilised around 0.8% until the end of 1982 when they increased sharply and were characterised by an increase in volatility. After 1984 the downward trend resumed. Movements in maturities tend to mirror those in spreads. Thus there was a large increase in maturities from 1977 to the beginning of 1980. Thereafter, maturities declined slightly.

---

[6] These are designed to prevent countries from practising favouritism, that is repaying some of their debts to certain banks but defaulting on others.

[7] If we take the interest rate in the Eurocurrency markets as determined exogenously by factors in the US, say, (for example US monetary policy as we argued in Chapter 7), then spreads and fees will be a good indicator of the bank's relative return on a syndicated loan. Spreads alone can be used as an indicator if falling spreads are not compensated for by rises in fees. Gibson (1989) finds little systematic relationship between spreads and fees either through time or cross-sectionally. She thus concludes that fees probably reflect administration costs. Hence spreads alone can be used as an indication of the return to the bank.

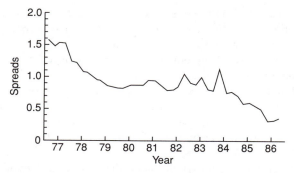

**Figure 9.6a.**   *All countries – quarterly average spreads, 1977–86*

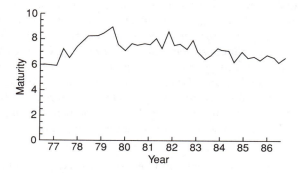

**Figure 9.6b.**   *All countries – quarterly average maturities, 1977–86*

These broad averages hide much variation in spreads between different groups of countries. In Figures 9.7–9.10 we plot the three-month moving average spreads from 1977 to 1986 for four country groupings: OECD major countries;[8] oil exporting developing countries; oil importing developing countries and the formerly centrally planned economies. Spreads for all four groups display the same general downward movement over the whole period. It is interesting that the OECD major countries experienced the same halt in the downward trend in mid-1980 along with the same volatility post-1982 that oil-importing and oil-exporting developing countries also experienced. This suggests that developments in certain segments of the market, namely the debt servicing problems of certain developing countries after 1982, affect not only other developing countries, but also the major industrial countries whose ability to service their debt was never in doubt.

A point illustrated in the graphs which is particularly interesting is that there is little evidence that banks increased spreads dramatically in anticipation of the debt crisis. For oil-exporting countries (Figure 9.8), spreads continued to fall right up until the middle of 1982. Yet many oil-exporting developing countries subsequently had repayment difficulties. For oil-importing developing countries, spreads did rise slightly after the second oil price shock in 1979, but by the end of 1981 they were falling again. Only well into 1982 did spreads begin to rise sharply. Overall, therefore

---

[8] OECD major countries are the group of five: US, UK, Japan, France and Germany.

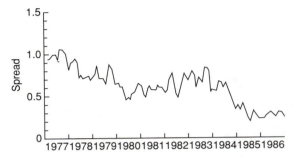

**Figure 9.7.** *OECD major countries – three-month moving average spreads*

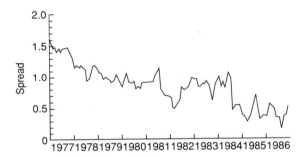

**Figure 9.8.** *Oil-exporting countries – three month moving average spreads*

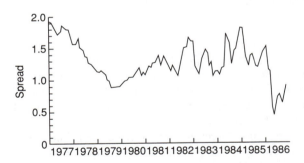

**Figure 9.9.** *Oil-importing countries – three month moving average spreads*

there is little evidence that the debt servicing problems which would subsequently arise were anticipated by banks by a tightening of spreads.

Figure 9.10 illustrates the situation in centrally planned economies. These countries have also had debt servicing problems since the 1980s.[9] Poland's debt servicing problems first became evident towards the latter half of 1980. As with oil-importing

[9] Cuba rescheduled in 1983 and 1984; Poland every year from 1981 to 1985; and Romania in 1982 and 1983.

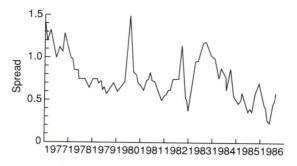

**Figure 9.10.**  *Centrally planned economies – three month moving average spreads*

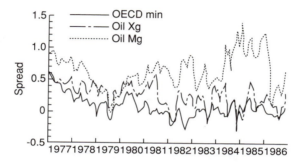

**Figure 9.11.**  *Deviations from prime risk (OECD major countries)*

*Note*: OECD min are OECD countries excluding the major 5; Oil Xg are oil-exporting developing countries; Oil Mg are oil-importing developing countries.

developing countries, there appears to have been little anticipation by the market of the Polish problems. Spreads were declining right up to the end of 1980.[10]

Our brief look at spreads suggests that the debt crisis of 1982 had a major impact on spreads. However, in the majority of cases, spreads did not anticipate the crisis. Only once the crisis occurred did spreads rise significantly and then the whole market was affected, including the major industrial countries. Figure 9.11 shows the deviations of each country group from the prime risk group (OECD major countries). One conclusion which can be drawn from this figure is that absolute risk differentials do not appear to operate in the market. Instead deviations from prime risk appear to be cyclical. In 1977, there was a clear hierarchy between the groups. Oil-importing developing countries paid the highest spreads, followed by oil exporting developing countries and the OECD minors. However, spreads by 1979 had converged on the prime risk group, before increasing towards the beginning of the debt crisis.

We argued in Chapter 8 that, in the presence of asymmetric information, banks would not simply use interest rates to control risk. In addition, they would also use

[10] It has to be noted that there are very few observations in each month and hence specific observations dominate. For example, the large spike in spreads in 1980 is entirely due to Poland. Other centrally planned economies were still able to get money at relatively low spreads if they came to the market.

credit rationing. Thus credit limits for particular borrowers are a third way which banks will seek to contain credit risk. We have argued that spreads did not appear to have been effective in ensuring that expected returns compensated borrowers for the risk undertaken. However, it might have been the case that banks reacted to their anticipation of the debt crisis by controlling the amount which they lent to individual countries. Some countries, which had previously had access to the international capital markets, were perhaps denied new funds. An interesting question, therefore, is whether credit limits were reached before the crisis occurred.

Evidence on whether credit rationing was effective is difficult to come by (Gibson, 1989). Banks do not reveal credit limits which are confidential. The only data which is available is *ex post* information on the extent of lending to individual countries. It is interesting to examine this data for, if credit limits were operational pre-1982, we would expect to see a decline in the actual volume of lending to countries most badly affected by debt servicing difficulties.

Table 9.4 shows the volume of new lending for various groups of countries as well as for some individual countries. Lending to countries which have subsequently experienced debt servicing difficulties appears to have continued right up until the first signs of trouble in 1982. This suggests that either country limits were continually being revised upwards or that they had not yet been reached. In either case, the figures suggest that banks were mistaken in their assessment of the risk involved.

It is notable that after 1982, the volume of new lending fell sharply.[11] Moreover, it fell not only to those countries which were initially experiencing difficulties, but to all countries. This suggests that banks reacted to the crisis by sharply cutting back on lending. Evidence from the group of socialist countries is particularly interesting here and serves to illustrate a wider point. The Polish crisis, as we have aleady noted, first became evident at the end of 1980. Lending fell sharply after 1981 to $3353 million in 1982 and $1046 million in 1983. But more importantly, this decrease in new money was not confined to those countries experiencing debt servicing difficulties. The only country in the group that continued to borrow normally after 1981 was the USSR and its borrowing was severely curtailed after 1982 when the general nature of the crisis became evident. This attitude of banks in cutting back lending to all countries which have been classified as part of a group can help to spread the crisis to other members of the group. Within the socialist countries, Hungary, for instance, was forced into debt servicing problems as a result of a decline in her ability to borrow because of the Polish crisis (Montagnon, 1983).

Thus credit rationing does not appear to have prevented the crisis. Instead new lending continued until the first signs of debt servicing difficulties appeared. Only after the crisis broke did rationing appear to become widespread. But, of course, by then rationing was the inappropriate response and official intervention sought to limit banks' freedom of action by forcing them to continue to lend to countries that had got into difficulties.

How can we account for the increased willingness of banks to take on greater risks towards the end of the 1970s? We argued in Chapter 8 that crises can develop in situations where information is scarce and costly to gather and where competition is intense. Both were features of the syndicated medium-term credit market in the later 1970s and early 1980s.

---

[11] We should note that this table includes new money negotiated along with rescheduling deals after 1982. Thus the table here overestimates the volume of voluntary new lending undertaken by banks after the crisis first broke. See Gibson (1989, Chapter 6) for a more detailed discussion of this issue.

*Table 9.4.*    Annual loan volumes ($ million, nominal amounts)

| | 1979 | 1980 | 1981 | 1982 | 1983 | 1984 | 1985 | 1986 |
|---|---|---|---|---|---|---|---|---|
| OECD | 34212 | 42789 | 111634 | 79497 | 61302 | 94076 | 177331 | 153485 |
| SOCIALIST | 8300 | 5006 | 4324 | 3353 | 1048 | 4849 | 4665 | 4758 |
| Poland | 901 | 1089 | 106 | 0 | 0 | 0 | 0 | 0 |
| Romania | 1100 | 458 | 337 | 0 | 0 | 0 | 150 | 0 |
| USSR | 1386 | 0 | 1147 | 2381 | 93 | 1048 | 1737 | 2071 |
| Hungary | 1047 | 550 | 573 | 458 | 647 | 1136 | 1234 | 1037 |
| GDR | 782 | 481 | 628 | 62 | 248 | 74 | 1100 | 1170 |
| Yugoslavia | 2291 | 1942 | 1522 | 439 | 2 | 82.7 | 48 | 32 |
| | | | | | | | | |
| OPEC | 13726 | 11228 | 14494 | 16448 | 8003 | 6652 | 4389 | 3350 |
| Algeria | 2164 | 300 | 500 | 507 | 1910 | 298 | 1271 | 1237 |
| Ecuador | 1054 | 1009 | 541 | 495 | 25 | 0 | 0 | 220 |
| Indonesia | 778 | 1152 | 1137 | 1686 | 2041 | 2467 | 457 | 1045 |
| Nigeria | 1972 | 768 | 3209 | 1495 | 978 | 0 | 0 | 0 |
| Venezuela | 6164 | 6903 | 6771 | 7852 | 146 | 0 | 352 | 110 |
| | | | | | | | | |
| LDC | 43873 | 28439 | 49347 | 42718 | 21100 | 17266 | 15167 | 10207 |
| Argentina | 2694 | 2307 | 3654 | 1398 | 250 | 0 | 0 | 85 |
| Bolivia | 47 | 0 | 424 | 7 | 0 | 0 | 0 | 0 |
| Brazil | 6883 | 5676 | 7060 | 6888 | 2010 | 3101 | 2689 | 228 |
| Chile | 666 | 885 | 2393 | 1258 | 107 | 0 | 0 | 37 |
| Colombia | 981 | 670 | 1181 | 629 | 519 | 480 | 1208 | 201 |
| Costa Rica | 272 | 168 | 0 | 0 | 0 | 0 | 0 | 0 |
| Cuba | 178 | 0 | 69 | 32 | 0 | 0 | 0 | 0 |
| Dom. Rep. | 195 | 220 | 76 | 0 | 0 | 0 | 0 | 0 |
| Honduras | 83 | 0 | 24 | 0 | 0 | 0 | 0 | 0 |
| Hong Kong | 1264 | 1736 | 3729 | 1674 | 1227 | 1195 | 1926 | 671 |
| Ivory Coast | 266 | 265 | 605 | 666 | 85 | 0 | 40 | 15 |
| Jamaica | 130 | 0 | 182 | 20 | 84 | 0 | 0 | 0 |
| Korea | 3246 | 2065 | 3979 | 4984 | 3848 | 3200 | 4243 | 1833 |
| Liberia | 105 | 0 | 27 | 30 | 44 | 14 | 16 | 0 |
| Malawi | 50 | 12 | 0 | 0 | 0 | 0 | 0 | 2 |
| Malaysia | 118 | 1050 | 1621 | 2261 | 1667 | 1416 | 45 | 1104 |
| Mexico | 10927 | 5332 | 13376 | 9905 | 4269 | 3975 | 634 | 0 |
| Morocco | 552 | 455 | 923 | 471 | 112 | 242 | 107 | 50 |
| Panama | 185 | 225 | 629 | 442 | 39 | 105 | 0 | 0 |
| Peru | 612 | 392 | 815 | 945 | 0 | 0 | 0 | 0 |
| Philippines | 1972 | 1321 | 1535 | 1398 | 905 | 188 | 40 | 0 |
| Senegal | 0 | 0 | 8 | 41 | 0 | 0 | 0 | 0 |
| Sudan | 0 | 0 | 30 | 62 | 0 | 0 | 0 | 0 |
| Uruguay | 67 | 116 | 216 | 220 | 0 | 0 | 0 | 0 |
| Zambia | 28 | 60 | 212 | 245 | 140 | 175 | 0 | 0 |
| | | | | | | | | |
| TOTAL (all countries) | 101651 | 88427 | 181088 | 148499 | 94214 | 122843 | 201552 | 171800 |

With respect to the availability of information, country risk assessment was notoriously poor during the early years of lending. Initially the argument was that country risk was relatively low risk because 'countries could not go bankrupt' as the Chairman of Citibank, Walter Wriston, argued. However, this rather missed the point: long before a country goes bankrupt it may, as a sovereign entity, decide to cease repayments on its debts. The problem facing lenders is how to recover their assets when this occurs. For this reason country risk analysis is an important investment which the lender should make.

However, systems of country risk analysis were poorly developed in the initial stages of lending. This lack of a systematic framework for analysis was reflected in headline banking (which can be regarded as a manifestation of herd behaviour). Banks often lent to countries who had discovered natural resources. By contrast, strikes and political or civil unrest would result in a country's risk rating being immediately downgraded. There was little analysis of how these events might affect individual countries.

During the second half of the 1970s, a literature began to emerge on country risk analysis.[12] Initially it was highly judgemental, with banks basing their decisions on a few socioeconomic indicators. These indicators were eventually to become important in the quantitative approach to risk rating. Here a checklist of ratios[13] would be combined to generate a weighted average score for each country. However, it is not clear that we can identify critical values for many of the ratios, which if passed indicate that lending should cease. Additionally, the weights assigned to each ratio are necessarily subjective. Attempts to identify the factors that explain rescheduling in a more systematic manner led to the development of the econometric approach to risk rating. This it typified by the early work of Frank and Cline (1971) and Feder and Just (1977). They use logit and probit analysis to try to identify the characteristics which are common to a group of rescheduling countries and which are not shared by countries with no debt servicing problems.

The problem with these more quantitative approaches is that not all variables which influence country risk are quantifiable. Examples include political and social factors which might be as important in determining a country's willingness to service its debt as economic factors. This led a number of banks at the end of the 1970s to employ political analysts to help in country risk assessment. A quantitative/qualitative approach became popular where quantitative analysis of economic factors was accompanied by qualitative analysis of political and social life within the country.

A basic problem with all these approaches is that they seek to predict a country's ability and willingness to repay its debt in the medium to long-term using indicators which apply to the present. Additionally, the subjective elements which are present in most of the methods usually implies that there is a lot of room for the calculated probabilities of debt servicing difficulty to change over time. In particular, if competition becomes more intense, a revision of the risk of lending to particular countries downwards could easily occur.

How can we account for the movement in spreads and the lack of systematic credit rationing before 1982? Information relevant to sovereign lending was far from perfect and it is clear from our above account of country risk analysis that banks were involved in a process of learning-by-doing. Nonetheless risk assessment methods did become more sophisticated as the 1970s progressed and this might have been expected to lead, at least in retrospect, to higher spreads and more restrictive credit limits.

How then can we explain the role of bank behaviour in causing the debt crisis? We

---

[12] See Ensor (1981) and Nagy (1984) for a survey of developments in country risk analysis.

[13] Examples include the debt-service ratio, the debt-GNP ratio, export product concentration, imports of nonessentials as a percentage of total imports etc.

argued in Chapter 8 that increased competition within international banking markets might make it difficult for banks to price loans in a way that reflects their risk. Increasing confidence tends to reduce the perceived riskiness of any loan. The Group of Thirty (1982a,b), in their survey of international bank opinions, confirms that banks were becoming increasingly confident about international lending. Moreover, this confidence was being vindicated by the fact that the profitability of foreign lending, at least until 1982, was greater than that on domestic lending. Thus any one bank which sought to increase the spread to a particular borrower would simply have found itself priced out of the market. Similarly with respect to credit limits, competition prevented credit rationing from limiting the risks taken on by international banks. In short, it appears that there is some evidence which supports our hypothesis of Chapter 8 that increased competition in the presence of information deficiencies can lead to a propensity to crisis.

**The role of the debtors**

Assessing the responsibility of the debtors in the build-up of debt which occurred is a difficult issue. Developing countries are a much less homogenous group than banks and hence it is difficult to say anything very useful without going into specific cases. The use to which the money borrowed was put is clearly of relevance for assessing developing countries' role. How exactly domestic policies and factors outside the control of the developing countries interacted is likely to be complex and requires detailed case studies of particular cases. Clearly it is beyond the scope of this book to do this here.[14]

What can we say, therefore, at a general level? Most commentators argue that debtor countries did attempt to use the borrowed money for investment projects.[15] Stewart and Sengupta (1982, p.13) note that those countries which had access to the international markets in the 1970s (mainly the middle income countries) experienced growth in per capita income of 3.1% compared with 3.6% in the 1960s. In lower income developing countries, where access to international capital markets was denied, per capita growth in the 1970s fell to 0.9% compared with 1.6% in the 1960s. Moreover for those countries which could borrow, domestic investment did by and large increase. Table 9.5 illustrates this for the case of Latin American countries. It indicates that both investment growth and export growth remained high throughout the 1970s. This is at least indicative of the fact that the borrowed money was not primarily squandered on consumption.

There are, of course, some notorious examples of countries where the money was squandered on luxury consumption by the elite ruling class or simply embezzled. Often-quoted examples include the Philippines under Marcos, Nicaragua under Somoza and Zaire under Mobutu. But such instances cannot explain the widespread nature of the debt crisis.

Here we can point to two problems which developing countries in general face and which have important implications for borrowing from international capital markets. The first relates to the relationship between borrowing and investment (Stewart and Sengupta, 1982). We have argued that the quantity of investment undertaken by developing countries was high during the 1970s. But this gives us little indication of the quality. Investment financed by borrowing can pose significant difficulties for

[14] For case studies of policies in individual developing countries, see Thorp and Whitehead (1987), Griffith-Jones and Sunkel (1986) and Williamson (1990).
[15] See, for example, Marcel and Palma (1987); Stewart and Sengupta (1982); Allsopp and Joshi (1986).

*Table 9.5.* Annual growth rates of economic aggregates (1970–81)

|  | 1970–75 | 1975–79 | 1979–81 |
|---|---|---|---|
| Gross Domestic Product | 6.4 | 5.5 | 3.6 |
| Government Consumption | 6.0 | 5.5 | 4.2 |
| Private Consumption | 9.3 | 5.9 | 3.1 |
| Gross Investment | 3.4 | 5.1 | 3.1 |
| Exports | 9.2 | 9.8 | 7.1 |
| Imports | 6.4 | 7.3 | 7.9 |

*Source*: Marcel and Palma (1987, p.5)

developing countries. Often projects involve investment in infrastructure. Such projects may have a high social return but may not generate enough revenue to allow repayments to be met smoothly. Tax collection in developing countries is notoriously difficult (because of low income, tax evasion and the existence of large informal sectors). This does not imply that investments with large social returns represent mistaken development policies. On the contrary, often such investments are necessary before further investment takes place. Rather it is simply difficult to use medium-term borrowing from private international banks to finance these projects. But the problem does not stop with simply collecting the returns from the project so that repayments can be made. Repayments have to be made in foreign currency. Thus ultimately investments undertaken have to yield greater export revenues. However, such investments might not be the ones which offer the best route for long-term development.

The second problem which developing countries faced in the 1970s and 1980s is that of capital flight.[16] This occurs where private citizens of a country export large amounts of their wealth either legally or illegally to private bank accounts abroad. Its causes are complex, but can include either short-term factors such as the expectation of devaluation or more long-term factors such as lack of political and economic stability in the home country. Allsopp and Joshi (1986, p.xix) provide some measurement of the volume of capital flight as a proportion of total inflows for several Latin American countries. These figures are given in Table 9.6. They have to be taken with a large pinch of salt since measurement of capital flight is notoriously difficult. What these figures suggest is that in the case of Argentina, for example, in 1981 and 1982 for every $1 that flowed into the country, $0.64 flowed back out to private bank accounts. Thus much of the debt accumulated in the later 1970s and early 1980s simply financed capital flight. The impact of capital flight is to reduce the availability of foreign exchange and this reduces the ability of a developing country to import goods required for either consumption or investment.

Studies of the causes of capital flight in developing countries (see Cuddington, 1986) point to a large role for an overvalued exchange rate. In so far as domestic policies enhanced overvaluation, so they contributed to the problem of capital flight. However, it is possible to implement policies which limit capital flight. The case of Brazil is particularly instructive. Table 9.6 suggests that capital flight was much less of a problem in Brazil than in the other countries cited. This was a consequence of

---

[16] See Lessard and Williamson (1987) for a review of the issues involved.

*Table 9.6.*  Capital flight as a percentage of inflows (1981–82)

| | |
|---|---|
| Argentina | 64% |
| Brazil | 8% |
| Mexico | 40% |
| Venezuela | 137% |

*Source*: Allsopp and Joshi (1986, p.xix)

the fact that Brazil had reasonably effective capital controls preventing capital outflows. Capital controls do not completely eliminate capital flight (some wealth-holders will still find it profitable to transfer their funds abroad), but they can significantly reduce it as the Brazilian case illustrates.

It is difficult to come to any conclusions regarding the responsibility developing countries must take for the debt crisis. In a few cases, the blame clearly lies with corrupt individuals. However, such a conclusion can hardly be generalised to account for the widespread nature of debt servicing problems which developing countries have faced since 1982. Here we have mentioned two factors, one of which (capital flight) might indicate some developing country responsibility for the debt crisis. The capital flight issue can, in part, be attributed to poor policy choices in developing countries. The second issue, that is the ability of the developing country to generate returns to repay the debt incurred, is a more tricky one to deal with. Recognition of this problem raises the question of the appropriateness of private commercial bank lending to finance development strategies whose gestation period is often long. This is an issue to which we return in the conclusions to this chapter.

*Exogenous shocks to the world economy*

A number of authors have investigated the role of exogenous shocks to the world economy in the early 1980s as a major cause of the debt crisis.[17] In particular, these factors are often considered to have triggered the crisis. As we argued in the introduction to this section, these exogenous shocks hit all developing countries alike and can therefore be considered to be the systematic risk associated with lending to developing countries.

Cline (1984) calculates the impact of the macroeconomic shocks on the external debt of non–oil developing countries. His results are shown in Table 9.7. The figures indicate the per annum increase in debt (for 1981 and 1982) resulting from each shock. Overall, the picture is one of developing countries being subject to large adverse external influences during 1981 and 1982.

The second oil price rise, as we saw earlier, caused developing countries to move further into deficit. Cline estimates that this added $37 billion to non–oil developing country debt in each of the years 1981 and 1982. The fall in the oil price in the mid-1980s clearly benefited these countries. However, oil-exporting countries also accumulated large amounts of debt, partly to enable the exploitation of their oil reserves. Oil price rises benefit them, but the oil price fall had the opposite effect.

The world recession from 1980 to 1982 caused both export volumes from developing countries to decline as well as export prices. Cline estimates that the combined effect of these factors on debt was around $50 billion per annum. Between 1971 and 1980 real export volumes of non–oil developing countries had grown at an average of

[17] See, for example, Cline (1984); and Gibson and Thirlwall (1989; 1993).

*Table 9.7.*    Exogenous shocks and their impact on developing country debt (1981 and 1982)

| Shock | Increase in Debt (per annum) |
| --- | --- |
| Oil price rise in 1979 (relative to 1978) | $37 billion |
| Real interest rate increase (the excess over the 1961–80 average) | $20 billion |
| Terms of trade loss | $40 billion |
| Export volume loss due to recession | $10 billion |

*Source*: Cline (1984)

8.1% in real terms per annum. In 1981 growth was still high at 9.9%. In 1982, however, export volumes increased only by 1.8%. Commodity export prices are also highly correlated with economic activity. The index of commodity prices fell from 100 in 1980 to 90 in 1982. The combination of both these factors led to a fall in export earnings and hence made debt servicing more difficult.

The final exogenous shock to the world economy was the rise in real interest rates in the US. During the 1970s, real interest rates were low if not negative. The average real dollar interest rate over the period 1971 to 1980 was −0.8%.[18] By the beginning of the 1980s, the combination of tight US monetary policy and a loose fiscal stance led to substantial rises in nominal interest rates. At the same time, inflation was falling. The result was a sharp increase in real interest rates to 7.2% in 1981 and 11% in 1982. As we have already noted, developing country commercial debt is floating rate debt. The interest payments vary in line with market interest rates. Thus the sharp rise in interest rates in the early 1980s increased developing countries' debt servicing obligations.

Gibson and Thirlwall (1989; 1993) examine the impact of these factors on the debt service ratios of developing countries.[19] The debt service ratio (DS) is given by:

$$DS = [(i + a)D] / P_x X \qquad (9.2)$$

where i is the rate of interest; a is the amortisation rate; D is the volume of debt; $P_x$ is the price of export; and X is the volume of exports. Taking discrete rates of change of equation (9.2) allows us to decompose the change in the debt service ratio into its various components:

$$dS/S = di/i(I/P) \pm da/a(A/P) + dD/D - dP_x/P_x - dX/X \pm \text{interaction term} \qquad (9.3)$$

where I/P is the share of interest payments in total debt service payments and A/P is the share of amortisation payments. Table 9.8 summarises some of their results by continent.

The results in Table 9.8 confirm Cline's findings that declining export earnings and rising interest rates worsened the position of developing countries in the period 1980–82. The results here are interesting in that they point to the wide variety of country experience within that overall conclusion. In Table 9.8 we provide the results by continent and some interesting differences show through. First, Latin and

[18]  This is calculated as LIBOR minus the change in the US wholesale price index.
[19]  The 1989 paper considers the contribution of changes in interest rates, amortisation rates, debt volume and export earnings to the change in the debt service ratio between 1980 and 1985. The 1993 paper conducts a similar analysis for the period 1986 to 1990 when debt service ratios actually fell.

Central America experienced the largest rise in the debt service ratio in the period 1980 to 1982. The decomposition suggests that the change in the debt service ratio was partly the result of rising interest rates and falling export earnings, but also a rising debt volume. By contrast, in the period 1982 to 1985, falling US interest rates benefited Latin and Central America since most of its debt is floating rate private debt.

The second factor which is illustrated in Table 9.8 is the small role that interest rates played in the change in the debt service ratio in African countries. This results from the fact that most debt to African countries is non-commercial and hence the impact of the interest rate rises in the early 1980s was least felt by them. By contrast, declining export revenues affected Africa in both periods. This reflects the dependence of African countries on primary commodities.

The final point we can make is that SE Asian countries were least affected by a fall in export earnings. This result, however, hides some variation between countries. Gibson and Thirlwall (1989, p.85) note that those countries with a larger proportion of primary commodity exports experienced a fall in export earnings, whereas those with a more diversified export base experienced a rise in export earnings.

In conclusion, there appears to be quite a bit of support for the idea that exogenous shocks triggered the debt crisis in the early 1980s. However, it is clear that these exogenous shocks were not the only factors contributing to the increased instability of international financial flows. The analysis conducted suggests that a debt crisis would have occurred at some point because the build-up of debt was clearly too much relative to what developing countries could successfully service. This conclusion is strengthened by the fact that the improvement in world economic conditions in the later 1980s did not appear to restore the ability of developing countries to service their debt. The debt crisis has proved to be rather more permanent than many commentators in the first half of the 1980s suggested.

*Table 9.8.* Decomposition of changes in the debt service ratio, 1980–82 and 1982–85 (measured in percentage points)

| | change in the debt service ratio | Effect of change in: | | | | interaction term |
|---|---|---|---|---|---|---|
| | | i | a | D | $P_xX$ | |
| Africa | | | | | | |
| 1980–82 | +3.9 | −0.2 | +0.1 | +2.0 | +2.3 | −0.3 |
| 1982–85 | +4.1 | −0.8 | +0.6 | +3.9 | +0.7 | −0.3 |
| Latin/Central America | | | | | | |
| 1980–82 | +8.8 | +1.1 | −3.0 | +8.3 | +2.6 | −0.2 |
| 1982–85 | −4.1 | −4.4 | −7.9 | +9.8 | −0.5 | −1.1 |
| SE Asia | | | | | | |
| 1980–82 | +3.9 | +0.3 | −0.7 | +4.3 | +0.0 | +0.0 |
| 1982–85 | +8.8 | −1.1 | +2.9 | +7.7 | −0.6 | −0.1 |

*Source*: Gibson and Thirlwall (1989, p.86)

## The management of the debt crisis

The exposure of banks to highly indebted countries (see the first section of this chapter) clearly signalled that the debt crisis could prove to be a threat to the stability of the international financial system. This signalled a dramatic turnaround in the approach to international financial flows, from the market-led approach adopted pre-1982 to the highly managed approach post-1982. In particular, industrial country governments and international institutions have controlled carefully flows to developing countries and have sought to reimpose conditions regarding the appropriate policies developing countries should adopt alongside the rescheduling agreements.

In this section we focus on the way the crisis has been managed. We examine the features of the case-by-case approach which has dominated the industrial countries' approach to the problem. We also look at the Baker and Brady proposals which can be seen as some recognition that the debt crisis is more permanent than was initially envisaged.

Milivojevic (1985) provides an in-depth study of debt rescheduling in the initial aftermath of the declaration by Mexico in 1982. He notes that there were several common features to all of the negotiations between countries who were experiencing debt servicing problems and international banks. First, a bridging loan was supplied by the US government and the Bank for International Settlements (BIS). They covered the period between the onset of debt servicing problems and the disbursement of new money by the IMF and commercial banks. Secondly, the IMF played a leading role through the agreement of adjustment programmes[20] for rescheduling countries and in providing financial support. Essentially the approach was one where IMF lending to developing countries was used as a signal by commercial banks to do likewise. This pivotal role for the IMF in rescheduling continues to this day: countries are usually unable to negotiate rescheduling agreements if an adjustment programme has not been agreed with the IMF.[21] Finally, rescheduling was costly. Indeed, banks made large fees from the process and any rescheduling deal usually involved an increase in the spread paid by the country concerned. For example, Mexico rescheduled in 1983 at 2.25% above LIBOR compared with a spread of 1.75% pre-1982. Brazil rescheduled at 2.5% above LIBOR whereas spreads of 1.5% had been common in the early 1980s.

Cline (1984) identifies a number of problems which this approach to debt rescheduling had to encounter. With respect to banks, they were forced into involuntary lending. After 1982 banks no longer wished to make any new loans to developing countries. However, they were compelled to supply new finance by the IMF which threatened not to provide finance or assistance if banks did not co-operate. For example, the package negotiated by Mexico in 1983 involved all banks increasing their exposure by 7%. The advantage of new lending is that it might reduce the risk of default. If banks did not inject new money into countries with debt servicing difficulties, then those countries would have a large incentive to default.

There is, however, an incentive for banks to free-ride. For any individual bank A, the first best outcome is for all other banks to increase their lending (thus reducing the default probability) and for bank A to keep its exposure constant. This problem is particularly acute in rescheduling debt to developing countries because the syndicated loan procedure implied the involvement of numerous small banks. The IMF

---

[20] We discuss these in some detail in the following chapter.
[21] An alternative is a structural adjustment programme overseen by the World Bank.

was again crucial here: it co-ordinated the rescue packages and eliminated free riding by coercing all banks to lend more.

From the point of view of developing countries, the rescheduling packages have involved severe adjustment (which we discuss in more detail later). In the short-run, at least, there was a strong incentive for debtors to default. At its best, crisis management has sought to reduce the incentive to default. To understand why crisis management has influenced the incentive to default, we have to examine the costs and benefits of default for a debtor. The benefits of default are easy to ascertain: the country no longer has to meet its interest and principal payments on its debt. The costs of default are more nebulous. They include lack of access to new finance from international capital markets, at least in the near future as well as a possible disruption to trade as banks refuse to finance trade with the defaulting country. Given the severe and costly adjustment packages which countries have undertaken to try to keep up with their debt servicing obligations, the benefits from defaulting have been high. It is in this light that we can interpret IMF attempts to ensure that banks continue to lend to rescheduling countries. This clearly helps to increase the costs to the debtor should default occur.

Attempts to manipulate the costs and benefits of default can also be seen in the Baker and Brady proposals. The Baker plan was launched by the US Secretary of State, James Baker, at the IMF–World Bank meeting in Seoul in October 1985. The plan was a tacit recognition that the approach adopted up until then had not provided much success: the debt problem was growing rather than improving. The aim of the plan was to increase the amount of lending to highly-indebted countries[22] as well as softening the terms on which rescheduling took place (that is, lengthening maturities and lowering spreads). Banks were to increase their lending by $20 billion over the three succeeding years. At the same time, multilateral institutions would increase their lending by some $10 billion dollars and encourage fiscal correction, trade liberalisation and privatisation in the 15 (and later 17) Baker countries (Cline, 1995). In doing so, it was hoped that the negative growth rates experienced by highly-indebted countries could be reversed. In terms of the costs and benefits of default, the clear aim was to increase the costs of defaulting.

Baker essentially saw the debt crisis as a problem of illiquidity associated with the downturn in the world economy. The new money was aimed at helping these countries through a difficult period and thus to prevent their default. Once world economic conditions improved, it was assumed that normal debt servicing would resume (indeed Cline's (1984) projections suggested just that).

The success of the Baker plan in persuading banks to lend new money to the 15 countries targeted was strictly limited. Gibson and Thirlwall (1993) show that the Baker countries did worse than the average of all developing countries in their ability to attract new money – banks were clearly unwilling to commit the amounts which Baker envisaged. Kenen (1990) also notes that the banks did not meet the Baker targets.[23] Even when a number of banks put aside large reserves to meet the possibility

---

[22] The highly-indebted countries were known as the Baker 15 and included Argentina, Bolivia, Brazil, Chile, Colombia, Cote d'Ivoire, Ecuador, Mexico, Morocco, Nigeria, Peru, The Philippines, Uruguay, Venezuela and Yugoslavia. Costa Rica and Jamaica were considered by the World Bank also to merit treatment under the Baker plan.

[23] Cline (1995, Chapter 5) is less pessimistic. He argues that the banks eventually committed some two-thirds of the original target. Multilateral institutions, by contrast, fell well short of their target with the absence of IMF agreements being a contributing factor to this shortfall.

of nonrepayment by the debtors and Baker again asked for new lending, the banks were reticent to become involved.[24]

The effect of debt management (or the 'muddling through' as Dornbusch (1984) described it) on the economies of developing countries during the 1980s was severe. The most direct effect was the large amount of resources which were transferred from developing to developed countries during the 1980s. Table 9.9 provides a conservative estimate of these transfers which is calculated by measuring total interest and principal repayments minus new debt inflows for any period.

These large transfers were achieved at the cost of very poor economic performance in developing countries during the 1980s. GNP fell in 1982 by 1% in sub-Saharan Africa and 3.5% in Latin America and the Caribbean. In 1983, the falls were 3.5% and 4.6% respectively. It has been estimated that for Latin America as a whole, real per capita expenditure fell by 16.8%. In the southern cone, the figures are 29.3% for Argentina, 30.6% for Uruguay and 20.2% for Chile.

These falls in national income and expenditure have been matched by increases in unemployment and reductions in real wages. In 1983, for example, real wages fell in Peru by 20% and in Mexico by 30%. Sachs (1990) argues that, by early 1989, Latin America was in a 'dire situation'. Peru was experiencing 'economic, political and social collapse' with annual inflation of around 30,000% per annum and real GNP falling by more than 10% per annum. Venezuela, after years of falling income, experienced rioting and deaths on the streets after the announcement of a new orthodox austerity programme. In Argentina, hyperinflation in Spring 1989 led to rioting and deaths. Brazil was heading towards hyperinflation and Mexico facing political uncertainty.

Equally worrying in terms of the future prospects for indebted countries are the large falls in investment which occurred in the 1980s. Table 9.10 indicates that investment declined most in Latin America and the Caribbean and sub-Saharan

*Table 9.9.* Negative net transfers (US$ billion)

|  | Developing Countries | Highly-indebted developing countries |
|---|---|---|
| 1982 | 17.80 | 3.85 |
| 1983 | 7.10 | −7.50 |
| 1984 | −7.30 | −17.50 |
| 1985 | −20.80 | −26.10 |
| 1986 | −30.70 | −24.90 |
| 1987 | −29.00 | −20.00 |
| 1988 | −40.98 | −20.94 |
| 1989 | −28.40 | −20.49 |
| 1990 | −12.72 | −3.98 |
| 1991 | −8.45 | −10.42 |
| 1992 | 13.06 | −15.75 |
| 1993 (projected) | 11.39 | −10.24 |

*Source*: World Bank, *World Debt Tables*, 1987–88 and 1993–94.

[24] Citibank, for example, put aside $3 billion as provisions against possible nonrepayment in 1987.

*Table 9.10.*    Investment in developing countries in the 1980s (%GNP)

|  | 1980 | 1981 | 1982 | 1983 | 1984 | 1985 | 1986 | 1987 |
|---|---|---|---|---|---|---|---|---|
| Sub-Saharan Africa | 20.4 | 20.8 | 18.3 | 14.6 | 11.4 | 12.2 | 14.3 | 16.1 |
| South Asia | 23.1 | 24.3 | 22.3 | 22.1 | 22.0 | 23.9 | 22.6 | 22.4 |
| East Asia | 30.1 | 29.4 | 28.9 | 29.3 | 29.3 | 30.8 | 29.7 | 29.7 |
| Latin America and the Caribbean | 24.4 | 23.6 | 21.4 | 16.8 | 16.7 | 17.5 | 17.4 | 18.2 |
| Highly indebted Countries | 25.3 | 24.8 | 22.3 | 17.8 | 16.6 | 17.6 | 18.6 | 19.4 |

*Source*: World Bank, *World Debt Tables* (1990).

Africa. By contrast, investment in South and East Asia, regions which have been far less affected by debt servicing problems, has held up to pre–debt crisis levels.

It can be argued that the basic problem with both the initial attempts at debt management and the subsequent Baker plan was their lack of recognition of the need to reduce the volume of debt in highly-indebted countries. By 1988, at the Group of Seven economic summit in Tokyo, industrial countries agreed to debt relief on the official debt of African (low-income) countries,[25] the argument being that debt levels were now so great that they were undermining attempts to restore growth. Middle-income debtors were not included in the benefits announced.

In March 1989, the idea of debt relief spread to the commercial debt of middle-income countries. Incoming US Treasury Secretary, Nicholas Brady, proposed a new debt programme. The programme was primarily an extension of the rather *ad hoc* agreements which had been emerging between debtors and the banks. These agreements followed a menu approach to debt reduction. For example, debt could be swapped for equity; it could be converted into bonds of lower value than the original debt; or it could simply be bought back in the secondary market at a discount.[26] The Brady initiative developed this menu approach but with the added incentive of US backing for the proposals. This was the first time debt reduction had received official backing and hence the Brady proposals can be seen as something of a turning point in the official treatment of the debt problem.

The World Bank notes that by the end of 1993, seven countries had successfully negotiated debt rescheduling agreements under the Brady Plan (World Bank, *World Debt Tables*, 1993–94). These were Mexico, The Philippines, Costa Rica, Venezuela, Uruguay, Nigeria and Argentina. Brazil was to conclude a deal in April 1994. At the same time, the International Development Association (IDA) of the World Bank adopted a similar menu-driven approach to commercial debt reduction, helping to

---

[25] Official debt is money owed to industrial countries. It has usually been lent on concessionary terms with low interest rates and long maturities. Most African debt to low-income countries is official debt because these countries were unable to gain access to the international capital markets.

[26] See Devlin (1990) for a discussion of the various approaches.

fund agreements in Niger, Mozambique, Guyana and Uganda.[27] Cline (1995) notes that the average amount of relief in these programmes is around 32% of the debt eligible for reduction (that is, private commercial bank debt). These are similar to the sorts of figures obtained by the World Bank.[28]

## Implications of the debt crisis for the international financial system

In any discussion of solutions to the debt crisis it is useful to think of solutions which deal with the existing volume of debt and those which represent long-term solutions to the problems of balance of payments imbalances and the need for development finance. We conclude this chapter by considering each of these in turn.

With respect to the existing debt, it is the so-called debt overhang which has more recently occupied writers on the debt crisis.[29] There are two approaches to arguing for debt relief. The first has been put forward by Krugman (1989a). He argues that the debt overhang reduces efficiency through two channels. First, debt service payments keep taxes high and hence discourage investment and a repatriation of capital flight. Secondly, debt service adds to government budget deficits and hence raises money supply growth and inflation. Debt reduction can therefore raise economic efficiency in developing countries and hence raise debtors' real income and reduce the probability of default.

An alternative viewpoint is put forward by Kenen (1990). He argues that the rationale for debt reduction can be better understood within the Eaton and Gersovitz (1981a,b) analysis which examines the costs and benefits of default. Debt reduction in this framework can be seen as tilting the balance of costs and benefits in such a way as to increase the willingness of countries to repay.

These two views are by no means incompatible. Krugman emphasises more the issue of the ability of developing countries to repay. Given our analysis in the previous section regarding the economic performance of major debtors in the 1980s, an increase in ability to repay can only be welcomed. Kenen, by contrast, views the problem as one of willingness to repay and debt reduction clearly reduces the benefits of default and hence makes continued debt servicing more likely. Both ability and willingness to repay are aspects which we noted are relevant for sovereign debt in Chapter 8.

Up until now, debt reduction has been voluntary, even with the implementation of the Brady plan. However, Sachs (1990) argues that voluntary debt reduction is not effective: it implies only a small reduction in debt and moreover it encourages free riding by banks. In addition, banks are often reluctant to grant too much relief for debtor countries for fear of setting a precedent. They do not want to encourage borrowers to assume that debt servicing difficulties will automatically lead to negotiations for debt reduction.

In order to understand the possible mechanics of debt reduction we discuss one particular proposal put forward by Kenen (1990). This scheme, like the Brady plan, makes use of the large discounts at which developing country debt is traded in the

---

[27] Those interested should consult the World Bank, *World Debt Tables*, which are published annually by the World Bank, for details regarding individual programmes. See also Cline (1995, Ch. 5) for a comprehensive survey of developments in the strategy of debt reduction.

[28] A large controversy reigns regarding the welfare value of such buybacks. Bulow and Rogoff (1988) argued that debt buybacks benefit only the creditors – debtor countries experience a net welfare loss. Others, such as Williamson (1988) have been critical. See Cline (1995) for a good survey.

[29] See, for example, Sachs (1990) and Kenen (1990). It should be noted, however, that some authors were arguing that debt volumes should be reduced in the mid-1980s. See, for example, Kenen (1983), Rohatyn (1983), Griffith-Jones (1986) and Guttentag and Herring (1985).

secondary market.[30] He argues that there are two possible means by which these discounts can be exploited. First, debtor countries could simply purchase the old debt at a discount with available resources. Buybacks for cash, however, are rare: highly-indebted countries simply do not have the resources to buy back debt using cash. Buybacks using debt–equity swaps also have their problems. Debtors are often highly ambivalent about foreign direct investment. Moreover, there is always the worry that developing countries are simply subsidising direct investment which would have occurred anyway.

These problems with the use of available resources leads Kenen to argue that a second method for exploiting discounts must be encouraged. This involves buying old debt by issuing new debt and is often referred to as defeasance. One advantage of this is that in issuing new debt, a greater variety of debt instruments can be used. A problem with the existing stock of debt which has been widely identified is that it all takes one form: medium-term syndicated loans (see Llewellyn, 1990a). The problem, however, with issuing new debt is that there is little guarantee that interest payments will be met on this debt given that they were not on the old debt.

For this reason, Kenen proposes that a new international organisation be set up whose role would be the guaranteeing of new debt using capital subscribed by its sponsors (the industrial countries). The International Debt Discount Corporation (IDDC), as Kenen calls it, would be entrusted with the task of buying up the old debt at a discount (negotiated with the banks). The bonds issued by the IDDC to finance these purchases would be long-term with an interest rate equal to the US government bond rate plus some spread. The bonds should be marketable and hence a secondary market in the new debt should be encouraged. In order to reduce the incentives for debtors to increase the discount they receive by following poor policies, the IDDC should agree the discount in advance and could perhaps offer higher discounts for countries pursuing 'tighter policy conditions'.

Neither banks nor debtors would be obliged to deal with the IDDC. However, in the case of banks, if they did decide to participate, then relief would have to be granted to all countries. Debtors would be required to have an IMF or World Bank programme in place before they would be allowed to participate.

At present participation by banks is voluntary, although governments and the IMF have been strongly encouraging banks to participate. Sponsoring governments could further seek to encourage participation by the banks by allowing them to amortise the losses made gradually. This need for industrial countries to change banking regulations in order to encourage banks to pursue policies of debt reduction is something which is discussed in some depth by Griffith-Jones (1989). She emphasises the need for tax deductibility of loan losses to be maintained only if banks actually participate in debt reduction. At present, loan losses are tax deductible in Europe whether the bank is participating in debt reduction or not. In the US loan loss provisions are not tax deductible.

Such changes could allow industrial countries to promote bank participation in

[30] A secondary market in debt grew up in the 1980s. However, as Guttentag and Herring (1985) have argued, this market is not like other secondary markets. Banks essentially sell subparticipations in loans to other banks at a discount. Often the borrower is unaware that the transaction has taken place. Moreover the legal status of these subparticipations is rather unclear since the original lender still retains the title on the loan. Guttentag and Herring argue for the need for an above board secondary market where quoted prices are published and transactions less opaque. See Cohen and Portes (1990) for an analysis of pricing in the market.

debt reduction schemes. This is important because of the potential free rider problem that these schemes face. Banks can gain if they do not participate but all other banks do: the reduced debt overhang will increase the probability of repayment for not only participating banks but also those which do not participate. Kenen suggests that nonparticipants be required to value their remaining debt at market value and be denied the ability to amortise their losses over a longer period. In this way the free rider problem is reduced.

Even if the problem of the current debt overhang is reduced significantly and developing countries economic performance improves, there is still the question of future flows of finance to developing countries. Some argue for the continued participation of banks in lending to developing countries (Guttentag and Herring, 1985; Llewellyn, 1990a). This also appears to be the view of the major international institutions and industrial country governments. Guttentag and Herring, for example, propose that banks should be forced to mark their external assets to market (that is, value them according to a market-determined price rather than the book value used presently). In this way, they argue, banks and borrowing countries will be constrained in their behaviour before any debt build-up becomes excessive. Such a view requires the encouragement of a secondary market in developing country debt. The problem is that this proposal assumes that markets are somehow less likely to generate crises than institutions such as banks. This may be too sanguine a view: markets can easily promote financial instability through their propensity for rational speculative bubbles (noted in Chapter 8).

Instead, our analysis suggests that development finance is perhaps not best provided primarily by the private sector. There are three possible reasons why banks are ill-suited to this task. First, developing countries require debt at much longer maturities than banks can safely offer. Unless banks are willing to enter into a long-term relationship with a country, staying with it through both good and bad times, then it is not surprising that debt servicing problems arise. History has taught us that the process of development is a long one, requiring capital inflows over a long period. However, where banks face pressure from shareholders to invest in the assets which maximise short-run returns, then such long-term relationships are difficult to establish.

Secondly, even in the competitive and easy lending conditions of the 1970s, there were only a small number of countries which were able to get access to bank finance, even if only for a short period. Hence to entrust development and balance of payments financing to banks simply deprives a large number of developing countries access to funds. It is notable that growth in Sub-Saharan African countries, whose access to funds was limited in the 1970s, was only 1.6% per annum (compared with growth rates of over 3% for Latin American countries). Hence, if the private international capital markets have a role to play, then it would only ever likely be a limited one. Intervention by official international institutions would still be required for investment in countries with no access to the international markets.

The final problem is that it is not clear that banks can adequately monitor the use to which loans are put. This seems evident from the debt crisis itself since in some cases, as we have already noted, funds borrowed were not used for investment, but rather consumed or even embezzled. Monitoring in general is, of course, costly. It requires time to be spent gathering information and, more specifically in the case of loans made in other countries, in learning about the country concerned. Moreover, for every bank to do this for all the countries to which they lend is surely an inefficient use of resources – information gathered could surely be shared. Again, therefore, we come back to the inevitable conclusion that some forms of international lending require a much greater degree of support from international institutions than has hitherto been seen if they are to be successful. Involvement of international institutions only during the crisis phase is not the optimum use of their resources.

For these reasons, a greater role for official institutions in the provision of development finance and in the organisation of recycling is required. As Allsopp and Joshi (1986, p.xxxii) have argued:

> . . . the experience of the 1970s and 1980s raises serious questions about the future of development finance. The fashion of laissez-faire in this area is relatively recent and contrasts with attitudes in the 1950s and 1960s. Many of the difficulties . . . provide a *prima facie* case for public intervention and control. Now that the problems are coming to be appreciated, attitudes to official lending also need to change. It seems inevitable that official flows of one kind or another will have to play a large role.
>
> (Allsopp and Joshi, 1986, p.xxxii)

But what form should these flows take and what role should international institutions play? We already have two major international institutions, the World Bank and the IMF, who undertake some lending. Is there therefore any need for change? To answer this question, we examine the role of the IMF in the following chapter.

## References

**Allsopp, C.J. and Joshi, V.** (1986) 'The assessment: the international debt crisis', *Oxford Review of Economic Policy*, 2: 1, i–xxxiii.

**Bird, G.** (1982) *The International Monetary System and Less Developing Countries.* Macmillan, London.

**Bulow, J. and Rogoff, K.** (1988) 'The buyback boondoggle', *Brookings Papers on Economic Activity*, 2: 675–92.

**Cline, W.R.** (1984) *International Debt: Systematic Risk and Policy Response.* Institute for International Economics, Washington, D.C.

**Cline, W.R.** (1995) *International Debt Reexamined.* Institute for International Economics, Washington, D.C.

**Cuddington, J.T.** (1986) 'Captain Flight', *Princeton Studies in International Finance*, 58.

**Devilin, R.** (1990) 'The menu approach', *Institute of Development Studies Bulletin*, 21: 2, 11–16.

**Eaton, J. and Gersovitz, M.** (1981a) 'Debt with potential repudiation: theoretical and empirical analysis', *Review of Economic Studies*, 48: 289–309.

**Eaton, J. and Gersovitz, M.** (1981b) 'Poor country borrowing in private financial markets and the repudiation issue', *Princeton Studies in International Finance*, 47, June.

**Ensor, R.** (1981) *Assessing Country Risk.* Euromoney Publications, London.

**Feder, G. and Just, R.E.** (1977) 'A study of debt servicing capacity applying logit analysis', *Journal of Development Economics*, 4: 25–38.

**Frank, C.R. and Cline, W.R.** (1971) 'Measurement of debt servicing capacity: an application of discriminant analysis', *Journal of International Economics*, 1: 327–44.

**Gibson, H.D.** (1989) *The Eurocurrency Markets, Domestic Financial Policy and International Instability.* Macmillan, London.

**Gibson, H.D. and Thirlwall A.P.** (1989) 'An international comparison of the causes of changes in the debt service ratio, 1980–85', *Banca Nazionale del Lavoro Quarterly Review*, 168, 73–95.

**Gibson, H.D. and Thirlwall, A.P.** (1993) 'An analysis of changes in the debt service ratio for 96 countries, 1986–90', *Banca Nazionale del Lavoro Quarterly Review*, 184, March, 31–47.

**Griffith-Jones, S.** (1986) 'Ways forward from the debt crisis', *Oxford Review of Economic Policy*, 2: 1, 39–61.

**Griffith-Jones, S.** (1989) 'European banking regulations and Third World debt: the technical, political and institutional issues', Institute of Development Studies, University of Sussex, Discussion Paper 271, December.

**Griffith-Jones, S. and Sunkel, O.** (1986) *Debt and Development Crisis in Latin America: the end of an illusion*. Clarendon Press, Oxford.

**Group of Thirty** (1982a) *How Bankers See World Financial Markets*, Group of Thirty, New York.

**Group of Thirty** (1982b) *Risk in International Bank Lending*. Group of Thirty, New York.

**Guttentag, J.M. and Herring, R.J.** (1985) *The Current Crisis in International Lending*. Studies in International Economics, Brookings Institution, Washington, D.C.

**Kenen, P.** (1983) 'Third world debt: sharing the burden', *New York Times*, 6 March.

**Kenen, P.** (1990) 'Organising debt relief: the need for a new institution', *Journal of Economic Perspectives*, 4: 1, 7–18.

**Krugman, P.R.** (1989a) 'Market-based debt reduction schemes', in J.A. Frenkel, M.P. Dooley and P. Wickham (eds) *Analytical Issues in Debt*. International Monetary Fund, Washington, D.C.

**Lessard, D.R. and Williamson, J.** (1987) *Capital Flight and Third World Debt*. Institute for International Economics, Washington, D.C.

**Llewellyn, D.R.** (1990a) 'The international capital transfer mechanism of the 1970s: a critique', in G. Bird (ed.) *The International Financial Regime*. Surrey University Press in association with Academic Press, London.

**Marcel, M. and Palma, G.** (1987) *The Debt Crisis, The Third World and British Banks*. Fabian Research Series, 350. The Fabian Society, London.

**Milivojevic, M.** (1985) *The Debt Rescheduling Process*. St Martin's Press, New York.

**Montagnon, P.** (1983) 'Eastern Europe: is it coming back to the market?', *The Banker*, October, 41–4.

**Nagy, P.J.** (1984) *Country Risk*. Euromoney Publications, London.

**Rohatyn, F.** (1983) 'A plan for stretching out global debt', *Business Week*, 28, February.

**Sachs, J.D.** (1990) 'A strategy for efficient debt reduction', *Journal of Economic Perspectives*, 4: 1, 19–29.

**Stanyer, P. and Whitley, J.** (1981) 'Financing world payments imbalances', *Bank of England Quarterly* Bulletin, 21: 2, June, 187–99.

**Stewart, F. and Sengupta, A.** (1982) *International Financial Cooperation: a framework for change*. Pinter, London.

**Thorpe, R. and Whitehead, L.** (eds) (1987) *Latin American Debt and the Adjustment Crisis*. Macmillan, London.

**Williamson, J.** (1988) *Voluntary Approaches to Debt Relief*. Institute for International Economics, Policy Analyses in International Economics, 25, Washington, D.C.

Williamson, J. (ed.) (1990) *Latin American Adjustment: how much has happened? Institute for International Economics*, Washington, D.C.

World Bank, *World Debt Tables*. Various years, World Bank, Washington, D.C.

# 10 THE IMF AND THE PROVISION OF FINANCE

The International Monetary Fund (IMF) was set up as part of the Bretton Woods agreement to deal not only with exchange rate arrangements in the world economy, but also to aid in the financing of balance of payments deficits. The imbalances which manifested themselves in the world economy following the first and second oil price shocks offered a role for the IMF in mediating these imbalances. However, as we have seen in the preceding chapters, balance of payments imbalances were financed during the 1970s and early 1980s by private international capital markets – the role of the IMF was limited, at least initially. Only after the emergence of the debt crisis did the IMF become prominent.

In Chapter 1 we noted that at the Bretton Woods conference there was a disagreement between Keynes (the UK representative) and White (the US representative). Keynes favoured a much wider role for the IMF in recycling finance from surplus to deficit countries. The US, who importantly was the major provider of funds to the IMF, disagreed, fearing that deficit countries would simply delay adjustment if finance were readily available. As a result, the IMF has rarely had enough funds of its own and has never had the right to raise funds compulsorily from surplus countries to enable it to act in the way that Keynes envisaged.

The size of the imbalances which emerged after the oil shocks was too large to allow the Fund to intermediate to any great extent. Instead, private finance was mobilised, as we have seen, to deal with the task. The IMF did not even play a role at this time in the distribution of private finance, preferring to leave the whole process to the banks. But this move towards private financing of imbalances had its drawbacks. In particular, we have argued that the tendency for banks to overlend to a selected group of countries without proper monitoring can be seen as a major factor in causing the debt crisis.

Following this experience with private international finance in the 1970s, it seems appropriate to examine what role a public international institution such as the IMF might take to alleviate the problems of private finance. In order to do this, we need to examine the role of the IMF at present in the World Economy. We focus here on its role in providing finance to developing countries, since this has formed a major part of its activities. By doing so, we hope to shed some light on any reforms which might be required to allow the IMF to assume a more active role in the international financial system.

The main thrust of the argument is two-fold. First, we suggest that the role of the IMF in the world economy in the 1980s and 1990s extends far beyond its provision of finance. With the emergence of the debt crisis and the need by the banks to enter into rescheduling agreements with debtor countries, the IMF took centre stage.

Banks, by and large, were unwilling to negotiate rescheduling agreements unless the country concerned had agreed a stabilisation programme with the IMF.[1]

Secondly, we argue that the IMF is in need of reform if it is to undertake seriously the important role of mediating between deficit and surplus countries. In investigating the role of the IMF in developing countries, we note that the relationship between these two parties has deteriorated substantially since the IMF first began to involve itself with issues relating to development in the 1960s. We suggest that not only is there a need for a change in the *modus operandi* of the IMF but that there is also a need for a change in the focus of the actual conditions usually entailed in an IMF stabilisation programme. In short, only through reform will the IMF become an attractive public institution mediating payments imbalances.

The chapter is organised as follows. In the first section, we outline the role of the IMF and describe the various facilities which exist for countries facing balance of payments problems. In the second section we go on to discuss the content of IMF stabilisation programmes, that is, the conditions attached to many of the loans granted by the IMF. The third section examines the rationale behind these conditions and investigates (as far as is possible) their impact on developing countries. A critique of the role of the IMF is offered in the fourth section. Finally, the fifth section concludes.

## The role of the IMF

The IMF has a number of facilities which members can draw on.[2] The amounts involved are directly related to the size of a members' quota (which, in turn, depends on the size of the country).[3] When a member borrows, it purchases foreign currencies from the IMF with its own currency. Repayment, where the member buys back its own currency with a foreign currency acceptable to the IMF, takes place at some agreed time in the future.

The basic facility offered by the IMF is the so-called General Resources Account. Access to the first tranche of this facility is usually fairly automatic. However, as members borrow progressively more and move into higher tranches, so the conditions attached to the loan increase. At the highest level, the IMF requires the country to sign a 'Letter of Intent' which outlines the stabilisation programme to be followed and the conditions to be met.

In addition to the General Resources Account, the IMF has introduced a number of special facilities. As Bird (1984b, p.146) notes, the creation of these facilities from the 1960s onwards marked a shift in the attitude of the IMF towards developing countries. Before the 1960s, the IMF had no specific focus on the problems of developing countries, although clearly developing countries benefited from the finance available through the IMF. This focus on developing countries can be contrasted strongly with the Fund's relationship with industrial countries – they rarely make

---

[1]  We should note here that banks would often accept a World Bank Structural Adjustment Programme as an alternative. The World Bank is the other main source of finance to developing countries. Its *raison d'être* in the past has been the promotion of development. In recent years, the kind of programmes designed by both institutions have been becoming more similar: the World Bank has moved from a provider of mainly project finance to agreeing major structural adjustment programmes (including liberalisation of markets, a reduction in the size of the state, etc.) with countries to whom it lends. Moreover, in practice, to qualify for a Structural Adjustment Loan, the World Bank requires that countries have an agreement with the IMF under the Extended Fund Facility (Killick *et al*, 1984).

[2]  See Bird (1982, Chapter 7; 1984b; 1985) for more detailed accounts of the facilities offered by the IMF. The IMF Annual Reports also offer a useful summary of new facilities and any changes in the way existing facilities operate.

[3]  See Chapter 1.

use of the facilities available and the IMF has little role to play in the kind of policies they pursue. In 1963 the Compensating Financing Facility was set up to help developing countries with the problem of export earnings instability. In 1969 the Buffer Stock Financing Facility was established to help countries to finance their contributions to international buffer-stock schemes, designed to help moderate price fluctuations of primary products. With the rise in oil prices in 1973–4, the Oil Facility and Subsidy Account was designed as a short-term facility (with a life of only two years) to help with the current account implications of the oil price rise.

The facilities focus mainly on the provision of short-term finance. In the 1970s and 1980s, the IMF established a number of facilities designed to provide medium-term assistance to developing countries. These include the Extended Fund Facility (1975), the Trust Fund (1976), the Structural Adjustment Fund (1986) and the Extended Structural Adjustment Fund (1988). Their aim is to promote more long-term, structural change in developing countries. All these facilities, with the exception of the Trust Fund,[4] carry the highest level of conditionality on any borrowing.

Figure 10.1 graphs the total amount of credit outstanding (and disbursed) by the IMF from 1963 to 1993. Credit to African countries and the Western Hemisphere (which includes Latin and Central America) is also illustrated.[5] The first striking feature shown in the figure is the rather insignificant amounts involved. At the peak of its lending in the mid 1980s the IMF had only around 37 billion SDRs (equivalent to 54 billion US dollars at 1994 exchange rates) compared to the total debt of developing countries of almost 1,000 billion US dollars in 1985. Thus, at least in terms of the

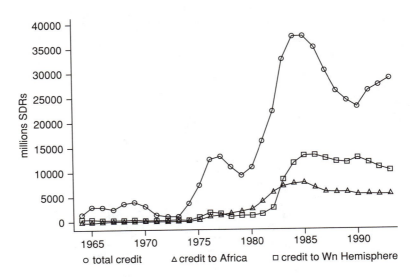

**Figure 10.1.** *IMF credit outstanding*

[4] The Trust Fund was set up with resources from gold sales by the IMF and is designed to make finance available to countries with the lowest *per capita* incomes. The finance is granted on concessional terms.
[5] The country groupings both in this figure and Figure 10.2 follow the IMF definitions (see any IMF publication for more details).

amounts involved, the IMF is a small lender to developing countries. The second feature of Figure 10.1 is the sharp increase in borrowing following the first oil price shock and more particularly the second oil price shock and the debt crisis. Finally, the figure indicates that lending to Latin and Central American states (Western Hemisphere) rose substantially only after 1982 when private capital markets were reluctant to lend further.

Figure 10.2 illustrates the net credit position (that is, lending minus repayments in any one year) of the IMF since 1980. Whereas Figure 10.1 paints a picture of the stock of borrowing from the IMF, Figure 10.2 gives us an indication of its role in the flow of funds in any given period. Thus the figure illustrates the large positive flow of funds to developing countries and Latin American countries after the second oil price shock and the start of the debt crisis. By contrast, the period since 1986 has been characterised by a number of years where the flow of funds has been negative (that is, countries were repaying more than they were borrowing).

These figures are clearly highly aggregative and do not give an indication of individual country experiences. Moreover, over the long-term we would expect net credit distributed by the IMF to be close to zero. This is true because the IMF's funds are supposed to be revolving in nature (that is, funds are borrowed, then repaid, then lent to another country), something which the IMF is continually stressing in its official pronouncements. However, the fact that, at a time of very poor economic performance in developing countries (a point we shall highlight later in this chapter), the IMF has been a *negative* net lender to significant groups of countries should cause some concern, not least because at the same time developing countries have had negative net credit from private borrowers.

Not surprisingly, given that the more a country borrows, the greater the conditions attached, the increasing use of IMF facilities has been accompanied by growing conditionality. In the late 1970s, borrowing which attracted high conditionality amounted to some 42.9% of total borrowing; by the early 1980s, this figure had

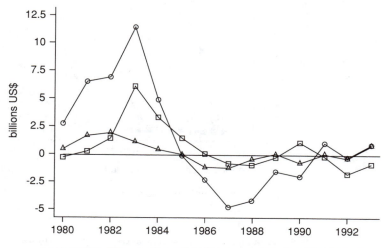

**Figure 10.2.**   *Net credit from IMF*

increased to 66.8%.[6] If we add to this the observation that rescheduling countries necessarily have an IMF programme in place, then it is clear that the role of the IMF in developing countries is higher nowadays than at any time in the past. However, its standing with developing countries might be said to be at an all-time low, with particular discontent over the kind of conditions it imposes on borrower or rescheduling countries. It is for this reason that we now examine in some detail the content of IMF stabilisation programmes.

**The content of IMF stabilisation programmes**

One problem associated with assessing the content of IMF stabilisation programmes is the confidentiality of the 'Letter of Intent' which describes the conditions attached to the loan. Moreover, not all the conditions which the IMF requires to be met are included in the 'Letter': in many cases, certain preconditions have to be met before the IMF will actually consider approving the programme itself. This makes it rather difficult for non-IMF researchers to identify accurately what exactly an IMF stabilisation programme is and they have to rely to a certain extent on IMF policy pronouncements as well as the incomplete accounts of any particular programme which might be made public.

One particularly good source of information on the conditions is provided by Killick (1984a). He makes substantial use of questionnaires which he sent out to IMF staff[7] and which relate to conditions imposed by the IMF in upper credit tranche programmes. The answers provided represent a very systematic account of IMF programmes and we draw on his work substantially in this section.

An important question which arises before discussing the actual content of IMF programmes is what the IMF considers to be their goals. According to the Articles of Agreement, a country has to show that it has a balance of payments problem before it can get access to finance from the IMF. Hence one of the main objectives of the IMF is a viable balance of payments. We should note that this need not imply that the current account need be in balance. The country could run a deficit on its current account provided that a sustainable inflow of funds can be attracted to finance it.

Whilst a viable balance of payments might be the ultimate goal of the IMF, often stabilisation programmes include targets for inflation and growth and there is some evidence that they are becoming more important. Killick (1984a, Statistical Appendix, Table B) notes, for example, that whereas only 20% of programmes had an inflation target over the period 1964–69, the figure rises to 30% between 1970 and 1973 and 70% between 1974 and 1979. Bradshaw and Wahl (1991) note the increased concern of the IMF with economic growth and the physical quality of life in recent years.

The causes of the balance of payments problems are clearly critical for understanding the type of policies followed by the IMF. Table 10.1 provides a summary of the results of Killick's questionnaires and illustrates several points. First it is clear that expansionary demand policies are seen as a major cause of balance of payments problems. Khan (1990, p.195) concurs, arguing that deficits are the result of

6  The figure of 42.9% is an average over the period 1976–79 and hides quite a large variance. The figure of 66.8% is the average over the period 1981–83. The figures are derived from IMF Annual Reports which list the amount disbursed under each facility.
7  Even with these questionnaires the IMF were keen to protect the confidentiality of their programmes. Killick (1984a, pp.183–4) notes, for example, that the exact wording of the questionnaire was chosen by the IMF itself. Every attempt was made to protect the identity of the countries concerned by allowing the IMF to choose a sample of countries in order to answer the questions posed.

*Table 10.1.*  The causes of balance of payments problems as identified by the IMF

|  | 1964–69 | 1970–73 | 1974–79 |
|---|---|---|---|
| 1. Expansionary demand policies | 7 | 7 | 6 |
| 2. Cost and price distortions |  |  |  |
| (a) related to the exchange rate | 4 | 2 | 5 |
| (b) other prices and wages | 2 | 3 | 9 |
| 3. Exogenous causes |  |  |  |
| (a) decline in export volumes | 2 | – | 2 |
| (b) deterioration in the terms of trade | 3 | 1 | 5 |
| (c) non-economic | 3 | 3 | 5 |
| 4. External debt servicing problems | 2 | 4 | 5 |

Note: the numbers refer to the number of programmes for which a particular policy was included. The maximum number of observations for each entry is 10.

*Source*: Killick, 1984a, Table 6.1

imbalances between aggregate demand and supply in the economy and 'often such imbalances can be traced to inappropriate policies that expand aggregate demand too rapidly relative to the growth of the productive capacity of the economy'.

The second factor which is clear from the table is the increased importance during the 1970s attached to price distortions in the economy. Balance of payments deficits might be associated with an overvalued real exchange rate resulting from a policy of fixing the nominal exchange rate whilst inflation is still high. In addition, other price and wage distortions are identified which refer usually to the structure of subsidies in the economy.

The final interesting conclusion which can be drawn is the fact that exogenous causes (that is causes beyond the control of the countries themselves) are thought to be of secondary importance. This tendency to identify domestic causes as the source of balance of payments problems not surprisingly impinges greatly on the kinds of policies which the IMF seek to suggest as part of their stabilisation programmes. However, as we noted in Chapter 9 when discussing the debt crisis, factors beyond the control of developing countries themselves can often impact hugely on their economic performance. In particular, developing countries appear to be highly sensitive to conditions in industrial countries with recessions in the latter causing declines in their terms of trade as well as a reduction in the demand for their exports.

IMF programmes themselves comprise a set of preconditions as well as various targets to be met and specific policies to be carried out. Preconditions are measures which have to be adopted before the agreement is approved by the IMF Executive and are not necessarily included as part of an IMF package. Killick (1984a) notes that the main preconditions found in IMF programmes include exchange rate devaluations, interest rate increases and changes to pricing policy more generally (the removal of subsidies, etc.).[8]

The targets to be met are known as the performance criteria and these determine a country's continued access to credit. The IMF disburses any agreed loan in various stages (only a certain proportion is released up front), and hence it is important for a

[8] We can note that devaluation rarely appears in the actual performance criteria (see later in text) in IMF programmes even although they are a policy most commonly associated with such programmes. This is because it is usually included as a precondition.

country to meet the performance criteria if the total loan is to be granted. Killick (1984a) finds that the most common criteria employed are credit ceilings with targets for a deceleration of credit expansion to both the public and private sector as well as in aggregate (total domestic credit). In addition, restrictions on the accumulation of external debt as well as balance of payments tests (usually expressed in terms of a minimum level of foreign exchange reserves) have become more frequent.

The remainder of the programme, on which continued access to finance does not depend, includes various and often wide-ranging policies designed to meet the targets set in the performance criteria. Killick's questionnaires reveal that there is usually a large fiscal content to programmes (changes to subsidies and taxes as well as reforms to the tax administration).[9] In addition, pricing policies of both state and private enterprises are often singled out for reform as is the efficiency of the administration of state-owned companies.

An interesting question is what exactly motivates countries to carry out the policies when they are not critical for the disbursement of further money. One easy answer to this question is that, whilst the policies are not compulsory, the IMF will not sign an agreement if it believes that they will not be carried out. Moreover, often these policies represent the only option for meeting the performance criteria. Thus, for example, if targets have to be met within a year on credit granted to the public sector, the only option available is to decrease government spending – increasing tax revenues through reform of the tax system usually take longer to realise.

In conclusion, therefore, IMF programmes place special emphasis not only on the achievement of a viable balance of payments, but also a reduction in inflation through the imposition of credit ceilings. Indeed, the prevalence of credit ceilings in most IMF programmes reflects the underlying belief of the IMF that balance of payments deficits in developing countries are largely the result of inappropriate aggregate demand policies. Moreover, Killick (1984a) notes that even where external causes are recognised as contributing significantly to the balance of payments problem, the IMF still imposes policies which have a deflationary impact on the economy. How exactly do the IMF account for such concentration of a specific group of policies? It is to this question and the rationale for IMF programmes in general to which we now turn.

## The rationale for IMF programmes

It could be argued from the description of the policies employed by the IMF that its general economic philosophy is monetarist in outlook and favours the freeing up of markets over state intervention. This is reflected in its concentration on controlling inflation by use of credit ceilings as well as by its broader policies on prices including the exchange rate and interest rates. The IMF is quick to reject this criticism arguing that its policies are flexible depending on the situation in any country and that they get on just as well with governments of more socialist leanings as they do with more right-wing ones. An examination of the rationales presented for the policies pursued provides, however, substantial support for the view that the IMF favours free-market monetarist economics. In support of this argument we look here at three main areas of policy: the relationship between credit ceilings and inflation; the role of devaluation; and the use of other pricing policies particularly interest rate liberalisation.

Inflation is seen by the IMF as an important impediment to growth in developing countries. This is based on simple correlation coefficients between growth and infla-

9  For a detailed account of the fiscal content of IMF programmes, see Beveridge and Kelly (1980).

tion which turn out to be negative.[10] The obvious weakness with such an approach is that correlation should not be taken as evidence of causality. Yet, as Killick and Sharpley (1984, p.45) suggest the IMF is sometimes guilty of exactly that. But there is a further problem with examining correlation coefficients which is that growth is clearly affected by factors other than the potential effect of inflation. Excluding these factors from any analysis of the relationship between growth and inflation could render the results invalid. In other words, a multivariate approach, where inflation is included as one of a number of possible influences on growth, should be preferred.

Nonetheless, in spite of the weak empirical evidence, there might be good theoretical reasons for supposing that inflation has a negative effect on growth. Higher inflation than that of trading partners may lead to falling competitiveness if the nominal exchange rate is fixed and hence output and growth might be affected. High inflation might also reduce savings and investment and hence affect growth. However, as Killick and Sharpley (1984, p.46) note, it could equally well be argued that higher growth causes lower inflation since higher growth expands the productive capacity of the economy and hence reduces bottlenecks which may be inflationary.

In addition to thinking that inflation is bad for economic growth, the IMF also appears to believe that inflation is largely the result of expansionary demand policies and that it can be controlled through the application of credit ceilings on the domestic component of the monetary base. Such a policy conclusion has its intellectual roots in the Polak model, a monetary model of the balance of payments, which is particularly relevant for an open developing country which fixes its nominal exchange rate (Polak, 1957).

Sharpley (1984) provides a very simple explanation of the Polak model.[11] Assume a constant velocity of money and that all domestic income is spent (that is, there is no hoarding). Under these conditions it will be true that income in period t, $Y_t$, can be written as:

$$Y_t = Y_{t-1} + X_t + F_t + \Delta DA_t - M_t \qquad (10.1)$$

where $Y_{t-1}$ is income last period; $X_t$ is exports; $F_t$ is net capital inflows; $\Delta DA_t$ is net domestic credit expansion; and $M_t$ is imports. In other words, this period's income is equal to last period's income plus injections (X, $\Delta DA$ and F) minus leakages (M).

If we rearrange equation (10.1) by taking $Y_{t-1}$ over to the left-hand side, then we derive the following:

$$Y_t - Y_{t-1} = \Delta Y_t = X_t + F_t + \Delta DA_t - M_t \qquad (10.2)$$

If we have a fixed exchange rate, then $(X_t + F_t - M_t)$ is equivalent to the change in international reserves (exports and net capital inflows increase reserves whereas imports reduce them). Hence the change in income can be rewritten as:

$$\Delta Y_t = \Delta FA_t + \Delta DA_t = \Delta MS_t \qquad (10.3)$$

where $\Delta FA_t$ is the change in international reserves and $\Delta MS_t$ is the change in the total money supply.[12]

---

[10] See IMF, *World Economic Outlook*, 1982.
[11] See also Ghatak (1981), Chapter 6.
[12] An alternative way of arriving at the fact that $\Delta Y_t = \Delta MS_t$ is from the quantity theory of money. $MV = Py = Y$ where M is the money supply, V is the velocity of circulation, P is the price level, y is real income and Y is nominal income. Taking changes on both sides of the quantity equation generates the following: $\Delta M + \Delta V = \Delta Y$. Since we are assuming that velocity is fixed here, $\Delta Y = \Delta M$ which is equation (10.3).

Assume now that the country has a current account deficit with $M_t > X_t$. This implies that $\Delta FAt < 0$ (for a given $F_t$). In other words, a deficit implies that foreign assets held by the central bank are declining. In the absence of sterilisation, this automatically leads to a decline in the money supply in total and hence a reduction is the excess demand which has caused the deficit. This is the familiar monetary theory of the balance of payments result that balance of payments deficits are self-correcting. Moreover the reduction in the rate of growth of the money supply causes inflation to fall.

How then can we explain the need for a ceiling on domestic credit expansion. If a ceiling is put on domestic credit expansion ($\Delta DA$), then the central bank cannot sterilise the impact of the fall in foreign exchange reserves on the monetary base by increasing the domestic component of the money supply. Hence the ceiling on domestic credit expansion ensures that the rate of growth of the money supply will fall.

Whilst this explains the rationale for domestic credit ceilings, it does not explicitly indicate why it might be desirable within that to have a limit on the fiscal deficit (or credit expansion to the public sector). To understand this we have to note that in developing countries markets in government bonds are frequently underdeveloped. Hence fiscal deficits are often financed by the seigniorage the government derives from printing money. Thus the fiscal deficit can impinge on the domestic credit expansion target and hence fiscal deficit reduction is often desirable.

Devaluation does not fit easily with the monetary approach to the balance of payments, since if the balance of payments automatically adjusts then devaluation is superfluous. The IMF argue that devaluation is appropriate in order to try to boost the traded goods sector. In many developing countries the real exchange rate is overvalued as a result of a fixed nominal exchange rate and higher inflation than trading partners. This acts as a tax on the export- and import-competing sectors. Devaluation under these circumstances could be beneficial. A further rationale for devaluation is given by Johnson and Salop (1980). They argue that if inflation and the current account deficit are being brought under control through demand reduction, then sticky wages and prices may lead to a deterioration in output and employment. Under such conditions, devaluation changes relative prices in favour of the country and hence moderates the deflationary effects of demand reduction.

A final policy involved in IMF programmes, that has become particularly popular over the 1980s, is that of financial liberalisation and in particular allowing the interest rate to settle at a level that will clear the market for savings and investment.[13] Such a strategy is seen as crucial for promoting growth. The rationale for financial liberalisation stems from the work of McKinnon (1973) and Shaw (1973).[14] They argued that economic growth was being hampered by low nominal interest rates in developing countries with the consequence that real interest rates were often negative. As a result savings are low and hence investment is credit-rationed. By contrast, a policy of raising real interest rates would enhance savings and hence lead to higher investment and growth.

[13] Policies such as financial liberalisation and devaluation can be seen as part of pricing policy in general. The approach of the IMF in this area is to persuade governments to allow more prices to be determined by the market. In this section we focus on the rationale for allowing the interest rate and the exchange rate to be market-determined since they happen to be two critical prices in any economy.
[14] See Gibson and Tsakalotos (1994) for a survey of the extensive literature in this area.

The argument is illustrated in Figure 10.3. II is the investment schedule which varies negatively with the rate of interest. $S(g_1)$ is the savings schedule associated with the initial growth rate $g_1$. It varies positively with the interest rate. Assume initially that the interest rate is fixed at $r_1$. Although investment demand in the economy is given by $r_1B$, only $r_1A$ amount of savings are forthcoming because of the low interest rates. Investment is thus credit rationed by an amount AB. Allowing interest rates to rise will encourage greater savings, and thus allow some of the unsatisfied investment demand to be met. This, in turn, raises growth and shifts the savings function further to the right, allowing even more investment. Finally the economy settles at the new equilibrium E which is characterised by a higher level of savings, investment and hence growth.

Thus, in conclusion, the rationale for the type of policies pursued by the IMF can certainly be said to be closely linked to monetarist ideas and a preference for the free operation of markets. The IMF would strongly resist such a classification pointing in their defence to instances of policy which do not fit easily with the monetarist approach (devaluation might be seen as one). However, whilst it is certainly the case that often programmes contain policies other than ones motivated by the monetarist or free market tradition, it is clear from our discussion of the rationale of IMF policies that they lie nearer that tradition than any other.

## A critique of the IMF approach

The criticisms of the IMF's approach to stabilisation have been numerous[15] and, moreover, have been directed at all aspects of IMF intervention. In this section we want to review these criticisms and at the same time to discuss the effects of IMF programmes. Can stabilisation as offered by the IMF promote the desired changes in economic performance in developing countries? Given the breadth of material we

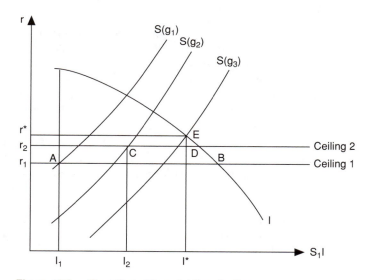

**Figure 10.3.**    *The effect of financial liberalisation*

---

[15] See, for example, Killick (1984a, b), Spraos (1984), Stewart and Sengupta (1982), Brett (1985) and Körner *et al.* (1984) to name but a few.

plan to cover in this section, it will facilitate the discussion greatly if it is organised under the following headings:

(i)   the rationale for conditionality of any kind;
(ii)  the total volume of resources available and the balance between high and low conditionality;
(iii) the burden of adjustment;
(iv)  the objectives of the IMF;
(v)   the hypothesised cause of balance of payments problems;
(vi)  the content of stabilisation programmes;
(vii) the effects of stabilisation programmes.

*The rationale for conditionality of any kind*

It can be argued that conditionality represents an infringement of sovereignty and, moreover, that it is impossible for conditionality to be politically neutral. Such arguments perhaps suggest that the problem lies with conditionality itself. However, there is little support in the literature for the view that conditions should not be attached to loans granted by international institutions. Loans are after all designed to be repaid at some time, allowing the resources then to be used to make new loans to other countries in need. In addition, the IMF would not act as a catalyst for funds from other sources (e.g. commercial banks) were not conditions of some kind adopted. Hence some monitoring is desirable. As Brett (1985, p.265) argues, when discussing the rationale for an increase in the amount of resources available to institutions such as the IMF:

> The demand for an increase in 'financing' cannot therefore be for entirely unconditional flows, since, in a world still characterised by unacceptable levels of scarcity and want, those who provide them are bound to wish to satisfy themselves that they are going to be put to positive use. Thus, what is at issue is not the problem of policy conditionality *per se*, but of the particular forms it should take.
>
> (Brett, 1985, p.265)

One important reform to make conditionality more acceptable and to deal at least partly with the infringement of sovereignty implied by an IMF stabilisation programme would be a change in the voting structure of the IMF. In particular, allowing developing countries more of a say on the policy stance of the IMF may help to make conditionality more acceptable to them.

The power structure of the IMF at present is determined by the quota system, that is, the contribution which each member makes to the IMF's resources. This structure reflects the political balance of power at the end of World War II (as we noted in Chapter 1), with the US having just under 20% of the total vote and the other nine countries in the Group of Ten having 35%. Any major policy changes can thus be vetoed by the US since they require at least 85% of votes to be in favour.[16]

The result of this domination by the US has resulted in increasing hostility towards the IMF from developing countries. They argue that they have no effective voice in decision-making within the IMF. This hostility has been reflected in a

---

[16] A good example of this domination by the IMF is given in Killick (1984a) where he catalogues the change in the IMF's approach to conditionality at the end of the 1970s. Killick argues that the change at the end of the 1970s was a move away from traditional demand management to more emphasis being given to the productive structure of the economy. The election of the Reagan Administration in November 1980 caused this policy change to be abruptly halted, albeit with a time lag, in 1982.

reluctance on the part of developing countries to use the IMF except under dire circumstance. Thus for example the low level of usage illustrated in Figure 10.1 in the 1970s reflects the fact that only countries without access to the international capital markets used the IMF (see also Stewart and Sengupta, 1982, p.119). An increase in the representation of developing countries is required if such feelings are to be overcome. Stability can only be achieved when those involved feel that they have a say in the decision-making process.

Thus whilst the issue of conditionality *per se* is rarely in question, the way in which important policy decisions within the IMF are taken would benefit from reform which would allow developing countries a greater say in the kind of conditions which should be attached to IMF loans. Only in this way could the IMF perhaps take on the role of helping countries before their situation become desperate: in other words, it could assume an important function in preventing crises from occurring rather than simply dealing with them once they have become evident.

## The total volume of resources available and the balance between high and low conditionality

The real value of resources available to the IMF has dramatically declined in real terms since the Bretton Woods settlement. Although quotas have been periodically increased, they have not succeeded in keeping in line with inflation. We can look at the importance of quotas relative to imports since they represent one measure of the size of international trade and hence the potential for balance of payments problems. In 1948 quotas averaged about 16% of total imports; by 1980, it was only 3%. This decline in resources available is compounded by the fact that average imbalances increased in the 1970s and 1980s compared to the period of the 1950s and 1960s (something we noted in Chapter 9).

The shortage of resources overall is linked to the rise in the proportion of high conditionality loans which are granted (we noted this fact earlier in the chapter, see also Helleiner, 1992). Were more resources to be made available, then the proportion of loans made with low or zero conditionality would also rise since the intensity of conditionality is related to the amount borrowed relative to a country's quota.

In addition extra resources might also allow the IMF more room to extend the time period over which loans are granted and also to write off or reduce the arrears which have accumulated on loans from the IMF to very low income countries. Helleiner (1992), for example argues that gold reserves of the IMF could be sold to finance an increase in the resources available, given the reluctance of industrial countries to increase their quotas.

## The burden of adjustment

In Chapter 1 we noted that under the Bretton Woods system, the burden of adjustment to balance of payments imbalances was supposed to be equally shared between deficit and surplus countries alike. The IMF, as the overseer of this system, was entrusted with the charge of ensuring this was so. However, as we saw in Chapter 1, such symmetry in adjustment responsibility was not forthcoming in practice. The scarce currency clause, one of the means by which symmetry would be enforced, was never invoked. As a result, the process of adjustment became compulsory for the deficit (debtor) country and voluntary for the surplus (creditor) country.

The question of symmetry has also arisen in connection with IMF adjustment programmes. It can be argued that a country could be experiencing a deficit on its balance of payments not as a result of excess demand at home, but rather because of a structural surplus abroad. Why in this case should the deficit country be the one to be forced to adjust via an IMF stabilisation programme? Demand reduction may reduce the deficit and hence also the surplus, but at the cost of a deflationary effect on the world economy.

Thus it is often argued that the IMF should seek to impose conditions on surplus countries not only on those with deficits. However, this has never occurred. Perhaps this can be explained by the fact that countries with structural surpluses tend to be strong as a result of the market domination of their producers. This position of strength allows them to block any change in such a direction (Bird, 1984b; Brett, 1985).

*The objectives of the IMF*

There is some debate in the literature on the extent to which the IMF see the balance of payments as a target. Killick *et al.* (1984) argue that the balance of payments is often the overriding target of the IMF, to the detriment of other objectives which individual governments may legitimately have. However, as we saw above, the IMF tends to base its assessment of whether or not to grant additional credit on the basis of whether credit ceilings are met. This leads Spraos (1984) to argue that this emphasis on credit ceilings is misplaced because it confuses targets and instruments.

The target, Spraos argues, should be a viable balance of payments. The instruments include a variety of policies of which credit controls may be appropriate if the cause of the deficit is demand inflation. The advantage of such an approach, as seen by Spraos, is that if the IMF merely sets a balance of payments target, the country could use whatever policies it wished to bring about that target. In this way, political neutrality would be easier to achieve.

Such an argument is highly appealing given the nature of the criticism which has been levelled at the IMF. However, on closer inspection, it might not be quite so neutral as first appears. A number of points can be made. First, how much should the current account deficit target be? In other words, how do we calculate a viable balance of payments target for developing countries? Should private capital flows be included even although they can often be withdrawn very quickly, something which was very clear during the Mexican crisis of 1994–5. Moreover, at present, developing countries need to run a surplus on their current account in order to finance the net repayment of debt accumulated in the 1970s and early 1980s. Would this be considered an appropriate target?

The second point which can be made relates to the nature of policies which would be considered capable of meeting the balance of payments target. Given the timescale and the amount of resources available to the IMF, often the only way of meeting a balance of payments target is through demand deflation. Demand deflation operates far more speedily on an economy than alternative supply-side structural reforms. Hence it may not just be a matter of setting a balance of payments target and letting developing countries meet it in whatever way they wish, reform of other areas might also be necessary if developing countries are to have a policy choice.

Killick *et al.* (1986) stress a different solution to the problem of objectives. They argue that there should be less emphasis on quantitative targets and more emphasis by the IMF on achieving a policy consensus in any particular country. That is, it should aim to get general agreement on what kind of policies might be appropriate. Such an approach has also been proposed by Körner *et al.* (1984) who argue that there is a need for public debate on IMF conditions within each country before agreement is reached. In this way the programme has a greater chance of success, since those groups that may bear the immediate costs of the programme will at least feel that their sacrifice has been recognised and moreover that they have participated in the process of programme formulation.[17]

**The hypothesised cause of balance of payments problems**

The IMF argues that the cause of the balance of payments deficit is not important. Rather the question is one of whether the deficit is temporary or permanent. If it is temporary, then it can be financed; if permanent, then adjustment is required. This view reflects the revolving nature of IMF funds as well as the tendency for the Articles of the IMF to emphasis that their role is to finance temporary balance of payments deficits.

Such a stance is, however, completely unrealistic. This is true for the very simple reason that programme design reflects causes. In other words, the kinds of policies that are proposed in the programme must inevitably be linked to what the IMF believes to be the causes of the problem. As we have already noted, it is clear from both the stabilisation programmes themselves and also from the answers by IMF staff to Killick's (1984) questionnaires that domestic policies within developing countries themselves are the most commonly identified cause – monetary and fiscal mismanagement. Hence there is a concentration in IMF programmes on demand deflation and on the relation between the fiscal deficit, monetary mismanagement and general price distortions which prevent free markets from working.

The structuralist school, however, would emphasise rather different causes of developing country deficits.[18] They argue that developing country deficits are a structural problem associated with development. They traditionally export primary commodities with low price and income elasticities of demand. At the same time, their imports include goods with low price elasticities of demand but often high income elasticities (including, for example, capital goods, fuel, etc.). Under these circumstances, it is unlikely that growth will be accompanied by balance on the current account.

Exogenous factors are also emphasised by the structuralist school, including the long-term deteriorating terms of trade for primary commodities as well as export earnings instability. Such exogenous falls in export earnings and the associated balance of payments deficit are associated with monetary imbalance as the monetary approach suggests. From the national accounts it is true by definition that a fall in income below absorption will be associated with an excess supply of money. However, the monetary imbalance is not the *cause* of the deficit but rather the *consequence* of the exogenous shock.

If the causes originate more on the supply-side rather than demand mismanagement by the domestic authorities, then IMF programmes would have to be somewhat differently designed and the timescale extended. The IMF might argue that more recently it has recognised that some developing countries require structural change and a longer time period in which to do it. That is precisely what the

[17] Such an approach relies to a great extent on the nature of democratic discourse in developing countries. However, there is evidence from industrial countries that such a consensual approach to decision-making in the face of the need for adjustment to external conditions is well worth the effort. Industrial countries with a greater degree of consensus adjusted more easily (in terms of inflation, unemployment, investment, growth etc.) to the oil price shocks than those with more confrontational modes of policy-making (see Henley and Tsakalotos, 1991; 1993).

[18] On the structuralist school and their critique of orthodox IMF stabilisation programmes, see Taylor (1988) and the references to WIDER research contained therein. See also Bird (1984a) on other causes of balance of payments problems.

IMF's Extended Fund Facility and then subsequently the Structural Adjustment Fund/Extended Structural Adjustment Fund were set out to facilitate. However, the policies which accompany conditionality on these programmes, namely the freeing of markets, are hardly what structuralists, who in their writings would emphasise market failures, would consider desirable.

*The content of stabilisation programmes*

As we have indicated, there is a broad range of policies which appear in stabilisation programmes. In addition to devaluation and credit controls (which appears in almost all programmes), there are a variety of measures which often seek to allow markets to operate more freely and reduce the role of the state. A comprehensive evaluation of all the policies which the IMF have used is clearly well beyond the scope of one chapter, requiring as it would, at the very least, a whole book. Hence here we want to focus on three particular policies which as we have shown are common to all IMF programmes: credit controls and their link with inflation; devaluation; and, as a representative policy from the vast array of market liberalisation measures, financial liberalisation.

As we have seen, the rationale for credit ceilings is based on the Polak model – a monetary model of the relationship between credit and the balance of payments. However, one of its weaknesses is the strong set of assumptions on which it is based. The monetary approach assumes, for example, that the demand for money is stable (the inverse of the assumption of constant velocity) and that the supply of money is controllable. In countries where inflation is high and variable, the demand for money is often unstable as agents economise on currency holdings (by far the largest part of the money supply) in periods of high inflation. Control over the supply of money is notoriously difficult in practice in most developed economies.[19] In developing countries it can be even more difficult for a number of reasons (Ghatak, 1981, pp.111–13). First, there is a large non-monetised sector in developing countries on which monetary control has no impact. Secondly, the narrowness of financial markets implies that the traditional monetary transmission mechanism does not operate. Central Banks cannot simply control domestic credit by influencing short-term interest rates and then allowing substitution effects to raise long-term rates.[20] A common short-term interest rate which Central Banks control is that on short-term government bonds (the interest rate on these is determined by the Central Bank by its influence over the price at which government bonds are sold). The lack of a well-developed market in government securities in developing countries can make this method of monetary control rather difficult.

A second criticism of the Polak model is that it ignores any impact of domestic credit ceilings on the rate of growth of output and unemployment. Implicitly underlying the interpretation put on it by the IMF is the view that money is neutral. Reducing the rate of growth of the money supply (or domestic credit) only affects inflation – output remains at its natural rate. In a world where output does not

---

[19] See, for example, Dow and Saville (1990) who provide an extensive discussion on the practical aspects of controlling the money supply in the UK.

[20] The method through which this operates is as follows. If the Central Bank increases short-term interest rates, then this initially creates a differential between short-term rates and long-term rates. Bond holders shift funds to short-term instruments and sell long-term ones. The act of selling long-term bonds reduces their price and so increases their interest rate. In this way long-term interest rates are raised and the rate of growth of domestic credit slowed.

remain at its 'natural rate', the economic costs of a sharp deflation can be quite severe (Killick, 1984b, p.218)

A final point about the use of credit controls relates to their relationship with inflation. For the IMF, inflation is a monetary phenomenon and can be controlled in developing countries by slowing the growth of domestic credit. However, the structuralist school would strongly refute this. Taylor (1988) argues that inflation in developing countries is a consequence of distributional conflict between wage earners and the owners of capital. Conflict can lead to 'excess' wage demands as workers seek to protect or raise their real standard of living. Increases in wages feed directly into prices, either because employers seek to protect their mark-up in the face of rising wages or because there is wage indexation, something which becomes engrained into the system either automatically or by governmental law.

If inflation is the result of such structural factors in developing countries, then controlling domestic credit will only affect inflation through its effect on the level of unemployment. Higher unemployment associated with disinflation reduces workers' bargaining strength and hence can help to moderate wage demands. However, this is hardly a long-term nor efficient solution to inflation.

We now turn to the role of devaluation in IMF programmes. Devaluation is intended to make imports more expensive (in domestic currency) and exports cheaper (in foreign currency). As a result the increase in competitiveness improves the trade balance, that is, the deficit is reduced. In addition, there may be output benefits which counter the contractionary effects of domestic credit restraint.

The simplest critique that has been made of this approach is that the price elasticities of demand for imports and exports are not sufficiently large to ensure that devaluation improves the current account. In other words, the Marshall–Lerner condition is not met. Bird (1984a), for example, notes that most developing countries export commodities for which there is a world price (set, for instance, in US dollars). Devaluation does nothing to affect this world price and hence devaluation will simply increase the profitability of exporting in domestic currency. Even if the domestic price of imports rises following devaluation, demand will not fall if these imports are necessary and there exist no domestic substitutes. Thus there may be good reasons for thinking that devaluation will not improve the current account in developing countries.

A second criticism of devaluation is that it can be inflationary. Devaluation increases the price level in the economy directly by its impact on the domestic price of imports. But it also has an indirect effect by increasing the cost of imported inputs. If firms have mark-up rules, this will soon be passed on to consumers in terms of higher prices for domestically-produced goods. If workers then resist the cut in real wages implied, a new round of inflationary wage claims will be forthcoming which will transmit themselves through the economy via the propagation mechanism already outlined. Hence devaluation is likely to make inflation targets more difficult to achieve, thus necessitating even tighter monetary targets with their consequent economic cost in terms of output and employment.

A final side-effect of the devaluation which is of particular importance at the present time is its impact on the domestic currency value of foreign debt. If a firm has acquired foreign currency liabilities, then a devaluation will increase their domestic currency value. This can lead to large deteriorations in firms' balance sheets and eventually possible bankruptcy (Taylor, 1988, pp.35–6). The recessionary impact of this can be quite large and can only be forestalled by the state bailing these companies out. But that, in turn, makes it more difficult for the government to meet the ceilings on credit expansion to the public sector.

Thus whilst an overvalued exchange rate can be damaging for a country and essentially act as a tax on exports (by making them more expensive), a policy of devaluation can have severe short-term costs and can jeopardise the ability of the country to meet the performance criteria laid down by the IMF.

The final IMF policy which we want to examine is that of financial liberalisation, one example from the more extensive programme of market liberalisation found particularly in the conditions attached to IMF longer-term loans. The advantage of financial liberalisation being conducted at the same time as macroeconomic stabilisation is that the output effects of deflationary monetary policy may be offset by the expansionary effects of financial liberalisation which we have already outlined (Kapur, 1976; Mathieson, 1979; 1980).

However, just as there is a vast literature devoted to the benefits of financial liberalisation, so there has been much written about its limitations. In particular, it is argued that the financial liberalisation literature overlooks the problems of severe market failures which are a common feature of credit markets. Thus credit rationing will exist even in liberalised credit markets because of problems of asymmetric information – the borrower always knows more about the project than the lender (Stiglitz and Weiss, 1981).[21] This can lead to sectors or groups in the economy being starved of finance because banks cannot distinguish within the sector/group between good and bad borrowers. In the past, this has been the rationale for government intervention in the form of directed credit. Such policies were successfully adopted in Japan (just after World War II) and more recently by countries such as South Korea (Gibson and Tsakalotos, 1994). In other words, certain interventions in credit markets can be seen as a response to market failure, rather than an example of financial repression.

More catastrophic, at least in the short run, is the potential for increased fragility of the financial system following liberalisation. In Chapter 8, we developed a model in which bank crises arose under conditions of intensified competition combined with the market failures which affect credit markets. Such a model explains quite well the experience of financial liberalisation in a number of developing, particularly Latin American, countries. For example, Chile began its process of liberalisation in the mid-1970s. By 1976–7 a serious financial crisis emerged as a result of the failure of a large bank. Liberalisation continued after this hiccup but crisis returned in 1981–2[22] when a number of large banks again got into difficulty following repayment difficulties of a number of large conglomerates.

What can we conclude therefore about the contents of IMF programmes? Our discussion here has been rather brief since the scope of IMF policies is rather wide to cover adequately. However, the discussion is intended to give readers a flavour of the vast array of criticisms which have been levelled at IMF programmes. It is certainly true that the type of stabilisation programme undertaken by the IMF tends to rely on a large number of assumptions which seem dubious. There are thus good theoretical reasons for rejecting this type of conditionality and for suggesting alternatives.

---

[21]  See Chapter 8 for a discussion of credit rationing under asymmetric information.
[22]  See Diaz–Alejandro (1985) on the rather similar liberalisation experiences of Chile, Argentina and Uruguay.

*The effects of stabilisation programmes*

Until now we have been discussing the impact of IMF stabilisation programmes without much reference to any studies investigating their actual effect on developing countries. Yet a most obvious way to test the ideas behind the programmes as well as the criticisms of them is to examine the impact of the programmes themselves and determine whether or not this might shed some light on the debate over IMF conditionality. There have been a number of studies in this area[23] and we examine their findings here.

The main difficulty with an assessment of any programme is the definition of the counterfactual. In other words, with what do we compare the actual performance of the economy? The most satisfying from a theoretical point of view would be if we could compare the performance of the economy having undertaken the programme with what would have happened had it not undertaken it. Clearly, however, this is impossible in practice since the latter is never observed. Khan (1990) offers a useful summary of the various approaches which have been used in the literature and assesses their advantages and disadvantages. There are four possible methods.

First, there is the 'before and after' approach which examines what happens during and after the programme in comparison with what went before. The obvious problem with this approach is that it is not only the IMF programme which characterises the second period but not the first. The economic environment in which the country operates will also have altered from one period to the next. Thus it is difficult to isolate the impact of IMF alone.

A second approach is the 'with–without' method. Here a group of countries who are not undergoing a stabilisation programme are used as a control group. These countries are similar to those being studied who have a stabilisation programme and, in this way, external conditions are controlled for. Before and after changes are then compared in both the control group and the Fund programme group. The problem with this approach is that there is a sample selection bias: countries with IMF programmes are inevitably doing much more poorly than those without the programme. Hence their performance would be expected to be weaker than that of the control group. Furthermore, although we control for external conditions using this method, we cannot control for factors internal to different countries which might affect their ability to deal with external shocks (for example, the structure of labour markets, financial markets, etc.).

Thirdly, there is the 'actual versus targets' approach which compares the actual performance of the country with the IMF targets. This method of evaluation has the disadvantage that it could induce the IMF to set a country easy targets so that in evaluations it appeared to be doing a good job. Clearly, however, the evaluator is interested in whether the stabilisation programme has actually done some good rather than just whether certain targets have been met. Moreover, restricting the study to examine only those factors which were targeted clearly prevents the evaluator from examining the performance of other economic variables which might just as legitimately have been targets. In view of the disagreements over what exactly the IMF should target, this seems a particularly important point.

The final method is the 'simulation' approach where IMF policies are simulated and compared with other policies. Small econometric models are estimated over a

[23] See, for example, Killick (1984b); Khan (1990); Johnson and Salop (1980); Faini and de Melo (1990); Bradshaw and Wahl (1991); and the WIDER (World Institute for Development Economics Research) country studies which are summarised in Taylor (1988).

sample of countries and then, using the coefficients obtained, different policies are simulated. A problem with such an approach is that different macroeconometric models can give different results (even when estimated for the same country) depending on their structure and the theory that underlies their structure.[24]

Killick (1984b) notes a second general methodological difficulty with any evaluation of an IMF programme and that is the time element. Over what time period should the programme be evaluated? Most studies examine their impact within a one to three year period from the inception of the programme. In this way, the evaluation follows what is expected of IMF programmes (given their timescale), namely a very quick turnaround in the performance of the economy. However, if one believes that IMF programmes may have a degree of short-term success with respect to the immediate variables of interest, yet they do little to solve the balance of payments problem over the longer term, then such a short time horizon might be inappropriate.

What can we conclude therefore with respect to the methodology used in evaluating IMF programmes. It is clear that none of the four approaches discussed is without its problems. As a result, we were probably too optimistic when we suggested that empirical studies might allow us to decide between the competing points of view regarding the suitability of IMF programmes. It is likely that each of the methods will shed light on some aspect of evaluating the stabilisation programme. What is important is that researchers are aware of these problems when assessing their results.

Bearing these points in mind, we can now turn to examine some of the studies which have sought to evaluate IMF programmes. In doing so we begin first with the impact of the programmes on some immediate variables of interest: inflation, the current account, the government deficit etc., before going on to examine some of the studies which have taken a longer-term perspective by examining the impact on investment, growth, income distribution and so on.

Let us examine first the record with respect to the balance of payments. The most up-beat results are found by Donovan (1981; 1982) who uses the 'with–without' approach to assess programmes over the period 1970–80. He finds evidence that export growth and balance of payments performance was better in IMF countries compared to the control group. Other studies show a less favourable outcome. Reichmann and Stillson (1978), using the 'before–after' approach, find little evidence of any change in the balance of payments when examining some 79 programmes over the period 1963–79. The same is also true for Killick (1984b) and Connors (1979). Khan (1990) investigates a more recent period (1973–88) and uses both the 'before–after' and the 'with–without' approaches. The results of each approach are similar: although the balance of payments improves in IMF countries the improvement is not statistically significant.

A second important policy target in IMF programmes is inflation. Again Donovan (1981; 1982) derives the only results which support IMF programmes. He finds that the increase in inflation is less in countries which had a programme than it was in the control group. Reichmann and Stillson (1978), Connors (1979) and Khan (1990) find little differences in either pre- and post-IMF performance or between the

[24] For example, if one looks at macroeconomic models in the UK, then one can get a variety of simulated outcomes from the same policy depending on which model is chosen. This results from the hypothesised linkages within each model which are usually closely related to a particular view of the economy. Thus Patrick Minford's new classical model of the UK economy will give rather different results from the more Keynesian model at National Institute of Economic and Social Research.

performance of IMF countries and the control group. Killick (1984) finds that whilst inflation falls in the first year of the programme's inception, it accelerates in the second year. Taylor (1988) quotes some results on inflation from the various country studies carried out by WIDER (World Institute for Development Economics Research) which suggest that only in a few cases was inflation reduced by an IMF programme (Ghana, The Philippines and India). By contrast a failure to cut inflation occurred in most Latin American countries, South Korea and Tanzania despite fiscal deficits being reduced.

A target often included by the IMF relates to a country's fiscal position and the growth of domestic credit to the public sector. Killick (1984) uses the 'actual versus target' approach and finds that on the whole targets were missed in programmes occurring over the period 1978–80. A failure to cut or slow public sector access to credit was particularly evident in Extended Fund Facility programmes.

Finally, we can examine the results with respect to growth during the operation of any IMF programme. The results here are very similar. Reichmann and Stillson (1978), Connors (1979), Killick (1984), Taylor (1988) and Donovan (1981; 1982) all find that IMF countries have a poorer or similar growth performance (either relative to what they had before; or relative to other countries). However, none of these results are statistically significant (where significance tests were carried out). Taylor (1988) interestingly contrasts the medium-term growth record of countries who had undertaken IMF programmes with South Korea and Brazil who had used more expansionary policies (in particular, higher public investment, export subsidies, easier credit and so on). These results suggest that the latter group of countries had much better medium-term growth rates than did the countries which had undertaken IMF stabilisation programmes. Bradshaw and Wahl (1991) also provide support for this view: they use a panel of countries over the period 1975 to 1987 and find that IMF programmes (indicated by a dummy variable) have a strongly negative effect on growth.

Thus, overall and irrespective of which methodology is used, the overwhelming conclusion is that IMF programmes make little significant difference to the balance of payments overall, the current account, inflation and the fiscal position. With respect to growth there is some evidence that IMF programmes will generate poorer results for a country over the medium-term. It is perhaps interesting to ask why Donovan's (1981; 1982) results seem to provide consistently greater support for some positive effect from IMF programmes. This result is somewhat misleading as he does not apply any significance tests, whereas the other authors surveyed are careful to do so.

The impact of IMF programmes has so far concentrated on those factors which the IMF itself would consider important, at least as indicated in their programme targets. It is also interesting, however, to ask what effects IMF programmes have, if any, on other economic indicators. Faini and de Mello (1990) examine the impact of IMF programmes on investment in developing countries over the 1980s. They explicitly seek to test for a positive production effect from devaluation. Recall that the usual argument put forward by the IMF is that devaluation will induce a shift in relative prices, make resource allocation more efficient over the medium-term and hence be beneficial for growth. By contrast, structuralists often argue that devaluation could well be contractionary. This result can come through a number of routes: higher import costs for capital goods could choke off investment; a higher price level reduces the real volume of credit in the economy and hence could raise interest rates;

or if devaluation results in an income redistribution from lower to higher incomes, then the propensity of save will rise reducing aggregate demand.[25] To adjudicate between these two competing hypothesis they estimate a supply equation using an unbalanced panel of countries over the period 1965–85.[26] Their results indicate a significant and negative effect from real depreciation on output. This output effect, not surprisingly, negatively affects investment. In addition, devaluation (through an increase in the cost of capital) and increased uncertainty (as captured by the debt service ratio) also have a negative effect on capital accumulation. They argue that these results do not bode well for growth in the future, in particular since the decline in investment does not seem to have been offset by any rise in its efficiency.

A criticism often levelled at the IMF is that their programmes worsen income distribution in developing countries, in particular because it is often the lower income groups which bear the brunt of the programmes.[27] Killick (1984) quotes evidence from Argentina, Brazil, Chile and Uruguay which shows that stabilisation programmes lead to large declines in real wages and a sharp rise in unemployment. What data is available on income distribution suggests that during the stabilisation periods there was an increasing concentration of income. However, further research in this area is severely hampered by a lack of data, particularly over longer periods so that trends can be identified.

What can we conclude therefore about the success of IMF stabilisation programmes? There is little evidence which suggests that they achieve their goals of improving the balance of payments, increasing growth and reducing inflation. Moreover, over the longer run there is evidence that growth and living standards might actually be harmed. Such a conclusion is supported to a great degree by the fact that it is the same countries which consistently return to the IMF for support. Thus at the very least the Fund appears to be failing in its duties to help countries in balance of payments difficulties.

It is rather difficult to draw any strong conclusions with respect to the causes of this failure. Failure could result from poor policies, lack of implementation or even the problems of evaluating the programmes precisely (Killick, 1984, pp.250–64). Killick concludes that there is little evidence that failure results from lack of implementation. Instead he points to problems arising from a lack of developing country government commitment to IMF stabilisation programmes as well as weaknesses in the programme design. This latter point is perhaps not surprising in view of the theoretical criticisms of the IMF's approach which we have already outlined.

**Conclusion**

We began this chapter by noting that the IMF provides little finance itself relative to other sources such as the international capital markets. However, we noted that the adoption of a programme has become increasingly significant in the 1980s as a catalyst for negotiating rescheduling agreements and perhaps also receiving new money flows from the international markets.

However, the IMF has come under severe criticism for the kind of policies which are included in its stabilisation programmes. We have provided some support in this

25  This latter effect may arise because lower income groups are less able to protect themselves from the real income implications of devaluation.
26  An unbalanced panel is one where the number of years for each country differs. In this case, a minimum of 4 years of data was required before a country was included.
27  See Johnson and Salop (1980) for a review of the likely distributional implications of IMF programmes.

chapter for the view that the IMF adopts a rather monetarist view of the way in which economies operate and favours a less interventionist approach to development in general. As such its programmes emphasis the role of excess demand in causing balance of payments problems and prescribe a reduction of inflation and a liberalisation of markets as a means of restoring growth. There is little doubt that many areas of developing countries require reform: financial markets are often poorly developed, weak fiscal systems make the provision of collective goods very difficult and the state sector is often grossly inefficient. However, as we indicated by examining the case of financial markets, liberalisation is not necessarily the only answer – building strong and appropriate institutions to deal with markets failures is also important. Reform, by all means, is necessary and indeed we did not doubt the need for conditionality *per se*. It is the nature of the reform which is in question.

Authors with a variety of opinions[28] believe that a lasting solution to the recurrent balance of payments crisis and poor growth performance of developing countries requires a greater emphasis to be given to supply-side factors rather than simply demand deflation. Indeed, even the IMF with its longer-term funds directed at supply-side reform seems to concur. However, the important question which arises is what kind of supply-side reforms. Liberalisation is unlikely to provide the answer. Instead, a much greater degree of attention should be paid to the construction of new and reform of existing institutions in developing countries.

But it is perhaps not only developing country institutions which are in need of reform. We argued in this chapter that the IMF itself might benefit from some institutional reform itself, particularly in the area of the voting system and the dominance of the US. This theme of the reform of institutions both at country level and at international level is one to which we return in the concluding chapter.

## References

**Beveridge, W.A. and Kelly, M.R.** (1980) 'Fiscal content of financial programs supported by stand-by arrangements in the upper credit tranches, 1969–78', *IMF Staff Papers*, 27: 205–249.

**Bird, G.** (1984a) 'Balance of payments policy', in T. Killick, (ed.) *The Quest for Economic Stabilisation: The IMF and the Third World*. Overseas Development Institute, Gower, Aldershot.

**Bird, G.** (1985) *World Finance and Adjustment*. Macmillan, London.

**Bradshaw, Y.W. and Wahl, A.** (1991) 'Foreign debt expansion, the international monetary fund, and regional variation in third world poverty', *International Studies Quarterly*, 35: 251–272.

**Brett, E.A.** (1985) *The World Economy since the War: the politics of uneven development*. Macmillan, London.

**Connors, T.A.** (1979) 'The apparent effects of recent IMF stabilisation programs', International Finance Discussion Paper, 135, Board of Governors of the Federal Reserve System, Washington, D.C.

**Diaz-Alejandro, C.F.** (1985) 'Good-bye financial repression: hello financial crash', *Journal of Development of Economics*, 19: 1–2, 1–24.

**Donovan, D.J.** (1981) 'Real responses associated with exchange rate action in

---

[28] See, for example, Killick *et al.* (1984) and Taylor (1988). Taylor is much more critical of the IMF than Killick *et al.*, yet both argue that there is a case for reform of IMF programmes along the lines of increasing the time element and also placing a greater emphasis on the supply-side.

selected upper credit tranche stabilisation programs', *IMF Staff Papers*, 28, December, 698–727.

Donovan, D.J. (1982) 'Macroeconomic performance and adjustment under Fund-supported programs: the experience of the 1970s', *IMF Staff Papers*, 29, June, 171–2–3.

Dow, J.C.R. and Saville, I.D. (1990) *A Critique of Monetary Policy: theory and the British Experience*. Oxford University Press, Oxford.

Faini, R. and De Melo, J. (1990) 'LDC adjustment packages', *Economic Policy*, October, 491–519.

Ghatak, S. (1981) *Monetary Economics in Developing Countries*. Macmillan, London.

Gibson, H.D. and Tsakalotos, E. (1994) 'The scope and limits of financial liberalisation in developing countries', *Journal of Development Studies*, 30: 3, 578–628.

Helleiner, G.K. (1992) 'The IMF, the World Bank and Africa's adjustment and external debt problems: an unofficial view', *World Development*, 20: 6, 779–92.

Henley, A. and Tsakalotos, E. (1991) 'Corporatism, profit squeeze and investment', *Cambridge Journal of Economics*, 15:4.

Henley, A. and Tsakalotos, E. (1993) *Corporatism and Economic Performance*. Edward Elgar, Aldershot.

IMF (1982) *World Economic Outlook*. International Monetary Fund. Washington, D.C.

Johnson, O. and Salop, J. (1980) 'Distributional aspects of stabilisation programs in developing countries', *IMF Staff Papers*, 27, 1–23.

Kapur, B.K. (1976) 'Alternative stabilisation policies for less-developed economies', *Journal of Political Economy*, 84: 4i, 777–95.

Khan, M.S. (1990) 'The macroeconomic effects of fund supported adjustment programs', *IMF Staff Papers*, 37: 2, 195–231.

Killick, T. (1984) *The Quest for Economic Stabilisation: the IMF and the Third World*. Overseas Development Institute, Gower, Aldershot.

Killick, T. (1984a) 'IMF stabilisation programmes', in T. Killick (ed.) (1984) 183–226.

Killick, T. (1984b) 'The impact of fund stabilisation programmes', in T. Killick (ed.) (1984) 227–269.

Killick, T. and Sharpley, J. (1984) 'Extent, cause and consequences of disequilibria', in T. Killick (ed.) (1984) 15–54.

Killick, T., Bird, G., Sharpley, J. and Sutton, M. (1954) 'Towards a real economy approach', in T. Killick (ed.) (1984) 270–320.

Korner, P., Maass, G., Siebold, T. and Tetzlaff, R. (1986) *The IMF and the Debt Crisis*. English translation by P. Knight, Third World Books, London.

Mathieson, D.J. (1979) 'Financial reform and capital flows in a developing economy', *IMF Staff Papers*, September, 450–89.

Mathieson, D.J. (1980) 'Financial reform and stabilisation policy in a developing economy', *Journal of Development Economics*, 7: 3, 359–95.

McKinnon, R.I. (1973) *Money and Capital in Economic Development*. The Brookings Institution, Washington, D.C.

Polak, J.J. (1957) 'Monetary analysis of income formation and payments problems', *IMF Staff Papers*, November.

Reichman, T.M. and Stillson, R.T. (1978) 'Experience with programs of balance of payments adjustment: standy-by arrangements in the higher credit tranches', *IMF Staff Papers*, 25, June, 293–309.

Sharpley, J. (1984) 'The potential of domestic stabilisation measures', in T. Killick (ed.) (1984) 55–85.

Shaw, E.S. (1973) *Financial Deepening in Economic Activity*. Oxford University Press, New York.

Spraos, J. (1984) 'IMF conditionality: a better way', *Banca Nazionale del Lavoro Quarterly Review*, 151, December, 411–21.

Stewart, F. and Sengupta, A. (1982) *International Finance Cooperation: a framework for change*. Pinter. London.

Stiglitz, J.E. and Wiess, A. (1981) 'Credit rationing in markets with imperfect information', *American Economic Review*, 71: 3, 393–410.

Taylor, L. (1988) *Varieties of Stabilisation Experience: towards sensible macroeconomics in the third world*. Clarendon Press, Oxford.

Taylor, M.P. (1988) 'An empirical examination of long-run PPP using cointegration techniques', *Applied Economics*, 20: 1369–82.

# 11 CONCLUSIONS

We have sought in this book to raise a number of important aspects to do with the operation of the international financial system. In Chapter 1 we stressed the fact that the international financial system has to address two crucial issues. It has to deal with the problem of adjustment of balance of payments imbalances and the related question of the role of the exchange rate. And it has to provide some form of international liquidity and financial flows which contribute to the (short-term) financing of payments imbalances as well as oiling the wheels of international trade in goods, services and assets. Different systems have different means of dealing with the two issues. But whatever system is adopted, each requires different institutions with their own 'rules of the game'. Member countries of the system have to adhere to these rules if the system is to operate smoothly.

A key feature of the period since the 1970s has been the adoption of floating, or perhaps more precisely managed (to different degrees), exchange rates. One of the key advantages which flexible exchange rates are supposed to confer is that they allow a country an automatic means of adjustment (through automatic changes in the exchange rate) as well as conferring policy independence. We have spent some time in this book in examining the determinants of exchange rates. We noted that exchange rates (both real and nominal) have been rather volatile since the advent of the floating era and that models of exchange rate determination have found it difficult to explain their movements. Economic fundamentals seem much more stable than exchange rates and exchange rate models often prove to have poor explanatory power and poor forecasting ability.

What is clear is that in modelling exchange rates we need to go far beyond the traditional models which examine only their role in balancing the current account (the elasticities and traditional absorption approaches). Asset market models suggest that exchange rates are driven primarily by the huge volume of capital movements which characterise the world economy nowadays. But exchange rate changes can still have detrimental effects on the real economies of countries. Prolonged periods of overvaluation or undervaluation can distort the traded/nontraded sectors as the UK's experience in the early 1980s has shown.

The tendency for floating exchange rates to exhibit both volatility and misalignment, along with their seeming inability to correct balance of payments imbalances, has led to a growing interest in some form of exchange rate management. At the level of the Group of Seven (G7) industrial countries, the Plaza and Louvre agreements of the later 1980s sought to co-ordinate both exchange rate and macroeconomic policies between these countries. More concretely, there is the European experience with monetary integration through the European Monetary System (EMS) and the debate over the path towards Economic and Monetary Union (EMU). In Chapter 4 we outlined some of the theoretical issues involved in exchange rate management. In particular we examined how a particular type of exchange rate management, the so-called target zone idea, might work in practice. Both the EMS and the G7 experience can be considered forms of target zones, with the former obviously much more strict than the latter.

But, of course, management of the exchange rate cannot occur in a vacuum with individual countries continuing to pursue their own preferred economic policies. Countries cannot conduct policy independently of each other if they are targeting the exchange rate. Instead, exchange rate management requires some co-ordination of policies, the degree of which will be dependent on the tightness of the exchange rate target. Events in Europe in 1992 and 1993 highlighted this clearly. But co-ordination of economic policy requires an institutional structure which can mediate the differences between the countries who have agreed to exchange rate co-operation. The alternative is that smaller countries simply peg their currencies to a larger one and accept the consequences in terms of their economic policy. This is what smaller developing countries do when they peg their currencies to the dollar, SDR, sterling or French franc. Such a form of exchange rate management is unlikely to be accepted by the major industrial countries: indeed, we argued that pressures within the EMS came exactly from the reluctance of member countries to continue to accept the direction of German monetary policy when their own economies would have benefited from a change. Thus if exchange rate management is to be successful, a structure which reconciles the differing policy goals of the participating countries and which allows discussion over the conduct of economic policy in general and monetary policy in particular is crucial.

Moreover, such co-ordination of policy has to be believable. We noted that target zones have a tendency to experience speculative attacks. Financial markets are very quick nowadays to undermine exchange rate arrangements should disagreements between participants surface. This was most clearly evident during the EMS crises in 1992 and 1993. Only if international financial flows are controlled (by throwing some 'sand in the wheels') can speculative attacks in the face of policy disagreements be forestalled. If countries are unwilling to control financial flows, then the institutional structure of the agreement is even more crucial.

The role of capital movements brings us to the second major aspect of the international financial system which we have emphasised throughout this book, namely the related issues of liquidity and financial flows in the international system. These issues formed the core of Chapters 6 to 10. We argued that liquidity in the international system can no longer be thought of as simply international reserves held by countries to finance balance of payments deficits. The growing importance of private financial flows implies that we now have to think of a broader definition of international liquidity: to include both privately and officially *held* liquidity as well as privately and officially *provided* liquidity. We categorised and explained the growth of the private flows in some detail, examining their implications in several areas.

First, we noted their role in increasing interdependence in the world economy. Recognition of this leads us back once again to the question of policy co-ordination. If spillovers are increasing as a result of financial flows, then the case for co-ordination of policy is even greater, irrespective of the exchange rate system adopted.

Secondly, we noted the tendency for these increased private flows to generate a propensity for financial crisis (or, at least, financial disturbances) in the world economy. We examined in particular the role of *bank* lending and the associated debt crisis, arguing that market failures make banks unsuited to lending on such a scale as they did in the 1970s and early 1980s, especially without adequate monitoring of their loans. After the debt crisis, in the later 1980s, private international financial flows took the form of portfolio investment in developing countries rather than bank lending.[1] But as the Mexican crisis of late 1994 and early 1995 illustrated, this form of finance has proved to be as fragile as bank lending was. At the slightest hint that all was not well with the Mexican economy, a huge volume of funds were withdrawn. Moreover, problems were not confined only to Mexico. In addition, a number of emerging stock markets found investors withdrawing their funds as part of the 'flight to quality'. Only through intervention by the US and other countries in the form of a support loan for Mexico was the crisis prevented from becoming even more severe.

This issue of the fragility of the world economy seems closely related to the question of recycling. How recycling is organised is a question which we highlighted at the start of this book as crucial to the design of any international financial system. It was a topic of much debate at the Bretton Woods conference, with Keynes favouring a more automatic mechanism of recycling through international institutions. With the advent of flexible exchange rates in the 1970s, it was hoped that recycling would become automatic. But the two oil shocks doubled the magnitude of balance of payments imbalances in the world economy and recycling remained one of the major issues in the 1970s and 1980s.

A pertinent question which might arise is to ask is where was the IMF during this period? What role did it play since it was designed in the Bretton Woods agreement to play a significant part in this area? In our examination of financial flows in the 1970s and 1980s, it is clear that the IMF was not at the centre of the recycling issue. Instead, it concentrated more on developing countries and even then was only used by those countries when private sources of finance were unavailable. In other words, it acted as a kind of lender of last resort.

It is clear that with the growing importance of private international flows the IMF is more likely to play a greater role in developing countries than in industrial countries. The latter find it easier to borrow private finance to finance any payments imbalance that might arise from an excess of investment over domestic savings. But, as we argued in Chapter 10, the IMF has to change considerably if it is to have a more positive influence in developing countries. At present, developing countries feel that the IMF simply imposes policy changes on them, without adequate discussion within the country concerned. Moreover, developing countries believe they have little impact on the kinds of policies which conditionality entails since they have little voting power. Similar arguments also apply to the World Bank, the other major international institution responsible for lending to developing countries. Thus reform of international financial system, must also include changes to the organisation of international institutions. It is not simply good enough to increase their role.

Where do all our arguments leave the international financial system? What should be clear is that the old debates which occupied researchers of the international financial system (adjustment, the role of exchange rates, liquidity and financial flows) are as important today as they have ever been. The debate over the type of exchange rate system is reflected today in the disintegration of the world economy into regional

---

[1] See Rohatyn (1994) for an interesting account of these developments and their implications for the world economy.

blocks which co-operate over trade, exchange rates and other economic policies. The debate on financial flows has centred on the role of private finance in contrast to finance provided by international institutions in the financing of imbalances. And as part of this debate there is the question of the extent to which private finance should be controlled through a tax on short-term transactions.

The main thrust of this book in these debates has been for the need to develop strong institutions at the international level. It is not good enough to leave the international financial system merely to the operation of markets. But such an argument covers a whole range of potential proposals for reform of the international financial system. At one end of the spectrum, institutional change could be quite radical such as the setting up of a clearing union more along the lines suggested by Keynes at the Bretton Woods conference (Davidson, 1993) to deal with the recycling problem. Other, less radical, reforms might follow the proposals for a loose exchange rate target zone proposed by Williamson and Miller (1987).[2]

What is clear from our discussion of the problems of the international financial system is that a liberal approach will not lead to optimal outcomes. History, especially since the 1970s, has taught us that much. The challenge for the 1990s – especially as we are now 50 years after the Bretton Woods conference – will be to reconsider the organisation of the international financial system. It improvement is crucial not only to the prospects for growth in developing countries but also for continued prosperity in the more developed countries of the world economy.

## References

Davidson, P. (1993) 'Reforming the world's money', *Journal of Post-Keynesian Economics*, 15: 2, 153–79.

Rohatym, F. (1994) 'The risks to the world economy', *New York Review of Books*, XLI: 13, July 14, 48–53.

Williamson, J. (1993) 'On designing an International Monetary System', *Journal of Post-Keynesian Economics*, 15: 2, 181–92.

Williamson, J. and Miller, M.H. (1987) 'Targets and Indicators: a blueprint for the international coordination of economic policy', *Policy Analyses in International Economics*, 22, Institute for International Economics, Washington, D.C.

[2] See also Williamson (1993).

# INDEX